The
L/L Research
Channeling Archives

Transcripts of
the Meditation Sessions

Volume 5
February 19, 1982 to September 25, 1982

Don
Elkins

Jim
McCarty

Carla L.
Rueckert

ISBN: 978-0-945007-79-1

Published by L/L Research
Box 5195
Louisville, Kentucky 40255-0195

E-mail: contact@llresearch.org
www.llresearch.org

About the cover photo: *This photograph of Jim McCarty and Carla L. Rueckert was taken during an L/L Research channeling session on August 4, 2009, in the living room of their Louisville, Kentucky home. Jim always holds hands with Carla when she channels, following the Ra group's advice on how she can avoid any possibility of astral travel.*

Dedication

These archive volumes are dedicated to Hal and Jo Price, who faithfully and lovingly hosted this group's weekly meditation meetings from 1962 to 1975,

to Walt Rogers, whose work with the research group Man, Consciousness and Understanding of Detroit offered the information needed to begin this ongoing channeling experiment,

and to the Confederation of Angels and Planets in the Service of the Infinite Creator, for sharing their love and wisdom with us so generously through the years.

Table of Contents

INTRODUCTION

Welcome to this volume of the *L/L Research Channeling Archives*. This series of publications represents the collection of channeling sessions recorded by L/L Research during the period from the early seventies to the present day. The sessions are also available on the L/L Research website, www.llresearch.org.

Starting in the mid-1950s, Don Elkins, a professor of physics and engineering at Speed Scientific School, had begun researching the paranormal in general and UFOs in particular. Elkins was a pilot as well as a professor and he flew his small plane to meet with many of the UFO contactees of the period.

Hal Price had been a part of a UFO-contactee channeling circle in Detroit called "The Detroit Group." When Price was transferred from Detroit's Ford plant to its Louisville truck plant, mutual friends discovered that Price also was a UFO researcher and put the two men together. Hal introduced Elkins to material called *The Brown Notebook* which contained instructions on how to create a group and receive UFO contactee information. In January of 1962 they decided to put the instructions to use and began holding silent meditation meetings on Sunday nights just across the Ohio River in the southern Indiana home of Hal and his wife, Jo. This was the beginning of what was called the "Louisville Group."

I was an original member of that group, along with a dozen of Elkins' physics students. However, I did not learn to channel until 1974. Before that date, almost none of our weekly channeling sessions were recorded or transcribed. After I began improving as a channel, Elkins decided for the first time to record all the sessions and transcribe them.

During the first eighteen months or so of my studying channeling and producing material, we tended to reuse the tapes as soon as the transcriptions were finished. Since those were typewriter days, we had no record of the work that could be reopened and used again, as we do now with computers. And I used up the original and the carbon copy of my transcriptions putting together a manuscript, *Voices of the Gods*, which has not yet been published. It remains as almost the only record of Don Elkins' and my channeling of that period.

We learned from this experience to retain the original tapes of all of our sessions, and during the remainder of the seventies and through the eighties, our "Louisville Group" was prolific. The "Louisville Group" became "L/L Research" after Elkins and I published a book in 1976, *Secrets of the UFO*, using that publishing name. At first we met almost every night. In later years, we met gradually less often, and the number of sessions recorded by our group in a year accordingly went down. Eventually, the group began taking three months off from channeling during the summer. And after 2000, we began having channeling meditations only twice a month. The volume of sessions dropped to its present output of eighteen or so each year.

These sessions feature channeling from sources which call themselves members of the Confederation of Planets in the Service of the Infinite Creator. At first we enjoyed hearing from many different voices: Hatonn, Laitos, Oxal, L/Leema and Yadda being just a few of them. As I improved my tuning techniques, and became the sole senior channel in L/L Research, the number of contacts dwindled. When I began asking for "the highest and best contact which I can receive of Jesus the Christ's vibration of unconditional love in a conscious and stable manner," the entity offering its thoughts through our group was almost always Q'uo. This remains true as our group continues to channel on an ongoing basis.

The channelings are always about love and unity, enunciating "The Law of One" in one aspect or another. Seekers who are working with spiritual principles often find the material a good resource. We hope that you will as well. As time has gone on the questions have shifted somewhat, but in general the content of the channeling is metaphysical and focused on helping seekers find the love in the moment and the Creator in the love.

At first, I transcribed our channeling sessions. I got busier, as our little group became more widely known, and got hopelessly behind on transcribing. Two early transcribers who took that job off my hands were Kim

Howard and Judy Dunn, both of whom masterfully transcribed literally hundreds of sessions through the eighties and early nineties.

Then Ian Jaffray volunteered to create a web site for these transcriptions, and single-handedly unified the many different formats that the transcripts were in at that time and made them available online. This additional exposure prompted more volunteers to join the ranks of our transcribers, and now there are a dozen or so who help with this. Our thanks go out to all of these kind volunteers, early and late, who have made it possible for our webguy to make these archives available.

Around the turn of the millennium, I decided to commit to editing each session after it had been transcribed. So the later transcripts have fewer errata than the earlier ones, which are quite imperfect in places. One day, perhaps, those earlier sessions will be revisited and corrections will be made to the transcripts. It would be a large task, since there are well over 1500 channeling sessions as of this date, and counting. We apologize for the imperfections in those transcripts, and trust that you can ascertain the sense of them regardless of a mistake here and there.

Blessings, dear reader! Enjoy these "humble thoughts" from the Confederation of Planets. May they prove good companions to your spiritual seeking. ♣

For all of us at L/L Research,

Carla L. Rueckert

Louisville, Kentucky

July 16, 2009

YEAR 1982

FEBRUARY 19, 1982 TO SEPTEMBER 25, 1982

L/L RESEARCH

L/L Research is a subsidiary of
Rock Creek Research &
Development Laboratories, Inc.

P.O. Box 5195
Louisville, KY 40255-0195

www.llresearch.org

Rock Creek is a non-profit
corporation dedicated to
discovering and sharing
information which may aid in
the spiritual evolution of
humankind.

THE LAW OF ONE, BOOK IV, SESSION 78
FEBRUARY 19, 1982

Ra: I am Ra. I greet you in the love and in the light of the one infinite Creator. We communicate now.

Questioner: Was there some problem with the ritual we performed that made it necessary to perform the ritual twice?

Ra: I am Ra. There was a misstep which created a momentary lapse of concentration. This was not well.

Questioner: What was the misstep?

Ra: I am Ra. It was a missed footing.

Questioner: Did this have any detrimental effect on the instrument?

Ra: I am Ra. Very little. The instrument felt the presence it has come to associate with cold and spoke. The instrument did the appropriate thing.

Questioner: Could you tell me the condition of the instrument?

Ra: I am Ra. The physical complex is as previously stated. There is some slight loss of vital energy. The basic complex distortions are similar to your previous asking.

Questioner: The instrument would like for me to ask if there is any problem with her kidneys?

Ra: I am Ra. This query is more complex than its brevity certifies. The physical complex renal system of this instrument is much damaged. The time/space equivalent which rules the body complex is without

flaw. There was a serious question, due to psychic attack, as to whether the spiritual healing of this system would endure. It did so but has the need to be re-enforced by affirmation of the ascendancy of the spiritual over the apparent or visible.

When this instrument began ingesting substances designed to heal in a physical sense, among other things, the renal complex, this instrument was ceasing the affirmation of healing. Due to this, again, the healing was weakened. This is of some profound distortion and it would be well for the instrument to absorb these concepts. We ask your forgiveness for offering information which may abridge free will, but the dedication of the instrument is such that it would persevere regardless of its condition, if possible. Thusly we offer this information that it may persevere with a fuller distortion towards comfort.

Questioner: What was the experience that caused the healing of the time/space kidney?

Ra: I am Ra. This experience was the healing of self by self with the catalyst of the spiritual healer whom you call Pachita.

Questioner: Thank you. In utilizing the energetic displacements of thought-forms energizing the instrument during contact most efficiently, what specifically could we do?

Ra: I am Ra. Each of the support group has an excess of love and light to offer the instrument during the working. Already each sends to the instrument love, light, and thoughts of strength of the physical, mental, and spiritual configurations. These sendings are forms. You may refine these sendings until the fullest manifestations of love and light are sent into the energy web of this entity which functions as instrument. Your exact sending is, in order to be most potent, the creature of your own making.

Questioner: Thank you. I am going to go back to an earlier time, if you could call it that, in evolution to try to establish a very fundamental base for some of the concepts that seem to be the foundation of everything that we experience so that we can more fully examine the basis of our evolution.

I am guessing that in our Milky Way Galaxy (the major galaxy with billions of stars) that the progress of evolution was from the center outward toward the rim and that in the early evolution of this galaxy the first distortion was not extended down past the sub-Logos simply because it was not thought of or conceived of and that this extension of the first distortion, which created polarization, was something that occurred in what we would call a later time as the evolution progressed outward from the center of the galaxy. Am I in any way correct in this statement?

Ra: I am Ra. You are correct.

Questioner: We have the first, second, and third distortions of the Law of One as free will, love, and light. Am I correct in assuming that the central core of this major galaxy began to form with the third distortion? Was that the origin of our Milky Way Galaxy?

Ra: I am Ra. In the most basic or teleological sense you are incorrect as the one infinite Creator is all that there is. In an undistorted seed-form you are correct in seeing the first manifestation visible to the eye of the body complex which you inhabit as the third distortion, light, or to use a technical term, limitless light.

Questioner: I realize that we are on very difficult ground, you might say, for precise terminology. It is totally displaced from our system of coordinates for evaluation in our present system of language.

These early Logoi that formed in the center of the galaxy wished, I assume, to create a system of experience for the one Creator. Did they then start

with no previous experience or information about how to do this? This is difficult to ask.

Ra: I am Ra. At the beginning of this creation or, as you may call it, octave there were those things known which were the harvest of the preceding octave. About the preceding creation, we know as little as we do of the octave to come. However, we are aware of those pieces of gathered concept which were the tools which the Creator had in the knowing of the self.

These tools were of three kinds. Firstly, there was an awareness of the efficiency for experience of mind, body, and spirit. Secondly, there was an awareness of the most efficacious nature or, if you will, significator of mind, body, and spirit. Thirdly, there was the awareness of two aspects of mind, of body, and of spirit that the significator could use to balance all catalyst. You may call these two the matrix and the potentiator.

Questioner: Could you elaborate please on the nature and quality of the matrix and the potentiator?

Ra: I am Ra. In the mind complex the matrix may be described as consciousness. It has been called the Magician. It is to be noted that of itself consciousness is unmoved. The potentiator of consciousness is the unconscious. This encompasses a vast realm of potential in the mind.

In the body the matrix may be seen as Balanced Working or Even Functioning. Note that here the matrix is always active with no means of being inactive. The potentiator of the body complex, then, may be called Wisdom for it is only through judgment that the unceasing activities and proclivities of the body complex may be experienced in useful modes.

The Matrix of the Spirit is what you may call the Night of the Soul or Primeval Darkness. Again we have that which is not capable of movement or work. The potential power of this extremely receptive matrix is such that the potentiator may be seen as Lightning. In your archetypical system called the tarot this has been refined into the concept complex of the Lightning Struck Tower. However, the original potentiator was light in its sudden and fiery form; that is, the lightning itself.

Questioner: Would you elucidate with respect to the significator you spoke of?

Ra: I am Ra. The original significators may undifferentiatedly be termed the mind, the body, and the spirit.

Questioner: Then we have, at the beginning of this galactic evolution, an archetypical mind that is the product of the previous octave which this galaxy then used as and acts upon under the first distortion so as to allow for what we experience as polarity. Was there any concept of polarity carried through from the previous octave in the sense of service-to-others or service-to-self polarity?

Ra: I am Ra. There was polarity in the sense of the mover and the moved. There was no polarity in the sense of service-to-self and service-to-others.

Questioner: Then the first experiences, as you say, were in monochrome. Was the concept of the seven densities of vibration with the evolutionary process taking place in discrete densities carried through from the previous octave?

Ra: I am Ra. To the limits of our knowledge, which are narrow, the ways of the octave are without time; that is, there are seven densities in each creation infinitely.

Questioner: Then I am assuming that the central suns of our galaxy, in starting the evolutionary process in this galaxy, provided for, in their plans, the refinement of consciousness through the densities just as we experience it here. However, they did not conceive of the polarization of consciousness with respect to service-to-self and service-to-others. Is this correct?

Ra: I am Ra. This is correct.

Questioner: Why do the densities have the qualities that they have? You have named the densities with respect to their qualities, the next density being that of love and so on. Can you tell me why these qualities exist in that form? Is it possible to answer that question?

Ra: I am Ra. It is possible.

Questioner: Will you please answer that?

Ra: I am Ra. The nature of the vibratory range peculiar to each quantum of the octave is such that the characteristics of it may be described with the same certainty with which you perceive a color with your optical apparatus if it is functioning properly.

Questioner: So the original evolution then was planned by the Logos but the first distortion was not extended to the product. At some point this first distortion was extended and the first service-to-self polarity emerged. Is this correct and if so, could you tell me the history of this process of emergence?

Ra: I am Ra. As proem let me state that the Logoi always conceived of themselves as offering free will to the sub-Logoi in their care. The sub-Logoi had freedom to experience and experiment with consciousness, the experiences of the body, and the illumination of the spirit. That having been said, we shall speak to the point of your query.

The first Logos to instill what you now see as free will, in the full sense, in its sub-Logoi came to this creation due to contemplation in depth of the concepts or possibilities of conceptualizations of what we have called the significators. The Logos posited the possibility of the mind, the body, and the spirit as being complex. In order for the significator to be what it is not, it then must be granted the free will of the Creator. This set in motion a quite lengthy, in your terms, series of Logos's improving or distilling this seed thought. The key was the significator becoming a complex.

Questioner: Then our particular Logos, when it created Its own particular creation, was at some point far down the evolutionary spiral of the experiment with the significator becoming what it was not and, therefore, I am assuming, was primarily concerned in designing the archetypes in such a way that they would create the acceleration of this polarization. Is this in any way correct?

Ra: I am Ra. We would only comment briefly. It is generally correct. You may fruitfully view each Logos and its design as the Creator experiencing Itself. The seed concept of the significator being a complex introduces two things: firstly, the Creator against Creator in one sub-Logos in what you may call dynamic tension; secondly, the concept of free will, once having been made fuller by its extension into the sub-Logoi known as mind/body/spirit complexes, creates and re-creates and continues to create as a function of its very nature.

Questioner: You stated previously that The Choice is made in this third-density and is the axis upon which the creation turns. Could you expand on your reason for making that statement?

Ra: I am Ra. This is a statement of the nature of creation as we speak to you.

Questioner: I did not understand that. Could you say that in a different way?

Ra: I am Ra. As you have noted, the creation of which your Logos is a part is a protean entity which grows and learns upon a macrocosmic scale. The Logos is not a part of time. All that is learned from experience in an octave is, therefore, the harvest of that Logos and is further the nature of that Logos.

The original Logos's experience was, viewed in space/time, small; Its experience now, more. Therefore we say, as we now speak to you at this space/time, the nature of creation is as we have described. This does not deny the process by which this nature has been achieved but merely ratifies the product.

Questioner: After third density, in our experience, social memory complexes are polarized positively and negatively. Is the interaction of social memory complexes of opposite polarity equivalent, but on a magnified scale, to the interaction between mind/body/spirit complexes of opposite polarity? Is this how experience is gained as a function of polarity difference in fourth and fifth densities?

Ra: I am Ra. No.

Questioner: This is a hard question to ask, but what is the value experientially of the formation of positive and negative social memory complexes, of the separation of the polarities at that point rather than the allowing for the mixing of mind/body/spirit complexes of opposite polarity in the higher densities?

Ra: I am Ra. The purpose of polarity is to develop the potential to do work. This is the great characteristic of those, shall we say, experiments which have evolved since the concept of The Choice was appreciated. Work is done far more efficiently and with greater purity, intensity, and variety by the voluntary searching of mind/body/spirit complexes for the lessons of third and fourth densities. The action of fifth density is viewed in space/time the same with or without polarity. However, viewed in time/space, the experiences of wisdom are greatly enlarged and deepened due, again, to the voluntary nature of polarized mind/body/spirit action.

Questioner: Then you are saying that as a result of the polarization in consciousness which has occurred later in the galactic evolution, the experiences are much more intense along the two paths. Are these experiences each independent of the other? Must there be action across the potentiated difference between the positive and negative polarity, or is it possible to have this experience simply because of the single polarity? This is difficult to ask.

Ra: I am Ra. We would agree. We shall attempt to pluck the gist of your query from the surrounding verbiage.

The fourth and fifth densities are quite independent, the positive polarity functioning with no need of negative and visa-versa. It is to be noted that in attempting to sway third-density mind/body/spirit complexes in choosing polarity there evolves a good bit of interaction between the two polarities. In sixth density, the density of unity, the positive and negative paths must needs take in each other for all now must be seen as love/light and light/love. This is not difficult for the positive polarity which sends love and light to all other-selves. It is difficult enough for service-to-self polarized entities that at some point the negative polarity is abandoned.

Questioner: The choice of polarity being unique as a circumstance, shall I say, for the archetypical basis for the evolution of consciousness in our particular experience indicates to me that we have arrived, through a long process of the Creator knowing Itself, at a position of present or maximum efficiency for the design of a process of experience. That design for maximum efficiency is in the roots of consciousness and is the archetypical mind and is a product of everything that has gone before. There are, unquestionably, relatively pure archetypical concepts for the seven concepts for mind, body, and spirit. I feel that the language that we have for these is somewhat inadequate.

However, we shall continue to attempt to investigate the foundation for this and I am hoping that I have laid the foundation with some degree of accuracy in attempting to set a background for the development of the archetypes of our Logos. Have I left out anything or made any errors, or could you make any comments on my attempt to lay the foundation for the construction that our Logos used for the archetypes?

Ra: I am Ra. Your queries are thoughtful.

Questioner: Are they accurate, or have I made mistakes?

Ra: I am Ra. There are no mistakes.

Questioner: Let me put it this way. Have I made missteps in my analysis of what has led to the construction of the archetypes that we experience?

Ra: I am Ra. We may share with you the observation that judgment is no part of interaction between mind/body/spirit complexes. We have attempted to answer each query as fully as your language and the extent of your previous information allow. We may suggest that if, in perusing this present material, you have further queries, refining any concept, these queries may be asked and, again, we shall attempt adequate rejoinders.

Questioner: I understand your limitations in answering that. Thank you.

Could you tell me how, in the first density, wind and fire teach earth and water?

Ra: I am Ra. You may see the air and fire of that which is chaos as literally illuminating and forming the formless, for earth and water were, in the timeless state, unformed. As the active principles of fire and air blow and burn incandescently about that which nurtures that which is to come, the water learns to become sea, lake, and river offering the opportunity for viable life. The earth learns to be shaped, thus offering the opportunity for viable life.

Questioner: Are the seven archetypes for mind a function of or related to the seven densities that are to be experienced in the octave?

Ra: I am Ra. The relationship is tangential in that no congruency may be seen. However, the progress through the archetypes has some of the characteristics of the progress through the densities. These relationships may be viewed without being, shall we say, pasted one upon the other.

Questioner: How about the seven bodily energy centers? Are they related to archetypes in some way?

Ra: I am Ra. The same may be said of these. It is informative to view the relationships but stifling to insist upon the limitations of congruency. Recall at all times, if you would use this term that the archetypes are a portion of the resources of the mind complex.

Questioner: Is there any relationship between the archetypes and the planets of our solar system?

Ra: I am Ra. This is not a simple query. Properly, the archetypes have some relationship to the planets. However, this relationship is not one which can be expressed in your language. This, however, has not halted those among your people who have become adepts from attempting to name and describe these relationships. To most purely understand, if we may use this misnomer, the archetypes it is well to view the concepts which make up each archetype and reserve the study of planets and other correspondences for meditation.

Questioner: It just seemed to me that since the planets were an outgrowth of the Logos and since the archetypical mind was the foundation of the experience that the planets of this Logos would be somewhat related. We will certainly follow your suggestion.

I have been trying to get a foothold into an undistorted perception, you might say, of the archetypical mind. It seems to me that everything that I have read having to do with archetypes has been, to some degree or another, distorted by the writers and by the fact that our language is not really capable of description.

You have spoken of the Magician as a basic archetype and that this seems to have been carried through from the previous octave. Would this be in order—if there is an order—the first archetypical concept for this Logos, the concept that we call the Magician?

Ra: I am Ra. We would first respond to your confusion as regards the various writings upon the archetypical mind. You may well consider the very informative difference between a thing in itself and its relationships or functions. There is much study of archetype which is actually the study of functions, relationships, and correspondences. The study of planets, for instance, is an example of archetype seen as function. However, the archetypes are, first and most profoundly, things in themselves and the pondering of them and their purest relationships with each other should be the most useful foundation for the study of the archetypical mind.

We now address your query as to the archetype which is the Matrix of the Mind. As to its name, the name of Magician is understandable when you consider that consciousness is the great foundation, mystery, and revelation which makes this particular density possible. The self-conscious entity is full of the magic of that which is to come. It may be considered first, for the mind is the first of the complexes to be developed by the student of spiritual evolution.

Questioner: Would the archetype then that has been called the High Priestess, which represents the intuition, be properly the second of the archetypes?

Ra: I am Ra. This is correct. You see here the recapitulation of the beginning knowledge of this Logos; that is, matrix and potentiator. The unconscious is indeed what may be poetically described as High Priestess, for it is the Potentiator of the Mind and as potentiator for the mind is that principle which potentiates all experience.

Questioner: Then for the third archetype would the Empress be correct and be related to disciplined meditation?

Ra: I am Ra. I perceive a mind complex intention of a query, but was aware only of sound vibratory statement. Please requestion.

QUESTIONER. I was asking if the third archetype was the Empress and was it correct to say that this archetype had to do with disciplined meditation?

Ra: I am Ra. The third archetype may broadly be grasped as the Catalyst of the Mind. Thus it takes in far more than disciplined meditation. However, it is certainly through this faculty that catalyst is most efficiently used. The Archetype, Three, is perhaps confusedly called Empress although the intention of this number is the understanding that it represents the unconscious or female portion of the mind complex being first, shall we say, used or ennobled by the male or conscious portion of the mind. Thus the noble name.

Questioner: The fourth archetype is called the Emperor and seems to have to do with experience of other-selves and the green-ray energy center with respect to other-selves. Is this correct?

Ra: I am Ra. This is perceptive. The broad name for Archetype Four may be the Experience of the Mind. In the tarot you find the name of Emperor. Again this implies nobility and in this case we may see the suggestion that it is only through the catalyst which has been processed by the potentiated consciousness

that experience may ensue. Thusly is the conscious mind ennobled by the use of the vast resources of the unconscious mind.

This instrument's dorsal side grows stiff, and the instrument tires. We welcome one more query.

Questioner: I would like to ask the reason for this session having been longer than most previous sessions and also if there is anything that we can do to make the instrument more comfortable or to improve the contact?

Ra: I am Ra. This instrument was given far more than the, shall we say, usual amount of transferred energy. There is a limit to the amount of energy of this type which may, with safety, be used when the instrument is, itself, without physical reserves. This is inevitable due to the various distortions such as we mentioned previously in this working having to do with growing dorsal discomfort.

The alignments are fastidious. We appreciate your conscientiousness. In order to enhance the comfort of the instrument it might be suggested that careful manipulation of the dorsal area be accomplished before a working.

It is also suggested that, due to the attempt at psychic attack, this instrument will require warmth along the right side of the physical complex. There has been some infringement but it should not be long-lasting. It is, however, well to swaddle this instrument sufficiently to ward off any manifestation of this cold in physical form.

I am Ra. I leave you, my friends, in the love and in the light of the one infinite Creator. Go forth, therefore, merrily rejoicing in the power and in the peace of the one infinite Creator. Adonai. ☘

L/L RESEARCH

L/L Research is a subsidiary of Rock Creek Research & Development Laboratories, Inc.

P.O. Box 5195
Louisville, KY 40255-0195

www.llresearch.org

Rock Creek is a non-profit corporation dedicated to discovering and sharing information which may aid in the spiritual evolution of humankind.

SUNDAY MEDITATION
FEBRUARY 21, 1982

(C channeling)

I am Hatonn, and am now with this instrument. Tonight we were enjoying the sounds of your laughter, but will refrain from attempting to indulge in joke-telling, for we feel we are too long out of practice to be able to adequately bandy about your puns. Tonight we wish to speak a few words about compassion, feelings that you experience in regard to your fellow entities, your planet. In your illusion, my friends, you are constantly faced with choices, and each affects, not only you, but also indirectly or sometimes directly affects those around you. These choices, as you develop, may at times seem very clear and shall be easy for you to do that which will aid you the most in your journey, but in your illusion few things are simple. Your illusion is such that in no case can the line clearly be drawn between serving of others, the serving of the self.

My friends, each of you must flow, each of you must act in the way that you deem most appropriate. In your illusion you become intertwined closely with various other entities in relationships, just friendship, family, ties that you call blood ties, connections that intertwine, that complicate each and every decision made, with relationships always [being] connected by choices. The choice is made with these relationships weighing very heavily upon the decision. You will find that you will tend to take relationships, bring them ever increasingly into your choices as you slowly progress in your journey as they are brought ever closer, the bonds strengthen and the ways in which you view these is ever more with a more focused love.

These entities, as you grow you may find that they take place … as you think and act first for them instead of first for you. As you continue to grow, this love/compassion will extend beyond your immediate relationships and reach further and further to others on your planet. Few begin … begin to place all others first in their choices, as you see it how they should be made.

My friends, the choices are hard, but through meditation you may find your mind so much clearer and the choices perhaps a little easier. No one but you may make your decision. The choice is always yours; no matter what acts upon you, you choose.

We are known to you as Hatonn, and we are always grateful to be able to speak a few humble words to you to aid in what ways we can. We can no more make your decisions than can any other catalyst you may encounter. We hope that through our few humble words love and light may serve you in your journey. We say this to emphasize that we do not, in your words, make decisions for you. Remember always choice, the decisions are yours.

We would, at this time, transfer this contact to another instrument. I am Hatonn.

(Carla channeling)

I am Hatonn, and am now with this instrument. We would continue briefly. My friends, there are many lonely people who do not believe that each person has a free choice of action at each moment in his life. The philosophy of such among your peoples is that first the parents instruct and must be obeyed, then society instructs and codes of social behavior must be followed, then, perhaps at some point, there is a marriage and the mate requires certain behavior and responsibilities ensue because children are forthcoming, and there are behaviors which are the responsibility of parents, and so from birth to death some people feel there is no freedom, but only a sometimes happy and sometimes dreary round of fitting in, doing your duty, and remaining within the law.

On the other side of the scale, my friends, there are those among your peoples who have listened to their inner voices and who say, and quite rightly, "All that I need to know is already within me. I do not need experience. Why should I accept sometimes being happy and sometimes sad and always involved with others who certainly seem to cause complications when I already know all that there is to know, when I am already aware of love, when I already feel the light of the Creator governing my footsteps? With my inner voice to guide me, what need have I for further experience in [the] outer world?"

Between these two systems of thought, my friends, there lies, as we have said, choices, a lifetime full. Those who believe that they are not free to make choices are lazy. Any number of clever statements can be made concerning such things as a prison, times wherein there is no choice as to the location of your physical vehicle, situations in which it would seem obvious that an action must be followed, but, my friends, the essence of choice is the use of the mind to discriminate between that which is worthy, true and beautiful in one's immediate environment and that which is not. There is no situation so limiting that you do not have full choice over your own mind, your own attitude, your own ability to radiate the love and the light of the infinite Creator.

To address those whom, far from feeling pent in by a society which seems to predetermine their destinies, feel instead that they have no need for experience, we can only suggest to each of you that you look back over a significant time period of your past, as you have experienced it in this lifetime. Are you indeed the same person that you were? Have not the choices that you have made, one by one, added up to a transformed person that sits in meditation in this domicile this evening with this group of people? Not some other group, not some other activity, not some other message. No matter that the universe is potentially complete within you. You must choose to know yourself, and there are so many things that you cannot know without experience. In happy times and in sad you know yourself better and better, and if you use the powers of your mind to determine what you have learned from the happy times and the sad ones, you will became more and more able, as a person, to, shall we say, stand upon your own two feet, within yourself surer, but able also to offer yourself to those about you as a listener, as an understander and as one who is seeking to be of aid.

Your first aid, my friends, is to yourself, so that you may be a person capable of aiding others. This aid is to know yourself, not to know what other people think of you; not to know what society expects of you; not to know what is legal, but to know what you think, what you feel and who you are. To suggest that you put into action, without discrimination, all those things that you are would be foolish, for, my friends, each entity has a light side and a dark one. To know yourself is the important thing, to know, to accept, and to love yourself, that which you consider good, that which you consider bad, is to became ready to know, to love and to accept others.

As always, we suggest the regular period of meditation, in order that those things which are too deep for conscious thought within yourself may be contacted and used, for you have a vast storehouse within you which will be of great aid as you seek the light of the infinite Creator.

At this time, we would pause so that our brothers and sisters of Laitos and we might move among you, offering to each our vibration, that you may feel our presence in a gentle manner, and if you wish, strengthen your own meditative state. I am Hatonn.

(Pause)

I am again with this instrument. I am Hatonn, and I thank you for your patience. We of the Confederation have begun working with many of those present and we greatly welcome each opportunity to touch their vibrations in a meeting such as this one. We would close now through another instrument. I am Hatonn.

(C channeling)

I am Hatonn, and I am once again with this instrument. We had experienced difficulty earlier in establishing contact with this instrument, and were attempting to strengthen contact this time. We now feel that contact has been improved and is more easily recognizable to this instrument. We shall now leave this group so that our brothers and sisters of Latwii may serve you by attempting to answer any questions you may have. We are Hatonn. Adonai, my friends.

(Carla channeling)

I am Latwii. I am with you in the love and the light of the infinite Creator, and am once again in the position of having to speak through this instrument in order to break up a little party going on up here between two of the instruments in the room who are playing a game which they call Alphonse and Gaston. My friends, each of these instruments is crackerjack. We would be happy to speak through either. Perhaps they should get together and decide whether one of them will actually allow us to speak, or whether we should just go home.

I am Latwii and will again attempt to contact somebody who can answer questions. I thank this instrument for allowing us to ring her chime, however briefly.

(L channeling)

I am Latwii, and I greet you, my brothers and sisters, in the love and the light of the infinite Creator. Now that we have the opportunity to express a few words to those present, we would gladly offer to attempt the service of answering …

(Side one of tape ends.)

(L channeling)

Now, then. Are there any questions that we may attempt to feel, so to speak?

M: If nobody has one, I have one for you, Latwii. Would you address the polarization or depolarization potential of taking another entity's life?

I am Latwii. I am aware of your question. My brother, we are surprised at this question, merely because we had assumed that your earlier conversation had managed to cover nearly every conceivable detail and variation upon that subject. If we may be allowed the pun, we had assumed that the concept of putting an other self into the ground had already been run into the ground.

M: If you'd like to make it brief, that's fine Latwii.

However, my brother, we shall attempt to add whatever commentary we can before the case or grave is closed. My brother, the taking of an other self's life is a task that, of course, should never be approached feverously, yet at times, if this situation occurs, you will find that you have very little opportunity for philosophical discussion prior to making the decision. We would suggest, my brother, that the same storehouse of information available for the lengthy philosophical discussion is also available for a quick service version of analysis. There is a capacity within each individual to evaluate a situation, not upon the details of the illusion, but rather upon the climate of wisdom and compassion within that same individual. It is not merely a matter of evaluating the details of the external situation, but rather of evaluating the details of your own orientation toward action or inaction. Therefore, my brother, we would simply offer the suggestion that while looking at the situation one should also include a brief effort toward looking at one's own motivations. More succinctly, let your conscience be your guide.

May we answer further, my brother?

M: No, thank you.

We thank you. Is there another question?

Carla: I have a question. Part of the time I feel very full of faith, and have a very good feeling about life in general and what I'm doing in particular, and this has been true ever since I was born. I can't remember a time when I didn't, at least part of the time, have a good deal of faith. At other times I feel very empty and full of doubts as to whether my life is worth anything or the work that I'm doing is valuable due to a strong desire to carry on, based on the observation that people who don't are usually even more unhappy than ones who do.

I continue, for the most part, acting as if the things that I believe in part of the time, I believed in all the time, and the actions that I do with a full heart part of the time, I'm doing with a full heart all the time.

What's the relative value of those things done with a full heart and with no effort, and things done when I really almost feel like I'm being a hypocrite, because I'm simply trying when I don't feel—when I have doubts?

I am Latwii. I am aware of your question. My sister, what would be the relative value of the individual who, upon finding an injured stranger abandoned on the road, chose reluctantly to attempt to save the life, as compared to that individual who found value in spending the waking hours of their day patrolling the roads attempting to locate someone who needed saving?

Again, my sister, we would reflect back to you the concept of the state of mind with which the effort is attempted, rather than the value of the effort itself. The accomplishment of expressing care, of offering compassionate attention when one might prefer to be involved in other pursuits, is difficult, yet the fact that the challenge exists of attempting these efforts as a service to others when one might prefer a more pleasurable occupation, is indicative of the dedication toward service necessary to attain polarization.

Those efforts which come easily are the result of the accumulation of past efforts which came with much more difficulty. Those efforts which come with difficulty are the initial steps of a journey that will come more easily as time passes. Do not be dismayed by suspicions of hypocrisy within yourself, rather, be attentive to the fact that your presence on this plane is due to a need to complete your polarization so as to attempt the next density. If all came with ease, my sister, we would suggest that you, perhaps, had misplaced your density.

May we answer you further?

Carla: No, thank you. That was most clarifying.

Is there another question?

(Pause)

I am Latwii. As there seem to be no more questions in the offing, so to speak, we shall ourselves be offing. We leave you, my brothers, and sisters, embraced in our love. Know that we are available to you upon request, and desire to be of service whenever we may be so. We leave you now. I am Latwii. ✤

L/L Research is a subsidiary of
Rock Creek Research &
Development Laboratories, Inc.

P.O. Box 5195
Louisville, KY 40255-0195

L/L Research

www.llresearch.org

Rock Creek is a non-profit
corporation dedicated to
discovering and sharing
information which may aid in
the spiritual evolution of
humankind.

ABOUT THE CONTENTS OF THIS TRANSCRIPT: This telepathic channeling has been taken from transcriptions of the weekly study and meditation meetings of the Rock Creek Research & Development Laboratories and L/L Research. It is offered in the hope that it may be useful to you. As the Confederation entities always make a point of saying, please use your discrimination and judgment in assessing this material. If something rings true to you, fine. If something does not resonate, please leave it behind, for neither we nor those of the Confederation would wish to be a stumbling block for any.

The Law of One, Book IV, Session 79
February 24, 1982

Ra: I am Ra. I greet you in the love and in the light of the one infinite Creator. We communicate now.

Questioner: Could you first give me the condition of the instrument?

Ra: I am Ra. It is as previously stated.

Questioner: The instrument would like to ask if there is any danger in the instrument receiving too much transferred energy in her present condition?

Ra: I am Ra. No.

Questioner: She would like to know the function of the energy transfer during the session?

Ra: I am Ra. The function of this energy transfer is a most helpful one in that it serves to strengthen the shuttle through which the in-streaming contact is received. The contact itself will monitor the condition of the instrument and cease communication when the distortions of the instrument begin to fluctuate towards the distortions of weakness or pain. However, while the contact is on-going the strength of the channel through which this contact flows may be aided by the energy transfer of which you spoke.

Questioner: We have been ending our banishing ritual prior to the session by a gesture that relieves us of the magical personality. I was just wondering if we should maintain this personality and omit that gesture while we are walking the Circle of One and then relinquish the magical personality only after the circle is formed or after the session? Which would be more appropriate?

Ra: I am Ra. The practice of magical workings demands the most rigorous honesty. If your estimate of your ability is that you can sustain the magical personality throughout this working, it is well. As long as you have some doubt it is inadvisable. In any case it is appropriate for this instrument to return its magical personality rather than carry this persona into the trance state, for it does not have the requisite magical skill to function in this circumstance and would be far more vulnerable than if the waking personality is offered as channel. This working is indeed magical in nature in the basic sense. However, it is inappropriate to move more quickly than one's feet may walk.

Questioner: I would like to question about the third-density experience of those entities just prior to the original extension of the first distortion to the sub-Logoi to create the split of polarity. Can you describe, in general, the differences between the third-density experience of these mind/body/spirits and the ones who have evolved upon this planet now?

Ra: I am Ra. This material has been previously covered. Please query for specific interest.

Questioner: Specifically, in the experience where only the service-to-others polarity in third density evolved, was the veil that was drawn with respect to knowledge of previous incarnations, etc., in effect for those entities?

Ra: I am Ra. No.

Questioner: Was the reincarnational process like the one that we experience here in which the third-density body is entered and exited numerous times during the cycle?

Ra: I am Ra. This is correct.

Questioner: Is it possible to give a time of incarnation with respect to our years and would you do so if it is?

Ra: I am Ra. The optimal incarnative period is somewhere close to a measure you call a millennium. This is, as you may say, a constant regardless of other factors of the third-density experience.

Questioner: Then prior to the first extension of the first distortion the veil or loss of awareness did not occur. From this I will make the assumption that this veil or loss of remembering consciously that which occurred before the incarnation was the primary tool for extending the first distortion. Is this correct?

Ra: I am Ra. Your correctness is limited. This was the first tool.

Questioner: Then from that statement I assume that the Logos first devised the tool of separating the unconscious from the conscious during what we call physical incarnations to achieve its objective? Is this correct?

Ra: I am Ra. Yes.

Questioner: Then from that statement I would also assume that many other tools were conceived and used after the first tool of the so-called veil. Is this correct?

Ra: I am Ra. There have been refinements.

Questioner: The archetypical mind of the Logos prior to this experiment in veiling was what I would consider to be less complex than it is now, possibly containing fewer archetypes. Is this correct?

Ra: I am Ra. We must ask your patience. We perceive a sudden flare of the distortion known as pain in this instrument's left arm and manual appendages. Please do not touch this instrument. We shall examine the mind complex and attempt to

reposition the limb so that the working may continue. Then please repeat the query.

(Ninety second pause)

I am Ra. You may proceed.

Questioner: Thank you. Prior to the experiment to extend the first distortion how many archetypes were there at that time?

Ra: I am Ra. There were nine.

Questioner: I will guess that those nine were three of mind, three of body, and three of spirit. Is this correct?

Ra: I am Ra. This is correct.

Questioner: I am going to guess that in the system of the tarot those archetypes would roughly correspond to, for the mind, the Magician, the Emperor, and the Chariot. Is this correct?

Ra: I am Ra. This is incorrect.

Questioner: Could you tell me what they correspond to?

Ra: I am Ra. The body, the mind, and the spirit each contained and functioned under the aegis of the matrix, the potentiator, and the significator. The significator of the mind, body, and spirit is not identical to the significator of the mind, body, and spirit complexes.

Questioner: I now understand what you meant in the previous session by saying that to extend free will the significator must become a complex. It seems that the significator has become the complex that is the third, fourth, fifth, sixth, and seventh of the mind, the tenth on of the body, and the seventeenth on of the spirit. Is this correct?

Ra: I am Ra. This is incorrect.

Questioner: Could you tell me what you mean by "the significator must become a complex"?

Ra: I am Ra. To be complex is to consist of more than one characteristic element or concept.

Questioner: I would like to try to understand the archetypes of the mind of this Logos prior to the extension of the first distortion. In order to better understand that which we experience now I believe that this is a logical approach.

We have, as you have stated, the matrix, the potentiator, and the significator. I understand the matrix as being that which is what we call the conscious mind, but since it is also that from which the mind is made, I am at a loss to fully understand these three terms especially with respect to the time before there was a division in consciousness. Could you expand even more upon the Matrix of the Mind, the Potentiator of the Mind, and the Significator of the Mind, how they differ, and what their relationships are, please?

Ra: I am Ra. The Matrix of Mind is that from which all comes. It is unmoving yet is the activator in potentiation of all mind activity. The Potentiator of the Mind is that great resource which may be seen as the sea into which the consciousness dips ever deeper and more thoroughly in order to create, ideate, and become more self-conscious.

The Significator of each mind, body, and spirit may be seen as a simple and unified concept. The Matrix of the Body may be seen to be a reflection in opposites of the mind; that is, unrestricted motion. The Potentiator of the Body then is that which, being informed, regulates activity.

The Matrix of the Spirit is difficult to characterize since the nature of spirit is less motile. The energies and movements of the spirit are, by far, the most profound yet, having more close association with time/space, do not have the characteristics of dynamic motion. Thusly one may see the Matrix as the deepest darkness and the Potentiator of Spirit as the most sudden awakening, illuminating, and generative influence.

This is the description of Archetypes One through Nine before the onset of influence of the co-Creator or sub-Logos' realization of free will.

Questioner: The first change made then for this extension of free will was to make the communication between the Matrix and the Potentiator of the Mind relatively unavailable one to the other during the incarnation. Is this correct?

Ra: I am Ra. We would perhaps rather term the condition as relatively more mystery-filled than relatively unavailable.

Questioner: The idea was then to create some type of veil between the Matrix and the Potentiator of the Mind. Is this correct?

Ra: I am Ra. This is correct.

Questioner: This veil then occurs between what we now call the unconscious and conscious minds. Is this correct?

Ra: I am Ra. This is correct.

Questioner: It was probably the design of the Logos to allow the conscious mind greater freedom under the first distortion by partitioning, you might say, this from the Potentiator or unconscious which had a greater communication with the total mind, therefore, allowing for the birth of uneducated, to use a poor term, portions of consciousness. Is this correct?

Ra: I am Ra. This is roughly correct.

Questioner: Could you de-roughen it or elucidate a bit on that?

Ra: I am Ra. There is intervening material before we may do so.

Questioner: OK. Was then this simple experiment carried out and the product of this experiment observed before greater complexity was attempted?

Ra: I am Ra. As we have said there have been a great number of successive experiments.

Questioner: I was just wondering since this seems to be the crux of the experiment, the large breaking point between no extension of the first distortion and the extension of the first distortion, what the result of this original experiment was with respect to that which was created from it. What was the result of that?

Ra: I am Ra. This is previously covered material. The result of these experiments has been a more vivid, varied, and intense experience of Creator by Creator.

Questioner: Well I was aware of that. I probably didn't state the question correctly. It's a very difficult question to state. I don't know if it's worth attempting to continue with but what I meant was when this very first experiment with the veiling process occurred, did it result in service-to-self polarization with the first experiment?

Ra: I am Ra. The early, if we may use this term, Logoi produced service-to-self and service-to-others mind/body/spirit complexes immediately. The harvestability of these entities was not so immediate and thus refinements of the archetypes began apace .

Questioner: Now we are getting to what I was trying to determine. Then at this point were there still only nine archetypes and the veil had just been drawn between the Matrix and the Potentiator of the Mind?

Ra: I am Ra. There were nine archetypes and many shadows.

Questioner: By shadows do you mean the, what I might refer to as, birthing of small archetypical biases?

Ra: I am Ra. Rather we would describe these shadows as the inchoate thoughts of helpful structures not yet fully conceived.

Questioner: Would The Choice exist at this point during the creation of the first service-to-self polarity?

Ra: I am Ra. Implicit in the veiling or separation of two archetypes is the concept of choice. The refinements to this concept took many experiences.

Questioner: I'm sorry that I have so much difficulty in asking these questions, but this is material that I find somewhat difficult.

I find it interesting that the very first experiment of veiling the Matrix of the Mind from the Potentiator of the Mind and visa-versa created service-to-self polarity. This seems to be a very important philosophical point in the development of the creation and possibly the beginning of a system of what we would call magic not envisioned previously.

Let me ask this question. Prior to the extension of the first distortion was the magical potential of the higher densities as great as it is now when the greatest potential was achieved in consciousness for each density? This is difficult to ask. What I am asking is that at the end of fourth density, prior to the extension of free will, was what we call magical potential as great as it is now at the end of fourth density?

Ra: I am Ra. As you understand, if we may use this misnomer, magic, the magical potential in third and fourth density was then far greater than after the change. However, there was far, far less desire or will to use this potential.

Questioner: Now, to be sure that I understand you: prior to the change and the extension of free will, let's take specifically the end of fourth density,

magical potential for the condition when there was only service-to-others polarization was much greater at the end of fourth density than at the end of fourth density immediately after the split of polarization and the extension of free will. Is that correct?

Ra: I am Ra. Magical ability is the ability to consciously use the so-called unconscious. Therefore, there was maximal ability prior to the innovation of sub-Logoi's free will.

Questioner: OK. At the present time we are experiencing the effects of a more complex or greater number of archetypes and I have guessed that the ones we are experiencing now in the mind are as follows: We have the Magician and High Priestess which correspond to the Matrix and Potentiator with the veil drawn between them which is the primary creator of the extension of the first distortion. Is that correct?

Ra: I am Ra. We are unable to answer this query without intervening material.

Questioner: OK. Sorry about that.

The next archetype, the Empress, is the Catalyst of the Mind, that which acts upon the conscious mind to change it. The fourth archetype is the Emperor, the Experience of the Mind, which is that material stored in the unconscious which creates its continuing bias. Am I correct with those statements?

Ra: I am Ra. Though far too rigid in your statements, you perceive correct relationships. There is a great deal of dynamic interrelationship in these first four archetypes

Questioner: Would the Hierophant then be somewhat of a governor or sorter of these effects so as to create the proper assimilation by the unconscious of that which comes through the conscious?

Ra: I am Ra. Although thoughtful, the supposition is incorrect in its heart.

Questioner: What would be the Hierophant?

Ra: I am Ra. The Hierophant is the Significator of the Body [Mind[1]] complex, its very nature. We may note that the characteristics of which you speak do have bearing upon the Significator of the Mind complex but are not the heart. The heart of the

---

[1] Ra corrected this error in Session #80. The Hierophant is the Significator of the Mind.

mind complex is that dynamic entity which absorbs, seeks, and attempts to learn.

Questioner: Then is the Hierophant that link, you might say, between the mind and the body?

Ra: I am Ra. There is a strong relationship between the significators of the mind, the body, and the spirit. Your statement is too broad.

Questioner: Let me skip over the Hierophant for a minute because I am really not understanding that at all and just ask if the Lovers represent a merging of the conscious and the unconscious or the communication of the conscious and unconscious?

Ra: I am Ra. Again, without being at all unperceptive, you miss the heart of this particular archetype which may be more properly called the Transformation of the Mind.

Questioner: Transformation of the mind into what?

Ra: I am Ra. As you observe Archetype Six you may see the student of the mysteries being transformed by the need to choose betwixt the light and the dark in mind.

Questioner: Would the Conqueror or Chariot then represent the culmination of the action of the first six archetypes into a conquering of the mental processes, even possibly removing the veil?

Ra: I am Ra. This is most perceptive. The Archetype Seven is one difficult to enunciate. We may call it the Path, the Way, or the Great Way of the Mind. Its foundation is a reflection and substantial summary of Archetypes One through Six.

One may also see the Way of the Mind as showing the kingdom or fruits of appropriate travel through the mind in that the mind continues to move as majestically through the material it conceives of as a chariot drawn by royal lions or steeds.

At this time we would suggest one more full query for this instrument is experiencing some distortions towards pain.

Questioner: Then I will just ask about the one of the archetypes which I am the least able to understand at this point if I can use that word at all. I am still very much in the dark, so to speak, in respect to the Hierophant and precisely what it is. Could you give me some other indication of what that is?

Ra: I am Ra. You have been most interested in the Significator which must needs become complex. The Hierophant is the original archetype of mind which has been made complex through the subtle movements of the conscious and unconscious. The complexities of mind were evolved rather than the simple melding of experience from Potentiator to Matrix.

The mind itself became an actor possessed of free will and, more especially, will. As the Significator of the mind, the Hierophant has the will to know, but what shall it do with its knowledge, and for what reasons does it seek? The potentials of a complex significator are manifold.

Are there any brief queries at this working?

Questioner: Only is there anything that we can do to make the instrument more comfortable or to improve the contact?

Ra: I am Ra. All is well. For some small portion of your future the instrument would be well advised to wear upon the hands those aids to comfort which it has neglected to use. There has been some trauma to both hands and arms and, therefore, we have had to somewhat abbreviate this working.

I am Ra. You are conscientious, my friends. We leave you in the love and in the light of the one infinite Creator. Go forth, therefore, rejoicing in the power and the peace of the One Glorious infinite Creator. Adonai. ☥

L/L Research is a subsidiary of Rock Creek Research & Development Laboratories, Inc.

P.O. Box 5195
Louisville, KY 40255-0195

L/L Research

www.llresearch.org

Rock Creek is a non-profit corporation dedicated to discovering and sharing information which may aid in the spiritual evolution of humankind.

INTENSIVE MEDITATION
FEBRUARY 25, 1982

(Unknown channeling)

I am Laitos, and am with this instrument. [I] greet you, as always, in the love and in the light of the one infinite Creator. We are happy, as always, to be allowed the chance to help those who seek to serve in the capacity of channels for [the] humble message of the Confederation. Each voice that is lent is greatly appreciated and aids more than can be hoped for. As each receives and speaks the words, the thoughts, each will in their own way express these as their store of *(inaudible)*. Each speaks as his orientation allows. Each channels vocabulary, background knowledge. Each has their own forms of expression, their own ways of conceiving the message that is transmitted to them. Each message may sound a bit different from one channel to another, but the differences in the presentation of the words are not as important as the basic meanings of the whole. While one may be able to use words not in your peoples' common vocabulary, they say no more than the one whose knowledge of words is small.

As each channel remains open, [flowing], that channel will speak an uncontaminated message in their own way. Each of those present at this time has totally different backgrounds, varying interests, individual phrases, mannerisms—yet each in their own way, style, is able to transmit the message they receive in more than acceptable clarity and preciseness. One may not feel they [are omitting] or changing the message if they do not use the words, the phrases, used by others. Each is unique, and each has their purpose. Each speaks, acts, in their own unique way. We are indeed privileged to have so many who actively seek to serve the channeling capacity within this group. We are privileged indeed to be able to work with you and any others seeking to serve as channels. We of Laitos are always at hand and will join with you in your meditations whenever asked. You need but call and we shall be with you.

I will leave you now, as always, in the love and the light. I am Laitos.

(Unknown channeling)

I am Hatonn, and greet you all in the love and in the light of the infinite Creator. We are honored to be asked to join your meditation this afternoon, and to offer ourselves in the capacity of answering questions which those present may have. May we at this time answer any questions?

Questioner: Hatonn, I think that the question that was on my mind was pretty well answered by Laitos. But I have been wondering about whether or not I was fully able to channel an acceptably unpolluted message. I have been having troubles recognizing your vibration and felt several times as I began to speak that a good contact had not been made. Have I been possibly picking up your presence as you attempted to contact another? And, if I have, when I spoke was I able to transmit the message fairly clearly?

I am Hatonn, and am aware of your question, my brother. To respond, may we say that as a new instrument which is gaining in experience, that you are progressing in a manner which is quite similar to other instruments along this similar path, shall we say. The quality or clarity of your transmission of those concepts which are sent to you is well within the range of acceptability. We may also say that your concern about the clarity of your contact is also well within the range of acceptability, for it is necessary to be aware that a contact can become, shall we say, swayed towards the bias of the one serving as instrument, but to be overly concerned in this area does then present problems of another nature. Those problems are more your current concern.

Specifically, we speak now of your doubt which has caused you some concern in the area of perceiving the initial contact, recognizing it, and beginning the transmission at what you consider the proper time. We would suggest that you set a certain level of conditioning which when reached would be your signal from the Confederation entity attempting contact that contact is now ready to be verbalized. The conditioning vibration can be provided in any degree of strength or frequency, shall we say. When you have experienced the strength of the vibration which will assure you that you have made a good contact, then simply speak without concern for that which will follow.

The desire to be an instrument, we have found, is the key ingredient in this process of channeling, as you call it. We have found also that being overly concerned about the success, shall we say, being demonstrated by the new instrument is that ingredient which is most detrimental to the steady development of a new instrument. The channeling process is in fact much more easily accomplished than most of your peoples believe. We speak now of those who are aware of the process. There is at all times when communication occurs among your peoples a channeling which occurs during these contacts. This process is simply refined so that your own memory bank, shall we say, and subconscious is blended in an harmonious fashion with our thoughts. To simply speak them and allow these thoughts to be verbalized is all that is necessary.

We realize, of course, that each time you endeavor to do this you are in fact playing the fool, for you are out on a limb, so to speak, without assurance that the limb will hold you. We can only suggest at this point in your development that you release your doubts and simply take part in the process. Speak the thoughts as you become aware of them and you shall clear the way for the thoughts which follow, and the limb shall indeed support you as it has thus far.

May we answer you further, my brother?

Questioner: No. Thank you. I do have one more thing. As I sit in meditation, especially when I'm channeling, I'm usually seeing various cloud-like shapes in front of me—sometimes in color, sometimes just dark shapes. But today as I was doing it, after several clouds of green went by, there was a small bright—it almost seemed like an opening that I could see. What was I experiencing?

I am Hatonn, and an aware of your question, my brother. To give you the specific nature and meaning of this experience would not be proper, in our estimation. We can only suggest that you investigate in further meditations the sensations that accompany such visual images, and let these sensations and images be the food for your further meditation, thereby opening, shall we say, yet another channel within your being for a fuller expression of that which seeks to make itself known to your conscious mind.

May we answer you further, my brother?

Questioner: No. Thank you very much.

I am Hatonn. Is there another question at this time?

Carla: I have a question. Would it be within the boundaries of the Law of Confusion for you to be able to give me some rough estimate of how many of this planetary population call the portion of the Confederation that is channeled at our Sunday night meditations and at Intensive meditations such as these?

I am Hatonn, and am aware of your question, my sister. We shall attempt a rough estimate of these figures, for it is quite harmless information. Your Sunday night, as you call them, meditations are more, shall we say, in line with the general Confederation philosophy, that being the transmission of the concept of the original Thought of the Creator which became that which you know of as the creation, and the need for meditation to gain knowledge of this thought, and the further need for the cultivation of love within the heart of each being. This type of calling is expressed by approximately six hundred million entities upon your planet. The type of calling which occurs during the normal intensive parts of your Sunday night meditation, that being the question and answer session as well as …

(Side one of tape ends.)

(Unknown channeling)

I am Hatonn, and am again with this instrument. To continue. The more intensive portions of your meditations represent a calling for that which may be described as wisdom, or light. The significantly representative portion of your planetary population which asks for this type of illumination [at all] approaches two hundred million of your peoples.

There are, in addition, a session when your meditation group is of such a configuration that entities of finer or, as you would say, higher vibrations are also called upon. This occurring most recently during your Christmas celebrations and meditations when the entire planetary population does, for a brief period, raise the mass vibration quite significantly.

May we answer you further, my sister?

Carla: Yes, please, Hatonn. This strengthens my feeling that it would be good to take advantage of the offer of one of our friends to attempt to make available some of the material from Sunday night meditations. Would we have the permission of you and all those members of the Confederation who speak to our group to publish this information? And edit it as necessary to remove mechanical portions of the content?

I am Hatonn, and am aware of your question, my sister. We of the Confederation are honored to share our simple and humble messages whenever requested, and we do so on a freely given basis, so to speak. What you choose to do with this information is completely your decision. Many simply bathe in the moment of the message only to be washed free of it shortly thereafter. Others choose to, shall we say, soak in more of the message so that it might be carried within the being. Yet others choose to take that which has become part of the being and radiate

it to others who have not had the opportunity of firsthand hearing, shall we say. The range of possibilities is quite wide. And we of the Confederation are quite pleased at any choice, and would gladly consent to any use which you might make of these humble offerings.

May we answer you further, my sister?

Carla: Yes, Hatonn. We of Rock Creek do not intend to be evangelistic in any way and will not attempt to push information such as this down anyone's throat, but merely to make it available to those who ask. We would like to know if it would be permissible for us to use your names, as you have given them to us, of your planetary being in the messages?

I am Hatonn, and once again, my sister, the choice is completely yours, for we have chosen certain names for the sole purpose of making ourselves known to you on a regular and recognizable basis. Names are not important for any other reason in our own estimation. Therefore, to use our name is quite acceptable.

May we answer you further, my sister?

Carla: No, thank you, Hatonn.

I am Hatonn. Is there another question at this time?

(Pause)

I am Hatonn. We have been greatly honored to have been asked to join our vibrations with yours during this meditation. We ask each present to remember that we are always available for such aid as we may give during your meditations. Simply request our presence and we shall gladly join you at the throne of the Creator. We leave you now at that throne and in the love and in the light of the one infinite Creator. We are Hatonn. Adonai, my friends. Adonai vasu borragus.

(Unknown channeling)

I am Oxal, and I greet you in the love and the light of the infinite Creator. It is a privilege to be with this meditation group. We take this opportunity to make the one known as C aware of our vibration. [We] will at this time condition this new instrument and give him the opportunity [to] speak a few words. Ours is not a wideband contact such as our brothers and sisters of Hatonn, and therefore reception is somewhat different. We will attempt not to cause discomfort in the contact. If discomfort is felt, please, mentally request adjustment. I am Oxal.

(C channeling)

I am Oxal, and I am now with this instrument. Our contact is somewhat discomforting to this instrument, but he wishes to fully experience our contact in order that he may more easily recognize us at another time. We are adjusting and now are able to ease some of the initial discomfort of contact. Our contact answers similarly to another this instrument has known, but [is centered] slightly different from the other he thinks he would confuse it with. We seldom speak, but we at times desire to speak when group configurations are such that our method of communicating the message of the Confederation is desired. We, as do all Confederation members, welcome the opportunity to make our vibration known to those who wish to act as what you call channels. We will work with this channel and will be with him when requested. We are known to you as Oxal. We will leave you now in love and light. Adonai, my friends. ☙

L/L RESEARCH

L/L Research is a subsidiary of Rock Creek Research & Development Laboratories, Inc.

P.O. Box 5195
Louisville, KY 40255-0195

www.llresearch.org

Rock Creek is a non-profit corporation dedicated to discovering and sharing information which may aid in the spiritual evolution of humankind.

ABOUT THE CONTENTS OF THIS TRANSCRIPT: This telepathic channeling has been taken from transcriptions of the weekly study and meditation meetings of the Rock Creek Research & Development Laboratories and L/L Research. It is offered in the hope that it may be useful to you. As the Confederation entities always make a point of saying, please use your discrimination and judgment in assessing this material. If something rings true to you, fine. If something does not resonate, please leave it behind, for neither we nor those of the Confederation would wish to be a stumbling block for any.

CAVEAT: This transcript is being published by L/L Research in a not yet final form. It has, however, been edited and any obvious errors have been corrected. When it is in a final form, this caveat will be removed.

FRIDAY NIGHT
FEBRUARY 26, 1982

(Carla channeling)

I am Hatonn, and I greet you, my brothers and sisters, in the love and the light of the Creator. My friends, my loved ones, it was with great pleasure that we shared the thoughts with which you opened your sharing, and it is the oneness of all of creation that is the objective toward which you strive. That oneness, my brothers and sisters, is contained within the love and the light described in those verses, for the light of the Creator is that from which all life, all energy, extends, and it is the love of that Creator that binds all together into a single unity.

The individual known to you as Jesus Christ, known to himself as Am Ne Ra, came to your race, to your planet, many of your years ago. He sought not to found a religion, a dynasty, or a kingdom on Earth but rather to be of service to those who sought to free themselves from the illusion that had begun to bind them so tightly. It may be said that this man was no greater than any other that has walked your planet, for his accomplishment was, in simple terms, to do that which he intended upon entering your density. My brothers, my sisters, was this not the same purpose for which you yourselves entered this density?

The accomplishment of setting oneself a task and striving toward its completion, although significant, does not place one beyond the realm within which the individual functions or has functioned. Rather, it more clearly defines the realm in which others of that race or density may accomplish their own set tasks, and more clearly illuminates the falsehood of accepting one's supposed limitations.

My friends, our purpose is not in saying these things to belittle the accomplishment of an individual, but rather to place it within a perspective, a perspective which we hope will enable you to understand that all of which he attained is within your grasp at this moment. He once said, "All of these things you shall do and more." Yet, most often it is convenient to ignore such statements as this, for they come uncomfortably close to reminding us of the truth of the understanding within our souls. It is far easier to establish a towering pedestal upon which to place such leaders, such lovers, far beyond our reach and far out of our sight, that we may not be uncomfortably reminded of our potential for attainment.

My friends, the possibility exists at this moment for each of you to destroy the pedestal, to realize that the accomplishments of this man and others like him who walked your planet are not safely out of reach and unattainable but rather within your grasp, within your attainment, for those individuals are yourselves and their attainment is your own. My friends, have confidence, have faith in yourselves. You are as that scripture stated, yourselves, Sons of

God, portions of the Creator, not merely children but each a unit of light within itself.

It is elsewhere said within that same book, my brothers, that the Creator formed each of you as a likeness of Himself. If this is true, my friends, then who but yourselves are responsible for what you have created? My friends, the temptation exists to point at others of accomplishment and say, "Yes, I will be like that some day, but not yet." Be like that today, my friends. I am Hatonn.

(Unknown channeling)

I am Laitos, and I greet you also, my brothers, in the love and the light of that Creator, of which we are all a part. It is our desire, dear friends, to share with you at this time our conditioning vibration that we may be of service in assisting the acquisition of a more effective meditational state. If there are those among you who would desire that we be of service in this manner, simple mentally request our assistance and we will be greatly honored to provide this small service. I am Laitos.

(Unknown channeling)

I am Latwii, and I greet you impatiently in the love and the light of the Creator. My brothers and sisters, now that our brothers of Hatonn and Laitos have performed their very worthy but time-consuming functions, it is now our turn to be of service, and we might add, to enjoy the pleasure of your company. At his time we would like to open the floor, so to speak, for any questions, for such is the service that is our honor and privilege to offer, even though our responses may not be as ponderous or dramatic as those of our brother, Hatonn.

Are there any questions?

S: I have some questions, but let me say that you are one of my favorite entities, and it's good to feel your thoughts again after such a break, as I call it, from the last times. To get to my questions. The first one is, Monday night, a week ago, I experienced astral projection, and it was either Monday or Tuesday night of this week I felt like I was in a classroom of some kind, learning things in which I only remembered two things, what I thought were two galaxies, Vale and Cyclops. Could you tell me if I was in a classroom trying to learn something?

I am Latwii. My brother, first we would express our appreciation for the affection that has enabled us to

attain placement within your "Top 40," so to speak. In answer to your question, my brother, if you were to reflect, would it occur to you that you have yet to leave the classroom?

May we answer you further?

S: Well, I understand your analogy that in my life here on Earth I'm here to learn lessons. I've always realized this even when I started learning more. But, could I have projected again and gone to a more specialized classroom away from Earth?

I am Latwii. My brother, the area within which you have chosen to invest your energies is the area which will attract fulfillment for your seeking. The experiences you describe are your own interpretation of learning experiences that are assembled or constructed to provide a functional analogy for your own purposes or meditation. It is difficult to ponder the subject of fruit without generating a mental image of one type of fruit or another upon which to focus one's attention. In a like manner, my brother, as it is your desire for education within this specific area, it is suitable that you should translate your learning experience into symbols that you are familiar with for the purpose of meditation and study.

May we answer you further?

S: Let me ponder that answer, and I may ask for clarification later. My second question is, the Tribunal of Saturn has always fascinated me, and along with the Guardians is there anything you can tell me now that in the past they have been unwilling to reveal to us?

I am Latwii. My brother, we must admit that these subjects fascinate us also, as they are a portion of our learning experience. An amount of difficulty lies in attempting to answer your question, for, if you will reflect, you will perceive that for you to answer truthfully about ongoing learning experiences within your own density is quite difficult, as it is not often until far later that you begin to develop a glimmer of understanding of what you were doing when you thought you knew what you were doing. The situation for ourselves as participants in our density in our response presents the same problem. It would be very difficult for us to describe to you what we think we're doing while we're doing it, for as with yourselves, we have not developed total awareness of our actions and intentions.

We are hesitant to offer information about conditions or events upon your own density. First, because we do not desire to establish biases within your perceptions. In addition, you must remember that our so-called predictions are simply evaluations of percentages and therefore always have a reluctance to come true 100% of the time.

On the subject of the Guardians, my brother, we are in all honesty at loss as to where to begin discussing them with one another within our density, for just as it is difficult for those of your density to attain understanding of our own, which is relatively close to your own, we find the Guardians to be quite difficult to understand for ourselves, which may be why we are within our density and they are within a much higher density. They do seem, we would estimate, to have a much higher level of development than our own. Beyond this, my brother, we can only say that we find great pleasure in studying them and their communications to us, in hopes that we may someday understand what they are trying to tell us.

May we answer you further?

S: No, that answers those pretty well, and I understand what you're trying to explain. Thank you.

We thank you, my brother, and we, in all humility, hope that at some point we will be able to understand what our teachers have been trying to explain to us. Is there another question?

(Pause)

I am Latwii. The silence in the room indicates either that all questions have been answered or that our eloquence has stricken you speechless. Rather than attempt to determine which of the two it is, we will simply accept the compliment and bid you all a loving farewell.

My brothers, my sisters, it is the message of all of our brothers and sisters of the Federation that our services are available at any time, at any place; that there is no task or unit of time that is too small to be worth our attention. It is our desire to be of service in our small ways, and we await the honor and privilege of your request for that service. My friends, we bid you adonai. I am Latwii.

(Carla channeling)

I am Nona. There is present within this group a strong desire for a healing, and we come in the love and the light of the Creator in answer to that calling. If [there are] those desiring to see loved ones blessed with our healing vibration or desire that for themselves, we ask that you offer a brief prayer for that person's healing, and then picture that person as whole and complete.

(Tape ends.) ♣

L/L Research

L/L Research is a subsidiary of Rock Creek Research & Development Laboratories, Inc.

P.O. Box 5195
Louisville, KY 40255-0195

www.llresearch.org

Rock Creek is a non-profit corporation dedicated to discovering and sharing information which may aid in the spiritual evolution of humankind.

ABOUT THE CONTENTS OF THIS TRANSCRIPT: This telepathic channeling has been taken from transcriptions of the weekly study and meditation meetings of the Rock Creek Research & Development Laboratories and L/L Research. It is offered in the hope that it may be useful to you. As the Confederation entities always make a point of saying, please use your discrimination and judgment in assessing this material. If something rings true to you, fine. If something does not resonate, please leave it behind, for neither we nor those of the Confederation would wish to be a stumbling block for any.

The Law of One, Book IV, Session 80
February 27, 1982

Ra: I am Ra. We greet you in the love and in the light of the one infinite Creator.

Before we initiate this working we would wish to correct an error which we have found in previous material. That Archetype Five which you have called the Hierophant is the Significator of the Mind complex.

This instrument is prey to sudden flares towards the distortion known as pain. We are aware of your conscientious attempts to aid the instrument but know of no other modality available to the support group other than the provision of water therapy upon the erect spinal portion of the physical body complex, which we have previously mentioned.

This instrument's distortions of body do not ever rule out, shall we say, such flares during these periods of increased distortion of the body complex. Our contact may become momentarily garbled. Therefore, we request that any information which seems garbled be questioned as we wish this contact to remain as undistorted as the limitations of language, mentality, and sensibility allow.

We communicate now.

Questioner: Thank you. Could you please give me the condition of the instrument?

Ra: I am Ra. This instrument is experiencing mild fluctuations of the physical energy complex which are causing sudden changes from physical energy deficit to some slight physical energy. This is due to

many, what you may call, prayers and affirmations offered to and by the instrument offset by continual greetings whenever it is feasible by the fifth-density entity of whom you are aware.

In other respects, the instrument is in the previously stated condition.

Questioner: I had to leave the room for a forgotten item after we performed the banishing ritual. Did this have a deleterious effect on the ritual or the working?

Ra: I am Ra. Were it the only working the lapse would have been critical. There is enough residual energy of a protective nature in this place of working that this lapse, though quite unrecommended, does not represent a threat to the protection which the ritual of which you spoke offers.

Questioner: Has our fifth-density visitor been less able to affect the instrument during our more recent workings?

Ra: I am Ra. We shall answer in two parts. Firstly, during the workings themselves the entity has been bated to a great extent. Secondly, in the general experiential circumstances of your space/time experience this fifth-density entity is able to greet this entity with the same effectiveness upon the physical body complex as always since the inception of its contact with your group. This is due to the several physical complex distortions of the instrument.

However, the instrument has become more mentally and spiritually able to greet this entity with love thereby reducing the element of fear which is an element the entity counts as a great weapon in the attempt to cause cessation, in any degree, of the Ra contact.

Questioner: What is the reason for the fact that the entity is able to act through physical distortions that are already present as opposed to being unable to act upon an entity who has no physical distortion at all?

Ra: I am Ra. The key to this query is the term, distortion. Any distortion, be it physical, mental, or spiritual in complex nature, may be accentuated by the suggestion of one able to work magically; that is, to cause changes in consciousness. This entity has many physical distortions. Each in the group has various mental distortions. Their nature varies. The less balanced the distortion by self-knowledge, the more adeptly the entity may accentuate such a distortion in order to mitigate against the smooth functioning and harmony of the group.

Questioner: As Ra well knows, the information that we accumulate here will be illuminating to a very minor percentage of those who populate this planet simply because there are very few people who can understand it. However, it seems that our fifth-density visitor is, shall we say, dead set against this communication. Can you tell me why this is so important to him since it is of such a limited effect, I would guess, upon the harvest of this planet?

Ra: I am Ra. Purity does not end with the harvest of third density. The fidelity of Ra towards the attempt to remove distortions is total. This constitutes an acceptance of responsibility for service-to-others which is of relative purity. The instrument through which we speak and its support group have a similar fidelity and, disregarding any inconvenience to self, desire to serve others. Due to the nature of the group the queries made to us by the group have led rapidly into somewhat abstruse regions of commentary. This content does not mitigate against the underlying purity of the contact. Such purity is as a light. Such an intensity of light attracts attention.

Questioner: What would our fifth-density visitor hope to gain for himself if he were to be successful in eliminating this contact?

Ra: I am Ra. As we have previously stated, the entity hopes to gain a portion of that light; that is, the

mind/body/spirit complex of the instrument. Barring this, the entity intends to put out the light.

Questioner: I understand this up to a point and that point is if the entity were successful in either of these attempts of what value would this be to him? Would it increase his ability? Would it increase his polarity? By what mechanism would it do whatever it does?

Ra: I am Ra. Having attempted, for some of your space/time with no long-lasting result, to do these things the entity may be asking this question of itself. The gain for triumph is an increase in negative polarity to the entity in that it has removed a source of radiance and, thereby, offered to this space/time the opportunity of darkness where there once was light. In the event that it succeeded in enslaving the mind/body/spirit complex of the instrument it would have enslaved a fairly powerful entity, thus adding to its power.

Questioner: I am sorry for my lack of penetration of these mechanisms and I apologize for some rather stupid questions, but I think we have here a point that is somewhat central to what we are presently attempting to understand. Some of my next questions may be almost unacceptably stupid, but I will attempt to try to understand what this power that our visitor seeks is and how he uses it. It seems to me that this is central to the mind and its evolution.

As our visitor increases his power through these works, what is the power that he increases? Can you describe it?

Ra: I am Ra. The power of which you speak is a spiritual power. The powers of the mind, as such, do not encompass such works as these. You may, with some fruitfulness, consider the possibilities of moonlight. You are aware that we have described the Matrix of the Spirit as a Night. The moonlight, then, offers either a true picture seen in shadow or chimera and falsity. The power of falsity is deep as is the power to discern truth from shadow. The shadow of hidden things is an infinite depth in which is stored the power of the one infinite Creator.

The adept, then, is working with the power of hidden things illuminated by that which can be false or true. To embrace falsity, to know it, and to seek it, and to use it gives a power that is most great. This is the nature of the power of your visitor and may shed some light upon the power of one who seeks in order to serve others as well, for the missteps in the night are oh! so easy.

Questioner: Are you saying, then, that this power is of the spirit and not of the mind or of the body?

Ra: I am Ra. The work of the adept is based upon previous work with the mind and the body, else work with the spirit would not be possible on a dependable basis. With this comment we may assert the correctness of your assumption.

Questioner: The fifteenth archetype is the Matrix of the Spirit and has been called the Devil. Can you tell me why that is so?

Ra: I am Ra. We do not wish to be facile in such a central query, but we may note that the nature of the spirit is so infinitely subtle that the fructifying influence of light upon the great darkness of the spirit is very often not as apparent as the darkness itself. The progress chosen by many adepts becomes a confused path as each adept attempts to use the Catalyst of the Spirit. Few there are which are successful in grasping the light of the sun. By far, the majority of adepts remain groping in the moonlight and, as we have said, this light can deceive as well as uncover hidden mystery. Therefore, the melody, shall we say, of this matrix often seems to be of a negative and evil, as you would call it, nature.

It is also to be noted that an adept is one which has freed itself more and more from the constraints of the thoughts, opinions, and bonds of other-selves. Whether this is done for service to others or service to self, it is a necessary part of the awakening of the adept. This freedom is seen by those not free as what you would call evil or black. The magic is recognized; the nature is often not.

Questioner: Could I say, then, that implicit in the process of becoming adept is the seeming polarization towards service to self because the adept becomes disassociated with many of his kind?

Ra: I am Ra. This is likely to occur. The apparent happening is disassociation whether the truth is service to self and thus true disassociation from other-selves or service-to-others and thus true association with the heart of all other-selves and disassociation only from the illusory husks which prevent the adept from correctly perceiving the self and other-self as one.

Questioner: Then you say that this effect of disassociation on the service-to-others adept is a stumbling block or slowing process in reaching that goal to which he aspires? Is this correct?

Ra: I am Ra. This is incorrect. This disassociation from the miasma of illusion and misrepresentation of each and every distortion is a quite necessary portion of an adept's path. It may be seen by others to be unfortunate.

Questioner: Then is this, from the point of view of the fifteenth archetype, somewhat of an excursion into the Matrix of the Spirit in this process? Does that make any sense?

Ra: I am Ra. The excursion of which you speak and the process of disassociation is most usually linked with that archetype you call Hope which we would prefer to call Faith. This archetype is the Catalyst of the Spirit and, because of the illuminations of the Potentiator of the Spirit, will begin to cause these changes in the adept's viewpoint.

Questioner: I didn't intend to get too far ahead of my questioning process here. The positively or negatively polarized adept, then, is building a potential to draw directly on the spirit for power. Is this correct?

Ra: I am Ra. It would be more proper to say that the adept is calling directly through the spirit to the universe for its power, for the spirit is a shuttle.

Questioner: The only obvious significant difference, I believe, between the positive and negative adepts in using this shuttle is the way they polarize. Is there a relationship between the archetypes of the spirit and whether the polarization is either positive or negative? Is, for instance, the positive calling through the sixteenth archetype and the negative calling through the fifteenth archetype? I am very confused about this and I imagine that that question is either poor or meaningless. Can you answer that?

Ra: I am Ra. It is a challenge to answer such a query, for there is some confusion in its construction. However, we shall attempt to speak upon the subject.

The adept, whether positive or negative, has the same Matrix. The Potentiator is also identical. Due to the Catalyst of each adept the adept may begin to pick and choose that into which it shall look further. The Experience of the Spirit, that which you have called the Moon, is then, by far, the more manifest of influences upon the polarity of the adept. Even the most unhappy of experiences, shall we say, which seem to occur in the Catalyst of the adept, seen from the viewpoint of the spirit, may, with the discrimination possible in shadow, be worked with until light equaling the light of brightest noon descends upon the adept and positive or service-to-others illumination has occurred. The service-to-self adept will satisfy itself with the shadows and, grasping the light of day, will toss back the head in grim laughter, preferring the darkness.

Questioner: I guess the nineteenth archetype of the spirit would be the Significator of the Spirit. Is that correct?

Ra: I am Ra. This is correct.

Questioner: How would you describe the Significator of the Spirit?

Ra: I am Ra. In answer to the previous query we set about doing just this. The Significator of the Spirit is that living entity which either radiates or absorbs the love and the light of the one infinite Creator, radiates it to others or absorbs it for the self.

Questioner: Then would this process of radiation or absorption, since we have what I would call a flux or flux rate, be the measure of the adept?

Ra: I am Ra. This may be seen to be a reasonably adequate statement.

Questioner: Then for the twentieth archetype I'm guessing that this is the Transformation of the Spirit, possibly analogous to the sixth-density merging of the paths. Is this in any way correct?

Ra: I am Ra. No.

Questioner: Sorry about that. Can you tell me what the twentieth archetype would be?

Ra: I am Ra. That which you call the Sarcophagus in your system may be seen to be the material world, if you will. This material world is transformed by the spirit into that which is infinite and eternal. The infinity of the spirit is an even greater realization than the infinity of consciousness, for consciousness which has been disciplined by will and faith is that consciousness which may contact intelligent infinity directly. There are many things which fall away in the many, many steps of adepthood. We, of Ra, still

walk these steps and praise the one infinite Creator at each transformation.

Questioner: Then I would guess that the twenty-first archetype would represent contact with intelligent infinity. Is that correct?

Ra: I am Ra. This is correct, although one may also see the reflection of this contact as well as the contact with intelligent energy which is the Universe or, as you have called it somewhat provincially, the World.

Questioner: Then by this contact also with intelligent energy can you give me an example of what this would be for both the contact with intelligent infinity and the contact with intelligent energy? Could you give me an example of what type of experience this would result in, if that is at all possible?

Ra: I am Ra. This shall be the last query of this working of full length. We have discussed the possibilities of contact with intelligent energy, for this energy is the energy of the Logos, and thus it is the energy which heals, builds, removes, destroys, and transforms all other-selves as well as the self.

The contact with intelligent infinity is most likely to produce an unspeakable joy in the entity experiencing such contact. If you wish to query in more detail upon this subject, we invite you to do so in another working. Is there a brief query before we close this working?

Questioner: Is there anything that we can do to improve the contact or to make the instrument more comfortable?

Ra: I am Ra. The alignments are most conscientious. We are appreciative. The entity which serves as instrument is somewhat distorted towards that condition you call stiffness of the dorsal regions. Manipulation would be helpful.

I am Ra. I leave you, my friends, glorying in the light and the love of the one infinite Creator. Go forth, therefore, rejoicing in the power and in the peace of the one infinite Creator. Adonai. ✦

L/L Research is a subsidiary of
Rock Creek Research &
Development Laboratories, Inc.

P.O. Box 5195
Louisville, KY 40255-0195

L/L RESEARCH

www.llresearch.org

Rock Creek is a non-profit
corporation dedicated to
discovering and sharing
information which may aid in
the spiritual evolution of
humankind.

SUNDAY MEDITATION
FEBRUARY 28, 1982

(Unknown channeling)

[I am Hatonn.] This evening *(inaudible)* which is somewhat difficult to approach within the context of your daily lives within the illusion which you now experience. You experience each entity *(inaudible)* as one simple *(inaudible)* you experience the creation as something separate, and above all my friends, you experience portions of yourself as being separate from each other.

In one of your Holy Books, the situation was described which has been called by your peoples, "The Transfiguration." The teacher known to you as Jesus was seen to be illuminated, brightened, as those about this teacher heard a voice that said, "This is my beloved Son, listen to him."

My friends, as you progress in your search to find your own relationship to the Creator, you must at one point along the way come to grips with the fact that within you lies a portion of that same consciousness which the one known as Jesus exemplified.

You must then be able at some point to see that every individual has that same relationship to the Creator, and that the creation itself—wood and flower, bird and bush—are sons and daughters of the Creator.

But, my friends, do you listen to the Creator when It speaks to us? This is the great important part of experience, that is, the opportunity to listen. We have followed your *(inaudible)*.

As we were saying … to listen, to inwardly digest, and to transfer each word, thought and vision you see into that which shows you a face, an aspect of the one infinite Creator. How difficult it is *(inaudible)* to change your perceptions, for your illusion is a harsh one. It is nearly impossible to believe that the entities seated within this domicile are all one being, for can you not touch each other and feel the difference between you? Can you not speak together and never know the outcome until it has already been manifested? And yet, my friends, this very experience is an experience of unity. And if you can maintain the overview that you are indeed speaking to yourself, that you, as a portion of the creation, speak only to other portions of the creation, transformation of your life will occur as what you call time reveals to you the beauty and the harmony of those about you of the creation. And most of all, my friends, of yourself.

It is easier for many of you to see the beauty of *(inaudible)*, to appreciate the radiance of perfection of another's being than to appreciate the perfection of your own. How many times this day have you been dissatisfied not with others, my friends, but with yourself?

And yet, the voice said, "This is my son, listen to Him." Listen to yourself, my friends, as well as to all the profound works of inspiration; all those others and all of creation. Listen to your body, listen to your mind, listen to your seeking, and find the unity and the perfection at the heart of all these things. And try to be pleased with the portion of creation that is yourself.

Please do not [cease], my friends, to open yourself up to the radiance that lies waiting for the one who has ceased quibbling with the self and has instead offered the self, imperfect as though it may seem, to the Creator, as a channel for love, *(inaudible)*.

At this time, *(inaudible)*, and therefore we shall close through this instrument. We thank the one known as *(inaudible)* for his service, and will be with him again.

(Unknown channeling)

[I am Hatonn.] My friends, to remain in this illusion is such a waste of your time. Even with your physical eyes you can see such a vastness of space, of light, of beauty. And within yourself you can find such imagination what will take you on voyages far beyond this illusion. May we suggest that you continue to discipline yourself to remove yourself from this illusion, from the needs of eating and sleeping and providing that with which you purchase those things you may need. May we suggest that you enter meditation with joy, for it is a freedom that you may never find within this illusion.

Time is a prison. Space, a jail. All these things that your, as you would call it, society expects of you are the warden's clanking of keys as they walk past your cell. Even those that love you the most expect things of you, and you expect things of them. And so, in small ways, you within your evolution are jailed and act as jailer, putting those about you in prisons of your expectations. This, my friends, is for a reason.

You have elected to enter into a very valuable personal relationship that you might gain experience. My friends, do not let this experience go to waste. Do not remain in prison. Not in thought, and not in action. Go instead, into that infinite space, that infinite time which is the kingdom.

Meditate and listen [to] all those things which can be imagined to be more beautiful, more full of fine quality, more happy than you can within the prison describe. Now open yourselves too. And you shall be in a goodly company. For many there are who dream the dream of the Creator. *(Inaudible)*.

I am known to you as Hatonn. And I leave you in that love, that light, that freedom I mentioned. I leave you in unity, the unity of the one Creator of which each is an infinitively valuable *(inaudible)*.

(Unknown channeling)

I am Latwii, and I greet each of you in the love and the light of the one infinite Creator. We are always happy to be asked to perform what simple tasks we might in conjunction with your call. This evening we find a simpler task for our, shall we say, ping-pong partner is not present. Therefore, we have only one target for the evening. May we at this time ask if there might be a question which we could attempt to answer?

Questioner: Yes, tonight as Carla channeled I felt Hatonn's presence very strongly *(inaudible)* and really do not feel the *(inaudible)* to the degree that I should be able to channel but when the attempt was made to transfer, the contact was lost. As Carla began to channel again, I once again felt the presence of the conditioning and at this moment [am] still experiencing the conditioning. Could you please explain the role Latwii plays in the ability to channel?

I am Latwii, and I am aware of your question, my brother. In this regard may we say that when we speak of the many variations in the levels of consciousness of your peoples, we speak of an area which is infinite in its range. That which you experience as your conscious waking state seems by most accounts to be quite homogeneous. But upon careful observation, it is discovered that this state does contain within the seeming homogeneity many ranges of perception. These are a result of the interactions of the self with other selves and the Creator's universe which results, as we have hinted, in different levels of perception. Which is another way of saying the sharpness of your perception may be influenced by what you have called fatigue, the fatigue having been created by the experience of the self on levels. This evening you have experienced yet another level of perception, another interaction of the fatigue or the wear of your experience upon your consciousness. When you attempt to be that which you have called an instrument to channel the words, the concepts, of Confederation entities, you, shall we say, zero in on a particular frequency, that which is used to communicate the thoughts by, in this case, the entities known as Hatonn.

You have experienced the subtler level of fatigue that is a result of an inner seeking, a desire to know the finer levels of the self, the finer levels of the Creator and to blend this seeking in an effort to serve as an instrument for Confederation contact. Your own inner seeking does therefore at times provide you with the experiences which are necessary for your inner growth, but which may also at times provide a certain fatiguing of that same inner channel that is used both for the inner seeking and the contact with Confederation entities.

This inner channel is exercised many times during your waking consciousness and your, shall we say, less conscious or sleeping periods as well. And its exercise may create a certain fatigue of which the conscious mind is not completely aware. It is not a matter of great concern, it is more frequently experienced by the new instrument and may be allowed to run its course without concern and upon the next attempt at contact may be completely absent. It is, shall we say, a random effect which you have experienced this evening. The entities of Hatonn are continuing their work with you by providing their conditioning vibration so that you might be assured that their vibration has been perceived by your instrument and shall be available to you at any time in what you call your future.

May we answer you further, my brother?

Questioner: Not on that particular subject. But I do have something that is troubling me, it has been for the last few weeks. I've been experiencing periods of depression, and periods of inability to interact in anything near a harmonious way to the people around me. I know I've not been following a rigorous program of meditation. At times I've let it slip altogether. But, here this last week when I did attempt to sit and meditate, I've come out of it feeling tired, and in a worse frame of mind than when I sat down to begin. I know, that of late, I've been shutting myself off quite frequently, as if something inside is slowly rebelling, at least momentarily rebelling against an influx of outside stimulus, and not until today have I experienced any form of inner peace. I'd like, if you will say some words on my mistakes in my current meditations, and if you would say a few words on dealing with that state of mind we refer to as depression.

I am Latwii, and I am aware of your question, my brother. First of all, may we say that in truth there can be no mistakes, for this illusion you find yourself within, each of you, is an experience which has the purpose of teaching. Each of you, in some way, seeks to learn the lessons of love. These lessons, in the particular case of which you now speak, concern learning to love the self. Learning to accept the self, as the self is and expresses daily. Learning to forgive the self, for that which is felt to be less than desired. The state of mind which you call depression is simply the realization consciously, [that] the self has not been accepted.

Again we say, there are no mistakes. You have each moment that you experience in your daily round of activities an opportunity to see yourself in many reflections, to see yourself [in] the faces of those you meet. To see yourself in the activity which you undertake. To see yourself within your own mind and your own heart. To accept yourself, to love yourself, to know that at the core of your being lies perfection, lies the creation, lies the infinite love and light that binds all of creation. You have presented to you, with each waking moment, an infinite array of opportunities to see this unity of self evolve. In order to see that unity, it is most frequently necessary to first be presented with the illusion of separateness, the illusion of the self which is not perfect, the illusion of the self which is filled with mistakes, and the illusion of the feeling and inability to accept the self.

To learn the lesson most fully, to drive it the deepest within the heart of your being, it is necessary first to experience the opposite of what is true, the illusion of imperfection of separateness. In your meditations, attempt then to see the perfection of being, attempt to see how each opportunity you have encountered, each thought of a depressing nature you have welcomed, has presented you an opportunity both ways, as imperfect and as perfect. See the choices that you have made, and *(inaudible)* have been swayed towards the imperfect; see then the opportunity for the perfection. For does not each opportunity teach? Have you not noticed each opportunity's lessons? Indeed, you have. For you have noted your own failures, as you call them. But look at them in another light.

Have they not shown you the depth of your being, the range of your feelings? The possibilities of your learning? To be alive and aware in your illusion is a state of mind and perception which few among your people enjoy. For they have been, shall we say, deadened to the world about them, and the world within them. Therefore, rejoice in the feelings which surge within your being, and see therefore the other side of the illusion which is the truth of your own perfection, your oneness, and the love/light that dwells with you. Attempt then, in your waking hours to continue the feeling you develop in your meditations so that a new light is shed on the experiences which you encounter. Do not forget you can have it an illusion. Do not forget it has but one purpose, to teach that you are whole, and perfect, acceptable, and loved.

May we answer you further, my brother?

Questioner: No, thank you very much. I do have one more question, then I'll be through. I know that when I do meditate, I have a definite distraction. The cause, as I go deeper and deeper into mediation, I attempt to leave my body to some degree to come to the point where I enjoy the experience, the feelings of the separation, no matter how slight. But I know this has a draining effect on me. Any suggestion on how to better center my thoughts so that [I will] not as often make the attempt for the separation?

I am Latwii, and I am aware of your question, my brother. We feel that you have yourself discovered the key to this, being very simply the centering of the self in separation for one purpose, and one purpose alone. To do more than one thing when you meditate is to split your consciousness and your effort so that you do neither thing well.

Therefore, we would suggest that at those times which you wish to use for the centering of the self, the seeking of the one Creator, in the quiet, the peacefulness, the heart of your being, that you attempt no other activity at this time. That if at another time you wish to attempt those activities which you have described as the separating of the bodies that this be done at another time. We do not suggest that great emphasis be placed upon, shall we say, the tricks of your illusion or your ability to manipulate the bodies. This is, shall we say, a side effect, random in nature, which of itself provides but little catalyst for the learning of the love of the creation and of the self.

May we answer you further, my brother?

(No further query.)

I am Latwii. We thank you greatly. Is there another question at this time?

(Pause)

(Unknown channeling)

I am Latwii, and am with this instrument. We have been most honored to be able to share a few of our simple thoughts with this group this evening. We look forward to such engagements with glee and hopeful anticipation for few are the times which we are able to join our vibrations with your peoples. We find a great and special excitement and opportunity at such times, for we learn as much if not more as do each of you during each of the occasions. For it is our special pleasure and privilege to see within each entity gathered here this evening a fuller, a deeper, and a richer array of the Creator's handiwork and unique expression, and this always brings up joy. We leave each of you and this group at this time, in that joy and the love and the light of the one infinite Creator. We are known to you as Latwii. Adonai, my friends. Adonai. ✣

L/L RESEARCH

L/L Research is a subsidiary of
Rock Creek Research &
Development Laboratories, Inc.

P.O. Box 5195
Louisville, KY 40255-0195

www.llresearch.org

Rock Creek is a non-profit
corporation dedicated to
discovering and sharing
information which may aid in
the spiritual evolution of
humankind.

FRIDAY NIGHT
MARCH 5, 1982

(Unknown channeling)

I am Hatonn. I greet you, my brothers and sisters, in the love and light of the infinite Creator. My friends, as always, it is a great pleasure to be amongst you once again to be able to share with you our thoughts, our advice, imperfect though it may be. It is a great service to us on your part to allow us to attempt service in return.

My friends, tonight we would share with you a small story concerning a lamb which had strayed from the flock, from its mother, from the shepherd whose efforts to ensure the lamb's safety within the flock were circumvented by the lamb's curiosity. You see, my friends, the lamb, realizing that among the flock there was simply retracing the steps already covered by those around it, chose to wander further and further toward the edge of the flock, seeking experience beyond what could be and often was narrated by its elders.

Eventually, as the lamb progressed toward the edge of the flock, the lamb began to notice that those around seemed to be somewhat different than those at the core. They were sheep, it was true, but they were of a more unencumbered nature. Their seeking for the close, shoulder to shoulder relationship that sheep seem to enjoy was less prevalent, and often one would stop, snatch a bite, look about a moment and have to gallop to regain the safety of the flock.

Indeed, those at the perimeter were a different breed of sheep.

But the lamb was not satisfied with a mere change of scenery, so to speak, and upon reaching the edge of the flock, chose to continue beyond the flock, beyond the shepherd, beyond all of that which was known and familiar. Gradually, the sound of the flock diminished, and the lamb was alone, having abandoned its past. Perhaps at this point, one would assume that the lamb should be afraid, for it's well known that the Earth contains those which would prey upon one another or upon the innocent, upon those which would try and extend themselves beyond the edge of the flock. Yet the lamb, possessing the wise *naiveté* of the fool, was not troubled, for the lamb simply sought to know.

My friends, at this point, in your minds we find the question concerning the eventual conclusion of our story. We wonder what happened to the lamb. My friends, the lamb is still wandering further and further from the crowded security it left behind where the decisions are made by caretakers. My friends, the lambs within your souls seek only to learn, and it is that craving for knowledge, for new experience with which to grow, that has brought you here this night. There is a meekness in knowledge, my friends, for an early and constant lesson upon that path is the awareness that one's knowledge is sorely lacking. The path extends ever onward to that knowledge that is without end.

One might ask, "To what purpose do we wander that path if there is no reward at the end, no pot of gold at the terminus of our rainbow. Why should we leave the flock? Is it not safer within the confinement of the crowd? Are we not protected from those that would prey upon us?" My friends, you are wanderers of the path, and to do other than that would betray your real nature. Accept this in yourselves and be not afraid, for though the predators exist, so also does that force within your world that knows of each bird in flight, of each tree desiring to bloom, of each flower striving through the soil toward the sun.

My friends, follow your path consciously and joyfully, and if you find other lambs upon your path be grateful for the God that walks beside you, for each of you, my friends, is of the Creator, is a facet, a particle of that which you call God, and each of you follow that path which guides you back to your Creator self, my friends.

At this time our brothers and sisters of Latwii desire to offer to assist you in your meditation. If those of you desiring this service would simply relax and within your minds offer a request for the vibrations of our brothers and sisters of Latwii, they will pass among you and be honored to perform their service. I am Hatonn.

(Unknown channeling)

I am Latwii, and we greet you, our brothers and sisters, in the love and light of the infinite Creator. My friends, it is with great honor that we take credit for the work performed by our brothers of Laitos. However, we would remind this instrument that although our names are similar, our functions are somewhat different, and that the vibrations imparted by our brother Laitos are much more effectively administered if the instrument would concentrate more fully, and get our names correctly.

Now then, we are, of course, present to perform our unworthy service of attempting to answer your questions. This is a role we enjoy because not only are we afforded the opportunity of sharing conversation with yourselves whom we find much more lively than some of our more overly serious brothers and sisters of other densities, but also we receive the opportunity of learning through the verbal interchange. So, without further ado, we

would offer ourselves for this service. Are there any questions which we may undertake to answer tonight?

Questioner: *(Inaudible).*

I am Latwii. My brother, we would assay the pun that no light can be shed, since all of Creation sheds its own light. However, we would attempt to answer your question in this fashion. There are a number of Federation members whose services are very specific in that they receive the honor of being assigned to working with specific individuals or very small groups of individuals, some of those being on your planet. A number of these Federation members are involved in working on your planet. Some of those are of the group you mentioned.

May we answer further?

Questioner: *(Inaudible).*

I am Latwii. My brother, we are somewhat at a loss to respond to your question, in that we would humbly suggest it was somewhat vaguely phrased, and we are reluctant to offer unrequested information. Would it be possible to more accurately phrase your question?

Questioner: *(Inaudible).*

I am Latwii. I am aware of your question. My brother, a difficulty encountered in the contacts which you refer to as "kindling" are that the instruments have certain biases that open the instrument to confusion of communication or the interjection of inaccurate material by entities who would seek to confuse or disrupt the message being conveyed. It is not on our agenda, so to speak, to conduct any landings at this time. The process which you described as "energy rings" is unfamiliar to us in the context with which your question was posed. We would offer the suggestion that perhaps the communication was misunderstood.

May we answer you further?

Questioner: *(Inaudible).*

I am Latwii. My brother, your perception is excellent. We would, as a friend, also remind you that we ourselves, being less than infallible, should also be taken with a grain of salt, to use your phrase. Our intention is to be of service, but we desire to perform the service of a loving advisor, not as an oracle which would accurately define your future for you or save you the difficulty of performing your own learning.

May we answer you further?

Questioner: *(Inaudible).*

As always, my brother, we thank you. Is there another question?

(Pause)

I am Latwii. We of Latwii are aware that there are questions of a more personal nature, as this instrument would say, which some present would desire answered, but are hesitant to verbalize. It is our desire to be of service, however, it is not our desire to force the issue. At this time we would once more offer ourselves as willing to attempt to respond to any questions which you may desire to verbalize.

S: I did have another question. *(Mostly inaudible. There was an analogy made between a book having to do with a being called the Watcher and the Guardians.)*

I am Latwii. My brother, we sincerely and deeply wish that we could answer your question, for questions like that are to an extent objects of our own learning process. The Guardians to us are primarily an unknown. They are entities which perform the service to us of assisting in our learning experience, and, as you may surmise, are at this time beyond our intellectual grasp.

We would suggest, however, that the image which you interpret as the Guardians, or as you refer to it, as the Watcher, is one that is prevalent within the subconscious mind of your gradually developing social memory complex. It is an archetypical concept which stems from a subconscious awareness that each of us as the Creator stands in a position of the overseer of Creation, an overseer who would find it possible to alter facets of the illusion within which the individual learns its lesson but realizes that to do so would be improper. A comparable term to your Watcher might be the expression "oversoul" or "higher self."

May we answer you further?

S: *(Inaudible).*

I am Latwii. My brother, the Guardians are entities who are far more fully self-realized than our humble selves, and therefore are beyond our current conscious understanding. We would suggest to you

that quite often your own understanding or interpretation of our advice stems from your subconscious, and the process of subsequent meditation upon the subjects of your interest would be quite beneficial to a more [full] understanding.

May we answer you further?

S: No, thank you.

Again, we thank you, my brother. Is there another question?

A: *(Inaudible).*

I am Latwii. My sister, we thank you for the opportunity to attempt to answer your questions, for we know the difficulty that your striving has encountered lately. To borrow an expression from this instrument, we would remind you that life is but a dream. It is possible within your illusion to exist within a very unconscious state that is sadly characteristic of a substantial number of your race. This state of existence, my sister, is analogous to the type of dreams within which a certain amount of entertainment is derived, similar to that produced from your video communication devices, and we would advise that one not take this type of dream too seriously, for its purpose is simply to entertain the mind as you sleep.

There are other types of dreams, however, just as there are other manners in which one may function consciously within the illusion within which you exist. For example, in a group such as this there are individuals who attempt to be conscious of the manner within which they perform their daily tasks, seeking both polarization and catalysts that they may advance upon the path of learning and polarization. These types of lives are analogous to those types of dreams within which specific types of work are performed under the direction of the higher self seeking to provide growth at the request of that portion of the mind/body/spirit complex which you might refer to as the conscious mind or the striving.

Other dreams also perform service to the individual, such as those dreams within which a catalyst may be provided, such as communication from entities such as Federation members, resulting from a calling within the individual that the individual may not be quite conscious of but nonetheless is communicating. These dreams being of a semiconscious point of origin, are in themselves less fully remembered, and often possess a very vague and indistinct memory trace after the mind/body/spirit complex has reawakened within the physical illusion.

May we answer you further?

A: *(Inaudible).*

I am Latwii. My sister, your terminology is beautifully precise. The calmness is resultant from the vibration experience during the learning process, the confusion resultant from the fact that the subconscious was the major recipient of the educational process.

We would also add that there is a further range of dreams that are generally referred to as nightmares among your race. These, in the same manner, may be the result of an entertainment of the mind or the result of an unpolarized individual requesting contact with a polarized entity whose vibrations they rapidly find very uncomfortable.

May we answer you further?

A: *(Inaudible).*

I am Latwii. My sister, we would suggest that the most effective manner within which one may receive communication that is consciously requested would be through the active use of the conscious mind in the area of meditation. The function of sleep in part is to assist those who do not have adequate control of the conscious mind to receive such communication. This is a facet of the sleep tool which you may desire to use, but we have found that the conscious awake mental meditational state is a much more precise form of communication and reception, and we would highly recommend its usage for conscious calling.

May we answer you further?

A: *(Inaudible).*

As always, my sister, we are grateful to be of service to one such as yourself.

Is there another question that we may answer?

(Pause)

I am Latwii. It seems that either the questions have been sufficiently answered or the previous discussion has managed to instill the dream state in all present. In either case, we shall consider our service to be completed at this point in time and shall communicate to you that we look forward to a further opportunity to be of service to you at any time, just as all members of the Confederation would offer. My friends, in the love and the light of our Creator, we bid you adonai. I am Latwii.

L/L Research is a subsidiary of
Rock Creek Research &
Development Laboratories, Inc.

P.O. Box 5195
Louisville, KY 40255-0195

L/L RESEARCH

www.llresearch.org

Rock Creek is a non-profit
corporation dedicated to
discovering and sharing
information which may aid in
the spiritual evolution of
humankind.

SUNDAY MEDITATION
MARCH 7, 1982

(Unknown channeling)

I am Hatonn, and I greet you, my brothers and sisters, in the love and the light of the infinite Creator. My friends, it is our great pleasure to perform this small service of addressing you this evening, and it is our desire that it be known that if our service be desired at any time, by any member or members of this group, you need only ask. Mentally request our presence and we shall be with you.

My friends, tonight we would share with you a few thoughts on the subject of purity. It is difficult to conceive of purity within the realm of your illusion, for as your illusion is permeated with indecision, as your illusion is the point at which the individual must select—correction—elect to polarize in one direction or the other, there is a strong tendency to accept a proximity to purity as the totality itself.

At this point, my brothers and sisters, the question occurs to a number of you, "What type of purity is being discussed?" My friends, in using the word purity we refer to the non-resistance to the outward reflectance of light from an individual. As you well know, every molecule, every atom, every portion of substance within your universe, being a facet of the Creator, [is] imbued with the light of the Creator and is capable of projecting that light in all directions. However, the influence of the individual—correction—individualized

consciousness which organizes the various molecules into a physical vehicle for the purpose of experiencing this density, exerts a controlling influence over the amount of light emitted from the total vehicle.

More briefly, my friends, you have the ability to restrict the amount of light which you are capable of emitting. The ramification of this act is that the energy level of your planetary sphere is being controlled by those entities upon that sphere yourselves. In restricting the amount of spiritual light and energy which you are capable of exuding, you reduce the amount of energy and therefore the vibratory level of your surroundings. When taken in terms of your race, the effect is to reduce the vibratory level of your planet, which results in the physical and emotional traumas that your planet and its populace continually experience.

My friends, the statement in your holy texts which decry the attempt to hide one's light beneath a basket refer to this type of choice. It is within the realm of your abilities to restrict the light-energy that you would choose to return to the Creator. It is also within the realms of your ability to restrict your own growth and that of your brothers and sisters. My friends, we are aware that on your planet there is pressure from those about you to conform, to avoid standing out in a crowd. But we would request that you consider whether a greater service [is] performed in [being] willing to be brave enough to allow your light to shine forth fully. The service that you would perform for your brothers and sisters in attempting this in your day-to-day actions is immense, for there is no being in existence who is capable of resisting the beneficial effects of this action. We would suggest, dear friends, that this be an object of consideration as you live within the confines of your illusion.

At this time, it is our desire to transfer this contact to another instrument, that we may accomplish the exercising of those who have made themselves available for this purpose. I am Hatonn.

(Unknown channeling)

I am Hatonn, and I am now with this instrument. We greet you once again in the love and in the light of the one infinite Creator. Within your illusion, one who stands out from the crowd is often isolated, scorned, ignored. But each is unique and each has their own rate of growth. And each has the choice. As you progress, you will find that at times you will be alone in the crowd, for as you grow and gain knowledge—become more aware—that which you have learned will be harder and harder to hide. You shall find that you will be more content with your particular place on your planet. Each works upon oneself.

Each self, each being *(inaudible)* will begin to see that though they are experiencing difficulties in relating to others on the planet, that they also become closer, for they will begin to see that which makes them brothers, one in the love and the light of the Creator. Though you will experience difficulties, they will be but lessons; the acceptance of others but mainly acceptance of oneself. The light is ever within *(inaudible)*. It is all things and it will shine, it will glow, as one becomes more aware of its presence. The knowledge that you gain grows increasingly brighter, warmer, feels more and more comfortable *(inaudible)* your being. My friends, as you grow, as you sit within meditation, allow yourself to feel. Experience the light. Allow it to glow. Be that which is you. Allow yourselves to be.

My friends, we are with you and shall be, whenever asked. For we wish in whatever humble way we can to aid you as you search, as you seek to experience, as you become aware and grow. For we are one with you, as all is one. *(Inaudible)* you're not you as *(inaudible)*. We will leave now this group so that

another of the Confederation may be with you. I am Hatonn.

(Unknown channeling)

I am Latwii. I greet you, my friends, in the love and the light of the infinite Creator. We speak briefly through this instrument in order to thank each of you for the privilege of being allowed to share our humble thoughts with you, and, with our brothers and sisters of Laitos and Hatonn, to offer as wide a variety of the types of Confederation energizing which we can at this time. We are aware that there are those of you who would wish to use this vibration for aid in deepening the meditation state, others who simply wish to feel the sensation of our presence, others who are working to become local channels. Please take from this band of vibrations that which you personally would find most helpful.

We shall pause at this time and pass among you that you may become aware of our presence and may be aided insofar as we will aid you with our vibrations. I am Latwii.

(Pause)

I am Latwii, and am again with this instrument. We are sorry that we are heating some of you up. We will attempt to adjust for your comfort and close the message through this instrument, that we may transfer to another. We would like for you to notice that we are not shouting through this instrument. We are very proud because we have finally figured out how to do that.

My friends, we would only offer a few foolish thoughts which we would ask you not to take any more seriously than necessary. We would like for you to think of what has been said by the brothers and sisters of Hatonn.

The concept of purity is one which pertains not to all of those foolish things that your peoples find so interesting, but rather to a quality which is as simple as light. If you would gaze out of your window, my friends, in the early morning hours, you will find the tiny crocuses moving upwards towards the still cool spring sun. They are pure. You will find the squirrels chasing the birds from the seed you have put out, their bright eyes darting back and forth, their tails moving quickly and cleverly as they maintain their balance. You hear the song of the birds, and all these things, my friends, are pure. They are pure because they are not conscious of themselves. They are creatures of the creation of the Father. And they are what they are without question.

But all, my friends, have you not been given a complicated task? To find again that beingness, that feeling of being a part of the Creation with no effort, while you are conscious of yourself? Your greatest task, my friends, is to stay out of your own way, for that which you are will shine, and all that might obstruct it is that which you might do. Some obstruct the light on purpose. But, my friends, many, many others in their efforts to increase their helpfulness, actually confuse the quality of that vibration of beingness, which we have so often described to you as the original Thought of the one infinite Creator. You are already a being of perfect love and light. To stay out of your way is a tremendous service to yourself and to others. All of the intelligence and analysis that you can produce through the time of your incarnation cannot yield up one more iota of light than is the totality of your being to begin with.

So, my friends, go within and trust that that which you are to be—do—is least of all a function of that mind which analyses and far more nearly a function of your ability to feel comfortable being one who is loved totally by the Creator. If you are loved you can then love, no matter what other function you may have in this illusion. Love, my friends, is the heart of your gift to those about you, and to yourself.

We are very happy to have used this instrument. We do not often receive the requisite amount of call to offer a little sermon, but are most grateful to you for allowing us to share these thoughts with you.

We would now transfer the contact to another instrument in order that we might attempt to field any questions that you might have at this time. I leave this instrument, in the love and the light of the infinite Creator. I am Latwii.

(Unknown channeling)

I am Latwii, and am with this instrument, and greet you all once again in love and light. May we at this time attempt to answer any questions which those present might have for us?

Questioner: Latwii, I have a question. If you are willing to, I would like for you to give me some feedback on the effectiveness of the channeling on the Friday night sessions, specifically the accuracy of the channeling.

I am Latwii, and am are aware of your question, my brother. May we say in this regard that your attempts to be of service during your meditations on the evenings have been quite successful. We have been very pleased with the quality of thoughts transmitted and received by your group. We have found an unusually receptive audience at your Friday evening gatherings, and for this reason have been able to provide information which has been called for, and which has been transmitted with accuracy.

May we answer you further, my brother?

Questioner: Yes, is there any advice you could offer as to the manner in which we could improve?

I am Latwii, and am aware of your question, my brother. In this regard, may we say that the seeking, the desire of each entity within your group, is that quality which, when taken as an unit, is responsible for the quality of both your meditation and the information which is received. The desire which has caused this group to be formed is of a high quality, therefore, to suggest the improvement of attuning, shall we say, this desire might be at this time too much to ask, for we feel each does present to the group the fullest amount of desire and will to seek the one Creator which is possible at this time, though it is always the nature of the pilgrim to continue the journey in ever a greater degree of depth and purity, and this refining of your purity shall, we are certain, also continue.

May we answer you further, my brother?

Questioner: You have answered me fully. Thank you.

I am Latwii. We are most grateful to you. Is there another question at this time?

Questioner: Are you the same entity that has been contacting us in Nova Scotia, in our group there?

I am Latwii, and am aware of your question, my sister. We of Latwii have had the privilege of making contact with your group on some few occasions. We of Latwii have not been able to make contact with many groups upon your planet, for the information which we have to offer is not often sought by such groups as this. We have been honored to join you on these occasions of which you are familiar, and do offer our thanks and our appreciation of this opportunity.

May we answer you further, my sister?

Questioner: No, we offer our thanks to you for joining us.

I am Latwii. We see that there is a great abundance of joy and thanksgiving, and for this we offer additional thanks. May we answer yet another question at this time?

Questioner: I had a question that occurred to me while you were speaking through me. And I just wondered—you were speaking of purity and you said something about the purity, the way people think of purity on this planet, isn't very helpful. I guess what most people think of as purity has to do with living …

(Side one of tape ends.)

Questioner: … that it is not actual purity, or that it is not conducive to development of actual purity, or that it is just not relevant, or what?

I am Latwii, and am aware of your question, my sister. May we say that, in general, you have expressed some degree of our perception of purity. Those of your people who have considered the concept of purity have quite frequently chosen to whittle away at their being in order to find the purity which they sense must be achieved by the removing of, shall we say, the catalysts of your illusion. By this we mean to say that the world which surrounds the self is too often seen as being of no value, and is too often removed from the experience of the entity, so that the entity seeking purity does isolate the self in what might be described as rigid and strict guidelines and frameworks and perceptions of the way purity must be expressed.

This, of course, is the free-willed choice of each entity, and does have the lessons to teach. The concept of purity which we have perceived as being, shall we say, more natural in its beingness is that concept which recognizes that you are pure and perfect as you are, without removing any ingredient from your experience. That indeed, each experience about you has a value to you, for it can teach you—a pure and perfect expression of the one Creator—are quite capable of learning each lesson that is made available to you by the world in which you find yourself immersed.

We do not, in our perception, see a need for living what might be called the monkish existence of the ascetic, for this type of perception quite frequently does further confuse the seeker. For if the world about one is seen to have no value, then part of the Creator is seen to have no value. If the entity is aware of the self as part of the Creator, the feeling of worthlessness then does intrude upon the consciousness and the perception of the entity seeking union with the Creator, which has part of its being that is of no value.

We instead would suggest the seeing of the Creator within all creation, within each other self that one encounters in the daily round of activities, and within the self as well. And we further suggest the attempt to discover the value of each experience, the lesson which does wait within each experience, which will point ever more accurately to the heart of your being which you seek, the heart of your being which is perfect, which is pure and which, when allowed to express itself to its fullest, will purely reflect the one infinite Creator.

May we answer you further, my sister?

Questioner: I think I understand pretty much exactly what you're saying, Latwii. What you're saying is, for instance, instead of removing sex from one's life, as do monks, you would instead request of [one]self the most careful search for the Creator in the truest of love within this experience, and instead of removing money from the experience, you would instead accept whatever amount of supply that you had within your station of life, and see what you could do with that money, to be of service as a part of the Creation. Is this what you're saying?

I am Latwii. My sister, we have indeed attempted to express thoughts similar to these. We would also add that we cannot speak specifically for any entity for each must make these choices as a result of the free will, and in this regard, we can only speak in general and express these thoughts which you have accurately reflected.

May we answer you further, my sister?

Questioner: No, thank you Latwii, that was very inspiring.

I am Latwii. We are most grateful to you as well. Is there another question at this time?

Questioner: I'm curious about angels. Are there angels, or beings, that can be helpful to us if we request it? That can help take care of us, or guard us or be with us to lend support and love, if we request it? I've always felt there were. I'm just curious.

I am Latwii, and am aware of your question, my sister. There are beings within the inner planes, shall we say, of this planetary influence which many of your peoples have described as being of an angelic nature. For their nature has been perceived [as] of great and intense love and light. These being do serve, shall we say, as guardians for entities upon this planetary sphere.

Each entity upon this planet has a number of such angelic presences which have as their honor and duty the guidance of individuals who have incarnated within this third-density illusion. Each entity may, therefore, call upon a variety of beings which reside within the inner planes. Each entity may determine the means by which the call is made, and the light and the being is invoked. It may be a simple ritual, a prayer of meditation, a simple sentence mentally asking assistance. It is helpful for each entity desiring this assistance to meditate upon the guides and beings which are in charge, shall we say, of the protection of the entity.

Attempt, then, in your meditation, to discern some aspects of the entity whose assistance you seek. Whatever aspects you are able to perceive—be it their form, their face, their color, shall we say, their tone, their quality, or their purpose—use this aspect as a part of your calling for their assistance. When this technique of seeking their nature is refined to a great enough extent you may receive additional descriptions, shall we say, of such beings, and eventually come to know their name and their form, and be able to call them by the visualization of either.

May we answer you further, my sister?

Questioner: Are they allowed to work with us, or must we request it? What form of aid are they allowed to give?

I am Latwii, and am aware of your question, my sister. The assistance which such beings render is that assistance which is called for by the entity, either consciously or subconsciously. Each entity upon this planet does call for some type of assistance, whether it is consciously recognized and verbalized, or whether it be subconsciously expressed. Each calling is answered. The degree of desire, the conscious seeking and strengthening of

this desire, is that key which shall determine how the call is answered.

Many calls, shall we say, are answered in sleep and dreams, providing inspiration and answers to problems. May calls are answered by intuitive hunches or inspirations of the moment, which seem to occur and appear out of the blue, shall we say. Other answers are of what might be called the coincidental or synchronistic nature, where you may wish to proceed along a certain path, to undertake a certain activity, and do not know exactly how this should be done, and within a short period of time an answer appears in the form of another self with a proposal, or with a part of your solution, or a situation which fulfils your needs.

Many are the ways in which calls are answered. Each entity which calls does take part in the answering of the call by making the call, by desiring the answer, and by arranging the, shall we say, landscape of the inner being, so that the proper sequence, or scene of events, might be painted upon that landscape.

May we answer you further, my sister?

Questioner: So the more in harmony we are with the creation, with the Creator, the more—the better landscape we provide for working with these entities?

I am Latwii. We perceive this statement to be basically correct, with the addition that at all times is each entity in harmony with the Creator. That variable which does change is the conscious awareness of this harmony and the ability to learn those lessons which have been provided in each opportunity.

May we answer you further, my sister?

Questioner: One more question. Do you ever work with these entities in your service here on this planet to us?

I am Latwii, and am quite happy to answer that at this time we do so.

Questioner: Thank you.

We are most grateful to you as well. Is there another question at this time?

Questioner: Yes. I've read a lot in the last few months and it's been very inspirational, and in fact sometimes it's given me a sense of real joy and bliss, and my question is, should I try to share this? At this point I don't know anybody who's got a listening ear and I don't know whether I have any responsibility in this respect.

I am Latwii, and am aware of your question, my sister. In this regard, may we say that the experiences which each entity such as yourself encounters are those experiences which are programmed by the self so that certain lessons might be learned for the evolution of the mind and the body and spirit of the entity. Part of this process of learning includes not only the evolution of the self but at some point in that evolution the radiating of this information, this inspiration, and this feeling of oneness to others. The sharing of such inspiration with other selves is that experience which then allows additional learning to become part of the experience of growth which each seeks.

The sharing of this information does require a careful balancing, shall we say, for few are the entities you shall meet that will request that which you have to share that is of a spiritual nature. To share such information when it is not requested is not the most efficient type of service to provide. Therefore, as, shall we say, a simple guide, we might suggest the full experience of this illusion in the way which is most beneficial to your own growth and the natural flowing of this exuberance for life through your being when you feel the proper moment has presented itself to you.

May we answer you further, my sister?

Questioner: In other words, unless there is a request or fairly obvious opportunity, then I don't make any real outward attempt at sharing what I experience?

I am Latwii, and am aware of your query, my sister. To refine our previous statement may we say that each moment in your existence is part of the one Creator, as is each entity. Each seeks the union with the Creator. Each moment, then, does present the opportunity to make the self available; for the sharing of that which is most dear to the self with an other self is that which is most helpful to the growth of both.

To become the evangelist, which requests and requires the open ear and mind, is that activity which shall prove to provide for results. To make the self available at each opportunity is most helpful, whether the opportunity be a simple smile, the granting of the right of way at one of your

intersections, the listening to the sorrows of a friend or stranger, the sharing of your deepest insights, or offering of a simple piece of advice when asked for. Each is an opportunity to share that which is the love and compassion for the self and each that self will meet.

May we answer you further, my sister?

Questioner: No, that's an excellent answer. Thank you very much.

I am Latwii. We thank you. Is there another question at this time?

Questioner: I have a question. Mostly out of curiosity. What causes and what are actually déja vu experiences?

I am Latwii, and am aware of your question, my sister. Each entity upon your planet, as we have said many times, is a part of the fabric of the one creation and the one Creator, and by their very nature, therefore, have the ability to become aware of other parts of the creation. Within your third-density illusion, the forgetting is in sway, and this unity with the creation is, shall we say, a more foggy part of your being. There are times, however, as the rhythms of your being change frequency, that you may become aware of a possibility which does exist for what you would describe as a future occurrence. This is one of many possibilities.

Each entity does have such insights, shall we say, whether they be dreams during sleep, daydreams in waking consciousness, or random thoughts floating through the mind. Most do not occur, for they are possibilities which were not taken, roads which were not traveled. There are, however, times when the thought, the daydream, the dream during sleep, does coincide with that road which was taken in what is perceived to be the future. It is at such times that the entity then becomes aware that the previous conscious knowing has transpired. This you have called the déja vu experience.

May we answer you further, my sister?

Questioner: Yes, but on another subject. This is pretty much a personal question. I spoke in another session of dreams and didn't ask this question. In such a dream I spent time with an individual that I did not know, but it was on a one-to-one contact and he was teaching me lessons and I was wondering if you could enlighten me who that was?

I am Latwii, and am aware of your question, my sister. To speak specifically to your query would be, in our humble opinion, [an] infringement upon your own free will, for the seeking of the solution to this riddle is of necessity for you at this time to accomplish through your own efforts.

You have been quite successful in remembering these experiences. Your dreaming experience can be quite valuable, if you wish it to be so. If you wish to return to this place and this entity, it is quite possible for you to do so, for the dreaming experience is one which offers a wider latitude, shall we say, for the entity which seeks to learn certain lessons. These lessons might be more difficult to experience within this third-density illusion and are more easily expressed and perceived in the state of consciousness which you have called the dreaming state.

May we answer you further, my sister?

Questioner: No, you answered another question in answering the first question. Another question, in dealing with people at school I am finding I am trying hard to be myself around them, and in doing so am getting rejected by many. I am at the point of quitting and not trying to work with them anymore. I'm having a hard time figuring out if that's right.

I am Latwii. We have listened to your description and assume that your question is whether you should proceed in one direction or another, and find that we cannot give this advice, for to travel your path for you is to remove the opportunities for growth that wait upon it for you, and this we do not feel to be a service at his time.

May we answer you further, my sister?

Questioner: No thank you. I'll be figuring it out …

I am Latwii. We are most grateful as well to you.

Is there another question at this time?

Questioner: When we see people that we know in dreams and deal with them, working out problems, are we actually speaking to that entity on a different plane or is it just working out problems in our minds?

I am Latwii. My sister, may we say that each possibility which you have mentioned is indeed possible. The state of consciousness which you call the dream state, as we have mentioned before, does lend to the entity a greater scope of experience.

Most often the experience of the dream state does include realms beyond that which you might consider the normal range of being. These realms do include the conscious awareness of other selves, which you are in contact with during your daily existence. In such dreams the work of experiencing the catalysts of this illusion might be more easily accomplished, and the conscious mind might therefore be apprised of those lessons which are most in need of concentrated effort. In many such dream experiences, the conscious mind is seeded with the necessary information which will allow the waking entity to experience those lessons which are, shall we say, pregnant within the being. The conscious mind, then so fertilized, shall we say, does provide the focus of attention in these areas by its very consideration of the dream and its possible meaning.

The dream state is far more varied and, shall we say, multi-dimensioned than it has been imagined by most of your peoples. To give an accurate description of what is possible within this dream state is, in our humble opinion, not possible, for the possibilities are infinite, since the conscious mind does not have its limiting perceptions to reduce the effectiveness of the learning, shall we say, during this dream state.

May we answer you further, my sister?

Questioner: No, thank you.

I am Latwii, we are most grateful to you as well. Is there another question at this time?

Questioner: I read a book written by a psychic that talked about walk-ins. People that want to leave this earth—this is nothing personal, this doesn't apply to me—about people who want to leave this earth and beings who had something to accomplish and did not want to go through childhood would take their place and fill out their life and then go on to accomplish in this particular body. Have you heard of walk-ins?

I am Latwii, and am aware of your question, my sister. This phenomenon which you have described as the walk-in is indeed that situation which has occurred upon your planet but which is not usual, shall we say. The integration of the mind, the body, and the spirit in the evolutionary progress of union with the Creator is that process which is most necessary for each entity to accomplish upon this planet at this time. This process is most carefully watched over by those entities we have previously described as being the guides, the guardians, the angelic presences.

There are rare occurrences in which an entity incarnates with many lessons to learn. The lessons are of such a nature that the integration of the mind, the body, and the spirit is not harmoniously achieved. Such an entity, quite frequently upon your planet, will then engage in that activity which your peoples have called the taking of the life, or the suicide. For those entities which have faced the great difficulties in the learning of the lessons, and which have not been able to achieve a satisfactory integration of mind, body and spirit, and which, in addition, do not have the desire to end their own existence, are those entities which then do make themselves available to beings or another entity to complete for them …

(Tape ends.) ♣

L/L Research

L/L Research is a subsidiary of Rock Creek Research & Development Laboratories, Inc.

P.O. Box 5195
Louisville, KY 40255-0195

www.llresearch.org

Rock Creek is a non-profit corporation dedicated to discovering and sharing information which may aid in the spiritual evolution of humankind.

Friday Night
March 12, 1982

(Unknown channeling)

I am Hatonn, and greet you, my brothers and sisters, in the love and the light of the infinite Creator. My friends, it is difficult at times to share with one another our feelings of confusion or sorrow, for these emotions stem from an awareness that we are somehow unable to balance within ourselves our perceptions of the universe within which we live. As these emotions, therefore, are based upon confusion it is understandably difficult to attempt to describe to one another these feelings. We of Hatonn are aware that your illusion can often be dismaying and may lead one to accept within one's emotional mass of perceptions this type of imbalance and although we may say that we can sympathize with this difficulty, we would emphasize to you, my friends, that the responsibility for clarifying this confusion resides with the individual. If it is your desire, dear friends, to perceive your illusion clearly then it is your responsibility to insure that your perceptions stem from reality and not from your illusion.

At this time we would like to relinquish our verbal contact with this group so that our brothers of Laitos may pass among you and offer his service to those who would mentally request his vibration. I am Hatonn.

(Pause)

(Unknown channeling)

I am Hatonn. I am again with this instrument. My friends, we cannot emphasize strongly enough that your perceptions of your reality substantially affect the manner in which you interrelate with your other selves and thereby achieve the results of your efforts toward service and polarization. It is essential to develop within oneself the ability to control your emotional reflexes, so to speak. The emotions that you experience are tools which may aid or retard your development depending upon your willingness and skill to learn to make use of these tools. As you become more adept, you will realize that in your recent past you were in the position of the malleable iron being hammered into a convoluted shape by the tools of emotion instead of being able to use those same tools for the development of your service orientation.

My brothers and sisters, we of Hatonn would encourage you to be conscious of your use of these tools, for like many of those of your manipulation of the physical role they may cause harm as well as good in the hands of the unskilled.

At this time we would relinquish our use of this instrument to our brothers and sisters of Latwii that they may perform their service of attempting to answer questions that you might choose to pose. I am Hatonn.

(Unknown channeling)

I am Latwii, and I greet you, my brothers and sisters, in the love and the light of our Creator. It is a great pleasure, as always, to be able to be among you and to share your various vibrations, to perceive the intricate artwork, so to speak, as they interweave and meld into one common vibration, thus uniting your group. However, as we are aware that you are probably not overly interested in psychic tapestry, we shall proceed with the original purpose of our visitation, to wit, are there any questions?

K: I have a request. Could you speak to the idea of tolerance for someone who does something and you wish that they would do, say, the opposite? How to achieve that tolerance of a person's difference?

I am Latwii. I am aware of your question, my sister. First we would suggest that the question as stated be examined further in view of the potential desire to manipulate another individual into performing in a desired mode of behavior. My sister, although this may be an attractive idea, it is not necessarily conducive toward your own personal growth to either act as the manipulator or to, in an effort to remain passively involved, wish for some form of catalyst to occur to perform the manipulation for oneself and hopefully exclude oneself from the responsibility for that manipulation.

We would suggest that a better route might be to examine the behavior pattern that is regarded as an irritant and to try to attain an understanding of why the action or inaction stimulates one to generate within oneself an unpleasing emotion. It is difficult in your dimension to acquire emotional and spiritual distance from the lessons that one attracts to oneself, for they will quite literally pursue you about the face of the Earth until you are willing to accept the catalyst that you have requested.

We would therefore, my sister, encourage you to look within your own soul for an understanding of the origin of these negative feelings and to attempt to convey forgiveness to the one whose actions are construed as in some manner wronging oneself.

May we speak further on the subject?

K: No, thank you.

As always, we thank you for the opportunity to provide our meager service. Is there another question?

S: I have a question having to do with the planets coming within close proximity of one another in our solar system. Did they cause any changes upon our Earth, and when they realign in the future, is there a possibility of any changes happening then in the form of earthquakes or any tremors or volcanic activity?

I am Latwii. My brother, there is always the possibility of any event, however unlikely, occurring. However, to more specifically answer your question, we would remind you that the major cause for the physical upheavals of your planetary surface are not the celestial bodies but rather the occupants of the physical bodies who so heavily populate your planet. It is the vibration level prevalent upon your planet that is in conflict with your planet's transition into the fourth density and therefore results in physical upheavals and redistribution as your conflicting vibrations strive to achieve a balance. This will, in most likelihood, continue to occur and to increase in frequency unless your peoples' vibration level alters substantially. This is the major effector and in comparison the celestial bodies to which you refer are considerably insignificant.

May we answer you further?

S: Do you see any high probability of an earthquake happening in a certain location on the Earth from these vibrations at this time?

I am Latwii. My brother, we might succinctly answer your question "yes," but to provide the further information that we are allowed in this case, we would remind you of our inability, so to speak, to make specific projections due to the potential disruptions to the individual's right to choice or confusion depends upon your perception of this requirement.

May we answer you further?

S: No, I understand, and I should have realized that before. In the past Hatonn has suggested we pray specifically for certain areas of the Earth. At one time it was for Red China when there was a conflict between China and Russia. Besides in general praying for the Earth and its problems are there specific areas where we could send energy?

I am Latwii. I am aware of your question. My brother, there are many areas to which a specific application of love and light could be beneficial. However, we are reticent on this subject due to the fact that again we seek to avoid making specific predictions or sharing with you knowledge that we possess that you do not, therefore altering substantially your own efforts toward growth. We would suggest as an alternative, my brother, that one might seek the answer within one's own soul and find the appropriate response therein.

May we answer you further, my brother?

S: No, thank you.

Again, we thank you, my brother. Is there another question?

G: I have a question. Sometimes when I meditate, I become really afraid. Could you instruct me toward how to overcome those fears?

I am Latwii. My sister, there is within your society a traditional perception of the individual possessing a sanctified protective entity whose efforts are solely concerned with a vague, indescribed protection of the individual, these entities being referred to as "guardian angels." Unfortunately, my sister, there are also a less prevalent breed of entities who achieve polarization through the disruption of efforts such as those of your own which you describe as meditation, and it may be said that these particular entities patiently wait for the opportunity to attempt to disrupt efforts toward positive polarization made by certain individuals.

It is your gift, my sister, to be quite perceptive to the psychic communication often referred to as intuition, however, each such gift is a twin-edged sword, and in your case you are also susceptible to the influence by those who would attempt to interrupt your efforts by psychic projection of fear or disruptive thoughts. We would encourage you, my sister, when these efforts begin to manifest themselves in your consciousness, to direct love and light to whatever individual or individuals are sending you their gift of disruption. We believe that you will find after a short period of time that these disruptions will reduce in frequency and intensity as your return gift is quite uncomfortable for its recipients.

May we answer you further?

G: No, thank you.

I am Latwii. We thank you as well, my sister. Is there another question?

(Pause)

I am Latwii. We would like to at this time thank our brothers and sisters of this group for inviting us to share your vibration and your learning. It is our desire that you understand that we ourselves, in addition to our other brothers and sisters of the Confederation, seek to be of service to you whenever possible in your lives. There is no task too small or unreasonable that we would be unwilling to offer our assistance [to].

Therefore, we would encourage you to contact us, if only briefly, that we might attempt to be of some service to you. At this time we will take our leave. Adonai, my friends. I am known to you as Latwii. ☙

L/L RESEARCH

L/L Research is a subsidiary of
Rock Creek Research &
Development Laboratories, Inc.

P.O. Box 5195
Louisville, KY 40255-0195

www.llresearch.org

Rock Creek is a non-profit
corporation dedicated to
discovering and sharing
information which may aid in
the spiritual evolution of
humankind.

SUNDAY MEDITATION
MARCH 14, 1982

(C channeling)

I am Hatonn, and I am with this instrument. We greet you, as always, in the love and the light of the one infinite Creator. We are once again extremely glad to be able to reach so many. It is indeed a great honor to speak to those who seek to become more aware of the love and the light of the infinite Creator.

My friends, on your planet the season has changed. New life will soon begin, entities growing, developing, each seeking the light, each wishing its own place in the whole of the Creation. The new life depends on a fragile balance of those things necessary for life in your illusion, the need for water, for food, for light, but each also needs a guide, a hand, whether it is advantage of more suitable genetic traits, such things as plants, or the aid of one more older [as] entities aid the young of your animal life or for the lives of the human.

Each new entity that is now incarnating on your planet has an excellent chance of reaching a state in their development to make what we refer to as the harvest. These entities are those with the greatest chance. These entities will have an impact on your planet and upon the entities thereupon. These entities also will have a need for guidance, for aid, that will exert great demand on those entities around it and who interact with it. These new entities will begin their lives as a very strong catalyst [to] those around them. They will teach as well as be taught. They will be as a beautiful flower if they be nurtured and allowed to grow. Those on your planet who have chosen the role of parent have taken upon themselves a task, a lesson that will be hard for many. The ideas, customs, habits that have been ingrained on each for generations before will be sent before them in such a way that many of the concepts will be seen as a light that before was not seen, not felt. The new entities, the children, are and will be a new light, [who] will help to illuminate the world around them. Hopefully, those around them may see this, may learn from it and continue to grow, become aware and themselves be awakened from the sleep or aided in seeking.

Cherish the new life, for each life is a beginning and a means for all to see. We of Hatonn wish to aid any who may need with the times that are to come, that are here, are filled with ever increasing lessons, ever more difficult. We need but hear your call, whether faint or loud, whether consciously or not, we shall aid when needed.

We would now transfer this contact. We are Hatonn.

(L channeling)

I am Hatonn, and I am now with this instrument. At this time, my friends, we would like to give our brothers and sisters of Laitos the opportunity to perform their service of passing among you and sharing their vibration with those who request this. If it is your desire that our brothers and sisters of Laitos should share their vibration with you, simply mentally request this service and they shall be performing it. We shall now pause that this may be accomplished. I am Hatonn.

(Pause)

(L channeling)

I am Hatonn. I am again with this instrument. My friends, my brothers and sisters, in your society, within your race, there are many variations, many opinions on the subject often referred to as the rearing of children. It is thought that those who perform the role of parent are in some manner performing the role of one who makes entries on a slate that was once blank and in doing so construct the mind and behavior of their offspring. It is difficult for one raised in such a society to disregard this concept, to allow the newly arrived entity the respect and understanding that would be accorded to an individual of physically mature years on your planet who was, for some reason, temporarily unable to communicate or adequately control one's physical functions, yet was obviously intelligent, knowledgeable and possessed of large amounts of experience.

My friends, if you would benefit those new lights among you, then we would suggest that an effort be made to perceive that these new lights are in many ways old lights that have been among you periodically since time within your dimension itself has begun, that these who enter during the final days are very likely entities with great experience and learning prior to their entry into your physical realm. Be aware, my friends, that those whom you would teach may have come to perform the service of assisting you to learn, of aiding you in achieving the necessary level of service for harvest. Be attentive to your lessons, for they have much to share with you. It is said on your planet that the child is the father to the man. There are many depths of meaning within this statement. We would encourage those present who would understand the process of aiding newly entered entities to meditate upon this statement.

I am known to you as Hatonn.

(Carla channeling)

I am now with this instrument. I am Hatonn, and I greet you once again in the love and in the light of our infinite Creator. Each of you, my friends, has a memory of being a small and defenseless being under the protection of those seemingly very large and almost godlike entities which were called grownups, and more especially, parents, and then, my friends, we as children find that illusion called time passing us by, and as we glance about ourselves we discover that we have become those very large beings whose impervious nature and iron rule was once totally accepted, and we find, my friends, that we are only large. We have not become omniscient or impervious or full of wisdom.

But, my friends, although we share with you this humorous situation, as we of Hatonn also have children and see to their raising, we may affirm to you that it matters not that you are often wrong, impatient, slow to understand and quick to speak. It does not matter any more than any other behavior matters if that behavior is the offspring of the moment. My friends, none small or large is infallible, but, my friends, there is one thing that can be done, and we speak not only for those who work with young ones, we speak for all. That one thing is always the seeking of the original Thought of the one infinite Creator. In seeking this heart within yourself and within the creation you bring sunshine into a life which otherwise may seem quite random and completely uninteresting.

You may look at your own being as that which is woven. There are those who go to the market and select that which is offered. Some buy cheaply and some for style, but few there are, my friends, who plan the design and the pattern of their leaving and then go select the yarns. If you but can weave your inner life slowly and thoughtfully, the pattern that will emerge will speak far loudly—we correct this instrument—far more loudly to child, to friend, or to stranger than any momentary behavior.

Let us look again at the arrangement itself. If you are faced with the instrument which you call the piano, and you think of a lifetime as that which can be played on the piano, you again have many choices. You can, if you are very lazy, choose to ignore the learning of this art and simply sit upon the keys. This will produce a lifetime, a noise, a jangle, a disharmony. You may play what this instrument calls "Chopsticks" over and over and over. You may be the last one tired of that particular tune. You may choose to learn to accompany yourself in popular singing and be an entertaining and light influence, or, my friends, you may choose to acquaint yourself with the literature of the piano, and, having the technique to play that which you wish and knowing that literature, you may then select the tune which carries your life in its breath.

We have spoken to you a great deal this evening about children because the children being born within this group, and, indeed, among your peoples in general at this time are souls that have by their very nature both a great deal to give and a great deal to ask. There are many who have chosen incarnation here in order to attempt to graduate from third density. There are others who have chosen to incarnate as shepherds to aid at this time in this harvest, in this transition, and at this time, my friends, there are those who are now being born who are commencing their work in the density of love into which your planet now revolves. To deal with such experienced, knowledgeable, old souls is not always, shall we say, child's play. However, these entities have chosen their parents and you they, and you are together for very specific reasons—to comfort each other, to teach each other and above all, my friends, to love each other.

All those who live at this time can be parents in the metaphysical sense, nurturing those whom you meet, comforting, accepting and loving. Do not find yourself displeased with yourself because of any momentary lapse from behavior you require of yourself, as a parent or as a person, for, my friends, the great gift you give is always yourself, your carefully woven tapestry of being, the lovely lilting melody that you have chosen to play with your lives in this illusion.

I thank you, my friends, with all my heart, that you have allowed those of Hatonn to speak with you this evening. It has been the greatest privilege for us, and we hope that we have been of some small service. We are always with you if you mentally request it. We leave you now. Soft and gentle as the raindrops which we may hear through this instrument's ears is the love that surrounds you. We leave you in that love and in the light of the one infinite Creator. Adonai vasu borragus.

(Jim channeling)

I am Latwii, and greet you all in love and light. We have been called to this group once again and have responded in joy and feel it a great honor to be allowed to present our simple service to this group. That service, as each of you know, is the attempt to answer the questions which might be of value to those present. Is there a question at this time?

L: I have two questions, Latwii. The first is, is it possible for the instrument who is channeling you to also ask questions of you?

I am Latwii, and am aware of your query, my brother. In this regard we may say that it would in some few cases be possible to do this, but we do not feel that the level of, shall we say, mental dexterity and discipline is properly advanced in any present …

(Side one of tape ends.)

(Jim channeling)

I am Latwii, and am once again with this instrument. As we were saying, there is a great deal of discipline that is necessary for the performing of such an activity, for unlike the simple changing of the recording device which this instrument has just accomplished, the framing of a question and the subsequent answering of the question does then blend the consciousness of the instrument and of those entities being channeled in such a way that doubt might enter the instrument's mind as to what the source of the query and the answer might be. It might be easy, shall we say, to ask the query. The answer received might present some problem for the instrument in the determining of its source and thereby increase doubt.

May we answer you further, my brother?

L: You've answered me fully on that subject. I have one other question I'd like to pose. I've noticed in the past two or three weeks that I feel constantly physically exhausted. Is there any information you could give on the cause of this and how to get beyond it?

I am Latwii, and am aware of your query. We cannot answer simply, for this query has many potential answers; to speak in general, then, is our lot. One potential source of weariness in the case of entities who have opened themselves to the seeking of that known as the evolution of mind, body and spirit is that the opening of the self to such seeking does then, as the magnet, attract that which is sought. Such seeking then does attract the necessary configuration of energies that will serve as catalyst for the learning necessary for such evolution.

Entities seeking with great will, with great desire, do then attract greater amounts of such energies and experiences, and may, as the over-eager college student signing up for classes, bite off, shall we say, more than can be comfortably chewed. There are also at this time many energies of a more general nature which affect each entity upon your planet, no matter of the degree of seeking present within the entities; that is the movement of your entire planet into a new configuration of vibrations and of energies which have been called by many the energies of your New Age.

The increased vibratory level of each particle of your creation, of your being and your experience is an increase in the, shall we say, channeling of these energies through each vehicle or the blocking of these energies by various vehicles of mind/body/spirit complex nature. These energies are available to each upon your planet. Many in their seeking and many unconsciously are not able to accommodate these new energies, for they have not yet built the proper foundation for their experience, and, therefore, their experience of these energies becomes somewhat of a deadening effect, which does then serve to protect the entity from being, shall we say, blown out as a circuit unable to accommodate the increased vibrations.

Therefore, we may say in general that there are specific reasons for each entity's experiencing of that which is known as weariness and tiredness, and there are general reasons at this time having to do with the increase in vibration upon the personal and planetary level.

May we answer you further, my brother?

L: No, you've given me a great deal to look at. Thank you.

I am Latwii. We thank you most humbly. May we answer another question at this time?

M: Yes. Edgar Cayce had an interesting skill, ability to read someone's aura. How can that skill be developed?

I am Latwii, and am aware of your question, my brother. To develop such a skill as this is the work of

many of, what you call, your years for most entities who would attempt it. Few there are who have what might be called a natural ability to do this, though there are such entities, as you are aware. To become able to perceive the patterns of the personality, shall we say, as they are expressed in the aura of any entity it is necessary to develop what might be called an inner vision, [which] might be most simply defined as the ability to perceive patterns of energy and to view these patterns in relation to the incarnational experience which has set them in motion.

The ability to read such patterns must, as we have said, in most cases be consciously pursued. The meditative state, of course, is of greatest value to the beginner, for within the meditative state does the entity then became aware of those patterns of energy within its own being. To aid the beginner, contemplation is rec … we continue—is recommended for the beginner, the contemplation of those sensations, experiences, cravings and patterns of thought which pass like a stream through the being of each entity, after an entity has been able to become more aware of such patterns within its own being. Then the entity may begin—and we stress, begin—to attempt to become aware of those patterns in others by the use of what might be called training aids.

One such aid might be what you have called the pendulum. An entity may, by the use of this training aid, determine the location and level of activity of the major energy centers within an other self. Continued practice at this activity will then allow the entity to move on to those secondary and tertiary centers within an other self. The continued practice of this activity and the use of this training aid will then allow the entity to begin to develop this inner vision or inner sense which not only views the energy centers and their activity within an other self, but also begins to sense the nature of this activity, its source, its movements, its characteristics.

With enough patience and practice such efforts to establish the inner vision then do bear fruit, for each desire does draw unto the one which has the desire that which is desired.

May we answer you further, my brother?

M1: No, thank you. That was very complete.

I am Latwii, and we thank you as well. Is there another question at this time?

M2: I have two questions. L's question about being tired two weeks, I would like to elaborate into a lifetime of being tired. Would you further tell me any more about the tiredness?

I am Latwii, and am aware of your question, my sister. We again can speak only in general terms, for to speak specifically to the causes of an entity's condition is to then take the lessons of that learning from the entity and delay their learning. Such an experience as you describe may again have many possible causes. We have spoken previously of those who have incarnated to learn the lessons that will allow graduation into the density of love. The time, as you describe it, remaining for these lessons to be learned grows short, therefore those incarnating at this time do attempt to learn that which is necessary for the graduation. These lessons may be few, these lessons may be many. To attempt what is necessary may be a large undertaking or a moderate one, but to allow those patterns of experience to be available to the entity for the learning may involve what you might call a constant state of near overload. This may result in the physical vehicle of such an entity to experience that which is known as weariness.

To elaborate upon this somewhat, let us say that the feeling of the weary state is not in itself to be dismissed or relegated as less than useful or desirable. There may, in such a situation, be yet another purpose for such a condition, for each condition experienced by each entity has a purpose. There are some who limit themselves in some way so that they shall not dissipate their energies in avenues which shall produce no learning. There are some who limit themselves so that they shall be more likely to direct their efforts in ways which shall be fruitful.

We might, in general, suggest the meditation upon this particular situation in your life condition, and thereby discover for yourself the most likely explanation, shall we say, for this condition. It is not by chance that such has occurred.

May we answer you further, my sister?

M2: I think you've answered that question sufficiently, but I would like to know the difference in some people. Same people have such a zest for living and want to stay here on earth indefinitely, and other people are not quite comfortable here and feel like they're serving a sentence and are not a bit unhappy about leaving. Why is there that variation?

I am Latwii, and am aware of your query, my sister. Many are the sources of origination of those of your peoples at this time. Many are not native to this planet. Many have come to be of service, and yet, as they forget their mission, do enter into that known as incarnation and do proceed through the life with the feeling of some purpose, but also with the feeling of not quite being at home, these—what might be called—bleed-through memories which have lingered through the forgetting process, as they are basic to the nature of the entity.

Some upon your planet feel the zest of life in its fullness, for it is perhaps their purpose and to their mission to be active and to radiate those resources that are theirs to others, that they might be of a service of a certain nature. Some radiate in yet another manner, without the overt physical manifestations, and experience vitality. The experience of vitality and of health which your peoples have described as optimal for the physical existence is an experience which does not in itself have any meaning or value, but does when applied to a specific individual then and only then take on meaning. Many are the ways in which the people of your planet have chosen to be of service. Many are the ways and the lessons to learn these ways of service. For each there is a purpose. For each there is a mission.

May we answer you further, my sister?

M2: You feel, then, that people who are not quite comfortable and who are not unhappy about leaving may have quite a bit of bleed-through. Is that correct?

I am Latwii. We believe that you have grasped the heart of our response.

May we answer you further?

M2: You have. I'm finished with the question.

C: Following right along in the same vein, do some people spend a lifetime of sickness for a purpose?

I am Latwii. My sister, may we say this is, indeed, quite true. It might be the preincarnative choice of an entity who experiences that known as sickness and ill health. To experience such a condition, to balance those experiences which have been distilled from previous incarnations, as you call them, it might be, for instance, that an entity has been of great service in previous incarnations, has given much selflessly, has been able to share a great deal of that which was available to it as love and light, and it might then be necessary for it to learn that others might also give unto it in like manner, and thereby choose an incarnation which would be full of that known as sickness so that the opportunity for others to give unto it would be established and perpetuated in its motion.

There are, of course, an infinite number of reasons for that known as sickness and ill health. We have given but one.

May we answer you further, my sister?

C: What about a condition known as paranoia? Would any entity ever choose such a state as that?

I am Latwii, and am aware of your query. May we say that the preincarnative choices are made from a plane of existence which is far removed from that which you now experience. Those various distortions such as the mental aberrations, the physical sickness and the spiritual yearning, each of these having certain desirable and undesirable traits, is seen from this plane of experience as simply an experience which may teach a certain lesson. The preincarnative state then does select those situations which will produce the catalyst necessary for learning of certain lessons.

A certain state of mind [such as] that which you have described as paranoia may be chosen for a certain period of time for a certain lesson, then, when that lesson is learned, may be discarded as the shoes are discarded at the end of the day. It may also be that such a state has resulted from the entity's inability to learn those lessons programmed. There are no mistakes, but there are occasional detours and delayings of the learning. It cannot be said that any mental, physical or spiritual state of being denotes only one purpose, for each offers an infinite array of opportunities for learning.

May we answer you further, my sister?

C: No, thank you. That answered it.

I am Latwii. May we answer another question at this time?

Carla: I just wanted to clarify what you said about the last entity—hi, Latwii, how are you? Then, you think that mental illness in general, which I've often wondered about, since the person is too enrapt to know what's going on, is perhaps a little bit like an electrical circuit blowing a fuse, so that just the fuse goes instead of the whole circuit. It's a safety valve to save the individual, while it isn't quite integrated. Is that sort of what you're saying?

I am Latwii, and we greet you, my sister, and we thank you for your query, and we may in general agree with your supposition. We do, however, wish to add that such a safety valve, as you have called it, is not the only particular, shall we say, cause or result of the entity's protective measures which it used to ensure the continuation of the mind/body/spirit complex. There are numerous protective measures or safety valves which entities may utilize for such a purpose. The mental condition which your peoples describe as neurotic or schizophrenic, and even that known as catatonic may be used for various purposes, as we have mentioned previously. Their greatest use, however, as you have mentioned, is that of providing a mechanism whereby the entity may be put into a holding pattern until the stabilization of the catalyst and experience of the entity is achieved. At that time further lessons may be undertaken.

May we answer you further, my sister?

Carla: No, thank you.

I am Latwii. We thank you, as well. Is there another question at this time?

C: Yes. May I pursue that just a little further? From having worked in a mental hospital, I got the feeling that such mental aberrations are childlike in nature, and an attempt to escape responsibility, but you indicate that it may be a holding pattern instead of an escape. Do I get that right?

I am Latwii, and am aware of your query. We might use either term, but have chosen to use the term "holding pattern," for it does not have the characteristic of judgment which that term "escape" carries with it. The entity has, in many cases, experienced some degree of difficulty in assimilating the lessons of its incarnation, and then does, with the assistance of what might be called the higher self, place itself in a pattern of experience which, indeed, is likened unto the child, in that further growth is not attempted, but is delayed until those patterns that have caused the difficulty can be stabilized, and further growth then attempted.

May we answer you further, my sister?

C: No, thank you. That answers my question.

I am Latwii. We thank you. Is there another question at this time? I am Latwii. We have been most honored to have been asked to join your group this evening. We feel a great joy at each opportunity, and we remind each that a simple request is all that is necessary for our joining your meditations, whether in group or in private. We are most honored to join you at any time for any length of that which you know of as time.

We leave this group at this time rejoicing with each in the love and in the light of the one infinite Creator. Go forth, then, peacefully. I am known to you as Latwii. Adonai vasu borragus. ⚜

L/L Research is a subsidiary of
Rock Creek Research &
Development Laboratories, Inc.

P.O. Box 5195
Louisville, KY 40255-0195

L/L Research

www.llresearch.org

Rock Creek is a non-profit
corporation dedicated to
discovering and sharing
information which may aid in
the spiritual evolution of
humankind.

Sunday Meditation
March 21, 1982

(C channeling)

I am Hatonn, and I am now with this instrument. We greet you, my friends, as always, in the love and light of the one infinite Creator. We are always happy to hear your voices as they seek to harmonize with one another, to bring forth song. Each sings the same words, yet each feels and expresses those same words, [in] sometimes subtle and at other time very distinct ways, which differ from their brothers and their sisters. From the one Source came many variations, for each, while part of a whole, is different, feels, thinks, reacts differently, for they are their own individual entity, each looking at your illusion through eyes that reflect the unique experiences, lessons.

Each is here to become aware, if that which each needs is not the same. Each of you see, yet as you know, each is very different. Each treads their own paths, though you be one in spirit. You need not feel lacking, or doubt your growth or ability to do so, if you are not doing as you see your other brothers or sisters. Your path is your own. Follow it as it may lead. Stray not right nor left, but keep your eyes forward and go as the light leads. Your path will cross those of many others and at times may be shared. These times are always joyous, for they serve to show that you are not alone. There are others who will help, whom you may help, but worry not if the paths diverge. Walk on. Share when you may. Give what you can. Be not proud and deny what others wish to share. You are always in harmony if the light is your guide and though there be differences in the light and the love of the Creator they provide harmony which is most beautiful. Be not afraid, look ahead. If the need be felt, raise your voice in chorus with others, but be not afraid to stand alone and sing.

We shall now transfer this contact to another instrument. I am Hatonn, and I transfer now.

(Carla channeling)

I am Hatonn, and I am now with this instrument. We were attempting to contact the one known as L, but discovered that one of our sisters in the Confederation is conditioning this instrument. Therefore, we shall allow this process to take place while we speak through this instrument.

We greet you once again, my friends, in the love and the light of our infinite Creator. "Be not afraid" is a statement, an injunction most easy to say and at times not so easy to do, and as you came together in this domicile at this time to listen to our humble message, we are aware that in many ways you come seeking to find whole that which has been broken, to find in a larger amount that which you feel you have not in great enough quantity. Perhaps, my friends, you are seeking faith. Perhaps you are seeking the grace with which to do good works. Perhaps you are seeking wisdom. All these are gifts of a consciousness which some call the spirit and which we choose to call love, that one great original Thought of the one Creator, and, my friends, as you seek in a group this gift of love, as you seek to feel the wholeness, the purity of this love, and to find yourself mended as well, it may seem to you that this group is absolutely necessary in order to experience this wholeness, this purity, and this love, but we say to you, my friends, this gathering is for the purpose of sending you forth alone into a world sorely in need of the wholeness and purity of the love of the infinite Creator.

You may experience it here. You may identify it with being with the group, but, my friends, you are only resonating each with one common vibration, that great original Vibration of light, and this can be taken with you, and as you follow your path in the light, in service, remembering the Creator, so you take with you this wholeness, and without saying any word or making any gesture you are then, yourself, an offering to the world of the manifestation of this enormous creative love.

You cannot do this yourself, for you are as you are in this illusion, but there is that within you which is more yourself than that self which you now know, and that deeper self can do all these things that you may wish to do. It can love. It can show forth patience and understanding, and, my friends, it can sing alone in the darkness and offer to those who grope, the seeking for love, that beacon which may guide them to their own paths, toward light.

You came together in a faith. This faith is a great blessing, and we thank you for desiring to hear these words enough to generate the faith and the seeking which leads you to this point in your existence. You may feel that this faith and this desire is simply not enough, but we ask you, my friends, to remember the workings of one of your great teachers, for the one known as Jesus sought to teach. Many gathered about this entity and his disciples were uneasy, for they wished to make these thousands of seekers comfortable, and yet had little food and less money, and therefore could not be generous and offer sustenance.

The one known as Jesus broke and scattered what seemed to be not enough, and it was more than enough. You, my friends, are also filled with this bread. It has been called the bread of heaven, and it may seem to you that it is not enough, but oh, my

friends, what an infinity of bounty you possess. As you go from this place, then, trust in the plenty and the bounty of love and find it in meditation again and again, that you may do those things which you wish to do in wholeness, in purity, in love, that you may sing your song with a glad and cheerful heart.

We thank you for allowing us to share these thoughts with you, and would now leave this instrument, that our sister that has been working with the one known as L might exercise that instrument.

I am known to you as Hatonn. Peace, my friends. I leave you in the love and in the light of our infinite Creator. Adonai vasu borragus.

(L channeling)

I am Laitos, and I greet you, my friends, in the love and the light of the infinite Creator. My brothers and sisters, it is, as always, a great pleasure for us to be able to share our vibration with those of this group. At this time it is our desire to pass among you and share our conditioning vibration with those of you who desire this experience. If you would simply mentally request that this sharing occur, it will be our privilege to perform this service for you. I am Laitos.

(Pause)

I am Laitos. I am again with this instrument. My friends, there are those of your planet who would say that your efforts are in vain, that those experiences which you share with one another do not exist, that the sensations that you experience are imaginary. My friends, your presence here is as seekers of truth and your experience is the result of your knowledge of that same truth. The facets of your illusion produce doubt and uncertainty in the best of your race, for such is the purpose of your illusion and for this the forgetting did occur.

My friends, concentrate not on whether your illusion is reality, on whether the voices conveyed through these instruments carry the thoughts of the instrument or of other entities. These are merely distractions. Your purpose, my friends, in this illusion is to determine your path, to choose the direction upon which your growing will occur. Concentrate on that, my friends. Choose well, and follow your choice, and do not let the facets of your illusion distract you from your purpose or occupy your attention.

It may be said that these thoughts so kindly conveyed through those who serve as instruments are unquestionably illusion, for are we not, in some ways, a part of your illusion? Therefore, my friends, accept the need for your choice and follow it, but place not too heavy an emphasis upon words of advice or encouragement from ourselves or others of your realm, for we are no more gods than you, and our advice, no matter how well intentioned, can never supplant that knowledge which stems from your own soul. A wise man of your realm spoke thusly: "Peace be with you, my peace I give unto you." My friends, my loved ones, we cannot improve upon that and such is our wish for you.

At this time we would relinquish our use of this instrument, for he is experiencing some unusual sensations that are distracting from the channeling process. Therefore, we will relinquish both this instrument and the floor, that our brothers and sisters of Latwii may speak. Adonai, my friends.

(Jim channeling)

I am Latwii, and I greet each of you in the love and in the light of the one infinite Creator. It is our joy to be able to blend our vibrations with this group at this time and once more to be able to offer ourselves as humble messengers of light. At this time if there be any light which we may be able to shed on those darker areas of your questions may we then begin? Is there a question at this time?

M: Latwii, the Book of Revelations talks about the second coming of Christ. How does that fit in with the harvest, and is there a second coming of the entity, the spiritual entity of Christ consciousness?

I am Latwii, and am aware of your query, my brother. We may respond by saying that, indeed, there is what you might call a second coming which is occurring upon your planet. Many have spoken of this coming. Many have spoken in a variety of ways of the nature of this coming. It is our understanding that as each of your peoples begins to seek in ever deeper patterns and fashions, that the opening made in each entity's consciousness does allow the energies of what you might call the fourth dimension of love and of understanding to enter that entity's complex of mind, of body, and of spirit. As this awakening occurs within each entity who does so seek for this awakening, there is a coming into the entity of that consciousness which was manifested as a pattern of being by the one known as Jesus of Nazareth, who

did achieve that consciousness during his incarnation for the purpose of setting the pattern so that those who would follow this entity might have an inspiration by which the entity would then evolve in a similar fashion.

The one known as Jesus is not, to our knowledge, to again incarnate upon your plane, but shall communicate to various instruments the message which shall serve as a beacon to many, and when this cycle has been appropriately ended there shall be those entities of like vibration awaiting to greet those of your plane who have made what you have called the graduation, or the transition from the illusion which you now inhabit, to the density of love and understanding.

May we answer you further, my brother?

M: Not at this time, thank you. I'll stew on that for awhile, Latwii.

I am Latwii. We hope we have not given you indigestion, my brother. We do thank you. Is there another question at this time?

C: Yes. In our healing practices, especially in the area known as surgery, there is a—they use, they replenish a person's blood with that of others, and over the years I've been giving blood for such purposes, but of late I've seen material from various groups which refuse, even at the point of ceasing existence, to accept blood from another due to a passage from somewhere in the Bible instructing then not to partake of blood. Is there any harmful effect to the acceptance of blood from another? I see it as merely a giving of life from one to another. I can't see any harm in the practice.

I am Latwii, and am aware of your question, my brother. In response, may we say this is not a simple matter, for indeed one who is approaching the limits of what you know as life and does, therefore, require what is called the transfusion of blood, such a practice might be deemed quite helpful, for indeed it is one means of prolonging the incarnation and might be the only means for many upon your planet, for their knowledge does not yet include other means.

In such cases it cannot be said to be other than helpful if each party does wish to aid in the prolonging of life which grows short. On the other hand, there are situations which mitigate against the transferring of that known as blood from one entity to another if the entities are not involved in what you call the …

(Side one of tape ends.)

(Jim channeling)

I am Latwii, and am once again with this instrument. As we were saying, there are instances which are not favorable to such a transfer of this vital fluid from one entity to another, for there are various, shall we say, patterns or parts of an entity's pattern of being of the bodily complex which are transferred in this process that may be detrimental to another.

We speak of areas now which are little known to your peoples, and are, therefore, most likely to be somewhat confusing, but we shall continue. Each entity does through the power of mind before incarnation create the pattern of the physical vehicle which it shall inhabit. This vehicle, in each cell of its substance, does contain the complete blueprint of the entity, much as a hologram. This is true also of the fluid known as blood. The state of being of health, shall we say, to use somewhat of a misnomer, is clearly reflected in the blood and each cell of that fluid. The transfer of such vital fluid to one entity from another does then transfer the patterns of being or of health from one entity to another, these patterns having a great complexity of interrelationship from the experience of the entity who has provided the blood for transfusion.

Therefore, the one receiving such blood shall be receiving not just a simple bodily fluid, but shall be receiving the patterns of the very being of the entity who served as donor, and shall, therefore, be creating a tie between the two entities in which some of which you know of as karma, shall be shared. This appears quite insignificant when the entity is facing what you call the life and death situation, but does grow in significance as the entity does continue its incarnation and as the entity which served as donor does also continue its incarnation. It is then left to what might be called higher levels of the being of both entities to complete the balancing of the karmic patterns which have been set in motion by this transfer.

We realize that we have said much which is confusing, but we hope that we have been able to transfer to you a basic understanding of this phenomenon.

May we answer you further, my brother?

C: In the case where one receives, say, a pint of blood, which is the usual unit, is the amount of the being of the donor that is received by the individual a sufficient enough amount to actually interfere with the being of the person receiving?

I am Latwii. My brother, we feel that you have correctly stated the situation. The amount is not significant—we correct this instrument—the amount is significant in that it serves as what you might call a ratio, a blending the beingness of the sources of blood, both of the donor and the one receiving the donation.

May we answer you further, my brother?

C: Yes. In our bodily systems, cells are constantly being used up and replaced. After a period of time would that amount of beingness be slowly removed from the blood of the one receiving?

I am Latwii, and am aware of your question, my brother. We may say in this case, in general, that this is not correct, for the reproduction of the blood fluid is by the existing ratio of blood, and this existing ratio does then reproduce itself much as what you have called the cloning mechanism does reproduce an exact duplicate of itself. The dilution, shall we say, of the donor's karmic patterns may occur in another manner, this being the balancing of the patterns of behavior of the one which has received the donation, and also of the one which has served as donor.

May we answer you further, my brother?

C: Yes. I don't mean to bore anybody, but it's something that's been on my mind for awhile. I just want to explore a few points. In the transference of blood from one to another there's a series of matching up, what we refer to as types of blood and RH factors of blood. Is there some basic tie between individuals who have what we refer to as the same blood type and RH factor?

I am Latwii, and am aware of your question, my brother. In this regard we may agree that there is indeed such a tie, but the tie is most general and gross in nature, similar to the relationship between those entities possessing brown hair or red hair or blue eyes, etc. Though the relationship between those with the similar types of blood is somewhat more complex, it is quite similar in nature. The matching of blood types does match the factor which is most easily recognizable by your peoples of the nature of blood, but does not take into account, as we mentioned previously, factors of greater complexity which are at present unknown to your peoples.

May we answer you further, my brother?

C: This is leaving great deal of confusion in my mind. I was considering going and donating again tomorrow, but I don't want to interfere with another's beingness or create a problem for them, and yet I feel drawn to do it for I feel that it's a giving thing to give of oneself to someone who may need, and I know you can't say yes, you should or no, you shouldn't, and I don't expect you to, but if you could speak to me just in general of whether or not the giving—I'm not quite sure how to say this, because I don't want to interfere with anyone else, yet, to me, I feel as if I'm serving others by giving of the life fluid we call blood, and still feel drawn to do so. I just wondered if you can speak to me in general if I would be creating unnecessary problems by doing so.

I am Latwii, and an aware of your question, my brother. We may say in beginning to answer this question in general terms that it is not a simple situation. As each entity proceeds on its chosen path of service few are the types of service that it will find which are purely of one nature or another—service to others or service to self. Even as we speak these words to you, to this group, we realize that we partake in that which is not a simple matter, for as we attempt to share that which we feel to be true in our own experience, we know that by the very nature of the words and the language that we use that we shall distort that which we intend to share, and therefore shall provide some confusion to those who listen. When you undertake an activity, whatever the nature, you shall find that you are unable to make clear distinctions in most cases, for there is, in truth, no way that you can avoid influencing another or infringing in some way upon another's free will, for each entity is most closely related to each other entity, not just in the actions and interactions which you share, but in your very beingness, for are not all one, and can any part of the one act without affecting another part?

When you engage in the giving of the life fluid which you call blood you do engage in an action which is like any other action. You provide a service, yet also do you influence or infringe in some way, however large or small, upon another being. This is the nature of being, for all entities share the experience of being and though each proceeds on a uniquely chosen path it has well been said that no entity is an island, and each does mingle with each other in some fashion. The confusions that you feel in such decisions are those factors which shall provide the necessary stimulus for careful thought, and always do we encourage your thoughts and feelings and innermost being be consulted as the final arbiter in your decision.

May we answer you further, my brother?

C: I want to say one more thing, then I'll stop. It's just the thought as you were speaking came to my mind that somewhere there's someone who in the planning, or in our planning coming into this illusion, that somewhere along the line there's—it was set up for him to receive part of my being as part of our growth, our pattern of incarnation, and it's all—my mind gets confused because I know there are no mistakes and that we really are fulfilling roles that were mapped out before incarnation, and I just feel like, to me, I have the feeling that there's someone waiting for this part of me, and that I should make that part of me available.

I'm not really asking a question or expecting an answer. I'm just more or less talking right now. But I just have that feeling that this part of my being I should share, and I want to thank you for your words tonight. They were very helpful.

I am Latwii. Our gratitude is with you as well, and as you have well stated, each possibility within this illusion has been carefully mapped out, and there is an infinite array of such possibilities that exist. Look about you in your world and you shall see many of them occurring as planned, for nothing occurs by chance.

May we answer yet another question at this time?

Carla: Before we leave this sanguine subject, I'd like to check a couple of hunches. Is it true that the link between patterns of the entities works precisely both ways?

I am Latwii. Yes, my sister, we do recognize this to be true in our understanding of such matters.

May we answer you further?

Carla: Yes. Hunch number two. Is this link the time/space portion of this very central fluid which is called blood, that is magical in nature, and is this why some of the more primitive of our tribes peoples have used blood to become blood brothers and things like this, why even as children we do things like that? Does this have a magical potential in the time/space portion of its reality?

I am Latwii, and again we find agreement with your statement, that the portion known as the time/space portion or metaphysical portion of the entity is that which is affected in what you have described as a magical nature.

May we answer you further, my sister?

Carla: That's very interesting. My last hunch had to do with blood types. I wondered if various planetary influxes of entities into this third-density experience may have at least a preponderance, a majority, of one blood type as opposed to another? I realize this crosses all racial boundaries, and thought perhaps this might be one large classification.

I am Latwii, and am aware of your question, my sister. We find that the answer to this query is in the affirmative when using the rather gross measurements of your peoples, but does become somewhat more difficult to assess and tends towards the negative when looking at the vital fluid in more refined manners.

May we answer you further, my sister?

Carla: No, thank you very much Latwii.

I am Latwii. We are thankful as well to you. Is there another question at this time?

C: Yes, while we're on the subject. If the pattern of beingness in each self … what of the situation as in our, in the drinking, in the partaking of blood orally as opposed to taking it into the veins directly, if ingesting the cells of another being, whether flesh or blood, do you still pick up the beingness?

I am Latwii, and am aware of your question, my brother. Again, we find that the general response can be somewhat misleading, for such an action as you have described would have far different results with different types of entities. Those most likely to accomplish such an action would be those who have begun the practice of what you might call the black magical arts and such an adept then would gain power, the power of the one whose vital fluid it

consumed. An entity who had no training in these arts and rituals would simply gain those karmic ties in the time/space or metaphysical portion of your existence.

May we answer you further, my brother?

C: I was just curious because in our legends of creatures such as vampires, they're always able to remove the being and leave just a shell, more or less, though animated, no longer expressing that which it was, and I was just curious as to the source of that idea, whether there was some truth behind it.

I am Latwii, and am aware of a general query. We may respond by saying that your legends in this regard have distorted greatly the foundation of facts in such situations, but have reflected some of that which is more nearly true. The magical nature of the fluid you call blood has been reflected in such stories and legends, for indeed the entity whose blood has been removed in some degree is only a shell of the former self, the greater portion having passed to the entity consuming the blood, the greater portion of power also passing with that consuming.

May we answer you further, my brother?

C: No. I think I shall take my leave of the subject. At least for now. There are other thinks floating around in my head, but I think I've sufficiently beleaguered the point for tonight or grossed out for the night …

M: You've bled it to death!

C: Wait! One more thing, one more … Many, even still, peoples have had a basic belief that the partaking of the blood of a particular creature, they could gain the attributes of that other creature, such as the partaking of the blood of the lion for fierceness, things of that nature, and I was just trying to picture where the, whether they received this information from a contact or whether it was just something they knew somewhere back in their lives before the forgetting that the beingness of another can be received through the blood.

I am Latwii, and am aware of your question, my brother. In this regard we may say that throughout the history of the peoples of your planet there have been those small groups located in various places upon your planet's surface who have, throughout time, sought the various means of gaining personal power. Such a seeking does then serve as a calling, and attracts those entities of what you might call a negative nature, who in their desire to serve the self do respond to this calling much as we respond to your calling, and they do make contact with these entities, and in, shall we say, a trade, do provide information which allows these entities to gain personal power, if these entities then shall do the bidding of those who have answered their call.

Such information as you have discussed this evening concerning the nature of blood and its magical properties is then given so that power might be concentrated in the hands of a few who then do owe their allegiance to a number of lesser, or entities of fewer numbers, but, shall we say, greater power.

May we answer you further, my brother?

C: No, thank you. I shall now cease the questions on the subject. Thank you very much.

I am Latwii. We are grateful to you as well, though this is somewhat of a distasteful subject. Is there another question at this time?

L: Yes. It seems to me every coin has two sides, There is a rather substantial number of people on this planet who currently are involved in a ritual partaking of blood. In their belief a transubstantiation occurs in which wine is metaphysically converted into blood of the one we knew as Jesus Christ. I realize you've no desire to get into a religious discussion, but could you speak in general upon this subject and the possible benefits resulting, if there are any.

I am Latwii, and am aware of your question, my brother. Again, we may return to the magical nature of that which is known as blood, but we now move to the time/space or metaphysical portion when discussing that activity which is known to your peoples as the Holy Communion.

The entity known as Jesus did possess a knowledge that was deep upon the subject of the magical transfiguration, shall we say, of its source of enlightenment or power unto those whom it desired to serve. It was well aware that the ritual of communion would provide those entities revering it with a means of making an opening within the time/space portion of their beings for the love and light of the one Creator to fill that opening, depending upon how efficiently the entity had prepared its being to receive this vital energy, much as a transfusion, if we may continue our analogy.

This particular type of ritual does focus, then, upon the aspects which you might call positive in the transferring of the power of the magical nature of life fluids and life energies which course through all creation. This type of ritual known as the Holy Communion does, then, allow each who partakes of it to drink of the life-giving beingness of the Father, so that those transfers of energy and of power are those which seek to serve the others of the being so that there is an increase in the level of awareness of the unity of all creation within those who partake within the ritual of communion.

May we answer you further, my brother?

L: Yes. In the accomplishment of this ritual, communion, is there any special significance to wine as opposed to any other substance? Does wine have a particular value that other substances do not possess that aids this transubstantiation?

I am Latwii, and am aware of your query, my brother. In this regard we may say that to those who first began the ritual with the use of that known as wine there was a purpose which allowed this substance to serve most efficiently for them. It is not necessary to use any particular substance. It is only necessary that whatever substance is used be given by those who use it, the trappings, shall we say, or the belief in its ability to serve as a pattern or symbol for that vital energy which is being channeled through it.

May we answer you further, my brother?

L: I have a couple of questions of a more personal nature. I was experiencing some intense conditioning earlier by Laitos. I would like to know if you can tell me the purpose for this, and why it seemed distinctly different from other conditioning I've received?

I am Latwii. In this case, my brother, we may say that the conditioning which you received this evening was aimed at the further deepening of your own channel which has been, of late, able to receive a wider band of information. In this regard we mean to convey the concept that your particular tuning has been increasing in its ability to perceive a wider array of contacts, including those of a narrower band and those of wider band, and this conditioning was, therefore, carried out with more vigor, shall we say, so as to continue the process of expansion which has already begun.

May we answer you further, my brother?

L: Yes. Is there any way, aside from continued requests …

(Tape ends.) ♣

L/L Research is a subsidiary of
Rock Creek Research &
Development Laboratories, Inc.

P.O. Box 5195
Louisville, KY 40255-0195

L/L Research

www.llresearch.org

Rock Creek is a non-profit
corporation dedicated to
discovering and sharing
information which may aid in
the spiritual evolution of
humankind.

Intensive Meditation
March 22, 1982

(Carla channeling)

[I am Hatonn, and] I greet this group in the love and in the light of the one infinite Creator Whom we all serve and in Whose love we all grow and breathe. We have been with this instrument for some time conditioning this instrument while attempting to reach the one known as C. We are aware that this instrument has had difficulty perceiving our contact, as it is intended to be a broader range contact and therefore easier to receive. It is therefore less easy to receive by one such as the one known as C which has become very sensitive to a somewhat narrower band of sensation preceding contact. We therefore would initiate, to the best of our ability, a simple opening of the mouth—somewhat as a yawn, as you call it, would feel, although, unlike a yawn, the need to breathe deeply and exhale deeply is not present—as a signal that the instrument has been contacted by the one known to you as Hatonn. We hope that we are able to effect this simple mechanical movement, and that this in turn will give the instrument the confidence which it desires.

There has been good contact at all times, however, it is very meritorious that the instrument not speak if there is doubt as to the origin of the contact. It is far better to remain tuned and silent than to accept a possible detuning by channeling an entity of whose identity you are not sure. We will again attempt to contact the one known as C using this recognition mechanism as a conditioning mechanism. We hope that it will be gentle without being so gentle that it is impractical. We transfer now. I am Hatonn.

(C channeling)

I am Hatonn, and I am now with this instrument. We feel that he now feels more comfortable and that the signal we mentioned will be felt [by] him in our attempt to contact this instrument. We are aware that this signal is somewhat similar to the way in which this instrument receives our brothers and sisters of Laitos, but we feel that our signal will be somewhat stronger and will not be confused when used.

We are Hatonn. We are more than grateful and happy to work with those who wish to be of service as vocal channels and with any who wish our help of the deepening of their meditation in their search to become more aware of the love and the light of the infinite Creator.

My friends, to speak to you for what to you has been a long period of time has been a great source of joy and of learning for us. We feel privileged that you request us so often to hear the message that we have, the message that is always the same. But always a new facet is shown that you may take each one and study and meditate upon it and add it to the others you have seen and become aware that by summation of the parts you may see that the whole is greater than the sum of the parts can ever be.

The love and the light of the infinite Creator is beyond meaning that your language can give, beyond that we or you now see. You become aware in your vision of only a small part of that light and love but as with all things in your illusion, beyond the first step needs to be taken, the choice must begun to be made, the path chosen. Now take what may be said to be equivalent to your first baby steps, the first few steps along the long but joyous path back to the One. Remember always that there is ever so much more to learn than you can see in your illusion. You perception is limited by physical vehicles and by the amount of your mental faculties that have been activated. But you shall know, you shall learn, you shall be aware. Take your steps carefully, and if you stumble and fall be not proud and refuse the help of others. If help is needed, allow them to help you, to stand once again that you continue to take the small but important steps. You are not alone, as we are not alone. There are countless kindred souls who reach out, who wish to help, who wish to give. They are not too proud to receive. They are with you, brothers and sisters. We are known to you as Hatonn, but also as brother and sister, as friend, as student, as teacher, as all those things that you want, that we all want. We rejoice with you as you step, to each as you go about that step.

We now close. Adonai, my friends. Adonai vasu borragus.

(Jim channeling)

I am Latwii, and greet you all in love and light. We have been waiting patiently for the opportunity to present our humble service to this group once again. We, as always, are overjoyed at the possibility of lending some light in whatever amount to those areas which are in some doubt and about which you have questions. At this time we would ask if any present would have a question?

C: D and I both have requests. We both know that children tend to reflect back those things that they see, experience, especially from the parents when they are a young age, but of late—well, really, for some time now—we've noticed that our son does not readily take up the roles that many in our society expect of children to take. In his preschool and even with other children in the area where we live, he

tends to draw people to him both older and younger but he does not easily, is not easily able to form any type of relationship, but tends to remain to himself. He tends not to try to fully utilize abilities that he has or that those who work with him know he has, at least not in their or in our way of thinking that he should use them. And I really would just like you to tell me anything that you could about our son within the limitations that I know that you must follow.

I am Latwii, and am aware of your request, my brother. To this regard may we say that it is correct to assume that the young child, as you call it, will in its younger years tend to reflect those behaviors, thoughts and patterns of its family and friends. But after a certain period of experience has been gained, and the young entity has begun to feel its own individual sense of being, then there shall begin to be those expressions of the young entity which the entity his incarnated for the purpose of expressing. It is to be noted in this regard that at this time there are many factors which govern the process and pattern of incarnations for entities upon your plane. As you know, this is the time of the harvest. Those entities having the greatest opportunity and potential for polarizing, shall we say, sufficiently, their own conscious beings may through catalyst experienced in an incarnation achieve that which is known as the graduation. Never before have so, shall we say, pure a group of entities been incarnate upon your plane. Which means that there shall be the individual expression of beingness in great variety and the illusion which you inhabit shall more fully provide the catalyst which these beings need in order to learn the lessons that will allow graduation.

The illusion which you inhabit has certain expectations, shall we say, of the entities which comprise it and move about in it. These expectations, roles and patterns of behavior are not in themselves that which is …

(Tape ends.) ♣

L/L Research is a subsidiary of
Rock Creek Research &
Development Laboratories, Inc.

P.O. Box 5195
Louisville, KY 40255-0195

L/L RESEARCH

www.llresearch.org

Rock Creek is a non-profit
corporation dedicated to
discovering and sharing
information which may aid in
the spiritual evolution of
humankind.

THE LAW OF ONE, BOOK IV, SESSION 81
MARCH 22, 1982

Ra: I am Ra. I greet you in the love and in the light of the one infinite Creator. We communicate now.

Questioner: Could you first tell me the condition of the instrument?

Ra: I am Ra. The physical complex energy is in deficit at this particular space/time nexus due to prolonged psychic accentuation of pre-existing distortions. The remainder of the energy complex levels are as previously stated.

Questioner: Is this the reason for the instrument's feeling of uninterrupted weariness?

Ra: I am Ra. There are portions of your space/time in which this may be said to be symptomatic of the psychic greeting reaction. However, the continual weariness is not due to psychic greeting but is rather an inevitable consequence of this contact.

Questioner: Why is this an inevitable consequence? What is the mechanism of this contact that creates this weariness?

Ra: I am Ra. The mechanism creating weariness is that connection betwixt the density wherein this instrument's mind/body/spirit complex is safely kept during these workings and the altogether variant density in which the instrument's physical body complex resides at this space/time. As the instrument takes on more of the coloration of the resting density the third-density experience seems more heavy and wearisome. This was accepted by the instrument, as it desired to be of service. Therefore, we accept also

this effect about which nothing of which we are aware may be done.

Questioner: Is the effect a function of the number of sessions, and has it reached a peak level or will it continue to increase in effect?

Ra: I am Ra. This wearying effect will continue but should not be confused with the physical energy levels, having only to do with the, as you would call it, daily round of experience. In this sphere those things which are known already to aid this instrument will continue to be of aid. You will, however, notice the gradual increase in transparency, shall we say, of the vibrations of the instrument.

Questioner: I didn't understand what you meant by that last statement. Could you explain it?

Ra: I am Ra. Weariness of the time/space nature may be seen to be that reaction of transparent or pure vibrations with impure, confused, or opaque environs.

Questioner: Is there any of this effect upon the other two of us in this group?

Ra: I am Ra. This is quite correct.

Questioner: Then we would also experience the uninterrupted weariness as a consequence of the contact. Is this correct?

Ra: I am Ra. The instrument, by the very nature of the contact, bears the brunt of this effect. Each of the support group, by offering the love and the light of the one infinite Creator in unqualified support in these workings and in energy transfers for the purpose of these workings, experiences between 10 and 15 percent, roughly, of this effect. It is cumulative and identical in the continual nature of its manifestation.

Questioner: What could be the result of this continued wearying effect after a long period?

Ra: I am Ra. You ask a general query with infinite answers. We shall over-generalize in order to attempt to reply.

One group might be tempted and thus lose the very contact which caused the difficulty. So the story would end.

Another group might be strong at first but not faithful in the face of difficulty. Thus the story would end.

Another group might choose the path of martyrdom in its completeness and use the instrument until its physical body complex failed from the harsh toll demanded when all energy was gone.

This particular group, at this particular nexus, is attempting to conserve the vital energy of the instrument. It is attempting to balance love of service and wisdom of service, and it is faithful to the service in the face of difficulty. Temptation has not yet ended this group's story.

We may not know the future, but the probability of this situation continuing over a relatively substantial period of your space/time is large. The significant factor is the will of the instrument and of the group to serve. That is the only cause for balancing the slowly increasing weariness which will continue to distort your perceptions. Without this will the contact might be possible but finally seem too much of an effort.

Questioner: The instrument would like to know why she has a feeling of increased vital energy?

Ra: I am Ra. We leave this answer to the instrument.

Questioner: She would like to know if she has an increased sensitivity to foods?

Ra: I am Ra. This instrument has an increased sensitivity to all stimuli. It is well that it use prudence.

Questioner: Going back to the previous session, picking up on the tenth archetype, which is the Catalyst of the Body, the Wheel of Fortune represents interaction with other-selves. Is this a correct statement?

Ra: I am Ra. This may be seen to be a roughly correct statement in that each catalyst is dealing with the nature of those experiences entering the energy web and vibratory perceptions of the mind/body/spirit complex. The most carefully noted addition would be that the outside stimulus of the Wheel of Fortune is that which offers both positive and negative experience.

Questioner: The eleventh archetype would then be the Experience of the Body which represents the catalyst which has been processed by the mind/body/spirit complex and is called the Enchantress because it produces further seed for growth. Is this correct?

Ra: I am Ra. This is correct.

Questioner: We have already discussed the Significator, so I will skip number thirteen. The Transformation of the Body is called Death, for with death the body is transformed to a higher vibrational body for additional learning. Is this correct?

Ra: I am Ra. This is correct and may be seen to be additionally correct in that each moment and certainly each diurnal period of the bodily incarnation offers death and rebirth to one which is attempting to use the catalyst which is offered it.

Questioner: Finally, the fourteenth, the Way of the Body is called the Alchemist because there is an infinity of time for the various bodies to operate within to learn the lessons necessary for evolution. Is this correct?

Ra: I am Ra. This is less than completely correct as the Great Way of the Body must be seen, as are all the archetypes of the body, to be a mirror image of the thrust of the activity of the mind. The body is the creature of the mind and is the instrument of manifestation for the fruits of mind and spirit. Therefore, you may see the body as providing the athanor[2] through which the Alchemist manifests gold.

Questioner: I have guessed that the way to enter into a better comprehension of the archetypes is to

---

[2] athanor: an oven; a fire; a digesting furnace, formerly used in alchemy, so constructed as to maintain a uniform and constant heat.

compare what we experience now, after the veil, with what was experienced prior to that time, starting possibly as far back as the beginning of this octave of experience, to see how we got into the condition that we are in now. If this is agreeable I would like to retreat to the very beginning of this octave of experience to investigate the conditions of mind, body, and spirit as they evolved in this octave. Is this acceptable?

Ra: I am Ra. The direction of questions is your provenance.

Questioner: Ra states that it has knowledge of only this octave, but it seems that Ra has complete knowledge of this octave.

Can you tell me why this is?

Ra: I am Ra. Firstly, we do not have complete knowledge of this octave. There are portions of the seventh density which, although described to us by our teachers, remain mysterious. Secondly, we have experienced a great deal of the available refining catalyst of this octave, and our teachers have worked with us most carefully that we may be one with all, that in turn our eventual returning to the great all-ness of creation shall be complete.

Questioner: Then Ra has knowledge from the first beginnings of this octave through its present experience and what I might call direct or experiential knowledge through communication with those space/times and time/spaces, but has not yet evolved to or penetrated the seventh level. Is this a roughly correct statement?

Ra: I am Ra. Yes.

Questioner: Why does Ra not have any knowledge of that which was prior to the beginning of this octave?

Ra: I am Ra. Let us compare octaves to islands. It may be that the inhabitants of an island are not alone upon a planetary sphere, but if an ocean-going vehicle in which one may survive has not been invented, true knowledge of other islands is possible only if an entity comes among the islanders and says, "I am from elsewhere." This is a rough analogy. However, we have evidence of this sort, both of previous creation and creation to be, as we in the stream of space/time and time/space view these apparently non-simultaneous events.

Questioner: We presently find ourselves in the Milky Way Galaxy of some 200 or so billion stars and there are millions and millions of these large galaxies spread out through what we call space. To Ra's knowledge, can I assume that the number of these galaxies is infinite? Is this correct?

Ra: I am Ra. This is precisely correct and is a significant point.

Questioner: The point being that we have unity. Is that correct?

Ra: I am Ra. You are perceptive.

Questioner: Then what portion of these galaxies is Ra aware of? Has Ra experienced consciousness in many other of these galaxies?

Ra: I am Ra. No.

Questioner: Has Ra experienced or does Ra have any knowledge of any of these other galaxies? Has Ra traveled to, in one form or another, any of these other galaxies?

Ra: I am Ra. Yes.

Questioner: It's unimportant, but how many other of these galaxies has Ra traveled to?

Ra: I am Ra. We have opened our hearts in radiation of love to the entire creation. Approximately 90 percent of the creation is at some level aware of the sending and able to reply. All of the infinite Logoi are one in the consciousness of love. This is the type of contact which we enjoy rather than travel.

Questioner: So that I can just get a little idea of what I am talking about, what are the limits of Ra's travel in the sense of directly experiencing or seeing the activities of various places? Is it solely within this galaxy, and if so, how much of this galaxy? Or does it include some other galaxies?

Ra: I am Ra. Although it would be possible for us to move at will throughout the creation within this Logos, that is to say, the Milky Way Galaxy, so-called, we have moved where we were called to service; these locations being, shall we say, local and including Alpha Centauri, planets of your solar system which you call the Sun, Cepheus, and Zeta Reticuli. To these sub-Logoi we have come, having been called.

Questioner: Was the call in each instance from the third-density beings or was this call from other densities?

Ra: I am Ra. In general, the latter supposition is correct. In the particular case of the Sun sub-Logos, third density is the density of calling.

Questioner: Ra then has not moved at any time into one of the other major galaxies. Is this correct?

Ra: I am Ra. This is correct.

Questioner: Does Ra have knowledge of any other major galaxy or the consciousness of anything in that galaxy?

Ra: I am Ra. We assume you are speaking of the possibility of knowledge of other major galaxies. There are Wanderers from other major galaxies drawn to the specific needs of a single call. There are those among our social memory complex which have become Wanderers in other major galaxies. Thus there has been knowledge of other major galaxies, for to one whose personality or mind/body/spirit complex has been crystallized the universe is one place and there is no bar upon travel. However, our interpretation of your query was a query concerning the social memory complex traveling to another major galaxy. We have not done this, nor do we contemplate it, for we can reach in love with our hearts.

Questioner: Thank you. In this line of questioning I am trying to establish a basis for understanding the foundation for not only the experience that we have now but how the experience was formed and how it is related to all the rest of the experience through the portion of the octave as we understand it. I am assuming, then, that all of these galaxies, this infinite number of galaxies that we can just begin to become aware of with our telescopes, are all of the same octave. Is this correct?

Ra: I am Ra. This is correct.

Questioner: I was wondering if some of the Wanderers from Ra in going to some of the other major galaxies, that is, leaving this system of some 200 billion stars of lenticular shape and going to another cluster of billions of stars and finding their way into some planetary situation there, would encounter the dual polarity that we have here, the service-to-self and the service-to-others polarities?

Ra: I am Ra. This is correct.

Questioner: You stated earlier that toward the center of this galaxy is what, to use a poor term, you could call the older portion where you would find no service-to-self polarization. Am I correct in assuming that this is true with the other galaxies with which Wanderers from Ra have experience? At the center of these galaxies only the service-to-others polarity exists and the experiment started farther out toward the rim of the galaxy?

Ra: I am Ra. Various Logoi and sub-Logoi had various methods of arriving at the discovery of the efficiency of free will in intensifying the experience of the Creator by the Creator. However, in each case this has been a pattern.

Questioner: You mean then that the pattern is that the service-to-self polarization appeared farther out from the center of the galactic spiral?

Ra: I am Ra. This is correct.

Questioner: From this I will assume that from the beginning of the octave we had the core of many galactic spirals forming, and I know that this is incorrect in the sense of timelessness, but as the spiral formed then I am assuming that in this particular octave the experiment of the veiling and the extending of free will must have started, roughly, simultaneously in many, many of the budding or building galactic systems. Am I in any way correct with this assumption?

Ra: I am Ra. You are precisely correct. This instrument is unusually fragile at this space/time and has used much of the transferred energy. We would invite one more full query for this working.

Questioner: Actually, I don't have much more on this except to make the assumption that there must have been some type of communication throughout the octave so that, when the first experiment became effective, knowledge of this spread rapidly through the octave and was picked up by other budding galactic spirals, you might say. Is this correct?

Ra: I am Ra. This is correct. To be aware of the nature of this communication is to be aware of the nature of the Logos. Much of what you call creation has never separated from the One Logos of this octave and resides within the one infinite Creator. Communication in such an environment is the communication of cells of the body. That which is learned by one is known to all. The sub-Logoi, then, have been in the position of refining the discoveries of what might be called the earlier sub-Logoi. May we ask if we may answer any brief queries at this working?

Questioner: Only if there is anything that we can do to make the instrument more comfortable or to improve the contact?

Ra: I am Ra. It is difficult to determine the energy levels of the instrument and support group. Of this we are aware. It is, however, recommended that every attempt be made to enter each working with the most desirable configurations of energy possible. All is well, my friends. You are conscientious and the alignments are well.

I am Ra. I leave you in the love and the light of the one infinite Creator. Go forth, therefore, rejoicing in the power and in the peace of the infinite Creator. Adonai. ♣

L/L RESEARCH

L/L Research is a subsidiary of
Rock Creek Research &
Development Laboratories, Inc.

P.O. Box 5195
Louisville, KY 40255-0195

www.llresearch.org

Rock Creek is a non-profit
corporation dedicated to
discovering and sharing
information which may aid in
the spiritual evolution of
humankind.

FRIDAY NIGHT
MARCH 26, 1982

(Unknown channeling)

I am Hatonn. It is a great pleasure and privilege to join you in your simultaneous acts this evening of service and pleasure. We are privileged to be admitted into your presence in this creative time for it is too seldom on your planet that members of your race are capable of perceiving the pleasure and satisfaction resultant of service, but rather perceive only sensations of discord, jealousy or doubt as they find that their efforts too often are grudgingly given under the suspicion that they may be actually allowing themselves in some manner to be taken advantage of.

My friends, it is no small achievement to be able in your illusion to lovingly give of yourselves in this manner. It is our pleasure tonight to share with you some thoughts on the subject of giving. It is appropriate to understand the reasons for which this service is performed if one is to seek attainment through the use of giving as a tool. Too often giving is regarded as a finite act, a sort of stopgap effort similar to that of a gear on a watch which at regular intervals detains a rotating wheel or gear for an increment of time as to prevent a surge of energy to burst out of control, accomplishing nothing as the hands of the watch spin uselessly at a high rate of speed. Many on your planet regard giving as a way of temporarily preventing their life from spinning

uselessly out of control by the periodic application of spiritual brakes, so to speak.

My friends, giving extends much further than service to self. There is a point at which the act of giving can be regarded as finite, thus limiting the effect of the action. There is also a point at which the same act of giving may produce an infinite amount of effects, all oriented toward the service to one's brothers and sisters. It is said on your planet that it is better to give than to receive. This is because the act of receiving is a simple service to another, yet the act of giving can and should be a constant and daily process as one performs those tasks necessary for participation within your illusion.

For example, many of those present serve in the capacity as assistants for the physical, emotional and educational maturation of recently arrived members of your race. It is quite easily understood that one who serves as a mother, for example, may spend an entire day engrossed in the function of giving to those recently arrived entities in that their requirements for physical and emotional attention are quite stringent. The pattern of giving then becomes not a simple jerky stopgap which punctuates the parents' day, but rather flows continuously from early morning until late night, and as we have noticed, regrettably, late into the night and early into the morning as well. It is one of the lessons of your experience within this illusion that this example of a continuous flow of giving of service may be extended beyond the more obvious requirements of the young child to the more subtle needs of those individuals—often strangers—which one encounters through the passage of one's waking hours.

It is possible to spend an entire waking day performing a myriad number of services for literally hundreds of individuals within your developing social/memory/complex, thus reinforcing those developing ties which will eventually link each individual to his or her fellow members of that developing complex. As this in itself is a major accomplishment for those currently in physical existence upon your planetary surface and as the development of positively-oriented social memory complexes is beneficial on a more grand scale to the entirety of creation, it may be understood that the simple act of wishing good morning to a stranger, holding a door open, picking up an object that another has dropped, may all be combined into a major accomplishment. That which unifies these seemingly insignificant individual events, my friends, into a continuous flow of giving is the conscious, although generally non-verbal, expression of love for those one encounters during the day combined with the loving acceptance of those same individuals.

The statement has been made on your planet that one should judge not lest one be judged. This is significant, my friends, in that the act of judgment is the act of simultaneously separating oneself and the self of another individual from that developing complex as one chooses to place themselves in a role of judicial separateness and the recipient of the judgment in the role of being detected as a portion of the complex which has attained insufficiently in certain aspects so as to no longer be capable of full participation. My friends, this act of judgment in separating both yourself as judge and your subject as an inadvertent victim of your judgment from that same developing social memory complex toward which your striving could possibly be more focused.

Therefore, my friends, we urge you to abandon the seat of judgment to those less suited for the position of a loving member of a family, that family being the unified group which struggles to attain the necessary levels of unification of intention, wisdom and compassion to accomplish a unified polarization.

At this time, my friends, we of Hatonn will leave this instrument, that our brothers and sisters of Laitos may in turn communicate with those present. Adonai, my friends. Adonai vasu borragus.

(Unknown channeling)

I am Laitos. I am with this instrument, and I greet you in the love and light of our infinite Creator. My friends, we too thank you for the opportunity to share in your efforts this evening. We are aware that there has been a calling for our vibration within those members of your group this evening, and at this time it is our desire to share our conditioning vibration with those of you present who wish to experience our contact. If it is your desire, simple mentally request that you might receive our conditioning vibration and we will gratefully perform this service to the best of our ability. At this time we desire to pass among you for this service. I am Laitos.

I am Laitos. I am again with this instrument. We are grateful for the opportunity to provide our small service and desire to remind you that we are available for this same purpose to any of you who might request our aid, no matter how brief the period of time you might have available to you. We thank you for providing us this opportunity to perform our small service. At this time we in turn shall relinquish this instrument that our brothers and sisters of Latwii might perform their service of answering whatever questions are within their abilities and limitations to answer. Again, we thank you. I am Laitos.

(Jim channeling)

I am Latwii, and I greet you, my brothers and sisters, in the love and the light of the infinite Creator. My friends, we are very happy to be here tonight for we have been observing your actions this evening and we must say that they seem from our vantage point to be quite enjoyable and you, in turn, seem to be taking full advantage of the opportunity to be enjoying your experience, and for this, my friends, we congratulate you for far too many of your brothers and sisters of your planet seem to take advantage of opportunities when among others of your race to pursue the path of boredom or superficiality or moroseness. Fortunately, we do not find it necessary to extend more than a passing glance in those directions as the calling for our services are very, very limited in those situations.

Again, we are grateful that we are called to such a pleasant atmosphere and wish to thank you for that reason. At this time we would open the floor, so to speak …

(Side one of tape ends.)

(Jim channeling)

I am Latwii. We are again with this instrument and with you. Are there any questions we might attempt to answer at this time?

S1: I have a question. I read about a young man a couple of years ago by the name of Carlos Castaneda. He was doing some research work with an Indian brujo in Mexico, supposedly using some hallucinogenic drugs to communicate with the gods, so to speak. Could you shed a little light, on the ancient Indian rituals and how they came about?

I am Latwii. I am aware of your question. My sister, we would with your permission attempt to answer your query in several segments as we feel that there are some implied queries within your statement that we would like to answer as well as your phrased question. So, with your permission, we will answer as follows.

First, the performance of rituals or the ingestion of any substance is not necessary to accomplish a communication with the gods. It is very common on your planetary surface for individuals of even the more conservative religious groups to acknowledge communication with that which they conceive as an omnipotent spiritual being. There seems to be some disagreement as to whether the communications for the masses of participants [is] one-way or two-way but there seems to be a general consensus among those leaders of those groups that the communication between those leaders and that which they refer to as a "God" is definitely both ways.

We will not attempt to evaluate the accuracy to this form of communication, rather we would choose to emphasize communication with that concept referred to as a "God" is considered quite common on your planet in many forms. We would add on this subject, prior to exhausting it, that if you wish to communicate with the Creator, simply address, whether yourself, your brother, or sister or any object within reach, for all are a part of the Creator. The rituals developed by the ancients of your race were developed to attain the state of spiritual

closeness or oneness with the Creator because the understanding of the Creator and the universe for these individuals was somewhat limited. The tool of ceremony and its lesser tools of drugs, instruments, drawings, etc., were all to serve the purpose of assisting the individuals and establishing and maintaining a contact with the creative consciousness of your universe.

The duplication of these rituals [or] the ingestion of the previously described substances would not be recommended for one who is seeking this same contact any more than driving a motorized vehicle or facing oneself for a period of time beneath the surface of a body of water to perform a ritual for that same purpose. The purpose of any ritual is simply to function as a tool and the tool generally is designed and selected by its owner to fulfill his or her specific need.

May we answer you further, my sister?

S1 No, I think not. Thank you.

As always, my sister, we thank you for the opportunity of being of service. Is there another question?

S2: *(Inaudible).*

I am Latwii. It is our desire, my brother, that you would attempt to clarify your question. There are limitations upon our ability to answer on this particular subject without further clarification of your inquiry.

S2: *(Inaudible).*

I am Latwii. I am aware of your question. My brother, you must understand that the limitations under which we function include a restriction against revealing to an individual that which is more appropriately learned by the individual as a portion of their educational experience while participating within this illusion. It is possible to explain to you, my brother, that the ability to receive this image reveals within you an ability in the area normally referred to as clairaudience which may be developed and refined. However, we are unable to divulge to you the significance of the image you have received for that is more appropriately an answer to be sought within your own self.

May we answer you further, my brother?

S2: Would you explain the concept of clairaudience?

I am Latwii. Clairaudience may be described as the ability which all possess but most in an unrefined state to perceive mentally the communication of other entities such as the instrument's channeling. The clairaudience may be of a conscious nature—as again in the example of channeling—or of an unconscious nature in which the individual does not recognize that communication is being received but rather recognizes only the sudden perception of hunches or ideas that are actually the revelation of information from an outside source without the individual perception of the information as a communication.

May we answer you further?

S2: No, that answers that. My second question is, I've tried to ask before about what I believe to have been a UFO sighting when I was five years old. Can you tell me now, would it be any different, was what I saw a UFO?

I am Latwii. I am aware of your question. My brother, the function of various elements of information may possibly be to act as keys in the unlocking of areas of understanding. There are the times when the key may be given from one to another. There are other times when the individual already possesses the key and must locate and use that key which is already possessed. We would not desire to make a factual statement but rather an evaluation or opinion in saying that we believe your situation in reference to the subject you described is of the latter group and that the likelihood of an outside source revealing to you that which should be revealed from within is very nominal.

We would suggest that further development in the area of meditative communication with oneself might be beneficial. We would also suggest, my brother, that it is not always beneficial to constantly focus one's attention on past events, for this often prevents one from extending their attention to that which occurs presently. We would therefore suggest that in your particular case, benefits might be achieved in the pursuit of understanding of the lessons which you currently are experiencing rather than lessons which may have occurred or may not have occurred at a period of time of approximately twenty of your years ago.

May we answer you further, my brother?

S2: Well, if I could just explain. It has puzzled me about the path that I've taken in my life, and the specialized studies that I've taken all my life, that has brought me to this time, and I've often felt that that might have been the start of it, by that one occurrence of seeing the UFO, and it's always puzzled me how I've been on an almost directed path, and I've felt this path was within me all along, and the deeper desire to study these specialized areas was always there. That's why I question it. I realize you're saying that I should devote more energy to the area of the future, which I'll try to do, but it still feels like something has guided me to this. Maybe it's what is referred to as my higher self. I really don't know. It will remain a question.

I am Latwii. My brother, we can empathize with the thoughts that you have expressed. We would concur with you that the guiding force of your life is not an outer force or external entity but rather that which you refer to as the higher self. We would also suggest to you, my brother, that many events in one's life are like signposts which assist one in following a predetermined route. Occasionally one may pass a signpost and either correctly or incorrectly read that which is presented. Often the misconceived signpost functions very well in guiding the traveler along the route that the subconscious, in its wisdom, prefers to that which the conscious mind thinks it prefers. In other cases, the signposts are read correctly and followed with great diligence to a consciously perceived objective. The experiences of most individuals, regrettably, are to travel in small circles, not realizing that the signposts exist.

We would encourage you, my brother, in following your path in the diligent manner that you have displayed. However, we would again suggest that the signposts be perceived as just that, and that one might better concentrate on the road which one's attention is focused forward [on] instead of on signposts of the past.

May we answer you further?

S2: That's good advice. One other thing that has puzzled me that you probably couldn't tell me is I've often wondered if maybe I've been what is sometimes referred to as a wanderer, that I've come from a higher density to assist the people of this density to reach a higher density. Is that within the realm of possibility or should I just continue thinking about your advice following more on the present and future than the past?

I am Latwii. My brother, it is correct to assume that all things are within the realm of possibility. It is not our privilege to define the number or identity of those individuals known to you as wanderers for the simple reason that the path …

(Tape ends.) ❧

L/L Research is a subsidiary of
Rock Creek Research &
Development Laboratories, Inc.

P.O. Box 5195
Louisville, KY 40255-0195

L/L Research

www.llresearch.org

Rock Creek is a non-profit
corporation dedicated to
discovering and sharing
information which may aid in
the spiritual evolution of
humankind.

ABOUT THE CONTENTS OF THIS TRANSCRIPT: This telepathic channeling has been taken from transcriptions of the weekly study and meditation meetings of the Rock Creek Research & Development Laboratories and L/L Research. It is offered in the hope that it may be useful to you. As the Confederation entities always make a point of saying, please use your discrimination and judgment in assessing this material. If something rings true to you, fine. If something does not resonate, please leave it behind, for neither we nor those of the Confederation would wish to be a stumbling block for any.

The Law of One, Book IV, Session 82
March 27, 1982

Ra: I am Ra. I greet you, my friends, in the love and in the light of the one infinite Creator. We communicate now.

Questioner: Could you first please give me the condition of the instrument?

Ra: I am Ra. It is as previously stated.

Questioner: Is there anything at all that we could do that we are not doing—besides eliminating the contact—to increase the physical energy of the instrument?

Ra: I am Ra. There is the possibility/probability that the whirling of the water with spine erect would alter, somewhat, the distortion towards what you call pain which this entity experiences in the dorsal region on a continuous level. This in turn could aid in the distortion towards increase of physical energy to some extent.

Questioner: I would like to consider the condition at a time or position just prior to the beginning of this octave of experience. I am assuming that, just prior to the beginning of this octave, intelligent infinity had created and already experienced one or more previous octaves. Is this correct?

Ra: I am Ra. You assume correctly. However, the phrase would more informatively read, infinite intelligence had experienced previous octaves.

Questioner: Does Ra have any knowledge of the number of previous octaves; if so, how many?

Ra: I am Ra. As far as we are aware we are in an infinite creation. There is no counting.

Questioner: That's what I thought you might say. Am I correct in assuming that at the beginning of this octave, out of what I would call a void of space, seeds of an infinite number of galactic systems such as the Milky Way Galaxy appeared and grew in spiral fashion simultaneously?

Ra: I am Ra. There are duple areas of potential confusion. Firstly, let us say that the basic concept is reasonably well-stated. Now we address the confusions. The nature of true simultaneity is such that, indeed, all is simultaneous. However, in your modes of perception you would perhaps more properly view the seeding of the creation as that of growth from the center or core outward. The second confusion lies in the term, 'void'. We would substitute the noun, 'plenum'.

Questioner: Then, if I were observing the beginning of the octave at that time through a telescope, say from this position, would I see the center of many, many galaxies appearing and each of them then spreading outward in a spiraling fashion over what we would consider billions of years, but the spirals spreading outward in approximately what we would consider the same rate so that all these galaxies began as the first speck of light at the same time and then spread out at roughly the same rate? Is this correct?

Ra: I am Ra. The query has confusing elements. There is a center to infinity. From this center all spreads. Therefore, there are centers to the creation, to the galaxies, to star systems, to planetary systems, and to consciousness. In each case you may see growth from the center outward. Thus you may see your query as being over-general in concept.

Questioner: Considering only our Milky Way Galaxy at its beginnings, I will assume that the first occurrence that we could find with our physical apparatus was the appearance of a star of the nature of our sun. Is this correct?

Ra: I am Ra. In the case of the galactic systems the first manifestation of the Logos is a cluster of central systems which generate the outward swirling energies producing, in their turn, further energy centers for the Logos or what you would call stars.

Questioner: Are these central original creations or clusters what we call stars?

Ra: I am Ra. This is correct. However, the closer to the, shall we say, beginning of the manifestation of the Logos the star is, the more it partakes in the one original thought.

Questioner: Why does this partaking in the original thought have a gradient radially outward? That's the way I understand your statement.

Ra: I am Ra. This is the plan of the one infinite Creator. The One Original Thought is the harvest of all previous, if you would use this term, experience of the Creator by the Creator. As It decides to know Itself It generates Itself, into that plenum full of the glory and the power of the one infinite Creator which is manifested to your perceptions as space or outer space. Each generation of this knowing begets a knowing which has the capacity, through free will, to choose methods of knowing Itself. Therefore, gradually, step by step, the Creator becomes that which may know Itself, and the portions of the Creator partake less purely in the power of the original word or thought. The Creator does not properly create as much as It experiences Itself.

Questioner: What was the form, condition, or experience of the first division of consciousness that occurred at the beginning of this octave at the beginning of this galactic experience?

Ra: I am Ra. We touch upon previous material. The harvest of the previous octave, was the Creator of Love manifested in mind, body, and spirit. This

form of the Creator experiencing Itself may perhaps be said to be the first division.

Questioner: I was interested specifically in how this very first division showed up in this octave. I was interested to know if it made the transition through first, second, third, fourth, etc. densities? I would like to take the first mind/body/spirit complexes and trace their experience from the very start to the present so that I could better understand the condition that we are in now by comparing it with this original growth. Could you please tell me precisely how this came about as to the formation of the planets and growth through the densities, if that is the way it happened, please?

Ra: I am Ra. Your queries seem more confused than your basic mental distortions in this area. Let us speak in general and perhaps you may find a less confused and more simple method of eliciting information in this area.

A very great deal of creation was manifested without the use of the concepts involved in consciousness, as you know it. The creation itself is a form of consciousness which is unified, the Logos being the one great heart of creation. The process of evolution through this period, which may be seen to be timeless, is most valuable to take into consideration, for it is against the background of this essential unity of the fabric of creation that we find the ultimate development of the Logoi which chose to use that portion of the harvested consciousness of the Creator to move forward with the process of knowledge of self. As it had been found to be efficient to use the various densities, which are fixed in each octave, in order to create conditions in which self-conscious sub-Logoi could exist, this was carried out throughout the growing flower-strewn field, as your simile suggests, of the one infinite creation.

The first beings of mind, body, and spirit were not complex. The experience of mind/body/spirits at the beginning of this octave of experience was singular. There was no third-density forgetting. There was no veil. The lessons of third density are predestined by the very nature of the vibratory rates experienced during this particular density and by the nature of the quantum jump to the vibratory experiences of fourth density.

Questioner: Am I correct, then, in assuming the first mind/body/spirit experiences, as this galaxy progressed in growth, were those that moved through the densities; that is, the process we have discussed coming out of second density. For instance, let us take a particular planet, one of the very early planets formed near the center of the galaxy. I will assume that the planet solidified during the first density, that life appeared in second density, and that all of the mind/body/spirit complexes of third density progressed out of second-density on that planet and evolved in third density. Is this correct?

Ra: I am Ra. This is hypothetically correct.

Questioner: Did this in fact happen on some of the planets or on a large percentage of the planets near the center of this galaxy in this way?

Ra: I am Ra. Our knowledge is limited. We know of the beginning but cannot asseverate to the precise experiences of those things occurring before us. You know the nature of historical teaching. At our level of learn/teaching we may expect little distortion. However, we cannot, with surety, say there is no distortion as we speak of specific occurrences of which we were not consciously a part. It is our understanding that your supposition is correct. Thus we so hypothesize.

Questioner: Specifically, I am trying to grasp an understanding of the process of experience in third density before the veil so that I can better understand the present process. As I understand, it the mind/body/spirits went through the process of what we call physical incarnation in this density but there was no forgetting. What was the benefit or purpose of the physical incarnation when there was no forgetting?

Ra: I am Ra. The purpose of incarnation in third density is to learn the ways of love.

Questioner: I guess I didn't state that exactly right. What I mean is, since there was no forgetting, since the mind/body/spirits had, in what we call the physical incarnation, their full consciousness, they knew the same thing that they would know while not in the physical incarnation. What was the mechanism of teaching that taught the ways of love in the third-density physical prior to the forgetting process?

Ra: I am Ra. We ask your permission to answer this query in an oblique fashion as we perceive an area in which we might be of aid.

Questioner: Certainly.

Ra: I am Ra. Your queries seem to be pursuing the possibility/probability that the mechanisms of experience in third density are different if a mind/body/spirit is attempting them rather than a mind/body/spirit complex. The nature of third density is constant. Its ways are to be learned the same now and ever. Thusly, no matter what form the entity facing these lessons, the lessons and mechanisms are the same. The Creator will learn from Itself. Each entity has unmanifest portions of learning and, most importantly, learning which is involved with other-selves.

Questioner: Then prior to the forgetting process there was no concept of anything but service-to-others polarization. What sort of societies and experiences in third-density were created and evolved in this condition?

Ra: I am Ra. It is our perception that such conditions created the situation of a most pallid experiential nexus in which lessons were garnered with the relative speed of the turtle to the cheetah.

Questioner: Did such societies evolve with technologies of a complex nature, or did they remain quite simple? Can you give me a general idea of the evolvement that would be a function of what we would call intellectual activity?

Ra: I am Ra. There is infinite diversity in societies under any circumstances. There were many highly technologically advanced societies which grew due to the ease of producing any desired result. When one dwells within what might be seen to be a state of constant potential inspiration, that which even the most highly sophisticated, in your terms, societal structure lacked, given the noncomplex nature of its entities, was what you might call will or, to use a more plebeian term, gusto, or élan vital.

Questioner: Did such technological societies evolve travel through what we call space to other planets or other planetary systems? Did some of them do this?

Ra: I am Ra. This is correct.

Questioner: Then even though, from our point of view, there was great evolutionary experience it was deemed at some point by the evolving Logos that an experiment to create a greater experience was appropriate. Is this correct?

Ra: I am Ra. This is correct and may benefit from comment. The Logos is aware of the nature of the third-density requirement for what you have called graduation. All the previous, if you would use this term, experiments, although resulting in many experiences, lacked what was considered the crucial ingredient; that is, polarization. There was little enough tendency for experience to polarize entities that entities repeated habitually the third-density cycles many times over. It was desired that the potential for polarization be made more available.

Questioner: Then since the only possibility at this particular time, as I see it, was a polarization for service to others, I must assume from what you said that even though all were aware of this service-to-others necessity they were unable to achieve it. What was the configuration of mind of the mind/body/spirits at that time? Why did they have such a difficult time serving others to the extent necessary for graduation since this was the only polarity possible?

Ra: I am Ra. Consider, if you will, the tendency of those who are divinely happy, as you call this distortion, to have little urge to alter or better their condition. Such is the result of the mind/body/spirit which is not complex. There is the possibility of love of other-selves and service to other-selves, but there is the overwhelming awareness of the Creator in the self. The connection with the Creator is that of the umbilical cord. The security is total. Therefore, no love is terribly important; no pain terribly frightening; no effort, therefore, is made to serve for love or to benefit from fear.

Questioner: It seems that you might make an analogy in our present illusion of those who are born into extreme wealth and security. Is this correct?

Ra: I am Ra. Within the strict bounds of the simile, you are perceptive.

Questioner: We have presently an activity between physical incarnations called the healing and review of the incarnation. Was anything of this nature occurring prior to the veil?

Ra: I am Ra. The inchoate structure of this process was always in place, but where there has been no harm there need be no healing. This too may be seen to have been of concern to Logoi which were aware that without the need to understand, understanding would forever be left undone. We ask your

forgiveness for the use of this misnomer, but your language has a paucity of sound vibration complexes for this general concept.

Questioner: I don't grasp too well the condition of incarnation and the time in between incarnations prior to the veil. I do not understand what was the difference other than the manifestation of the third-density, yellow-ray body. Was there any mental difference upon what we call death? I don't see the necessity for what we call the review of the incarnation if the consciousness was uninterrupted. Could you clear up that point for me?

Ra: I am Ra. No portion of the Creator audits the course, to use your experiential terms. Each incarnation is intended to be a course in the Creator knowing Itself. A review or, shall we say, to continue the metaphor, each test is an integral portion of the process of the Creator knowing Itself. Each incarnation will end with such a test. This is so that the portion of the Creator may assimilate the experiences in yellow, physical, third density, may evaluate the biases gained, and may then choose, either by means of automatically provided aid or by the self, the conditions of the next incarnation.

Questioner: Before the veil, during the review of the incarnation, were the entities at that time aware that what they were trying to do was sufficiently polarize for graduation?

Ra: I am Ra. This is correct.

Questioner: Then I am assuming that this awareness was somehow reduced as they went into the yellow ray third-density incarnative state even though there was no veil. Is this correct?

Ra: I am Ra. This is distinctly incorrect.

Questioner: OK. This is the central important point. It seems to me that if polarization was the obvious thing that more effort would have been put forward to polarize. Let me see if I can state this differently. Before the veil there was an awareness of the need for polarization towards service to others in third density by all entities, whether incarnate in third-density, yellow-ray bodies or in between incarnations. I assume, then, that the condition of which we earlier spoke, one of wealth you might say, was present through the entire spectrum of experience whether it might be between incarnations or during incarnations and the entities just simply could not manifest the desire to create this polarization necessary for graduation. Is this correct?

Ra: I am Ra. You begin to grasp the situation. Let us continue the metaphor of the schooling but consider the scholar as being an entity in your younger years of the schooling process. The entity is fed, clothed, and protected regardless of whether or not the schoolwork is accomplished. Therefore, the entity does not do the homework but rather enjoys playtime, mealtime, and vacation. It is not until there is a reason to wish to excel that most entities will attempt to excel.

Questioner: You have stated in a much earlier session that it is necessary to polarize more than 50% service-to-others to be harvestable fourth-density positive. Was this condition the same at the time before the veil?

Ra: I am Ra. This shall be the last full query of this working.

The query is not answered easily, for the concept of service to self did not hold sway previous to what we have been calling the veiling process. The necessity for graduation to fourth density is an ability to use, welcome, and enjoy a certain intensity of the white light of the one infinite Creator. In your own terms at your space/time nexus this ability may be measured by your previously stated percentages of service.

Prior to the veiling process the measurement would be that of an entity walking up a set of your stairs, each of which was imbued with a certain quality of light. The stair upon which an entity stopped would be either third-density light or fourth-density light. Between the two stairs lies the threshold. To cross that threshold is difficult. There is resistance at the edge, shall we say, of each density. The faculty of faith or will needs to be understood, nourished, and developed in order to have an entity which seeks past the boundary of third density. Those entities which do not do their homework, be they ever so amiable, shall not cross. It was this situation which faced the Logoi prior to the veiling process being introduced into the experiential continuum of third density.

May we ask if there are any brief queries at this working?

Questioner: Is there anything that we can do to improve the contact or make the instrument more comfortable?

Ra: I am Ra. All parameters are being met. Remain united in love and thanksgiving. We thank you for your conscientiousness as regards the appurtenances.

I am Ra. I leave you in the love and in the light of the One Infinite Glorious Creator. Go forth, therefore, rejoicing merrily in the power and the peace of the one Creator. Adonai. ☥

L/L Research is a subsidiary of
Rock Creek Research &
Development Laboratories, Inc.

P.O. Box 5195
Louisville, KY 40255-0195

L/L Research

www.llresearch.org

Rock Creek is a non-profit
corporation dedicated to
discovering and sharing
information which may aid in
the spiritual evolution of
humankind.

The Law of One, Book V, Session 82, Fragment 42
March 27, 1982

Jim: Ra mentioned a number of times that impatience is one of the most frequent catalysts with which the seeker must work. When a general outline of the path of evolution is seen it is often too enticing to resist jumping ahead of one's actual place upon the path and making quickly for the goal. This was the case for me as I queried about the steps of accepting the self which I had discovered in my own seeking. Ra's suggestion to carefully place the foundation of one's house before hanging the roof seems sound. It brings to mind the old saying, "There is never time enough to do a thing right the first time, but there is always time enough to do it over."

Note also how any thought and action, when carefully scrutinized, can lead one to the basic distortions or lessons that one is working on. Thus any portion of the life experience can be seen as a holographic miniature of the entire incarnational plan for an entity as layer upon layer of meaning is discovered behind the smallest surface of things. As we discovered in Book Four, this is not because the events in our world are naturally filled with layers of meanings—though this is also true—but because we subconsciously color the events in our lives in the way that we have pre-incarnatively decided will provide us with the opportunities to learn what we wish to learn. That's why different people see the same catalyst in different ways—often wildly varying. As we work with these colorations/distortions/reactions in a conscious

manner we begin to accept ourselves for having them because we begin to see the purpose behind them. This acceptance draws to us the balancing attitudes for our distortion so that our viewpoint expands and we are able to accept and love another part of the Creator which was previously not accepted and loved. Love, then, is the potential product of any distortion.

Carla: The course of spiritual seeking is often unclear, and seekers are always looking hopefully for some single point of clarity to hold against the universe as yardstick. Certainly, the remembrance of Love Itself suffices in this wise. But this remembrance comes slowly when we are caught up in our reactions. We each have these hooks that catch us up, and there is some time that passes before we are reoriented. We wish we were more alert! But we are not always attentive, no matter how abreast of things we hope to be. I like Ra's insistence that we continue to catch ourselves in the act, rather than swinging around in a supposed short cut that keeps us from seeing into why we got caught. It is a real breakthrough for me every time I see myself GETTING caught. This moment reveals to us that inner distortion we've been looking for! Once we can see the mechanism, we can far more effectually work on its release. I think the goal here is not to be without error, but to see our errors more clearly. We are human: we will err. It is impossible not to. But we can, slowly, learn ourselves well enough to do the erring during inner processes, rather than upon the outer world stage. Perhaps, one day, all the "buttons" from childhood and other traumas might become released, and we be clear. And perhaps not. I don't think this matters nearly as much as how much we have loved.

Session 82, March 27, 1982

Questioner: Jim has a personal question that is not to be published. He asks, "It seems that my balancing work has shifted from more peripheral concerns such as patience/impatience, to learning to open myself in unconditional love, to accepting my self as whole and perfect, and then to accepting my self as the Creator. If this is a normal progression of focus for balancing, wouldn't it be more efficient once this is discovered for a person to work on the acceptance of the self as Creator rather than work peripherally on the secondary and tertiary results of not accepting the self?"

Ra: I am Ra. The term efficiency has misleading connotations. In the context of doing work in the disciplines of the personality, in order to be of more full efficiency in the central acceptance of the self, it is first quite necessary to know the distortions of the self which the entity is accepting. Each thought and action needs must then be scrutinized for the precise foundation of the distortions of any reactions. This process shall lead to the more central task of acceptance. However, the architrave must be in place before the structure is builded. ❧

SUNDAY MEDITATION
MARCH 28, 1982

(C1 channeling)

I am Hatonn, and I am now with this instrument. We greet you, brothers and sisters, in the love and the light of the one infinite Creator.

Tonight we would speak a few words on compassion, a term not fully understood by your peoples and difficult to express with words. Each of you here is on a path of service to others and each has felt lacking at times in relation to the ability to help others, may see the difficulties that others may face as they learn or try to learn the lessons chosen or that they have chosen. As each seeks to be of service each need not treat themselves harshly if at times they come short of their expectations of how they should help others, or if others fail to respond to your attempts at service as you would have expected them to. The attempt is often worth more if it is tried without the expected results occurring, for in these times you are afforded the opportunity to reflect on reactions, the attempts, and can learn to deal with oneself softly. As you do this you are better able to touch another softly, for as you know the softness, the touch, the warmth conveyed tends to be a more direct linking and the other is grabbed, pulled, pushed. One need but be open, flowing in order to more fully be in touch with another, to be able to see more clearly from the perspective of the other.

So often in your illusion the urge to take charge of a given situation often creates more blockages than existed prior to that situation. As you learn to be soft the walls become less high, narrower, and open slowly and allow the touching and exchange. The softness is something that you learn, though it has always been within you. It is something you must learn to develop, to be sought, to be able to see as others see. Though being soft, touching may lead at times to hurt, for as you touch you are brought closer and share the feelings, emotions. This sharing, even through the hurt, is a very valuable lesson. Be soft, my friends, gentle. Be open to experiences and those of others. Lay judgment aside *(inaudible)*. We too are learning to be soft. We join with you *(inaudible)*.

I am known to you as Hatonn, and will at this time transfer this contact to another. I am Hatonn.

(Carla channeling)

I am Hatonn, and I greet you once again in the love and light of the infinite Creator. I and my brothers and sisters of Laitos would at this time pause in order that we may move among you, and if you request it may offer you the vibration that is known to you as conditioning. If you wish to be made aware of our presence, please mentally request it at this time and we shall be with you. I am Hatonn.

(Pause)

I am Hatonn, and am once again with this instrument. We thank you for allowing us to be of service to you. It is a great privilege to work with each of you and if, at any time, you might desire the same conditioning vibration, mentally request this and we shall be with you. If at any tine as you are experiencing conditioning you are in any way in discomfort we ask that you mentally request that we adjust the conditioning or remove it completely. We shall do so immediately. We shall continue now, with your kind permission.

Let us tell you a small story, a story in which the hero is a man bent upon learning the meaning of compassion. He seeks first a very, very famous and successful mental and spiritual guide to many. This famous man greets our hero. His home is palatial, his manner most civilized. His entire being radiates a sureness of character and the confidence of wealth and yet, so many who are themselves influential in the ways of your society have spoken highly of this gentleman, but our hero feels perhaps he will know the meaning of compassion, having helped so many.

"Ah," the rich man says, "all these things that I own are necessary in order that I may offer my services to those who in turn have the power to help so many others. True compassion is knowing whither to put your energies, and I have offered my aid to those who will be able, in turn, to be of the greatest help to the greatest number."

Our hero moves from this interview understandably unsatisfied and walks into the middle of the city, into the meaner portions of its dark streets, passes warehouses, bolted windows, and those among your peoples who have not a supply of money for protection against the elements, and he comes to a terribly dirty, falling down storefront which is marked, "Mission." Inside, there is a rather gaunt woman ladling soup for those indigents who have no money and he asks her with hope in his eyes and in his voice, "Can you tell me what compassion is?"

"Certainly," says the woman, lifting her tired eyes from the kettle. "Compassion is a plate of soup for a hungry man. Compassion is seeing beauty and perfection in those things which are apparently not lovely, in seeing love in that which is not loved."

"How many do you serve in this manner?" asked our seeker.

"I do not know," replies the gaunt woman. "As many as I can supply with soup. Not many, I suppose," she says, "but it is all that I can do."

Our seeker by this time is quite confused. The two faces of compassion both seem so compelling. One is logical, one moves the heart. Both seem to be a means of comforting those who seek comfort, and is that not what compassion is?

Wandering aimlessly in the bright sun of the mid-afternoon, the young man spies a tree in the midst of a small park. There is a circular seat beneath it and he is tired and without thinking he goes to it and rests upon it that he may consider what compassion might be. After spending some time in aimless and unproductive musing, he glances to one side and then the other. Upon one side sits a most wealthy man busy with his work, the signs of wealth in his dress and his accouterments. Upon our hero's other side rests one of those from the soup kitchen, a man unable to function within the limits of society based upon money.

The seeker looks up at the tree and suddenly knows what compassion is, for the tree is shading all three entities from the harshness of the afternoon sun.

My friends, in compassion there is no judgment. The actions that you may take because of your compassion are many and various, for you have many faculties of mind and spirit at your command and your actions are yours to discriminate, but the love that is within you, if you wish to be compassionate, shall shine as gently as sunlight filtered through the living green of the shading leaves of a great tree.

As always, we cannot emphasize enough to you our perception and our belief that it is not to be expected of each entity that it be able to have such compassion without aid, and, as always, the aid which we suggest is that of meditation, for you have these things as a birthright which you seek. They are locked within you as treasure within a chest and meditation is the key. We ask you to be gentle with yourselves as well as with others, and to allow the process of compassion to work its magic within your own life.

If you wish to radiate to others you must first allow the radiance within you to come forth, and if you block this radiance by some feeling of disappointment within yourself, then you must stop and return to meditation until you can see that in the view of love it matters not what mistakes, what conditions, what experiences you may have had. It matters only that you are a portion of the infinite Creator. This is your reality. The remainder is illusion. We ask you to feel as we leave you the joy and the freedom of a lack of judgment for yourself and for others. Not a lack of judgment that implies a lack of discrimination, for it is only by discrimination that you can learn better how to be of service, but as you attempt to be of service lay the judgment aside and as the tree gives shade, let your love and the love that shines through you gently touch each and every entity about you with the glorious oneness.

I am Hatonn. It has been a great privilege to be able to greet each of you. We thank you for allowing us to share our thoughts with you. And at this time we leave you through this instrument in the love and the light of the infinite Creator. I am known to you as Hatonn, Adonai, my friends. Adonai.

(Jim channeling)

I am Latwii, and I greet each of you in the love and in the light of the one infinite Creator. We are greatly honored to once again be able to join this group and to be asked to partake, as always, in the capacity of attempting to answer those queries which those present may have the value in asking. At this time we would open this working to questions. Are there any questions at this time?

C1: I'll try not to get into anything as lengthy as I did last week, but here of late D's had some aches and pains and I've tried to use touch to alleviate them and it seems to be working fairly well, but one night after we'd gone to bed—I was told of this, I remember none of it—as she was experiencing a muscle cramp, and then I used touch to alleviate it and spoke with her without ever fully waking up, because I have no knowledge myself what happened, just what I was told, and I was wondering if you could explain to me a little bit about what takes over in your sleeping that you can operate in that capacity?

I am Latwii, and am aware of your query, my brother. In this regard we might suggest that this particular situation is one which reflects not so much another aspect taking over your conscious being, but your conscious awareness removing itself from your unconscious. Therefore, this allows those latent abilities which you are attempting to develop to make themselves more apparent and they do become more apparent because you have consciously sought to develop them and at that particular moment of which you speak the unique situation occurred in which your conscious mind was laid to rest and those belief patterns which inhibit such activity normally were not in effect.

May we answer you further, my brother?

C1: Is this type of activity a common thing? I know that—I mean that I've been told about it, but I really don't remember—for quite a number of years a functioning while being what we refer to as asleep. Is this something that is common or is it something that in particular happens to work with me?

I am Latwii. May we say in this regard that such activities as you have described are common to a great number of your peoples, but are less commonly expressed as you have expressed them. The ability of each entity to function within the state commonly called the hypnogogic state is well known and widespread while the entity sleeps. To manifest this condition in what seems to be a waking state to those present and witnessing the action is not so common but does occur on occasions for entities who have prepared their minds, shall we say, in a certain manner which meditation does allow. This is to say, there is an opening, or a channel made between the conscious and unconscious minds, a piercing, shall we say, of the veil which divides these two portions of your mind complex. This, then, allows the communication between the two portions of your mind to flow more easily without the restrictions common to those of your peoples who have yet to seek the mysteries and their solutions.

(Side one of tape ends.)

C1: Today I was with some others as they were trimming a tree, and at this time of year, especially as the weather gets warm, there's a lot of—the sap starts to run. Today, as the tree was trimmed, it ran freely, almost as if rain dripping from the tree, but this is not really what seemed unusual to me, but at this same time another tree some ten feet away from the first which had been trimmed several weeks before began also to run as the one being trimmed today began, and I was curious because there are times when we refer to people having sympathy pains, as when one of a mated pair is suffering or experiencing discomfort, then the other does. I was wondering, if in second density that this same thing can occur?

I am Latwii, and am aware of your query, my brother. We may agree that in the second density of your plants and your animals there is quite frequently that relationship which is sympathetic and as one entity vibrates, so does the other harmonically resonate in sympathy. In the situation of which you speak it is more likely that it was simply the time for the movement of the fluid which you call the sap of the tree to progress in an upward fashion as the season of your year beckons it thusly, and because there were wounds upon both trees then the sap did emanate from these wounds. This is not to say that these particular entities which you call the trees were not also resonating with an harmonic vibration, for both were experiencing the same flow of the fluid called sap and had also experienced the same removal of lower limbs and then did share two experiences quite closely.

May we answer you further, my brother?

C1: In this situation, in the time between today and when this first tree was trimmed, there was much warmer weather more conducive to sap flow, but it did not occur until the—it occurred as the other tree was being cut. Today the sap was not flowing until the wounding of the tree today, which seems to be one of those chance situations that happened too simultaneously to be solely chance.

I am Latwii. We have not perceived a clearly stated query. May we ask if there is a further question along this line, my brother?

C1: No, I really guess not. I have a bad tendency to talk and not really formulate a distinct question, and at times it helps me think in motion, so to speak. Since being really connected with these meditations I've begun to see what I used to refer to as coincidence and become more aware that there are reasons behind such things and that there's more pattern than I was aware of previously, and I guess I was thinking aloud. Thank you for your answer, and I'm sorry I couldn't get a question formulated, but my ramblings sometimes help me, so have patience with me at times.

I am Latwii. We are most grateful to you, my brother, for your patience with us as well, for often we also tend to ramble. May we ramble upon another subject?

C2: Yes. My husband has lost his mother in the last couple of months, and they were very attached to each other, and he's having a very hard time. I wonder what I can do to help him that I'm not doing.

I am Latwii, and am aware of your query, my sister. In such cases where a dearly loved friend does pass from this illusion to another it is often the case that the one remaining shall suffer that which may be described as grief, loneliness and pain, for the one which has passed meant a great deal to the one which remains. In such cases it is often difficult to move the perspective beyond the immediate feeling of loss and grief, but if it is possible to do so we may suggest the enlarging of the perspective by compassionate communication with the grieving entity so that this entity does begin to perceive a larger pattern in the flow of life, so that there is seen not the loss, but a gain, so there is seen not the pain of the passing, but the joy in the passing.

In this regard we would suggest that in such a situation the beliefs of the entity remaining be discussed in such a fashion that the basic view of life is uncovered and the view is then allowed to progress in such a way as to include the possibility that each incarnation which is experienced is likened unto a class in a great school of learning, that each experience of each incarnation does provide those lessons which shall allow the entities to prepare for the great graduation, the graduation into that density of love and of compassion which awaits those who have completed their lessons within this illusion.

If an entity can realize that this illusion is but an eye blink in eternity, and that it has helped another to learn the lessons that will permit graduation, then the entity remaining might see with clearer perspective that there is only the feeling of joy as a residue to be felt when a loved one has learned the lessons programmed before the incarnation and has joyfully passed the test, shall we say, and passed through that transition which is called death. In such a situation we would also suggest that the joy and feeling of gratitude at having experienced the incarnation and the love and the learning with the entity which has passed be felt by the one which remains and that this feeling of joy and gratitude be sent daily to the one who has passed from this illusion by the one which has remained to learn further lessons, for it is necessary for the loved ones of those passing to release the hold, shall we say, the emotional and psychic bonds which bind those who are close in the incarnation, so that when the passing has been achieved there might be the free movement to the next level of lessons without the calling back to the classroom which has been left.

May we answer you further, my sister?

C2: No, that was very good. I thank you. Now, one other question. I've had a spinal curvature all my life and I've lived with [it] and I've had a great deal of pain. I have pain now. Is there anything I can do that I'm not doing to relieve the back pain?

I am Latwii, and am aware of your query, my sister. We might suggest that there could be benefit gained from the use of what you might call the swirling water upon the erect spine to relax those muscles which attempt to hold the misplaced curvature, shall we say. There might also be benefit gained from the manipulation which is called massage to deeply move these muscles so that once again they might be relaxed from their tight grip. There is also the possibility of benefit to be gained from the mild exercise of the walking on a daily basis.

May we answer you further, my sister?

C2: No. Thank you. That helps.

I am Latwii. May we ask if there is another question at this time?

Questioner: Yes. I would like to know if you ever appear in visual form to those requesting it?

I am Latwii, and am aware of your query, my sister. We of Latwii, as members of the Confederation of Planets in the Service of the Infinite Creator, do occasionally appear in dream states and less frequently in meditative states to those who have requested our presence or the presence of entities which are willing and able to provide a certain type of lesson. It is often the case that an entity so requesting will not remember the appearance in the dream state, for there are certain necessities, shall we say, of maintaining the free will of such entities. This is not always the case. Quite often there will be a remembering of such a dream or vision, and it will be remembered as a situation which was quite inspiring to the one requesting.

May we answer you further, my sister?

Questioner: In a dream state is it the message received in symbolic form or literally?

I am Latwii. In this case of the dream appearance the message is given in whatever form the entity requesting the message is able to receive it. Those entities able to receive a clear transmission are then aware of less symbolic imagery. Those not able to assimilate a directly transmitted message will be given those symbols which will serve as *(inaudible)* or somewhat of an enigmatic mantra for the mind.

May we answer you further, my sister?

Questioner: Does the entity of Jesus ever speak through dream state?

I am Latwii. In this particular query we find that the answer is in the affirmative, and is not limited to only the dream state. Many entities of the Confederation do appear in this dream state in meditation, and do provide messages of a wide variety of contents to those requesting such messages.

May we answer you further, my sister?

Questioner: Thank you. You've answered my questions.

I am Latwii. We are most grateful to you as well. Is there another query at this time?

M: Could you discuss how a person could find a small degree of happiness?

I am Latwii. My sister, we find that your query does reflect the great desire to penetrate, shall we say, the grosser nature of this illusion which each of your peoples inhabit. Each entity on your planet moves in its daily round of activities seemingly unaware of the meaning for the movement. Each completes a seemingly prescribed set of tasks. Each feels a multitude of feelings. Each rides the roller coaster of pain, joy, sorrow, boredom, etc. Few seek the reason for the ride. Few seek to find that which is loosely defined as happiness. Most feel that happiness can be bought. Some feel it can be worn. Some feel it can be traded for. Some have given up all hope of finding happiness. Most have no concept of what it might be composed of.

We of Latwii can only suggest to one such as yourself who seeks deeper meaning of this life in which you experience each moment, that in the meditative state you might come closer to that which is poorly called happiness, for what, my sister, could make one happier than to know that one is an integral part of all Creation, and more—the one Creator. What could make an entity more fulfilled than to know the heart of love resides within its own being? What could fulfill one more than to know that the plan of the one Creator is not complete without the participation of the one who seeks that known as happiness?

We can only suggest that the palest shadow of happiness can be found in the daily round of activities. Remove for but a moment each day yourself from this round of activities which too often confuses and distracts, and place your being within the silence and peace of meditation. Seek within this state to know that which you wish to know. Seek within your being that which you called happiness. That which you have called happiness can only be found at the depths of your heart, for there the Creator which is yourself has planted a seed that needs the nourishment of your seeking and your attention to grow into the tree of life that will sustain the fruits of your incarnation.

May we answer you further, my sister?

M: Thank you. You've answered me very well.

I am Latwii. We are most grateful, as well, to you. Is there another question at this time?

C2: Yes. We read in the New Testament that Jesus said that it was necessary for him to leave in order for a Comforter to come, and we interpret that as the Holy Spirit, of course. Is the entity known as Jesus looking over the planet today in its distress? Does he still have responsibility for the happenings on this planet?

I am Latwii, and am aware of your query, my sister. The entity known to your peoples as Jesus of Nazareth does continue its vigil over this planet, as do countless souls who are members of the Confederation of Planets in the Service of the One Infinite Creator. There are those of this Confederation, such as the one known as Jesus, who have become much more well known to your peoples than have great multitudes of the heavenly hosts which have never ceased their surveillance and compassionate caring for those of your peoples who have sought their service. No entity upon your planet is without such aid. Each who calls for the service of love, of light, of unity, is answered in some

way. Those of your peoples who are most familiar with the entity known as Jesus are also answered by this entity in whatever manner they are capable of understanding, for it is the understanding of each entity within this Confederation that your peoples must have their free will respected fully, and all responses to calls for service must be made in such a way as to allow the entity so called to be aware within the limits of its perception that the call has been answered.

May we answer you further, my sister?

C2: Paul talks about a crowd of witnesses. That's the way I'm remembering it right now. He said something about seeing that you are encompassed about with a great crowd of witnesses. Now, is that what he's talking about? Say you're referring to members of the Confederation, is that what Paul's talking about when he talks about a crowd of witnesses?

I am Latwii. That is correct, my sister. May we answer you further?

C2: No, thank you. That answers the question very well.

I am Latwii. May we ask if there is another question at this time?

Questioner: Yes. I would like to inquire about an (inaudible) master, Saint Germaine, and a group called the Brotherhood of the Royal Teton. Are they in contact in physical form with entities on this Earth?

I am Latwii, and am aware of your question, my sister. The entity known to you and to your peoples as St. Germaine has made contact through various entities and organizations, as you call them, for the purpose of providing the services which have been requested, most usually dealing with the ability to open the heart of being in love and compassion for the entities surrounding one. This entity has maintained a constant vigil, shall we say, and shall continue in its serving of those entities who called. We cannot be more specific and state whether this or that organization has been in contact with this or that entity, for we do not wish to infringe upon any entity's free will, and direct their attention towards or away from any organization.

May we answer you further, my sister?

Questioner: No, that will be all. Thank you.

I am Latwii. Is there another question at this time?

C2: Yes. One short question. Does Buddha still assume some care and responsibility for the planet also?

I am Latwii, and am aware of your query, my sister. Each master, shall we say, that has blended its vibrations with this planet at any time in its evolutionary history does by that shared experience create the bond, shall we say, which persists until the lessons which must needs be learned have been learned by those who were the students of the teacher. This is true in every case of which we are aware.

May we answer you further, my sister?

C2: No. That's very comforting.

I am Latwii. Is there another question at this time?

Carla: L has a question. L has a two year old boy, and he realizes that in the past his son has been too restless to take part in these meditations, and would like to know if it would be possible for the child to take part in meditations at this time, or follow still the recommendation that the child wait until he can more fully grasp and desire the information? L wants to attend the meditations.

I am Latwii. We greet the one known as L in absence, shall we say, and do look forward to his returning to this group. In response to the query of whether or not it is possible at this time for the young entity known as A to attend these sessions, we can only suggest that until an entity such as this young child is able to perceive the basic contents of these meditations it is not advisable for such an entity to be present, for it is our foremost desire not to infringe upon the free will of any entity of your peoples. The young child spoken of is not yet able to perceive those concepts which are most likely to be shared in this group, therefore it would not be included in the level of understanding which is necessary for the partaking in these meditations.

We of Latwii, as do each Confederation member speaking at these meetings, wish to include as purely and as closely as possible each entity which joins this group. We attempt in our messages and responses to queries to construct our message in such a way as to be available to each entity which is present. This requires, shall we say, a certain skill which we are unable to perfect to the degree necessary to allow an entity of limited vocabulary and concept understanding to participate within. We are always attempting to expand our own capacities in presenting these messages, but at present are unable to include an entity which is of the configuration of mind of the one known as A.

May we answer you further, my sister?

Carla: Yes, just a sideline. We have a couple of newborns in the group and it seems to make no difference whatsoever that the newborn who does not understand the language and doesn't care where it is as long as mama is there is included. Is this due to the fact that the faculty of will has not been activated?

I am Latwii, and am aware of your query, my sister. In general, we would agree that you have correctly stated the situation. The newborn entity has, shall we say, a self-contained world which does not extend very far from its own physical vehicle. It, therefore, is unaware of the activities of the other entities within the same room and is therefore not infringed upon when present at such a meeting as this. An entity which has begun the concept and practice of moving beyond its own immediate being and has begun to interact with those around it then has developed the will to expand its field of perception and experience, and therefore must be accounted for by those present in the room with it, and this then requires our attention as well, for such an entity is seeking with the group in that instance.

May we answer you further, my sister?

Carla: No, thank you, Latwii. How are you tonight?

I am Latwii, and we are doing quite well with our abilities to verbalize in your language this evening and feel a great joy at having our state of being queried. We thank you for your interest, as always, and do always look forward to the lighter side, shall we say, of the queries.

May we answer another query at this time?

C2: One quickie. We talk about accidental death. Is there ever an accidental death?

I am Latwii, and am aware of your query, my sister. Within the illusion which you inhabit there appear to be many accidents. There are, in reality, very few accidents. There are what appear to be random occurrences, but with such a situation as you would describe as the death of any nature, it is very unlikely that such a situation would occur truly by accident, for there is a far greater comprehension, shall we say, of the total life pattern, by that portion of the self known to you as the higher self, than can be perceived by most entities of your plane of experience. There is at the level of the higher self seen the great road map of the being and its progression through the incarnation. Each entity does, before incarnation, make certain agreements and preparations for the incarnation with each of those with whom it shall experience the illusion. It is, therefore, highly unlikely that the passing from the illusion would occur …

(Tape ends.) ♣

L/L Research is a subsidiary of
Rock Creek Research &
Development Laboratories, Inc.

P.O. Box 5195
Louisville, KY 40255-0195

L/L RESEARCH

www.llresearch.org

Rock Creek is a non-profit
corporation dedicated to
discovering and sharing
information which may aid in
the spiritual evolution of
humankind.

ABOUT THE CONTENTS OF THIS TRANSCRIPT: This telepathic channeling has been taken from transcriptions of the weekly study and meditation meetings of the Rock Creek Research & Development Laboratories and L/L Research. It is offered in the hope that it may be useful to you. As the Confederation entities always make a point of saying, please use your discrimination and judgment in assessing this material. If something rings true to you, fine. If something does not resonate, please leave it behind, for neither we nor those of the Confederation would wish to be a stumbling block for any.

CAVEAT: This transcript is being published by L/L Research in a not yet final form. It has, however, been edited and any obvious errors have been corrected. When it is in a final form, this caveat will be removed.

FRIDAY NIGHT
APRIL 2, 1982

(Unknown channeling)

I am Hatonn, and I greet you, my brothers and sisters, in the love and the light of the infinite Creator. My friends, we welcome the sounds of your laughter, of your pleasure in sharing the company of one another this evening. It is a great blessing that you are able to share your love for one another, your thoughts, your beliefs, your conversation, just as the sharing described in the text which was previously read, the music spoken of in those words, the sharing of love, the awareness of oneness and the acceptance of the blessings which originate from the Creator. Too often those of your race and others find these blessings difficult to accept, for they have strayed far from their original intention and in seeking to reflect the will and the awareness of the Creator by developing themselves as independent yet equal co-Creators, they forget the original intention to return to their source.

My friends, it is the blessings of the Creator that draw you to seek one another's companionship, to share that light that joins you, that makes a oneness of your individual alonenesses. It is the sharing of His love that makes your illusion bearable, for it is true that the sharing of the Creator's love, although greatly misunderstood, is perhaps the primary driving force of all striving, both spiritual and physical, upon your plane of existence. It is often the case among your peoples that that desire for

reception of the light of the Creator and the light which it engenders becomes transmuted into a lesser form, just as an alchemist might inadvertently transmute gold back to lead. Those who experience this difficulty find themselves seeking the light of the Creator yet perceiving that light as the love given by or drawn from another individual of your species.

My friends, realize and be aware of the source of the love which can permeate your lives. Understand that in loving another you love yourself. Is it your desire to imprison within the bonds of promises about the future made with no awareness thereof? Or is it your desire to fashion a permanence of an emotion by establishing a rigid outer form, a structure for that emotion similar to words or pictures carven into stone that persist long after that it represents has passed to its appropriate conclusion?

My friends, give and accept love with the awareness that it is a precious gift which may be neither owned nor held but simply experienced and be grateful for this experience as one encountering a wild flower growing freely and beautifully in one of your forests. Seek not to define but rather appreciate the beauty that exists. It is a tradition on your planet to establish bonds that link individuals together for the purpose of establishing a permanence within which responsibility may be shared. This is the custom of your race and exists to serve a purpose. Although this custom itself does no harm, but being a tool can serve or hinder its master.

We would encourage you, my brothers and sisters, to realize that the tool is meant to serve and not to command, that the role established by the tool is but a fleeting image within the imagination of your race and is simply form without substance if it does not serve the purpose of being a conduit through which love may flow freely in all directions. My friends, we urge you to give freely of your love to all who would receive it. Be generous, my friends, with yourselves, for indeed these brothers and sisters are but yourselves.

At this time we would pause that our brothers and sisters of Laitos might pass among you and extend their conditioning vibration to those of you who would mentally request this service. I am Hatonn.

(Pause)

(Unknown channeling)

I am Hatonn. I am again with this instrument. My friends, my loved ones, your illusion appears often to you to be an entrapment, an endless complexity within which you have managed somehow to ensnare yourselves. We are aware of the difficulty that you encounter as we are also aware of the challenges you face. But, my friends, be aware those difficulties, those challenges, are also reflections of love, that their existence is due in part to those conditions established by yourselves among many others prior to this incarnation that you might learn to choose to be of service to one another and in so doing attempt and accomplish the reunification of your race into a single consciousness of love.

There are many of your race who despair of this accomplishment, who finally throw up their hands and fly to the desolate areas, and there find the means to continue their loving in a more suitable manner. There are others for whom the proper method of loving is to immerse themselves into the greatest densities of population or corruption of your race and thereby strive to achieve a maximized effect by loving where love is sorely lacking. Both can be paths of service, my friends, and of accomplishment. Your own paths will be that portion of the spectrum within which you are best able to serve. Therefore, do not concern yourselves overly with worries of the fitness of your service or comparisons between

yourselves and others. Rather, find your path and strive confidently to follow it.

I am known to you as Hatonn. Adonai, my friends. Adonai vasu borragus.

(Unknown channeling)

I am Latwii, and I greet you, my brothers and sisters, in the love and the light of the infinite Creator, and may I say that we are very happy both to be able to address this group, and if we might say so, to balance the somber tones of our beloved brother of Hatonn with our somewhat lighter and somewhat frivolous, but no less loving, tones. At this time we would attempt to provide answers to any questions that might be asked, even if their total number exceeds the total number of two. Are there any questions?

S: Yes, I have a couple of questions. To keep it a little short tonight, my first question is more of a personal nature, and I know that normally you cannot answer specific things, but maybe if you could give me some advice. At this time in my life I'm going through a great deal of stress in trying to decide what my future will be like—to work or to stay in school or maybe having to leave Louisville. Can you give me some advice to help me through this?

I am Latwii, and we would love, so to speak, to give you some advice on this or any other subject, for doing so is one of the easiest paths of extending love we are aware of, and we love to love by speaking. To respond more succinctly to your question, we would remind you that your decision was made in this area prior to your incarnation, and therefore rather than concentrating on remaking the same decision your energy might be more comfortably and appropriately focused on understanding what your decision was and following it.

May we answer you further?

S: Interesting. I feel like I'm at a crossroads but you tell me I've made the decision previously. Why is it I feel, in one respect, dead set in my decision on staying in Louisville—I have to think about this. How would you recommend I rediscover what my future will be?

(Side one of tape ends.)

(Unknown channeling)

I am Latwii. I am again with this instrument and we must say the sensations we experience as the instrument fumbles in the dark are quite novel. However, to return to your question. We would draw an analogy if you would permit us. If you were to decide to go to the grocery to purchase a food product you might elect to travel in a motorized vehicle to a grocery at some distance from your residence. In performing this task, there are probably a number of routes you might elect to follow, and in choosing one you're in essence duplicating the accomplishment that would be attained by any of them, in that each would entice you to stray in different directions from the direct course, but all would eventually lead you to your objective and the sustenance you seek.

If, en route, you were to momentarily lose track of your objective, or forget entirely, it is likely that you might drift for a while to one direction or another or to several until the calling for sustenance recalls to you your objective and aids you in redetermining the best path to follow to that target. In a like manner, my friend, there are many objectives before you seemingly, but there is one primary objective that will provide for you the sustenance that you seek on a spiritual level, and although you may meander in one direction or another, you will return to the path you originally selected, for that path leads from your pre-incarnate self to your post-incarnate self.

It will be your task and pleasure to determine which of the routes you are examining will most lovingly deliver you to your objective. The best way, of course, that we can recommend to determine that objective, and therefore the best route, is through meditation, for in the act of meditation, the higher self is more able to communicate to your conscious mind through the link established during meditation between the subconscious mind and the conscious mind, and in doing so will assist you in answering your questions.

In the meantime, may we answer you further?

S: No, that will help me and I see the logic. I've tried meditating on this. I've had some problems concentrating, but that will help. My second question is: I was looking over some material I have on past contactees during the 1950's. I've been fascinated with the different groups that have contacted the human race in the past, and what their purposes are. What groups were primarily contacting in the '50s? They claim to be from Venus. Could you explain a little more about that?

I am Latwii. I am aware of your question. My friend, there are a number of groups which have been contacting your planet, not only [during] the span which you mentioned, but during the greater part of your race's existence on this same sphere. For example, those of the Federation on occasion will use the physical vehicle that is referred to as a UFO for specific purposes when a physically perceivable structure is beneficial. The same might be said for those of the group referred to as the Orion group, which also have their own purposes which they desire to accomplish.

There are also those entities which are referred to as "constructs," which although not actual entities in themselves, are functional creations that are brought into being and have occasionally visited your planet for the accomplishment of specific purposes before they are again allowed to dissipate back into the raw material from which they were constructed.

There are also occasional visitations of your planetary sphere from entities of other planets and solar systems, however, we would explain that those entities of the planet Venus are not of your density and therefore would not figure prominently in any physical manifestation grouping for your planet.

May we answer you further?

S: Was their purpose in contacting us during the '50's similar to your purpose in preparing the human race for the passage from the third to the fourth density?

I am Latwii. To answer this question, my brother, both we and yourself would need clarification of the word "they," for a multitude could be interpreted within this grouping which could be at cross-purposes.

S: I was thinking of those primarily who claim to be Venusians. I believe they were in contact with George Adamski.

I am Latwii. There are a number of factors within this situation that you have described that we are unable to discuss because of the possible infringement upon the free will of those who are involved or interested. However, we would suggest in general that frequently a communication is often either distorted by the previous positions of that individual receiving the telepathic communication or by those entities which would consciously choose to attempt such distortion so as to produce confusion, thereby serving themselves.

May we answer you further?

S: No, I think that explains that. One last quick question. In the past I asked to be able to see a UFO again—preferably from the Confederation—and I was told it would be against my will and I think perhaps against the Law of Confusion. Would it be possible now for me to see another one?

I am Latwii. My brother, that which prevents your perception is not of our doing, but of your own. It is your higher self that generates the experiences that you will encounter, and it is within that realm that the interdiction exists. It is not within our own system of restrictions, if you will, to work in such a manner as to oppose your growth, which acting in opposition to your higher self's will would accomplish.

May we answer you further?

S: So are you saying to see another UFO would be against the wishes of my higher self?

I am Latwii. We would rephrase your statement slightly and respond as such. For you to physically perceive a vehicle in the manner you desire is in opposition to conditions established by that higher self. These conditions are established for the purpose of your growth and accomplishment and therefore considerable wisdom has been used in establishing these conditions.

May we answer you further?

S: Yes, so my higher self feels for me to see a UFO that it would be a distortion of my learning at this time?

I am Latwii. My brother, it is not our place or desire to speak for that higher self, for in doing so we could only hope to provide a distortion of the original intention. However, [if] we might again be permitted the use of an analogy, we would provide the following analogy. There are many of your race who follow a religious sect or grouping that refer to themselves as Christians, and whose lives are based upon the attempt to follow the teachings of that one we know as Am Ne Ra. If we might pose a question to you we would do so as follows. If for these

individuals a visitation by Am Ne Ra occurred at each point of difficulty or temptation, would a substantial amount of growth occur within those individuals, or if a service which you refer to as a miracle would occur to remove this difficulty for them without the necessity of their faith or firmness of purpose being tested, would this be that which you would regard as beneficial or loving service?

S: Not really. I understand your analogy here, and I'm starting to understand better why it would not be beneficial for me to have an occurrence like that. Thank you.

As always, my brother, we thank you. Is there another question?

G: I have a question. I'm having problems meditating. I feel like I'm just sitting thinking, not really meditating when I'm meditating alone. Would you give me some help?

I am Latwii, and we would say first of all, my sister, that we are greatly pleased to receive your question, and hope you would not feel inhibited in asking one or even more than one question of us, for such is a service we enjoy providing.

We would have you understand, my sister, that the mind is a servant to the individual that must be trained just as an animal such as dog can be trained to behave or allowed to run amuck. The training process is a slow process, and immediate success in conquering this frolicsome creature is seldom encountered. However, consistent practice is always beneficial to the accomplishment of the taming of the beast, so to speak. To this end, we would suggest using one or more of several tools, the greatest and most effective of which is consistence. It is important to be consistent in your demands of your mind, in that the frequency of your attempts toward meditation and the scheduling of those same attempts with consistency are both beneficial to accomplish your purpose.

If you were to attempt to meditate daily at a specific time you might find that your dominance over your mind was more easily accomplished. While in your meditative attempt we would suggest that you begin with the concentration upon a specific—correction, that was not part of our statement. To return to the subject momentarily abandoned by the instrument—we would suggest the use of a tool for focusing the concentration rather than attempting to blank out the mind entirely, which is more difficult. Many find it beneficial to use a specific prayer as an object of meditation. There are also those phrases which this instrument identifies as mantras for this same purpose.

Finally, you might choose to meditate on a particular symbol such as those used in your various religious groups or upon a particularly uplifting phrase or expression. These and many other similar tools are most effectively used by concentrating upon the object of concentration, and when one finds one's mind has drifted away, do not punish or berate oneself, but simply return to the original thought …

(Tape ends.) ♣

L/L RESEARCH

L/L Research is a subsidiary of
Rock Creek Research &
Development Laboratories, Inc.

P.O. Box 5195
Louisville, KY 40255-0195

www.llresearch.org

Rock Creek is a non-profit
corporation dedicated to
discovering and sharing
information which may aid in
the spiritual evolution of
humankind.

ABOUT THE CONTENTS OF THIS TRANSCRIPT: This telepathic channeling has been taken from transcriptions of the weekly study and meditation meetings of the Rock Creek Research & Development Laboratories and L/L Research. It is offered in the hope that it may be useful to you. As the Confederation entities always make a point of saying, please use your discrimination and judgment in assessing this material. If something rings true to you, fine. If something does not resonate, please leave it behind, for neither we nor those of the Confederation would wish to be a stumbling block for any.

CAVEAT: This transcript is being published by L/L Research in a not yet final form. It has, however, been edited and any obvious errors have been corrected. When it is in a final form, this caveat will be removed.

SUNDAY MEDITATION
APRIL 4, 1982

(Carla channeling)

I am Hatonn, and I greet you, my friends, in the love and in the light of the one Creator. We extend our love and our greeting to each of you as you can receive it, and we especially thank the instrument known as L for his recent increased dedication to service as a channel for our thoughts and those of the Confederation other than ourselves. We were attempting to begin the evening with a few thoughts using that instrument but understand the instrument's desire to listen rather than channel and will, therefore, speak through this instrument and offer again an opportunity at a later time.

My friends, there is a cave that is a subterranean maze full of darkness, half-darkness, and into this cave, this cavern, your mind so often travels. There are so many among your peoples who fear these travels that they constitute an enormous majority, and their fear of these deep and secret places of their minds is such that they would do anything which can be done to avoid these places, to not think, to not search, to not be awake. And thus you see around you, my friends, many whose intellects you know to be above adequate who are working quite hard to distract themselves from that great cavern of being which lies below the surface of the comfortable, everyday illusion, and we share with you, my friends, the perception that this search through the mind for truth is risky. One does not

stumble upon love, illumination, enlightenment, and blinding joy within ten days after saying, "I shall seek the truth, or your money back." Indeed, there is never a time, no matter how many times you have been into the dark places of your mind and come through them safely when you are not potentially at the entrance to another blind alley, another difficult station, another mistaken perception, another point in your growth when it will seem to you that all has come to zero and that there is no more use in seeking, that there is no more hope for love and laughter and easiness of heart.

My friends, those who seek shall indeed be given what they seek, but the truth of your being is such an enormous and gigantic truth that it is difficult to accept. The truth of your being is a truth of unity—not apparent unity, not conditional unity, but unity with the dark and with the light, with the shadow and with the angel. One love created all. One love creates you. One great Thought is you and all else in the creation. Do you wish to know yourself? You have many choices to make, for again and again it will be easier to decide to know nothing more than to again affirm your desire to know. And each affirmation will bring with it a resolution, a lightening, and often that sudden burst of joy.

We speak to you, my friends, not of those things that are apparently occurring about you, for you may apparently be most contented and comfortable or most unsettled, but of those tides which ebb and flow in the heart of your being. We can offer to you only the comfort that you could offer a child, for you are as children, and as you grow there are not only scrapes and bruises but very real dangers, most of which work out quite, quite well. See yourself in your inner journey as a child. Know yourself as naive, unsophisticated. Yet know that you are not alone, for there is always guidance, and this guidance is with you constantly.

It is not our place to give to this particular group inspiration without a more serious note, for you have gone too far on this road. You know that the comfort of unity is not an illusion, and you have experienced much, but as you experience you experience also that which is most painful and that, my friends, is transformation. We, therefore, stand beside you as brothers and sisters, not wishing to inspire and then send you upon your way, but wishing instead to inspire in a deeper sense and be with you. Each of you is strong, and in quiet times may feel that strength.

Seek ye then, my friends, the times of quiet, for all truly shall be well. Even in a night when there are no candles, the dawn comes. We offer to you by these thoughts a root, that which is below the surface, just as in your conversation you spoke of the planting of flowers. The bloom comes and goes, and so your transitory experiences bloom and fade ever so quickly, and whether the blooming is effortless or labored, it passes and your true essence goes down again into the roots to be nurtured, to be affirmed, and to be fed by your desire, by your faithfulness to the will to seek the love of the Creator.

We would pause at this time, and, with those of Laitos, move among you that we way share our vibrations with each of you. If you will mentally request our presence we shall be with you at this time. I am Hatonn.

(Pause)

I am Hatonn, and I am again with this instrument. We thank you for the opportunity of working with each of you and would now, at this time, transfer the contact to another instrument. I am Hatonn.

(L channeling)

I am Hatonn, and I greet you again, my brothers and sisters, in the love and in the light of the infinite Creator. My friends, it is often difficult to find the stimulation to proceed forward. Inspiration seems to wax and wane and yet the path is ever present. It is quite easy to become discouraged, to feel that one is willingly falling by the wayside when the lack of inspiration seems to encourage one's feet to tarry or to stumble or even to stop. My friends, my loved ones, discouragement, anticipation, joy, and depression are all emotions. They are but tools that you may call upon in your quest for growth and learning.

Therefore, when you sense discouragement, disillusionment, perceive these emotions for what they are. They are the instruments which are available for your use to evaluate your progression, to adjust, if necessary, those facets of your being that appear to be retarding your progression, and, most important of all, they may be used to detect, to discern those areas within which adjustments of perception must be accomplished that your growth may continue.

Therefore, when these emotions become evident to you, experience and discern that which is being revealed. But just as one would not, in a suddenly non-functioning motor vehicle, state to oneself, "I am a dead car," do not take the identity of the tool upon your self with the acceptance in the manner of, "I am discouraged." Rather, experience the sensation with the awareness of, "I sense discouragement within my self," and make use of this powerful tool to further your striving.

My friends, the power of a group of a sharing such as this one is little realized by its members, yet who among you has not, many times during your days, discerned suddenly dramatic differences between your individual self and those other-selves with which your life is shared away from this group. My friends, realize that as each of you is like a molecule of which the cell of your group is composed, so also is your group a cell among many of which a larger entity is composed. These cells composing a hand within your individual body can accomplish little on their own, yet perceive for a moment the marvelous instrument their composition achieves. In your moments of discouragement or disillusionment, my friends, when you sense yourself as somehow failing to meet your desires or expectations, pause for a moment and realize what a mighty force is accomplished through your own will aligned with that of your loved ones. There is no failure, my friends. Those who set foot on the path do so by choice, the choice to seek the light. It is a choice not made lightly and, once made, cannot be abandoned, for how may a child among your people decide at one moment never again to grow, never more to learn?

Therefore, my friends, believe in yourselves, love yourselves, and continue confidently in your efforts. I am Hatonn.

(L channeling)

I am Latwii, and I greet you, my brothers and sisters, in the love and in the light of the infinite Creator. My friends, it is, as usual, a great privilege and pleasure for us to be here in that we both enjoy the sensation of your group's vibration, and also because we have been impatiently waiting for our somewhat stodgy brother of Hatonn to finish his dissertation. At this time we would offer our services, inadequate though they may be, to attempt to answer any questions you may desire to pose. Are there any questions?

R: Yes, Hatonn. What can you tell me of witchcraft?

I am Latwii. I assume that your question was directed to me, in that Hatonn does not seem capable of answering it at this time, so I will attempt to answer the question for him, or for me, as the case may be.

R: Forgive me.

[I am Latwii.] We are all forgiven, my brother. At this point I will attempt to answer your question. Witchcraft can consist of many different attempts to perform specific tasks. There are facets of the general subject referred to as witchcraft which are functional, and, as you may suspect, other facets which do not seem to accomplish a great deal. Those that tend to accomplish their desired ends may be further divided into the areas generally referred to as white magic or black magic. We assume that black magic is the subject of your interest and will address that topic.

Just as your own group is endeavoring to progress along a path of service to others, so are there also individuals who desire to progress along a path of service to self. This, of course, you are aware of. What you perhaps are not aware of is the fact that the desire to exert one's will upon another or a number of other individuals is one of the strong suits, shall we say, of those involved in that effort, and there are many facets or fields of study within

that realm through which the will of an individual may be projected in dominance over the wills of others. There are many rituals that can be used as tools to assist in this endeavor, those rituals being valuable solely in the effort of enabling the aspiring magician to focus his will and intention.

May we answer you further, my brother?

R: I don't really know how to phrase what I am thinking, but I am curious if people who practice that, whether it be white or black, are basically doing the same thing that we are doing here, with it all leading towards the same thing, the same goal, just different methods?

I am Latwii. My brother, consider the individual who desires to progress from what we shall describe [as] point A to point B in as rapid a manner as possible. The individual who is endeavoring to serve others would most likely choose a route which will disturb or endanger as few as possible whereas the individual who is engrossed in service to self might choose to drive the vehicle which you refer to as a tank through a crowded stadium in an effort to achieve his goal. Both have progressed from A to B, but by substantially different methods and with substantially different results, due to their orientation. We hope that this might clarify the distinction between groups such as this and those who would, in an effort to serve themselves, exert their will over other individuals to accomplish personal growth.

May we answer you further?

R: No, thank you, Latwii.

As always, we thank you. Is there another question?

K: What about the "Moral Majority"? It seems to me that they try very hard to force their wills on other people, and yet they seem like they are trying to accomplish good ends. Could you speak to that?

I am Latwii. It is difficult to address this question in that it refers to a specific group of individuals, and there are limitations upon the amount of information we are allowed to give due to the possible infringement upon your freedom of choice. It is always possible to select specific groups that seem to be significant because of the stridency of their voices and regard these groups as being perhaps more significant than they are. We would simply say that the majority of the true accomplishment performed on your planet is seldom accomplished through groups which deal with the illusion but rather through the efforts of groups that deal beyond the illusion, such as this group, or through the efforts of special individuals whose responsibility to strive toward certain objectives was taken on prior to incarnation.

May we answer you further?

K: No. That's answered the question. Thank you.

As always, we thank you. Is there another question?

Carla: I wouldn't mind mopping up a little bit on that one because it was an interesting one. …

(Side one of tape ends.)

Carla: … potential as far as the potential for service of any kind?

I am Latwii. I am aware of your question. My sister, picture, if you will, that form of blanket or coverlet which is woven of yarn and referred to often as an afghan. If there are individuals who require the warming comfort of such an object to sleep comfortably, it would be an act of service for one or more people to lift that object and remove it to the location where the one desiring the comfort of warmth may have it placed upon them. However, if a number of individuals are all desiring to move that comfort in different directions to serve different purposes, although each has a hand on the blanket and claim honestly in his or her heart to be attempting an act of service, the conflicting desires may result in a composite accomplishment of service that borders on nothing, although each truly sought to act in service.

The difficulty within your illusion that is constantly encountered by groups of any sort desiring service is not the heartfelt desire to serve but rather the lack of communion between its members within which dissension evaporates in the light of common purpose.

May we answer you furthers my sister?

Carla: Well, you haven't plumbed the depths of that one, but I'll let it be. I have a couple of questions from S in Denver. She would like to know first about the comparison, if it is possible for you to give one, between an experience she had while under age regression hypnosis into another life where she was initiated in a temple, and the experience of the initiate in the Queen's chamber as described by Ra. Could you comment on any similarities between those two experiences?

I am Latwii. I am aware of your question. The desire of the individual originating the question was to be assured, first of all, of the linearity or congruence of the two individual types of experience, and indeed there are similarities between the two. The experiences are both what may be referred to as illuminations in which the common factors of consent, rituals and devices are shared to accomplish a specific balancing and attunement of those areas known as chakras.

In each situation the structure within which the illumination occurred serves a specific purpose in focusing the channeled light energy due to the configuration of the structure. The facet referred to as consent of course was necessary in the experience recalled during the regression as it also is in the Queen's chamber experience. The ritual aspect of both is to serve the purpose of allowing individuals of attainment to assist in the illumination process for the individual. The result in both cases is the opening and balancing of those areas referred to as chakras due to the individual's acceptance of the light energy which is funneled through the individual.

May we answer you further, my sister?

Carla: I'll let S see this, and see if she has any other questions.

Her other question was probably much shorter and easier to answer because it is sort of a yes or no question. She wanted to know if the higher self could have two instead of one mind/body/spirit complexes on the same plane of being in the same density at the same time, and, if so, if they could be as close as mother and daughter or father and son?

I am Latwii. The higher self referred to is associated with not only the specific individual at the unique time and place within your illusion but of course also the various incarnations of that particular individual throughout his incarnate experiences. It must be remembered that all individuals are a part of a larger, unified self, and that although the higher selves are associated only with specific individuals, they are more attuned to the consciousness of their unity than the mind/body/spirit complex within your illusion tends to be.

It is often the case that individuals will repeatedly incarnate over a period of several incarnations so as to encounter and re-encounter, that the recognition might be a stimulus to the desire to extend one's consciousness beyond the limits of the forgetting. This can be a very powerful tool toward assisting both individuals to recall their purpose in incarnating, thus receiving an earlier stimulus toward a focusing of their effort.

May we answer you further?

Carla: No. Again, I thank you for S. I still see very rich ground for discussion on the subject of how the various groups [who] think so much alike and feel so much alike and believe so much alike and have so much community are the very ones who judge and are so abrasive in their contact with those who don't think as they do.

I will save that for another week because I am sure that the instrument is getting very tired. I'll just ask, how are you, Latwii?

I am Latwii. I am in the condition referred to as fine, and thank you both for your salutation, and the heartfelt affection that we are aware initiated the salutation, and we also hope that your condition is similar to our own.

Carla: I am fine too.

That is well. Is there another question we may answer?

K: You can probably answer this with a yes or a no. I've recently read two books by Capra. One was *The Tao of Physics*, and the other was *The Turning Point*, which I haven't quite completed. Is Capra being used by the Confederation to guide and help the planet?

I am Latwii. My sister, there are many definitions and many titles for those areas of assistance or tools for that purpose that are perceived by those of your planet. It is wise perhaps to recall that all originates with the Creator and regardless of what name is attached to a particular object of interest or definition, the source is the same.

May we answer you further?

K: No. I'll accept that answer.

We thank you. Is there another question?

(Pause)

I am Latwii. As there is a reluctance to pose further questions due to concern for the wellbeing of the instrument we shall take our leave and hope for the opportunity to serve in answering those questions at a future time. Adonai, my friends. Adonai vasu borragus. I am Latwii. ☙

L/L Research is a subsidiary of
Rock Creek Research &
Development Laboratories, Inc.

P.O. Box 5195
Louisville, KY 40255-0195

L/L RESEARCH

www.llresearch.org

Rock Creek is a non-profit
corporation dedicated to
discovering and sharing
information which may aid in
the spiritual evolution of
humankind.

THE LAW OF ONE, BOOK IV, SESSION 83
APRIL 5, 1982

Ra: I am Ra. I greet you in the love and in the light of the one infinite Creator. I communicate now.

Questioner: Could you first please give me the condition of the instrument?

Ra: I am Ra. It is as previously stated.

Questioner: Could you please tell me why the instrument now gains weight after a session instead of losing it?

Ra: I am Ra. To assume that the instrument is gaining the weight of the physical bodily complex due to a session or working with Ra is erroneous. The instrument has no longer any physical material which, to any observable extent, must be used in order for this contact to occur. This is due to the determination of the group that the instrument shall not use the vital energy which would be necessary since the physical energy complex level is in deficit. Since the energy, therefore, for these contacts is a product of energy transfer the instrument must no longer pay this physical price. Therefore, the instrument is not losing the weight.

However, the weight gain, as it occurs, is the product of two factors. One is the increasing sensitivity of this physical vehicle to all that is placed before it, including that towards which it is distorted in ways you would call allergic. The second factor is the energizing of these difficulties.

It is fortunate for the outlook of this contact and the incarnation of this entity that it is not distorted towards the overeating as the overloading of this much distorted physical complex would over-ride even the most fervent affirmation of health/illness and turn the instrument towards the distortions of illness/health or, in the extreme case, the physical death.

Questioner: Thank you. I'm going to ask a rather long, complex question and I would request that the answer to each portion of this question be given if there was a significant difference prior to the veil than following the veil so that I can get an idea of how what we experience now is used for better polarization.

What was the difference before the veil in the following while incarnate in third density: sleep, dreams, physical pain, mental pain, sex, disease, catalyst programming, random catalyst, relationships, and communication with the higher self or with the mind/body/spirit totality or any other mind, body, or spirit functions before the veil that would be significant with respect to their difference after the veil?

Ra: I am Ra. Firstly, let us establish that both before and after the veil the same conditions existed in time/space; that is, the veiling process is a space/time phenomenon.

Secondly, the character of experience was altered drastically by the veiling process. In some cases such as the dreaming and the contact with the higher self, the experience was quantitatively different due to the fact that the veiling is a primary cause of the value of dreams and is also the single door against which the higher self must stand awaiting entry. Before veiling, dreams were not for the purpose of using the so-called unconscious to further utilize catalyst but were used to learn/teach from teach/learners within the inner planes as well as those of outer origins of higher density. As you deal with each subject of which you spoke you may observe, during the veiling process, not a quantitative change in the experience but a qualitative one.

Let us, as an example, choose your sexual activities of energy transfer. If you have a desire to treat other subjects in detail please query forthwith. In the instance of the sexual activity of those not dwelling within the veiling each activity was a transfer. There were some transfers of strength. Most were rather attenuated in the strength of the transfer due to the lack of veiling.

In the third density entities are attempting to learn the ways of love. If it can be seen that all are one being it becomes much more difficult for the undisciplined personality to choose one mate and, thereby, initiate itself into a program of service. It is much more likely that the sexual energy will be dissipated more randomly without either great joy or great sorrow depending from these experiences.

Therefore, the green-ray energy transfer, being almost without exception the case in sexual energy transfer prior to veiling, remains weakened and without significant crystallization. The sexual energy transfers and blockages after veiling have been discussed previously. It may be seen to be a more complex study but one far more efficient in crystallizing those who seek the green-ray energy center.

Questioner: Let's take, then, since we are on the subject of sex, the relationship before and after the veil of disease, in this particular case venereal disease. Was this type of disease in existence prior to the veil?

Ra: I am Ra. There has been that which is called disease, both of this type and others, before and after this great experiment. However, since the venereal disease is in large part a function of the thought-forms of a distorted nature which are associated with sexual energy blockage the venereal disease is almost entirely the product of mind/body/spirit complexes' interaction after the veiling.

Questioner: You mentioned that it existed in a small way prior to the veil. What was the source of its development prior to the veiling process?

Ra: I am Ra. The source was as random as the nature of disease distortions are, at heart, in general. Each portion of the body complex is in a state of growth at all times. The reversal of this is seen as disease and has the benign function of ending an incarnation at the appropriate space/time nexus. This was the nature of disease, including that which you call venereal.

Questioner: I'll make this statement and you can correct me.

As I see the nature of the action of disease before the veil, it seems to me that the Logos had decided upon a program where an individual mind/body/spirit would continue to grow in mind and the body would be the third-density analog of this mind. The growth would be continual unless there was an inability, for some reason, for the mind to continue along the growth patterns. If this growth decelerated or stopped, what we call disease would then act in a way so as to eventually terminate this physical experience so that a new physical experience would be started, after a review of the entire process had taken place between incarnations. Would you clear up my thinking on that, please?

Ra: I am Ra. Your thinking is sufficiently clear on this subject.

Questioner: The thing I don't understand is why, if there was no veil, the review of the incarnation after the incarnation would help the process since it seems to me that the entity should already be aware of what was happening. Possibly this has to do with the nature of space/time and time/space. Could you clear that up, please?

Ra: I am Ra. It is true that the nature of time/space is such that a lifetime may be seen whole as a book or record, the pages studied, riffled through, and re-read. However, the value of review is that of the testing as opposed to the studying. At the testing, when the test is true, the distillations of all study are made clear.

During the process of study, which you may call the incarnation, regardless of an entity's awareness of the process taking place, the material is diffused and over-attention is almost inevitably placed upon detail.

The testing upon the cessation of the incarnative state is not that testing which involves the correct memorization of many details. This testing is, rather, the observing of self by self, often with aid as we have said. In this observation one sees the sum of all the detailed study; that being an attitude or complex of attitudes which bias the consciousness of the mind/body/spirit.

Questioner: Now before the veil an entity would be aware that he was experiencing a disease. As an analogy would you give me, if you are aware of a case, a disease an entity might experience prior to the veil and how he would react to this and think about it and what effect it would have on him?

Ra: I am Ra. Inasmuch as the universe is composed of an infinite array of entities, there is also an infinity of response to stimulus. If you will observe your peoples you will discover greatly variant responses to the same distortion towards disease. Consequently, we cannot answer your query with any hope of making any true statements since the over-generalizations required are too capacious.

Questioner: Was there any uniformity or like functions of societies or social organizations prior to the veil?

Ra: I am Ra. The third density is, by its very fiber, a societal one. There are societies wherever there are entities conscious of the self and conscious of other-selves and possessed with intelligence adequate to process information indicating the benefits of communal blending of energies. The structures of society before as after veiling were various. However, the societies before veiling did not depend in any case upon the intentional enslavement of some for the benefit of others, this not being seen to be a possibility when all are seen as one. There was, however, the requisite amount of disharmony to produce various experiments in what you may call governmental or societal structures.

Questioner: In our present illusion we have undoubtedly lost sight of the techniques of enslavement that are used since we are so far departed from the pre-veil experience. I am sure that many of service-to-others orientation are using techniques of enslavement even though they are not aware that these are techniques of enslavement simply because they have been evolved over so long a period of time and we are so deep into the illusion. Is this not correct?

Ra: I am Ra. This is incorrect.

Questioner: Then you say that there are no cases where those who are of a service-to-others orientation are using techniques of enslavement that have grown as a result of the evolution of our social structures? Is this what you mean?

Ra: I am Ra. It was our understanding that your query concerned conditions before the veiling. There was no unconscious slavery, as you call this condition, at that period. At the present space/time the conditions of well-meant and unintentional slavery are so numerous that it beggars our ability to enumerate them.

Questioner: Then for a service-to-others oriented entity at this time meditation upon the nature of these little-expected forms of slavery might be productive in polarization I would think. Am I correct?

Ra: I am Ra. You are quite correct.

Questioner: I would say that a very high percentage of the laws and restrictions within what we call our legal system are of a nature of enslavement of which I just spoke. Would you agree with this?

Ra: I am Ra. It is a necessary balance to the intention of law, which is to protect, that the result would encompass an equal distortion towards imprisonment. Therefore, we may say that your supposition is correct. This is not to denigrate those who, in green and blue-ray energies, sought to free a peaceable people from the bonds of chaos but only to point out the inevitable consequences of codification of response which does not recognize the uniqueness of each and every situation within your experience.

Questioner: Is the veil supposed to be what I would call semi-permeable?

Ra: I am Ra. The veil is indeed so.

Questioner: What techniques and methods of penetration of the veil were planned and are there any others that have occurred other that those planned?

Ra: I am Ra. There were none planned by the first great experiment. As all experiments, this rested upon the nakedness of hypothesis. The outcome was unknown. It was discovered, experientially and empirically, that there were as many ways to penetrate the veil as the imagination of mind/body/spirit complexes could provide. The desire of mind/body/spirit complexes to know that which was unknown drew to them the dreaming and the gradual opening to the seeker of all of the balancing mechanisms leading to adepthood and communication with teach/learners which could pierce this veil.

The various unmanifested activities of the self were found to be productive in some degree of penetration of the veil. In general, we may say that by far the most vivid and even extravagant opportunities for the piercing of the veil are a result of the interaction of polarized entities.

Questioner: Could you expand on what you mean by that interaction of polarized entities in piercing the veil?

Ra: I am Ra. We shall state two items of note. The first is the extreme potential for polarization in the relationship of two polarized entities which have embarked upon the service-to-others path or, in some few cases, the service-to-self path. Secondly, we would note that effect which we have learned to call the doubling effect. Those of like mind which together seek shall far more surely find.

Questioner: Specifically, by what process would, in the first case, two polarized entities attempt to penetrate the veil, whether they be positively or negatively polarized? By what technique would they penetrate the veil?

Ra: I am Ra. The penetration of the veil may be seen to begin to have its roots in the gestation of green-ray activity, that all-compassionate love which demands no return. If this path is followed the higher energy centers shall be activated and crystallized until the adept is born. Within the adept is the potential for dismantling the veil to a greater or lesser extent that all may be seen again as one. The other-self is primary catalyst in this particular path to the piercing of the veil, if you would call it that.

Questioner: What was the mechanism of the very first veiling process? I don't know if you can answer that. Would you try to answer that?

Ra: I am Ra. The mechanism of the veiling between the conscious and unconscious portions of the mind was a declaration that the mind was complex. This, in turn, caused the body and the spirit to become complex.

Questioner: Would you give me an example of a complex activity of the body that we have now and how it was not complex prior to the veil?

Ra: I am Ra. Prior to the great experiment a mind/body/spirit was capable of controlling the pressure of blood in the veins, the beating of the organ you call the heart, the intensity of the sensation known to you as pain, and all the functions now understood to be involuntary or unconscious.

Questioner: When the veiling process originally took place, then, it seems that the Logos must have had a list of those functions that would become unconscious and those that would remain consciously controlled. I am assuming that if this occurred there was good reason for these divisions. Am I in any way correct on this?

Ra: I am Ra. No.

Questioner: Would you correct me, please?

Ra: I am Ra. There were many experiments whereby various of the functions or distortions of the body complex were veiled and others not. A large number of these experiments resulted in nonviable body complexes or those only marginally viable. For instance, it is not a survival-oriented mechanism for the nerve receptors to blank out unconsciously any distortions towards pain.

Questioner: Before the veil the mind could blank out pain. I assume then, that the function of the pain at that time was to signal the body to assume a different configuration so that the source of the pain would leave, and then the pain could be eliminated mentally. Is that correct, and was there another function for the pain prior to the veiling?

Ra: I am Ra. Your assumption is correct. The function of pain at that time was as the warning of the fire alarm to those not smelling the smoke.

Questioner: Then let's say that an entity at that time burned its hand due to carelessness. It would immediately remove its hand from the burning object and then, in order to not feel the pain any more, its mind would cut the pain off until healing had taken place. Is this correct?

Ra: I am Ra. This is correct.

Questioner: We would look at this in our present illusion as an elimination of a certain amount of catalyst that would produce an acceleration in our evolution. Is this correct?

Ra: I am Ra. The attitude towards pain varies from mind/body/spirit complex to mind/body/spirit complex. Your verbalization of attitude towards the distortion known as pain is one productive of helpful distortions as regards the process of evolution.

Questioner: What I was trying to indicate was that the plan of the Logos in veiling the conscious from the unconscious mind in such a way that pain could not so easily be controlled would have created a system of catalyst that was not previously usable. Is this generally correct?

Ra: I am Ra. Yes.

Questioner: In some cases it seems that this use of catalyst is almost in a runaway condition for some entities in that they are experiencing much more pain than they can make good use of as far as catalytic nature would be considered. Could you comment on that?

Ra: I am Ra. This shall be the last query of this working of a full length. You may see, in some cases, an entity which, either by preincarnative choice or by constant reprogramming while in incarnation, has developed an esurient program of catalyst. Such an entity is quite desirous of using the catalyst and has determined to its own satisfaction that what you may call the large board needs to be applied to the forehead in order to obtain the attention of the self. In these cases it may indeed seem a great waste of the catalyst of pain and a distortion towards feeling the tragedy of so much pain may be experienced by the other-self. However, it is well to hope that the other-self is grasping that which it has gone to some trouble to offer itself; that is, the catalyst which it desires to use for the purpose of evolution. May we ask if there are any brief queries at this time?

Questioner: I noticed you started this session with "I communicate now" and you usually use "We communicate now." Is there any significance or difference with respect to that, and then is there anything that we can do to make the instrument more comfortable or to improve the contact?

Ra: I am Ra. We am Ra. You may see the grammatical difficulties of your linguistic structure in dealing with a social memory complex. There is no distinction between the first person singular and plural in your language when pertaining to Ra.

We offer the following, not to infringe upon your free will, but because this instrument has specifically requested information as to its maintenance and the support group does so at this querying. We may suggest that the instrument has two areas of potential distortion, both of which may be aided in the bodily sense by the ingestion of those things which seem to the instrument to be desirable. We do not suggest any hard and fast rulings of diet although we may suggest the virtue of the liquids. The instrument has an increasing ability to sense that which will aid its bodily complex. It is being aided by affirmations and also by the light which is the food of the density of resting.

We may ask the support group to monitor the instrument as always so that in the case of the desire for the more complex proteins that which is the least distorted might be offered to the bodily complex which is indeed at this time potentially capable of greatly increased distortion.

I am Ra. We thank you, my friends, for your continued conscientiousness in the fulfilling of your manifestation of desire to serve others. You are conscientious. The appurtenances are quite well aligned.

I am Ra. I leave you, my friends, in the love and in the light of the one infinite Creator. Go forth, therefore, rejoicing merrily in the power and in the peace of the one infinite Creator. Adonai. ♣

FRIDAY NIGHT
APRIL 9, 1982

(Carla channeling)

I am Hatonn, and I greet you, my brothers and sisters, in the love and light of the infinite Creator. My friends, my loved ones, this is a day traditionally associated on your planet with the remembrance of one known to you as Jesus, Joshua, or known to us as Am Ne Ra. The mission and accomplishments of this entity while on your planet have been greatly misunderstood by most, in that an effort was made by a number of your people to interpret his words and actions within the framework of that which was earlier understood and yet was so sorely lacking as to require his sojourn upon your planet.

The interpretations of his words and actions were by some misunderstood while in others a conscious effort was made to misrepresent those words to create confusion and augment the numbers on your planet who would either polarize in what you describe as a negative sense or would fail to polarize due to confusion. However, my friends, it is never possible for confusion to overwhelm knowledge, just as darkness, being but the absence of light, is unable to overwhelm light.

My friends, there is always one source of information that you may draw upon, and that is that still, quiet voice that speaks to you from the depths of your soul when presented a heartfelt question. It is often difficult to perceive that voice behind the clamorings of those voices of the mind, and for this reason, among others, we encourage strongly the frequent use of that tool which you call meditation, for it is only through the attainment of skill with this tool that the voice may be perceived and thereafter recognized.

My friends, the attainments of Am Ne Ra are worthy of your attention and emulation, for he was able to accomplish much of which on your planet was long overdue, yet it is important, my friends, that you realize that his accomplishments are not unattainable to yourselves; if anything, they are more attainable as a result of his efforts. Seek, my friends, and you shall find. Knock, and it shall be open to you, and if you but ask, that for which you ask you shall receive, for such is the way of the universe.

These are not merely grand statements deprived of an eloquence of a man thought to be two thousand years dead, but rather statements of fact, of simple laws that guide the functioning and development of your universe. If it is your will to attain that growth which was achieved by that man, Jesus, if you would have his knowledge, if you would share his wisdom, then, my friends, these goals are within your grasp, these answers will be given. This wisdom will be obtained if you but constantly seek, my friends, if you but constantly ask. If your knock at the door of knowledge is ceaseless, if your maintain your hunger, refusing to be satisfied with that of which you are aware and continue to strive toward that which is still unknown, then, my friends, your quest will be fulfilled, just as that of the one you call Jesus.

You may recall, my friends, the final statement attributed to him on the day that you are recalling. That statement, "It is consummated[3]." My friends, give yourselves to your striving, do not yield to distraction, to boredom, or to the influences of those who do not understand your seeking, but maintain your efforts and do not be satisfied until you have reached that point where you may confidently acknowledge that your task of learning on this plane has been completed.

At this time we would pause that our brothers and sisters of Laitos might pass among you and share their vibration with those of you who might request it. I am Hatonn.

(Pause)

I am Hatonn, and I am again with this instrument. We of Hatonn would like to thank you for your patience while we have spoken. We are aware that at times our words are ponderous and unyielding, yet we would ask you to be aware that our intention is but to serve, just as the one who fiercely and seemingly without compassion braided himself a whip and drove those which you call money changers from a place of worship. The eyes can't see it but the heart can recognize the love within the action and the love within our communication when we attempt to share our thoughts with you.

We will now relinquish the use of this instrument that our brothers and sisters of Latwii may share their thoughts with you. I am Hatonn.

(Jim channeling)

I am Latwii, and I greet you in the love and the light of the infinite Creator. My friends, as always, it is a great pleasure to be able to perform our small service for those of you who desire to ask questions from this unworthy source of information. Is there a question that we may attempt to answer tonight?

S1: As always, I have a question. What would our life probably be like in the fourth density?

---

[3] From the *Holy Bible*, the Gospel of John, 19:30, "When Jesus had received the vinegar, he said, 'It is finished,' and he bowed his head and gave up his spirit."

I am Latwii, and, as always, I have an answer. My friend, we assume that your question deals with the everyday details of your fourth-density existence, and not with the physical structures or bodies involved therein, and, my friend, we would very candidly answer you by saying, my friend, your life will be what you make of it. There is no defined society, no cities, no interstates awaiting your arrival. However, as you may have surmised, there will be a great quantity of love and light within the larder so that you will not feel completely abandoned.

May we answer you further, my friend?

S1: Yes, from what I've learned in the past, we will probably leave the Earth to go to another destination. Is this correct?

I am Latwii, and I would answer your question by replying that this is correct for certain entities who have not fully polarized, and for others who will fully polarize by the time of harvest but will polarize in such a fashion that their service-to-self orientation will require their removal from this planet. The remaining entities will initiate their fourth-density experience upon this planet, although it will be substantially altered by that time.

May we answer you further?

S1: Well, I'm curious. I will probably still have my physical body at that time. What will happen to the physical carrier, and will I have a physical carrier during and after the change?

I am Latwii. My brother, we are going to answer your question with reticence, for it is not our intention to violate your free will by revealing to you details about your personal future. We will therefore speak in general, and caution those present against making broad assumptions about their personal future based upon generalized statements.

There is what may be referred to as a fourth-density body which will be for those in fourth density a carriage or physical vehicle, but for those in third density this same carriage or vehicle would be invisible and completely indistinguishable. Those entities who are alive and functioning, you might say, in fourth density will be doing so solely in this type of body. There will be a transition period in which certain entities who currently are in existence in a third-density vehicle will be in the process of a transformation, for they are also at this time simultaneously in possession of a fourth-density vehicle of which they are unaware, and a process will be experienced by which the butterfly will shed its cocoon and leave it behind. It remains to be seen by yourself, however, as to your own personal future.

May we answer you further?

S1: You may not be able to tell me this because of it being a violation of my free will. Am I on the right path to being able to graduate to the fourth density?

I am Latwii. My friend, there is no wrong path for attainment to fourth density or any other density for all paths lead in one direction. The object of your concern, however, might be the sufficient polarization of a chosen polarity and the maintaining of that condition so as to be sufficiently polarized to attain harvest on the particular occasion as opposed to several harvests down the road.

May we answer you further?

S1: Will I be harvested at the next harvest or do you think it will be further on?

(Side one of tape ends.)

(Jim channeling)

I am Latwii, and apologize for the delay and lack of coordination of the instrument. Our intention was not to keep you in suspense, my brother, until the next episode. As you surmised, my friend, that is a question we may not respond to in any fashion that would imply to you or identify any level of accomplishment that you have attained or failed to attain, for to do so could drastically affect your polarization and efforts thereto.

May we answer you further?

S1: I may have asked you this in the past. Besides meditating more often, is there anything else I can do toward polarizing more positively than I already am so that I can attempt to make harvest?

I am Latwii. My brother, if we may paraphrase one who has previously spoken on your planet, we would suggest that you love all that is of the Creator and love your brothers as yourself. Beyond this there is very little else that can be accomplished that will affect your polarity in the direction in which you currently strive.

May we answer you further?

S1: Well, if I could just make a comment. I hope that I will be able to reach polarization. I may not understand things too well, but I feel that having these lifetimes in the physical carrier is a waste of time in a way because when you're born you forget all you've accomplished in a previous life on a conscious level. Like right now I wish I could finish my third density so that I would not have to go through another lifetime and possible mess everything up. Do you understand my frustration here?

I am Latwii, and we are aware of your question. My brother, we are aware of your feelings and we counsel you in this fashion. There are no mistakes within the will of the Creator. If it is your quest to attain the level of polarity necessary to successfully be harvested as a fourth-density positively-polarized entity, as our brother Hatonn pointed out, your sustained seeking will attain fruition. The efforts and accomplishments of those who are unable to sustain a seeking will result in a confused response to a confused seeking. We would not suggest for those present that either is the case, for only in each entity's heart is [there] an awareness of their performance and their level of desire, for we would suggest that there are no mistakes within creation, and each will attain at the harvest that end toward which his striving has led him.

May we answer you further?

S1: It takes a moment for all of this to sink in. I'm trying to realize all of what you've said. Maybe it's that I'm very happy with my present situation. I've been going through a lot of questioning in my environment right now trying to decide what my future will be in my interactions in my daily life. That was just an observation I made. I feel that my major striving should be to help myself and others in their spiritual paths, and trying to keep this thought in mind while considering the daily interaction, trying to understand how to put that in perspective in my immediate future. Do you understand sort of what I'm going through right now?

I am Latwii. My brother, moments ago you spoke of your lack of understanding of the Creator's will and the waste of time involved in experiencing a physical incarnation. My brother, for the edge of a sword to remain keen it must first be stressed and tempered, for that which comes easily is easily lost, while that which is bought dearly is dearly held.

My brother, we understand that your polarization and that of all others is dearly bought and often seems to be of unfair cost. We can only reply, my friend, that you shall not, at a future date, reminisce and wonder at what point your polarity was obtained and strive to recall the foggy details, for your past striving and attainments will ever be a lamp that you will proudly hold high and shine brightly as a sword whose edge was painfully brought to keenness or even as the pearl described for which the individual sold all that he had so as to obtain it.

May we answer you further, my brother?

S1: No, I'm understanding that better. I guess I'll have to learn more patience in this area, and just keep trying re-learning my lessons, and keep trying to polarize myself so that when the time comes I'll be ready for whatever the Creator has set forth for me. Thank you for your help, and it helps to talk to someone that I feel has all the answers that I don't have. Thank you.

I am Latwii. My brother, we would sincerely respond that we find great pleasure in our ability to learn with you and from you as well as to share what meager advice we might offer, and for this, my brother, we thank you and urge you to contact us at any time for however brief a time that we may, with our presence, attempt to sustain you in your striving.

Is there another question?

G: Yes, I have a question. My son, T, is having difficulty in school maintaining average grades, and I'm pushing and he seems to be resisting. Is there another way to go about helping him get better grades or do the younger children realize nowadays that that's just not their goal?

I am Latwii. My sister, you must first understand that we are restricted in our ability to respond to your question due to the nature of your question itself, in that we do not wish to imply a certain decision must be made. However, with the understanding that we speak in general terms we would respond that those entities which are currently incarnating into your world are more aware of the transience of their incarnation, in that a subconscious knowledge exists of the relatively small period of time remaining until the harvest occurs. For this reason there is difficulty in performing the large number of nominal and repetitive tasks that are associated with your educational systems.

However, we would also suggest that those entities who incarnate in your illusion do so to experience fully that illusion and to experience the illusion with an attitude of, "We will selectively experience those parts which are enjoyable but not those parts which are less desirable," is not as prone to stimulate growth as another approach might be.

May we answer you further, my sister?

G: No, thank you.

As always, it is a pleasure to be of service to you. Is there another question?

S2: Yes, I have a question, Latwii. Could you explain the chakras and their activation a little for me, please?

I am Latwii. I am aware of your question. My sister, as you consider the progression of light energy through the physical body then you must first examine the path which is followed. The energy traditionally associated with the Earth follows generally in a path up the legs, the base of the spine and up the spine itself to the skull. This may seem misleading in reference to light energy but nonetheless this is the path that is followed as all of creation exudes light in a 360 degrees, and that light is not limited to solar bodies such as your Sun.

The various energy centers, or chakras, may be regarded as contact points between the physical vehicle and what might be referred to as the spiritual body, each contact point representing a stage of development akin to levels on a staircase. As the light progresses through each stage it will stimulate a retention of light or emittance of light through each of these centers. The proper configuration for a fully developed entity would be a configuration in which each of the chakras is unblocked and fully emitting light energy that it is receiving as described previously.

The sequence of the chakras in receiving light corresponds to the learning experience sequence generally encountered by those in your illusion. For example, the first chakra, being primarily involved in the survival of the single entity, would take progression in sequence before that of the development of interpersonal relationships. The difficulty in the light flow through the chakras which is referred to as blockages are the results of the individual choosing to reduce or deny the admission of light to the individual center or centers or the refusal to emit light through those centers for whatever reasons the individual possesses. These reasons may be involved with particular emotions or may be the result of experience received by the entity which must be balanced in the entity's perceptions. These are but two explanations of many effectors of the energy centers or chakras.

May we answer you further, my sister?

S2: Not at this time Latwii. Thank you.

We thank you. Is there another question?

(Pause)

I am Latwii. As there seems to be no further questions we will relinquish our use of this instrument, and will leave you to your own devices, so to speak. We would, however, caution a number of those present against the levitation by hand of many of those devices that, what is referred to as *(inaudible)*, as this seems to result in certain inconsistencies within the structural framework that supports your vehicle, and although we recognize the pleasure derived from assisting one another in readjusting of the structural frameworks[4], we are always reluctant to see those dear to us experience physical pain, however minor. With this reminder we would bid you farewell 'til our next …

(Tape ends.) ♣

---

[4] Carla: I may have been walking on L's back to ease his back pain. At this remove of time, I am not sure, but I did that frequently for him, as at that time I weighed about 80 pounds.

L/L Research is a subsidiary of
Rock Creek Research &
Development Laboratories, Inc.

P.O. Box 5195
Louisville, KY 40255-0195

L/L Research

www.llresearch.org

Rock Creek is a non-profit
corporation dedicated to
discovering and sharing
information which may aid in
the spiritual evolution of
humankind.

SUNDAY MEDITATION
APRIL 11, 1982

(C channeling)

I am Hatonn, and I am now with this instrument. We greet you, as always, in the love and the light of the one infinite Creator. For many of your peoples this is a holy time of your year, a time in which hope and faith is renewed, as they remember the one known to you as Jesus and how he overcame what you term death to live. My friends, each in his own fashion finds as they forget, as they begin anew to learn, as each as they incarnate, are reborn begin to experience again a start of the road that will take them back, and will enable them to remember that forgotten. Each of you has begun to see a small part of that which was forgotten, each seeing that which they need. Awareness of forgetting. It is a valuable step for your journey. Your life will …

We are experiencing difficulty with our contact with this instrument and will now, at his request, transfer this contact. I am Hatonn.

(L channeling)

I am Hatonn. I am now with this instrument, and I again greet you in the love and light of the infinite Creator. My friends, that which you celebrate at this time of your year is a rebirth and reemergence of life upon your planet and within your souls. It is fitting that the death in the physical form of that one which you call Jesus coincides with this time of rebirth, for just as a change in form occurs throughout those areas of your planet experiencing what you call Spring in that an old form, that of the concealed, that of the waiting, that which seems withered and dead externally but merely conceals and protects the life within, is suddenly abandoned and a new life leaps forth, a life form which was unseen and inconceivable in its previous incarnative form. A new life spreads literally with the speed of light across your planet, for is it not light that summons the new life forth and feeds, nourishes and sustains it as the trees and flowers begin to grow, climbing ever higher ever further, extending their buds as arms and hands reaching to grasp the light, almost as if desiring to take hold of it and pull it back into the center of their souls.

My friends, accept, recognize and celebrate your spring. Let your growth proceed in harmony with the flower and grasses that surround you and let your hearts climb ever higher, striving to obtain that light, to ingest it, to make it ever a part of you. There is in your need—correction—in your world a need for this substance, and just as on the physical realm the light is passed through the food chain from plant to animal, from animal to animal, in truth from brother to brother, so also within the spiritual realm, my friends. Be aware of your need to share your light and of your brother's need to partake of your light that you may both be sustained.

At this time we would pause that our brothers and sisters of Laitos might pass among you and extend their conditioning vibration to those of you who mentally request it. I am Hatonn.

(Pause)

I am Hatonn. I am once again with this instrument. My friends, it is our desire at this time to take our leave that our brothers and sisters of Latwii might perform their service of answering your questions. Adonai, my friends. I am Hatonn.

(Carla channeling)

I am Latwii, and I greet you, my friends, in the love and the light of the one infinite Creator. I am very, very pleased to be with you this evening, and very pleased that we are able to say a few words through this instrument before we get to the task at hand which is our great privilege.

We are always pleased to be able to use this instrument. My friends, we would like you to consider an aspect of this which you call the resurrection of an entity known to you as Jesus of Nazareth. To some extent this occasion has been upon each of your minds this day, and we take this opportunity to use this story to the purpose for which it was intended, as example for your consideration. My friends, what would you feel if one to whom you were very devoted had been killed in a most barbarous manner and his body placed in a cave behind a great rock? It is daybreak, my friends, and you go to tend the dead. You are mourning yet you know death, for it comes to all, but there is no corpse. What do you feel, my friends, when a being whiter than any normal being, and more full of light says to you, "He is not here. He is alive."

My friends, there were reasons why the women did not disbelieve the livingness of their beloved. Undoubtedly, your first impulse would be to say, "There is trickery involved here and someone has robbed a grave," but if you knew that the dead one was now alive, what would you feel? My friends, the women were afraid and most troubled in mind, because the possibility of life had suddenly been presented to them. My friends, we ask you why are you afraid of dying and take your living for granted? Would it not be more helpful to you to have a fear and awe and a wonder of the living that you are somehow miraculously doing?

So many of your peoples, my friends, pass through this life in a dream, scarcely waking 'til they die. Let your life became less familiar to you. Try to see how totally amazing it is. Find that which has been called in your holy works "life more abundant." Because, my friends, there is so much to do, to see, to feel. There is so much joy in the universe. Why waste a day, a moment, upon indifference? We rejoice with you that we share consciousness. You are all alive and you shall be now and forever. Stand in awe of the great consciousness of the Creator and try not to slip too quickly into indifference.

I shall, at this time, leave this instrument that we may proceed with any questions which you may wish to ask at this time. I leave this instrument in the love and the light of the Creator. I am Latwii.

(Jim channeling)

I am Latwii, and I greet you all once again in the love and the light of the one Creator. It is now our privilege to begin the question and answer portion of this meeting. May we at this time ask if there are any questions?

C: As I began to channel tonight the contact was good but I realized after it started that I assumed a position too close to a heating vent and felt some physical discomfort. But tonight I had—when I usually channel it seems I have concept with words. It's sort of like it had a little caption there, and I see the words as I try to speak them, but tonight I had a concept, but it seemed there were no words and I felt a bit of nervousness, that I felt like I had no words to express the concept, and I was just wondering if tonight Hatonn was trying to help me further develop as a channel by having me draw upon myself more, or whether the contact was just weakened by me being—my attention being distracted by physical discomfort.

I am Latwii, and am aware of your question, my brother. We might suggest that your latter assumption is more nearly correct, for the mind which is divided does not pay the necessary attention to the concepts which are presented to it.

May we answer you further, my brother?

C: No, thank you.

We thank you. Is there another question at this time?

R: Yes. Can you tell us if the Easter Shroud of Turin is the actual burial cloth of Christ? And also what created the image on it?

I am Latwii, and am aware of your query, my brother. We shall, we are afraid, have to invoke that great Law of Confusion at this time, for we do not feel it would be appropriate for us to answer the riddle which is presented by this artifact which you have called the Shroud of Turin, for such mysteries are most important to your peoples at this time in their evolution. Such mysteries pose questions of the eternal for the conscious minds to consider. Each entity upon your planet now seeks in ever greater degree to proceed with its evolutionary path, and such mysteries as this one do serve as a stimulus to provoke the questioning and increase the seeking.

May we answer you further, my brother?

R: No, thank you.

We thank you. Is there another question at this time?

L: Yes, first for myself and those present I'd like to wish you a happy Easter. Beyond that, I've noticed in myself that my dedication, if you wish to call it that, tends to wax and wane with no particular stimulus or lack of stimulus that I can discern. Would you discuss this subject?

I am Latwii, and am aware of your question, my brother. We would first of all thank you for your Easter wishes, and hope that we do not lay any eggs this evening. We now address your query. The seeker shall, as it proceeds on what you might call the path of enlightenment, discover those light areas and those dark areas in its seeking. These may be likened unto times when the seeker is most clearly aware that it is seeking and might feel some pride, shall we say, in the success of the seeking. There might be the comparison of current attitudes, thoughts and desires with those of the entity's past, and there might be some, shall we say, rejoicing at the progress that has been made. There are other times when the entity is not aware that progress has been made in other areas of its being. There might be, for instance, the repeating of patterns of thoughts, desires and behaviors which do not satisfy the entity, for they seem the same as always, and no growth is there apparent.

We can only suggest to the ardent seeker that in each instance the estimation which we have rendered

might be just the opposite, for in those times in which the seeker feels the progress has been made, it might indeed be true that the progress has been made, but in that area for the present moment there is no further growth, the growth having been accomplished. In the area in which the seeker feels the frustrations and disappointments at the, shall we say, maintenance of the status quo, there is yet the growth in motion and in potential, and there is the possibility for the developing of new thoughts and behaviors.

To summarize our somewhat lengthy statement, may we say that at each moment the seeker shall be experiencing some facet of the growth process, but in your illusion you shall not be fully appraised of the exact nature of your growth until it is well behind you, for the illusion which you inhabit is quite dense, and does provide many times of confusion, many opportunities for growth, and as you seek the light you seek the darkness of your own forgetting that is necessary to propel you towards the light.

May we answer you further, my brother?

L: I desire to question you on a different subject, the subject of healing. I am aware that certain procedures that I have developed in the past were simply tools or constructs that were for the purpose of enabling me to develop a rudimentary understanding of the process so as to work with it, and I'm aware that those constructs are but tools and not the reality itself. My understanding of the reality of healing is incomplete. I do know that there are points in time where I can apparently generate or tap into a form of energy and apparently can project this, but I do not understand how it works or what purpose it accomplishes, in that to my understanding the actual purpose of the healer is simply to act as a go-between, a focusing object, or the person desiring healing and intelligent infinity. I realize this is a pretty vague introduction for the question, but would you discuss the subject of healing in relation to this?

I am Latwii, and am aware of your query, my brother. We are also aware that this is quite a large subject, but we shall attempt to make some general statements that we hope may be of service to you.

First of all, we shall begin with the normally accepted realm of healing as it is experienced within your density, this known as the allopathic method of healing, where the healer assumes the greatest amount of responsibility for the one to be healed and its healing process. You may see this as an action from outside of the one to be healed and as some kind of salve upon the wound, the presence of the healer therefore being necessary in order for what is loosely described as the healing process to occur. Now we move to that realm of healing which has just begun to surface in the conscious knowledge of this group, that being the contact with intelligent infinity, by which the healer offers to the one to be healed the opportunity to accept a new configuration of mind/body/spirit more congruent with that configuration known as health. In this process the healer has no will, but offers itself as an instrument or a channel for the intelligent infinity present in each entity to …

(Side one of tape ends.)

(Jim channeling)

I am Latwii, and am once again with this instrument. To continue—this shell, then, having been pierced, the one to be healed then has the opportunity to accept the new configuration that offers health, shall we say. This process then having been successfully completed does then allow for what you call the healing to occur.

Between these two types of healing lie many steps. Those seeking to become healers travel this path that joins these two points. At each step along this path the healer does become transformed so that it does practice upon itself what you might call the healing process, so that the injunction which is old among your peoples of physician, "Heal thyself," is indeed accomplished. This healing of the one desiring to become a healer does then allow this entity to provide other entities with this same opportunity. As this process continues, as the healer does become what is called healed or—what might be more clearly defined as—balanced in its energy centers, and balanced in mind, body and spirit, then [it] is able to provide this opportunity to other selves.

At one point more closely associated with the contact with intelligent infinity, yet short of this point, there does come about a transformation, shall we say, which might be described as contact with intelligent energy, which is more known among your peoples as action at a distance, and does include the ability of the entity to utilize powers of the mind which have not been well known among your

peoples. The entity then is able to provide more energy, shall we say, of its own abilities to the one to be healed, and then does affect the one to be healed, but to a lesser extent than does the allopathic healer.

May we answer you further, my brother?

L: Yes. One last question. In seeking to heal, obviously one of the prime requisites would be to assist in whatever manner possible the person desiring healing to identify the novel condition that is projected from intelligent infinity. Obviously this is something I need to do for myself as well. Have you any advice on how to go about this?

I am Latwii. My brother, we would wish to correct what we believe to be a misapprehension, and that is that the one seeking to be a healer is one wishing to serve the one Creator without a will of its own, making its will subservient to the will of the Creator. Therefore, the one seeking to be the healer does not aid the one to be healed in the preparation of the configuration of the mind of the one to be healed, for this is the task solely of the one to be healed, and the one seeking to be that known as a healer then offers itself for whatever the outcome as a catalyst, shall we say, for the healing to occur or not to occur.

May we answer you further, my brother?

L: No. I thank you for your assistance and your patience.

I am Latwii. We are most grateful to you, as always. Is there another question at this time?

K: Yes. I hesitate to ask this question, and I'll certainly understand if the answer is not appropriate. When I was in my 30's, as I can recall, I had a completely overwhelming experience in a classroom during the worship service. The classroom was in another building even from the worship service, and I was totally overwhelmed with a presence in that room and I certainly did not understand the experience, and I had no one to whom I could go that did understand, and I've lived with that—still am—without understanding it. I felt a pain in the heart for years and [wonder,] if it's appropriate, would you comment on that?

I am Latwii, and am aware of your query, my sister. We may speak in general upon this subject, for such experiences are not as unusual among your peoples as many would believe, for this seeming random contact with what we have called intelligent infinity does from time to time make itself known to various entities for a great variety of reasons. In your particular case, the pain which you have felt within the heart of your being acts much like the grain of sand within that creature you call the oyster. It does motivate you, shall we say, to ask the reasons for this occurrence, the meaning of this occurrence, and does in some way then affect the way in which you seek. The sand is likened unto the pain, and produces that likened unto the pearl of great price, and as you seek the meaning of this occurrence, you shall, within your being, produce that pearl which you have incarnated to produce.

May we answer you further, my sister?

K: Well, it was so very, very painful and overwhelming that I tried to forget it for a long time, and it comes back to me from time to time. Would you comment on why I insisted on forgetting it?

I am Latwii, and again may speak only generally. It is often the case that an experience which is so overwhelming and out of the ordinary shall be too intense for an entity to consider at once and must needs be spread out, shall we say, over the period of the lifetime for its meaning to be fully revealed.

May we answer you further, my sister?

K: No, thank you. That's fine. Thank you very much.

I am Latwii. We are grateful to you, as well. Is there another question at this time?

M: Yes. Could you tell me how one becomes an instrument?

I am Latwii, and may suggest that the desire to be that known as an instrument is the greatest factor in becoming such. There is within this group a practice which allows such entities to devote a specific period of time to developing this ability, and we might simply refer you to those entities present which will aid you in this process if it should be your desire. The process is quite simple and requires the attaining of the meditative state with the desire to receive such information after the tuning in a group has been accomplished, as it has been this evening, and the beginning transmissions experienced.

May we answer you further, my sister?

M: You've answered me. Thank you.

I am Latwii. Is there another question at this time?

L: Latwii, as there do not seen to be any more questions, I would just like to say that in view of the fact that this is Easter, that your answers have been "eggsactly "what we've been "dyeing" to hear, and we shall look forward to hearing from you again.

I am Latwii, and am most pleased with these puns, and we shall file them for future reference.

L: I hope you enjoyed my "yolks."

We are very pleased to have other groups with which to share them, and shall give this group the proper credit. May we ask if there are any questions before we leave this group? We are not always able to provide answers which are as potentially enlightening, shall we say, as those questions this evening have elicited, and we would not wish to leave any question unanswered.

K: Yes. One other question. The sixties and the seventies—I've lived a long time, and I think I'm aware of this, but the sixties and the seventies have been, it seems to me, times of reappraisal, and a kind of an awakening or at least a seeking. Is that true?

I am Latwii, and am aware of your query, my sister. We are in agreement with your estimation, and may comment somewhat further by suggesting that as this cycle of learning is ending for your peoples those entities incarnating are incarnating for what may well be the last opportunity for completing the lessons of this cycle, and therefore have programmed before the incarnation a great deal of learning which it is hoped shall occur during the incarnation. This fact is increased in its intensity when it is realized that the entities now incarnating are also those entities most likely to achieve the graduation, the, shall we say, cream of the crop which your planet has produced in its cycles of evolution, and this fact added to the previous fact does then increase that experience which occurs in the incarnative state. The periods of years which you have described are an accurate reflection of the increased vibratory rates of the peoples of your planet and the learning which is being attempted, and you might be prepared, shall we say, for the future years being of an increased vibratory nature as well, as both polarities seek to make their graduations upon your planet.

May we answer you further, my sister?

K: Yes. I've had some friends in the seminary who think that the year 2000 is a climatic time, and is that an accurate statement also?

I am Latwii, and am aware of your query, my sister. When speaking of time periods it is increasingly difficult to accurately describe the time in which any event shall occur the further the event is from that you call the present. You may see your present situation as a point in space and time with an infinity of possibilities surrounding that point—possibilities for future events. You may also see the course which has been traveled by your peoples and its direction of further travel, but to project that force further into your future becomes more and more difficult, for each entity upon your planet fully exercises that known as free will, and as this is exercised the possibility of predicting its course becomes more and more difficult as what you call time progresses.

It might be generally stated that the year 2000, and subsequent years following that year, are more likely to be decisive points, and become that culmination of points of experience which is often called the graduation or the harvest for your peoples.

May we answer you further, my sister?

K: When you talk about the harvest—we use the concept of the end of a dispensation or is that the same?

I am Latwii, and we find that there are many terms which have been applied to this which is loosely called the harvest by many of your peoples over great periods of what you call time. When we speak of harvest we are speaking of the end of this planet's third density experience and the beginning of its fourth-density experience, that experience which is likened unto a quantum leap in evolution.

May we answer you further, my sister?

K: No. That helps a lot. Thank you.

I am Latwii. We are most grateful to you as well. Is there another questions at this time?

M: Yes. I have a friend that is disgustingly happy all the time, and she doesn't seem to have much depth. Now, I don't know whether or not to envy her happiness or whether I feel sorry for her because she takes everything, what seems to me, lightly or maybe it's because I'm not as happy. Is her happiness good or not?

I am Latwii, and am aware of your query, my sister. We can respond to this query most helpfully, we believe, by suggesting that the response depends upon one's point of view. In truth, it has been said there is no right or wrong, no good or evil, but only the experience of the Creator by the Creator. Each entity [as] a portion of the one Creator incarnates to learn certain lessons. Some lessons require the application of a great amount of what you might call pain and difficult experience in order to get the attention, shall we say, of the self which is attempting these lessons. Other lessons may not require so great an application of the pain. It cannot be said without knowing the full scope of an entity's preincarnative choices whether the entity is learning the lessons programmed, or whether these lessons are being ignored, or whether they have indeed been learned. There are an infinite array of lessons, of portions of the one Creator and experiences available within the one creation. Each is a portion of the Creator, and is experienced by the Creator.

May we answer you further, my sister?

M: No. I think you have answered the question.

I am Latwii. Is there another question at this time?

M: Maybe you can tell me a little bit more about her. She paints happy faces on everybody around her and [that] makes her happy, and is she ignoring the misery around her or is it a good idea to paint happy faces on people?

I am Latwii, and am aware of your query, my sister. Again we must respond by suggesting that it is not possible to say whether an action such as this is good or not good, but can only be seen as an experience of the Creator in which lessons are being attempted. Within your illusion each entity has his or her own set of biases, of preferences, of their definitions of what is good and what is not good. These are an illusion, as we have said, for there is no good or evil in truth, but these are necessary illusions to provide the catalyst for growth among your peoples. As you meet entities in your daily round of activities such as this entity, you shall view such an entity through the framework of your own preferences and biases. You shall, therefore, interact with this entity in a manner which does then produce a catalyst for experience and growth. You shall see the entity in such and such a manner, and the entity shall see you likewise. This shall produce an interchange and interplay of thoughts, ideas, behaviors and feelings for both of you and those surrounding you. All of these thoughts and feelings shall either add to the biases which you have, or shall in some way produce the balancing effect, so that that concept which is known to you as judgment is evened or smoothed in its effect and acceptance of the other self. The other self's behavior and your own self is then aided, for this is the greatest lesson of your illusion, the acceptance of all entities including yourself, the acceptance of all experience, for all is the experience of the one Creator.

May we answer you further, my sister?

M: Well, I'm not sure. I think I would like to find some of her happiness, but I don't particularly like shallowness if it has to go with it. Can happiness and shallowness be separated?

I am Latwii, and am aware of your query, my sister. We may suggest that those distortions which you have called happiness and shallowness are two facets of the jewel of the one creation and Creator, and are not greater or lesser than any other experience. Each then does provide a lesson. All lessons aid the Creator in knowing Itself, and aid each portion of the Creator in knowing the Creator.

May we answer you further, my sister?

M: Well, if she's getting as much out of it as I am, then I think I would like to have some of her happiness. From what you're telling me, she's accomplishing just as much. Am I understanding that correctly?

I am Latwii, and am aware of your query, my sister. Depending upon one's point of view, this is entirely correct. It is difficult to know whether an entity is accomplishing what it set out to accomplish before its incarnation during its incarnation, but whether or not lessons are learned, there is an infinity of time for each entity to learn all lessons and all lessons are lessons which aid the Creator and the entity.

May we answer you further, my sister?

M: No. I think you have answered the question at this time as much as I can understand.

I am Latwii. May we ask if there is another question at this time?

(Pause)

I am Latwii. We are most grateful to each present this evening for extending to us the opportunity to speak this capacity of attempting to answer your queries. We realize that each seeks the solution to many inner mysteries. We of Latwii do not presume

to be able to answer these queries fully. We hope in our answers that you might find further stimulus for seeking within the true solutions to each mystery. We can only offer directions and comments, for any answer we give contains the distortions which are inherent in any language which attempts to convey thoughts in words which are unable to hold the thoughts. Therefore, we ask each entity present to remember that we are also seeking solutions to mysteries which we share with you.

We would at this time take our leave of this group. We leave each of you in the love and in the light of the one infinite Creator. We shall be with you again in what you call your future, and look forward to each opportunity to be with you in your meditations. I am known to you as Latwii. Adonai, my friends. Adonai vasu borragus. ƺ

L/L Research is a subsidiary of
Rock Creek Research &
Development Laboratories, Inc.

P.O. Box 5195
Louisville, KY 40255-0195

L/L Research

www.llresearch.org

Rock Creek is a non-profit
corporation dedicated to
discovering and sharing
information which may aid in
the spiritual evolution of
humankind.

The Law of One, Book IV, Session 84
April 14, 1982

Ra: I am Ra. I greet you, my friends, in the love and in the light of the one infinite Creator. We communicate now.

Questioner: Could you first please give me the condition of the instrument?

Ra: I am Ra. The physical complex energy level of the instrument is in sizable deficit. The vital energies are well.

Questioner: In the last session you mentioned the least distorted complex protein for the instrument since its body complex was capable of greatly increased distortion. Would you define the protein of which you spoke and in which direction is the increased distortion, towards health or ill-health?

Ra: I am Ra. We were, in the cautionary statement about complex protein, referring to the distortions of the animal protein which has been slaughtered and preservatives added in order to maintain the acceptability to your peoples of this non-living, physical material. It is well to attempt to find those items which are fresh and of the best quality possible in order to avoid increasing this particular entity's distortions which may be loosely termed allergic.

We were speaking of the distortion towards disease which is potential at this space/time.

Questioner: The instrument asked the following question: Ra has implied that the instrument is on the path of martyrdom, but since we all die are we not all martyred to something, and when, if ever, does martyrdom partake of wisdom?

Ra: I am Ra. This is a thoughtful query. Let us use as exemplar the one known as Jehoshua. This entity incarnated with the plan of martyrdom. There is no wisdom in this plan but rather understanding and compassion extended to its fullest perfection. The one known as Jehoshua would have been less than fully understanding of its course had it chosen to follow its will at any space/time during its teachings. Several times, as you call this measure, this entity had the possibility of moving towards the martyr's place which was, for that martyr, Jerusalem. Yet in meditation this entity stated, time and again, "It is not yet the hour." The entity could also have, when the hour came, walked another path. Its incarnation would then have been prolonged but the path for which it incarnated somewhat confused. Thusly, one may observe the greatest amount of understanding, of which this entity was indeed capable, taking place as the entity in meditation felt and knew that the hour had come for that to be fulfilled which was its incarnation.

It is indeed so that all mind/body/spirit complexes shall die to the third-density illusion; that is, that each yellow-ray physical-complex body shall cease to be viable. It is a misnomer to, for this reason alone, call each mind/body/spirit complex a martyr, for this term is reserved for those who lay down their lives for the service they may provide to others. We may encourage meditation upon the functions of the will.

Questioner: The instrument asked if the restricted, unpublishable healing information that was given during the first book could be included in Book Four since readers who have gotten that far will be dedicated somewhat?

Ra: I am Ra. This publication of material shall, in time, shall we say, be appropriate. There is intervening material.

Questioner: Going back to the previous session, you stated that each sexual activity was a transfer before the veil. Would you trace the flow of energy that is transferred and tell me if that was the planned activity or a planned transfer by the designing Logos?

Ra: I am Ra. The path of energy transfer before the veiling during the sexual intercourse was that of the two entities possessed of green-ray capability. The awareness of all as Creator is that which opens the green energy center. Thusly there was no possibility of blockage due to the sure knowledge of each by each that each was the Creator. The transfers were weak due to the ease with which such transfers could take place between any two polarized entities during sexual intercourse.

Questioner: What I was getting at, precisely, was, for example, when we close an electrical circuit it is easy to trace the path of current. It goes along the conductor. I am trying to determine whether this transfer is between the green energy centers (the heart chakras). I am trying to trace the physical flow of the energy to try to get an idea of blockages after the veil. I may be off on the wrong track here, but if I am wrong we'll just drop it. Can you tell me something about that?

Ra: I am Ra. In such a drawing or schematic representation of the circuitry of two mind/body/spirits or mind/body/spirit complexes in sexual or other energy transfer the circuit opens always at the red or base center and moves as possible through the intervening energy centers. If baffled it will stop at orange. If not, it shall proceed to yellow. If still unbaffled it shall proceed to green. It is well to remember in the case of the mind/body/spirit that the chakras or energy centers could well be functioning without crystallization.

Questioner: In other words, they would be functioning but it would be equivalent in an electrical circuitry to having a high resistance, shall we say, and although the circuit would be complete, red through green, the total quantity of energy transferred would be less. Is this correct?

Ra: I am Ra. We might most closely associate your query with the concept of voltage. The uncrystallized, lower centers cannot deliver the higher voltage. The crystallized centers may become quite remarkable in the high voltage characteristics of the energy transfer as it reaches green ray and indeed as green ray is crystallized this also applies to the higher energy centers until such energy transfers become an honestation[5] for the Creator.

Questioner: Would you please correct me on this statement. I am guessing that what happens is that when a transfer takes place the energy is that light energy that comes in through the feet of the entity and the voltage or potential difference is measured between the red energy center and, in the case of the green ray transfer, the green energy center and then must leap or flow from the green energy center of one entity to the green energy center of the other, and then something happens to it. Could you clarify my thinking on that?

Ra: I am Ra. Yes.

Questioner: Would you please do that?

Ra: I am Ra. The energy transfer occurs in one releasing of the potential difference. This does not leap between green and green energy centers but is the sharing of the energies of each from red ray upwards. In this context it may be seen to be at its most efficient when both entities have orgasm simultaneously. However, it functions as transfer if either has the orgasm and indeed in the case of the physically expressed love between a mated pair which does not have the conclusion you call orgasm there is, nonetheless, a considerable amount of energy transferred due to the potential difference which has been raised as long as both entities are aware of this potential and release its strength to each other by desire of the will in a mental or mind complex dedication. You may see this practice as being used to generate energy transfers in some of your practices of what you may call other than

---

[5] honestation: *n.* adornment; grace. [Obs.]

Christian religious distortion systems of the Law of One.

Questioner: Could you give me an example of that last statement?

Ra: I am Ra. We preface this example with the reminder that each system is quite distorted and its teachings always half-lost. However, one such system is that called the Tantric Yoga.

Questioner: Considering individual A and individual B, if individual A experiences the orgasm is the energy, then, transferred to individual B in a greater amount? Is that correct?

Ra: I am Ra. Your query is incomplete. Please restate.

Questioner: I am trying to determine whether the direction of energy transfer is a function of orgasm. Which entity gets the transferred energy? I know it's a dumb question, but I want to be sure that I have it cleared up.

Ra: I am Ra. If both entities are well polarized and vibrating in green-ray love any orgasm shall offer equal energy to both.

Questioner: I see. Before the veil can you describe any other physical difference that we haven't talked about yet with respect to the sexual energy transfers or relationships or anything prior to veiling?

Ra: I am Ra. Perhaps the most critical difference of the veiling, before and after, was that before the mind, body, and spirit were veiled, entities were aware that each energy transfer and, indeed, very nearly all that proceeds from any intercourse, social or sexual, between two entities has its character and substance in time/space rather than space/time. The energies transferred during the sexual activity are not, properly speaking, of space/ time. There is a great component of what you may call metaphysical energy transferred. Indeed, the body complex as a whole is greatly misunderstood due to the post-veiling assumption that the physical manifestation called the body is subject only to physical stimuli. This is emphatically not so.

Questioner: After the veil, in our particular case now, we have, in the circuitry of which we were speaking, what you call blockages. Could you describe what occurs with the first blockage and what its effects are on each of the entities assuming that one blocks and the other does not or if both are blocked?

Ra: I am Ra. This material has been covered previously. If both entities are blocked both will have an increased hunger for the same activity, seeking to unblock the baffled flow of energy. If one entity is blocked and the other vibrates in love, the entity baffled will hunger still but have a tendency to attempt to continue the procedure of satiating the increasing hunger with the one vibrating green ray due to an impression that this entity might prove helpful in this endeavor. The green-ray active individual shall polarize slightly in the direction of service to others but have only the energy with which it began.

Questioner: I didn't mean to cover previously covered material. What I was actually attempting to do was discover something new in asking the question, so please if I ask any questions in the future that have already been covered don't bother to repeat the material. I am just searching the same area for the possibility of greater enlightenment with respect to this particular area since it seems to be one of the major areas of experience in our present condition of veiling that produces a very large amount of catalyst and I am trying to understand, to use a poor term, how this veiling process created a greater experience and how this experience evolved. These questions are very difficult to ask.

It occurs to me that many statues or drawings of the one known as Lucifer or the Devil are shown with an erection. Is this a function of orange-ray blockage, and was this known in a minimal way by those who devised these statues and drawings?

Ra: I am Ra. There is, of course, much other distortion involved in a discussion of any mythic archetypical form. However, we may answer in the affirmative and note that you are perceptive.

Questioner: With respect to the green, blue, and indigo transfers of energy, how would the mechanism for these transfers differ from the orange-ray mechanism in making them possible or setting the groundwork for them? I know this is very difficult to ask and I may not be making any sense, but what I am trying to do is gain an understanding of the foundation for the transfers in each of the rays and the preparations for the transfers or the fundamental requirements or biases and potentials for these transfers. Could you expand on that for me please? I am sorry for the poor question.

Ra: I am Ra. We would take a moment to state in reply to a previous comment that we shall answer each query whether or not it has been previously covered for not to do so would be to baffle the flow of quite another transfer of energy.

To respond to your query we firstly wish to agree with your supposition that the subject you now query upon is a large one, for in it lies an entire system of opening the gateway to intelligent infinity. You may see that some information is necessarily shrouded in mystery by our desire to preserve the free will of the adept. The great key to blue, indigo, and finally, that great capital of the column of sexual energy transfer, violet energy, transfers, is the metaphysical bond or distortion which has the name among your peoples of unconditional love. In the blue-ray energy transfer the quality of this love is refined in the fire of honest communication and clarity; this, shall we say, normally speaking in general, takes a substantial portion of your space/time to accomplish although there are instances of matings so well refined in previous incarnations and so well remembered that the blue-ray may be penetrated at once. This energy transfer is of great benefit to the seeker in that all communication from this seeker is, thereby, refined and the eyes of honesty and clarity look upon a new world. Such is the nature of blue-ray energy and such is one mechanism of potentiating and crystallizing it.

As we approach indigo-ray transfer we find ourselves in a shadowland. We cannot give you information straight out or plain, for this is seen by us to be an infringement. We cannot speak at all of violet ray transfer as we do not, again, desire to break the Law of Confusion.

We may say that these jewels, though dearly bought, are beyond price for the seeker and might suggest that just as each awareness is arrived at through a process of analysis, synthesis, and inspiration, so should the seeker approach its mate and evaluate each experience, seeking the jewel.

Questioner: Is there any way to tell which ray the transfer was for an individual after the experience?

Ra: I am Ra. There is only a subjective yardstick or measure of such. If the energies have flowed so that

love is made whole, green-ray transfer has taken place. If, by the same entities' exchange, greater ease in communication and greater sight has been experienced, the energy has been refined to the blue-ray energy center. If the polarized entities, by this same energy transfer experience, find that the faculties of will and faith have been stimulated, not for a brief while but for a great duration of what you call time, you may perceive the indigo-ray transfer. We may not speak of the violet-ray transfer except to note that it is an opening to the gateway of intelligent infinity. Indeed, the indigo-ray transfer is also this but, shall we say, the veil has not yet been lifted.

Questioner: Did most Logoi plan, before the veil, to create a system of random sexual activity or the specific pairing of entities for specific periods of time, or did they have an objective in this respect?

Ra: I am Ra. This shall be the last full query of this working.

The harvest from the previous creation was that which included the male and female mind/body/spirit. It was the intention of the original Logoi that entities mate with one another in any fashion which caused a greater polarization. It was determined, after observation of the process of many Logoi, that polarization increased many fold if the mating were not indiscriminate. Consequent Logoi thusly preserved a bias towards the mated relationship which is more characteristic of more disciplined personalities and of what you may call higher densities. The free will of each entity, however, was always paramount and a bias only could be offered.

May we ask if there may be any brief queries before we leave this instrument?

Questioner: Is there any way that we can make the instrument more comfortable or to improve the contact?

Ra: I am Ra. We would ask that each of the support group be especially vigilant in the, what you would call, immediate future due to this instrument's unbidden but serious potential for increased distortion towards illness/health.

You are most conscientious. We thank you, my friends, and leave you in the glorious light and love of the one infinite Creator. Go forth, therefore,

rejoicing in the power and in the peace of the one
infinite Creator. Adonai. ☙

L/L Research is a subsidiary of
Rock Creek Research &
Development Laboratories, Inc.

P.O. Box 5195
Louisville, KY 40255-0195

L/L RESEARCH

www.llresearch.org

Rock Creek is a non-profit
corporation dedicated to
discovering and sharing
information which may aid in
the spiritual evolution of
humankind.

THE LAW OF ONE, BOOK V, SESSION 84, FRAGMENT 43
APRIL 14, 1982

Jim: The first portion of Session 84 is mostly nuts and bolts maintenance of the instrument. Her primary exercise each day was one hour of brisk walking, and when her feet began to suffer injury we tried alternating two different kinds of shoes hoping that each would aid one portion of the injury without aggravating another portion.

Don also asked Ra about information concerning earth changes which Andrija Puharich had received from one of his sources. Instead of responding directly to the query and risking infringing upon the free will of Dr. Puharich, Ra chose to speak to the subject of earth changes as representative of one of two choices that a person may make in the search for truth.

Between that response and the last question and answer that you see was a portion of information concerning a person's encounter with a UFO which Ra asked us to keep private. The question and answer that you do see is in reference to this same UFO contact and reveals the general way in which many face-to-face encounters between our third-density population and extraterrestrial entities occur. What is actually remembered by the third-density entity is a product of its expectations and what its subconscious mind fashions as an acceptable story that will allow the entity to continue functioning without losing its mental balance. This is the nature of the positive contact in which the third-density entity is being awakened to seek more clearly the

nature of not only the UFO encounter but the life pattern as well. Negative contacts, however, utilize the concepts of fear and doom to further separate and confuse the Earth population.

Carla: My poor feet! Rheumatoid disease is notorious for its depredations upon one's extremities, and perhaps my hands, feet and neck have suffered the worst from its progression. Thirteen operations on my hands and six on my feet have staved off total dysfunction, but the old digits are not what they once were. During these sessions, they suffered far more than normal, because when I was in trance, I did not move at all. Those of Ra did not know how to make my body move very well, and so whatever aches and pains I had became rapidly very hard to bear. It was easy for me to be discouraged. I can remember asking the Creator, with some asperity, what It had in mind when it gave me these gifts! How inconvenient! Especially in terms of this contact, which we all knew was special, I tended to feel that I had let down the side by these sore joints' taking time away from the sessions in length. Feeling unworthy in the first place, I felt sheepish that I was, by these distortions, lessening the content of each working. At this latter day, however, I have ceased to rail against whatever comes my way. I am just glad to be here. And if I can still channel, fine. But I think all of us have one main job, and that is just to be who we are, living in an open-hearted love of the creator and His creation.

Ra's zinger of an answer to Puharich's question about coming earth changes is worth pondering in depth. The answer concerning the person's remembrance of a close encounter of the third kind, being on board a craft, is also pithy. We really have a great deal to do with how we experience events of an archetypal nature, and this bleeds through into the everyday. So much of what we receive from the world is set by what we give to it. Ra's comments are provocative in suggesting how we can view that ineffable thing called sanity.

Session 84, April 14, 1982

Questioner: What disease in particular were you speaking of and what would be its cause?

Ra: I am Ra. One disease, as you call this distortion, is that of the arthritis and the lupus erythematosus. The cause of this complex of distortions is, at base, pre-incarnative. We refrain from determining the other distortion potential at this space/time due to our desire to maintain the free will of this group. Affirmations may yet cause this difficulty to resolve itself. Therefore, we simply encourage the general care with the diet with the instructions about allergy, as you call this quite complex distortion of the mind and body complexes.

Questioner: Could you make any suggestions about the instrument's feet or how they got in the bad shape that they are in, and if alternating the shoes would help?

Ra: I am Ra. The distortion referred to above; that is, the complex of juvenile rheumatoid arthritis and lupus erythematosus acts in such a way as to cause various portions of the body complex to become distorted in the way in which the instrument's pedal appendages are now distorted.

We may suggest care in resumption of the exercise but determination as well. The alternation of footwear shall prove efficacious. The undergarment for the feet which you call the anklet should be of a softer and finer material than is now being used and should, if possible, conform more to the outline of those appendages upon which it is placed. This should provide a more efficient aid to the cushioning of these appendages.

We may further suggest that the same immersion in the waters which is helpful to the general distortion is, in general, helpful to this specific distortion as well. However, the injury which has been sustained in the metatarsal region of the right pedal appendage should be further treated for some period of your

space/time by the prudent application of the ice to the arch of the right foot for brief periods followed always by immersion in the warm water.

Questioner: I am sure that we are getting into a problem area with the first distortion here with a difficulty with a bit of transient material, but I have questions from a couple of people that I would like to ask. The first one especially is of no lasting value. Andrija Puharich asks about the coming physical changes, specifically this summer. Is there anything that we could relay to him about that?

Ra: I am Ra. We may confirm the good intention of the source of this entity's puzzles and suggest that it is a grand choice that each may make to, by desire, collect the details of the day or, by desire, seek the keys to unknowing.

Questioner: I can't help but be interested in the fact that this other entity to whom we were previously referring reported being taken on board a craft. Could you tell me something about that?

Ra: I am Ra. The nature of contact is such that in order for the deep portion of the trunk of the tree of mind affected to be able to accept the contact, some symbology which may rise to the conscious mind is necessary as a framework for the explanation of the fruits of the contact. In such cases the entity's own expectations fashion the tale which shall be most acceptable to that entity, and in the dream state, or a trance state in which visions may be produced, this seeming memory is fed into the higher levels of the so-called subconscious and the lower levels of the conscious. From this point the story may surface as any memory and cause the instrument to function without losing balance or sanity. ☙

L/L Research is a subsidiary of
Rock Creek Research &
Development Laboratories, Inc.

P.O. Box 5195
Louisville, KY 40255-0195

L/L RESEARCH

www.llresearch.org

Rock Creek is a non-profit
corporation dedicated to
discovering and sharing
information which may aid in
the spiritual evolution of
humankind.

INTENSIVE MEDITATION
APRIL 15, 1982

(Carla channeling)

I am Hatonn, and I greet you in the love and light of our infinite Creator. It is a great privilege, as always, to be with you. Our brothers and sisters of Laitos have been with you, and have been conditioning each. However, we wished to work with the one known as S if this is agreeable to that instrument. We should first condition that instrument and then speak a few words through that instrument if she would relax. I am Hatonn.

(Pause)

(Carla channeling)

I am Hatonn, and am again with this instrument. We apologize for disturbing your pet. We shall speak a few general thoughts through this instrument before we leave as we know that there are many things upon your minds, and it is sometimes possible that by turning over in the mind a few concepts, a path may become remarkably clearer than previously seen.

We would like to observe the seeming delicacy of all that surrounds you, the extreme delicacy of the parameters which guard the ability of your physical vehicles to dwell in safety upon this sphere in space, the fragile chain of life which the creation of the Father has provided for all creatures from the smallest to the greatest. Yet we would like to point out that this seeming fragility houses an imponderably huge and immense role of an evolution which goes so far beyond the evolution of the physical form that there are no words to describe this everlasting evolution. It may seem at times that each is a fragile and easily wounded and torn entity, yet there is no possibility of true harm, for there is no ending to consciousness. Physical death cannot touch it, and any experience can only aid it.

Moreover, it may seem that in addition to fragility the third-density experience has a great loneliness, a great separation of being from being, brother from brother, Creator to Creator. We have often said that this can be gone beyond, shall we say, in the depths of meditation, that the roots of being and of consciousness can be seen to be one. But, my friends, even in your everyday existence, in the greatest illusion possible, you may see signs of the oneness of all things. How many times, my friends, just when you thought that this illusion held no ideals, have you heard of some entity who acted in such a way that the light of the one infinite Creator and the love of this marvelous unity radiates to the world?

You may see stories upon stories of the difficulties and the travails of your planet, and travails there will be, for this is the proper time for such to occur. Yet in the midst of these you will see again and again the story that you are lucky enough to hear of one just such as yourself, who has turned from being the sheep and has awakened into the shepherd, and tends the flock. What might this flock be? It might be a person defending the beauty of an ideal against those who would misuse it for money's sake or for power. It might be a person who has given much to aid a group or a cause at great personal sacrifice, or it might be one person who serves one other person with such selflessness that all who see it may marvel. This is the creation of the Father. The illusion can be pierced.

Now, just as you have the ideals within you which are your birthright, you have also these things which are called travails by the world. Accept them in yourself and in the world, these seeming imperfections, and, no matter how great the error, attempt to see yourself in each circumstance that comes before your vision. Imagine yourself in the place of one who has greatly erred, and then forgive yourself, for although you have been wrong, yet you are still the child of an infinite Creator and there is time enough and more to mend any error.

We thank you, my friends, for providing us with the great service of your presence and the blessing of your vibrations. We would at this time make room for our brothers and sisters of Latwii. Consequently, we leave this instrument, wishing all about you the love and the light of the infinite Creator. I am Hatonn. Adonai, my friends. Adonai vasu borragus.

(Transcript ends.) ♣

L/L Research is a subsidiary of
Rock Creek Research &
Development Laboratories, Inc.

P.O. Box 5195
Louisville, KY 40255-0195

L/L RESEARCH

www.llresearch.org

Rock Creek is a non-profit
corporation dedicated to
discovering and sharing
information which may aid in
the spiritual evolution of
humankind.

SUNDAY MEDITATION
APRIL 18, 1982

(C channeling)

I am Hatonn, and I am now with this instrument.
We were listening to the sounds that surround you,
the singing of your birds which has begun again in
your season of spring. The cycle has turned, new life
begins. The world echoes the sounds of nature—
beautiful, musical peace. My friends, if you would
but take a little extra of your time to sit and quietly
listen, the world around will speak of many things
and you, if you listen, may begin to become more
aware of the simple, the profound lessons that the
world around you offers. My friends, you are part of
an illusion and learning experience that allows you
to became aware of the love and light of the Creator.
In your illusion, as awareness is slowly achieved, a
balance will become more and more evident to you
as you begin to find your place in the workings of
your world. Each person has a place on the scale, a
scale that has many of your years been unbalanced,
ever teetering, but is slowly begun to change this as
more and more seek to be a part of the world instead
of centered simply on what they perceive as their
physical needs. This scale, though leveling, is still
unbalanced, yet your world, you, are slowly riding
this. Each of you, as you become aware, aid the
planet and your own self in your growth in this
period of transition. We join you and would aid in
whatever way that we may. You need but call and we

shall be with you in your meditations. We are your
brothers and sisters.

We would now at this time pause to allow our
brothers and sitters of Laitos to pass among you so
that those who wish may feel their conditioning
vibration. We will pause now, and then will transfer
to another instrument. I am Hatonn.

(Carla channeling)

I am Hatonn, and I greet you, my friends, in the
love and in the light of our infinite Creator. I
continue through this instrument. I and my brother
Laitos thank you for the opportunity of blending our
vibrations with yours. It is a great blessing to share
consciousness with you. Please know that if this
sharing is of value to you, you need only ask for it at
any time.

To conclude our thoughts for this evening we would
continue to speak upon the subject of those times
that are in what you call your immediate future. We
are aware that this topic is upon the minds of many,
and we wish to thank each of you that you have not
single-mindedly attempted to discover details of
prophecy concerning specific events which are part
of your planetary entry into the full dimension of
love.

My friends, it is not that we cannot speak to you of
these things. We would take this opportunity to

attempt to express to you our perceptions of the difficulties involved in the transference of specific information through conscious channeling. The contact such as we have through this instrument is a free will contact. This instrument receives impressions of concepts of a crystalline nature, that is, they are below or other than words. This instrument then cloaks these concepts in the vocabulary with which this instrument is most comfortable. In any free will contact of this nature we expect and encourage a certain amount of communication by the instrument through the instrument, as well as communication by the Confederation through the instrument. This portion by the instrument consists of those biases, concepts and ways of approaching subjects that are unique to that instrument, and, therefore, make our very simple message more varied, more inspiring, and more interesting to those who seek and who listen to these communications.

This same free will, my friends, causes specific information to be quite difficult to transmit, for as we transmit we ourselves are functioning in free will. We cannot know that which is the future to you, but can only know probabilities, for it is your free will which determines which future your peoples shall achieve. Therefore, when an instrument is repeatedly asked for specific information, for dates, for places, and for plans of catastrophe, there are others willing to be less than truthful, willing to give specific dates and places and plans, and so we lose our instrument.

It is a gradual process and one which we are very glad has not yet begun with this group at this time, for, my friends, there are important concerns in your immediate future, as you call it, that have to do only peripherally with the undoubted fact that the topography of your earth will change somewhat as a result of the stresses within it at this time as it must adjust to the new vibrations of the New Age, as you call it. That which is important to you, my friends, is your own inner balance, your own inner awareness of your identity, your essence, and your beingness, for as long as you breathe the air of this planet you will be able to offer under any circumstances whatever that beingness, that essence, that identity.

One of your great poets, many, many of your years ago wrote, "Yea, though I walk through the valley of death, I shall fear no evil." This was, of course, a translation from another language, but the concept, my friends, is infinitely important compared to the details of Earth changes. We ask you to be aware that at each moment presences guard you in life and in death. Your consciousness is not subject to this death. You have, before incarnation, chosen some things which you may wish to do. You did not make these plans with the intention of knowing them ahead. You made these plans knowing that at each point that something was required of you, you would have the free will to choose the manner of your beingness. We realize that in your daily illusion the events, the cataclysms, the mounting strangeness of the times in which you live, may well seem to be far more important than your own disciplined understanding of who you are, but, my friends, your seeking of that understanding is the only burden to carry in those days to come, for the more of your identity that you are able to fathom, the greater your light will shine in a very dark world, and like the great lighthouse which guides the ships to harbor and warns of a craggy rock and a dangerous gale, those within the view of your simple beingness will gain a kind of safe harbor until they themselves can begin to seek for themselves.

The days to come, my friends, are indeed a life and death situation, but these are the ingredients of which your illusion has always been made. That which is different is that the harvest is upon you. Prepare that part of yourself, therefore, which shall endure. Prepare not for catastrophe, but for joy; not for darkness, but for light; not for fear, but for hope, and never doubt that you are one with many, many brothers and sisters who share with you the hope of love and light for all of the peoples of the Earth.

I am Hatonn. I leave you, my friends, in the love and the light of our infinite Creator. Adonai vasu borragus.

(Jim channeling)

I am Latwii, and I greet each of you in love and light. We have been waiting patiently for our opportunity to speak to this group, and this evening our wait has been much easier than usual, for we also have been most engrossed in the message our brothers and sisters of Hatonn have shared with your group. We, at this time, would hope that our encore, shall we say, shall be of equal value or some value approaching that of the message you have heard this evening. We would now ask if there would be any questions which we may attempt to answer this evening?

M: Yes. I have one, I believe. It is not terribly important, but a curiosity. It seems that a few years back the messages of then were that the harvest was coming and that there was very little time, not very many people were going to make it, and for the first time I can recall Hatonn spoke to us about the balance, and more and more people were going to the other side, understanding what this experience was all about. Is this in fact accelerating our people of the Earth understanding our purpose more?

I am Latwii, and am aware of your query, my brother. The people of your planet are now experiencing those times which have long been foretold by those whom you call prophets, the so-called last days of your great cycle of evolution. It is during these days that the experiences, the catalyst and the opportunities for growth shall be increased manyfold so that each entity upon your planet who seeks in any degree might have available to him or her much more of a fulcrum of energy, so to speak, that shall act as a lever within the consciousness and move it great distances in comparison to where it was and where it could have been moved prior to this time.

The reason for this is, as many of you know, manyfold. The entities now incarnating on your planet have, for some period of time, maximum possible polarization. Those entities who were nearest the harvest—for the time grows short and only those entities could benefit by now being incarnate on your planet—this fact, when combined with the fact that the inconveniences, shall we say, have well begun and do themselves provide much more opportunity for the seeking—creates a situation in which if an entity wishes to know the truth of its being, this truth is ever closer and less veiled, shall we say, to the entity who seeks it, for those experiences which seem to be of major or minor cataclysmic effect, those experiences of the, shall we say, sagging economy, of the threats of nuclear war, of the prophecies of great Earth changes, of the difficulties in interpersonal relationships, in the confusions of the personal journey of seeking, all these experiences and events magnify for an entity who seeks the truth the ability to find that truth, for each such experience does pose the question for the entity, the question being, "What is the meaning of this life in which I experience and see these events?"

May we answer you further, my brother?

M: No, thank you, Latwii.

I am Latwii and we thank you. Is there another question?

Carla: I have a question from L. L was asking if gypsies were a race apart from others, and perhaps like the Chinese who come from Deneb, from a certain star system or a certain origin that was different than the other peoples of the Earth?

I am Latwii, and am aware of your query, my sister. To recount the origins of those whom your peoples call the gypsies is indeed a difficult task, for one aspect of these entities that those here are aware of, that being the wandering nature, is a facet which has colored these entities for their entire history, shall we say, upon your planet. These entities, therefore, are of many roots, the majority of which coming from the areas of your Mediterranean sea, have from times long passed been the caretakers of the codes and systems of secret knowledge, that which follows the mystic path.

Many schools of seeking the one Creator have evolved upon your planet in its past. Each path has been fortified more or less, and its tenets have been propounded within the walls of the secret schools. There have been, from time to time, attempts by other forces to purge various cultures of these mystery schools and their secret rites, for they were considered other than a normally accepted society, and as is the case even unto this day in your own society such entities who are too far removed from normal acceptance are often shunned and ostracized.

Therefore, these entities known to you as gypsies have as their origins a variety of lands in the area which borders the Mediterranean Sea, some of these lands being Egypt, Turkey and Greece. When these mystery schools were attacked and when efforts were made to cease their functioning, those in charge of the teachings would remain viable and could be passed on in what is called the future to other entities also seeking the same truth.

Therefore, those who you call the gypsies have been wandering from home to home and land to land and from age to age throughout the history that has been written upon your planet, and few there are of these entities remaining true to the teachings which they sought to preserve unto this day, for all teachings are subject to distortion, to loss, and to forgetting.

May we answer you further, my sister?

Carla: Yes. Two questions. If I remember my Ra correctly, Turkey was a repository both of people from Mu and for people from Atlantis after both of those lands sank, but mysteries schools were Atlantis' strong suit. It would be logical, then, to suspect that it is Atlantean mystery schools that were the basis of the gypsies' store of knowledge. Is this correct?

I am Latwii, and am aware of your question, my sister. This is basically correct, for the lineage of most of these mystery schools is traced to the Atlantean era, its middle and latter portions, though some few of these schools were in existence as a result of other cultural influences, specifically speaking now of the Egyptian culture, which was able to maintain an identity unique even in the times of the Atlantean culture.

May we answer you further, my sister?

Carla: Yes. The other question is the teachings of these systems which are called mystery schools. Are they at heart a purely service-to-others oriented school of teaching?

(Side one of tape ends.)

(Jim channeling)

I am Latwii, and am once more with this instrument. These mystery schools may be generally classified under the areas which you are already familiar with as the tarot, the astrology, and the Tree of Life, or that which is more commonly known as ritual magic. Each attempt at codification of the path of seeking the one Creator has as its foundation the service-to-others polarization. Through the ages each system has undergone various distortions as those in whose trust they were placed have altered these teachings, some alterations also being of service-to-others polarization, others being of the negative polarization, what you would call the service-to-self polarization.

The amount of distortion within each system presents the greatest difficulty to the student of the system, for many other additions, shall we say, or fields of knowledge, have been blended with each of these three systems, and has resulted in a system in each case which is quite far removed from the original, therefore, both the distortions present in each system and specific distortions of negative orientations present the student of each system with the greatest difficulties in penetrating the symbolism involved in each way of knowing.

May we answer you further, my sister?

Carla: No, thank you, Latwii. I think I've caught right up with you.

I am Latwii, and we are pleased that we have not left any in our ancient dust. May we ask if there be another question at this time?

M: Yes. I have a question. Why is it that some people I know are so afraid of the supernatural or the unknown? They feel that somehow it's something evil, and to me it's just knowledge. Why do we have that different opinion?

I am Latwii, and am aware of your query, my sister. The unknown, to those who do not seek it, is a great mystery, a great challenge, and represents to such an entity the part of its own being which is yet unexplored, and is unexplored, for there is some reason within this entity to fear that part of itself which it has not chosen to explore.

For each entity holding the view [that] that which you call the supernatural is evil there is an unique reason for this view. Many entities fear that which they have begun to find within their own being, that which expresses to them some ramification of this supernatural realm, but which they have had some difficulty in comprehending.

Many entities have had some kind of experience of a supernatural nature early in their incarnation, and have been unable to assimilate its occurrence and its meaning within their being and this new information has so overwhelmed their ability to assimilate it that they have, in fact, shoved it aside and forgotten it on the conscious level, yet it remains in their unconscious as a possibility for further exploration, if only they would journey that path, yet the fear of further journey remains, and only this fear filters into the conscious mind so that the similar experience of another will again trigger this fear within their own being.

May we answer you further, my sister?

M: Well, they don't really fear evil, they just fear fear itself. Is that it?

I am Latwii, and am aware of your query, my sister. The fear is the result of the difficulty with the experience at a previous time, and that which is feared might also be forgotten so that only the fear surfaces. The fear, over a long period of time, might itself begin to fade so that only the coloration of what the entity then describes as evil remains. That which is feared is most often called by your peoples evil.

May we answer you further, my sister?

M: Thank you. You've answered me.

I am Latwii. We thank you. Is there another question at this time?

(Pause)

I am Latwii. We find this group rather quiet this evening, and we also enjoy your peaceful vibrations. We thank each for allowing us to enter this group and to blend our vibrations with each. We look forward to each encounter. We leave this group now, rejoicing in love and light. We leave you in that love and light of the one Creator. We shall be with you again. I am Latwii. Adonai vasu borragus.

(C channeling)

I am Nona, and am now with this instrument. We have been called, for there is concern of those who are close, a part of this group who are at this time experiencing difficulties with their physical vehicles, and we are called for concern of this group for your planet and the conditions faced in this period of your time.

(C continues to channel Nona.)

L/L Research is a subsidiary of
Rock Creek Research &
Development Laboratories, Inc.

P.O. Box 5195
Louisville, KY 40255-0195

L/L Research

www.llresearch.org

Rock Creek is a non-profit
corporation dedicated to
discovering and sharing
information which may aid in
the spiritual evolution of
humankind.

INTENSIVE MEDITATION
APRIL 22, 1982

(Unknown channeling)

… Hatonn. I greet you, my friends, in the love and in the light of [our] infinite Creator. We thank you for being patient with [us] while we work with the instrument now receiving. We were attempting to make ourselves reliably known to this instrument that she may in the future be able to initiate contact without a *(inaudible)* experienced instrument. We thank the new instrument for her dedication to serve others and at this time we greatly appreciate the opportunity to share a few of our thoughts with you through *(inaudible)*.

We would now transfer this contact. I am Hatonn.

(Pause)

(Unknown channeling)

I am Hatonn, and [am] with this instrument. We are pleased to greet you once again in the love and in the light of the one infinite Creator. We are happy to speak through this instrument at this time and assure her of her ability to recognize our conditioning as it becomes more obvious to her. We are pleased to join our vibrations with those who are gathered today in their seeking. It is a beautiful experience for us. We are always pleased to be of service to those who call upon us to do so. We are pleased at the [feelings]—correction—feelings of those who are gathered together and share the same

space at the same time. We are sometimes in awe of the warmth *(inaudible)* from this group. It is a great honor to share this with you and we are indeed privileged to be able to blend our vibrations with yours. It is an uplifting experience for us and reassures us that there is indeed a great deal on your planet to be thankful for. We are often overwhelmed by the misery or callousness that is often present, but when we are joined with groups such as this we are uplifted and grateful to be a part of this meditation. We are grateful for your calling and are grateful to be of service, as we are also serving in our way by helping those who are seeking.

We wish to be able to speak to you through another instrument at this time. Thank you my friends. I am Hatonn.

(Unknown channeling)

I am Hatonn, and *(inaudible)* with this instrument. We are indeed most grateful to you for the sharing of our vibrations which adds so much richness to our experience and enables us to learn as well as hopefully offer some thoughts that may teach to some limited extent. We are aware, my friends, that many times those thing which we say may seem to have an almost a transparent quality, as if the [ideas], concepts and the very light of which we speak were the illusion, compared to the solid reality of your daily difficulties and trivialities.

We do not change our message to you, because regardless of the great potential that our message has for being ignored because it seems so nearly irrelevant, it is, nevertheless, the only message which we have to share with you, which in our humble opinion does not partake so heavily of an illusion and instead rests itself within the framework of that which is not an illusion.

From within the illusion, my friends, it would hardly seem possible that all the things that you experience at this time are transparent in quality and can be pierced through as one would pierce through a veil. What has occurred to you this day, my friends? As you share these memories with yourself you are aware of the strength of your various feelings and thoughts and patterns of behavior and of the interactions between yourself and others. All of these things did not seem transparent to you; this is for a reason. If they were transparent to you, you could not learn from them. But resting now in meditation as we join our vibration with you …

(Tape ends.) ♣

L/L RESEARCH

L/L Research is a subsidiary of
Rock Creek Research &
Development Laboratories, Inc.

P.O. Box 5195
Louisville, KY 40255-0195

www.llresearch.org

Rock Creek is a non-profit
corporation dedicated to
discovering and sharing
information which may aid in
the spiritual evolution of
humankind.

SUNDAY MEDITATION
APRIL 25, 1982

(Carla channeling)

I am Hatonn, and I greet you, my friends, in the love and in the light of our infinite Creator. What a blessing and privilege it is to be with you this evening. We especially send our greetings to the one known as S, whom we have not spoken to through this instrument for some time. We thank you for your patience, my friends. We are again with this instrument. We wished to delay for some brief moments while each of you is made more comfortable.

This evening we would speak to you of your rainbow beings and that which you call sin. As you proceed in your meditations and in your reflections upon your daily lives you will no doubt grasp the fact that when you achieve something in your inner life it does not seem to be apparent on the outer planes of manifestation. This self-judgment is not only unnecessary but in some cases unhelpful. When you are in meditation you are within a point of light such as you visualized at the beginning of this session. This white light, so full of love and purity, enfolds you with peace and calmness, and, indeed, does lift up your consciousness into a realm which may be considered to be the kingdom of heaven. When you return from this state to your daily life you return to a dazzling rainbow of experience. All the colors of experience, all the hues of feeling and emotion are available to you. The white light has

been splintered into a visible range of a variety of experiences.

The nature of what you call sin is twofold. Firstly, there is that which the entity which you may call your society names as sin. We examine this instrument's mind. Within this instrument's mind it is a sin to wear checked material with patterned material when donning the clothes which your peoples feel are necessary to cover their bodies. This, my friends, is an apparent sin which has no meaning whatsoever. Many, many of those things which you do which are not acceptable to others fall in this category, having no spiritual reality.

The other category of what you call sin is inherent of the nature of your rainbow being. You must understand yourself as containing everything. Whatever you see about you or hear in one of your news programs is a mirror to yourself. Do you hear of a rapist? You are he. Do you watch the trial of a murderer? You stand with that person waiting to be sentenced. Do you see about you those whose argumentative qualities are such that trouble follows them as a wake follows a fast-moving ship? You see the ripples of your being also.

Each entity is potentially capable of all things. It is a function of your biases, your preferences, and the circumstances of your particular situation as to what will test you and what will call forth from you the reactions which you will later judge. In all cases it is undeniable that each entity will at some point fail to polarize totally towards service to others. We speak not only of those in this room. We speak of all those in your density. All will fail from time to time. It is as understandable as one who enters your school system as a young child and is asked to count two plus two. The child works upon its fingers and says the answer is five. This is the nature of what you call sin. It is an error. There is no judgment necessary for an error.

We would ask, my friends, that as you look at yourselves instead of judging yourselves you simply make note of any errors that you feel you may have committed, any defaults that you may have sustained in striving towards love and light, so that at the next testing you will not repeat the error. And yet, my friends, if you repeat the error again you are only exhibiting one hue of a magnificent rainbow. You are still a portion of the Creator. You still have the birthright of the great wholeness and perfection of that white light, and you can at any moment, by an act of will and faith, remove your consciousness from that of judgment of self and others into that vision of the white light which sees all things as whole.

My friends, it is written in the holy work that you call the Bible that the master known as Jesus was an advocate for your sins. This sentence, and those like it, have caused many among your peoples to fear greatly the great array of possibly sinful acts, and to put their trust and their hope in one who was both man and Christ consciousness. We offer to you the possibility for your consideration that the entity known to you as Jesus, being the perfect example of one who saw the white light during a great portion of his life, may then offer to you the shining lodestar, that which may be seen as example and inspiration, for this Christ consciousness, as you may call it, is within you also just as all the errors and all the mistakes have their place in your being.

You may call, in your mind, upon an outside influence. You may put your trust and your faith outside of yourself, but we say to you, my friends, to the best of our understanding all is within yourself including the master known to you as Jesus. Why is it that among your peoples it is so easy for you to see yourselves as sinful, which is true within the bounds of your language, and is so difficult for you to see

yourselves as perfect, which is also true within your language?

Have you looked kindly upon yourself this day, my friends? And have you looked kindly upon others? Have you seen the rainbow? Ah, my friends, the colors are so lovely and beautiful, and it is with the greatest love that we rejoice in each of you just as you are in what you would call an imperfect state. Let yourselves too rejoice in the uniqueness of your being and doggedly and quietly and confidently continue that patient path of finding the white light that has been splintered into every color that you see about you.

At this time we would like to exercise the one known as S. If he would relax, we shall work with him at this time. I am Hatonn.

(S channeling)

I am Hatonn. I wish only … I wish only to say a few words so that the one known as S can develop his confidence in his service to others. I am Hatonn.

(Carla channeling)

I am Hatonn, and am again with this instrument. We thank the one known as S for making himself available to us. We assure him that we shall continue to work with him. Before we leave this group we would like to work briefly with each who wishes the conditioning wave. We ask that each mentally request this wave if you would wish it, and we and our brothers and sisters of Laitos will be with you. I am Hatonn.

(Pause)

I am Hatonn, and am again with this instrument. We shall leave you with this thought. You are rainbow beings. You may consider yourself as you wish. You may spend your life concerning yourself with how far you have fallen short of the perfection of the Creator. You may scold yourself unceasingly, and, having made yourself miserable, may spend a most productive life creating misery for others. Or you may look deeper. How deeply do you wish to look within the colors and the hues? Do you fear that you will find darkness? Be unafraid. You are creatures of the one infinite Creator, creatures of the light that is so powerful that the universe is one and you are one with it. How then can you fear? Whatever you do and have done and whatever you shall do does indeed fall short of yourself. How many people vary from your requests of them. Look closely and deeply and carefully and find the source of the rainbow. Every cell of your body is greatly composed of water. Infused with the white light that surrounds you, how brightly shall you radiate rainbows of being?

I leave you now, my brothers and sisters, in the love and the light of our Creator. I am known to you as Hatonn and speak only as we hope and trust the Creator has given us to speak. Do with these words what you will, for we are but fallible beings, yet we offer them to you along with our love. I am Hatonn. Adonai vasu borragus.

(Jim channeling)

I am Latwii, and greet each of you in the love and the light. It is our privilege once again to join this group to offer our service in attempting [to] answer the questions which each of you have brought with you this evening. We would now ask if there might be a question which we might attempt to answer?

K: Yes, let's talk about the white light. If I judge myself because I have failed in something, and if I judge my fellow man, I understand that I diminish the white light about me and I am somehow of a negative influence as I move about people. Do I understand that pretty well?

I am Latwii. My sister, we may say that in general your grasp of this concept is correct, and we may comment further by suggesting that the activity that you may call judgment does provide a barrier through which efforts to proceed in the evolutionary process are halted for as long as that barrier restrains them by its existence. By this we mean to say when an entity judges the self or any other entity, the entity, then, is affirming the illusion of separation in that the entity is saying one person or activity is less than another and is to be shunned, when in truth all beings and activities are one. To accept the self, no matter what the activity or behavior or thought, is to accept the self or another entity as part of the one Creator.

This is not to say that certain behaviors or thoughts cannot be improved upon to reflect, ever more closer, the unity with all beings, but is to say whatever the experience an entity encounters, whether within the self or within an other self, the entity is seeing the Creator experiencing Itself. The entity is seeing the opportunity for growth into

further realization of that unity presented. To fully utilize that opportunity for growth one must, if one travels the positive path, accept the activity, the self, and any other self involved, for this acceptance then reaffirms the unity of all creation.

May we answer you further, my sister?

K: No. That's a good answer. Thank you.

I am Latwii. We are most grateful to you as well. Is there another question at this time?

J: Lately I have been having dreams that have been coming true, and I was wondering maybe if I may have a certain ability. Could you explain this a little to me?

I am Latwii, and am aware of your question, my sister. We may comment only generally upon this most interesting topic. We might suggest that, indeed, as does each entity, you have certain abilities. These abilities are focused about the general concept of being of service to others. In your particular case, you have a certain openness, a certain receptivity, to messages from planes of existence which are normally considered outside the one which you presently inhabit. You are now developing this receptivity in order to be of service to those about you, and this development is, shall we say, making itself known in certain ways which are becoming more familiar to you, but these ways are not themselves the heart of your ability, but only reflections of that ability, much as though one would see a scene reflected in a mirror.

Your abilities lie deeper within your being, and are of a nature which shall be most helpful in your future, as you would call it, as you begin to bring through certain inspirations and ideas from deeper parts of your own being and other realms, shall we say.

May we answer you further, my sister?

J: No. I think I understand. Thank you very much.

I am Latwii. We thank you very much. Is there another question at this time?

S: I have a question. I need some information about this and I also would like to have your recommendations on this about a friend of mine who I believe to have a contact with the Orion group. Could you explain to me how I should encounter him or interact with him in daily activities and explain to me what his contact is?

I am Latwii, and am aware of your query, my brother. First of all, we may not, shall we say, engage in judgment of the source of any type of contact such as that which you now speak of, for to do so would be to lend an heavy, shall we say, opinion upon the mind of another entity and weight the judgment or discernment in such a fashion as to abridge the entity's free will.

Concerning the second portion of your query, we might suggest when you meet any entity which is of special concern to you that you treat such an entity as being your own self, which is to say the acceptance of such an entity is of paramount importance. If you feel, in your daily round of activities and interactions with this entity that you might be of service by sharing those concepts which are cherished by your own being, this you may do. There might be some suggestion concerning your understanding of how information can be helpful to entities hearing it. You might share, as with any entity, those feelings which are part of your being but all the while remembering that you speak to yourself, you speak to the Creator, and all words have only the value which the ear hearing them gives them, and each ear and each entity has the right to hear and to act according to its own desires, for each entity is the one Creator experiencing the creation and learning those lessons it deems important.

May we answer you further, my brother?

S: That's helpful, what you have said so far. I have another query in the same area. Should I feel any kind of fear in this interacting towards—I was reading in the Ra work about a possible lessening of our positivity because of this interaction. Should I be afraid of that or should I look at this as possibly a catalyst in helping myself learn and possibly this other individual?

I am Latwii, and we are aware of your question, my brother. To begin, there is no need for fears for fear is that energy which is most used and fed upon by those entities you describe as negative. The method or means of interaction with any entity, to be most helpful to all concerned, must needs be that action which reflects love, acceptance and compassion for all concerned, for this reaffirms the path of positivity, the reality of the unity of all creation. To fear is to assume that the illusion of separation is

correct, for to fear is to engage in that separation by feeling some part of the unity stands apart from yourself and is other than yourself and has some intention of harming you. Though there are those within the creation of the Father which pursue this path and would intend such harm, it is but an illusion to those who travel the path of positivity, for those on this path, within the heart of their beings, [know] that all is one and that there is no need for fear of the self.

May we answer you further, my brother?

S: That's a big help. Is there, by interacting with this individual—will any harm come to our group?

I am Latwii, and am aware of your question, my brother.

(Side one of tape ends.)

(Jim channeling)

I am Latwii and am once again with this instrument. To continue. We may not predict your future, for we are unable to determine the path which an entity may take. Therefore, the effect is unknown, though we might suggest the chances are quite small, given your present orientation, that there would be any deleterious effect on this group.

May we answer you further, my brother?

S: Thank you. It helps a lot.

I am Latwii. We are most grateful to you as well. May we ask if there might be another question at this time?

K: Would you comment on the prevalence of cancer? I have so many friends who have died of cancer and there seems to be no cure that we know of so far. Why so much cancer?

I am Latwii, and am aware of your query, my sister. The cycle of evolution which is now ending upon your planet shall be finished, shall we say, by those entities which have the greatest chances of graduating from this cycle into the next. These entities now incarnate and have been incarnating upon your planet for some time. Such entities, before incarnation, realize that there is a certain distance, shall we say, that must be traveled, certain lessons that must be learned before the graduation may be achieved.

Therefore, these entities are most likely to program great opportunities for learning into their incarnations. These opportunities serve as catalysts for growth in a great variety of ways. At this time upon your planet there are catalysts of great intensity being provided by such entities for the learning of the lessons needed for graduation. One of these catalysts, as those who have read further in what you term the Ra material have discovered, is that catalyst known as cancer. The cancerous growth is usually a result of an entity's inability to balance the emotion which you call anger with the emotion that you call love. Those entities who feel the anger, the frustration, the heat of the emotion of separation for any other entity or for the self, or even a situation, are providing themselves with the catalyst known as cancer.

If the entity is unable to accept, forgive and love that entity or situation for which the anger was first felt, the anger is like the cells within the body which begins in one location. Fed by the great reservoir of energy known as anger the cells begin to grow and spread, nourished by the heat of the anger, and when this anger, then, is not balanced with love the cancerous condition does begin to consume the entity which first began the generation of anger, for each entity upon your planet is every other entity, and when anger is felt toward any it is reflected to the self, and this reflection of the heat of anger does then begin to consume the entity which began it. The simple cure, as you would call it, for that catalyst known as cancer, then, is the acceptance, the forgiveness, the loving [of] that which first felt the anger.

May we answer you further, my sister?

K: No. I had a notion that that was true but I have a lot more insight now. And one further. It's almost a follow-up on this question. Because I have had this back pain for so long—sometimes worse, sometimes better—I asked the Christ consciousness a couple of weeks ago to remove it and heal my body because the New Testament indicates that that is possible. And the thought came, "Heal yourself." Would you comment on that?

I am Latwii, and am aware of your query, my sister. Any ailment, be it physical, mental or even that known as spiritual has a lesson to teach. The lesson most generally has to do with the acceptance of the creation, some aspect of yourself, some aspect of the creation with which one is intimately concerned. Certain ailments reflect those lessons which have

been programmed before the incarnation to serve as, shall we say, training aids so that the entity might not forget the need to learn that lesson. Other ailments are, when in the physical vehicle, simply symbolic representations of the frame of mind which has not yet been able to accept a portion of itself. In each case the injunction to heal the self is another means of saying to the self that there is some portion of the self that needs to be accepted as part of the self, whole and perfect, and when this acceptance is made deep within the heart of the being, then the entity shall realize the unity of that portion with the self and with all creation and shall be healed [of] that known as the ailment which served to point out that which needed to be accepted.

Oftentimes, all that is necessary is the faith, shall we say, in an entity known as a healer. At other times it is necessary that more work be done upon the self by the self. The intensity of the lesson to be learned determines the intensity of the effort necessary for the entity wishing to be healed to make.

May we answer you further, my sister?

K: That's what I thought, but you've given extra information. That's helpful. Thanks a lot.

I am Latwii. We thank you. Is there another question at this time?

S: I have a couple of other questions that won't take too long. The first question is that for the last day or so I have felt extremely warm and my hands have gotten real cold, and this has happened on other occasions and I have wondered if somehow I might be sending light because of the Falkland Island crisis. In the past I have felt extreme warmth when the President had that assassination attempt and the other time when there was an assassination attempt on him.

Is this warmth somehow sending light to these crisis situations?

I am Latwii, and am aware of your query, my brother. Though each entity has its own unique means of dealing with those situations which your peoples call crises, we may not comment upon the particular means of any specific entity in its response to such a situation, for it is most important for each entity to look upon those experiences of its complex of mind, body and spirit for its own inner guidance. We may suggest beginning with the supposition which you have just articulated in your meditative state and allowing that supposition to travel its own path in your mind, thereby revealing to your own awareness the cause of the sensations which you have explained.

May we answer you further, my brother?

S: That explains that. Thank you on that. I have another question. I was reading in the Ra materials about blockages that occur in our energy centers. This will probably be in violation of my free will and you can't answer it, but can you tell me if I have any major blockages now?

I am Latwii, and am aware of your query, my brother. We may begin by agreeing that to comment upon the specific configuration of an entity's energy centers would be an infringement, for each entity must find these blockages and begin the process of balancing through its own efforts, otherwise, there would be no reward for the entity to reap. The reward, then, would go to our complex, and we would not wish to take this from another.

We might suggest in general that if an entity exists upon your planet in the third density the entity has blockages in the energy centers, for this is simply another way of expressing the fact that each entity has incarnated to learn certain lessons. Before a lesson can be learned there must needs be the distortion called a blockage of the knowing or the learning of that lesson. A bias must exist in one direction before it might be balanced with a bias in another direction. Each entity, therefore, seeks to learn what configuration of blockages is unique unto its own being. When an entity becomes consciously aware that it seeks to evolve in mind, body and spirit then the entity is ready to travel that path through the energy centers which shall reveal to the entity those areas that are blocked, those areas that are open, and shall reveal to the entity the path of its own unique spiritual journey.

May we answer you further, my brother?

S: As a start towards discovering my blockages or maybe analyzing these biases better, which I recognize right away that I've had them, that I consciously recognized this in the past—probably through my daily meditation I can better understand these blockages and study these biases.

As for my third question—in the Ra materials it talks about one of the ways the Confederation makes contacts now is through the dreams, what we call

dreaming, and I was wondering—a friend of mine this week … The last couple of months I have noticed a very definite spiritual growth and this last week he did some sleepwalking and woke up with somewhat of a positive message. Was this an example of what I referred to in the Ra materials?

I am Latwii, and am aware of your query, my brother. We do not mean to be short, shall we say, of information but again find it an infringement to comment upon a specific experience, for experiences of this nature occur to entities for the very purpose of providing a mystery which must be solved. The entity so experiencing this mystery, then, hopefully shall be intrigued to pursue the mystery to its solution. The path of pursuing this mystery does then provide the entity with an exercising of the spiritual desire to seek the truth. To exercise this desire is to strengthen it, and in the seeking shall come the fruits of the seeking, and when the mystery has been solved then that portion of the seeking will have served its purpose for the entity.

We might suggest in general that experiences such as this experience are those which can be used by Confederation entities, by personal guides, shall we say, and by other portions of the entity's own being, those portions being within the subconscious mind. Each of these particular types of communication has a purpose in that it provides a mystery which then inspires the seeking further.

May we answer you further, my brother?

S: I just want to thank you.

I am Latwii. We thank you. Is there another question at this time?

M: I have a question. I should be grateful because I never have any physical pains, but I would like to get more energy. Is there any particular pattern or method that a person can use to obtain more energy?

I am Latwii, and am aware of your query, my sister. That which you seek as the increase of the energy level of your complex of mind, body and spirit has many potential sources of increase. We could spend a great deal of time explaining each but this would be the work of many sessions such as this one. In general, we may comment by suggesting that the care of the vehicle that you inhabit in its physical and mental forms by the proper and unique configuration of food intake, of rest, of exercise, and of the stimulation of the mind complex in its developing of a framework for the spiritual energies to pass through are, of course, the most general and helpful means of increasing the energy levels of your complex of mind, body and spirit.

As an entity undertakes the path of the spiritual seeker these general suggestions may be altered, for each entity shall experience those sensations of the vehicle which it inhabits which reflect the, shall we say, efficiency of learning those lessons which it has incarnated to learn. Therefore, as an entity becomes more conscious of its own spiritual seeking those suggestions which we have given as general guidelines might be greatly altered depending upon the entity's unique means of learning lessons and upon the entity's success in learning those lessons.

For example, it might be that as an entity becomes more sensitive to its environment as it becomes more attuned to the unity of all creation that certain foods in their grosser forms might need to be eliminated from the diet, when in the beginning stages of the seeking these foods were felt to be most helpful and provided the necessary ingredients for the energizing of the vehicle.

Therefore, we cannot say specifically what would be most helpful for increasing the energy levels of your own complex of mind, body and spirit, for to do this would be an infringement upon your own seeking which you now undertake. We may comment in general upon your desire to increase this level of energy by suggesting that within your meditative state you may be able to discern those means of increasing that energy level by certain activities. This type of meditation might begin by viewing the entity which is yourself as it proceeds through its day and encounters that known as fatigue and view this process as a series of lessons that are being attempted. By gaining the overview, shall we say, of your particular means of learning you may also increase those levels of energy you now feel are in deficit.

May we answer you further, my sister?

M: No. Thank you for answering me very well. Thank you.

I am Latwii. We thank you. Is there another question at this time?

(Pause)

I am Latwii. We are most gratified to have been able to speak with your group this evening. We thank each entity present for allowing us to attempt to respond in our meager way to those concerns that are upon your minds. We wish each to know that we value greatly each query for our possible response. We know that each entity present brings these queries as treasures of their own being [in] which they feel there is lack of completeness and which they seek to complete in perfection. We wish each entity to know that the perfection of the being which you are at the heart of your seeking is that perfection which has always existed within your being and shall always be there. The questions which you ask are simply the means by which you shall eventually realize that perfection. We are honored that you have asked us to join you in that seeking, and we ask each entity to remember that the true answers to any question that you may ask already exist within the heart of your being and you shall find them as you continue to ask your questions.

We leave this group now in the love and in the light of the one infinite Creator. We shall look forward to being with you again. We are known to you as Latwii. We leave you now. Adonai vasu borragus. ♣

L/L Research is a subsidiary of
Rock Creek Research &
Development Laboratories, Inc.

P.O. Box 5195
Louisville, KY 40255-0195

L/L RESEARCH

www.llresearch.org

Rock Creek is a non-profit
corporation dedicated to
discovering and sharing
information which may aid in
the spiritual evolution of
humankind.

THE LAW OF ONE, BOOK IV, SESSION 85
APRIL 26, 1982

Ra: I am Ra. We communicate now.

Questioner: Could you first give me the condition of the instrument?

Ra: I am Ra. We ask your permission to preface this answer by the inclusion of the greeting which we use.

Questioner: That is agreeable.

Ra: I am Ra. We greet you in the love and in the light of the one infinite Creator. We were having some difficulty with the channel of energy influx due to pain flare, as you call this distortion of the physical body complex of this instrument. Therefore, it was necessary to speak as briefly as possible until we had safely transferred the mind/body/spirit complex of this instrument. We beg your kind indulgence for our discourtesy which was appropriate.

The condition of this instrument is as follows. The necessity for extreme vigilance is less, due to the somewhat lessened physical complex energy deficit. The potential for distortion remains and continued watchfulness over the ingestion of helpful foodstuffs continues to be recommended. Although the instrument is experiencing more than the, shall we say, normal, for this mind/body/spirit complex, distortions towards pain at this space/time nexus the basic condition is less distorted. The vital energies are as previously stated.

We commend the vigilance and care of this group.

Questioner: What is the current situation with respect to our fifth-density, service-to-self polarized companion?

Ra: I am Ra. Your companion has never been more closely associated with you than at the present nexus. You may see a kind of crisis occurring upon the so-called magical level at this particular space/time nexus.

Questioner: What is the nature of this crisis?

Ra: I am Ra. The nature of this crisis is the determination of the relative polarity of your companion and your selves. You are in the position of being in the third-density illusion and consequently having the conscious collective magical ability of the neophyte, whereas your companion is most adept. However, the faculties of will and faith and the calling to the light have been used by this group to the exclusion of any significant depolarization from the service-to-others path.

If your companion can possibly depolarize this group it must do so and that quickly, for in this unsuccessful attempt at exploring the wisdom of separation it is encountering some depolarization. This shall continue. Therefore, the efforts of your companion are pronounced at this space/time and time/space nexus.

Questioner: I am totally aware of the lack of necessity or rational need for naming of entities or things, but I was wondering if this particular entity had a name just so that we could increase our efficiency of communicating with respect to him. Does he have a name?

Ra: I am Ra. Yes.

Questioner: Would it be magically bad for us to know that name, or would it make no difference?

Ra: I am Ra. It would make a difference.

Questioner: What would the difference be?

Ra: I am Ra. If one wishes to have power over an entity it is an aid to know that entity's name. If one wishes no power over an entity but wishes to collect that entity into the very heart of one's own being it is well to forget the naming. Both processes are magically viable. Each is polarized in a specific way. It is your choice.

Questioner: I am assuming that it would be a problem for the instrument to meditate without the hand pressure from the other-self at this time because of the continued greeting. Is this correct?

Ra: I am Ra. This is correct if the instrument wishes to remain free from this potential separation of its mind/body/spirit complex from the third density it now experiences.

Questioner: Since our fifth-density companion has been monitoring our communication with Ra it has been made aware of the veiling process of which we have been speaking. It seems to me that conscious knowledge and acceptance of the fact that this veiling process was used for the purpose for which it was used would make it difficult to maintain high negative polarization. Could you clear up my thinking on that, please?

Ra: I am Ra. We are unsure as to our success in realigning your modes of mentation. We may, however, comment.

The polarization process, as it enters fourth density, is one which occurs with full knowledge of the veiling process which has taken place in third density. This veiling process is that which is a portion of the third-density experience. The knowledge and memory of the outcome of this and all portions of the third-density experience informs the higher-density polarized entity. It, however, does not influence the choice which has been made and which is the basis for further work past third density in polarization. Those which have chosen the

service-to-others [service-to-self[6]] path have simply used the veiling process in order to potentiate that which is not. This is an entirely acceptable method of self-knowledge of and by the Creator.

Questioner: You just stated that those who are on the service-to-others path use the veiling process to potentiate that which is not. I believe that I am correct in repeating what you said. Is that correct?

Ra: I am Ra. Yes.

Questioner: Then the service-to-others path has potentiated that which is not. Could you expand that a little bit so that I could understand it a little better?

Ra: I am Ra. If you see the energy centers in their various colors completing the spectrum you may see that the service-to-others(self) choice is one which denies the very center of the spectrum; that being universal love. Therefore, all that is built upon the penetration of the light of harvestable quality by such entities is based upon an omission. This omission shall manifest in fourth density as the love of self; that is, the fullest expression of the orange and yellow energy centers which then are used to potentiate communication and adepthood.

When fifth-density refinement has been achieved that which is not is carried further, the wisdom density being explored by entities which have no compassion, no universal love. They experience that which they wish by free choice, being of the earnest opinion that green-ray energy is folly.

That which is not may be seen as a self-imposed darkness in which harmony is turned into an eternal disharmony. However, that which is not cannot endure throughout the octave of third density and, as darkness eventually calls the light, so does that which is not eventually call that which is.

Questioner: I believe that there were salient errors in the communication that we just completed because of transmission difficulties. Are you aware of these errors?

Ra: I am Ra. We are unaware of errors although this instrument is experiencing flares of pain, as you call this distortion. We welcome and encourage your perceptions in correcting any errors in transmission.

---

[6] Ra corrects this error in the next two answers.

Questioner: I think that the statement that was made when we were speaking about the service-to-others path was incorrect. Would you check that, please?

Ra: I am Ra. May we ask that you be apprised of our intention to have spoken of the service-to-self path as the path of that which is not.

Questioner: I am interested in the problem that we sometimes have with the transmission since the word "others" was used three times in this transmission rather than the word "self." Could you give me an idea of this problem which could create a discrepancy in communication?

Ra: I am Ra. Firstly, we may note the clumsiness of language and our unfamiliarity with it in our native, shall we say, experience. Secondly, we may point out that once we have miscalled or misnumbered an event or thing, that referent is quite likely to be reused for some transmission time, as you call this measurement, due to our original error having gone undetected by ourselves.

Questioner: Thank you. Do you have use of all the words in the English language and, for that matter, all of the words in all of the languages that are spoken on this planet at this time?

Ra: I am Ra. No.

Questioner: I have a question here from *(name)*. It states: "As we see compassion developing in ourselves is it more appropriate to balance this compassion with wisdom or to allow the compassion to develop as much as possible without being balanced"?

Ra: I am Ra. This query borders upon that type of question to which answers are unavailable due to the free-will prohibitions upon information from teach/learners.

To the student of the balancing process we may suggest that the most stringent honesty be applied. As compassion is perceived it is suggested that, in balancing, this perception be analyzed. It may take many, many essays into compassion before true universal love is the product of the attempted opening and crystallization of this all-important springboard energy center. Thus the student may discover many other components to what may seem to be all-embracing love. Each of these components may be balanced and accepted as part of the self and

as transitional material as the entity's seat of learn/teaching moves ever more clearly into the green ray.

When it is perceived that universal love has been achieved the next balancing may or may not be wisdom. If the adept is balancing manifestations it is indeed appropriate to balance universal love and wisdom. If the balancing is of mind or spirit there are many subtleties to which the adept may give careful consideration. Love and wisdom, like love and light, are not black and white, shall we say, but faces of the same coin, if you will. Therefore, it is not, in all cases, that balancing consists of a movement from compassion to wisdom.

We may suggest at all times the constant remembrance of the density from which each adept desires to move. This density learns the lessons of love. In the case of Wanderers there are half-forgotten overlays of other lessons and other densities. We shall leave these considerations with the questioner and invite observations which we shall then be most happy to respond to in what may seem to be a more effectual manner.

Questioner: What changes of functions of the mind/body/spirits were most effective in producing the evolution desired due to the veiling process?

Ra: I am Ra. We are having difficulty retaining clear channel through this instrument. It has a safe margin of transferred energy but is experiencing pain flares. May we ask that you repeat the query as we have better channel now.

Questioner: After the veiling process certain veiled functions or activities must have been paramount in creating evolution in the desired polarized directions. I was just wondering which of these had the greatest effect on polarization?

Ra: I am Ra. The most effectual veiling was that of the mind.

Questioner: I would like to carry that on to find out what specific functions of the mind were most effectual and the three or four most effective changes brought about to create the polarization.

Ra: I am Ra. This is an interesting query. The primary veiling was of such significance that it may be seen to be analogous to the mantling of the Earth over all the jewels within the Earth's crust; whereas previously all facets of the Creator were consciously known. After the veiling, almost no facets of the Creator were known to the mind. Almost all was buried beneath the veil.

If one were to attempt to list those functions of mind most significant in that they might be of aid in polarization, one would need to begin with the faculty of visioning, envisioning, or far-seeing. Without the veil the mind was not caught in your illusory time. With the veil space/time is the only obvious possibility for experience.

Also upon the list of significant veiled functions of the mind would be that of dreaming. The so-called dreaming contains a great deal which, if made available to the conscious mind and used, shall aid it in polarization to a great extent.

The third function of the mind which is significant and which has been veiled is that of the knowing of the body. The knowledge of and control over the body, having been lost to a great extent in the veiling process, is thusly lost from the experience of the seeker. Its knowledge before the veiling is of small use. Its knowledge after the veiling, and in the face of what is now a dense illusion of separation of body complex from mind complex, is quite significant.

Perhaps the most important and significant function that occurred due to the veiling of the mind from itself is not in itself a function of mind but rather is a product of the potential created by this veiling. This is the faculty of will or pure desire.

We may ask for brief queries at this time. Although there is energy remaining for this working, we are reluctant to continue this contact, experiencing continual variations due to pain flares, as you call this distortion. Although we are unaware of any misgiven material we are aware that there have been several points during which our channel was less than optimal. This instrument is most faithful but we do not wish to misuse this instrument. Please query as you will.

Questioner: I will just ask in closing: is an individualized portion or entity of Ra inhabiting the instrument's body for the purpose of communication? Then, is there anything that we could do to improve the contact or to make the instrument more comfortable?

Ra: I am Ra. We of Ra communicate through narrow band channel through the violet ray energy center. We are not, as you would say, physically indwelling in this instrument; rather, the mind/body/spirit complex of this instrument rests with us.

You are diligent and conscientious. The alignments are excellent. We leave you rejoicing in the power and in the peace of the one infinite Creator. Go forth, then, my friends, rejoicing in the power and in the peace of the infinite love and the ineffable light of the one Creator. I am Ra. Adonai. ☙

L/L RESEARCH

L/L Research is a subsidiary of
Rock Creek Research &
Development Laboratories, Inc.

P.O. Box 5195
Louisville, KY 40255-0195

www.llresearch.org

Rock Creek is a non-profit
corporation dedicated to
discovering and sharing
information which may aid in
the spiritual evolution of
humankind.

INTENSIVE MEDITATION
APRIL 27, 1982

(Unknown channeling)

I am Latwii, and am once again with this instrument. To continue. We were saying that the density of eight is most normally, shall we say, used by entities in the review process of the incarnation just passed so that the distillations or learning from that incarnation might be seen within the wholeness of the love and the light of the one Creator, and the decisions for the next incarnation might be made. This is not a type of communication where the entity reviewing the incarnation is aware of another individualized being communicating a concept, but rather a type of all-embracing communication of the total of beingness or nature of the creation so that the life experience just passed might be seen in comparison to this wholeness and the further needs for learning might thereby be discerned.

May we answer you further, my sister?

Questioner: Then you are saying that the communications is light? A quality of light? Is that correct?

I am Latwii, and apologize for our interruption. We have so indicated because this is the means by which we feel this concept might be most easily understood. The communication, if it might be called that, is one which is of a total nature, and is experienced by the entity reviewing the incarnation as an experience of white light which might then shine upon the incarnation just completed, illuminating its various learnings and the efficiency of the learning so that future decisions can be made.

May we answer you further, my sister?

Questioner: No, thank you.

I am Latwii. We are most grateful to you, as always. Is there another question at this time?

Questioner: I am not sure if I understand the concept of an over-self or a higher self. Is that an entity that is with us? Or is that a part of us? Or is that *(inaudible)* coexist simultaneously in other dimensions?

I am Latwii, and am aware of your query, my brother. This is a most difficult concept to attempt to explain. We shall do our best, however, for we are not known for our reticence. The concept of simultaneity is one which is most confusing to entities inhabiting an illusion in which time seems to be experienced in a linear fashion with a past, a present, and a future. But if you would consider the possibility that all of the time and space which you are aware of exists in a solid 360 degree angle you might see this simultaneity as likened then to the solid sphere of infinite proportions and the path through this sphere or universe of evolution might then be chosen at any point and the further progress made in any direction. The [accumulation] of choices being seen during one lifetime, therefore, would appear to be linear. That portion of yourself which you know as the higher self, and that portion of yourself which you know of as your third density [waking] conscious self are quite closely allied portions of the one Creator as is each a portion of the creation.

You have provided for your experience portions of yourself which do exist in other, shall we say, locations besides that density which you are now inhabiting. The higher self, for example, does exist within the sixth density and serves as, shall we say, the kindly grandfather which oversees the progress of the grandchild. This higher self does provide a blueprint for your use in learning the lessons which are necessary for your evolution through each density. You as an individualized portion of this higher self then choose through free will the means of learning theses lessons, the speed with which they shall be learned, and you embellish upon these lessons as it meets your fancy. This higher self, which provides the framework in which you shall proceed, is also aided by another portion of itself and yourself which exist within the seventh density. Therefore, each entity within each part of the creation has resources and guides, shall we say, which might be called upon at any point in the incarnation and most especially between the incarnations, for guidance in the further learning of lessons which [accumulate] in each portion of the one Creator, joining once again the one Creator, bringing with it the fruits of the process of evolution.

May we answer you further, my brother?

Questioner: No, that was great, thank you.

I am Latwii, and am most grateful to you. May we answer another question at this time?

(No further queries.)

I am Latwii. We are once again quite honored to have been asked to join this group. We would remind each entity present that a simple request in meditation is all that is necessary for our joining each in private meditation. We would especially encourage those entities wishing to deepen their meditative states to call upon our services, for we feel that each entity present might be most aided at this time by a deepening of meditative states and each entity seems to be quite open to such an experience.

We would now leave this group and say once again that it is a most great honor to be with you. We leave you in the love and in the light of the one infinite Creator. I am Latwii. Adonai, my friends.

(Tape ends.) ❧

L/L RESEARCH

L/L Research is a subsidiary of Rock Creek Research & Development Laboratories, Inc.

P.O. Box 5195
Louisville, KY 40255-0195

www.llresearch.org

Rock Creek is a non-profit corporation dedicated to discovering and sharing information which may aid in the spiritual evolution of humankind.

FRIDAY NIGHT
APRIL 30, 1982

(Unknown channeling)

I am Hatonn, and I greet you, my brothers and sisters, in the love and the light of the infinite Creator. My friends, it is a great pleasure to be with you once again, and to be able to share with you the love that we extend in the name of ourselves and our brothers of the Confederation. We desire only to be of service to you in whatever manner may be allowed and are grateful to you for providing us this opportunity.

Tonight we would share with you a small story concerning an animal of your planet which is referred to by you as a squirrel. It is seemingly not a significant animal in that its contact with those of your race is very limited. It is generally regarded by many as simply an object of prey for consumption at their tables, yet as with all things of the Creator, it may serve the purpose by its example as being a teacher. The squirrel seemingly spends its life in the process of storing food away for the winter. It appears to be a very seriously minded creature, not prone to relax and allow the universe to provide its sustenance when and where it is desired, preferring rather to work constantly, taking responsibility for providing its own sustenance, trusting the future to no one.

Yet, my friends, the squirrel, in a larger sense, is similar to those who strive upon a spiritual path, for although one may often see the younger ones on a pleasant day indulging in playful frolics, chasing one another, clambering rapidly up and down their trees, the elder squirrels are not content to allow the world about them to provide for their needs, but rather constantly strive to improve upon their own situation, to acquire what is available at the moment, no matter how unnecessary the acquisition may momentarily seem, for they realize that that which may seem of questionable value, at this moment not worth pursuing, at a later date may be perceived as a jewel beyond comparison.

My friends, it is often difficult to understand the necessity for striving. It is convenient to casually glance about oneself and view that which is available with a cynical eye, telling oneself, "I do not need to learn this for it is of no use to me at this moment. Perhaps later at a more convenient time, at a time when the education appears more valuable, at that moment I will begin to learn what is offered." My friends, the difficulty one encounters when one approaches their life training session with this attitude is the fact that when the need appears it is often a need that arrives at a critical time, a point in your existence where one is unable to stop and say to yourself, "Now I will take the time to learn that which was available before."

My friends, you cannot count on the opportunity to leisurely pursue your growth at some later date, for that later date will suddenly be thrust upon you, born with the force of your indolence. For that lesson will be then coupled with another lesson for which you have called concerning your reluctance to undertake the process of spiritual growth. We say these words, my friends, not to chastise for you are deeply loved by us, and it is neither our place or desire to attempt to correct your path or to direct your growth, for there is but one teacher on each of your paths. That teacher is yourself.

It is our desire, however, to share with you, if possible, that which we have experienced ourselves and those experiences of our own in which from a retrospective viewpoint we find that our dedication was somewhat lacking. My friends, be conscious of the gifts that are given to you. Do not simply accept them and place them on a shelf or file them away until such time as your illusion presents that which you regard as the ideal situation under which to take them down from the shelf, dust them off, and begin to work with them. Rather, my friends, realize that the arrival of those lessons, those opportunities, is due to a calling on your part, a summoning of those lessons that they might be worked upon at that point in your life which is the ideal condition, the ideal time for those lessons.

At this time, our brother Laitos would pass among you, and to those who request it will extend their service of the conditioning vibration to those among you who desire this. I am Hatonn.

(Pause)

I am Hatonn. I am again with this instrument. At this time we desire to speak a few words through the instrument known as S. If he will relax and open his perceptions to our presence, we will speak through him. I am Hatonn.

(S channeling)

I am Hatonn. I am Hatonn. I wish at this time to be able to speak a few words so that the one known as S can begin to feel more comfortable with our presence. We wish at this time to allow our brothers of Laitos to provide their service of answering your queries. I am Hatonn. I wish at this time to transfer the contact to the one known as L. I am Hatonn.

(L channeling)

I am Hatonn. I am again with this instrument. We have experienced some minor difficulty in our

contact with the one known as S, but this is not a significant difficulty, and with time will [be] overcome by the instrument's increased familiarity with the process known as channeling.

At this time we will relinquish our use of this instrument so that our brothers and sisters of Latwii may make themselves available for the purpose of answering any questions that those present might desire to ask. I am known to you as Hatonn.

I am Latwii, and I greet you, my brothers and sisters, in the love and the light of the infinite Creator. My friends, it is a great pleasure to be back with you, for although we are always appreciative of a desire on anyone's part to have a brief vacation, [we] would point out to you that we did not get to go on vacation at the same time, and therefore we are glad to be back with you, for it was much like watching the shop when the shop was closed!

At this time we would make ourselves available for the wonderful opportunity to attempt to answer your harmless questions. May we answer a question for anyone present?

S: I have a question.

We have an answer.

S: About my attempted channeling. Hatonn said my performance tonight was not exactly a 100%, and there was some distortion on my part. Is this normal until I get more relaxed and have more confidence with channeling?

I am Latwii. Yes. To extend our answer further we would suggest that what our brothers and sisters of Hatonn stated was simply that some difficult was encountered, and were very consciously specific in not stating upon whose part. This is because our brothers and sisters of Hatonn tend to be tactful to the extreme. However, due to the fact that we posses less tact, we shall discuss the subject, for we feel that was the nature of your question however it was implied.

The difficulty as our brother Hatonn described it is of the nature of an individual who is channeling suddenly wondering if they are channeling. The next step, generally speaking, is then to wonder if they are channeling an entity or channeling themselves. This is a very normal and expected process in any individual who seeks the path of being an instrument. We would suggest, therefore, that the simultaneous pursuits of relaxation, practice and increased meditation would all be beneficial to your efforts. In particular, we would recommend at some point during your daily meditations, would you choose to meditate daily, we would suggest the services of our brothers and sisters of Laitos and their conditioning vibration, for this is very conducive to the process by which one refines their facilities, so to speak, as an instrument.

May we answer you further?

S: I have two questions. When I meditate, am I able to call Laitos for his assistance, being by myself?

I am Latwii. My brother, you are able at any time, at any moment, for any reason, to request the services of any member of the Confederation. It is not recommended to attempt to channel in the situation you describe, but to request the presence and assistance of any member of the Confederation is always within the realm of acceptable, and we would always suggest that for a person desiring to polarize in the direction that you refer to as positive polarization, this type of contact would be very beneficial.

May we answer you further?

S: The other thing was—you mentioned besides meditation …

(Side one of tape ends.)

(L channeling)

I am Latwii. My brother, the opportunity several minutes ago that you availed yourself of is a good example of practice. The presentation of oneself as an instrument being offered for the service of channeling at any of the co-minglings that you refer to as group meditation is an example of opportunity for practice.

S: That answers those question. There was something else I wanted to ask. I saw a movie this week on TV, and there were things in it that would be pretty much parallel to the things we've been receiving from the Confederation. I've been wondering if the person who wrote this might have been receiving the same type of contact.

I am Latwii. My brother, the individual to whom you refer has not been in contact with us in the manner that those in this room are at this time. However, we would point out that there are many types of calling by which your peoples seek the aid of entities such as ourselves or those entities referred to by your group as the Orion group, and the type of response is defined by the type of calling. For example, if an individual's calling was limited to those periods of time during which a nocturnal relaxation of the conscious mind is in process, then a response such as this one would not be possible, yet a response would occur.

May we answer you further?

S: No, that explains that. There was one other thing. At the beginnings of our meditations I feel Hatonn's presence very strongly. Should I as a rule, right now while I'm developing channeling, wait until I'm specifically called upon?

I am Latwii. My brother, it is neither our intent or responsibility to instruct you in the manner in which you perform your educational processes while you are existing within your illusion, for this would be an interference that is not permissible for entities such as ourselves. However, we would suggest that in general the adoption of fixed rules of conduct are not often beneficial. We would suggest therefore that each situation be viewed as a new learning experience with unique characteristics, and a response should be tailored to the situation. There would be no evil or badness that would result from one such as yourself acting as an instrument in the situation you describe, for the contact you experience is a result of your offering yourself for the service of providing an instrument for the entity you are aware of.

We would suggest in general that many opportunities for channeling can be made available to those who desire to channel if their desire is mentally expressed at the commencement of the session. However, as there is no particular value to being first off the line, so to speak, that a more efficient contact might result if the developing instrument is confident that the entity whom they sense is actually present and has previously identified itself and declared its desire to speak through the new instrument, for this can be beneficial to those who are experiencing difficulty resulting from lack of confidence or from self-analysis.

May we answer you further?

S: No, that answers those questions. Thank you.

We thank you, my brother, both for your questions, and for your desire for service, and we would suggest that those opportunities you seek will be made available as your desire persists.

Is there another question?

M: Yes, Latwii, I'd like some help and reflection on a social concept having to do with morals in our culture. For example, we have morals which guide us in how to live. One would be respect to our brothers, treating them as we would want to be treated ourselves, and our cultures has all types of morals which are generally common sense, and seem to deal in the vein of loving one another, until you get to sexual relationships, and then there suddenly seems to be a great deal of confusion that doesn't seem to follow common sense, and doesn't seem to follow in the vein of truly loving your fellow man. Why all the confusion around this part of our social make-up when it's not around other parts of it?

I am Latwii. My brother, to answer your question briefly we would simply suggest that the answer lies in your statement, in that the confusion is the purpose. There has been, in your past, a large amount of contact with many entities, for your current experiences in [this] area is not new to your race or to any of the races who have migrated to your planet and incarnated in your current form. The entities who have worked with your peoples throughout their history have all sought to sincerely aid those of your people in achieving a level of polarization. Unfortunately, there are two levels of polarization available, and a great deal of confusion has resulted from a sort of tug-of-war as both those oriented toward service to self and those oriented toward service to others attempt to aid the entities of your planet who extend a calling to the entities we have described.

The result is a set of conflicting rules which are the result of those of your planet attempting to set down in a fixed form methods of conduct based upon information received from both sources. For example, the entities who are oriented toward service to others might suggest that to love all people in such a manner as to regard each individual as being of equal value as to oneself would be in direct conflict with those entities who would suggest that the best way to love a person would be to control that person. The concept of being possessed as an object of someone's love is recognizable to yourself

and to those present as a very widely supported role that meets the approval of many on your planet. However, the act of possessing or being possessed by another person is not often very comfortable, and requires further restrictive rules to then limit the power exerted by the possessor. As the tug-of-war between the two opposite polarities and the recipients of their information continues, a mass of contradictory mores and laws becomes evident.

May we answer you further?

M: Well, perhaps. I understand the purpose of confusion, but what I don't understand is why there is so much more confusion in this area than in perhaps many of the other areas where social mores are clearly defined and seem to be more in line with loving one another.

I am Latwii. My brother, it is important to realize that the process of becoming a social memory complex takes place in your current density. The relationships that occur while in this density either accelerate or retard this process. Obviously, the retardation of this process is beneficial to those who seek to serve only themselves, while the acceleration of this process is beneficial to those who seek to serve others. The distinction between the two sexes is present not only in your density but in several others, and is always a focal point for much learning. When the focal point is in conjunction with the necessity to determine one's polarity in a density that has an increased emphasis upon relationships with other selves, the situation you have described is very likely to occur. The process of loving becomes saddled with the burden of loving while owning or being owned. The characteristic of owning or being owned being a definitive state then requires further definition so as to provide sufficient limitation and restriction in increased polarization for those seeking the negative polarization. This is a very valuable tool for those individuals who follow the path of service to self.

May we answer you further?

M: No, I think that will do for now, thank you.

We thank you. Is there another question?

(Pause)

I am Latwii. As there are no more questions we will relay some comments from some entities present— acting as a sort of instrument ourselves—that they are very pleased that the sun has recently risen again and were somewhat confused at the extended period of darkness in their aquatic world, for they were somewhat confused. They are grateful to whatever deity decided to return the sun to their world and give thanks. At this time we would bid you adieu, my friends. We thank you. Adonai, my friends. ☀

L/L RESEARCH

L/L Research is a subsidiary of Rock Creek Research & Development Laboratories, Inc.

P.O. Box 5195
Louisville, KY 40255-0195

www.llresearch.org

Rock Creek is a non-profit corporation dedicated to discovering and sharing information which may aid in the spiritual evolution of humankind.

SUNDAY MEDITATION
MAY 2, 1982

(C channeling)

I am Hatonn, and I am now with this instrument. I greet you, my brothers and sisters, as always, in the love and in the light of the one infinite Creator. We have been observing your planet for a long, long period of what you call time, and we find much happiness at this time of your year as your planet, with the light of your sun, renews its cycle. On your planet the cycles are short, your time, you'll find, is often short. In your nature, the shortness each season is used fully by your second-density creatures for their purposes. Their time, they realize, cannot be wasted. They exist with a purpose in mind to perpetuate themselves as best they can in the time that they have. They do not utilize choice as you do, though their free will may have an instinct that drives them.

You, my friends, with your increased awareness and utilization of choice, often do not realize the shortness of your time. Your lives are a small fraction of even a millisecond, to use your terms, in the universe. So often on your planet the time available in each incarnation is not used. So many wander aimlessly, not feeling the light, engrossed in attempting to gather as much physical comfort as they can, with little regard for that part of themselves that seeks, pushing it aside and falling back. Though the time is short you have ample time if you would but attempt to allow even a small portion of this short time for quiet thought and meditation, to allow your being to become aware of the light of the Creator.

The physical vehicle needs [to] be maintained, and no one can neglect it and hope to be able to utilize fully the spiritual self. They are connected, one affecting the other. But in caring for the physical self, the spiritual self also needs the caring, and needs to grow as does the physical. The growing is much like going from infanthood through the stages up to where, to use the analogy, adulthood is reached and you have achieved the level of awareness that is possible within this illusion. If you would but look around you can see people, other beings, who are wasting time. Worry not about their wasting, but stop and sit quietly and think and meditate of what you are doing with the time available to you.

On your planet, physical death awaits each. Not to interfere, but just merely a point in time which shows you that your time is limited, each incarnation is short. Use your time wisely. Take care of each part of yourself. Love each part of yourself. Strive to properly maintain the physical and spiritual. Allow time for each, for you exist in time and for you time is something to be aware of. So often your peoples have the habit of saying that they will begin at a later time; they have other concerns for now. My friends, if there is any doubt about when to begin, start then, even a small step, but begin. We do not mean to sound as though we are trying to scare or rush you, but for your planet time is growing increasingly short.

Many more of your peoples, becoming aware, are easily distracted, and do not follow up after the initial awareness begins. We hope that even more of your peoples become aware, but also hope they use what time is left wisely and truly begin the slow process of awakening, and truly become aware of the love and the light of the Creator.

We of Hatonn are always waiting to be of service to any who would but ask, for we are anxious to help. If you would but ask, on any level of your meditation, we shall be with you, as will any and all of your brothers and sisters of the Confederation. We grow as you grow, and are one with you.

We would at this time pause to allow the brothers and sisters of Laitos to pass among you and ask that each who wishes to feel their conditioning vibration would ask. We are known to you as Hatonn and now take our leave of this group. Adonai, my friends.

(Carla channeling)

I am Laitos, and I greet you, my friends, in the love and in the light of the infinite Creator. We would say but a few words to those of this group, for we know that our brother, Latwii, is waiting to speak to you. We were going to speak on the subject of the physical vehicle and its aid to you, and due to the member of your circle which is using its physical vehicle at this time for one of its functional uses we would choose this subject on which to speak.

We speak to you on the subject of sleep. This is an underrated activity of the physical vehicle. Indeed, my friends, many more of your peoples sleep in the waking state than achieve true unconsciousness while in the sleeping state. We ask you to picture your physical vehicle as it is, a creature of both time and space. Your physical vehicle has a great web of energy receptors which during the day are put to use to a degree which is governed by the desire of each entity. There are those whose desire to be sensitive to the incoming vibrations of all those things about it are such that it receives almost no positive value from the physical vehicle, and in addition receives many distortions of the incoming energies of planets, of stars, of the universe, and most of all, my friends,

of those other entities with whom you come in contact.

In fact, by the time that your day is done, and you are prepared to take your rest, nearly all entities have developed a certain system of distortions during that day, due to the free choice of various thoughts which are not in harmony with the energy influxes, primarily of other entities with whom you have come in contact. The more sensitive the entity, the more possible it is to avoid great distortion of these energy influxes.

However, when the physical body enters the sleep, the distortions that have occurred within the energy web of the body may be healed to a greater or lesser extent, depending upon the depth of sleep, the length of the sleep, and the manner with which sleep is respected. If it is a sleep of exhaustion, a sleep without gratitude, a sleep entered into without purpose, the positive functions of sleep are much less apparent, and it is possible to even awaken in a weary state.

The potential of sleep itself for lifting the distortions of the day are very great. We would suggest that as you enter sleep be aware that this function is tremendously helpful to you, for your physical body has great wisdom and in every cell is built a governing factor which will of itself control the proper functioning of the intake of the energies which are available. In sleep it is possible to affirm that the distortions of the day will be lifted. In sleep it is possible to request that those angelic presences who guide you shall be with you. Yes, my friends, thankfulness and gratitude and a certain amount of understanding of the functions of sleep will enable you to lie down to your rest with far less weariness, far more a sense of another portion of your learning experience upon which you are about to embark, which is every bit as valuable to you as your daily experience.

My brothers and sisters of Hatonn have spoken to you of the virtue of not wasting time. As you enter sleep, know that this, too, is time not to be wasted. For there is a great deal of healing and learning and a stretching of, shall we say, those inner muscles of self, which may be achieved during this blessed activity you call sleep.

We would at this time make way for the one known as Latwii. We thank you, my friends, for allowing us to speak through this instrument. It has been a great privilege. I am Laitos. Should you desire our companionship at any time, you have only to ask. I leave you in the love and in the light of the infinite Creator. I leave you in the great infinity of the one original Hope. Adonai, my friends. Adonai.

(Jim channeling)

I am Latwii, and greet you all in the love and in the light of the Creator. It is a great honor to once again be asked to join your group in meditation. At this time, as is our custom, we open this meeting to queries which those present may have brought with them. Is there a question at this time?

Questioner: Yes. To follow up with the idea of sleep, if I can make sense out of this. A couple of nights just this past week I had dreams that were frustrating. I couldn't quite remember them when I woke up, but they were dreams that left me frustrated, and I was tired, and the thought occurred to me in meditation that the dreams, or whatever caused the dreams, had blocked energy, and that was the reason I was tired. And so I thought if I unblocked this energy I would be able to release it, and I began to imagine that I was sending blessings to everybody I knew, and then extending it out to the ends of the Earth in meditation for maybe fifteen minutes, and tried to think or imagine this. And I was totally rested at the end of the meditation, and was rested all day. And my question is, did I unblock energy or what happened in that experience? That was the first time that a thought like that had come to me, that I had blocked the energy and I could release it.

I am Latwii, and am aware of your question, my sister. In responding, may we suggest that indeed when any entity sends that known as love, light and healing energies to any other entity it is opening within its own being a channel for the flow of life-giving energies to open such a channel. To be of service to others does have ramifications for the entity opening that channel, these being the energizing of that entity's mind, body and spirit complex of vehicles. Thusly, you may see that truly it is said, "To give is better [than] to receive." For in truth when one gives to others, oneself cannot help but receive.

This exercise may or may not have a connection with a particular dream experience. They may be two different experiences. Or they may be related in that the meditative sending of love and light and healing energy does then respond to the symbolic blockage experienced in the dream state. We can not be specifically accurate in this instance, for this is a matter for your own inner inquiry. But we might suggest that you did indeed open a pathway by sending the life-giving energies to others.

May we answer you further, my sister?

Questioner: As I did this, did others really benefit from this energy?

I am Latwii. My sister, when such an activity as you have described and carried out is effected, no matter the length of the visualization or the depth of the meditation, there is an increase in the vibratory level of your planet. There is a substantial increment in the amount of love, light and healing energies which is available to each entity so requesting. The amount may be small, but when engaged in as a periodic or regular activity by an entity, the action then is doubled with each sending, and when engaged in by more than one entity, the activity is doubled with each entity. Therefore, each sending does have its effect in raising the vibrations of your planet. The planet itself resounds with the joy of your effort.

May we answer you further, my sister?

Questioner: No. That's fantastic. That's all for right now. I'll have to live with that one a minute.

I am Latwii. Is there another question at this time?

Questioner: Is there ever a time when giving is not of benefit to people?

I am Latwii, and am aware of your query, my sister. There are a number of ways to look at this activity called "giving." If one looks at such an activity in, shall we say, a small frame of reference, one may see the giving of answers to another, which the other seeks, could be a disservice if the answers could have been found by the other's own efforts, for to find such answers by the effort of one's own seeking increases the strength of seeking. Yet, if one expands the frame of reference, in this instance, to consider a much larger view, it might be found that the effect upon the entity receiving such answers is but momentary, and shall lead to other lessons having to do with the seeking of answers, and the finding by one's own efforts. And therefore, it might be seen that this action has but minuscule effect on both entities.

There is no right or wrong behavior which one can engage in, in the larger view, for all experience teaches whether the lesson is planned as a part of that experience or not, for there is but one Creator and many portions of that one Creator, and there is but one experience, that of the Creator. Yet, that experience has many facets. Each entity, as a facet of the Creator, therefore, will look upon a situation, a thought, or an action in the frame of reference with which it is currently dealing and within which it experiences its lessons.

Most entities upon your planet at …

(Side one of tape ends.)

(Jim channeling)

I am Latwii. I am once again with this instrument. To continue. The incarnation, as you would call it, is that period of time [with] which entities upon your planet are primarily concerned, and therefore is that frame of reference which is usually considered as that frame which shall be used to discern that which is learned and that which is not well learned. This, then, provides the criterion for the discernment of the helpful nature of an action, and is primarily concerned with those lessons chosen before the incarnation. An entity in the waking state of an incarnation cannot know whether an action is helpful or not, unless it knows what lessons were programmed before the incarnation.

We apologize for taking this long route to arrive at that statement, but find that the subject is so large that some background is necessary to understand what the result of analysis in this area is.

May we answer you further, my sister?

Questioner: Are you saying that the experience of seeking is perhaps more meaningful than the result, that they're equal or …? I've said enough of the question. I thought I heard you say that experience of seeking was the most vital aspect of living in this incarnation and that the result was there were no right or wrong answers exactly. Am I understanding you correctly?

I am Latwii, and am aware of your query, my sister. We would agree that your basic assumption is correct, and would add that in reality the seeking and the result of the seeking are but parts of one process. That process is the experience of the Creator. For the seeking yields the result and the

result asks yet another question. For the process of that which you call learning has no end as far as we can tell. Therefore, there is an equality in the seeking and in that which is found. For each feeds the process of experience for the entity which is seeking the Creator within.

May we answer you further, my sister?

Questioner: The only part that I'm slightly unclear about is that there is the choice of either telling someone the answer, perhaps, or not giving them the answer, but allowing them to experience their life and come up with an answer. And I guess what I'm hearing you say is that it's OK. Is it preferable to encourage them to seek the process rather than to just give them the answer, as a sort of shortcut?

I am Latwii, and am aware of your query, my sister. We of the Confederation of Planets in the Service of the Infinite Creator take that view that to give answers to questions which might provide answers to the seeker by the seeker's own efforts is not a desired service. We use this frame of reference in dealing with groups such as this one, but also recognize—but from a much larger point of view, that of the Creator—that it matters [not] what we do or what any entity does, for all actions provide experience and all experiences teaches lessons.

May we answer you further, my sister?

Questioner: No, thank you. That is very clear. Thank you very much, Latwii.

I am Latwii. We are most grateful to you, and once again apologize for our occasional wordiness. We do enjoy these opportunities for expressing our humble understanding of the experience which each entity undertakes.

May we ask if there might be another question at this time?

Questioner: I have not a question, but a request. That is that you be available to my grandfather as he makes the transition from this world.

I am Latwii. My brother, we assure you that each entity which passes from this plane in that process which is known to your peoples as death does have a great number of those angelic beings which wait upon it: those entities known as guides, those dear souls which have been closely associated with the one transitioning this life in previous life experiences, and those entities of the Confederation which oversee such processes. Each entity which makes this transition is well protected and attended. And those entities which remain in the third density illusion might be of the greatest aid by wishing the entity "God speed," shall we say, and sending joy, love and light with the entity, and rejoicing at the process which allows the entity to move from one level of lessons to yet another level of lessons. Be ye therefore full of that joy and peace which is the result of each entity's unending existence within the one Creator.

May we ask if there might be another question at this time?

Questioner: I have a question. Are there new third-density beings and old third-density beings at the same time on this Earth?

I am Latwii, and am aware of your question, my sister. This situation has indeed occurred upon your planet for most of its time, as you call it, within this cycle which is now ending. At this time however, there are no "new," shall we say, third-density beings upon your planet, those being those entities passing from the second density into the third by virtue of their own graduation. This is the case since at this time upon your planet that process of incarnation by the seniority of vibration has been in effect for many, of what you call, the years, being necessitated by the ending of the cycle and the providing of the opportunity for those entities to graduate from this density to the next by virtue of their own lessons learned throughout many incarnations.

These lessons take a good deal of what you call time. Therefore, it would not serve an entity well who had just, shall we say, arrived in this density to incarnate at this time. Nor would it serve well those who might have an opportunity to achieve the graduation with but one further incarnation.

May we answer you further, my sister?

Questioner: Thank you. That answers the question.

I am Latwii. We are most grateful to you. Is there another question at this time?

Questioner: Yes. I have another question. I have a lot of friends who talk about the second coming of Christ. You talk about the harvest. Are these similar events? Can we talk about them—when we refer to the harvest, and refer to the second coming of Christ, are we talking about the same thing? I think this is what I'm trying to ask.

I am Latwii, and am aware of your query, my sister. Basically, this is correct, but there is an addition which we feel might be helpful. That known as the harvest, or the graduation, is a process which occurs at the end of each cycle of evolution upon your planet of 75,000 years. All entities at this time are harvested, for the planet itself has its own evolution, and will for a short period be unsuitable for third density existence. Therefore, each entity shall be given the opportunity to pass on to another level of existence, either in the positive orientation, that known as the service-to-others path, or the negative orientation, that known as the service-to-self path.

For these two groups there is also that known as the second coming of the Christ consciousness, which is the experience of each entity of the increase in vibration which accompanies the opening of the red, orange, yellow and green energy centers, for the positive vibrations, and the red, orange, yellow and momentary opening of blue, for the negative vibrations. This second coming of the Christ consciousness simply refers to the fourth-density level of understanding expressed in the entities who are being graduated to the next density of learning.

Those entities who have not achieved this level of understanding are between the polarities, shall we say, and though harvested have not experienced the second coming of the Christ consciousness, and therefore shall be allowed another great cycle of experience upon another third-density planet just beginning its 75,000 year cycle.

The one known as Jesus, the Christ, was the pattern for this experience of the coming, shall we say, of the Christ consciousness. This entity was able to open its energy centers, red through green, quite easily at an early age and spoke of this experience when it said, "The Father and I are One." Such an experience is available to any entity which truly seeks the one Creator, and shall be experienced by those who have achieved this goal, whether it be in the service-to-self or service-to-others polarization.

May we answer you further, my sister?

Questioner: Yes, you said this planet would not be—oh, I am not sure that I can repeat that—fit for habitation of third-density entities. Does that mean that no one will be living on this planet for a period of time?

I am Latwii, and am aware of your query, my sister. There will be those fourth-density positive service-to-other entities living on this planet who have either been graduated from the third-density cycle now ending upon this planet, or who have transferred to this planet from another third-density planet ending its cycle of evolution, after having achieved the graduation upon that planet. There shall not be third-density entities as you know them now, for it will take some period of what you call time for the fourth-density inhabitants of this planet to learn the ways of the density of love and compassion. It is necessary that such entities learn the ability to shield their physical vehicles from the sight or perception from any third-density entity such as yourself, for it is considered an infringement on the free will of a third-density entity to be aware of those experiences of density above third, for it is necessary upon your planet to make the choice of polarity, either the positive or the negative, and this choice must be made within the confines of the third-density experience only, uncontaminated by any density's experience which exceeds the third density.

After a period of what you call time the fourth-density entities who have been newly harvested, and who inhabit this planet shall be able to achieve the shielding effect, and at this time there shall be the reemergence of the third-density life experience as you know it now.

May we answer you further, my sister?

Questioner: No, I believe that answers the question, thank you.

I am Latwii. We thank you. Is there another question at this time?

Questioner: What becomes of people like Hitler who seem to have caused a lot of trouble on our planet?

I am Latwii, and am aware of your query, my sister. When such an entity is successful in pursuing the negative polarization to the degree which shows a great desire to serve the self at least 95% of the time, shall we say, then an entity is also able to achieve that known as the graduation in the negative, or service-to-self sense, and is then able to choose a planet of fourth-density negative vibration with which to join its vibrations in a social memory

complex of a negative nature. The entity which you have referred to, the entity known as Adolf, was not able to achieve this effect in his consciousness, and did suffer some depolarization and was unable to make the graduation during its previous incarnation, and has been undergoing a process of healing for some of what you call time within the middle astral planes of your planet.

May we answer you further, my sister?

Questioner: Yes. Do some people become negative and positive and go back and forth, or do the people that are negative tend to remain negative through all the densities?

I am Latwii, and am aware of your query, my sister. Within your third-density illusion, indeed most of your population swings between the positive and negative poles, neither polarizing in service to others or in service to self. These entities, therefore, must repeat the great cycle of learning now ending upon your planet, for it is necessary within this octave of creation for an entity to choose one path or the other in order that evolution might occur. After this choice has been made and successfully achieved in the degree of its purity, the entity then pursues that path of polarization for many of what you call years or time, and through a number of your densities.

Yet those of the negative path find that the path they pursue must join the positive path by the time the sixth density is achieved. At some point within the density there is the realization that the experience of what is called spiritual entropy occurs for the negative polarization, and therefore there must be a switch, shall we say, or a release of the negative potential so that the orientation becomes that known as the positive, for the negative path pursues that part of the illusion which is not, shall we say, for it is the understanding of negative entities that to manipulate and control others, even for their own good, is the best way to evolve in mind, body and spirit. Therefore, they omit that great universal love which is associated with the green-ray energy center, and this omission allows evolution to occur only up until the point of the mid-sixth density experience. At this time it is necessary to add this component if further evolution is desired.

May we answer you further, my sister?

Questioner: I think that is as much as I can comprehend at this time.

I am Latwii. We are most grateful for your query and hope we have not overtaxed your patience or your interest. May we ask if there is another query at this time?

Questioner: Just one more, and I don't want to wear you out. Recently in my meditations I have had most unusual thoughts come. And one that just sort of overwhelmed me was, "My mind is at home among the stars." I wrote it down, I was so overwhelmed with the thought. Where does such a thought come from?

I am Latwii, and am aware of your query, my sister. Such a thought comes from the heart of your being, for each entity upon your planet is indeed at home among the stars. Few there are, however, who become aware of that fact within their lifetime. Each lifetime has as one portion of its goal the realization of that truth. It is the birthright of each, and each incarnates to claim it.

May we answer you further, my sister?

Questioner: No, that's fine, thank you.

I am Latwii. We are most grateful. Is there another question?

Questioner: I have one more thing I want to talk about for a second, and that is I have a friend that I have loved for a long time, about four years, that I have had very much of a struggle becoming close to. And I'm about to leave her and probably never see her again. I feel like I want to reach her, and I'm really having a struggle with it. I don't know if there is anything you can tell me that would help, but I thought I would tell you about it anyway.

I am Latwii, and am aware of your concerns, my sister. Each entity upon your planet experiences those times of what is usually described as a difficult nature. Usually such difficulty occurs with a specific entity or a number of entities, for each entity has the ability to teach in relation to its ability to provide the opportunity for another to learn. Opportunities come most frequently with what you call problems, for, to learn, an entity must have something to push against, shall we say.

When an entity experiences the difficult times, the problems, and the disharmonies, these experiences then point out to the entity the areas where learning might be found, the learning to resolve the disharmony, the learning to solve the problem, the learning to make smooth that which is difficult, the learning to love, to accept, to forgive, to have compassion for another entity and for the self. When an entity experiences the difficult times, then deep within that entity's being comes the realization that the preincarnative choices for lessons has once again provided a means for being fulfilled. The yearning within the heart of being calls then to the conscious mind and points to the opportunity for learning so that the learning might be achieved. Your feelings of wishing to reach out are simply those feelings which describe to you your desire to learn, to love, and to accept.

May we answer you further, my sister?

Questioner: No. I think I have a better understanding now, thank you.

I am Latwii. We thank you. Is there another question at this time?

Questioner: Yes. I have often wondered where my husband went. He died four years [ago] and he was afraid to die. He had no idea where he was going, and as far as I know he had no beliefs. And although he was a good man, he hated the question why, and I don't think he ever asked himself why anything happened. Would a person like that probably be reincarnated before the harvest?

I am Latwii, and am aware of your query, my sister. It is most difficult from the perspective of your illusion to perceive the great variety of lessons which may lead to the graduation from this density, for each entity is a unique facet of the one Creator. And each entity has specific lessons which enable that entity to proceed in its own evolutionary process. It cannot be said even with a general statement where an entity such as your husband has incarnated next, whether it be this density or the next, for each entity does pursue those lessons which will allow it to achieve that graduation. For each entity upon your planet, and upon all planets in all densities, there is as much time and experience and incarnations as is necessary for the process of evolution to have its effect within the heart of being.

May we answer you further, my sister?

Questioner: No, I think that is sufficient.

I am Latwii. Is there another question at this time?

Questioner: Yes. One quickie. I'm full of questions tonight. In talking about service to others, is volunteer work, where—like, you're working in a hospital, where you're not particularly needed—service to others?

I am Latwii, and am aware of your query, my sister. Indeed, such an activity, when undertaken with the conscious desire to be of such service, is indeed service to others. It is a most difficult task to make the distinction between what is of service to others and what is not, for there is nothing but the one Creator, and all serve the one Creator. Therefore, all engage in service to others, and yet all engage in service to self. For are not all entities part of the one Creator?

The distinction to be most applicable to those within your density between service-to-others activity and that activity which is not of service to others needs to be considered within the light of what is the conscious choice. The entity which engages in activities by conscious choice that are of service to others, therefore does more effectually polarize in consciousness than does the activity which an entity undertakes with no conscious thought as to whether others are served or not. Therefore, it is not always an easy distinction to make. But we offer this framework of thought for your consideration.

May we answer you further, my sister?

Questioner: No, thank you.

I am Latwii. We thank you. Is there another question at this time?

(Pause)

I am Latwii. We are aware that this group has provided us with the queries most important for the current questioning, and are most grateful for this opportunity to be of whatever service it is possible for us to be in providing our meager responses, though [they are] always provided with enthusiasm. We hope each will realize that our responses are framed within a reference which is not all-knowing, but does have those elements which we consider to be the kernels of our truth, as we also seek the solutions to the mystery of being as do each of your entities on your planet, and within this meeting room. We are most grateful at each request, and at each question for the opportunity to blend our vibrations with yours, and to provide that service which it is our honor to provide. We remind each entity that a simple request for our presence within

the meditative state will bring us, rejoicing in our blending of vibrations within your own.

We would at this time take our leave of this group and leave each therefore in the love and in the light of the one infinite Creator, Who resides within the heart of all who chooses. We are known to you as Latwii. We leave you now. Adonai, my friends. Adonai vasu borragus. ♣

L/L Research is a subsidiary of
Rock Creek Research &
Development Laboratories, Inc.

P.O. Box 5195
Louisville, KY 40255-0195

L/L RESEARCH

www.llresearch.org

Rock Creek is a non-profit
corporation dedicated to
discovering and sharing
information which may aid in
the spiritual evolution of
humankind.

THE LAW OF ONE, BOOK IV, SESSION 86
MAY 4, 1982

Ra: I am Ra. I greet you in the love and in the light of the one infinite Creator. We communicate now.

Questioner: Would you first please give me the condition of the instrument?

Ra: I am Ra. The instrument's distortion towards physical energy complex deficit has slightly increased since the last asking. The vital energy levels have had significant calls upon them and are somewhat less than the last asking also.

Questioner: What was the nature of the significant calls upon the vital energy?

Ra: I am Ra. There are those entities which entertain the thought distortion towards this entity that it shall remove for the otherselves all distortions for the other-self. This entity has recently been in close contact with a larger than normal number of entities with these thought complex distortions. This entity is of the distortion to provide whatever service is possible and is not consciously aware of the inroads made upon the vital energies.

Questioner: Am I correct in assuming that you are speaking of incarnate third-density entities that were creating the condition of the use of the vital energy?

Ra: I am Ra. Yes.

Questioner: What is the present situation with our fifth-density service-to-self polarized companion?

Ra: I am Ra. The period which you may call crisis remains.

Questioner: Can you tell me anything of the nature of this crisis?

Ra: I am Ra. The polarity of your companion is approaching the critical point at which the entity shall choose either to retreat for the nonce and leave any greetings to fourth-density minions or lose polarity. The only other potential is that in some way this group might lose polarity in which case your companion could continue its form of greeting.

Questioner: In the last session you had mentioned the properties precipitating from the veiling of the mind; the first being envisioning or far-seeing. Would you explain the meaning of that?

Ra: I am Ra. Your language is not overstrewn with non-emotional terms for the functional qualities of what is now termed unconscious mind. The nature of mind is something which we have requested that you ponder. However, it is, shall we say, clear enough to the casual observer that we may share some thoughts with you without infringing upon your free learn/teaching experiences.

The nature of the unconscious is of the nature of concept rather than word. Consequently, before the veiling the use of the deeper mind was that of the use of unspoken concept. You may consider the emotive and connotative aspects of a melody. One could call out, in some stylized fashion, the terms for the notes of the melody. One could say, quarter note A, quarter note A, quarter note A, whole note F. This bears little resemblance to the beginning of the melody of one of your composer's most influential melodies, that known to you as a symbol of victory.

This is the nature of the deeper mind. There are only stylized methods with which to discuss its functions. Thusly our descriptions of this portion of the mind, as well as the same portions of body and spirit, were given terms such as "far-seeing," indicating that the nature of penetration of the veiled portion of the mind may be likened unto the journey too rich and exotic to contemplate adequate describing thereof.

Questioner: You have stated that dreaming, if made available to the conscious mind, will aid greatly in polarization. Could you define dreaming or tell us what it is and how it aids polarization?

Ra: I am Ra. Dreaming is an activity of communication through the veil of the unconscious mind and the conscious mind. The nature of this activity is wholly dependent upon the situation regarding the energy center blockages, activations, and crystallizations of a given mind/body/spirit complex.

In one who is blocked at two of the three lower energy centers dreaming will be of value in the polarization process in that there will be a repetition of those portions of recent catalyst as well as deeper held blockages, thereby giving the waking mind clues as to the nature of these blockages and hints as to possible changes in perception which may lead to the unblocking.

This type of dreaming or communication through the veiled portions of the mind occurs also with those mind/body/spirit complexes which are functioning with far less blockage and enjoying the green-ray activation or higher activation at those times at which the mind/body/spirit complex experiences catalyst, momentarily reblocking or baffling or otherwise distorting the flow of energy influx. Therefore, in all cases it is useful to a mind/body/spirit complex to ponder the content and emotive resonance of dreams.

For those whose green-ray energy centers have been activated as well as for those whose green-ray energy centers are offered an unusual unblockage due to extreme catalyst, such as what is termed the physical death of the self or one which is beloved occurring in what you may call your near future, dreaming takes on another activity. This is what may loosely be

termed precognition or a knowing which is prior to that which shall occur in physical manifestation in your yellow-ray third-density space/time. This property of the mind depends upon its placement, to a great extent, in time/space so that the terms of present and future and past have no meaning. This will, if made proper use of by the mind/body/spirit complex, enable this entity to enter more fully into the all-compassionate love of each and every circumstance including those circumstances against which an entity may have a strong distortion towards what you may call unhappiness.

As a mind/body/spirit complex consciously chooses the path of the adept and, with each energy balanced to a minimal degree, begins to open the indigo-ray energy center the so-called dreaming becomes the most efficient tool for polarization, for, if it is known by the adept that work may be done in consciousness while the so-called conscious mind rests, this adept may call upon those which guide it, those presences which surround it, and, most of all, the magical personality which is the higher self in space/time analog as it moves into the sleeping mode of consciousness. With these affirmations attended to, the activity of dreaming reaches that potential of learn/teaching which is most helpful to increasing the distortions of the adept towards its chosen polarity.

There are other possibilities of the dreaming not so closely aligned with the increase in polarity which we do not cover at this particular space/time.

Questioner: How is the dream designed or programmed? Is it done by the higher self, or who is responsible for this?

Ra: I am Ra. In all cases the mind/body/spirit complex makes what use it can of the faculty of the dreaming. It, itself, is responsible for this activity.

Questioner: Then you are saying that the subconscious is responsible for what I will call the design or scriptwriter for the dream. Is this correct?

Ra: I am Ra. This is correct.

Questioner: Is the memory that the individual has upon waking from the dream usually reasonably accurate? Is the dream easily remembered?

Ra: I am Ra. You must realize that we are over-generalizing in order to answer your queries as there are several sorts of dreams. However, in general, it may be noted that it is only for a trained and disciplined observer to have reasonably good recall of the dreaming. This faculty may be learned by virtue of a discipline of the recording immediately upon awakening of each and every detail which can be recalled. This training sharpens one's ability to recall the dream. The most common perception of a mind/body/spirit complex of dreams is muddied, muddled, and quickly lost.

Questioner: In remembering dreams, then, you are saying that the individual can find specific clues to current energy center blockages and may, thereby, reduce or eliminate those blockages. Is this correct?

Ra: I am Ra. This is so.

Questioner: Is there any other function of dreaming that is of value in the evolutionary process?

Ra: I am Ra. Although there are many which are of some value we would choose two to note, since these two, though not of value in polarization, may be of value in a more generalized sense.

The activity of dreaming is an activity in which there is made a finely wrought and excellently fashioned bridge from conscious to unconscious. In this state the various distortions which have occurred in the energy web of the body complex, due to the misprision with which energy influxes have been received, are healed. With the proper amount of dreaming comes the healing of these distortions. Continued lack of this possibility can cause seriously distorted mind/body/spirit complexes.

The other function of the dreaming which is of aid is that type of dream which is visionary and which prophets and mystics have experienced from days of old. Their visions come through the roots of mind and speak to a hungry world. Thus the dream is of service without being of a personally polarizing nature. However, in that mystic or prophet who desires to serve, such service will increase the entity's polarity.

Questioner: There is a portion of sleep that has been called REM. Is this the state of dreaming?

Ra: I am Ra. This is correct.

Questioner: It was noticed that this occurs in small units during the night with gaps in between. Is there any particular reason for this?

Ra: I am Ra. Yes.

Questioner: If it is of any value to know that would you tell me why the dreaming process works like that?

Ra: I am Ra. The portions of the dreaming process which are helpful for polarization and also for the vision of the mystic take place in time/space and, consequently, use the bridge from metaphysical to physical for what seems to be a brief period of your space/time. The time/space equivalent is far greater. The bridge remains, however, and traduces each distortion of mind, body, and spirit as it has received the distortions of energy influxes so that healing may take place. This healing process does not occur with the incidence of rapid eye movement but rather occurs largely in the space/time portion of the mind/body/spirit complex using the bridge to time/space for the process of healing to be enabled.

Questioner: You mentioned the loss of knowledge and control over the body as being a factor that was helpful in the evolutionary process due to veiling. Could you enumerate the important losses of knowledge and control of the body?

Ra: I am Ra. This query contains some portions which would be more helpfully answered were some intervening material requested.

Questioner: I'm at a loss to know what to request. Can you give me an idea of what area of intervening material I should work on?

Ra: I am Ra. No. However, we shall be happy to answer the original query if it is still desired if you first perceive that there is information lacking.

Questioner: Perhaps I can question slightly differently here. I might ask why the loss of knowledge and control over the body was helpful?

Ra: I am Ra. The knowledge of the potentials of the physical vehicle before the veiling offered the mind/body/spirit a free range of choices with regard to activities and manifestations of the body but offered little in the way of the development of polarity. When the knowledge of these potentials and functions of the physical vehicle is shrouded from the conscious mind complex, the mind/body/spirit complex is often nearly without knowledge of how to best manifest its beingness. However, this state of lack of knowledge offers an opportunity for a desire to grow within the mind complex. This desire is that which seeks to know the possibilities of the body complex. The ramifications of each possibility and the eventual biases thusly built have within them a force which can only be generated by such a desire or will to know.

Questioner: Perhaps you could give examples of the use of the body prior to veiling and after the veiling in the same aspect to help us understand the change in knowledge of and control over the body more clearly. Could you do this, please?

Ra: I am Ra. We could.

Questioner: Will you do this?

Ra: I am Ra. Yes. Let us deal with the sexual energy transfer. Before the veiling such a transfer was always possible due to there being no shadow upon the grasp of the nature of the body and its relationship to other mind/body/spirits in this particular manifestation. Before the veiling process there was a near total lack of the use of this sexual energy transfer beyond green ray.

This also was due to the same unshadowed knowledge each had of each. There was, in third density then, little purpose to be seen in the more intensive relationships of mind, body, and spirit which you may call those of the mating process, since each other-self was seen to be the Creator and no other-self seemed to be more the Creator than another.

After the veiling process it became infinitely more difficult to achieve green-ray energy transfer due to the great areas of mystery and unknowing concerning the body complex and its manifestations. However, also due to the great shadowing of the manifestations of the body from the conscious mind complex, when such energy transfer was experienced it was likelier to provide catalyst which caused a bonding of self with other-self in a properly polarized configuration.

From this point it was far more likely that higher energy transfers would be sought by this mated pair of mind/body/spirit complexes, thus allowing the Creator to know Itself with great beauty, solemnity, and wonder. Intelligent infinity having been reached by this sacramental use of this function of the body, each mind/body/spirit complex of the mated pair gained greatly in polarization and in ability to serve.

Questioner: Did any of the other aspects of loss of knowledge or control of the body approach, to any

degree in efficiency, the description which you have just given?

Ra: I am Ra. Each function of the body complex has some potential after the veiling to provide helpful catalyst. We did choose the example of sexual energy transfer due to its central place in the functionary capabilities of the body complex made more useful by means of the veiling process.

This instrument grows somewhat low in energy. We would prefer to retain the maximal portion of reserved energy for which this instrument has given permission. We would, therefore, ask for one more full query at this working.

Questioner: I would assume that the veiling of the sexual aspect was of great efficiency because it is an aspect that has to do totally with a relationship with an other-self. It would seem to me that the bodily veilings having to do with other-self interaction would be more efficient when compared with those only related to self, which would be lower in efficiency in producing either positive or negative polarization. Am I correct in this assumption?

Ra: I am Ra. You are correct to a great extent. Perhaps the most notable exception is the attitude of one already strongly polarized negatively towards the appearance of the body complex. There are those entities upon the negative path which take great care in the preservation of the distortion your peoples perceive as fairness/ugliness. This fairness of form is, of course, then used in order to manipulate other-selves. May we ask if there are any brief queries?

Questioner: Is there anything that we can do to make the instrument more comfortable or to improve the contact?

Ra: I am Ra. We are pleased that this instrument was more conscientious in preparing itself for contact by means of the careful mental vibrations which you call prayer. This enabled the channel to be free from the distortions which the contact fell prey to during the last working.

We would suggest to the support group some continued care in the regulating of the physical activities of the instrument. However at this nexus it is well to encourage those activities which feed the vital energies as this instrument lives in this space/time present almost completely due to the careful adherence to the preservation of those mental and spiritual energies which make up the vital energy complex of this entity. Each is conscientious. The alignments are good.

We would caution the support group as to the physical alignment of the appurtenance known as the censer. There has been some slight difficulty due to variation in the pattern of the effluvium of this incense.

I am Ra. I leave you rejoicing in the power and in the peace of the one infinite Creator. Go forth, then, rejoicing in the love and in the light of the one Creator. Adonai ✣

L/L RESEARCH

L/L Research is a subsidiary of
Rock Creek Research &
Development Laboratories, Inc.

P.O. Box 5195
Louisville, KY 40255-0195

www.llresearch.org

Rock Creek is a non-profit
corporation dedicated to
discovering and sharing
information which may aid in
the spiritual evolution of
humankind.

FRIDAY NIGHT
MAY 7, 1982

(Unknown channeling)

I am Hatonn, and I greet you, my brothers and sisters, in the love and the light of the infinite Creator. My friends, it is a great pleasure to share with you our thoughts, our aspirations, in the hope that they may be in some small way be of assistance to you in the accomplishment of your own objectives of growth, of love, of reunion with one another and the Creator. My friends, it is always a blessing to share oneness with our brothers, for so seldom on your planet does this occur. It might be said that each individual lives within a vacuum, that each isolates himself or herself from the other selves that surround them, and in fear and misunderstanding of the isolation that has been created, each as in a vacuum contracts into himself as if unable to contact the energy with which to expand outward and establish a reunion with those among [whom] one lives.

My friends, we are aware of the exhaustion that is characteristic of those who strive to overcome this spiritual vacuum, for it is a great struggle to constantly extend oneself, holding oneself open and extended, so to speak, in one's attempt to establish and maintain contact with those other selves that compose the single unit that your race has the potential of becoming. My friends, do not be discouraged. What will pass, will pass and what will occur, will occur. As your book [the Bible] states, for

every purpose, there is a season, and it is perhaps beneficial to remember that just as one cannot push a river upstream, one may not also be able to establish the desired reunification before its season arrives.

How then, you might ask, are those who strive to find acceptance of this statement? Is one to simply surrender to the overwhelming flow and simply wash downstream, relying upon chance occurrence or fate to establish the desired configuration between individual entities, or is one to take upon oneself the task of attempting to force the establishment of this interrelationship, even while being conscious of the fact that the task may not be accomplished until the season has arrived?

My friends, it is important to realize that the seed which is sown will first lie dormant just as each of you who initially entered this incarnation lay dormant for a period of time before awakening to the light of your inner fire. It is important for the seed, once awakened, to climb toward the light, to strive to reach it, but it is also important, my friends, that at the same time, the roots within the world be also established, for just as those entities that you so generally refer to as grass will strive simultaneously to reach the sun, and also intertwine its earthly roots with those of its brothers and sisters, so also must you realize that your contact with your world is not intended to be solitary and aloof, but rather one characterized by an entwined uplifting toward the light of the Creator.

My friends, do not cease to strive, for this is your path of growth, but be aware that not all seeds will germinate at the same moment in time. Be aware that the grass which firsts sprouts and successfully establishes and entwines its roots with those who sprout at the same time do not need to grasp their slower brothers by the hair or shoulders and attempt to rip them higher in a fanatic effort to assist. Rather, realize that as those younger seeds germinate and sprout forth that the soil has been conditioned by the older brothers and sisters who have retained the moisture and attracted those life forms which will provide the nutrients for the fledglings to follow.

My brothers and sisters, it is said on your planet that those serve who also sit and wait. My friends, realize the love that is necessary to sit and wait and be patient, for just as the parent awaits the younger child to cease sleeping that new tasks may be undertaken, so also is it important that you who go before be patient and support and protect those who will follow.

At this time we will close and allow our brothers and sisters of Laitos to pass among you and offer their conditioning vibration to those among you who would request it. I am Hatonn.

(Pause)

(Unknown channeling)

I am Latwii, and I greet you, my brothers and sisters, in the love and the light of the infinite Creator. My friends, as always, it is a great pleasure to be once again amongst you that we may perform our small service of answering any questions or puns that might be cast in our direction. Is there any question that we may attempt to respond to on this wonderful evening on your planet?

S: I have a question concerning nuclear explosions. What happens to an entity that is caught in one of these?

I am Latwii, and I am aware of your question, my sister. It is our assumption that your field of interest lies in the dissolution of [an] entity rather than the physical manifestation of nuclear explosion, and we shall attempt to answer the question on that perspective.

The entity which is within the most intense area affected by the disruption that you refer to as a nuclear explosion is affected thusly. The Word of the Logos Itself is disrupted, in the manner of a framework or structure on your planetary surface can be disrupted, to such a degree as to be rendered into particulate matter, and such is the effect upon an entity experiencing this dismantling, so to speak.

As the Logos is the force establishing the framework into a functional form within your particular density and galaxy, this disruption relinquishes the form, in effect canceling the structure which had been formed by the Logos. The raw material, so to speak, does not cease to exist, but rather ceases to retain its structured form, and to put it simply, returns to the Creators' raw material pile, so to speak.

We would hasten to point out that this occurrence is not limited to those entities of your own density, but also of those lesser densities occupying the same area of effect. Therefore, we would emphasize the responsibility taken on by those who would detonate such a device, in that the entities affected are not only your people, but also those first and second-density entities who occupy the same localities. We would refer to this as food for thought.

May we answer you further?

S: Maybe at a later date after I've had a chance to think about this. Thank you, Latwii.

[I am Latwii.] As always, we thank you for the opportunity to communicate with you in this fashion. Is there another question?

(Pause)

I am Latwii. As there are no questions, and as the energy and attunement within the group is rapidly dropping off, we would take our leave. We would offer the suggestion that the embodiment of those materials known to produce a state of somnolence is in general not beneficial to the communication of our thoughts, as the variations in tuning that occur so rapidly after the commencement strongly affect our ability to communicate. We would also refer [to] this as food for thought in future contacts. As always, my brothers and sisters, we leave you in the love and the light of the infinite Creator. Adonai vasu borragus. I am Latwii. ♣

SUNDAY MEDITATION
MAY 9, 1982

(L channeling)

I am Hatonn, and I greet you, my brothers and sisters, in the love and the light of the infinite Creator. My friends, as always, it is our pleasure to be able to join your group and participate with you in your meditations, and, as always, we are honored by the service you do us in requesting our service, small and insignificant as it may be.

There are many aspects, my friends, to the study of meditation, and for many these aspects are never readily perceivable, for there is seldom sufficient striving to attain the depth necessary for the perception of the distinctions between the types of meditation. For example, when one of your brothers or sisters who has not participated for a long period of time in a group such as this or in other forms of meditation, there is a sense of puzzled wonderment when the subject is raised. It may be assumed by many that the act of meditating is in some way the attainment of a mystical state that is available to but a few, and for that reason there is no reason for the individual to pursue the attainment as one would practice to achieve a level of attainment in a sport or other field of endeavor on your planet.

My friends, do not be dismayed by your perceptions, for perceptions are based upon a limited amount of knowledge, and only through your striving will the truth be opened to you. The attainments in meditation do not come painfully, but rather they come consistently. As one practices regularly and with frequency one begins to perceive the potential paths that open before oneself, as a fan of leaves open from the branch of a tree, each leading farther and farther in a different direction, but striving still in unity toward the light.

My friends, we do not speak on this subject as a lector or professor who will define and detail for you the various aspects of meditation, but rather as an encouraging participant or co-student who, having discovered a small amount of the splendor attainable, would rush back to share the surprise with his brothers or sisters. We cannot encourage you sufficiently, my friends, to undertake the regular practice of meditations for it is your sincere desire, we believe, to seek attainment, and find that this path above all others will enable you to achieve that end.

At this time we would transfer our contact to the one known as Jim.

(Jim channeling)

I am Hatonn, and greet you once again in love and light. It is our privilege to utilize this instrument, which we have not been able to speak through for some time. It is always, my friends, the lot of the seeker that the seeking shall be strewn with those situations which you call the difficulties. So it is with the method of seeking known as meditation. As one seeks in meditation there are a number of parameters, shall we say, that must be met which may offer that known as the difficulty from time to time, for the purpose of teaching the seeking entity how best to meet them.

The first parameter is the honing of the desire to actually make the time for meditation in the busy schedule. It seems so often that there is not enough time to accomplish those activities which acquire the attention in the outer world of the entity for its survival and sustenance. This is the basic requisite, shall we say, for the desire to seek in this manner must be of a certain strength before the seeking shall have the opportunity to begin. A meditator then finds that when time has been made for this activity that the outer world is not easily shed and remains, indeed, within the head or mind. Quieting this muscle of stray thoughts and leftover concerns from the day's activities then becomes the next step for the seeker in meditation.

This is approached by each entity in a unique fashion. Many use various means to quiet the mind: the chanting, the visualizing of a blank space, the seeing of the thoughts settling to the bottom of a pool, the watching of the thoughts as they pass through the mind's eye without giving them undue attention are some means that may be used. These thoughts shall continue in their progression for quite some time, shall we say, for each meditator, for each entity so seeking in meditation is always engaged in some degree in the outer world. For this outer world seems to be that which is most real and which requires the seeker's attention.

When a stillness of a sufficient nature has been achieved then the entity may utilize this stillness for a great variety of purposes. It may be that the meditator has a need which must be met in the spiritual, emotional or mental sense, which then might be the theme or topic of the meditation. This need might be allowed to travel its natural course, shall we say, as the seeker seeks its solution. It might be that the seeker would use this stillness to meditate upon a concept such as love, wisdom, mercy, etc. It might also be the case that the seeker simply wishes to remain in that stillness and feel the presence of its guides and the higher vibrations of these entities so that a subconscious sustenance or food might be gained.

A visualization of certain symbols sacred to the seeker might also be accomplished within the bounds of this stillness. These are but a few of those uses for the meditative state. Each seeker, whatever the use made of this state, does in some way seek the one Creator. Meditation can never fail, my friends. You may feel that your mind loses its concentration as often as a leaf in a wind, yet the very act of seeking in meditation carries a metaphysical charge or power, shall we say, which is always of aid to the seeker, though seldom perceivable.

We would at this time close this particular discussion through the entity known as C. We would now transfer this contact. I am Hatonn.

(C channeling)

I am Hatonn, and I greet you now through this instrument. We would but say that though [there are] those who do not understand and see meditation as a passive state, we would but remind [you of] the dynamics occurring for reaching, as you, through your meditations, become more in touch and activate those parts in you which aid as you seek and grow. We will join with you and aid in what ways we can. You need but request, and we shall be with you. We are known to you as Hatonn, and at this time we shall take our leave of this group that our brothers and sisters of Latwii may aid you in that which is their particular specialty, and answer as they may questions of those things that have begun to be turned over in your minds as you have become more aware of. We leave you now in the love and light of the one infinite Creator. Adonai, my friends.

(L channeling)

I am Latwii, and I greet you, my brothers and sisters, in the love and in the light of the infinite Creator. As always, we are very happy to be here, particularly on such a day that produces such wonderful feelings and contentment in those who attend the meetings, for we find it is much more pleasurable to share oneness with you when you are happy than when you are depressed or soggy.

At this time we would offer our services of attempting to answer any questions that you may choose to offer within our feeble realm of ability. Are there any questions?

Question: This week I attended a funeral and a practice sort of stuck in my mind that I was wondering the significance of. That is the practice of using incense as part of the ceremony. It seems to be something that is used worldwide, and I was just wondering what value the use of incense is?

I am Latwii, and am aware of your question. My brother, the substance that you describe as incense has the ability to perform tasks on several levels of perception. We would describe them as follows. First and most generally, the substance being recognized as a symbol within the physical realm of a religious event or occurrence has the ability to key both the conscious and subconscious mind to a particular state of mind. Such as, "I am at a funeral. I shall be attentive and solemn." We are sure that this is quite easy to understand.

However, we would offer also the information that just as certain sounds such as the chanting of the "om" may have an effect upon the subconscious mind in the performance of an attunement, so also may the sense of smell be activated in such a manner, and some of these substances generally referred to on your planet as incenses may perform this function.

There has been in your past a misunderstanding of these concepts and some confused loquation. These concepts were translated into the idea that an omnipotent entity somehow craved the odor of this substance. We would suggest that this seems quite unlikely to us, and is simply a misunderstanding of the concept that the Creator which is within and without all of us is desirous of reunification, and the state of mind which is signaled by the smelling of the substance incense is desirous for the Creator in us all.

May we answer you further, my brother?

Questioner: If I get all that right it is that incense is mainly a tool for focusing?

I am Latwii. That is primarily correct. It also functions in a metaphysical manner, but this is not the substance incense itself, but rather the process of using a tool to accomplish an end. It is very functional as a tool for certain purposes.

May we answer you further?

Questioner: Not at this time, thank you.

We thank you. Is there another question?

Questioner: I have a friend who I am very close to, and my brother and I explained to him a little of the

meditation, and he doesn't understand. He thinks it's all weird, and he says that it isn't right. Some people say it is, and I need a little help on it. I was wondering if maybe you could help me?

I am Latwii, and am aware of your question. My friend, it is often very difficult to be in the position of possessing some wonderful knowledge, and yet being unable to share that knowledge with those who are dear to us or whose companionship we desire. It is always appropriate to desire that a friend or loved one be enabled to attain this particular type of knowledge. However, it is important to remember that one must first ask before one receives. That one must knock before the door is opened. If this were not so then the gifts and the answers that are given would not be fully appreciated, and would very likely be disregarded. My friend, there are times when you will want to share your knowledge with others, and must hold back out of love for your friends, for to share with them too soon would reduce their appreciation of that knowledge because it is knowledge that they have not sought, and because they were not looking for it, they are not impressed or satisfied when they find it.

It is more easy to understand that they find this type of communication to be unusual or suspect it of being a deception or lies because for those who do not yet seek there are no answers yet provided. They have not yet been given the information that you have already discovered. If we could offer advice, my friend, we would simply say that rather than share your knowledge with those who may not [be] prepared to accept it, share instead your love, for that is a language which is always understood, and it is a form of communication that will not be seen by your friends as weird or somehow wrong. Love your friends, and should they ask of you at that point it would be better to share your knowledge, for by asking they will identify themselves to you as seekers.

May we answer you further?

Questioner: No, I think I understand and thank you for your advice.

My friend, we thank you for your question. Is there another question?

Questioner: Yes. As I see things, our own country as well as the world is in such a dilemma financially that there are no solutions, and I am assuming that because of the harvest being near that we'll have to muddle through until harvest time about the way we're going. Am I right in that assumption?

I am Latwii. We would state that you are incorrect in that there are an infinite number of solutions available at this time to the peoples of your planet. They might range from the solution of eradicating the problems by eradicating your planet, to sharing responsibility by solving your difficulties by sharing responsibility for distributing those forms of physical needs to the areas in which they lack, and in this way expressing love for one's other selves.

May we answer you further?

Questioner: Yes. Let me push that a little farther. For instance, in Africa, where people reproduce so fast, it seems that there is no way to meet that need. What do we do in cases like that?

I am Latwii. My sister, we might point out that the need is currently being balanced to a large extent by a substantially early withdrawal of many entities from your planet in a form you refer to as physical death, at often a very young age, from a lack of food substances. This is neither good nor bad, but simply that which occurs, and might be regarded by some as an acceptable solution to the problem.

We would extend our analysis of this answer even further to hazard the assumption that this is what your people are doing to solve the problem. This is very likely regarded by your people as an acceptable and workable solution to the problem. However, your planet and your people have at this time the capability to feed extremely well all of those who currently inhabit your planet. That is not a matter of finding the food, or finding locations within which to produce the food, but rather finding those people who will share what they have. It is also possible on your planet to control and regulate the population of your planet, and when this becomes a sufficiently desirable solution to some of your people who do not regard it as such at this time, it will likely be implemented in those areas.

May we answer you further?

Questioner: Is there any one form of government on the planet at this time that is capable of distributing wealth where it is needed?

I am Latwii. My sister, the distribution of substances can be accomplished by any group who are motivated by love. The effective distribution over substantially wide ranges may only be accomplished by a substantially large group motivated in this same manner. The form under which the group operates or the government under which this distribution takes place is not important. What is important is a sufficient number of sufficiently motivated people. Just as rocks may be worn away by the constant barrage of raindrops and grains of sand, so also can the most substantial problems be overcome with enough determination and with enough motivation.

May we answer you further?

Questioner: No, that is sufficient. Thank you.

We thank you. Is there another question?

Questioner: Yes. One other question. It's very personal. My grandson, D, is having a very hard time. Can you make any comments about his condition, or what his dad can do, or what we can do?

I am Latwii. My sister, is not permissible for us to speak in terms of particular individuals or, as you understand, this is antagonistic to our own purpose in communicating with you. In speaking generally, however, of relationships between those individuals who find difficulty in one another's presence, we would simply say that if the people desire to love and understand one another, if their desire is to extend love unconditionally without placing demands upon others, then their path would become much easier, and their companionship less abrasive. The difficulty lies not in the fact of loving or not loving, but rather in the placement of rules or limitations upon that loving. If one person says to another, "I will only love you if you do this, or I will cease to love you if you act in that manner," my friend, how valuable is love that can be bought and sold in such a fashion?

We would offer instead a suggestion that one attempt to view one's brothers and sisters with the understanding of, "If you do that, I will love you still. If you act in that manner, I will try to love you more, and I will try to understand. And if unable to understand, I will try to remember that your path is not mine, and that it is not my responsibility or right to guide your steps." For such is permissible only to the individual himself or herself. The journey must be made, but the direction and the speed can only be determined by he or she who walks the path.

May we answer you further?

Questioner: That's very good, thank you.

My sister, we thank you for the opportunity to offer our services, and we desire that you find peace in this manner.

Questioner: Thank you.

Is there another question?

(Pause)

I am Latwii. I am again with this instrument. As there are no further questions at this time, we will take our leave. May the love and the light of the Creator be ever in your awareness, my friends, just as you are always in their presence. Adonai vasu borragus. I am known to you as Latwii. ✣

THE LAW OF ONE, BOOK IV, SESSION 87
MAY 12, 1982

Ra: I am Ra. I greet you in the love and in the light of the one infinite Creator. I communicate now.

Questioner: Could you first please give me the condition of the instrument?

Ra: I am Ra. The distortions of the physical complex are unchanged. The vital energy levels are greatly enhanced.

Questioner: Thank you. In considering what was mentioned in the last session about the censer I have thought about the fact that the position of the origin of the smoke changes approximately six inches horizontally. Would it be better to have a censer in a single, horizontal smoking position?

Ra: I am Ra. This alteration would be an helpful one given that the censer is virgin.

Questioner: What would be the optimum geometrical arrangement of censer, chalice, and candle with respect to the Bible and table and the positions that we now have them in?

Ra: I am Ra. Both chalice and candle occupy the optimal configuration with respect to the book most closely aligned with the Law of One in the distortion complexes of this instrument. It is optimal to have the censer to the rear of this book and centered at the spine of its open configuration.

Questioner: Would a position directly between the chalice and the candle be optimum, then, for the censer?

Ra: I am Ra. This is not an exact measurement since both chalice and candle are irregularly shaped. However, speaking roughly, this is correct.

Questioner: Thank you. What is the present situation with respect to our fifth-density negative companion?

Ra: I am Ra. This entity has withdrawn for a period of restoration of its polarity.

Questioner: Would you expand upon the concept of the acquisition of polarity by this particular entity, its use, specifically, of this polarity other than the simple, obvious need for sixth-density harvest if this is possible, please?

Ra: I am Ra. We would. The nature of the densities above your own is that a purpose may be said to be shared by both positive and negative polarities. This purpose is the acquisition of the ability to welcome more and more the less and less distorted love/light and light/love of the one infinite Creator. Upon the negative path the wisdom density is one in which power over others has been refined until it is approaching absolute power. Any force such as the force your group and those of Ra offer which cannot be controlled by the power of such a negative fifth-density mind/body/spirit complex then depolarizes the entity which has not controlled other-self.

It is not within your conscious selves to stand against such refined power but rather it has been through the harmony, the mutual love, and the honest calling for aid from the forces of light which have given you the shield and buckler.

Questioner: What is the environmental situation of this particular fifth-density entity, and how does he work with fourth-density negative entities in order to establish power and control; what is his particular philosophy with respect to himself as Creator and with respect to the use of the first distortion and the extension of the first distortion to the fourth-density negative? I hope that this isn't too complex a question.

Ra: I am Ra. The environment of your companion is that of the rock, the cave, the place of barrenness, for this is the density of wisdom and that which is needed may be thought and received. To this entity very little is necessary upon the physical, if you will, or space/time complex of distortions.

Such an entity spends its consciousness within the realms of time/space in an attempt to learn the ways of wisdom through the utmost use of the powers and resources of the self. Since the self is the Creator, the wisdom density provides many informative and fascinating experiences for the negatively polarized entity. In some respects one may see a more lucid early attachment to wisdom from those of negative polarity as the nexus of positions of consciousness upon which wisdom is laid is simpler.

The relationship of such an entity to fourth-density negative entities is one of the more powerful and the less powerful. The negative path posits slavery of the less powerful as a means of learning the desire to serve the self to the extent that the will is brought to bear. It is in this way that polarity is increased in the negative sense. Thus fourth-density entities are willing slaves of such a fifth-density entity, there being no doubt whatsoever of the relative power of each.

Questioner: A reflection of this could be seen in our density in many of those leaders who instigate war and have followers who support, in total conviction that the direction of conquest is correct. Is this correct?

Ra: I am Ra. Any organization which demands obedience without question upon the basis of relative power is functioning according to the above described plan.

Questioner: One point that I am not clear on is the understanding and use of the first distortion by fifth and fourth-density negative entities in manipulating third-density entities. I would like to know how the first distortion affects the attempts to carry out the conquest of third-density entities and the attempt to add them, under the premise of the first distortion, to their social memory complexes. Would you expand on that concept, please?

Ra: I am Ra. This latter plan is not one of which fourth-density negative social memory complexes are capable. The fourth-density habit is that of offering temptations and of energizing preexisting distortions. Fourth-density entities lack the subtlety and magical practice which the fifth-density experience offers.

Questioner: It seems though that in the case of many UFO contacts that have occurred on this planet that there must be some knowledge of and use of the first distortion. The fourth-density entities have carefully remained aloof and anonymous, you might say, for the most part, so that no proof in a concrete way of their existence is available. How are they oriented with respect to this type of contact?

Ra: I am Ra. We misperceived your query, thinking it was directed towards this particular type of contact. The nature of the fourth-density's observance of the free will distortion, while pursuing the seeding of the third-density thought patterns, is material which has already been covered. That which can be offered of the negatively oriented information is offered. It is altered to the extent that the entity receiving such negative information is of positive orientation. Thus many such contacts are of a mixed nature.

Questioner: I'm sorry for getting confused on my question here in not asking it correctly. There is a philosophical point of central importance that I am trying to clear up here. It has to do with the fact that fourth-density negative seems to be aware of the first distortion. They are in a nonveiled condition, and they seem to use this knowledge of the first distortion to maintain the situation that they maintain in contacts with this planet. I am trying to extract their ability to understand the mechanism of the first distortion and the consequences of the veiling process and still remain in a mental configuration of separation on the negative path. I hope that I have made myself clear there. I have had a hard time asking this question.

Ra: I am Ra. The answer may still not satisfy the questioner. We ask that you pursue it until you are satisfied. The fourth-density negative entity has made the choice available to each at third-density harvest. It is aware of the full array of possible methods of viewing the universe of the one Creator and it is convinced that the ignoring and non-use of the green-ray energy center will be the method most efficient in providing harvestability of fourth density. Its operations among those of third density which have not yet made this choice are designed to offer to each the opportunity to consider the self-serving polarity and its possible attractiveness.

Questioner: It seems to me that this is a service-to-others action in offering the possibility of the self-serving path. What is the relative effect of polarization in this action? I don't understand that.

Ra: I am Ra. In your armed bands a large group marauds and pillages successfully. The success of the privates is claimed by the corporals, the success of corporals by sergeants, then lieutenants, captains, majors, and finally the commanding general. Each successful temptation, each successful harvestable entity is a strengthener of the power and polarity of the fourth-density social memory complex which has had this success.

Questioner: If one mind/body/spirit complex is harvested from third density to a fourth-density social memory complex is the total power of the social memory complex before the absorption of this single entity doubled when this entity is absorbed?

Ra: I am Ra. No.

Questioner: The Law of Doubling, then, does not work in this way. How much does the power of the social memory complex increase relative to this single entity that is harvested and absorbed into it?

Ra: I am Ra. If one entity in the social memory complex is responsible for this addition to its being, that mind/body/spirit complex will absorb, in linear fashion, the power contained in the, shall we say, recruit. If a sub-group is responsible, the power is then this sub-group's. Only very rarely is the social memory complex of negative polarity capable of acting totally as one being. The loss of polarity due to this difficulty, to which we have previously referred as of kind of spiritual entropy, is quite large.

Questioner: Then assuming that a single negatively oriented entity is responsible for the recruiting of a

harvested third-density entity and adds its polarity to his negative polarity and power, what type of ability or what type of benefit is this and how is it used by the entity?

Ra: I am Ra. The so-called pecking order is immediately challenged and the entity with increased power exercises that power to control more other-selves and to advance within the social memory complex structure.

Questioner: How is this power measured? How is it obvious that this entity has gained this additional power?

Ra: I am Ra. In some cases there is a kind of battle. This is a battle of wills and the weapons consist of the light that can be formed by each contender. In most cases where the shift of power has been obvious it simply is acknowledged and those seeing benefit from associating with this newly more powerful entity aid it in rising within the structure.

Questioner: Thank you. We noticed a possibility of confusion between the term "mind/body/spirit" and "mind/body/spirit complex" in the last session. Were there a couple of misuses of those terms in shifting one for the other?

Ra: I am Ra. There was an error in transmission. The use of the term "mind/body/spirit" should refer to those entities dwelling in third density prior to the veiling process, the term "mind/body/spirit complex" referring to those entities dwelling in third density after the veiling process. We also discover a failure on our part to supply the term "complex" when speaking of body after the veiling. Please correct these errors. Also, we ask that you keep a vigilant watch over these transmissions for any errors and question without fail as it is our intention to provide as undistorted a series of sound vibration complexes as is possible.

This entity, though far better cleared of distortions towards the pain flares when prepared by those mental vibration complexes you call prayer, is still liable to fluctuation due to its preincarnative body complex distortions and the energizing of them by those of negative polarity.

Questioner: Thank you. We will make the corrections[7]. In the last session you made the

---

[7] The text was corrected before publishing and now reads as it should.

statement that before the veiling, sexual energy transfer was always possible. I would like to know what you meant by "it was always possible" and why it was not always possible after the veiling, just to clear up that point?

Ra: I am Ra. We believe that we grasp your query and will use the analogy in your culture of the battery which lights the flashlight bulb. Two working batteries placed in series always offer the potential of the bulb's illumination. After the veiling, to continue this gross analogy, the two batteries being placed not in series would then offer no possible illumination of the bulb. Many mind/body/spirit complexes after the veiling have, through blockages, done the equivalent of reversing the battery.

Questioner: What was the primary source of the blockages that caused the battery reversal?

Ra: I am Ra. Please query more specifically as to the mind/body/spirits or mind/body/spirit complexes about which you request information.

Questioner: Before the veil there was knowledge of the bulb-lighting technique, shall we say. After the veil some experiments created a bulb lighting; some resulted in no bulb lighting. Other than the fact that information was not available on methods of lighting the bulb, was there some root cause of the experiments that resulted in no bulb lighting?

Ra: I am Ra. This is correct.

Questioner: What was this root cause?

Ra: I am Ra. The root cause of blockage is the lack of the ability to see the other-self as the Creator, or to phrase this differently, the lack of love.

Questioner: In our particular illusion the sexual potential for the male seems to peak somewhere prior to the age twenty and the female's peak is some ten years later. What is the cause of this difference in peaking sexual energy?

Ra: I am Ra. We must make clear distinction between the yellow-ray, third-density, chemical bodily complex and the body complex which is a portion of the mind/body/spirit complex. The male, as you call this polarity, has an extremely active yellow-ray desire at the space/time in its incarnation when its sperm is the most viable and full of the life-giving spermato. Thusly the red ray seeks to

reproduce most thickly at the time when this body is most able to fulfill the red-ray requirements.

The yellow-ray, chemical body complex of the female, as you call this polarity, must needs have a continued and increasing desire for the sexual intercourse for it can only conceive once in one fifteen to eighteen month period, given that it carries the conceived body complex, bears it, and suckles it. This is draining to the physical body of yellow ray. To compensate for this the desire increases so that the yellow-ray body is predisposed to continue in sexual congress, thus fulfilling its red-ray requirement to reproduce as thickly as possible.

The more, shall we say, integral sexuality or polarity of the body complex, which is a portion of the mind/body/spirit complex, does not concern itself with these yellow-ray manifestations but rather follows the ways of the seeking of energy transfer and the furthering of aid and service to others or to the self.

Questioner: In addition, why is the ratio of male to female orgasms so heavily loaded on the side of the male?

Ra: I am Ra. We refer now to the yellow-ray, physical body or, if you will, body complex. At this level the distinction is unimportant. The male orgasm which motivates the sperm forward to meet its ovum is essential for the completion of the red-ray desire to propagate the species. The female orgasm is unnecessary. Again, as mind/body/spirit complexes begin to use the sexual energy transfer to learn, to serve, and to glorify the one infinite Creator the function of the female orgasm becomes more clear.

Questioner: What was this ratio before the veil?

Ra: I am Ra. The ratio of male to female orgasms before the veil was closer to one-to-one by a great deal as the metaphysical value of the female orgasm was clear and without shadow.

Questioner: Is it meaningful to give this ratio in early fourth density and, if so, would you do that?

Ra: I am Ra. In many ways it is quite meaningless to speak of orgasm of male and female in higher densities as the character and nature of orgasm becomes more and more naturally a function of the mind/body/spirit complex as an unit. It may be said that the veil in fourth density is lifted and the choice has been made. In positive polarities true sharing is almost universal. In negative polarities true blockage so that the conqueror obtains orgasm, the conquered almost never, is almost universal. In each case you may see the function of the sexual portion of experience as being a most efficient means of polarization.

Questioner: In our illusion we have physical definitions for possible transfers of energy. We label them as the conversion of potential to kinetic or kinetic to heat and examine this with respect to the increasing entropy. When we speak of sexual energy transfers and other more basic forms of energy I am always at a loss to properly use, you might say, the terms since I am not understanding—and possibly can't understand—the basic form of energy that we speak of. However, I intuit that this is the energy of pure vibration; that is, at the basic level of our illusion, that vibration between the space and time portion of the space/time continuum and yet somehow is transferred into our illusion in a more basic form than that. Could you expand on this area for me, please?

Ra: I am Ra. Yes.

Questioner: Would you do that?

Ra: I am Ra. You are correct in assuming that the energy of which we speak in discussing sexual energy transfers is a form of vibratory bridge between space/time and time/space. Although this distinction is not apart from that which follows, that which follows may shed light upon that basic statement.

Due to the veiling process the energy transferred from male to female is different than that transferred from female to male. Due to the polarity difference of the mind/body/spirit complexes of male and female the male stores physical energy, the female mental and mental/emotional energy. When third-density sexual energy transfer is completed the male will have offered the discharge of physical energy. The female is, thereby, refreshed, having far less physical vitality. At the same time, if you will use this term, the female discharges the efflux of its stored mental and mental/emotional energy, thereby offering inspiration, healing, and blessing to the male which by nature is less vital in this area.

At this time may we ask for one more full query.

Questioner: Why is the male and the female nature different?

Ra: I am Ra. When the veiling process was accomplished, to the male polarity was attracted the Matrix of the Mind and to the female, the Potentiator of the Mind, to the male the Potentiator of the Body, to the female the Matrix of the Body. May we ask if there are any brief queries before we close this working?

Questioner: Is there anything that we can do to make the instrument more comfortable or to improve the contact?

Ra: I am Ra. We shall find the suggested readjustment of the censer helpful. The alignments are good. You have been conscientious, my friends. We leave you now in the love and in the light of the one infinite Creator. Go forth, therefore, rejoicing merrily in the power and in the ineffable peace of the one infinite Creator. Adonai. ☥

L/L RESEARCH

L/L Research is a subsidiary of
Rock Creek Research &
Development Laboratories, Inc.

P.O. Box 5195
Louisville, KY 40255-0195

www.llresearch.org

Rock Creek is a non-profit
corporation dedicated to
discovering and sharing
information which may aid in
the spiritual evolution of
humankind.

ABOUT THE CONTENTS OF THIS TRANSCRIPT: This telepathic channeling has been taken from transcriptions of the weekly study and meditation meetings of the Rock Creek Research & Development Laboratories and L/L Research. It is offered in the hope that it may be useful to you. As the Confederation entities always make a point of saying, please use your discrimination and judgment in assessing this material. If something rings true to you, fine. If something does not resonate, please leave it behind, for neither we nor those of the Confederation would wish to be a stumbling block for any.

CAVEAT: This transcript is being published by L/L Research in a not yet final form. It has, however, been edited and any obvious errors have been corrected. When it is in a final form, this caveat will be removed.

INTENSIVE MEDITATION
MAY 13, 1982

(Carla channeling)

[I am Laitos,] and I greet you, my friends in the love and in the light of our infinite Creator. We thank you for the privilege of having been called to this meeting, for it [is] our special delight to work with those who desire to familiarize themselves with the channeling vibration, and who serve as couriers of a very simple message, a message which has been available to your peoples for many, many of your years, but which in all times and places finds new ways of reaching those whose ears have not yet been opened to the words of love.

Before we begin to work with you, my friends, we would like to say a few words about this service of being a vocal channel, a messenger of love, a voice for those who serve the Creator with all their strength. First we wish to acquaint you with the concept that a messenger is a servant, one who is humble and who bows the knee before those to whom he speaks. A messenger is not involved in the outcome or the result of the message. The responsibility of the messenger is to the source of that message, that it may be given as truly and as well as the messenger has the capability of doing so.

Therefore, in any situation, all are messengers, all speak from a source. All are channels, my friends. You are offering to be a channel to aid the Confederation in the service of the one infinite Creator. [It] differs from these unconscious channelings of your race in that you have a conscious desire to focus your message in such a way that it reflects a deeper source, that you may speak more truly, and that your message may originate within the realms of service to others. This is indeed a very blessed decision, for the desire to serve will open the door to that service.

My friends, there is no question as to your ability to function as channels once your desire has been summoned. We have especially been aware for many weeks that the one known as D was contemplating a closer acquaintance with this service, but until this entity had concluded the decision-making process we felt that it would be an infringement to offer our services.

We would say one more thing before we begin, and ask you to consider this in your meditations. As you serve, you grow, and as you grow, it may seem to you that you have been blessed with more information, more depth of understanding, more realization of that great source of love which is within you, than some others. We ask that when these thoughts come to you, you bless them, and then release and remember instead that each understanding brings with it a responsibility. Each responsibility brings with it an understanding. Therefore, my friends, avoid either praising or not praising your progress. Simply continue to seek.

That service which has been prepared for you will be yours as you take it up moment by moment and day by day.

Again, we are so very happy to be working with you. We shall begin at this time with a period of conditioning concentrated in the area of the head, the face, and the throat. This is to make you aware of the presence of those of Laitos, and to give you a true feeling of our ability to communicate with you. We shall pause for this exercise at this time. I am Laitos.

(Pause)

I am Laitos, and am again with this instrument. We are beginning to blend our vibrations with yours, and would at this time like to work with the one known as S if she would relax. We will be sending one single thought. That is our identification. We ask that this entity to relax, allow her mind to rest undisturbed, and wait for the thought, "I am Laitos." We will repeat this several times in order to assure the one known as S that she is not creating this voice within her own being. I am Laitos.

(Pause)

(Carla channeling)

I am Laitos, and am again with this instrument. We have good contact with this instrument, but we find that the one known as S has some blockage due to some slight indecision about the actual speaking of our words. We shall continue to work with this instrument and return to this instrument after work with the one known as D, that it may consider what it wishes to do at this time. We are most happy to be of service, whether as offerers of the channeling vibration alone, or as offerers of thoughts. We thank the one known as S and would now work with the one known as D.

It would be suggested to the one known as D that quietness and a refraining from analysis be employed so that we may transmit our single thought, "I am Laitos." When the instrument thinks this particular concept, it will seem much like his own thought. That is the nature of our channeling process as we work within a deeper portion of the mind. Therefore, we ask the instrument not to attempt to analyze the source of the concept, but when the thought occurs, speak it without hesitation. We shall repeat the thought several times. We will now transfer to the one known as D. I am Laitos.

(Pause)

(Carla channeling)

We are adjusting our contact with this instrument to provide more comfort and efficiency and shall continue working with this instrument as we move back again to the one known as S, and attempt once more to make our vibrations available to her. We shall again offer the possibility of the simple channeling exercise. We transfer this contact at this time. I am Laitos.

(S channeling)

I am Laitos. I am with this instrument. I am Laitos. I am Laitos.

(Carla channeling)

I am Laitos, and am again with this instrument. It is with great joy that we make contact with this instrument. We realize the rush is a bit of an experience at first, but assure the instrument that the accompanying sensations subside to a far more pleasant configuration as we learn better how to channel the energy that we have been given through the physical vehicle of each instrument. Each instrument is unique and with each instrument we go through a process of adjustment.

We would at this time attempt again to speak through the one known as D in hopes that the adjustments we have been making have been helpful. Again we ask for the instrument to completely relax and to speak what comes into the mind spontaneously. We transfer now. I am Laitos.

(D channeling)

I am Laitos.

(Carla channeling)

I am Laitos, and am again with this instrument. We see that our adjustments have been in the right direction, and we shall continue to endeavor to make this contact more comfortable for the one known as D. Again, we assure the instrument that the experiences and sensations which accompany channeling do not remain at the level of intensity of first contact, for we do attempt to channel our vibrations in a way which enables the instrument to remain comfortable. Also, each instrument becomes more comfortable with the process, and thus a certain amount of what is experienced is dropped as the surprise element, shall we say, of our reality ceases to become a factor.

We are so very happy and pleased to be able to make contact with the one known as D and the one known as S. We are full of love for both instruments, and wish each to know that we shall be with you at any time you wish. We would advise, however, practicing the actual channeling of a vocal nature only in a group with a more experienced channel, for the tuning, as this instrument would call it, is quite important to the quality and content of the message received.

We have begun a journey, my friends. We greet you, and as we leave the shores, we rejoice in the power of that pilgrimage, which we all make together, to love and serve the one infinite Creator.

At this time I would transfer to the one known as Jim. I am Laitos.

(Jim channeling)

I am Laitos, and am now with this instrument, and greet you once again in love and light. At this time we would open this meeting to questions which those present may have on their minds. May we answer any question at this time?

D: Yes. The sensations that I felt I've been feeling for years. Is that possible?

I am Laitos. My brother, your experience with this group in its initial stages enabled you to become familiar with this type of vibration, and to become aware that the process which you have now begun was always possible, for many entities of the Confederation wish to avail themselves of the contacts such as this contact in order to make the philosophy of love and light and unity available to more people on your planet. Therefore, you have at this time tapped the potential which has been available to you since your beginning experience with this group.

May we answer you further, my brother?

D: No, that's fine.

We are most grateful for this opportunity. Is there another question which we might attempt to answer?

D: Yes. I have a question. In practicing …

(Side one of tape ends.)

D: … In practicing this type of thing, should I focus my consciousness or release?

I am Laitos. We would suggest, my brother, that you use whichever method is most helpful to you, for each has its strength and each has its weakness. Your own unique configuration of mind, body and spirit will determine through practice that technique which is most useful. The releasing of the attention so that a blankened focus of mind is achieved allows for the easier perception of the vibration for most entities, but also does allow for the random thought to be equally considered as well. The focused attention does allow for a more precise perception and is usually useful in the later stages of the channeling process. But many instruments find this is helpful at each beginning stage as well.

May we answer you further, my brother?

D: So, when I become accustomed to the conditioning vibrations, the focus will probably be better? Is this what you're saying?

I am Laitos. In general, this is correct, my brother. May we answer you further, my brother?

D: No, that's fine. Thank you.

I am Laitos. We thank you as well. Is there another question at this time?

S: Yes. You were saying that you used the energy in the physical vehicle to channel. Is there a way, the science through meditation, that this energy could be increased and directed?

I am Laitos. My sister, the technique of meditation is that technique which focuses the seeking of an entity so that the seeking might be used for a more refined purpose, in this case, the purpose of the vocal channeling. The refinement or enhancement of this type of focus of energy might be accomplished by any activity which the entity undertakes as a means of expressing the seeking, the desire to know the one Creator. Any activity, therefore, might aid this focus of energy. There are those activities such as meditation which are far more efficient, shall we say, in the focusing of this energy. One might also engage in that known as prayer, or that known as contemplation, or the philosophical discussion on an intellectual basis of those concepts which are felt to be crystallized portions of the understanding of the one Creator. Many are the ways which are available to the seeker to gain leverage, shall we say, in the application of this focus of energy.

May we answer you further, my sister?

S: No, not on that, but I do have another question. It seems that there are a lot of questions inside that I cannot seem to quite [get at.] Is there a reason for this? How can I go about unblocking these? It seems to me that meditation would be the best thing—the only thing—to do. Is this true?

I am Laitos. My sister, again we find another facet of the previous query, and again we would respond by saying that your assumption is correct, that meditation is the most efficient means of discovering those portions of the self which seek to make themselves known to the conscious mind so that the conscious mind might grow further in its grasp of understanding of unity with all that is. You may see these unformed queries in your mind as the seeds of your future growth, and you may see the practice of meditation, contemplation, prayer and the seeking in general as those means whereby the seeds shall receive the water of your attention, which is necessary for them to sprout and to bloom forth into their full glory, for they contain that part of yourself which is yet unborn, and which seeks to become born.

May we answer you further, my sister?

S: No, thank you.

I am Laitos. We thank you, as well. May we answer another question at this time?

Carla: I was surprised at the strength of energy that I felt when each of the new channels began to channel. I thought it was an unusually strong sensation. I wondered if you could comment on it?

I am Laitos. My sister, we would concur with your recognition of the strength of desire that is present this afternoon within this group, for the desire that has been manifested by the new instruments is a desire to be of service to others, and has within each entity had much of what you call time in which to be nourished and has now been manifested in the conscious actions which have been undertaken this day. We are always most honored to be able to participate in this process of the desire to serve finding a means whereby it might be fulfilled, and within this new grouping of instruments we find that desire is quite strong indeed.

May we answer you further, my sister?

Carla: No, thank you.

I am Laitos. May we attempt another answer at this time?

(Pause)

I am Laitos. We have been filled with joy this afternoon as each entity has participated in the process of serving as vocal instruments. We look forward to the continued progress of each new instrument, and assure each that we shall be with each in his and her meditations. A simple request for our presence is all that is necessary. Again, we remind each that the actual attempt to vocalize the thoughts which we send is best carried out within the parameters present, that is, the presence of an experienced instrument, so that tuning might be most helpful. We leave each entity at this time in the love and in the light of the infinite Creator. We thank each. I am Laitos. Adonai, my friends. ☘

L/L RESEARCH

L/L Research is a subsidiary of Rock Creek Research & Development Laboratories, Inc.

P.O. Box 5195
Louisville, KY 40255-0195

www.llresearch.org

Rock Creek is a non-profit corporation dedicated to discovering and sharing information which may aid in the spiritual evolution of humankind.

ABOUT THE CONTENTS OF THIS TRANSCRIPT: This telepathic channeling has been taken from transcriptions of the weekly study and meditation meetings of the Rock Creek Research & Development Laboratories and L/L Research. It is offered in the hope that it may be useful to you. As the Confederation entities always make a point of saying, please use your discrimination and judgment in assessing this material. If something rings true to you, fine. If something does not resonate, please leave it behind, for neither we nor those of the Confederation would wish to be a stumbling block for any.

CAVEAT: This transcript is being published by L/L Research in a not yet final form. It has, however, been edited and any obvious errors have been corrected. When it is in a final form, this caveat will be removed.

SUNDAY MEDITATION
MAY 16, 1982

(C channeling)

I am Hatonn, and I greet you, my brothers and sisters, in the love and light of the one infinite Creator. It is indeed a great privilege to be able to address so many who seek the love/light. It is not often that we have this opportunity, so we extend special greeting to those new to this group, and those who have been associated with us for some time now.

As we have said before, more and more of your peoples are beginning their search, beginning to feel that urge to know the love and the light, as conditions in which you now live begin to intensify, various lessons that each needs to experience as what you refer to as time begins to wind down. Your peoples are beginning to feel what many of them say is an urgency of need to quickly learn all, but we ask you to not rush, not grab and try to cram as if you were studying for one of your school tests. The awareness that you seek is something that develops slowly, but not always evenly. To begin to experience, to feel, you need to stop rushing and begin to take time to sit in quiet meditation, allow yourself to open, to begin to slowly expose your being to the light, to the love. This awareness may at times seem to come in the flash of a moment, but it is never a flash, it is built slowly. We do not simply request that! Though time as you know it may be winding down, you need not rush. Slow down, my friends, allow yourself to experience. Allow yourself to flow. It is not necessary to push or grab.

We would at this time pause for a moment to allow our brothers and sisters of Laitos to pass among you, and allow each the request to feel their conditioning vibrations. You would then resume through another instrument.

(Pause)

(L channeling)

I am Hatonn. I am now with this instrument, and I greet you again, my brothers and sisters, in the love and the light of the infinite Creator. My friends, in your race there is often a tendency to avoid the responsibility for one's own actions or lack of actions. It is frequently heard that an individual or a group is blessed. Those making the statement, not realizing that what they regard as blessings, distributed, perhaps, randomly by some external entity, are in reality the result of the individuals and their efforts. My friends, it may be said in the same manner that many in this group are blessed, in that their efforts find fulfillment, and, because as accomplishments on the spiritual plane are reflected on the physical plane, the fulfillments themselves are readily reflected and quite noticeable to those about them.

My friends, your desires are strong, as are your wills, and this is good. However, do not concern yourselves with the accomplishment of a certain level of attainment, for it is not in this manner that the spirit progresses. In the situation within which you exist, the choice is soon to be upon you which will determine the characteristics of your next incarnation, for the time remaining for your race is relatively brief. It is tempting when faced with this situation to attempt a frenzied effort in the manner referred to by your people as cramming, as if you are aware that the final examination is soon to be undertaken, and desire not to be found wanting.

My friends, this is not the path to development. Do not be frightened by the future. But, also do not be sustained in your efforts by something akin to fear, for this also is a stony ground upon which to attempt growth. Rather, my friends, accept that your drive for attainment, that your will to progress, that your striving to learn will sustain you, will nurture you in whatever incarnation is destined to be yours, and accept joyfully that that life which follows this life will be that which is most fit for your path of learning. Do not let the final examination be your goal, my friends, but rather let the final attainment be your goal.

At this time we would like to attempt to speak a few words through another instrument present, as there is a strong drive—correction—strong desire to be of service in this fashion, and we desire to exercise the instrument. I am Hatonn.

(S channeling)

I am Hatonn, and I greet you in the love and light of the Creator. My friends, we are aware that this instrument is …

(L channeling)

I am Hatonn. I am again with this instrument. We would like to thank the instrument known as S for her efforts in service of communicating our thoughts, and we would congratulate her for the successful transmission thereof. It is always encouraging to us to encounter one who possesses a strong drive for service in this fashion, as there are so very many who desire to hear the message that we attempt to convey, but there are so few who are willing to serve in the fashion of conveying these messages for us. For this reason, as one who would be mute without the service of another to speak for

them, we thank the instrument S, and all others who serve in this fashion for their efforts in service to us.

At this time we will take our leave so that our brothers and sisters of Latwii may perform their service of attempting to answer any questions you might care to offer. Adonai, my brothers and sisters, my loved ones. I am known to you as Hatonn.

(L channeling)

I am Latwii, and I greet you in the love and the light of the infinite Creator. My friends, it is always a pleasure to speak to this group, but it is especially a pleasure when there is such a large audience, for we must admit that there is a facet of our collective character that enjoys the limelight. For this reason we are especially grateful that this group has enabled us to strut our stuff, so to speak. Are there any questions we might attempt to answer?

S: Yes, Latwii. I have a question. This is kind of difficult to phrase. Is it a service to someone or an infringement upon them to force something on them that would help them in the long run, and would be of service to someone else by helping them? I guess what I'm trying to say is, do we have the right to take that decision in our hands, so to speak, or let them work out their catalyst?

I am Latwii, and I am aware of your questions. My sister, you must be aware that there are a number of parameters involved in answering the question as you pose it. For example, the parent in supervising the child exerts their will upon another individual, [and] can be viewed as being involved in service to self or may be viewed as involved in service to another in the same situation. The critical factor becomes the intention with which the action is performed. In a like manner …

(One of the tape recorders stops.)

We will pause in order that our priceless words may be ever maintained for posterity.

(Pause)

I am Latwii, and I am again with this instrument. The most critical factor in all potential situations of this nature is the intent with which the action is performed. That individual who attempts to pressure or manipulate another may do so for a variety of reasons, and although many of the reasons might be quite questionable when viewed from a standpoint of positive polarity, it would be safe to say that from the standpoint of negative polarity there are a larger number of situations with which this could be viewed as right.

In general, we might say that for one who desires to polarize positively, it is best when dealing with a child to be conscious of one's own intentions that one might avoid the potential for negative polarization while attempting to exert a—correction—an influence upon the offspring for the purpose of that individual's benefit. When the parameters no longer include the responsibility of assisting in the acclimatization of the newly returned entity, and involves the interaction of two of which you refer to as adults, it is very difficult to exert one's influence upon another in the manner you describe without a reduction in positive polarity. For this reason, if polarization in the positive direction is your intention, we would strongly suggest avoiding this situation.

May we answer you further?

S: No, thank you.

We thank you. Is there another question?

C: Yes. In our dealings with our fellow beings I'm well aware that we all have our own lessons and problems that we deal with, but many are complicated, or we have to interact with others around us, and in these interactions there are times when a particular individual seems to be of great need, and it's often a hard decision to know whether—as if they come when a sympathetic ear should be given, and when they should just be told to go and work on themselves, and instead of a pat on the back and say it's all right, to tell them that as you see things that they just need to stop seeking sympathy, and start straightening things out for themselves, and I was wondering if you'd just speak for a minute about such a situation.

I am Latwii, and I am aware of your question. My friend, there are many situations that you encounter in your manner of living in which the difficulties encountered by other individuals are readily apparent. If we might paraphrase one of your more renowned predecessors, we would suggest that the poor, those who are lacking in some manner, will be with us always. The question then becomes whether an individual desires to attempt to alleviate another individual's suffering or to recognize that suffering as a portion of a lesson that an individual desires not to

infringe upon. This, as you are well aware, is not an easy decision.

My friends, there is within each of you a portion of that whole which you call the Creator. If you but allow yourselves to listen, my friends, to that small, still voice you will not find that your questions are answered for you, for thus would be the antithesis of your learning. But, rather, you will encounter guidance that will be beneficial to you in your interactions with your brothers and sisters. There are many forms with which you might offer aid to a brother or sister, and in general we would suggest that to avoid infringing upon another's lessons, that the aid offered by yourselves be limited to the form requested by the entity who is suffering.

As you are aware, very often the sufferer requests upon two levels. Verbally, the individual may bewail their fate and desire nothing more than attention, yet the intention which brought them to seek the interaction with yourself often comes from a higher source which drives the individual to one who loves them, to chastise. This is as it should be. For that given with love can only be beneficial. In the situation you describe, my friend, that which you give lovingly, be it the pat on the back or the chastisement, can only be beneficial. Your lesson, however, is the selection of that which, in benefiting the individual most, will perform the best service.

May we answer you further?

C: Well, maybe. In this situation I spent a lot of time watching others deal with the individual of whom I'm speaking, and I noticed the difference in the way the individual interacts with them and how he, the individual, interacts with me, and it seems that the individual comes around more or less to have someone to mirror themselves back, and I find myself often, even before the contact is initiated, running the situation mentally, and more or less setting the situation in my own mind. I feel many times that instead of extending love to this individual by establishing the situation prior to the contact that I am really many times a self seeking to avoid any real meaningful interaction with this individual, so that each time contact is made I run the series of emotions about the situation, one where I'm acting out of love to help this person by mirroring themselves back—more or less by trying to chastise—instead of extending sympathy, and in the same moment I'll turn around and see myself as avoiding any real contact with this individual and more or less drawing into myself instead of extending myself to them. And earlier you spoke of the intent in each situation. Could you speak briefly about these doubts such as that I experience in my interactions with this particular individual?

I am Latwii. My brother, we would preface our remarks with the reminder that we are reticent to speak of individual learning experiences, as we do not wish to have our advice weigh in the balance. However, to speak in general on the subject, we would observe that quite often individuals who seek advice, in reality seek not advice but attention, and will manipulate others to this end. For this reason, the type of interaction which occurs is from their viewpoint not significant. What is significant is the duration and intensity of the interaction, for this is through manipulation an opportunity to exercise control of individuals such as yourselves toward the end of attaining negative polarity.

We do not intend to advise you in this area. We would suggest however that the responsibility for the individual's situation is their own, and that you do not bear even a portion of that load. Therefore, whatever your action be, let it be accomplished with love and the desire for an enlightenment of the interaction.

May we answer you further?

C: No, thank you very much.

As always, we thank you. Is there another question?

K: This thought has come to me several times. We read about sorcery, the evil eye. Some people you just simply can't seem to get along with very well, and I have known a few people who had a way of looking at you with the eyes that was just a little frightening. What is the evil eye? Can you make a comment about that if there is such a thing?

I am Latwii. My sister, it is a common tendency when attempting to exert influence over another individual to concentrate one's visual attention on that individual so as to enable oneself to exert the full strength of the conscious mind on the performance of this task. This serves the purpose both of concentrating the conscious mind and performing the specific ritual which in turn gives added strength to the creative effort of that person who is attempting to dominate or exert influence over another. It is also a common statement on your

planet that the eye is the window to the soul, and we would observe that the examination of another's eye can often be revealing as to the nature of that individual's intentions and polarity, as eye-to-eye contact is beneficial to the transmission [of] information.

May we answer you further?

K: Then, if a mother, for instance, used the eyes in a frightening way to control a child, and if the child accepts this control, would this then be likely to be someone who is negatively polarized? I don't think I made that very clear. Is the mother likely to be negatively polarized if she uses the eye in this way to control the child?

I am Latwii. My sister, it is not significant which instrument—the hand, the eye, the voice—is used in controlling the child, but rather the intention with which the instrument is used. If the parent, for example, sternly reprimands the small child for attempting to play with a sharp instrument, the parent's intention is quite likely to be oriented toward serving the child in this manner. In this situation we would suggest that there is no effort exerted toward dominance, but rather toward enabling the young individual to attain a safe level of independence. Therefore, we would reiterate that it is not the action undertaken, but rather the intention with which the action is undertaken that is significant.

May we answer you further?

K: No, that's fine, thank you.

We thank you. Is there another question?

M: Could you say a few words on the subject of suicide?

I am Latwii. My sister, it is not our intention or our right to stand in judgment over the actions of another entity. For this reason, we would strongly suggest that those present be aware that such an action is, although not positively polarizing in most cases, is an acceptable form of death for those who seek a different avenue of progress. We, being of a positive orientation, regard this as a detrimental action in that, as you are aware, it terminates the possibility of attainment before a number of lessons are offered. It also acts in a less than selfless manner upon the lives of others who had chosen to interact with the now dead individual for the purpose of that individual and their own learning. Again, this, as it exerts control and influences the learning progression of others, can be regarded as beneficial to those whose path lies in the direction of negative orientation. However, for those who seek positive polarization we, in the majority of cases, would strongly suggest avoiding this path.

May we answer you further?

M: No, I think you've answered me very well.

We thank you very much for the compliment, my sister. Is there another question?

R: Yes, I have a question. Latwii, could you tell me from the knowledge that you have to explain the mystery of the triune God?

I am Latwii. I am aware of your question. My sister, because of your own seeking for understanding in this area, we must be very reticent in this discussion, for to provide your learning for you would be a disservice to you that would be beyond our scope of allowed behavior, so to speak. If we might be permitted, however, we would suggest that the Creator exists not only in many forms but in all forms, for that which is not of the Creator does not exist.

The structures that men create in their efforts toward attainment often result in a structured form of Creator that enables the individuals concerned to better strive toward understanding. It may be said quite truthfully that the entity to which you refer as the triune God does exist, but it might be equally accurate to say that the Creator exists in all forms but is limited to no man's concept of a God.

May we answer you further?

R: No. Thank you very much.

We thank you, my sister. Is there another question?

K: Yes, the New Testament says that without the shedding of blood there is no remission of sin. And I have seen that most of my friends are church friends, and I hesitate to have much conversation with them any more for fear I'll offend in some way, and would you speak to that concept about … I have some friends who take that very seriously, that if Jesus had not shed his blood, and they also talk about salvation and so the shedding of blood and lostness and salvation gets pretty mixed up sometimes. Could you speak to that?

I am Latwii. With your permission, my sister, we will attempt to discuss the topics separately as we feel this will be more beneficial to communication. The concept of salvation is unfortunate in that it is broadly misunderstood to be a reference to either a point in time or a situation in which one passes the test with a sufficient grade, so to speak, or a point in time at which another entity performs the necessary actions to rescue another entity, thus enabling them to graduate to their concept of an eternal paradise. We would suggest an examination of this concept, that it might be somewhat limited, and if we might be allowed to submit a more accurate definition we would suggest that salvation might be regarded as a constant process by which the individual heals themselves of that which is in imbalance within themselves. As the individual attains greater spiritual development that individual will also attain greater spiritual perception of those progressively finer and finer imbalances within themselves that require the salve of healing that the individual may become perfected and one with the Creator.

The shedding of blood might be more accurately translated as the flowing of blood, which is a reference to the understanding that the blood acts as a carrier of experience. Just as the individual blood cell in your body might serve not only its physical purpose of delivering oxygen to each individual cell, it also serves the metaphysical purpose of conveying throughout the body the congregate of experiences, that the experiences may be absorbed and maintained by the body as an entirety.

The reference, therefore, is directed toward the fact that the remission of sin, or more correctly, the correction of imbalances, is accomplished through the experiences and their—correction—and the absorption of those experiences and their lessons throughout the entire body of the populace. In this manner the healing of the spiritual body of your planet, the—correction—of imbalances that you might refer to as salvation might be achieved.

May we answer you further?

K: So then, this statement that without the shedding of blood there is no remission of sins is really symbolic of what you have just explained. Is that—that's the way I'm understanding it. Is that correct?

I am Latwii. That is correct, in that the statements to which you refer are directed as advice or exhortation by the individual who originally spoke them, directed [to] those followers who were present as well as those to come, and not a reference to an individual action which had occurred in more than a metaphorical sense.

May we answer you further?

K: No. That helps a lot. Thanks a lot.

We thank you my sister. Is there another question?

R: I have another question. Latwii, when Jesus lived on this Earth and he established a church, my thoughts of what a church is is not what I'm seeing. My experience and concept of church is one that has a lot of power, hierarchical structure. I have found church to imprison and hold people in captivity, and I would like to know if you could comment on what Jesus' concept of church would be and when he said to Peter that, "Thou art Peter and upon this rock I will build my church and the gates of Hell will not prevail against it"?

I am Latwii, and I am aware of your question. The individual to whom you refer as Jesus, that who is known to us as Am Ne Ra, visited your planet for the purpose of assisting those present and to come in their attainments. The church that he sought to establish was not a structure either physical or theological, for those in many cases serve but as distraction and limitation as you are fully aware. The rock upon which the church was to be founded was that of willingness to serve one another, and the willingness to love one another. As you are aware, the statements which preceded the …

We will pause.

(Side one of tape ends.)

(L channeling)

As you are aware, the statements preceding the verbal founding of the church were the questions repeatedly, "Do you love me?" and the exhortation, "Feed my lambs, feed my sheep." Upon these two concepts, love and service, are that church founded. The accomplishment of these two efforts requires no structure. As you are again probably aware, the moment to which you refer took place out of doors and not within the confines of a building or regimented theological society. The social structures that you refer to as churches are not without love or service, and we would not imply that they are without value, however we would suggest that just as the communication that you receive this evening is

not appropriate for all entities on your planet, so also are the teaching and actions of these social structures inappropriate for some who are not benefited by these social structures. We would therefore suggest that that which is an occasion of discomfort, that which produces frustration or dissatisfaction, be avoided if the net result is not beneficial.

May we answer you further?

R: No, thank you.

We thank you, my sister. Is there another question?

M: Yes. I was reading about wanderers and how some of them cannot quite adjust to the third density and if they die in confusion, do they stay in the third density or do they go to their normal place?

I am Latwii. Generally speaking, those entities known as wanderers enter the density no better equipped for the most part than those who [are] originally of that density in that the wanderer, in experiencing the forgetting, is not allowed to draw upon the full resource of experiences. They are in essence playing the odds, so to speak, that their natural tendency toward positive polarization will exert itself, and they will be successful in both contributing to the welfare of those about them and the attainment of sufficient polarization to upon their physical death be presented the option of returning to their original density or progressing to another act of service.

However, the possibility occurs, as whenever one plays the odds, that the odds will not fall in the direction that seems most obvious, and in this situation the wanderer incurs some responsibilities or karmic debts, as you refer to them, that must be discharged, and if this is not accomplished during the first incarnation, additional incarnations may be required to accomplish this end.

May we answer you further?

M: Well, do they eventually go back to their fifth or sixth dimension? I mean density, or do they stay in the third density indefinitely, the same as a third-density person?

I am Latwii. The wanderers who discharge their acts of service without incurring further indebtedness are allowed to return to their original density or to take upon themselves further acts of service which may or may not require reincarnating in that same density on that same planet or reincarnating in that same density on a different planet, as that need exists.

May we answer you further?

M: I meant the ones that die confused. Do they have a choice or must they stay in the same density?

I am Latwii. The distinction between confusion and indebtedness is significant in that confusion does not affect the wanderer's attainment. The wanderer, upon experiencing physical death, once again passes through the veil of forgetting and recovers those forgotten memories. The significant factor is not confusion, but whether a karmic debt has been incurred during that incarnation. If this is the case, the wanderer must discharge the karmic debt before proceeding to his own density or further acts of service. If the wanderer has not incurred such indebtedness, he or she is free to return to the original density or elect to perform further acts of service in lesser densities.

May we answer you further?

M: I think that's enough at this time. Thank you.

We thank you. Is there another question?

A: I have two questions. One is about wanderers you were just speaking of, whether when they are incarnated in the third density, and go through the forgetting, whether or not during that incarnation they can lift the forgetting and do remember some of their experiences. Is that possible?

I am Latwii. I am aware of your question. There are certain situations in which this might occur and those, generally speaking, are based upon the intended acts of service that will be performed by the wanderer as a preincarnate condition for incarnating. For example, a wanderer might incarnate upon your planet, and later in life experience a hypnotic regression that enables the incarnate wanderer to recall certain experiences that occurred on different planets or in different densities. This generally is to serve the purpose of motivating the wanderer to initiate the acts of service previously agreed upon before incarnation. The remembrance in this situation is of a type that is somewhat vague and hazy, thus resulting in a lack of confirmed belief by the wanderer. The wanderer is aware that there is an amount of confusion or perhaps imagination involved in the memories. In this fashion the wanderer is motivated on cue, so to speak, but is

never given what might be called an unfair advantage in that the attainment of polarity accomplished in performing their service would be greatly lessened if the wanderer were operating under conditions of confirmed status as a wanderer. The wanderer therefore must always function in an atmosphere of some doubt so as to attain their own polarization.

Is there another question?

A: On the same lines, is it possible then when dealing with these situations of life given to us that in a meditation it is possible to remember something but not, you know, as if the subconscious remembers, the conscious might remember part of it, but not realize that it was from the past, and then use this to handle the situation. Is that possible?

I am Latwii. The situation you refer to is very possible. It is equally possible, however, that the individual is recovering or remembering a—correction—an experience from a previous life, and this type of remembrance does not define the individual as a wanderer, but simply as one who has incarnated previously.

May we answer you further?

A: This is the other question. I didn't fully understand the last time we spoke as to why you couldn't comment on the question of the circle of light. I was wondering if you could explain it again.

I am Latwii. My sister, to comment upon such a subject would be to add definitive information within a structure that has been determined by entities of your race. For example, we would not take it upon ourselves to discuss the relative values of the various religions on your planet. In like manner, we are reluctant to undertake the discussion of a clearly defined concept in that we are reluctant to imply evaluation of that same concept. If the question were rephrased so as to request information about specific details rather than the overall topic, it might be possible to offer additional information.

May we answer you further?

A: Well, since the topic is something I really know nothing about, I find it very hard to ask detailed questions about it. Let me just ask about the group [that] are part of the circle of light. I believe that everyone is a child of the circle of light, but there are those who are the circle of light. Does that make sense, and if so, say if I'm right or wrong.

I am Latwii. Again my sister, we must apologetically decline to answer. As you are aware, for us to define the spiritual activities or positions, so to speak, of various entities would not be an act of service.

May we answer you further?

A: No, thank you.

We would add, if we might, that meditation or the seeking of information on this subject might be beneficial to one such as yourself.

A: Thanks for that added bit.

We thank you, sister. Is there another question?

J: Yes, Latwii, I'd like to ask a question about the condition known as senility which occurs later in life to some people. Is this an opportunity for continued learning? It seems as if the person is kind of just absent, but is this an opportunity to actually to continue learning and becoming, and could you comment on that?

I am Latwii. That condition which you refer to as senility, generally speaking, is the focusing in the twilight years of physical life of one's attention upon those details which occurred in that life so as to reevaluate with the intent of balancing that which is imbalanced, correcting that which might be corrected, and absorbing in completion those lessons which occurred. It might be likened to the proofreading of a very significant paper before submitting it to the teacher. It is a sort of grace period to allow the individual to put a final polish, so to speak, on the efforts of a lifetime. The fact that the individual is quite unaware frequently of the details that occur in the contemporary setting is simply the result of the fact that the majority of lessons have been completed to whatever extent was possible, and that due to lack of conditions in the present—correction—lessons in the present, the attention of the individual is exerted upon scanning the lessons of a lifetime to glean what there is remaining from them.

May we answer you further?

J: Thank you. That's a beautiful answer. No, thank you.

We thank you. Is there another question?

K: Yes, let me just ask one step further. You mean that during this period of senility that one is reviewing your life, one can make corrections on past mistakes or one can balance the life that has already been lived?

I am Latwii. If we might offer examples, we would suggest that in certain situations the individual who has not forgiven himself or herself for actions taken previously in that incarnation might find it an opportunity to do so. One might also, in reviewing one's experiences, come to the awareness of a lesson which was overlooked but is still available for learning if one were simply to cast one's attention upon those experiences, whether they occurred yesterday or fifty years ago.

May we answer you further?

K: No, thanks. That's fine.

We thank you. Is there another question?

M: In one of the books of [the Law of] One they talk about some wanderers knowing they are wanderers, and others not knowing. Is it an advantage to know it or is it a disadvantage?

I am Latwii. My sister, that is defined by the responsibilities to be undertaken by the wanderer. There are those who are served in their efforts by the awareness of their past. There are others who are best served by ignorance of their past.

May we answer you further?

M: Thank you. That answers the question.

R: I have another question. The one we refer to as Jesus, is he the fullest manifestation of God's love? And also Jesus' relationship with his father, is that more than what our relationship is or can be?

My sister, the fullest manifestation of the Creator is yourself and others such as yourself, for the Creator loves in an infinite manner, and as you and all things are a part of that Creator, He loves all parts of Himself equally, and that is to an infinite degree. The relationship between the one you refer to as Jesus and the Creator was significantly different at the time of his incarnation than the relationships of the majority of the population of your planet and the Creator at that time, in that the entity you call Jesus was willing to allow the love of the Creator to flow unimpeded through him, whereas the majority of entities of your planet at that time would not allow this to occur, but rather blocked the love and light of the Creator. This, sad to say, still occurs, but to a lesser degree on your planet.

The relationship of the one known as Jesus with the Creator is often pictured as the entity Jesus loving the Creator and the Creator singling the entity Jesus out for a special type of love, but we would submit for your examination, my sister, that when the Creator's love for all parts of His creation are infinitely equal, is there the potential for special relationships?

May we answer you further?

R: I have another question. In the process of being and becoming, will one day—will we just be or will we always be becoming? Do you understand?

I am Latwii. My sister, as you grow so also does the Creator. The Creator learns and grows through the interaction of those portions of Himself with one another. This increases the Creator's awareness of Himself and his ability to love Himself, so to speak, in that He further appreciates those component parts, their actions, and their growth.

In answer to your question on that basis, we would suggest that you will always be becoming, but that you will never find yourself at the point of a spiritual exhaustion from constant striving, for as effort toward spiritual striving is exerted, so also does fulfillment become obtained.

May we answer you further?

R: No. Thank you very much.

We thank you for your questions, my sister. Is there another question?

R: I think I do have another question. Are we to become like God?

I am Latwii. My sister, you have never ceased to be like God. May we answer you further?

R: No, thank you.

Is there another question?

K: Yes, and this can be answered yes or no because I know it's getting too long. It seems to me that in the last ten or fifteen years, lots more people that I know believe in reincarnation. Yes or no? I'll take a yes or no.

(Laughter)

M: There go your degrees of freedom!

(Laughter.)

K: What I meant to say, I don't require a long, long answer.

I am Latwii, and, my sister, we thank you for the opportunity of laughter. We would answer your question: Yes.

(Laughter)

We would point out, however, the balance of potentially harvestable souls on your planet is constantly increasing as the point of termination draws nearer and the awareness of this concept is past work, as you might call it, for the majority of these entities, and they find it quite easily finally recognizable.

May we answer you further?

K: No. Thanks for the extra information.

And we thank you, my sister. Is there another question?

J: I have a question about an author named Ayn Rand, who died recently. She wrote books and she maintained a position in which she tried to persuade people that altruism was very bad for them and selfishness was very good for them. Was she an Orion-influenced person or simply a person of extreme negative polarity or just comment briefly on this person.

I am Latwii. My sister, we regret that we are limited in the discussion of such individuals. We would have you understand that to evaluate the individual would be to cast light upon the orientation of the individual's works which are significant in their effect upon the polarization of other people. For this reason we are unable to answer your question.

Is there another question?

J: No. And I realize that I really meant to ask about the significance of the works, but you say that you cannot respond to that, right?

That is correct.

J: Thank you.

We thank you, my sister. Is there another question?

(Pause)

I am Latwii, and we must say that we find the silence deafening. As there are no further questions, we will thank each of you again for the wonderful opportunity of sharing your joy and companionship, and for the opportunity to offer our service as slight as it may be. We bid you adieu for this time. I am known to you as Latwii. ♣

L/L RESEARCH

L/L Research is a subsidiary of
Rock Creek Research &
Development Laboratories, Inc.

P.O. Box 5195
Louisville, KY 40255-0195

www.llresearch.org

Rock Creek is a non-profit
corporation dedicated to
discovering and sharing
information which may aid in
the spiritual evolution of
humankind.

INTENSIVE MEDITATION
MAY 20, 1982

(Unknown channeling)

[I am Laitos.] I greet you, my friends, in the love and the light of our infinite Creator. We thank you for the precious gift of the meditation shared with us. While we work with each of you to deepen the meditative state we would ask you to walk with us a few steps into the light of the infinite Creator. Oh, my friends, even in the brightness of the noon day each mind, each heart, so often walks in shadow. As you walk into the white and limitless light, shed from yourself the shadows of this day. Has there been a harsh word? Take a step and leave it behind, and feel the light grow brighter. Have you felt inadequate to any task? Take a step into the light, and leave that feeling behind. Have you tried to reach out only to find yourselves lacking the right words, too shy to make the right choice? Take another step, my friends, and feel the light grow brighter. Drop away all those things about yourself that seem imbalanced, inadequate, limited. Have you felt helpless? Have you felt proud? You do not need these feelings, my friends, to be a child of the Creator. Remove these garments from your soul. Remove these bindings from your spirit.

As you walk into the fullness of light know that you are one, whole and perfect being. You and all in creation are this being, and without you this being could not exist. To feel yourself wrapped in the love and light of the infinite Creator. And that all else

(inaudible). All who seek may come to His light, but let it not be for comfort only, but as a source of inspiration and strength, that you may emerge from such moments prepared to walk in the remembrance of *(inaudible)*. For there is work for you to do and the means whereby you may do it, and for each entity the work is different. That the light, the love, and the strength are one.

At this time we transfer this contact to the one known as S.

(Pause)

(Unknown channeling)

We have a good contact with this instrument, and we ask only that the instrument speak forth without hesitation or questioning so that she may learn through practicing what our contact feels like. We transfer now. I am Laitos.

(Pause)

(S channeling)

I am Laitos, and I am with this instrument. Before she can *(inaudible)* she must learn to *(inaudible)* and speak words as they are given.

(Pause)

I am Laitos, and I am again with this instrument. If she would speak the words. If she would find it easier to believe that *(inaudible)* the words come from us and not from her. I am Laitos. I will now transfer this contact to another, and I would ask D if he would relax, and accept our vibrations he would find it easy to say the words of our message. I am Laitos.

(Pause)

(Unknown channeling)

I am Laitos and I am now with this instrument. May we express our extreme gratitude at being able to work with the one known as S. And [we] are pleasured at the rapid progress this instrument has made. We have at this time a good contact with the one known as D, but find that this entity is analyzing our concepts. Oh, my brother, the analysis of concepts is all-important to the examination of your moment to moment existence in order that you might find in each experience the love and the light of the Creator, and we applaud you for your ability to use the power of your mind in such a constructive way. It happens that in the service of offering yourself to be a vocal instrument for the Confederation of Planets in the Service of the Infinite Creator this particular gift of the mind is counterproductive due to the fact that our concepts are given to you in a somewhat subconscious manner that is awkward to your subconscious mind as concepts or thoughts not as words. Consequently, they seem to arise out of your own mind and the words come to you which are the clothing of these concepts. This is precisely the same manner in which you do your own conceptualizing and thinking. It is virtually impossible without some experience as a channel to examine for yourself the difference between our thoughts and your own thoughts.

Therefore, as a new channel you are instructed to lay aside the faculty of analysis and allow those thoughts which spontaneously come to you to be spoken without hindrance of any kind by your intellect. You will find that as you speak one thought another will come, and as you speak that thought, another. You will find that if you stop to examine a thought the entire process is halted. Therefore, as we transfer to you again we ask you to keep in mind that a lack of analysis is perhaps the most helpful thing which you could attempt at this time in order to foster our contact with you and our ability to communicate concepts of love with your instrument. I would at

this time transfer to the one known as D. I am Laitos.

(D channeling)

I am Laitos, and am with this instrument. I have been many times in intimate contact and found the way blocked This instrument is not aware of the *(inaudible)* but is so conscious. I am Laitos.

(Unknown channeling)

I am Laitos, and am with this instrument. We would like to say how pleased we are with the progress shown by the one known as D, for the speaking of our concepts without analysis is the first great hurdle, shall we say, that a new instrument must clear before being able to fully partake in the channeling process. It is one which is most difficult for those who have never experienced such type of meditation in their experience of meditation, for most entities as they partake in the meditative state are aware that many thoughts flow through the mind as debris upon the ocean, and think nothing of such thoughts' possible origins. When the channeling process is undertaken there is also seen by the new instrument the beginnings of our contact which appear as the debris of the mind even though configured in our normal greeting which is familiar to each, thereby adding to the conviction of being an instrument that there is nothing particularly special about our contact, nothing to differentiate it from the normal thoughts which proceed through the mind in meditation.

Indeed, our contact is most like your thoughts. This is the way it must be for free will to be maintained. Each part of this process which you have undertaken with rapid progress will require continued refraining from analysis, and the continued willingness to step out on the limb, shall we say, for there shall be no solid proof that this contact is indeed occurring, or such solid proof would be an infringement. Yet each instrument shall in its experience with the channeling process find that certain inner confirmations shall be made available so that the instrument might become more comfortable with the process. This is the most that can be done by any member of the Confederation when working with an instrument who serves as vocal channel, for it is most important that the free will of each entity be maintained.

We would at this time open this meeting to questions if any present might have a question for us. Is there a question at this time?

Questioner: *(Inaudible)* block things out?

I am Laitos. My brother, we find that your experience with the initial contact, a Confederation member has produced within your mind complex at the juncture, shall we say, between the conscious and the unconscious mind a pattern of recognition of this contact which you have been aware of for a long period of what you call time, and which has produced an unconscious or subconscious [shunting] of this contact so that it is not, shall we say, paid attention to. The many experiences which you have with this contact in your past has therefore accustomed your mind to the initial recognition, and since you have made no efforts to vocalize these contacts in the past but have ignored them, shall we say, or simply observed them and let them go their way, this pattern of behavior has reached the level of your unconscious mind, having been given to it by the conscious mind as an automatic response.

May we answer you further, my brother?

Questioner: Yes, is it you all the time that I have felt?

I am Laitos. We of Laitos have been among others of the Confederation, those presences which you have become familiar with throughout your past, as you call it. This is correct, my brother.

May we answer you further?

Questioner: How can I differentiate?

I am Laitos. The process which you are now undertaking is one which will allow you to become sensitized to the differences in the frequency of various Confederation members' contact. This of course takes practice, and must be pursued with a steady desire as any new skill which requires the learning of new patterns of thought and perception.

May we answer you further, my brother?

Questioner: Will experiencing these conditioning vibrations further on other days at these intensive meetings confuse things?

I am Laitos. At the times which you now refer to when conditioning vibrations are sought—and we underline the necessity for their being consciously sought in your meditations—then if you are perceptive and notice their effect upon your being you will be able to increase your ability to recognize the various Confederation members which are making their conditioning vibrations available to you, [and] then you may use meditations such as this meditation to confirm that a certain vibration was being felt.

May we answer you further my brother?

Questioner: Thank you very much.

I am Laitos, and we are most grateful to you. Is there another question that we might answer?

S: Yes, Laitos. I would just like to know if I was channeling your words or mixing some of my thoughts in with them?

I am Laitos. My sister, this question is the first question which most new instruments entertain, and we are quite pleased to note the progress which you and the one known as D have shown is the normal mixture, shall we say, for the new instrument, which is ranging between 60 and 70% of our transmission, the remainder being your own. This is how it should be, for we do not wish to control any instrument to the extent that it does not have a part in the process, for this would infringe upon free will. We are very pleased with the progress which you and the one known as D have shown this evening, and we encourage both new instruments to continue as the beginning as they may.

May we answer you further, my sister?

S: No, thank you.

I am Laitos. Is there another question?

Questioner: Yes, sometimes I seem to get messages that are undistorted and seem clear, and I was wondering if I fabricate those? Not here but at home.

I am Laitos, and, my brother, we find that there is a certain line which we may not cross in responding to this query, for it is messages such as these of which you speak that are most important to each seeker of love and light. May we respond in general by saying that each entity which seeks the love and light of the one Creator opens its being, its channel, shall we say, to the reception of messages from a great variety of beings. This receptivity is then able to make available to the seeker messages from the Confederation, from guides who are located in what you might call the inner planes of this planet's web of energy, and from the deeper levels of the being's own subconscious mind which also plays a most important role in the informing of the conscious mind as the being seeks ever more highly the tuning that will allow the unity with all that is.

It is then for the being who seeks to look at that which has been found, to ponder and meditate upon the meaning of the messages, their origins, and how they might be implemented in the life's activities. Thereby does the seeker find that which is sought. To lay the table out openly, shall we say, and reveal the source and meaning of each message is not that which we wish to do, for that would be a great infringement upon your free will, and [this] is your honor and privilege to pursue as part of your path to seeking.

May we answer you further, my brother?

Questioner: Did we get any conditioned vibrations from any other source?

I am Laitos. There has been present this evening those entities of our brothers and sisters at Hatonn who have been lending their conditioning vibrations to each member in this group. For those of Hatonn are those who, shall we say, are the elder statesmen who serve this group in the normal capacity of the channeling process, and you shall become familiar with their vibrations as well. As this process continues, in a very short time it appears as though each of the new instruments will be available to brothers and sisters of Hatonn for the vocal channeling process. Therefore it has been their honor and privilege to join us this evening in the making ready of each new instrument.

May we answer you further, my brother?

Questioner: *(Inaudible).*

I am Laitos, and we thank you. Is there another question at this time?

Questioner: Laitos, a very beloved friend of mine who is also one of the very best instruments for the Confederation that I have ever heard has virtually stopped channeling. It isn't until I read some of this instrument's transcriptions, and enjoy again the beauty of the channeling, that I realize how much I miss this channeling from this particular instrument. What makes such a beautiful instrument decide to cease offering themselves, and how can I accept it

and be helpful instead of wishing to hear the words again through that particular instrument?

I am Laitos, and, my sister, as you are well aware each instrument in the process of serving as an instrument encounters those opportunities for further seeking and further refining in the channeling process which provide the entity with a choice: the choice of whether to continue the process with the increased demands, shall we say, of inner surrender that are necessary for each transformation or to rest for awhile while the reserves of the inner being are focused in other areas, and are held, shall we say, in limbo in the particular area known as the channeling.

The entity therefore finds that the process of seeking in any direction will be [that] the channeling process, meditation in general, or any service to any other self, requires that there be made and remade and made again the inner dedication to continue refining the self in the fires of personal experience. It may be for some entities this process becomes too intense, and must be for a period laid aside so that there might be a regrouping, shall we say, and a rededication. For the progress that each entity makes is the result of the will to seek and to serve, and the will of each entity which serves in this manner is quite unique.

For one who wishes to hear once again the service of the channeling by an entity which has chosen for the moment to rest is a desire which must take into account the unique nature of each entity and the unique requirements that are made upon the resources which the entity calls the will. To wait until another has become once again available through transformation to provide this service is to recognize that each progresses at the proper rate for their own unique configuration of being. To offer yourself when asked as an advisor or supporter of this process in another is the most one can do. For we cannot, no matter how much we may wish to, help another proceed on his spiritual path faster than his feet can carry the entity.

May we answer you further, my sister?

Questioner: *(Inaudible).*

I am Laitos, and we thank you. Is there another question at this time?

(Pause)

I am Laitos. We are most honored to have been asked to join this group this evening. We thank each of you. Again we remind each new instrument that it is most helpful to request our conditioning in your private meditations but to reserve the actual vocal channeling for meetings such as this one with experienced instruments present. We commend each new instrument on the rapid progress that is being made, and look forward to the continuation of this service to each new instrument, and by each new instrument. We shall now take our leave of this group. We leave you in the love and the light of the one Creator. We are always one in spirit. I am Laitos. Adonai, my friends.

(Unknown channeling)

We are receiving an unspoken question and would like to send a concept to the one who asks at this time *(inaudible).*

(Pause)

I am Latwii. We thank you for your patience. Sometimes it is desirable that privacy be maintained, and this is not a question that we wish to verbalize the answer to. Is there another question at this time?

(Pause)

I am Latwii. My friends, we thank you. We would close through the instrument known as J. I will transfer at this time. I am Latwii.

(J channeling)

I am Latwii, and we would say in closing that the tasks which each of you have set for yourselves are worthy tasks, and we would aid you in every way that is possible for us to do so in the accomplishing of your tasks. Your work will not be easy but you will discover the greatest rewards in serving your brothers and sisters on your planet at this time. Your world has never needed your service more, and it is with this knowledge that you must go forth each in your own way, and be of whatever service you can be. I am known to you as Latwii, and I leave you in the light and love of our infinite Creator. Adonai, my friends. ☙

L/L Research is a subsidiary of
Rock Creek Research &
Development Laboratories, Inc.

P.O. Box 5195
Louisville, KY 40255-0195

L/L RESEARCH

www.llresearch.org

Rock Creek is a non-profit
corporation dedicated to
discovering and sharing
information which may aid in
the spiritual evolution of
humankind.

MONDAY MEDITATION
MAY 23, 1982

(Unknown channeling)

I am Hatonn, and I am now with this instrument. We greet you again in the love and in the light of the one infinite Creator. This indeed lessons to view the blessings in song, in harmony, with all of those present we see to the one divine purpose, see on the planet many people who are living the emotion you call fear. Many have begun to look too far ahead at things which might be, which could be [occurring]. You live in a time when the threat of what you call global destruction appears somewhere, someone, who does that one thing that start the dominoes to fall bringing an end to your world. Others live in the fear that the changes that your planet is undergoing, they fear those events occurring in nature will begin to intensify; the earthquakes, severe storms, volcanoes and other natural disasters as you call them, will sweep over your planet and bring great death and destruction.

All these things, my friends, may happen, they may not. The things that you do now are those things that *(inaudible)* of what you call the future. If one dwells too long on the things that have not yet happened, or even those things that have already passed, one runs the risk of not living the moment that they're in. My friends, each moment offers you choices. Each moment holds the lesson for you to see, to learn from. Each moment provides an opportunity to start the journey to begin seeking the [brightness] of the love and of the light. As you begin you will have an effect on your planet. Small *(inaudible)*, whether you be aware of it or not, it is the combined effects of your peoples which will help to shape the planet's future. In these times many of your planet have begun to journey, have begun to seek the Creator, the love, the light, and it's beginning, it's happening, it's [affecting]. But, as this effect is [pondered], also affecting the planet of those combined energies of those who dwell in a *(inaudible)* of darkness shall [dawn] who love like the same way those who seek to serve the *(inaudible)*.

There is at this time an ever shifting balance between these two effects. We ask that you remain with the moment. Allow yourself to experience, to feel the love and the light, [to allow for time] that you do not rush into the future. But allow yourselves to slowly be in each moment and deal with those things that are in the moment. We are Hatonn. Realize that to be in the moment in your illusion is indeed a difficult task. You've been living constantly bombarded by all the aspects of the world. You are constantly pressured by those who would attempt to sway the thinking but you are always free to examine and for yourself choose that which you do. We hope that you will allow yourself the time to be each love and light, to open yourself in your meditations to the love and the light and allow yourself love.

We would now transfer this contact to another instrument at this time. I am Hatonn.

(Carla channeling)

I am Hatonn, and I am with this instrument. We greet you once again, my friends, in the love and the light of the infinite Creator. We offered the contact to the one known as L but discovered that this instrument was too *(inaudible)* for the present. This is well, for this instrument has some *(inaudible)* and we thank this instrument *(inaudible)*.

We would continue with some thoughts for our subject which has been *(inaudible)* in the eyes of many of you at this time. We are aware, my friends, that you seek not only to know the truths of the one original Thought but also to establish a company with whom you make this pilgrimage *(inaudible)* companions on the way, support upon the journey.

The questions on how to structure a community which is centered in spiritual seeking is one which it is impossible for us to answer, for each group of entities is a unique blend of needs. However, our own community is one based upon just such things and therefore we may offer some thoughts which may aid you. We surely hope that this may be true.

As you sit in community in this domicile this evening, you are experiencing the height of that which community is. The shared experience, a shared ideal, a shared desire. As these means of unity pass and as you discover each other's individual needs, the community who comes as *(inaudible)* as the entities within it. There may be one who needs sympathy, an outstretched hand, there may be another who needs the understanding soul too and the support of that soul to be protection and yet these two entities are seeking the same idea. [All have] the same [privilege] of sharing the same experience. There are some who identify community with those who work closely together. There have been several within this group of companions who have striven to cause this to come about.

This sharing, rightly understood, is greatly helpful. But there is a sharing of periodical community— such as these meetings—which is also extremely helpful. And the structures necessary to offer this community then form the structures necessary to offer a completely common human experience. There is a greater community, the community of those who know that this group sits in circle and

shares the light. And my friends, these entities are *(inaudible)* and they form a community also. Shall we say, a community of *(inaudible)*. They accept with great thankfulness the products of the service which you offer, as you sit in meditation and share your energy in unity that channels such as this one may speak to you; and not only to you but to the larger community. And there is that one last great community without which no [ideal] community is complete and that is those who do not yet know of this community.

To have a structure available for those who wish to know about this community, this is service that aids greatly in a community's polarity towards service to others. It is well that this particular companionship is open to any who wish to attend. It is well that you ask only that simple preparations of reading and studying be accomplished. For there will be those attracted to this group and an entrance to be fashioned to greet them, one as full of friendliness, love and light as the one which greeted each of you.

We have spoken through instruments such as this upon the simple subject of the original Thought for many of your years and in that time many are those who have listened and have gone forth keeping the knowledge of these thoughts within their hearts. This is a great feat, a great bounty to us and it is well when you think of community not to look [at] the unity regardless of time for all those which have sat in this circle of shared experience, shared ideas, and shared seeking. As you seek, as you meditate, become sensitive to your needs, become sensitive to those who share your path at this time.

(A baby is heard crying.)

(Carla channeling)

I am Hatonn, we are sorry for the delay but they will *(inaudible)* an entity close to your group which did not adjust *(inaudible)*.

Become aware of the opportunities for community. Not as you would *(inaudible)* but as your ideals, your visions, and your love show you.

It has been written, my friends, that the kingdom of heaven is within. The community of that kingdom is one of the great blessings of the shared experience *(inaudible)*. Rejoicing *(inaudible)* rejoice in the strangers with whom you may share your love and your light and rejoice most of all because the comfort, the confidence, and the power which supports those who desire to love each other is abundant in every atom of the creation.

I would at this time leave this instrument. I am Hatonn. I leave you as a voice [upon the rooftop] that you must know, my friends, that we are always with you. As all of those who desire to wait and hearken to the call. We leave you in that great companionship, that great community that is yours for eternity. I *(inaudible)* now *(inaudible)* Hatonn. We leave you in the love and in the light of our infinite Creator. Adonai vasu borragus.

(Jim channeling)

I am Latwii, and I greet you all in the love and in the light of the one infinite Creator. We are most honored to be able to join your group this evening. We thank each of you for extending the invitation to us once again, to blend our vibrations with yours. We, as always, offer ourselves in the capacity attempting to answer those queries which have meaning to those requesting information. We would at this time therefore open this meeting to the questions. May we ask for the first question?

Questioner: What is meant in the New Testament, why the statement that if we resist the devil he will [slowly charm us]? And also what is meant by "devil"?

I am Latwii, and am aware of your query, my sister. We believe that this statement has been misstated in that reference in its effect. For it is our understanding, humble and simple though it be, that to resist that known as the devil, to resist any influence considered dark or evil, is to intensify the ability of that influence to make its effect felt upon the one resisting. The concept is based upon the fact that all is one and that those who pursue that path of darkness, or the serving of the self, are also part of that oneness and to resist, or fight against, propose an opposition against such a force is to reinforce that power of separation by reaffirming separation. The forces of darkness obtain their power by separation from and control over others. To resist, in any degree, is to affirm that there is a separation and therefore it is to affirm the base of power of which the forces of the darkness draw their being. Therefore it is more in conformity, shall we say, with the principle of unity to accept all entities that are of a dark or light nature as part of the self, recognizing the one Creator in all. Accepting, forgiving and loving these entities therefore provides the entity

with, what might be called, the shield of light, and does provide that protection which entities may seek in the resistance of that called evil.

The devil, my sister, is simply that dark portion of creation which seeks separation and pursues its path to the Creator by the separation from, and control over, other selves. But this, of course, is a path of limited light for it is not in total agreement with the underlying unity that is the fabric of all creation. And this path must therefore at some point, if it wishes to continue in evolution, join in the path that accepts all, loves all, forgives all, and sees all as the one Creator.

May we answer you further, my sister?

Questioner: Well, just let me see if I've got this clear. So the statement, resist the devil and he will *(inaudible)*. I'm not sure which one it is and he will [flee from you] so that's not really not a good path to follow, is that right?

I am Latwii. It is our suggestion that that path would not prove effective for those who would wish to be protected from the influence of negative forces. This is correct, my sister.

Questioner: Thank you.

I am Latwii, we thank you. Is there another question at this time?

Questioner: Do people who say that rosary and prayer wheels and other prayers for people, do they accomplish something?

I am Latwii, and am aware of your query, my sister. Such entities do indeed accomplish something. That which is wished to be accomplished, the aiding in love and light of another entity is that which is in some degree accomplished by the activities which you have described. The purity of the seeking to be of service and the strength with which the will is turned in this direction are the factors which determine the degree of success of this desire. There are, as you are aware of, many methods by which such service …

(Side one of tape ends.)

(Jim channeling)

… might be rendered, for the entity wishing to undertake such a service needs be most concerned with the will and the purity of the desire. The manner in which this is manifested is of concern only to those entities who wish to make this type of service a more refined and regularized, shall we say, offering of service. Such entities may then wish to employ other techniques.

May we answer you further, my sister?

Questioner: Thank you, you answered me very well.

I am Latwii, we thank you and we are pleased that we have been able to serve. May we ask if there is another question at this time?

Questioner: Yes, Latwii, would a major nuclear confrontation affect existence in other places, or other dimensions, or other worlds [of awareness] or would it be confined to this planet's third density?

I am Latwii, and am aware of your query, my brother. There is a unity, as each of you know, [and] when any portion of that unity is affected by any action, the rest of the unity is also affected, for are not all one? If such an action which you have described and discussed this evening were to be accomplished upon your planet as it has been accomplished elsewhere, even within your own solar system, there would indeed be an effect which would be felt and there would be certain balances that would be, for the moment, awry and would therefore need to be balanced by another action upon the various levels of what you call the creation.

May we answer you further, my brother?

Questioner: Yes, would the Confederation interfere in any way …? We were discussing information from various sources that it would not be allowed to happen. Is that true?

I am Latwii, and am aware of your query, my brother. We of the Confederation of Planets in Service to the Infinite Creator seek to be of service to those entities who call us. We see the creation as one thing, we see needs, we see perfection, we see the Creator knowing Itself in all activities and we see each portion of the Creator pursuing its path in reuniting with the one Creator. Each entity, each portion of the creation, must be allowed to pursue this path within free will insofar as this is possible. We see many possibilities on your planet at this time. Each possibility must be granted the opportunity to be expressed. For those entities now upon your planet have, at this time, many balances which are in the process of becoming complete.

There are, as you are aware, entities from a great number of planets which have found the necessity to repeat this third-density cycle. Many have found this necessity because they have experienced that which is now feared upon your planet—the destruction of the planet. These entities and these actions now are attempting to reach a reconciliation, a balance, if you will. And this activity must be allowed to become completed. Therefore, whatever choices your peoples make as they seek this balance, individually, in community, and in global terms, therefore, must be allowed to find full and free expression and shall be allowed to do so. The stage from which the drama is played is one part of the creation. It has evolved from many sources. Whatever its final curtain *(inaudible)* upon this planet, it shall continue in some manner and continue in its evolution of characters, of scripts, and expression of the one Creator. There is no end to the experience.

May we answer you further, my brother?

Questioner: No, thank you.

I am Latwii, we thank you. Is there another question at this time?

Questioner: Does the presence of entities from other planets which have destroyed themselves increase our chances of this type of thing happening here since they had to balance that experience somehow?

I am Latwii, and am aware of your query my brother. Indeed, this may be so, but it is also true that many of those entities that have experienced this destruction are also desirous now, upon the subconscious levels, to make a reconciliation for this action and it might then be said the possibilities of such an action could also be less. With some entities, their purposes being manipulation and control upon a conscious level, the likelihood then becomes increased; with other entities, who wish to make a balance in the actions—whether on a conscious or unconscious level—then is generated the possibility that such would not occur. But therefore are—we correct this instrument—therefore all possibilities continue as possibilities with some awaiting in favor of one activity at certain times, another activity at other times.

May we answer you further, my brother?

Questioner: No, thank you.

We thank you. Is there another question at this time?

Questioner: Are there any entities upon this planet presently who experienced the demise of Atlantis?

I am Latwii, and, my sister, there are many entities upon this planet which experienced that action. Indeed, almost every entity which was a part of the population of that continent known in your history as Atlantis now resides upon your planet.

May we answer you further, my sister?

Questioner: And I'm assuming they're both of the positive and negative polarity?

I am Latwii. In general, my sister, this is correct, although the greatest portion of your peoples have not yet chosen their polarity but swing back and forth between the two, both upon the conscious and unconscious levels.

May we answer you further, my sister?

Questioner: So then these entities really aren't helping us very much within the crisis we think we're in, is that right?

I am Latwii. May we ask for a more specific naming of the entities referred to?

Questioner: Are there more entities who have chosen the positive polarity than there are who have chosen the negative polarity?

I am Latwii. My sister, this is correct. The number of entities at this time who have chosen the positive polarity is quite small considered in relation to the entire population of your planet. Yet this number far exceeds those entities who have chosen the negative polarity. The entities, however, who have chosen the negative polarity are more to be seen in the positions of power, shall we say, for this is the natural habitat, shall we say, of such a negative polarity.

May we answer you further?

Questioner: Then I'm assuming some of them are rulers today? Or they're at least in government positions of power.

I am Latwii. This is correct, my sister, and to this we would only add that many such entities are not publicly visible, though many are. May we answer you further?

Questioner: No, thank you.

I am Latwii, we are most grateful to you. Is there another question at this time?

Questioner: Could you tell us something about yourself *(inaudible)*?

I am Latwii. As an introduction, may we say that we are most pleased to be asked about our meager existence—meager, shall we say, when compared with the great variety of experiences that your peoples now enjoy upon the surface of your planet. Our existence has become quite simplified for many thousands of your years and even greater spans of years have we been of one mind, shall we say. We of Latwii inhabit that density known to you as the density of light, the density of wisdom, numbering five. We seek the density of unity which will allow us to balance the compassion which we as a social memory complex gained in our experience of the fourth density. With the reason that we are now learning in its fullest extent. This attempt that we make at evolution has been aided greatly by our intense desire to seek the one Creator. For it has been our experience to know a great variety of the paths, shall we say, of evolution. For we of Latwii have *(inaudible)* of those you know of as wanderers to many parts of this galaxy and have become acquainted with a great array of planets, of peoples, and of processes of evolution. All this we have taken into our beings and have learned therefore that the one Creator is that experience of unity which all entities seek.

We of Latwii experience an illusion similar in some ways to your own in that we yet have much catalyst to work with and much experience to complete before our graduation to the next density. Yet our illusion is somewhat more finely constructed than is your own. For it is an illusion that is made of light, as are all illusions, but we are able to form that light at will so that our simple needs might be met by our own actions in a more easily observable fashion. This, of course, is true upon your own planet and within your own density, yet it's not so apparent to the peoples of your planet for they still dwell within the veil of the forgetting. We of Latwii have utilized this veil of forgetting in the third density and now proceed in our evolution at what might be considered a slower pace but a pace in which we are able to see that each part of our illusion is the fabric of our own creation.

We at times exist within what you would call a sun body but, being unable to balance wisdom and love at this time, we are not able to remain in that configuration for an extended period of what you would call time. Our normal environment, shall we say, is within the realms of light and consists of that focus of light which we find a need for in order to learn certain lessons—these lessons having to do with the refinement of wisdom. Therefore, our environment is not what you would call constant. We periodically make forays, shall we say, into other planetary environs such as your own in order to study the configurations of light that are the basis for a certain portion of the evolutionary process of your peoples and other peoples. We are what you might call more scientifically oriented than our brothers and sisters of Hatonn or Laitos who find philosophical explorations more to their liking and nature.

May we answer you further, my sister?

Questioner: Are they in the same density as you are?

I am Latwii. Though we are in the same creation, our density is one density removed from those of Hatonn and Laitos, their density being the fourth density—that of love and understanding.

May we answer you further, my sister?

Questioner: Thank you that was very *(inaudible)*.

I am Latwii. We thank you and are pleased that our chance to, shall we say, strut our stuff has pleased you. May we ask if there is another question at this time?

Questioner: Yes, would you evaluate the accuracy of the channeling that occurs on Friday nights?

I am Latwii, and am aware of your query, my brother. We prefer to make a general statement in this case for it is necessary for entities engaging in this process of refining the channeling process to seek such a refinement as a result of inner revelation. We would say in general that we are most pleased that we have been able to speak at your meetings held upon another evening and in another location as you call it, and are very happy to offer ourselves in this endeavor. We are happy that the entities engaging in this meeting process have asked for our services and that these entities continue to seek whatever stronger desire to know the one Creator.

We assure each this desire shall continue to refine that process which is now taking place.

May we answer you further, my brother?

Questioner: Yes, have you any suggestions to offer for our examination that would possibly lead to a more refined and accurate channeling?

I am Latwii. My brother, again we must speak generally. Each entity which wishes to refine the process of seeking may do so in any number of ways. The most important ingredient is the strengthening of the will and of the desire to seek. We have mentioned this many times. These are the foundation stones, shall we say, upon which the seeking of any entity rests. For as the entity seeks so shall they find, for the seeking is as the magnet which attracts the filings. You are part of one creation; as you seek, you respond. Your greater selves are aware that that portion of yourself which you project as a personality, through its desire thereby seeks greater illumination. Therefore, may we suggest simply the reaffirming of each moment of which you are conscious of your seeking of the desire to seek in ever more pure and ever more positively polarized matters. This is a suggestion which each may find aid in utilizing.

May we answer you further, my brother?

Questioner: I have a question on a different subject. I'm currently experiencing a lesson which involves the decision to whether it is best to communicate or not communicate with another self. I've reached what I feel is the best decision but I would be very interested in any advice that Latwii might be willing to offer on that.

I am Latwii. My brother, we can only advise you to do that which you feel is best to do. For within your own being resides those biases which seek the balance; and to advise an entity to do anything other than that which it wishes to do is to advise an entity to do that which will not aid its evolution as greatly as will its own volition. You cannot make mistakes, my brother. You can learn from all experiences.

May we answer you further, my brother?

Questioner: No, thank you for your answers.

I am Latwii. We thank you as well. Is there another question at this time?

Carla: I had to tie up about three questions that I had more questions about when you finished answering. First was L's question about channeling. I've wondered also what one could do to refine one's channel. Don has always talked about the possibility of what a teacher would call "master classes." That's when teachers teach other teachers. Would this sort of channelers' channeling meditation be of aid to the channels involved in refining the channels of those who desire to take part? Or can you comment?

I am Latwii. My sister, we can indeed comment. Our comment is, yes. May we answer you further?

Carla: Yes, to work on C's question a little bit more. I do understand your idea about not resisting evil because obviously if evil—or the devil if you want to personify it—being a part of yourself since we are the creation—is to be loved and accepted as a part of the self and thereby made non-powerful because it is a part of the self, it is understood, it is forgiven. I could understand that but many is the time when I've talked with someone who has a very specific problem like wanting to stop eating too much or wanting to stop smoking; or my own particular weakness is wanting to stop purchasing garments that I don't need to wear. It does seem to be a simple prayer "resist," will get me through one specific instance. Is there virtue in that limited kind of resistance or am I talking about evil or just the (inaudible) choices?

I am Latwii, and am aware of your query, my sister. There is a significant difference in those activities of which you speak having to do only with the self in relationship to the self and those activities which have to do with the self in relationship to other selves. As an entity seeks to balance its own biases and distortions, there are those activities which are subject to the will, which may be undertaken and prove efficacious in that balancing. It is possible to exercise the will to such an extent that the simple losing of the desire to do those things which are not deemed proper might be accomplished.

When dealing with an other self, on the other hand, it is not deemed proper for one wishing to proceed [on] the path of positive polarity to exercise the will in such a fashion over another entity if this entity has [been] seen to be that of what is called the negative polarity. For to do so is to engage in a battle which is a thought upon the negative entity's turf, shall we say, and is to engage in a contest of wills which will inevitably lead to the depolarizing of the positive entity. It is better for such an entity to not exercise the will in opposition to such an entity but to withdraw from the contest and, within the meditative state, seek to send the negative entity the love and the light which is truly felt for another part of the great self.

May we answer you further, my sister?

Carla: I believe I understand. What you're saying is that, for instance, when Jesus said, "Get thee behind me Satan," he was dramatizing not the reality of the devil but his ability to use his will to decide not to accept a certain temptation and then to pray for those who did persecute, as he did for the forty days before he went to be crucified. His statement then is misleading as it's written in the *Bible* which is basically saying because the emphasis is wrongly placed on the personification which seems to be evil instead of the rule to choose one thing instead of another.

Is this correct? Is this what you're saying?

I am Latwii, my sister. In general, we agree with your summary. We may comment further by suggesting that the entity known as Jesus, when speaking of that concept of negativity called Satan in your holy works, was speaking of those temptations that were being offered it by those forces which wished to depolarize the one known as Jesus so that its work would remain undone. The one known as Jesus, though it accepted fully those forces of negativity or darkness within its heart of being, loved them, forgave them, and had compassion for them, yet did it say to those forces that it wished to pursue another path and that those temptations which were being offered were not acceptable to this entity, though the entities offering them were indeed accepted, loved and cherished. Therefore, the entity known as Jesus was, in refusing these temptations, not opposing those forces of darkness but was loving them in the fullest while at the same time refusing their offerings.

May we answer you further, my sister?

Carla: Not on that subject, that was most helpful, thank you. I wanted to just pursue some questions that were asked about lots of UFO rumor mongering that's been going on—that's about the best I can call it—when the UFO research community, for years and years, ever since I've been involved in these meditations, the big rumor has always been the UFO involvement in what the *Bible* has called the rapture. This rapture business has been going on for the last eighteen hundred or so years and I've always been curious as to what germ of truth it held, the remnant that shall remain and the being taken up, whether it was simply the small harvest at the end of the cycle or what. And I've always figured when UFOs become a part of the scene it was only natural that UFO channels [who] were familiar with the *Bible* would then latch onto the idea of the rapture and figure that it was going to be accomplished by means of the mechanisms of spaceships. I wonder if you could comment on this for our group because I think that in many ways this whole concept has been a very damaging one in that it concerns people and it distracts them from your message. This whole idea of the mechanical salvation by UFOs?

I am Latwii, and I am aware of your query, my sister. We are very pleased to be able to make a comment upon this subject which we also have found to be quite disconcerting. The, shall we say, kernel of truth as we see it within this concept is the fact that there shall be those of the fourth-density vibration who shall greet those entities upon your planet who are harvested into the fourth density of love and compassion. These entities who shall serve as the greeters, the guides, and the teachers from the newly harvested of your planet, are those entities of the similar configuration to the one known as Jesus and shall be those who shall fulfill that known as the Second Coming in one aspect. That is the greeting. These entities stand ready at all times to greet those upon your planet who, in their daily round of activities, in their daily round of activates seek ever more purely the one Creator. Love and light is sent, a direction then possible is offered, and as your planet makes the appropriate passage into that density of love and understanding which it is now entering, these entities shall be those who make ready the passage and who …

(Tape ends.) ❧

L/L RESEARCH

L/L Research is a subsidiary of Rock Creek Research & Development Laboratories, Inc.

P.O. Box 5195
Louisville, KY 40255-0195

www.llresearch.org

Rock Creek is a non-profit corporation dedicated to discovering and sharing information which may aid in the spiritual evolution of humankind.

INTENSIVE MEDITATION
MAY 27, 1982

(Carla channeling)

[I am Laitos,] and I greet you, my friends, in the love and the light of our infinite Creator. We thank you for the great blessing you have offered us in asking us to come and work with those who have gathered here in the name of the Creator, the Source. We attempted for a time before we contacted this instrument to make contact with the one known as S1. We say this in order that this instrument may know those sensations that she was feeling were those of contact. We shall continue for a short period working with each instrument as we speak through this one.

My friends, in these groups in which we concentrate so much upon service, sometimes we of Laitos may stress too much that great pillar of "the life lived in knowledge of [8]," and forget to stress with the most abundant emphasis the joy that permeates the universe of this Creator Whom we serve. Too much we stress responsibilities connected with being a pilgrim and not enough do we share with you the reality of freedom that that service brings, for in each attempt to serve the Creator you have freed yourself from the opinion of a disillusioned illusion, you have removed yourself from a dimly lit, habitually angry and negative set of circumstances which persist despite all the beauties of the creation around you,

and you have with your eyes in your inner selves glimpsed the reality of an infinite merrymaking, an eternal joyousness, the love that is without end.

Because of the medium of speech, we do not seem to you to be constantly joyful, and because of those things which we wish to teach, those skills which we wish to share, we seem bent single-mindedly upon the great responsibilities of service, and it is true, my friends, that those who wish to become shepherds must rise up and take the shepherd's crook, and stand by the sheep in daytime and in dark, in safety and in peril. You do not know when you shall be called upon to channel in your own way. Consequently, we speak frequently on the service that is to be kept in mind. But, my friends, if we could but skip and jump and rejoice among you, laughing and shouting and making merry, for we are drunk on the very joy of the universe! We shall never be able to bring this into your language or your illusion, yet as you meditate, this feeling may come to you at any moment as you touch the Kingdom of the Father and His reality. As we charge you to meditate, to seek the truth, to attempt to be of service, if that is your desire, we invite you also to a grand party. Everyone is there. It is just, my friends, that some do not yet know it.

We would at this time again transfer this contact to the one known as S1. I am Laitos.

---

[8] Carla: The consciously lived life or the reviewed life.

(S1 channeling)

I am Laitos. I am with this instrument. She was afraid to speak before, thinking that it was her own thoughts and not ours she perceived, but this is not true. She was receiving our thoughts, and she will find it easier as she practices. I am Laitos. I will now at this time transfer this contact to the one known as D. I am Laitos.

(S1 channeling)

I am Laitos. I am again with this instrument. The one known as D did not wish this contact at this time. We will therefore, continue to work with him in hopes that he will in the future rely more on his feeling than his analysis. I am Laitos. I will transfer this contact to the one known as Carla. I am Laitos.

(Carla channeling)

I am Laitos, and I greet you again in love and Light. We would say to the one known as D that the brothers of Hatonn are joining us in twisting your arm, and we shall contact you again later [in the evening.]

We would at this time ask your patience as we wish to spend some time familiarizing the one known as M with our vibrations. We would attempt to speak a very, very simple phrase through this instrument in order that the words themselves do not constitute a difficulty, but merely the experience of channeling will be the focus of the experience. We shall repeat, "I am Laitos," and this repetition will seem as though it is the thought of the instrument. Nevertheless, my friends, none of you goes through life say to himself, "I am Laitos." This is not a normal thought.

Consequently, we ask the one known as M to comfort himself, and not to analyze this thought when it appears within his conscious mind. We urge him, rather, simply to speak this thought and then await another thought. We shall repeat this transmission several times in order to familiarize the instrument with the experience of speaking our concepts. We ask that the instrument relax and refrain in the most rigorous manner possible from analysis, as analysis will block our transmissions. We would at this time, with the permission of the instrument, transfer this contact to the one known as M. I am Laitos.

(M channeling)

I am Laitos. I am with this instrument. I am Laitos. I am Laitos. I am Laitos. I am with this instrument. We are glad to speak to this instrument. We have had a desire for a long time to work with the one known as M, but due to his reluctance we have not been able to do so. We are glad to be with this instrument. I am Laitos. I am Laitos. I am Laitos. I am Laitos. I am with this instrument. I am Laitos.

(Carla channeling)

I am Laitos. I am again with this instrument. We are extremely pleased to be able to make such rapid contact with the one known as M. The way has indeed been made plain for us by this instrument's desire. This instrument has an extremely strong ability to concentrate upon the tuning which is so great a part of this type of contact. For this, we are most grateful, also, for it shall greatly accelerate the speed with which we are able to open this particular channel. The one known as Hatonn has been conditioning the one known as D, and at this time we would step aside, that those of Hatonn may offer their greeting through this instrument. We would now leave this instrument temporarily. I am Laitos.

(D channeling)

I am Hatonn. I am with this instrument. It is with great difficulty we use this instrument, due to his concentration. I am Hatonn.

(Carla channeling)

I am Laitos, and I am again with this instrument. At this time we would like to share with the one known as J and the one known as R with the vibrations of ourselves and of Hatonn in order that we may deeply share in consciousness, and more deeply share in meditation. We now pause.

(Pause)

I am Laitos. I am Laitos. We would now exercise the instrument known as S2. It is with great pleasure that we move with this contact to that instrument. I am Laitos.

(S2 channeling)

I am Laitos. I am pleased to greet you once again with this instrument. It has been quite some time since we have been able to speak our words through her. She is most frequently used by those known to you as Hatonn and we are indeed happy that she has all us to be—correction—to speak through her today. We of Laitos are pleased with the progress of all those who are attempting to improve their abilities to speak our words, and are amazed at the speed with which all of you are beginning to, what you might call, grasp our thought out of thin air. It is often confusing to those who are not so experienced to distinguish between those thoughts of the instrument and those thoughts which we are attempting to send them. However, we wish to let you all know that you are correctly receiving these messages which you have been speaking.

We are aware of some of the difficulties you have when we are not able to direct our beam of thought in the precise manner in order to make a clear and concise contact. We are grateful for your patience with us, and we will try to zero in on each of you individually as we become more accustomed to your own particular frequency.

(Side one of tape ends.)

I am Laitos. We apologize for the interruption, but as you know, we were unable to speak momentarily. As we were saying, it is now with a great deal of pleasure that we would turn our contact over to those known to you as Latwii, as we know that there are many of you who are anxious to communicate with Latwii. We would leave you now, my friends, in the love and in the light which we arrived in. I am Laitos.

(Carla channeling)

I am Latwii, and I am surprising this instrument in the love and the light of the infinite Creator, for we wish to speak a few words through her, and also depart greatly from established custom in this group. However, there is one in this group which has been toying with the idea of attempting contact with the Confederation, and this particular instrument has its wiring strung somewhat delicately, and it was a thought, as we counseled together, those of us who serve you at this time, that the one known as A would perhaps best comfortably be able to communicate a few words with our particular vibration, which this instrument feels with a strength akin to the two-by-four, but which to other vibratory complexes is far more comfortable than even that vibration of old, easy-going Hatonn. Therefore, we would at this time ask your patience as we repeat with the one known as A the exercise of the repetition of our simple identity so that the one

known as A may have the experience, if she wishes it, of this channeling. We ask the instrument to relax, and to mentally inform us if there is discomfort, and we shall adjust accordingly our vibration. We would transfer at this time. I am Latwii.

(Pause)

(Carla channeling)

I am Latwii. I am again with this instrument. I fear that we have, shall we say, inadvertently blown some circuitry, even as we were attempting to be most careful not to. Also, the desire to be of service in this particular manner is not yet a fixed star, but rather one which twinkles on and off. So be it.

We thank the one known as A, and may we say to each of you, we shall, along with our brothers and sisters, be with you at any time you may wish to work with our vibrations. We leave this instrument now in order to get on with the answering of any questions that you may have. We leave this instrument in love and light. I am Latwii.

(Jim channeling)

I am Latwii, and greet you all once again in love and light. We are privileged at this time to be able to offer ourselves in the capacity of attempting to answer your queries, for we are aware that there are those questions upon some minds which might prove useful in the answering. May we at this time, therefore, ask if there is a question which we might attempt to answer?

R: Yes, Latwii, I've asked this before, and the answer is bothering me quite a bit. I'm curious, an experience I had—I'm wondering how much damage [there is] or how thwarted my abilities to receive mentally your conditioning, and conditioning in general [is] for the Confederation. Is there any way I can take care of that, or is there any way back, or do I just have to learn to function with whatever I have left of those abilities? Can I undo the damage?

I am Latwii, and am aware of your query, my brother. The experience of which you speak was one which was most intense on those minor circuits of your metaphysical body, shall we say. This body might be likened unto that which is not visible, and is that body which is activated at the times in which you are engaging in what you call meditation, a deep contemplation, and for many entities, the activity of prayer. It has been somewhat affected, shall we say, in its ability to make its manifestations known to your physical vehicle, as you are in the meditative state. The circuitry has suffered some impairment of connections. These connections might be most fruitfully repaired by your conscientious observance of regular periods of meditation, and the continued strengthening of your seeking of the one Creator.

The experience of which you speak has had beneficial effects as well, for it has made various portions of your metaphysical body more finely tuned, shall we say, and able to receive impressions and transmissions from other sources such as the Confederation. This occurred in, shall we say, somewhat of a premature manner, and therefore resulted in that impairment of the transmission of these perceptions to your physical conscious vehicle. But we are of the opinion that your continuation in strengthening your desire to seek the one Creator in the meditative state shall be most beneficial in the repairing of these circuits.

May we answer you further, my brother?

R: No. Thank you.

We thank you. Is there another question at this time?

Carla: We have a couple of friends that do work with crystals, and both of them seem to be good crystal healers to me. Would R's particular metaphysical difficulties be aided by this type of healing?

I am Latwii. My sister, we feel that the type of healing which you have referred to as crystal healing would have at best what might be described as short-term benefits, for the impairment of the circuitry connecting the metaphysical and physical vehicles is that which was made in free will, and which must also be repaired by that same free will. It is, of course, possible that this free will could seek an avenue of expression through a response in a positive nature to this crystal healing of which you speak. This is possible, though our recommendation for the continuation of the meditative periods and the strengthening of the desire to seek are our best suggestion.

May we answer you further, my sister?

Carla: No, thank you, Latwii. I believe I have you pegged. Take two meditations and call me in the morning.

I am Latwii. My sister, we hope you shall not report us for practicing without one of your licenses. May we answer another question at this time?

Questioner: Yes, Latwii. What can you tell me in general, and I won't mind if you're brief, about the benefits of going through hypnotic regression?

I am Latwii, and am aware of your query, my sister. The process of enhancing the memory of previous experiences through that which you have called the hypnotic regression is a process in which information is added unto an entity's conscious mind from those levels of the unconscious which are not normally available to the conscious mind. Therefore, information of this sort is usually of such an unique nature that its use is often not discovered until much of what you call time is passed. This is usually the case unless an entity has quite specific purposes for seeking information from previous incarnations. Most entities are unaware of the most beneficial type of information which could be sought. Therefore, the information which is received is usually not of much use.

Were an entity to look upon that life which is presently being experienced and see in that life those lessons which are being attempted, and attempt to trace those lessons in a previous incarnation so as to see their roots, then it might be possible for the entity to use that information in a more beneficial manner, for each bias which an entity develops during any incarnation shall at some time need to be what you call balanced with its opposite bias. This usually occurs in a future incarnation. Therefore, if one is able to look upon the current incarnation as a balancing effort set in motion by a previous incarnation's gaining of bias, then there might be information of a most helpful nature which could be obtained by using the tools of regressive hypnosis.

May we answer you further, my sister?

Questioner: Might I say, "Aha, that's exactly what I was after." Thank you very much.

I am Latwii. We thank you. Is there another question at this time?

M: Yes, Latwii. In recent months I've read volumes of back issues of meditations and something I've noticed in many of the question and answer periods are some extremely long answers to what sometimes seem as relatively simple questions, and as I read over these, it seems as though the length and some of the things you go into in your answer actually add confusion to the answers. Why are you not more concise more often?

I am Latwii, and am aware of your query, my brother. In responding, we may respond in two ways, hopefully with brevity. Firstly, the question which is asked by any entity has components which often reach into unspoken portions of inquiry. In order to be of the most service to such an entity, we feel a responsibility to speak to these portions which have not been verbalized, but have, shall we say, been tacked on in a nonverbal manner. Often we speak to another portion of the mind complex of the questioner. Secondly, the instrument through which we speak has an effect upon the upon the type of response, and even its length, for some instruments have certain strengths, certain characteristics and means of expressing thoughts. When we present our responses to queries, most often they are in a somewhat seed or crystallized form, not yet at the level of the spoken word. It is therefore up to the instrument to clothe these thoughts in the words considered most appropriate for their transmission. Some instruments feel more inadequacy, shall we say, in able—we correct this instrument—some instruments feel more inadequacy in being able to clothe our thoughts in the most precise words, and therefore use what might be called the shotgun approach on occasion, hoping that by expressing the thought in more than one way that it shall be correctly expressed in its total summation.

May we answer you further?

M: No, Latwii, that makes a lot of sense. I knew you had good reasons all along.

I am Latwii. We thank you, my brother, for your patience and your good humor. We hope that we shall be able to provide each entity with those thoughts which are most coherent and crystallinely pure as we respond to your queries. We realize that we are quite frequently unable to do this to the satisfaction of all present, yet we shall continue in our efforts, for we find great joy in being able to provide this service, even if it is occasionally clothed in more verbiage than the prevailing styles of speech would allow.

May we ask if there is another question at this time?

(Pause)

I am Latwii. We find that we have exhausted the questions, but hopefully have left your minds somewhat more intact. We appreciate the invitation to join this group, and we look forward to each meeting. We are with each of you in your meditations as requested. We remind each that a simple request will bring us in joy. We leave you now in the love and in the light of the one infinite Creator. We are known to you as Latwii. Adonai vasu borragus. ❧

L/L Research is a subsidiary of
Rock Creek Research &
Development Laboratories, Inc.

P.O. Box 5195
Louisville, KY 40255-0195

L/L RESEARCH

www.llresearch.org

Rock Creek is a non-profit
corporation dedicated to
discovering and sharing
information which may aid in
the spiritual evolution of
humankind.

© 2009 L/L RESEARCH

THE LAW OF ONE, BOOK IV, SESSION 88
MAY 29, 1982

Ra: I am Ra. I greet you in the love and in the light of the one infinite Creator. We communicate now.

Questioner: Could you first please give me the condition of the instrument?

Ra: I am Ra. The physical complex energy deficit is considerable at this space/time. There has been also a significant loss of the vital energies. However, these energies are still well within the distortion you may call strength.

Questioner: Of all of the things that you have mentioned before for replenishing these energies, at this particular space/time, which would be most appropriate for the replenishing of both of these energies?

Ra: I am Ra. As you note, there are many factors which contribute to the aiding of the strength distortions and the amelioration of distortions towards weakness in this instrument. We suggest to each that those many things which have been learned be conscientiously applied.

We would single out one physical distortion for discussion. The fourth-density negative minions which visit your group at this time are energizing a somewhat severe complex of imbalances in the manual appendages of this instrument and, to a lesser extent, those distortions of the thoracic region. We suggest care be taken to refrain from any unnecessary use of these appendages. As this

instrument will not appreciate this suggestion we suggest the appropriate discussion.

Questioner: I assume from this that our fifth-density negative companion is still on R and R. Is this correct?

Ra: I am Ra. Your fifth-density companion is not accompanying you at this time. However, it is not resting.

Questioner: Is the censer that we have provided all right? It does go out prior to the end of the session. Would it be better if it did not go out prior to the end of the session?

Ra: I am Ra. The new configuration of the censer is quite helpful to the more subtle patterns of energy surrounding these workings. It would be helpful to have a continuously burning amount of cense. However, the difficulty is in providing this without overpowering this enclosure with the amount of effluvium and physical product of combustion. Having to choose betwixt allowing the censer to finish its burning and having an overabundance of the smoke, we would suggest the former as being more helpful.

Questioner: The instrument has mentioned what she refers to as bleed-through or being aware, during these sessions sometimes, of the communication. Would you comment on this?

Ra: I am Ra. We have the mind/body/spirit complex of the instrument with us. As this entity begins to awaken from the metaphorical crib of experiencing light and activity in our density it is beginning to be aware of the movement of thought. It does not grasp these thoughts any more than your third-density infant may grasp the first words it perceives. The experience should be expected to continue and is an appropriate outgrowth of the nature of these workings and of the method by which this instrument has made itself available to our words.

Questioner: The instrument mentioned a recurrence of the need to go to the bathroom prior to the session. Is this because of the low vital energy?

Ra: I am Ra. It is part of the cause of the lowered vital energy level. This entity has been sustaining a level of the distortion you call pain which few among your peoples experience without significant draining of the energies. Indeed, the stability of the entity is notable. However, the entity has thusly become drained and further has felt other distortions such as those for a variety of experiences accentuated, for this is one means of balancing the inward-looking experience of the physical pain. Due to concern for this entity such activities have been discouraged. This has further drained the entity.

The will to be of service to the Creator through the means of offering itself as instrument in these working, therefore, was given an opportunity for the testing of resolve. This entity used some vital energy to fuel and replenish the will. No physical energy has been used by the instrument, but the vital energies were tapped so that this entity might have the opportunity to once again consciously choose to serve the one infinite Creator.

Questioner: Our publisher requests pictures for the book, The Law of One, that is going to press at this time. Would you comment on the advisability, the benefit, or detriment, magical or otherwise, of us using pictures of this particular setup, the instrument, and the appurtenances in the book?

Ra: I am Ra. The practical advisability of such a project is completely a product of your discrimination. There are magical considerations.

Firstly, if pictures be taken of a working the visual image must needs be that which is; that is, it is well for you to photograph only an actual working and no sham nor substitution of any material. There shall be no distortions which this group can avoid

any more than we would wish distortions in our words.

Secondly, it is inadvisable to photograph the instrument or any portion of the working room while the instrument is in trance. This is a narrow band contact and we wish to keep electrical and electromagnetic energies constant when their presence is necessary and not present at all otherwise.

Questioner: From what you … I'm sorry. Go ahead. If you meant to continue, continue. If not, I'll ask a question.

Ra: I am Ra. We wished to state, thirdly, that once the instrumental *(?)* is aware that the picture-taking will be performed, that during the entire picture-taking, whether before or after the working, the instrument be required to continuously respond to speech, thus assuring that no trance is imminent.

Questioner: From what you have told me, then, I have planned the following: We will, after the session is complete and the instrument has been awakened, and before moving the instrument, have the instrument continually talk to us while I take pictures. In addition to this I will take some other pictures as requested by the publisher. Is this the optimal filling of this requirement?

Ra: I am Ra. Yes. We ask that any photographs tell the truth, that they be dated, and shine with a clarity so that there is no shadow of any but genuine expression which may be offered to those which seek truth. We come as humble messengers of the Law of One, desiring to decrease distortions. We ask that you, who have been our friends, work with any considerations such as above discussed, not with the thought of quickly removing an unimportant detail, but, as in all ways, regard such as another opportunity to, as the adept must, be yourselves and offer that which is in and with you without pretense of any kind.

Questioner: Thank you. I would like to ask you as to the initial production of the tarot, where this concept was first formed and where the tarot was first recorded?

Ra: I am Ra. The concept of the tarot originated within the planetary influence you call Venus.

Questioner: Was the concept given to or devised for a training tool for those inhabiting Venus at that time or was it devised by those of Venus as a training tool for those of Earth?

Ra: I am Ra. The tarot was devised by the third-density population of Venus a great measure of your space/time in your past. As we have noted the third-density experience of those of Venus dealt far more deeply and harmoniously with what you would call relationships with other-selves, sexual energy transfer work, and philosophical or metaphysical research. The product of many, many generations of work upon what we conceived to be the archetypical mind produced the tarot which was used by our peoples as a training aid in developing the magical personality.

Questioner: I'll make a guess that those of Venus of third density who were the initial ones to partially penetrate the veil gleaned information as to the nature of the archetypical mind and the veiling process and from this designed the tarot as a method of teaching others. Is this correct?

Ra: I am Ra. It is so.

Questioner: I will also assume, and I may not be correct, that the present list that I have of twenty-two names of the tarot cards of the Major Arcana are not in exact agreement with Ra's original generation of the tarot. Could you describe the original tarot, first telling me if there were twenty-two archetypes? That must have been the same. Were they the same as the list that I read to you in a previous session or were there differences?

Ra: I am Ra. As we have stated previously, each archetype is a concept complex and may be viewed not only by individuals but by those of the same racial and planetary influences in unique ways. Therefore, it is not informative to reconstruct the rather minor differences in descriptive terms between the tarot used by us and that used by those of Egypt and the spiritual descendants of those first students of this system of study.

The one great breakthrough which was made after our work in third density was done was the proper emphasis given to the Arcanum Number Twenty-Two which we have called The Choice. In our own experience we were aware that such an unifying archetype existed but did not give that archetype the proper complex of concepts in order to most efficaciously use that archetype in order to promote our evolution.

Questioner: I will make this statement as to my understanding of some of the archetypes and let you correct this statement. It seems to me that the Significators of Mind, Body, and Spirit are acted upon in each of these by the catalyst. This produces Experience which then leads to the Transformation and produces the Great Way. This is the same process for the mind, the body, and spirit. The archetypes are just repeated but act in a different way as catalyst because of the differences of mind, body, and spirit and produce a different type of experience for each because of the difference in the three. The Transformation is slightly different. The Great Way is somewhat different but the archetypes are all basically doing the same thing. They are just acting on three different portions of the mind/body/spirit complex so that we can say that in making the Significator a complex basically we have provided a way for Catalyst to create the Transformation more efficiently. Would you correct that statement, please?

Ra: I am Ra. In your statement correctness is so plaited up with tendrils of the most fundamental misunderstanding that correction of your statement is difficult. We shall make comments and from these comments request that you allow a possible realignment of conceptualization to occur.

The archetypical mind is a great and fundamental portion of the mind complex, one of its most basic elements and one of the richest sources of information for the seeker of the one infinite Creator. To attempt to condense the archetypes is to make an erroneous attempt. Each archetype is a significant *ding an sich*, or thing in itself, with its own complex of concepts. While it is informative to survey the relationships of one archetype to another it can be said that this line of inquiry is secondary to the discovery of the purest gestalt or vision or melody which each archetype signifies to both the intellectual and intuitive mind.

The Significators of Mind, Body, and Spirit complexes are complex in and of themselves, and the archetypes of Catalyst, Experience, Transformation, and the Great Way are most fruitfully viewed as independent complexes which have their own melodies with which they may inform the mind of its nature.

We ask that you consider that the archetypical mind informs those thoughts which then may have bearing upon the mind, the body, or the spirit. The archetypes do not have a direct linkage to body or spirit. All must be drawn up through the higher levels of the subconscious mind to the conscious mind and thence they may flee whither they have been bidden to go. When used in a controlled way they are most helpful. Rather than continue beyond the boundaries of your prior statement we would appreciate the opportunity for your requestioning at this time so that we may answer you more precisely.

Questioner: Did Ra use cards similar to the tarot cards for training in third-density?

Ra: I am Ra. No.

Questioner: What did Ra use in third density?

Ra: I am Ra. You are aware in your attempts at magical visualization of the mental configuration of sometimes rather complex visualizations. These are mental and drawn with the mind. Another example well-known in your culture is the visualization, in your mass, of the distortion of the love of the one infinite Creator called Christianity, wherein a small portion of your foodstuffs is seen to be a mentally configured but entirely real man, the man known to you as Jehoshuah or, as you call this entity now, Jesus. It was by this method of sustained visualization over a period of training that we worked with these concepts.

These concepts were occasionally drawn. However, the concept of one visualization per card was not thought of by us.

Questioner: How did the teacher relay information to the student in respect to visualization?

Ra: I am Ra. The process was cabalistic; that is, of the oral tradition of mouth to ear.

Questioner: Then when Ra attempted to teach the Egyptians the concept of the tarot, was the same process used, or a different one.

Ra: I am Ra. The same process was used. However, those which were teach/learners after us first drew these images to the best of their ability within the place of initiation and later began the use of what you call cards bearing these visualizations' representations.

Questioner: Were the Court Arcana and the Minor Arcana a portion of Ra's teachings or was this something that came along later?

Ra: I am Ra. Those cards of which you speak were the product of the influence of those of Chaldea and Sumer.

Questioner: You mentioned earlier that the tarot was a method of divination. Would you explain that?

Ra: I am Ra. We must first divorce the tarot as a method of divination from this Major Arcana as representative of twenty-two archetypes of the archetypical mind.

The value of that which you call astrology is significant when used by those initiated entities which understand, if you will pardon the misnomer, the sometimes intricate considerations of the Law of Confusion. As each planetary influence enters the energy web of your sphere those upon the sphere are moved much as the moon which moves about your sphere moves the waters upon your deeps. Your own nature is water in that you as mind/body/spirit complexes are easily impressed and moved. Indeed, this is the very fiber and nature of your journey and vigil in this density: to not only be moved but to instruct yourself as to the preferred manner of your movement in mind, body, and spirit.

Therefore, as each entity enters the planetary energy web each entity experiences two major planetary influxes, that of the conception, which has to do with the physical, yellow-ray manifestation of the incarnation, and that of the moment you call birth when the breath is first drawn into the body complex of chemical yellow ray. Thus those who know the stars and their configurations and influences are able to see a rather broadly drawn map of the country through which an entity has traveled, is traveling, or may be expected to travel, be it upon the physical, the mental, or the spiritual level. Such an entity will have developed abilities of the initiate which are normally known among your peoples as psychic or paranormal.

When the archetypes are shuffled into the mix of astrologically oriented cards which form the so-called Court Arcana and Minor Arcana these archetypes become magnetized to the psychic impressions of the one working with the cards, and thusly become instruments of a linkage between the practitioner of the astrological determinations and divinations and the one requesting information. Oft times such archetypical representations will appear in such a manner as to have seemingly interesting results, meaningful in configuration to the questioner. In and of themselves, the Major Arcana have no rightful place in divination but, rather, are tools for the further knowledge of the self by the self for the purpose of entering a more profoundly, acutely realized present moment.

Questioner: Ra must have had, shall we say, a lesson plan or course of training for the twenty-two archetypes to be given either to those of third density of Ra or, later on, to those in Egypt. Could you describe this scenario for the training course?

Ra: I am Ra. This shall be the last full query of this working.

We find it more nearly appropriate to discuss our plans in acquainting initiates upon your own planet with this particular version of the archetypes of the archetypical mind. Our first stage was the presentation of the images, one after the other, in the following order: one, eight, fifteen; two, nine, sixteen; three, ten, seventeen; four, eleven, eighteen; five, twelve, nineteen; six, thirteen, twenty; seven, fourteen, twenty-one; twenty-two. In this way the fundamental relationships between mind, body, and spirit could begin to be discovered, for as one sees, for instance, the Matrix of the Mind in comparison to the Matrices of Body and Spirit one may draw certain tentative conclusions.

When, at length, the student had mastered these visualizations and had considered each of the seven classifications of archetype, looking at the relationships between mind, body, and spirit, we then suggested consideration of archetypes in pairs: one and two; three and four; five; six and seven. You may continue in this form for the body and spirit archetypes. You will note that the consideration of the Significator was left unpaired, for the Significator shall be paired with Archetype Twenty-Two.

At the end of this line of inquiry the student was beginning to grasp more and more deeply the qualities and resonances of each archetype. At this point, using various other aids to spiritual evolution, we encouraged the initiate to learn to become each archetype and, most importantly, to know as best as possible within your illusion when the adoption of the archetype's persona would be spiritually or metaphysically helpful.

As you can see, much work was done creatively by each initiate. We have no dogma to offer. Each perceives that which is needful and helpful to the self.

May we ask if there are any brief queries before we leave this working?

Questioner: Is there anything that we can do to improve the contact or to make the instrument more comfortable?

Ra: I am Ra. We, again, ward you concerning the distortions of the instrument's hands. The fourth-density influence upon them could be inconvenient in that, if allowed to proceed without abatement, what you call your surgery shall be almost immediately necessary.

The alignments are good. You have been fastidious. We leave you, my friends, in the love and in the light of the one infinite Creator. Go forth, therefore, rejoicing merrily in the power and in the glorious peace of the one infinite Creator. Adonai. ♣

L/L RESEARCH

L/L Research is a subsidiary of
Rock Creek Research &
Development Laboratories, Inc.

P.O. Box 5195
Louisville, KY 40255-0195

www.llresearch.org

Rock Creek is a non-profit
corporation dedicated to
discovering and sharing
information which may aid in
the spiritual evolution of
humankind.

© 2009 L/L RESEARCH

THE LAW OF ONE, BOOK V, SESSION 88, FRAGMENT 44
MAY 29, 1982

Jim: The gift of a crystal that has been charged by a friend is a very special gift. Apparently, it is also the kind of gift that creates a special connection between the one who gives it and the one who receives it, and because of this connection it would seem that a special care needs to be exercised by both the one who world give and the one who would receive such a crystal as a gift.

Carla: People like myself, who are sensitive to energy flow, often find that they simply cannot ignore certain crystals. I do not wear them at all, having found that their energy can disturb me, make me edgy. In these latter days of crystal technology, it is not surprising that crystals can be seen to have power. It is their magnetization by the people who have them, or give them, that makes them unique beyond their structure's singularity. They need to be handled with care, I think. I have been told many stories of the effects, good and bad, of such magnetized stones. If you receive one, or are drawn to one, be sure to cleanse it in salt water overnight, and then magnetize it for your own use by holding it during meditation and asking silently that it be blessed for service.

Session 88, May 29, 1982

Questioner: Is the small crystal that the instrument uses upon her during the session of any benefit or detriment?

Ra: I am Ra. This crystal is beneficial as long as he who has charged it is functioning in a positively oriented manner.

Questioner: Who charged the crystal?

Ra: I am Ra. This crystal was charged for use by this instrument by the one known as Neil.

Questioner: It would be an abridgment of the first distortion for you to tell us if he is still functioning in a positive manner, would it not?

Ra: I am Ra. We perceive you have replied to your own query. ♣

L/L Research is a subsidiary of
Rock Creek Research &
Development Laboratories, Inc.

P.O. Box 5195
Louisville, KY 40255-0195

L/L RESEARCH

www.llresearch.org

Rock Creek is a non-profit
corporation dedicated to
discovering and sharing
information which may aid in
the spiritual evolution of
humankind.

SUNDAY MEDITATION
MAY 30, 1982

(C channeling)

I am Hatonn, and I am now with this instrument. We greet you, my friends, as always in the love and in the light of the one infinite Creator. It is indeed a privilege tonight to be able to speak a few humble words to those who are new to this group. So often it seems that too few wish to become aware of the love and the light. So, as the time does begin to run short, more and more are trying their many ways to establish a contact with the Creator. There are still many who walk blindly and alone. That is why new ears are opened. We are more than happy to serve in what way we can. We would say, as we have before, that meditation is indeed the most useful tool at your disposal. In the quiet you may hear, you may feel those things which people in their hurried life pass by, give no heed to. Meditation—begin to touch that part of you that seeks, that wishes to stretch out, to experience the love and light.

Those few precious moments in which you allow yourself to open may have more effect than all the deliberate thought, all the logical methods of solving problems. So often people believe that everything may be rationalized, everything fits into those qualifications that they establish to fit the concepts of the solution. By doing so, people limit that which they may reach. We would remind that this is an illusion in which you exist, and this illusion does have its limits. It is for you to become aware that the love and the light of the Creator is infinitely more than your illusion. Through your meditations you may begin to pierce the illusion, to feel, to hear, to truly see the light. It is for you to grow, to learn, to experience. It is for you to choose whether you seek to be of service to others or seek to be of service to self. Your task is the same, to become aware of the light, the love.

We of Hatonn are always ready to aid any who would but request our aid in your meditations. You need but ask. We would at this time pause and allow our brothers and sisters of Laitos to pass among you and allow you to feel their conditioning vibration. If you would but request, they will work with you. We would then transfer this contact to another instrument. I am Hatonn.

(Pause)

(L channeling)

I am Hatonn, and I greet you once again, my brothers and sisters, in the love and the light of the infinite Creator. My friends, the desire for growth is strong among you. It is this desire that has brought you together. It is this desire that will continue to bring yourselves and many others—correction—many other selves into contact with one another as you progress through your illusion that you may achieve through interaction a fuller appreciation of the oneness of creation.

My friends, your illusion is perhaps the most complex facet of your universe. For although what you perceive as stars and planets, galaxies, constellations, all seem to exist in one manner to you, they actually exist in a much simpler form, as does indeed the rest of the universe which surrounds you. Those objects which you would call the manifestation of your God's creation are in complexity quite simple in comparison to that creation of your own within which you often feel as one who is drowning. My friends, realize that your creation is simply an illusion, and that, like the waters, one may elect to submerge oneself or one may simply make use of the waters, the illusion, to the scant degree necessary to accomplish physical survival. It is not necessary to remain submerged, my brothers. The choice is your own, just as the waters of your illusion are your own.

At this time it is our desire to exercise those other instruments present who are willing to perform this service. At this time we will transfer our contact to another instrument. I am Hatonn.

(Carla channeling)

I am now with this instrument, and I greet you once again in the love and the light of the infinite Creator. We are enjoying greatly the unity of this group, and have been attempting to contact each of the new instruments, but have found that each is somewhat reluctant to speak, fearing that the signal from us was not being perceived correctly. Therefore, we shall attempt to give a bit more aid. We would at this time transfer our contact to the one known as S. I am Hatonn.

(S channeling)

I am Hatonn. I am with this instrument, and I greet you once again, my brothers and sisters, in the love and the light of the infinite Creator. My friends, it is indeed wonderful to be able to speak through this instrument this evening and to so many that we love, to send forth our thoughts, but we know that many do not wish to hear. And so, when we are called upon to speak, it is indeed joyous to us. We thank you for this opportunity to speak to you, and wish only to send our vibrations to those who request it. And now we would transfer this contact. I am Hatonn.

(Carla channeling)

I am Hatonn, and am again with this instrument. We are most pleased at the excellent progress by which our channel through the instrument known as S is being opened. Those who wish to be of service are indeed a breed apart, my friends, and we cannot speak our gratitude enough. For it is only through the free will of those who wish to speak of the one original Thought of the infinite Creator that we may fulfill our mission as messengers of that thought of love.

We would at this time speak a few words through the one known as D, if he would relax and mentally request that that portion of the subconscious which governs memory be released and that trust be restored concerning those contents which this instrument has experienced in the past, but doubted. We have good contact with this instrument, but are very appreciative of the difficulties of such a blockage and can only suggest that a mental suggestion to the self and a refraining of analysis will enable a free flowing of our vibrations. We would now transfer to the one known as D. I am Hatonn.

(D channeling)

I am Hatonn, and am with this instrument. The blockages that occur, to adapt, the confusion, and the inability to accept this contact. Progress is being made in the ability to differentiate our thoughts from those that are his own. Will now transfer this contact. I am Hatonn.

(Carla channeling)

I am Hatonn, and am again with this instrument. May we thank the instrument known as D for having the courage to recognize desire and to pursue it despite many doubts and confusions. For who are we, my friends, that we should erase doubts and confusions as to our ability to exist and to speak through instruments? We cannot convince, nor would we wish to, for we come to speak of those things which can only subjectively be accepted or used. We have no proof to offer, and those who seek service by their desire to seek the Creator are taking a step which can never be justified in any intellectual manner as being a certain or sure method of acquiring or offering that which you call knowledge.

Ah, my friends, the mind of men on Earth is a fine and wonderful thing, and through its good graces, many a plan and many a life has been executed.

However, my friends, there is one great disadvantage to the workings of the conscious mind, and that is that even as the conscious mind seeks the truth, it seeks a quantity of truth. The mind finds the idea that there is no quantity of truth quite outrageous. It seems logical, does it not, my friends, that truth should be of a certain kind and of a certain quantity so that by knowing all of the truth one may come to the end of the truth and firsthand know the Creator. For is not the Creator truth, and should know love in its entirety, for is not the truth love?

And yet, my friends, we say to you that the mind of man will not know truth, will not know the Creator, and will not know love. And in our poor estimation, we come as messengers of a quality of thought— never a quantity. We come as messengers of one original Thought that is infinite. We cannot finish learning that unity. We do not know any end to the journey which you have begun. We know only that the journey is good, that the piercing of the illusion is inevitable, and that the desire to pierce that illusion, to find the truth, and to be of service in your own way, shall speed you upon that journey, and cause you to meet many an intimate stranger, and hear many a much needed word.

As you seek and as you desire, my friends, more and more of the illusion will resound with that which beneath the surface may be felt to have a meaning which you may use in your spiritual pilgrimage. It takes courage to come to the end of the intellect and leap forward into a true seeking for the infinite unity of the one original Thought. As you sit in meditation, you are in an extremely appropriate environment in which to seek that thought. We offer ourselves in any way that we may be of aid in your meditations, and through channels such as this one, and we thank each of you for your desire and the courage with which you pursue it.

We would at this time wish to close our message and would transfer this contact to the one known as M. We apologize for having offered to this instrument some, shall we say, interesting sensations as we are acclimating ourselves to the particular vibratory complex of this instrument. We believe we have adjusted appropriately at this time. If there is still discomfort, may we ask that the instrument known as M mentally request further adjustment. We would transfer at this time. I am Hatonn.

(M channeling)

I am Hatonn. I am with this instrument. We are pleased to be here with this instrument, and will close so that those of you that have questions can ask them of our brothers of Latwii. We are always happy to be among you, my friends. It is for only a short time, it seems, that we can be with you, but a joyous time for us, my brothers. We leave you now in the love and the light of the infinite Creator. I am Hatonn.

(Jim channeling)

I am Latwii, and I greet you, my friends, in the love and in the light of the one infinite Creator. It is a great honor to be asked to join your group this evening, and as always, it is our privilege to offer ourselves in the attempt to answer those queries which you have brought with you. Is there a question at this time?

Carla: I have a question, Latwii. It's from R, who couldn't be here this evening. He called and has a question that is very important to him right now. He's not the same person that he was when he began coming to this group and yet in his daily life, the work that he does as a disc jockey is based upon his ability to act out a persona which, up until he came to this group, matched his true personality. Now he has experienced a good many transformations and has a great desire to be of service in more ways than are available to a rock and roll disc jockey. He wishes to be able in his life to have some outward and visible signs of his inward and spiritual gifts, but he doesn't know how to bring them through into his daily life, and especially into his work …

(Side one of tape ends.)

Carla: … He would pretty much like to hear any comments that you might be able to make regarding this situation in his life.

I am Latwii, and am aware of this query, my sister. It is indeed a dilemma for each entity upon your planet who seeks the one Creator within the illusion within which the entity moves, for the Creator seems to be most difficult to pursue and to find. And yet, there is the finding in stages for each pilgrim, and with the joy of the awakening to another truth comes the responsibility of putting that truth into motion in the life, in the daily round of activities in which the entity finds itself. If this is not done, then the progress remains without movement and the seeking loses its drive. When the entity of which you speak began this particular portion of its seeking, its desire was quite strong and has resulted in that transformation of which you have spoken. Now the entity finds that the truth which is becoming more apparent within its inner being must needs be manifested without as well. To such an entity we might say that to seek to make this truth known to those about it is not only a noble effort, and one which requires courage, but is one which must be done with some finesse, shall we say. For to take that truth which has been dearly won and to lay it out for others plain, without their seeking for it, is not to provide the service which is possible. To be of the greatest service and to remain true to those gems of truth which have been found within requires of the entity a discernment to match the desire to be of service.

As you well know, we cannot speak specifically as to what this entity must do, for to do so would be to infringe upon this entity's free will. The choice must remain with the pilgrim. But, might we suggest in general those things which could be of use to any entity in such a situation. The seeking, my friends, began within. Within the states of meditation, the outer self comes to know and to blend with the greater self that lies within. It is also within these states of meditation that the path which now needs be traveled shall be revealed unto the inner eye. There is the tendency for seekers who have undergone transformations of any kind to become, shall we say, somewhat of in a panic as to how to manifest that truth and that transformation. Quite often it is forgotten how it was achieved.

May we say firstly that to continue the seeking in meditation is most important. Also to be encouraged is the contemplation of the possibilities which present themselves to such an entity within the frame of its daily round of activities. Each entity has been placed by its own choice in those situations which shall allow it the greatest expression of its own being and the truth which shines through it. Therefore, let the entity look upon that situation in which it has placed itself to see what new means of expression might be created for the sharing of the truth of the love and light of the one Creator which the entity wishes to offer. There is no problem without solution to this entity. May we simply suggest that its continued seeking in meditation, in contemplation, and in experimentation in its daily

round of activities shall provide those solutions to the problems which now beset it.

May we answer you further, my sister?

Carla: No. I thank you for R. I ask that you be with him, as I know he would ask, in the coming days as he works on this problem.

I am Latwii. We are with each when requested. May we ask if there is another question at this time?

C: Yes, I have a couple. When I began channeling, it was that I would see a flash of color as I started. The color I saw was green. The last few times I've channeled, the color has changed. More of a purplish color. Can you tell me anything about why I'm seeing something different or if it is anything at all?

I am Latwii, and am aware of your query, my brother. The channeling process, as you have called it, and as you are aware, is quite unique to each entity. As an entity offers itself as an instrument, there shall be those times wherein the tuning of the entity shall be of such and such a nature because of the concerns which the entity is attempting to work upon in balancing its own being. Therefore, when the conditioning vibration is offered to such an entity there is the necessity of blending the vibration with the entity's own unique configuration.

As you know, each of your energy centers are composed of an individual color. Those concerns which you are undertaking, therefore, are associated with these energy centers and the corresponding colors. As we blend our vibrations with any instrument, and this is true for each member of the Confederation, we must make an attempt to blend our vibration so that a match is made. Often this blending shall be visible to the entity's inner eye. The changing colors, therefore, my brother, are simply your changing concerns reflected in your own unique vibrations.

May we answer you further, my brother?

C: Yes, on another question, again dealing with channeling. In the beginning as I began to receive concepts, it seemed like I also was able to pick up words to help express them. As I have begun to channel more and have received more practice at it, it now seems that I get the concepts, and I feel I understand, but I feel now that I don't pick up any words with the concept. And I've been undergoing some fears that due to limits of my particular vocabulary that I'm not fully or totally accurately expressing the concept that I've received. Can you give me any idea of how accurately I am relaying these concepts?

I am Latwii, and am aware of your query, my brother. With new instruments it is most usually the practice to exercise more of that that you know as control so that each word is provided in order that the concept be expressed. As the instrument progresses in this process, the concepts are provided in more of a whole manner, and the instrument is therefore left more free to interpret these concepts. This is a natural progression of the channeling process of this nature, that is, the telepathic vocal contact. In your case, you have become able to discern the concepts with a great enough degree of accuracy to be able to choose your own descriptive terminology for them. As with all transitions, as we said previously, there comes the fear, shall we say, as to how to utilize the new information or ability. If at any time you should wish to return to the technique of perceiving the words in a more concrete manner, this may be accomplished with a simple request mentally. We appreciate your concern and assure you that your progress has been most rapid and accurate.

May we answer you further, my brother?

C: Thank you. That was very reassuring. I would ask one more question, again on a similar subject. I was wondering if you could speak a few words on the state of being we call depressed. It's something that seems to be very prevalent at this time.

I am Latwii, and am aware of your query, my brother. Entities upon your planet experience the depressed qualities of being when they have recognized within themselves, perhaps at a subconscious level, that they are not taking advantage of those opportunities for learning the lessons for which they incarnated, and therefore feel a drawing within the self so that the self might examine more carefully the purpose for the incarnation, and the lessons which are being presented to the self. This state of depressing the awareness within the being hopefully then, with guidance from others, will result in a new direction being chosen, and a new desire to proceed in that direction.

May we answer you further, my brother?

C: It seems that more and more who experience depression never really come out. People in such a state have turned to suicide, various other methods of totally escaping from the illusion. How may one best aid someone, who has gone to such an extreme, to stay?

I am Latwii, and am aware of your query, my brother. The aid that might be given to such an entity is an aid which can only point in the direction of the inward search. Each entity making that journey inward, whatever the motivation, shall find two paths, either of which might be chosen. There is that path that leads toward the light. This path looks at all which surround it—correction—looks at all which surrounds the entity as an opportunity to grow in understanding, and to use the illusion as a tool for evolution, and this path requires a certain maturity, as you are aware. It is a path frequently not chosen.

The other path which an entity discovers within is that path which you have called the escape. The escape from the illusion, the escape from the lessons, the escape from the ability to respond to the challenge. To aid an entity who has chosen this path most efficiently, we might suggest the recounting of those times within the past of your own being in which you have encountered the difficulties, and share your point of view as to how these difficulties aided your own growth. By providing an example or a pattern, if you will, to such an entity, you might once again allow the entity to see some glimmer of light, and to turn its feet to another path.

May we answer you further, my brother?

C: No. Thank you very much.

We thank you. Is there another question at this time?

J: Some people tend to block out believing in meditations and so on. How come most people tend to do this?

I am Latwii, and am aware your query, my sister. Each entity has complete free will as to how it shall seek the one Creator. Each entity therefore chooses those methods which seem most useful to it. Some of what you might call errors are occasionally made and other paths or methods then chosen. But it is necessary, my sister, that each entity be allowed the total free will choice as to how it shall seek, or if it shall seek the one Creator. It is necessary to understand that each entity is quite unique. It is this uniqueness that gives your illusion and your Creator the richest experience possible, for if all entities sought in the same way, then the variety, the richness, the depth of experience would be greatly reduced.

May we answer you further, my sister?

J: Why must we always choose between one thing and another, instead of all going on one path?

I am Latwii, and am aware of your query, my sister. To the best of our understanding, that which you know as the creation of the one Creator exists so that the one Creator might know Itself in as many ways as possible. Therefore, to each of Its portions has It given free will that choices might always be made in free will as to how to know the one Creator and how the one Creator might then know Itself. Never forget, my sister, that though the illusion which you inhabit seems to provide an infinite array of paths, all lead to the one Creator.

May we answer you further, my sister?

J: No, thank you very much.

I am Latwii. We are most grateful to you. Is there another question at this time?

M: I have one for my mother. Looking at your probability vortices, what are the chances of the Falkland situation expanding beyond its present scope?

I am Latwii, and am aware of your query, my brother. We perceive many possibilities with this particular situation. It is not possible to give you an accurate percentage for each, for there are many forces in motion at this time, and their choices are many and each choice therefore affects the possible outcome, and each choice affects other choices so that we might humbly say that all possibilities are viable at this time.

May we answer you further, my brother?

M: No, Latwii, thanks anyway.

I am Latwii. We thank you. Is there another question at this time?

D: I have a couple of questions, Latwii. First, it is my understanding that each of the members of the Confederation who work with the people on Earth have a particular area of responsibility of attention. Is this correct?

I am Latwii, and am aware of your query, my brother. Each Confederation entity has certain skills. It is these skills that determine where the services might be offered, and not the entities, the situations or the areas which determine the responsibility.

May we answer you further, my brother?

D: Yes. What are the skills of the entity, Oxal, that are brought into play when that entity is working with people on Earth?

I am Latwii, and am aware of your query, my brother. Our brothers and sisters of Oxal have a particular penchant for seeing and sharing the infinite perfection within all creation so that the entities which are contacted by Oxal might gain a greater insight into the workings of the one Creator. The entities of Oxal have chosen to offer their services to entities who wish to gain that which is known as wisdom in a balancing action with that known as love.

May we answer you further, my brother?

D: Yes. To what would you attribute the fact that the Friday Night group and this group are so seldom contacted by the entity, Oxal?

I am Latwii and am aware of your query, my brother. The entities of Oxal, as we have mentioned, have the service of wisdom in great purity to offer. Wisdom is, to our best understanding, the ability to see each entity, each situation, and each thought within your illusion as absolutely perfect and in no need of alteration of any kind. The ability to see each situation in this light is to some entities somewhat of a cold approach to your illusion and its needs, for those entities which gather in this group are greatly distorted towards compassion and understanding, that vibration known to you as love. The love vibration sees all creation as one thing, but sees the many portions of the Creator in various states of need of service, and within this understanding and compassion and love, then, is generated the desire to serve and alleviate what is seen as pain, sorrow, sickness, ignorance.

These same conditions, seen through the eyes of wisdom, are revealed as being the perfect situation for the entities inhabiting them to learn the lessons which they incarnated to learn. This group perceives the need for love at this time upon your planet, and seeks therefore the offerings of those entities of

Hatonn and Laitos and of our service in the answering of queries.

May we answer you further, my brother?

D: Yes, on a different, more personal subject. For about the last week, I've been experiencing some pains in the right half of my brain, and I have an amount of tenderness in an area surrounding my right eye. I don't recall doing anything to produce either of these effects. Could you explain to me what the causative agent is?

I am Latwii, and am aware of your query, my brother. We are afraid that we must invoke the great Law of Confusion so that we do not infringe upon your free will as you attempt to pursue that path which you have freely chosen. We can only suggest, as always in these cases, that inward meditation is that path which will reveal unto you the roots and the fruits of this affliction.

May we answer you further, my brother?

D: Yes. I don't want to try to browbeat you into giving me information, but could you answer this question, or perhaps I should say, would you evaluate the statement that I am on some level causing this myself for some reason?

I am Latwii, and am aware of your query, my brother. As all are one, this is quite true. May we answer you further, my brother?

D: No, and I commend you on your slickness. Thank you very much.

I am Latwii. We hope that we have not become too slippery. May we ask if there is another question at this time?

K: Yes. I was at a funeral this afternoon, and where is this entity now?

I am Latwii, and am aware of your query, my sister. When an entity passes from that which you call the incarnation and goes through that door known as death, there is a certain period in which the entity is somewhat, shall we say, disoriented, in that it is aware that its consciousness has continued, but its environment has greatly changed. At this time, the entity then begins a series of questions which resonate to the depths of its being, and cause those guides and angelic presences which watch over it to join it in whatever fashion it will allow itself to perceive them. The entity's conscious recognition of these guides and presences will allow it to utilize their service so that it might begin the review of the life which has just been completed. When this review has been accomplished, then there is the placement of the entity by its own choosing within the proper configuration of illusion, shall we say, until another attempt or incarnation is made to learn those lessons which it has agreed to undertake with the aid of its guides and higher self. The time spent in the condition of the confusion is entirely dependent upon the entity's grasp of this process, and its desire to seek a clearer understanding of its functioning. There may be a time, as you call it, required in healing certain imbalances and actions that were obtained in the preceding incarnation. This time is also dependent upon the nature and degree of the imbalances obtained.

May we answer you further, my sister?

K: Do I understand that the greater preparation we have made before death, and the better understanding we have before death helps in this period of disorientation? Is it possible for us to be prepared in such a way that the disorientation …

(Tape ends.) ❧

L/L Research is a subsidiary of
Rock Creek Research &
Development Laboratories, Inc.

P.O. Box 5195
Louisville, KY 40255-0195

L/L RESEARCH

www.llresearch.org

Rock Creek is a non-profit
corporation dedicated to
discovering and sharing
information which may aid in
the spiritual evolution of
humankind.

SENIOR CITIZENS INTENSIVE MEDITATION
JUNE 6, 1982

(Carla channeling)

[I am Hatonn,] and I greet you, my friends, in the love and the light of the one infinite Creator. We have observed your group with some humor as we attempted to speak through each of you, for each was unwilling to be an instrument due to the concern that the channeling would not be enough advanced for an advanced group. My friends, do not take yourselves too seriously. A carpenter may learn to drive a nail with ten blows, then six, then three, and then two, but he is still making a floor. When you were beginners, my friends, you were making a floor, a foundation of communication between the messengers that surround your planet and those upon the surface of your planet who have a desire at this time to seek beyond the illusion that this planet's culture offers. When you had gained some experience, you continued building that floor, and now you seek to become better carpenters. But, my friends, you are still attempting the same task. The message will forever be that which is designed by the Creator, to be made available to those within your density for the purpose of encouraging their seeking.

In order to improve the ability to drive the nail, we shall begin a story through this instrument and rather than finish it through one instrument, we shall several times change our instrument, and through several, tell one story.

My friends, there was once a great kingdom beneath the sea. Beneath the green waters and the sand lay golden doors. And some beings there were who under enchantment could enter that majestic world. In this world, my friends, there was no aging. There was no work. There was no ugliness or lack of any kind. All were beautiful. Each meal was a banquet, the only drawback being that the entities of this enchanted land could eat nothing.

We shall now transfer this contact. I am Hatonn.

(C channeling)

All was laid for the people. That which others could taste, select from, was denied. People found that though all was theirs, save this one thing, could not find contentment or peace for they could not have this one pleasure. Those who had lived within the kingdom for some time tried to ignore this thing. They went about their lives with one part missing. But for some, that which they did not know became ever heavier on their minds.

We now transfer.

(L channeling)

The people reacted to their difficulty in many ways. Some chose to respond in anger, choosing at first to blame one another for their deprivation. Others chose to feel within themselves antagonism toward the deprivation itself, and sought to destroy all that was associated with the untouchable, the unattainable. Others elected to attempt to forget that which they seemed unable to control. It became an accepted practice as time passed among these people, to ignore that which lay before their eyes, to pretend that it never had existed, and to belittle any reference on the subject as mythical, as childish fairy tale, as something absurdly illogical. "For if it were true," they said, "would we not all see it?"

We shall now transfer our contact.

(Jim channeling)

Years passed. Generations grew to maturity, died, and left to their children many stories of the forbidden and mythical prohibition. Entities soon came to feel a great confusion concerning this almost forgotten tale of the great banquet set before their ancestors which could not be had. And then there arose from time to time among these people a few entities who spoke of having some knowledge of this food. Their speakings were largely ignored. Some, however, felt a type of kinship for what was spoken, perhaps because they had retained childish ways, said many. Yet, did some knowledge continue to grow, and word spread on occasion that there was indeed such a banquet, and indeed were means known to some for partaking in its plenty.

We will now transfer.

(Don channeling)

After much persuasion, one of these who knew of the means of partaking of the banquet was able to bring others to the appointed place where such a banquet was said to have been many, many years past. To the great surprise of all present, magically a banquet appeared. One reached eagerly for the delicious food, but as he touched it, it vanished. One who said he knew the means for taking of this reached out and picked a piece of fruit from the table, held it in his hand, and gave it to the one that so eagerly reached for the vanished fruit. Amazed, he ate it.

I will now transfer this contact.

(Carla channeling)

This entity, tasting the delicious fruit, took the example of the first and offered food to another, and that third offered it to a fourth, and so on until each at the table, in feeding each other instead of themselves, was satisfied. For no food had ever been so delicious, so luscious, and so delectable.

My friends, those who seek dive in deep waters, and very quickly a golden door is opened unto them. All about the seeker who is in meditation there is glamour, there is nothing but beauty. In meditation, the seeker can look, can explore, can walk the universe, and every activity is wonderful. But, my friends, as the seeker does this, he has not yet found the fruits of his seeking.

I will now transfer this contact.

(C channeling)

Each who finds himself beginning to reach the table soon finds that as an entity, they are not alone. As each gets closer, we find that to truly reach forward, they need to share that which has been found. Each does so in their own manner. Each who has received will find the giving is indeed more fulfilling.

We will now transfer.

(L channeling)

My friends, each of you by now is aware of the fact that your own craving for spiritual sustenance cannot be satisfied by yourself alone. Each of you has chosen a path upon which your own sustenance is derived from the sustaining of others, that your own growth occurs as a result of the efforts of others. Consider for a moment, my friends, that structure which you call a pyramid. It is composed of a number of massive, powerful, unyielding blocks of stone, each of which to the observer is quite impressive, but each of which, my friends, is but form without function when standing alone. For it is only when each stands upon the shoulders of his other selves that the form is produced through which their purpose may be accomplished, through which their service may be performed. My friends, be aware that your sustenance comes to you as a result of your efforts to assist and sustain your brothers as they grow and change. Each of you must perform his or her tasks without the expectation of receiving the fruits thereof, for the fruits of service belong to another, and the fruits of their service, my brothers, will belong to you.

We will now transfer our contact.

(Jim channeling)

Your journey as seekers is indeed one which must be pursued in solitude within the deepest portions of your being, and as you travel this path you shall find that there is a greater responsibility which shall be necessary for you to assume in the sharing of the fruits which you find on that inward journey. The seeker cannot be aided in such a manner that work is done for it. Yet, as it travels this path and removes the distortions which separate it from understanding, there must needs be a sharing of this growing fruitfulness, else the path shall not be able to be continued. For this path, though traveled in solitude, is one which unites the seeker with all, and the reflection and manifestation of this unity then requires the seeker to go out into that world which is hungry and naked, sick and poor, to point out the direction to sustenance, clothing for the soul, and the support of Creator to Creator.

We shall now transfer this contact.

(Carla channeling)

In the world of the meditative journey, my friends, it is so entrancing that it is like some siren beckoning sailors from their course. It can be pursued endlessly, and all experiences are good. Never forget, my friends, the one thing that is missing in that kingdom beneath the waters of your illusion in the enchanted land where the illusion gives way to the first view of reality. That one thing, my friends, is the creation. To reach for it is to lose it. If you reach in solitude, to offer it to another is to manifest it, and in the world of manifestation does the enchantment become food and drink of the spirit.

May we thank you for having this opportunity to work through each of you. We leave you in the love and the light of our infinite Creator. I am Hatonn. Adonai, my friends. Adonai. ☥

L/L Research is a subsidiary of
Rock Creek Research &
Development Laboratories, Inc.

P.O. Box 5195
Louisville, KY 40255-0195

L/L RESEARCH

www.llresearch.org

Rock Creek is a non-profit
corporation dedicated to
discovering and sharing
information which may aid in
the spiritual evolution of
humankind.

THE LAW OF ONE, BOOK IV, SESSION 89
JUNE 9, 1982

Ra: I am Ra. I greet you in the love and in the light of the one infinite Creator. We communicate now.

Questioner: Could you first please give me the condition of the instrument?

Ra: I am Ra. It is as previously stated.

Questioner: I have two questions, the first of which is: during the last intensive meditation here the instrument experienced very strong conditioning from an entity which did not identify itself and which did not leave when she asked it to. Would you tell us what was occurring then?

Ra: I am Ra. We find the instrument to have been given the opportunity to become a channel for a previously known friend. This entity was not able to answer the questioning of spirits in the name of Christ as is this instrument's distortion of the means of differentiating betwixt those of positive and those of negative orientation. Therefore, after some resistance, the entity found the need to take its leave.

Questioner: Was this particular entity the fifth-density visitor that we have had quite often previously?

Ra: I am Ra. This is correct.

Questioner: Is he back with us at this time?

Ra: I am Ra. No. The attempt to speak was due to the vigilant eye of the minions of this entity which noted what one may call a surge of natural telepathic ability upon the part of the instrument. This ability is cyclical, of the eighteen-diurnal period cycle, as we have mentioned aforetimes. Thusly, this entity determined to attempt another means of access to the instrument by free will.

Questioner: Was this what I would refer to as an increased ability to receive telepathically over a broader range of basic frequencies so as to include not only the Confederation but also this entity?

Ra: I am Ra. This is incorrect. The high point of the cycle sharpens the ability to pick up the signal but does not change the basic nature of the carrier wave. Shall we say, there is greater power in the receiving antennae.

Questioner: This question may be meaningless but would a fifth-density entity of the Confederation who was positively polarized transmit on the same frequency as our negatively polarized fifth-density companion?

Ra: I am Ra. This is correct and is the reason that the questioning of all contacts is welcomed by the Confederation of Planets in the Service of the Infinite Creator.

Questioner: Question two: *(name)* has also felt some conditioning which was unbidden while channeling Latwii recently and in his personal meditations. Could you also tell us what occurred in these cases?

Ra: I am Ra. The entity which has been companion has a vibratory frequency but a small amount lesser than that of the social memory complex known as

Latwii. Also, Latwii is the primary Comforter of the Confederation for entities seeking at the vibratory complex level of the one known as *(name)*. Therefore, this same companion has been attempting the contact of this instrument also, although this instrument would have great difficulty in distinguishing the actual contact due to the lack of experience of your companion at this type of service. Nevertheless, it is well that this instrument also choose some manner of the challenging of contacts.

Questioner: How many of our years ago was Ra's third density ended?

Ra: I am Ra. The calculations necessary for establishing this point are difficult since so much of what you call time is taken up before and after third density as you see the progress of time from your vantage point. We may say in general that the time of our enjoyment of the choice-making was approximately 2.6 million of your sun-years in your past. However—we correct this instrument. Your term is billion, 2.6 billion of your years in your past. However, this time, as you call it, is not meaningful for our intervening space/time has been experienced in a manner quite unlike your third-density experience of space/time.

Questioner: It appears that the end of Ra's third density coincided with the beginning of this planet's second density. Is that correct?

Ra: I am Ra. This is roughly correct.

Questioner: Did the planet Venus become a fourth-density planet at that time?

Ra: I am Ra. This is so.

Questioner: Did it later, then, become a fifth-density planet?

Ra: I am Ra. It later became a fourth/fifth-density planet; then, later a fifth-density planet for a large measure of your time. Both fourth and fifth-density experiences were possible upon the planetary influence of what you call Venus.

Questioner: What is its density at present?

Ra: I am Ra. Its core vibrational frequency is sixth density. However we, as a social memory complex have elected to leave that influence. Therefore, the beings inhabiting this planetary influence at this space/time are fifth-density entities. The planet may be considered a fifth/sixth-density planet.

Questioner: What was your reason for leaving?

Ra: I am Ra. We wished to be of service.

Questioner: I have here a deck of twenty-two tarot cards which have been copied, according to information we have, from the walls of the large pyramid at Giza. If necessary we can duplicate these cards in the book which we are preparing. I would ask Ra if these cards represent an exact replica of that which is in the Great Pyramid?

Ra: I am Ra. The resemblance is substantial.

Questioner: In other words, you might say that these were better than 95% correct as far as representing what is on the walls of the Great Pyramid?

Ra: I am Ra. Yes.

Questioner: The way that I understand this, then, Ra gave these archetypical concepts to the priests of Egypt who then drew them upon the walls of one of the chambers of the Great Pyramid. What was the technique of transmission of this information to the priests? At this time was Ra walking the surface among the Egyptians, or was this done through some form of channeling?

Ra: I am Ra. This was done partially through old teachings and partially through visions.

Questioner: Then at this particular time Ra had long since vacated the planet as far as walking among the Egyptians. Is this correct?

Ra: I am Ra. Yes.

Questioner: I would like to question Ra on each of these cards in order to better understand the archetypes. Is this agreeable?

Ra: I am Ra. As we have previously stated, these archetypical concept complexes are a tool for learn/teaching. Thusly, if we were to offer information that were not a response to observations of the student we would be infringing upon the free will of the learn/teacher by being teach/learner and learn/teacher at once.

Questioner: You stated that Ra used the tarot to develop the magical personality. Was this done to mentally become the essence of each archetype and in this way develop the magical personality?

Ra: I am Ra. This is incorrect. The clothing one's self within the archetype is an advanced practice of the adept which has long studied this archetypical system. The concept complexes which together are intended to represent the architecture of a significant and rich portion of the mind are intended to be studied as individual concept complexes as Matrix, Potentiator, etc., in viewing mind/body/spirit connections and in pairs with some concentration upon the polarity of the male and the female. If these are studied there comes the moment when the deep threnodies and joyful ditties of the deep mind can successfully be brought forward to intensify, articulate, and heighten some aspect of the magical personality.

Questioner: You stated that each archetype is a concept complex. Would you please define what you mean by that statement?

Ra: I am Ra. Upon the face of it such a definition is without merit, being circular. A concept complex is a complex of concepts just as a molecule is a complex structure made up of more than one type of energy nexus or atom. Each atom within a molecule is its unique identity and, by some means, can be removed from the molecule. The molecule of water can, by chemical means, be caused to separate into hydrogen and oxygen. Separately they cannot be construed to equal water. When formed in the molecular structure which exemplifies water the two are irrefragably water.

Just in this way each archetype has within it several root atoms of organizational being. Separately the overall structure of the complex cannot be seen. Together the concept complex is irrefragably one thing. However, just as it is most useful in grasping the potentials in your physical systems of the constituted nature of water, so in grasping the nature of an archetype it is useful to have a sense of its component concepts.

Questioner: In Archetype One, represented by tarot card number one, the Matrix of the Mind seems to have four basic parts to the complex. Looking at the card we have, first and most obvious, the Magician and what seems to be an approaching star. A stork or similar bird seems to be in a cage. On top of the cage seems to be something that seems to be very difficult at (?) discern. Am I in any way correct in this analysis?

Ra: I am Ra. You are competent at viewing pictures. You have not yet grasped the nature of the Matrix of the Mind as fully as is reliably possible upon contemplation. We would note that the representations drawn by priests were somewhat distorted by acquaintance with and dependence upon the astrologically based teachings of the Chaldees.

Questioner: When Ra originally trained or taught the Egyptians about the tarot did Ra act as teach/learners to a degree that Ra became learn/teachers?

Ra: I am Ra. This distortion we were spared.

Questioner: Then could you tell me what information you gave to the Egyptian priests who first were contacted or taught with respect to the first archetype? Is this possible for you to do within the limits of the first distortion?

Ra: I am Ra. It is possible. Our first step, as we have said, was to present the descriptions in verbal form of three images: one, eight, fifteen; then the questions were asked: "What do you feel that a bird might represent?" "What do you feel that a wand might represent?" "What do you feel that the male represents?" and so forth until those studying were working upon a system whereby the images used became evocative of a system of concepts. This is slow work when done for the first time.

We may note, with sympathy, that you undoubtedly feel choked by the opposite difficulty, that of a great mass of observation upon this system, all of which has some merit as each student will experience the archetypical mind and its structure in an unique way useful to that student. We suggest that one or more of this group do that which we have suggested in order that we may, without infringement, offer observations on this interesting subject which may be of further aid to those inquiring in this area.

We would note at this time that the instrument is having almost continuous pain flares. Therefore, we ask that each of the support group be especially aware of any misinformation in order that we may correct any distortions of information the soonest possible.

Questioner: Now as I understand it, what you suggest as far as the tarot goes is to study the writings that we have available and from those formulate questions. Is this correct?

Ra: I am Ra. No.

Questioner: I'm sorry that I didn't understand exactly what you meant with respect to this. Would it be appropriate then for me to answer the questions with what I think is the meaning of the three items that you spoke of for Card Number One and then Card Eight, etc.? Is this what you mean?

Ra: I am Ra. This is very close to our meaning. It was our intention to suggest that one or more of you go through the plan of study which we have suggested. The queries having to do with the archetypes as found in the tarot after this point may take the form of observing what seem to be the characteristics of each archetype, relationships between mind, body, and spiritual archetypes of the same ranking such as Matrix, or archetypes as seen in relationship to polarity, especially when observed in the pairings.

Any observations made by a student which have fulfilled the considerations will receive our comment in return. Our great avoidance of interpreting, for the first time, for the learn/teacher various elements of a picture upon a piece of pasteboard is involved both with the Law of Confusion and with the difficulties of the distortions of the pictures upon the pasteboard. Therefore, we may suggest a conscientious review of that which we have already given concerning this subject as opposed to the major reliance being either upon any rendition of the archetype pictures or any system which has been arranged as a means of studying these pictures.

Questioner: All right; I'll have to do that. Ra stated that a major breakthrough was made when proper emphasis was put on Arcanum Twenty-Two. This didn't happen until Ra had completed third density. I assume from this that Ra, being polarized positively, probably had some of the same difficulty that occurred prior to the veil in that the negative polarity was not appreciated. That's a guess. Is this correct?

Ra: I am Ra. In one way it is precisely correct. Our harvest was overwhelmingly positive and our appreciation of those which were negative was relatively uninformed. However, we were intending to suggest that in the use of the system known to you as the tarot for advancing the spiritual evolution of the self a proper understanding, if we may use this misnomer, of Archetype Twenty-Two is greatly helpful in sharpening the basic view of the

Significator of Mind, Body, and Spirit and, further, throws into starker relief the Transformation and Great Way of Mind, Body, and Spirit complexes.

Questioner: Were some of Ra's population negatively harvested at the end of Ra's third density?

Ra: I am Ra. We had no negative harvest as such although there had been two entities which had harvested themselves during the third density in the negative or service-to-self path. There were, however, those upon the planetary surface during third density whose vibratory patterns were in the negative range but were not harvestable.

Questioner: What was Ra's average total population incarnate on Venus in third density?

Ra: I am Ra. We were a small population which dwelt upon what you would consider difficult conditions. Our harvest was approximately 6 million 500 thousand mind/body/spirit complexes. There were approximately 32 million mind/body/spirit complexes repeating third density elsewhere.

Questioner: What was the attitude prior to harvest of those harvestable entities of Ra with respect to those who were obviously unharvestable?

Ra: I am Ra. Those of us which had the gift of polarity felt deep compassion for those who seemed to dwell in darkness. This description is most apt as ours was a harshly bright planet in the physical sense. There was every attempt made to reach out with whatever seemed to be needed. However, those upon the positive path have the comfort of companions and we of Ra spent a great deal of our attention upon the possibilities of achieving spiritual or metaphysical adepthood or work in indigo ray through the means of relationships with other-selves. Consequently, the compassion for those in darkness was balanced by the appreciation of the light.

Questioner: Would Ra have the same attitude toward the unharvestable entities or would it be different at this nexus than at the time of harvest from the third density?

Ra: I am Ra. Not substantially. To those who wish to sleep we could only offer those comforts designed for the sleeping. Service is only possible to the extent it is requested. We were ready to serve in whatever way we could. This still seems satisfactory as a means of dealing with other-selves in third density. It is our feeling that to be each entity which one attempts to serve is to simplify the grasp of what service is necessary or possible.

Questioner: What techniques did the two negatively harvested entities use for negative polarization upon such a positively polarized planet?

Ra: I am Ra. The technique of control over others and domination unto the physical death was used in both cases. Upon a planetary influence much unused to slaughter these entities were able to polarize by this means. Upon your third-density environment at the time of your experiencing such entities would merely be considered, shall we say, ruthless despots which waged the holy war.

Questioner: Did these two entities evolve from the second density of the planet Venus along with the rest of the population of Venus that became Ra from second density to third?

Ra: I am Ra. No.

Questioner: What was the origin of the two entities of which you speak?

Ra: I am Ra. These entities were Wanderers from early positive fifth density.

Questioner: And though they had already evolved through a positive fourth density they, shall we say, switched polarity in the reincarnating in third density. Is this correct?

Ra: I am Ra. This is correct.

Questioner: What was the catalyst for their change?

Ra: I am Ra. In our peoples there was what may be considered, from the viewpoint of wisdom, an overabundance of love. These entities looked at those still in darkness and saw that those of a neutral or somewhat negative viewpoint found such harmony, shall we say, sickening. The Wanderers felt that a more wisdom-oriented way of seeking love could be more appealing to those in darkness.

First one entity began its work. Quickly the second found the first. These entities had agreed to serve together and so they did, glorifying the one Creator, but not as they intended. About them were soon gathered those who found it easy to believe that a series of specific knowledges and wisdoms would advance one towards the Creator. The end of this was the graduation into fourth-density negative of the Wanderers, which had much power of personality, and some small deepening of the negatively polarized element of those not polarizing positively. There was no negative harvest as such.

Questioner: What was the reason for the wandering of these two Wanderers, and were they male and female?

Ra: I am Ra. All Wanderers come to be of assistance in serving the Creator, each in its own way. The Wanderers of which we have been speaking were indeed incarnated male and female as this is by far the most efficient system of partnership.

Questioner: As a wild guess, one of these entities wouldn't be the one who has been our companion here for some time would it?

Ra: I am Ra. No.

Questioner: Then from what you say I am guessing that these Wanderers returned or wandered to Ra's third density possibly to seed greater wisdom in what they saw as an overabundance of compassion in the Ra culture. Is this correct?

Ra: I am Ra. This is incorrect in the sense that before incarnation it was the desire of these Wanderers only to aid in service to others. The query has correctness when seen from the viewpoint of the Wanderers within that incarnation.

Questioner: I just can't understand why they would think that a planet that was doing as well as the population of Venus was doing as far as I can tell would need Wanderers in order to help with the harvest. Was this at an early point in Ra's third density?

Ra: I am Ra. It was in the second cycle of 25,000 years. We had a harvest of six out of thirty, to speak roughly, of millions of mind/body/spirit complexes, less than 20%. Wanderers are always drawn to whatever percentage has not yet polarized, and come when there is a call. There was a call from those which were not positively polarized as such but which sought to be positively polarized and sought wisdom, feeling the compassion of other-selves upon Venus as complacent or pitying towards other-selves.

Questioner: What was the attitude of these two entities after they graduated into-fourth density negative and, the veil being removed, realized that they had switched polarities?

Ra: I am Ra. They were disconcerted.

Questioner: Then did they continue striving to polarize negatively for a fifth-density harvest in the negative sense or did they do something else?

Ra: I am Ra. They worked with the fourth-density negative for some period until, within this framework, the previously learned patterns of the self had been recaptured and the polarity was, with great effort, reversed. There was a great deal of fourth-density positive work then to be retraced.

Questioner: How is Ra aware of this information? By what means does Ra know the precise orientation of these two entities in fourth-density negative, etc?

Ra: I am Ra. These entities joined Ra in fourth-density positive for a portion of the cycle which we experienced.

Questioner: I assume, then, that they came in late. Is this correct?

Ra: I am Ra. Yes.

Questioner: I didn't mean to get so far off the track of my original direction, but I think that some of these excursions are enlightening and will help in understanding the basic mechanisms that we are so interested in in evolution.

Ra stated that archetypes are helpful when used in a controlled way. Would you give me an example of what you mean by using an archetype in a controlled way?

Ra: I am Ra. We speak with some regret in stating that this shall be our last query of length. There is substantial energy left but this instrument has distortions that rapidly approach the limit of our ability to maintain secure contact.

The controlled use of the archetypes is that which is done within the self for the polarization of the self and to the benefit of the self, if negatively polarized, or others, if positively polarized, upon the most subtle of levels.

Keep in mind at all times that the archetypical mind is a portion of the deep mind and informs thought processes. When the archetype is translated without regard for magical propriety into the manifested daily actions of an individual the greatest distortions may take place and great infringement upon the free will of others is possible. This is more nearly acceptable to one negatively polarized. However, the more carefully polarized of negative

mind/body/spirit complexes will also prefer to work with a finely tuned instrument. May we ask if there are any brief queries before we leave this working?

Questioner: I'll just make the statement that I perceive that a negative polarity harvest is possible with less negativity in the environment like Ra's environment than in the environment such as we have at present and ask if that is correct, and then is there anything that we can do to improve the contact or the comfort of the instrument?

Ra: I am Ra. Firstly, the requirements of harvest are set. It is, however, easier to serve the self completely or nearly so if there is little resistance.

In the matter of the nurturing of the instrument we suggest further manipulation of the dorsal side and appendages of this instrument and the whirling of the waters, if possible. The alignments are conscientious. We ask for your vigilance in alignments and preparations. All is well, my friends.

I am Ra. I leave you in the love and in the light of the one infinite Creator. Go forth, then, rejoicing in the power and in the peace of the one infinite Creator. Adonai. ❧

L/L Research is a subsidiary of
Rock Creek Research &
Development Laboratories, Inc.

P.O. Box 5195
Louisville, KY 40255-0195

L/L Research

www.llresearch.org

Rock Creek is a non-profit
corporation dedicated to
discovering and sharing
information which may aid in
the spiritual evolution of
humankind.

Intensive Meditation
June 10, 1982

(S channeling)

I am Hatonn. I am with this instrument and I greet you, my brothers and sisters, in the love and light of our infinite Creator. My friends, this is a great lesson, and we are happy to see that this instrument can perceive our thoughts and has the courage and love to serve the Creator to speak those thoughts and not think that by speaking those thoughts others would believe that those thoughts were not from us. We thank this instrument, and wish only to serve by speaking. We are Hatonn. We leave this instrument and transfer to the one known as Carla. I am Hatonn.

(Carla channeling)

I am Hatonn, and I greet you through this instrument in the love and the light of the infinite Creator. We thank the one known as S for the constancy with which this instrument pursues the desire to be of service to the infinite Creator by this means of what you call vocal channeling. We ask each to remember that all of us who call ourselves by the name of the Confederation of Planets in the Service of the Infinite Creator are but messengers, so that those who speak our thoughts are also messengers. That which comes through us and through you is, therefore, a sometimes simple and sometimes more complex rendering of one basic concept and its implications. The concept is the original Thought, its nature, its unity, and its creative power. Its implications are infinite, and are expressing themselves all about you and to the ends of the endless universe of the Father.

We do not speak with any remarkable powers, with absolute knowledge, but rather out of what we are aware is a limited grasp that is just a bit wider than your own. Therefore, we turn to you to aid you as you attempt a wider grasp of the original Thought of love. We would say to each instrument that desires to be of service that the mechanism by which we produce concepts through instruments is one which is not discernibly different than the method which your own deeper self uses to produce concepts which your conscious minds then clothe with words. As we send concepts to the higher regions of the subconscious levels of your mind, we release them to come forth into your conscious mind just as do your own thoughts, so that you with your unique background of experience of language and of attitude may clothe our simple thoughts in your own unique way so that our message may be offered to those who seek in an ever changing and ever varied manner.

And therefore, my friends, the very first concept to remember as you begin to work with our brothers and sisters of Laitos is the concept of non-analysis. We shall in the beginning be very careful to be specific in what it is that we intend to do in regard to using each as instrument. But then, my friends, because you have become familiar with our words, when you hear the familiar salutation rising to thought in your mind, you may analyze this thought and say to yourself, "I am making this up. I know that is what I should say, and so I shall not [say] it. I shall wait for further recognition." And yet, my friends, to do this is to completely block the contact, for unless you speak the first concept, the second shall not rise. When you speak the second, the third shall rise, and so forth, until you have spoken all that you may be capable of funneling through your instrument at a given time.

Just as a musical instrument in the hands of an inexperienced player may make only a few notes in the beginning, so you shall perhaps be able to only begin slowly, although, my friends, there are natural musicians who play well immediately and there are natural channels who speak fluently immediately. So, have no expectations of yourself, good or bad. Do not hesitate to speak if you hear in your mind the rising of the thought. Do not analyze, and do not be concerned, for each in this group is here to support this process, and we shall be with you as our brothers and sisters of Laitos work with each new instrument. We leave you for a while. I am Hatonn.

(Pause)

(Carla channeling)

I am Laitos, and I greet you, my friends, in the love and the light of the infinite Creator. What a pleasure to be with you this evening. We are grateful to this instrument for making itself available, for it is somewhat fatigued, and [we] would use it to commend itself on the constancy of its desire to serve in this manner.

We have been conditioning the one known as M, the one known as A, and the one known as K. If at this present moment there are physical discomforts connected with this channeling or vibration, we would request that you mentally ask for adjustment, and we shall immediately begin to alleviate any discomfort that you may have. We will pause for a moment in order to deepen our contact with each instrument.

(Pause)

(Carla channeling)

I am Laitos, and I am again with this instrument. We would at this time attempt to identify ourselves through the instrument known as M, if she would relax and allow her mind to remain calm. We shall identify ourselves by the phrase, "I am Laitos." We shall repeat this—in order that the instrument need not be concerned with only having one opportunity—several times. At this time we would transfer this contact to the one known as M. I am Laitos.

(M channeling)

I am Laitos. I greet you, my brothers and sisters, in the love and light of the infinite Creator. You have a beautiful day today. Did you appreciate it? You have a good planet. It's a shame there is so much turmoil. You personally need to learn to rejoice. I am now leaving this instrument.

(Carla channeling)

I am Laitos, and am again with this instrument. We thank the one known as M, and are most appreciative of the natural abilities of this instrument. With work, we look forward to a most fruitful collaboration in expressing the love of the infinite Creator.

We would at this time turn to the one known as A. We thank this instrument for the deep consideration it has given to the development of this form of service. We assure this instrument that this is only one of many types of service, and that we are most grateful that the instrument has chosen to avail herself for this particular service. If the instrument would relax and cease from analysis, we shall again make the repetition of the identification several times, that the new instrument may have several opportunities to perceive our presence and speak. I am Laitos.

(A channeling)

I am Laitos. I am Laitos, and [am] now with this instrument. I am Laitos. We greet you through this instrument. We are pleased that she … I am Laitos.

(Carla channeling)

I am Laitos, and I am again with this instrument. We thank the one known as A for remaining open to our contact after it had become somewhat uncomfortable and difficult to transmit. The ability to perceive our contact has been well established, and we are most pleased with this excellent beginning. We shall be adjusting for better comfort and clarity of contact at this time and in future meditations as the instrument requests adjustment.

We would now like to proceed to the one known as K who we also thank with a grateful heart for offering herself in this service. As your voices, my friends, are our only means of communicating to your people those thoughts which may aid them in the evolution which they seek, we cannot speak often or deeply enough of our gratitude to those who serve. Again, we remind the one known as K to cease from analysis and relax, as there is much supporting and tuned vibratory aid which protects and underlines our opening to the instrument and the instrument's opening to us. We ask the instrument to avoid analysis and to simply speak up when the thought rises. We shall again be identifying ourselves several times. I am Laitos. We transfer now.

(K channeling)

I am Hatonn, and am now with this instrument. My brothers and sisters, I greet you with the love and the light of the infinite Creator. I have been trying to get through for some time. I would just like to greet all of you, and I hope this instrument is comfortable with me. I have made contact. I now leave this instrument.

(K channeling)

I am Laitos. I am now with this instrument. I greet you, my friends, in the love and the light of the infinite Creator.

(Carla channeling)

I am Laitos, and am again with this instrument. My friends, how joyful we are that we have been able to contact all those who have sought to receive our words. We feel as though we are at a banquet and that the bounty is so great that our thanks could never be sufficient. We would say to the one known as K and to the one known as A that we shall be adjusting our contact and that those experiences which especially affected the one known as K are those to be expected because of the initial, shall we say, shock to the subtle electrical body of the power of the vibration which we use. It has a very uncomfortable affect upon some. Upon others it can produce a not unpleasurable, but certainly disruptive

influence at first. These sensations will subside as the instrument becomes more comfortable with our contact.

To all we ask that the practicing of the opening of the—we correct this instrument—that the opening of the instrument be attempted only when there is a supportive group of at least two other entities, one of which is preferably more experienced. We also suggest this thought to all. The one known as A and the one known as K verbalized thoughts which were almost totally from the Confederation. The one known as M, one of the natural instrumentalists of which we were hearing from our brothers and sisters of Hatonn, was able to speak a mixture of concepts, those of the self and those of the Confederation.

In all cases, what we desire is to obtain within each instrument the ability to speak that which is approximately seventy percent Confederation, thirty percent the instrument in content. In this way, my friends, we find it possible to keep ever new our simple message. Therefore, let all be comforted, for we were with each of you, and it was our vibrations that were perceived. Again, as we are full of praise to the Creator that we have been given the opportunity to serve, we are full of gratitude to you that we may be of service with your aid.

We would now turn the contact back to our brothers and sisters of Hatonn in order that any questions that may be upon your minds may be asked. I leave this instrument now, as always, in the love and light of the infinite Creator. I am Laitos. Adonai, my friends. Adonai vasu borragus.

(Jim channeling)

I am Hatonn, and greet each of you in the love and in the light of the one infinite Creator. It is our privilege at this time to be able to present ourselves in a capacity in which we have not been utilized by this group for some of what you call time. It is our privilege, therefore, to ask at this time if there might be any questions which we could attempt humble reply to?

A: I have a question out of curiosity. Why have the brothers and sisters of Latwii not spoken tonight?

I am Hatonn. We of the Confederation always attempt to serve in the manner which is requested. We have perceived this evening that the blended vibrations of this particular group ask for the type of service which is more distorted towards the concept of love and understanding. This is not unusual for those who are new instruments, for the desire to be an instrument of the Confederation is usually the type of desire which includes a great concern for that known as love. Each gathering in which you participate is quite unique and therefore each gathering shall have its unique calling. Often this calling falls within the vibrational levels of love and understanding, and other times it includes the level of light or wisdom, and at that time it is the honor of our brothers and sisters of Latwii to join this group.

May we answer you in any further way, my sister?

A: No, that was interesting. I think I understand. Thank you.

I am Hatonn. We are most grateful for your care and concern. May we ask if there is another question at this time?

M: Yes. Who is this silly, funny, happy, wonderful person that is contacting me?

I am Hatonn. My sister, an instrument such as yourself which has the natural capacity to receive and transmit the thoughts of entities such as those of the Confederation, is open, shall we say to a great variety of impressions. The natural vibration of your being, being that of a joyful and carefree nature in most instances, does then attract entities of like vibration. You will note that from time to time when you are in a meditative state and have opened your instrument to contact such as you have done this evening, that you shall experience a variety of impressions if you continue to leave your channel, shall we say, or your receiver, open. The entity which contacts you now is of no specific orientation, but merely greets you in joy. We would suggest that as you perceive various impressions or contacts that you develop some means of determining the nature of the contact, so that your instrument does not become utilized by entities which are of what might be called the negative nature.

Therefore, it is helpful for new instruments to ask of any entity which attempts to transmit through the channel a general type query which would ask if that entity desires to be of service to others, or is of positive polarity, or is of Confederation origin, or by some means the new instrument might utilize some form of challenge …

(Tape ends.) ❧

L/L RESEARCH

L/L Research is a subsidiary of
Rock Creek Research &
Development Laboratories, Inc.

P.O. Box 5195
Louisville, KY 40255-0195

www.llresearch.org

Rock Creek is a non-profit
corporation dedicated to
discovering and sharing
information which may aid in
the spiritual evolution of
humankind.

SUNDAY MEDITATION
JUNE 13, 1982

(C channeling)

I am Hatonn, and I am now with this instrument. We greet you, my friends, in the love and the light of the one infinite Creator. Tonight we have heard the sounds of your planet, and have felt many entities thereupon who are seeking to harmonize with it. The sounds of the harmonies is indeed a joyous chord, and as you sing, the sounds become stronger to the planet, and those entities singing grow together, become ever more aware of the love and the light. As you well know, at this time, while many sing, there are many who remain silent or who had hit the sour note. At this time upon your planet the lessons are becoming ever more demanding and all those entities on your planet are in many cases reacting to an emotional extreme. As they launch themselves with fever upon their various paths, many, drawn to uniting by means of the ties that are formed in groups, identify themselves as a nation, and sever many of the close ties which they have experienced when, in their youth, people were simply that—people—and not one of a particular country.

As you are well aware, all are one with the Creator, none better, none worse, not separated, not segregated by geography or religion or the ties of nationalities, of race. Each on your planet is in their own unique ways seeking the awareness of the love and light. Few are those who may totally shield their eyes, for the love and light is and surrounds us. Though you may attempt to shield [your] eyes, your being, the awareness and the learning is something that we all will face, and each at his own speed will learn. You need not be disheartened if in your seeking there are times when you seem to stumble or move backward, for the lessons are difficult, but not impossible. Each will learn and in these times that are upon you the lessons will not lessen in any degree.

To us it is hard to deal with your concept of time, but as we understand, yours is drawing ever shorter. Each of you need to utilize each moment, to allow yourself each moment, open yourselves to the love and the light, not grabbing, not running toward it, but allowing yourself to be within it. Though time does for you begin to run down, use and be in the moment when the moment is your time. Be with each as they occur. You need not plan far into the future, for one who looks too far ahead often loses his way upon the path, his own mind. But with the aid of meditation and dealing with the moment, your path may well become a little straighter and easier to follow.

We join you on your journey any time you request, to be of what aid we may. I am known to you as Hatonn. We leave you, as always, in the love and light. Adonai, my friends.

(M1 channeling)

I am Hatonn, and am now with this instrument. I greet you in the love and the light of the infinite Creator. Although your path seems hard, you have chosen to learn. If you accept your problems you will experience learning, you will not feel they are so personal. Meditation will help you solve your problems and understand them. You have chosen your path for specific reasons. Although it may seem hard, in looking back you will understand why it was so.

At this time I leave this instrument.

(K channeling)

I am Hatonn. I greet you, my friends, in the love and the light of the infinite Creator. I am unable to adjust this instrument right now and I transfer the contact to another.

(L channeling)

I am Hatonn. I am once again with this instrument. It is our desire at this time to further exercise those instruments who are relatively new. If those desiring to be of service in this manner will simply relax and listen with confidence for our words, we will pass from instrument to instrument that each in turn will be exercised. I am Hatonn.

(S channeling)

I am Hatonn. I am with this instrument and I greet you, as always, in the love and light of the one infinite Creator. My friends, it is with great joy that we are among you this evening, and we relish the chance to exercise the new channels so they may become more used to our vibration—correction—blended vibration, and so serve the Creator in a way that is both loving and loved. We speak only a few words through this instrument so she will become easier and more confident that she is receiving our thoughts, for we know the love and desire that is there that is hidden and locked at times, but given time and practice will be allowed to come forth, for are we all not brothers and sisters and a part of the one Creator? And remember, my friends, that in loving, so are we loved. I now transfer this contact. I am Hatonn.

(L channeling)

I am Hatonn. I am again with this instrument. It was our intention to exercise the instruments known as A and M2, but we found ourselves unable to sufficiently assure these individuals that we were indeed attempting to contact them. At this time, with their permission, we would again attempt to contact these instruments. First the instrument known as A, and second the instrument known as M2. We will now attempt these contacts. I am Hatonn.

(A channeling)

I am Hatonn, and we are now with this instrument. We greet you once again in the love and the light of the one infinite Creator. We are pleased at being able to speak through this instrument. We have been working at adjusting our vibrations so that she might more easily perceive our thoughts. We will now transfer our contact to the one known as M2. I am Hatonn.

(M2 channeling)

I am Hatonn. I am with this instrument. We are pleased to have had the opportunity to work with the one known as A. She has—she is progressing well in her attempts to channel our messages. We are pleased at every opportunity to work with the new channels. There is a great desire in this group to serve in this manner. We are pleased this is so. We are now going to transfer this contact to the one known as D. I am Hatonn.

(D channeling)

I am Hatonn, and am with this instrument. We have experienced difficulties in adjusting to this instrument also. Reassurances are needed to gain confidence even for a channeler. We will close tonight. Repeat that we enjoy working with the new channels and look forward to more in the future. I am Hatonn, and I leave this instrument. Adonai.

(M1 channeling)

I am Hatonn. I greet you with the love and the light of the infinite Creator. No experience is wasted. You who struggle hardest to get our message gain our respect. Sometimes the things that are hardest to achieve are the most valuable. We do not intend to give up. We hope that you will continue to try to receive our messages. I leave this instrument. I am Hatonn.

(L channeling)

I am Latwii, and I greet you, my brothers and sisters, in the love and the light of the infinite Creator. My friends, as always it is a great pleasure to join you, especially on such a lovely evening as you would call it, for we are aware that the sounds and the conditions which are prevalent outside your structure are somewhat pleasantly distracting, but as we are capable of sharing this pleasure, we too are grateful for the distraction. At this time we present ourselves for your enjoyment in answering or avoiding the answering to any of your questions which you may desire to pose. We would make you aware, however, that the instrument also has a craving for this form of intellectual satisfaction, and would be appreciative of an opportunity to transfer the contact at an appropriate point so that his appetite may be sated. Without further ado, is there another question—correction—is there a question?

C: Yes. Something that popped, came to my mind this week, as to what are those things we call solar flares, and what are their purpose, since they seem to have an effect upon this planet?

I am Latwii. The manifestations that you refer to as solar flares are obviously, on the physical plane as you would call it, sudden outbursts of …

(Side one of tape ends.)

(L channeling)

The solar flares, as you call them, are outbursts of visible energy. They are the result of creative expression, so to speak, within the individual sub-logos which you designate as your sun. The sun, being the physical point of origin of the manifestation of energy brought into your dimension, produces what appear to be violent outbursts or explosions of energy which are the result of metaphysical reordering of that which will become physical. There are also what you call solar flares that are the result of a need for forms of balancing on planets such as your own, which in their disruptive effect upon your communications and, incidentally, guidance systems of ballistic missiles, tend to serve a less understandable, but equally beneficial purpose.

May we answer you further?

C: Why is this energy then pouring into our—what is the reason for this input of energy?

I am Latwii. My brother, as you are aware, your planet is within a period of transition. Just as the surface of your planet has begun to react strongly to the resistance of those upon its surface to orderly change [in] thought and deed, so also does the remainder of the universe react to rectify the situation, just as a vacuum would soon be filled were it to exist anywhere in the universe. The alteration of your planet's vibration is also accompanied by a strong desire emanating from the hearts of your people to have the disease that your people call war or aggression to be corrected in whatever manner possible. In this case the universe, within the limitations of the sub-logo, is providing conditions which are less than favorable for the continuation of your race's aggressive tendencies.

May we answer you further?

C: So that when aggression is the highest, then activity, that inpouring of energy we call—that comes to us as solar flares, will increase?

I am Latwii. That is not necessarily the case, in that the specific form of the inpouring of energy may not always be the one to which you refer. However, we may confidently say that as the aggressive activity increases, so also will the number of aids provided by the universe to assist your race in reducing these same aggressive tendencies.

May we answer you further?

C: On a different subject, I could use some general words of advice. I know that for me when it comes time to begin accepting others after initial judgments have been made and labels put upon them, when it comes time to accept, and I have a tendency to throw up a wall and hide behind my ego, and just mentally to say I'm above such—the person—and work toward acceptance. And this does present quite a problem when the ones toward who I'm not accepting, my non-acceptance spills out beyond my interaction with this person into our children's actions towards one another, and mine, and this other person's actions toward the children. I would just feel grateful for any general words you could speak at this time upon such a situation.

I am Latwii. We would first preface our comments with the observation that the problem that you refer to is characteristic of individuals who have not yet attained unification with their other selves in the form of a social memory complex, but rather function as separate and substantially emotionally undisciplined individuals. This is not a criticism, but rather an observation that the fact that you are experiencing this difficulty might lead one to correctly assume that you are currently in third density. However, to provide advice in addition to the observation, we would suggest that often the faults that one perceives within an other self are those characteristics within one's own self that one finds least attractive. These same difficulties may be of the nature of problems that one feels that one has overcome, but is still aware that the problem within themselves simply lies dormant rather than has ceased to exist, and one tends to react strongly to that same problem when made visible within the reflection of an other self.

The difficulty to which you refer concerning offspring results from the parent's conscious effort to resist the transmission of the parent's own flaws or faults to a beloved offspring. In the same manner, when the other self possessing those same faults is perceived as—correction—is perceived to have an offspring, the faults are often perceived as having been transferred to the offspring. In effect, the mirror image is constructed of a dual reflection. The self perceives the other self in a darkly invested form. The self perceives its own offspring as untainted while perceiving the other self's offspring as already contaminated, and prepared to extend the courtesy to one's own offspring. As you are aware, when you are examining this within your own situation, the occurrence is quite unlikely, yet the fear still remains. We would simply remind you, my friend, that in both cases, the offspring is not a blank slate upon which anything might be inscribed, but rather a soul who possesses age equal to your own, experiences in many ways equal to your own, and although we would urge attention to protecting the offspring from undue influence, we would caution you that the young body contains the old soul to whom it is hard to present new tricks.

May we answer you further?

C: No. I had a pretty good idea of what I needed to work on. More than anything, I needed some confirmation so I could get started upon the right path to something that would be useful. Thank you for your words.

We thank you for the opportunity to speak, my brother. Is there another question?

M2: Will you transfer your contact so L can ask a question?

We will indeed do so, and the instrument is appreciative of this consideration. Is the instrument known as M2 willing to act in this service?

M2: I'll give it a shot.

(Laughter)

I am Latwii. We are grateful that you will undertake this service. We do not wish to mandate it upon you, however, if it is your desire, we shall transfer our contact. Is this your desire?

M2: I'll give it a try, Latwii.

We are grateful. We will leave this instrument at this time. I am Latwii.

(M2 channeling)

I am Latwii. I am with this instrument. Are there any questions?

L: In the past two weeks I have been experiencing some difficulty that I now attribute to being a draining or waning of my own psychic energy. Is this correct?

I am Latwii. We heard your question. My friend, we are unable to give you specifics about your condition, as you are aware, but to speak in a general sense, we might say that the activities which you have undertaken during this recent period of time have contributed to the state you find your physical vehicle in. If one takes better care of oneself, one might find that you would not experience this problem quite to the degree that you are experiencing now. We would perceive that you are suffering more from a physical exhaustion than from a lack of spiritual energy, my brother, for as well as we can determine, your spiritual energies are quite high.

Does this answer your question?

L: I have some further queries. Speaking only in general and not to the specific, is it possible for another—correction—is it possible for one individual either intentionally or unintentionally to in some manner drain or reduce psychic energy from another individual?

We understand your question. This is indeed a possibility. The degree to which this is likely would seem to be largely dependent upon an entity allowing another entity to share in these energies. We are not sure—correction—this is not necessarily a problem, for you normally share a great deal of energy with other selves in your day-to-day life. For example, as you might send a blessing of sorts to another self, are you not truly sharing your energies with them? And as for an other self to tap into your energies, this is quite possible if you allow it. You may choose, if you wish, to prevent someone from tapping into these energies by surrounding yourself with a shield of light, and concentrating—correction—focusing your energies upon yourself or some symbol which is meaningful to you.

Does this answer your question?

L: Yes. I thank you for your help.

Is there another question?

(Pause)

If there are no other questions, we shall leave this instrument at this time, before we, as this instrument would say, blow him away. I am Latwii. ✤

L/L RESEARCH

L/L Research is a subsidiary of Rock Creek Research & Development Laboratories, Inc.

P.O. Box 5195
Louisville, KY 40255-0195

www.llresearch.org

Rock Creek is a non-profit corporation dedicated to discovering and sharing information which may aid in the spiritual evolution of humankind.

INTENSIVE MEDITATION
JUNE 17, 1982

(S channeling)

[I am Hatonn.] I am with this instrument and I greet you, my brothers and sisters, in the love and light of the one infinite Creator. My friends, how wonderful to hear your voices raised in song this evening. It's great meditating with the one Creator, for it is pleasant to see such as yourselves striving to attain that oneness with the Creator no matter how difficult and distant the road is as it lies before you.

My friends, we are pleased this evening to see that the one known as S recognized our vibration and initiated this contact within the group. We are pleased at the progress of all [the entities] and urge each one to continue in their seeking of the one Creator. The roads are different, the paths not smooth at times, but yet with continued striving and love the object will be attained as all roads eventually lead to the Creator.

My friends, we would leave this instrument at this time and would transfer this contact to the one known as E. I am Hatonn.

(E channeling)

I am Hatonn, and we are now with this instrument. We greet you in the love and in the light of the one infinite Creator. We come here tonight to speak a few words through this instrument. She is doing well in picking up our vibration and is having some difficulty in not analyzing our thoughts. [If] she will just relax and speak a few words she perceives, it would be much easier. We would now transfer this contact to the one known as M. I am Hatonn.

(M channeling)

I am Hatonn. I am now with this instrument. I greet you in the love and the light of the infinite Creator. We can help you find a rhythm to relieve. So many of your people on your planet get caught in [longing]. They do not seem able to take *(inaudible)*. If you realize you are here to learn lessons you will not get over-involved and live your life in jerks. You will have a spirituality and will learn your lessons easily. I now leave this instrument. I am Hatonn.

(S channeling)

I am Hatonn. We are again with this instrument. We are pleased that she would initiate another contact. We would like to speak a few more words through her to build up her confidence because she had been feeling she had been making up the last contact. We will now transfer this contact so as to exercise the other instruments present. I am Hatonn.

(Unknown channeling)

I am Hatonn, and I greet you once again in the love and the light of the infinite One. We confirm for the one known as M that we were indeed attempting to contact that instrument, and further that we were attempting to put this instrument to work through the referral of the contact to the one known as D, and then to the one known as K, for these two instruments are still building confidence in the service they have offered to provide. Therefore, you were not receiving the beginnings of a message, for we were initiating a contact with you, my brother, in order to facilitate the exercising of other channels. We would appreciate the opportunity to work with you in this manner so that you may feel the ebb and flow of our contact, and become ever more confident in its initiation and in the guiding of other channels. Therefore, we would again attempt to contact the one known as M. We thank this instrument for his service and appreciate the confusion that must ensue in … The new instrument is beginning to achieve some experience at this service. I am Hatonn.

(Unknown channeling)

I am Hatonn. I am with this instrument. This is a contact. This instrument is experiencing some confusion or anxiety upon initiating the contact. This will pass with practice. We wish to speak a few words through another instrument at this time, and will transfer this contact to the one known as K. I am Hatonn.

(K channeling)

I am Hatonn. I am now with this instrument. I greet you, my brothers and sisters, in the light and the love of the infinite Creator. This instrument has been exceedingly reticent about this contact. It is due in part to past experiences at having seen others become terribly confused. Even though the desire is there, there has been ambivalence. With some practice this ambivalence will pass and great strength will come as a result. I am grateful for having had the opportunity to exercise this instrument, and I will now leave this instrument and transfer the contact to one known as D. I am Hatonn.

(D channeling)

I am Hatonn, and am with this instrument. This instrument, too, is experiencing confusion, not the sensation associated with this contact. We are now making adjustments with the contact.

(Pause)

My friends, experiences such as these require practice. It is natural for some to have some hesitation in initiating this contact, sensations in practice. This will develop. We are still experiencing some difficulty, and we transfer this contact to the one known as Carla. I am Hatonn.

(Carla channeling)

Firstly, my friends, we ask you to be aware and fully conscious of the mechanism of faith or belief, by which this contact is made far more accessible. Indeed, the faculty of faith has long since atrophied among many of your peoples, and it is understandable and to be appreciated that this faculty would be used cautiously and in many cases mistrusted. Whereas [when] we look about your peoples, my friends, we find that those who have exercised the faculty of faith have in many cases become overbalanced in the direction of that faith, and so have separated themselves from a great many other entities rather than using that faith to become one with their brothers and sisters.

Therefore, my friends, we ask you to use that faculty of faith as a tool, and later to feel perfectly free to fully use your powers of discrimination and intellectual analysis to consider those experiences which you have had and those thoughts which have been offered for your consideration. It has never been our desire to offer to your peoples any dogma or system of belief or faith which would bind or constrict that spirit within you which is in the process of growth. Each entity has its own needs, its own food, its own garb, and its own journey. What we then ask all [is] to find details upon which to agree. Could we expect this to be helpful? No, my friends. Our message is simple.

Then, secondly. We ask you that you be aware of the type and quality of service which you are attempting to provide. We ask you to cast your minds back to the first meeting of this kind which you attended, which spoke to you. We ask you to be aware that whoever the instrument …

(Side one of tape ends.)

(Carla channeling)

… over a period of time as you call to reach the point where you too wish to be of service as you were served. Each of you as a channel shall indeed be of a unique service, for each of you will interpret our concepts with different language, different examples, different experiences. For such is the nature of our contact that the use of your own personal vocabulary and memory is encouraged. Thus, that within you which is inspirational shall be added to our simple message. And you may one day find yourself thanked by yet someone else whose time it now is to have become aware of this particular kind of meeting, meditation and message.

Thirdly, my friends, we ask that you put no pressure upon yourselves of any kind. For although we are endlessly grateful for your service in this particular mode, we assure you that you cannot help being of service. It has been said by this instrument that anyone is of service, even those who serve as bad examples. And although this is a somewhat casual statement, it is the gist of what we wish to convey. My friends, by the way that you live and express your being you witness to those about you. And in that witnessing lies a great service, no matter what you witness, for there is an infinite variety and need both for positive and negative witness. Even in your very worst moment, as you would call it, you are offering someone the opportunity for understanding, for kindness, for anger, for irritation, for indifference, for some catalyst, and as each serves as catalyst for another person, so each has aided in the growth of that person.

Now, my friends, we realize that you do not wish to be of random service. We realize that you wish with all of your hearts and minds to be of positive polarized service. Do not ever think that such service begins and ends with any particular kind or degree of service. Do not feel that the service of being an instrument, of receiving material such as this instrument does, is the best or the finest service. My friends, your finest service is the very vibration that causes the atoms of your being to dance in their energy fields as you move in your own special way, through your own special light, moment by moment by moment. We rejoice in your company and give great praise to the Creator for this opportunity to share our thoughts with you, and to work with each channel.

At this time we would leave this instrument. It has been a great delight to work with you. We leave you in the love and the light of our infinite Creator. Adonai. Adonai vasu borragus.

(Unknown channeling)

I am Latwii, and greet each of you in the love and in the light of our infinite Creator. It is our privilege once again to be able to join your group as you seek the One, as is our custom. We offer ourselves at this time in the capacity of attempting to answer your queries. May we now ask if there might be a question which we could attempt to answer?

Questioner: All is quiet on the southeastern front, Latwii, but we do wish you well.

Questioner: Yes. I have a question, Latwii. In recent weeks I've just had a special feeling. It just keeps coming to me over and over that we're being prepared for some, shall I say, unknown event. And I'm torn between a little anxiety and anticipation. In other words, I feel that I'm being prepared for something, and I don't know what it is. Have you got any enlightenment on this subject? I'm assuming that lots of other people feel the very same way.

I am Latwii, and am aware of your query, my sister. We thank you, incidentally, for posing this query, for we were afraid that we had drawn, shall we say, a blank with this group for the first time in our memory. You are indeed being prepared for a great event. To some it will seem that this event is most unusual, even earth shaking, shall we say. We can only say to you that this event is that which each shall have—we correct this instrument—which each has incarnated to experience. The event, my friends, is the discovery of yourself. That which you know of as yourself in your present incarnation is but the tip of the iceberg, shall we say.

The self that you seek and that soon you shall know is much more than the great majority of your peoples have ever conceived of. The self which is now possible for many of your peoples to perceive is that great being known to your peoples as the one Creator. You as the Creator have chosen to play a masquerade in order that you shall know yourself more fully. To put on the mask of that which you know as the personality in your present incarnation, and in many past incarnations, aids the Creator in discovering facets of the Self which would have been unknown had not the free will to discover been granted through each portion of the Creator experiencing a forgetting.

You have forgotten much, and you have spent many incarnations remembering piece by piece those portions of yourself which, seen cumulatively, become the one Creator. It is now possible for many upon your planet to complete the puzzle, shall we say, and this feeling of anticipation, growing even unto anxiety, is within many of the hearts and minds of your peoples. It is your day of graduation. It is the day in which all that you are shall be revealed unto you. You shall know yourself as the Creator, and as all other selves. This is that for which you are now being prepared.

May we answer you further, my sister?

Questioner: OK. Let me just see if I can put this in my own words. This feeling that I have of this event, and sometimes it's joyous, and it's as I said, sometimes there's some anxiety about it. But it is nothing more than just self-discovery, is that what I understand? Is that right?

I am Latwii. This is correct, my sister. Each entity seeks the self through many means, and though there shall be many accompanying phenomena, many of which shall be most disturbing to those who still reside within the darkness and the ignorance of their self and their being, yet, for those who truly seek the self, the truth of the Creator, so shall these, the gems of your being, be revealed unto you.

May we answer you further, my sister?

Questioner: So this is what Socrates was talking about when he said, "Know thyself"?

I am Latwii. Yes. May we answer you further?

Questioner: No, thank you.

I am Latwii. We are most grateful to you. Is there another question at this time?

Questioner: I'd like to ask about the previous one just a bit more. The answer that you gave could be seen as a very uplifting way of looking at the physical death of the body. It could also be seen as having quite a bit to do with the particular incarnation's physical death which will undoubtedly tie in with the graduation from this density. Were you referring to either of these events tangentially?

I am Latwii, and am aware of your query, my sister. We were indeed referring to each of these events of which you have spoken. Indeed, it could be said that that great event which awaits each entity now upon your planet could be spoken of as that entrance into what has been called the New Age of being, of understanding, of love. For this, a great discovery of the self is that prime moving element which has set all that you see occurring upon the stage of your world in motion. Indeed, it has been well said that

all the world is a stage, and each entity upon this stage plays many parts in its time, with many exits and entrances, and yet the play is the thing. And the purpose of this play, my friends, is that you shall know yourself. For you have authored the play, and you sit in the audience; you raise the curtain, you sell the ticket; you are the critic and you are those who know not that a play is in progress.

You, my friends, shall discover yourself in all these positions and many more, for you are the Creator and all that is exists so that the Creator might know Itself. As your age ends there will be many events, many lives lived successfully, shall we say, so that the self is found, many deaths to be lamented in the respect that the self still remains hidden to the entity. All that shall occur will have but one purpose—that is, to aid in the revealing of the self to each entity who seeks the self.

May we answer you further, my sister?

Questioner: No, thank you.

I am Latwii. We are most grateful to you as well. Is there another question at this time?

Questioner: Yes. Will you clear up one other concept that has bothered me, and that's the meaning of love. It seems to me that in the English language we use it to mean so many different things, and most of the time it's just an emotional experience. Right now, I think of love as the unconditional or the total acceptance of the self, of all selves, shall I say. Would you comment on the meaning of love?

I am Latwii, and am aware of your query, my sister. It seems that this group has once again found its voice, and we are appreciative for the queries. Love, my friends, has many meanings among your peoples. The meaning which we would choose to share with you at this time is that type of love of which each of you is only dimly aware. It is an experience of acceptance, of being, and of the Creator, which may be approached through a surrender of the self to all that is. When an entity upon your planet surrenders the self to the experience of love, then the entity opens its being to knowing what forgiveness means, for all is seen as One and how can One hold anger for any when all is seen as the Creator? All is then accepted as the Creator knowing Itself.

Each entity is seen as the Creator. The self which is seen is also recognized as this Creator so that a band of unity binds each entity to each other entity and there is only seen the desire to be of service to the one Creator by serving the parts or portions known as other selves. The desire is great, for that which is known as love is felt for each. The pains and sorrows, the difficulties, are seen, and it is felt deep within the self that to minister to those selves feeling such pain is a great necessity. Therefore, an entity which seeks to know love, to know compassion, then does begin step-by-step to appreciate and to understand each other entity, as well as the self, as being the one Creator, and the great need is felt to be of service to the One through the many.

May we answer you further, my sister?

Questioner: No, that helps a lot. Thanks, thanks a lot.

I am Latwii. We thank you as well. Is there another question at this time?

Questioner: It seems as if almost everyone on our planet is anxious, and, I don't know whether I'm stupid or not, but it doesn't seem to bother me. Is there something lacking that I'm not anxious, that everybody else is worried about earthquakes and seems to be filled with tension? Am I missing something?

I am Latwii, and am aware of your query, my sister. We don't feel that you lack, rather, it might be said that those who feel anxiety are more apt to communicate the same anxiety than are those who feel less anxiety, perhaps even tranquility, likely to communicate tranquility. For the peace of mind is as it is and shares itself not in, shall we say, any ostentatious manner in which others are urged to feel what the self feels. Those of anxious hearts and minds feel a great desire burning within to alert others to that which has made the self anxious, and thus the anxiety is spread, much likened unto what you call disease. Those, on the other hand, who feel a tranquility by their very nature radiate, shall we say, the tranquility in a more passive means, serving as stabilizers within the field of entities which has become somewhat enmeshed in the anxiety. Therefore, those who feel the tranquility might at this time be of great service to their fellow beings when asked why they are not anxious.

May we answer you further, my sister?

Questioner: No. I believe that explains it. Thank you.

I am Latwii. We thank you. Is there another question at this time?

(Pause)

I am Latwii. We are most appreciative towards each entity for allowing us to speak our simple words this evening. We cannot speak without your participation, shall we say, and the service you provide us by the queries you bring is a service for which we cannot thank you for enough. At this time we shall take our leave of this group, and remind each that a simple request for our presence in your meditation is all that is necessary for us to join you there. We leave you now in the love and in the light of the One Who is All. I am Latwii. ☥

L/L RESEARCH

L/L Research is a subsidiary of Rock Creek Research & Development Laboratories, Inc.

P.O. Box 5195
Louisville, KY 40255-0195

www.llresearch.org

Rock Creek is a non-profit corporation dedicated to discovering and sharing information which may aid in the spiritual evolution of humankind.

THE LAW OF ONE, BOOK IV, SESSION 90
JUNE 19, 1982

Ra: I am Ra. I greet you in the love and in the light of the one infinite Creator. We communicate now.

Questioner: Could you first please give me the condition of the instrument?

Ra: I am Ra. The physical complex energy deficit is somewhat increased by continued distortions towards pain. The vital energy levels are as previously stated, having fluctuated slightly between askings.

Questioner: Could you tell me the situation with respect to our fourth and fifth-density companions at this time?

Ra: I am Ra. The fourth-density league of companions accompanies your group. The fifth-density friend, at this space/time nexus, works within its own density exclusively.

Questioner: By what means do these particular fourth-density entities get from their origin to our position?

Ra: I am Ra. The mechanism of calling has been previously explored. When a distortion which may be negatively connoted is effected, this calling occurs. In addition, the light of which we have spoken, emanating from attempts to be of service to others in a fairly clear and lucid sense, is another type of calling in that it represents that which requires balance by temptation. Thirdly, there have been certain avenues into the mind/body/spirit complexes of this group which have been made available by your fifth-density friend.

Questioner: Actually, the question that I intended was how do they get here? By what means of moving do they get here?

Ra: I am Ra. In the mechanism of the calling the movement is as you would expect; that is, the entities are within your planetary influence and are, having come through the quarantine web, free to answer such calling.

The temptations are offered by those negative entities of what you would call your inner planes. These, shall we say, dark angels have been impressed by the service-to-self path offered by those which have come through quarantine from days of old and these entities, much like your angelic presences of the positive nature, are ready to move in thought within the inner planes of this planetary influence working from time/space to space/time.

The mechanism of the fifth-density entity is from density to density and is magical in nature. The fourth density, of itself, is not capable of building the highway into the energy web. However, it is capable of using that which has been left intact. These entities are, again, the Orion entities of fourth density.

Questioner: You stated previously that fifth-density entities bear a resemblance to those of us in third density on planet Earth but fourth density does not.

Could you describe the fourth-density entities and tell me why they do not resemble us?

Ra: I am Ra. The description must be bated under the Law of Confusion. The cause for a variety of so-called physical vehicles is the remaining variety of heritages from second-density physical vehicular forms. The process of what you call physical evolution continues to hold sway into fourth density. Only when the ways of wisdom have begun to refine the power of what you may loosely call thought is the form of the physical complex manifestation more nearly under the direction of the consciousness.

Questioner: If the population of this planet presently looks similar to fifth-density entities I was wondering why this is? If I understand you correctly the process of evolution would normally be that of third density resembling that from which evolved in second density and refining it in fourth and then again in fifth density, becoming what the population of this looks like in the third density. It seems to me that this planet is ahead of itself by the way that its mind/body/spirit complex or body complex looks. What is the reason for this?

Ra: I am Ra. Your query is based upon a misconception. Do you wish us to comment or do you wish to requestion?

Questioner: Please comment on my misconception if that is possible.

Ra: I am Ra. In fifth density the manifestation of the physical complex is more and more under the control of the conscious mind complex. Therefore, the fifth-density entity may dissolve one manifestation and create another. Consequently, the choice of a fifth-density entity or complex of entities wishing to communicate with your peoples would be to resemble your peoples' physical-complex, chemical, yellow-ray vehicles.

Questioner: I see. Very roughly, if you were to move a third-density entity from some other planet to this planet, what percentage of all of those within the knowledge of Ra would look enough like entities of Earth so that they would go unnoticed in a crowd?

Ra: I am Ra. Perhaps five percent.

Questioner: Then there is an extreme variation in the form of the physical vehicle in third density in

the universe. I assume that this is also true of fourth density. Is this correct?

Ra: I am Ra. This is so. We remind you that it is a great theoretical distance between demanding that the creatures of an infinite creation be unnoticeably similar to one's self and observing those signs which may be called human which denote the third-density characteristics of self-consciousness, the grouping into pairs, societal groups, and races, and the further characteristic means of using self-consciousness to refine and search for the meaning of the milieu.

Questioner: Within Ra's knowledge of the third-density physical forms, what percentage would be similar enough to this planet's physical forms that we would assume the entities to be human even though they were a bit different? This would have to be very rough because of my definition's being very rough.

Ra: I am Ra. This percentage is still small; perhaps thirteen to fifteen percent due to the capabilities of various second-density life forms to carry out each necessary function for third-density work. Thusly to be observed would be behavior indicating self-consciousness and purposeful interaction with a sentient ambiance about the entity rather than those characteristics which familiarly connote to your peoples the humanity of your third-density form.

Questioner: Now in this line of questioning I am trying to link to the creations of various Logoi and their original use of a system of archetypes in their creation and I apologize for a lack of efficiency in doing this, but I find this somewhat difficult. For this particular Logos in the beginning, prior to its creation of the first density, did the archetypical system which it had chosen include the forms that would evolve in third density or was this related to the archetypical concept at all?

Ra: I am Ra. The choice of form is prior to the formation of the archetypical mind. As the Logos creates Its plan for evolution, then the chosen form is invested.

Questioner: Was there a reason for choosing the forms that have evolved on this planet and, if so, what was it?

Ra: I am Ra. We are not entirely sure why our Logos and several neighboring Logoi of approximately the same space/time of flowering chose the bipedal, erect form of the second-density apes to invest. It has been our supposition, which we share with you as long as you are aware that this is mere opinion, that our Logos was interested in, shall we say, further intensifying the veiling process by offering to the third-density form the near complete probability for the development of speech taking complete precedence over concept communication or telepathy. We also have the supposition that the so-called opposable thumb was looked upon as an excellent means of intensifying the veiling process so that rather than rediscovering the powers of the mind the third-density entity would, by the form of its physical manifestation, be drawn to the making, holding, and using of physical tools.

Questioner: I will guess that the system of archetypes then was devised to further extend these particular principles. Is this correct?

Ra: I am Ra. The phrasing is faulty. However, it is correct that the images of the archetypical mind are the children of the third-density physical manifestations of form of the Logos which has created the particular evolutionary opportunity.

Questioner: Now, as I understand it the archetypes are the biases of a very fundamental nature that, under free will, generate the experiences of each entity. Is this correct?

Ra: I am Ra. The archetypical mind is part of that mind which informs all experience. Please recall the definition of the archetypical mind as the repository of those refinements to the cosmic or all-mind made by this particular Logos and peculiar only to this Logos. Thus it may be seen as one of the roots of mind, not the deepest but certainly the most informative in some ways. The other root of mind to be recalled is that racial or planetary mind which also informs the conceptualizations of each entity to some degree.

Questioner: At what point in the evolutionary process does the archetypical mind first have effect upon the entity?

Ra: I am Ra. At the point at which an entity, either by accident or design, reflects an archetype, the archetypical mind resonates. Thusly random activation of the archetypical resonances begins almost immediately in third-density experience. The disciplined use of this tool of evolution comes far later in this process.

Questioner: What was the ultimate objective of this Logos in designing the archetypical mind as It did?

Ra: I am Ra. Each Logos desires to create a more eloquent expression of experience of the Creator by the Creator. The archetypical mind is intended to heighten this ability to express the Creator in patterns more like the fanned peacock's tail, each facet of the Creator vivid, upright, and shining with articulated beauty.

Questioner: Is Ra familiar with the archetypical mind of some other Logos that is not the same as the one we experience?

Ra: I am Ra. There are entities of Ra which have served as far Wanderers to those of another Logos. The experience has been one which staggers the intellectual and intuitive capacities, for each Logos sets up an experiment enough at variance from all others that the subtleties of the archetypical mind of another Logos are most murky to the resonating mind, body, and spirit complexes of this Logos.

Questioner: There seems to have been created by this Logos, to me anyway, a large percentage of entities whose distortion was towards warfare. There have been the Maldek and Mars experiences and now Earth. It seems that Venus was the exception to what we could almost call the rule of warfare. Is this correct and was this envisioned and planned into the construction of the archetypical mind, possibly not with respect to warfare as we have experienced it but as to the extreme action of polarization in consciousness?

Ra: I am Ra. It is correct that the Logos designed Its experiment to attempt to achieve the greatest possible opportunities for polarization in third density. It is incorrect that warfare of the types specific to your experiences was planned by the Logos. This form of expression of hostility is an interesting result which is apparently concomitant with the tool-making ability. The choice of the Logos to use the life-form with the grasping thumb is the decision to which this type of warfare may be traced.

Questioner: Then did our Logos hope to see generated a positive and negative harvest from each density up to the sixth, starting with the third, as being the most efficient form of generating experience known to It at the time of Its construction of this system of evolution?

Ra: I am Ra. Yes.

Questioner: Then built into the basis for the archetypes is possibly the mechanism for creating the polarization in consciousness for service to others and service to self. Is this, in fact, true?

Ra: I am Ra. Yes. You will notice the many inborn biases which hint to the possibility of one path's being more efficient than the other. This was the design of the Logos.

Questioner: Then what you are saying is that once the path is recognized, either the positive or the negative polarized entity can find hints along his path as to the efficiency of that path. Is this correct?

Ra: I am Ra. That which you say is correct upon its own merits, but is not a repetition of our statement. Our suggestion was that within the experiential nexus of each entity within its second-density environment and within the roots of mind there were placed biases indicating to the watchful eye the more efficient of the two paths. Let us say, for want of a more precise adjective, that this Logos has a bias towards kindness.

Questioner: Then you say that the more efficient of the two paths was suggested in a subliminal way to second density to be the service-to-others path. Am I correct?

Ra: I am Ra. We did not state which was the more efficient path. However, you are correct in your assumption, as you are aware from having examined each path in some detail in previous querying.

Questioner: Could this be the reason for the greater positive harvest? I suspect that it isn't, but would there be Logoi that have greater negative percentage harvests because of this type of biasing?

Ra: I am Ra. No. There have been Logoi with greater percentages of negative harvests. However, the biasing mechanisms cannot change the requirements for achieving harvestability either in the positive or in the negative sense. There are Logoi which have offered a neutral background against which to polarize. This Logos chose not to do so but instead to allow more of the love and light of the infinite Creator to be both inwardly and outwardly visible and available to the sensations and conceptualizations of mind/body/spirit complexes undergoing Its care in experimenting.

Questioner: Were there any other circumstances, biases, consequences, or plans set up by the Logos other than those we have discussed for the evolution of Its parts through the densities?

Ra: I am Ra. Yes.

Questioner: What were these?

Ra: I am Ra. One more; that is, the permeability of the densities so that there may be communication from density to density and from plane to plane or sub-density to sub-density.

Questioner: Then as I see the plan for the evolution by this Logos it was planned to create as vivid an experience as possible but also one which was somewhat informed with respect to the infinite Creator and able to accelerate the progress as a function of will because of the permeability of densities. Have I covered accurately the general plan of this Logos with respect to Its evolution?

Ra: I am Ra. Excepting the actions of the unmanifested self and the actions of self with other-self, you have been reasonably thorough.

Questioner: Then, is the major mechanism forming the ways and very essence of the experience that we presently experience here the archetypical mind and the archetypes?

Ra: I am Ra. These resources are a part of that which you refer to.

Questioner: What I am really asking is what percentage of a part, roughly, are these responsible for?

Ra: I am Ra. We ask once again that you consider that the archetypical mind is a part of the deep mind. There are several portions to this mind. The mind may serve as a resource. To call the archetypical mind the foundation of experience is to oversimplify the activities of the mind/body/spirit complex. To work with your query as to percentages is, therefore, enough misleading in any form of direct answer that we would ask that you requestion.

Questioner: That's OK. I don't think that was too good a question anyway.

When Ra initially planned for helping the Egyptians with their evolution, what was the primary concept, and also secondary and tertiary if you can name those, that Ra wished to impart to the Egyptians? In other words, what was Ra's training plan or schedule for making the Egyptians aware of what was necessary for their evolution?

Ra: I am Ra. We came to your peoples to enunciate the Law of One. We wished to impress upon those who wished to learn of unity that in unity all paradoxes are resolved; all that is broken is healed; all that is forgotten is brought to light. We had no teaching plan, as you have called it, in that our intention when we walked among your peoples was to manifest that which was requested by those learn/teachers to which we had come.

We are aware that this particular line of querying; that is, the nature and architecture of the archetypical mind, has caused the questioner to attempt, to its own mind unsuccessfully, to determine the relative importance of those concepts. We cannot learn/teach for any, nor would we take this opportunity from the questioner. However, we shall comment.

The adept has already worked much, not only within the red, orange, yellow, and green energy centers but also in the opening of the blue and indigo. Up through this point the archetypes function as the great base or plinth of a builded structure or statue keeping the mind complex viable, level, and available as a resource whenever it may be evoked. There is a point at which the adept takes up its work. This is the point at which a clear and conscious consideration of the archetypal mind is useful.

Questioner: I have an observation on Archetype Number One made by *(name)* and I request comment on it by Ra. I will read it, "The Matrix of the Mind is the conscious mind and is sustained by the power of the spirit as symbolized by the star which flows to it through the subconscious mind. It contains the will which is signified by the scepter of power in the Magician's hand. All of creation is made through the power of the will directed by the conscious mind of the Magician, and the bird in the cage represents the illusion in which the self seems trapped. The Magician represents maleness or the radiance of being manifested as the creation through which each entity moves."

Ra: I am Ra. As this instrument is becoming somewhat weary we shall not begin this considerable discussion. We would request that this series of observations be repeated at the outset of the next working. We would suggest that each concept be discussed separately or, if appropriate, a pair of concepts be related one to the other within the concept complex. This is slow work but shall make the eventual building of the concept complexes more smoothly accomplished.

Were we to have answered the observations as read by you at this space/time, as much space/time would have been given to the untangling of various concepts as to the building up of what were very thoughtful perceptions.

May we ask if there are any brief queries at this time?

Questioner: Is there anything that we can do to make the instrument more comfortable or to improve the contact?

Ra: I am Ra. It is well that the appliances for the arms were placed upon the instrument. We ask that continued vigilance be accorded these distortions which are, if anything, more distorted towards disease than at our previous cautionary statement.

All is well, my friends, You are conscientious and faithful in your alignments. We appreciate your fastidiousness.

I am Ra. I leave you now, rejoicing merrily in the love and the light of the one infinite Creator. Go forth, then, rejoicing in the power and in the peace of the one infinite Creator. Adonai. ♰

L/L Research is a subsidiary of
Rock Creek Research &
Development Laboratories, Inc.

P.O. Box 5195
Louisville, KY 40255-0195

L/L RESEARCH

www.llresearch.org

Rock Creek is a non-profit
corporation dedicated to
discovering and sharing
information which may aid in
the spiritual evolution of
humankind.

SUNDAY MEDITATION
JUNE 20, 1982

(Unknown channeling)

I am Hatonn. I greet you, my brothers and sisters, in the light and the love of the infinite Creator. My friends, we initially attempted to contact a number of the newer instruments, yet found ourselves unable to convince those individuals of the veracity of the contact. It is our desire in the future to attempt this often at further sessions so as to familiarize each instrument with our vibration that they might perceive and be confident in our initial contacts.

At this time, we desire to extend our vibration to the one known as A, that she might again experience the sensation and be able to compare the vibration with that which she experienced earlier and so better recognize our presence. At this time we will transfer our contact to the one known as A. I am Hatonn.

(A channeling)

I am Hatonn. I am now with this instrument and again we greet you in the love and the light of the infinite Creator. My friends, we would like at this time to speak a few words though this instrument.

You are all going through a time in which you are learning many lessons and we are well aware of the difficulties and the pain that is sometime felt from learning the lesson. But did you not choose to learn this lesson so that you might learn more and thereby experience the love and the light of the infinite Creator? We wish to say that you all are doing well in seeking the love and light of the infinite Creator. And at those times when you feel the lesson is too hard, remember you are not alone, but that you are one with the infinite Creator and therefore you will take on any challenge you face.

We will leave this instrument now so that we may exercise some of the other new instruments. We will now transfer this contact to the one known as [D1.] I am Hatonn.

(D1 channeling)

I am Hatonn. I am now with this instrument. I greet you with the love and the light of the infinite Creator.

Your life and your mind is like a stream. At times you feel it is dried up and cannot go on. But a torrent of ideas and events, as a torrent of rain, will send you further along the [path.] At times part of your mind will go into still ponds and you do not see the end, but part will still be in the main stream and will pull you down. As life goes on and the stream gets bigger, your ideas and your understanding become larger and you eventually will reach your destination. I now leave this instrument. I am Hatonn.

(Unknown channeling)

I am Hatonn. I am now with this instrument. I greet you, my friends, in the love and the light of the infinite Creator. It is well for us to remember that all of us are one in the Creator and that the least of us is as much a part of the Creator as those that may appear great. On your planet, you have a tendency to place people on different levels, but that is not necessary with [love,] because all are one and one is all.

You hear many distressing things day by day, but it is always well to remember that the Creator is indeed in all of us and you need have no concern for the things that bombard your ears day by day. We are pleased to have had the opportunity to exercise this instrument and will now transfer the contact. I am Hatonn.

(Carla channeling)

I am Hatonn. I am now with this instrument and once again greet you, my friends, in love and in light. If you will be patient, we will take a few moments to comment upon the work of the instruments that are now developing and their skills and then we shall share a few thoughts with you. During this time we shall be adjusting a contact with the one known as D1, that this instrument may have an opportunity to work with us under somewhat better circumstances. May we say to each that we are very grateful for the opportunities for delving into the treasures of each instrument's mind and experience offered to us. To the one known as A, we would say that although the progress made is very quick, it is to be relied upon and is a result of a desire which has, according to the nature of this individual, been carefully thought out. This clarity of desire is extremely helpful in preparing instruments for this or any positive service and we commend this instrument.

We commend also the instrument known as M and would only ask that this gifted instrument, that in contact with our vibration it refrain from closing the contact for a brief moment after each train of thought has been accomplished and communicated. The process by which we of the Confederation build concepts into meaningful relationships for these communications is one in which concept is built upon concept. Therefore, as the instrument begins to be aware of concepts it is then time for the instrument to be aware of the possibility that more than one concept may be prepared for communication. This was in this case a possibility. We offer this information in order that the instrument may grasp the nature of the sensations felt and may see the mechanism whereby the flow of our communication may be easily shut off at any junction at the desire of the instrument. We wish also to commend and thank the one known as K that [that] which we wished to communicate was well received.

Each of you, my friends, is progressing at a rapid rate and we are, along with our brothers and sisters of Laitos, in awe at the opportunity presented to us at this time and offer our thanks and our love to each. We are aware of a desire for some words at this time which may be of aid, for there are a majority among you whose questioning at this time is particularly keen in the area of the actual practicality or reality of living a life filled with the Creator while within an illusion of [that] which may seem harmless or may seem difficult, but certainly seems full of the unnecessary, the ambivalent, the humorous, and the ridiculous.

Where, then, is the profundity of the great love of the Creator? As you sit at your traffic lights, do you see the Creator? As you attempt to clean up after your ceaselessly disordering lives, filling your refuse pails and consuming the contents of brown paper bags, do you see the Creator? My friends, if you do not it is understandable, but it is also an area that needs work. Let us remove ourselves, not from the traffic lights or the places behind the wheels of automobiles. Not from the self as it consumes and creates garbage, but from the attitude that trivializes existence. Let us look at the atoms that make up the scene at the traffic light. Is not everything that is created a creation full of love? Indeed, where can you go to escape love? You tabernacle with love as you gaze into the blank faces that await the changing of a random traffic light. If you wish to ignore the temple that is about you, this you may do. It is not necessary. Do you find your lives trivial because in some portion there is a routine of maintenance and sustenance and the removing of the husks of this maintenance and sustenance? My friends, you physical vehicle was given to you because it is a marvelously sensitive mechanism for perceiving the Creator. Listen and learn from its perceptions and do not begrudge it its maintenance. For each thing that you must do in order to maintain life within the illusion may be reflected upon and learned from. My friends, meditation is extremely helpful, but you do not have to wait for meditation to seek the non-trivial in each moment.

You stand upon holy ground, as the one known as Moses in your holy works. Take the shoes from off your feet, take the numbness from you feelings about your self and about your routines. When you feel that presence, that love in the so-called trivial moment that you spend with yourselves, then, my friends, how much more ready you are to be of service to those about you. You may look for the Creator in genetic coding, in the furthest star, in the small, in the enormous. Look where you wish, my friends, your vision will not fail you. You will find the Creator that you seek, but begin by seeking where you are and within your own nature.

I would at this time, close this contact through the instrument known as [D2]. I am Hatonn.

(D2 channeling)

I am Hatonn. We have been making adjustments for contact with this instrument and find that he is constantly readjusting. The method of contact this time is not fully understood or accepted and has made it much more difficult.

(Long pause.)

At this time we have very good contact with this instrument and hope in the future he will remain open and accepting of our presence. This instrument has sensitive *(inaudible)* … We may need *(inaudible)*. This instrument does not accept the fact that we are, in effect, dissolving his defenses as his desire is greater than his own resistance. If he will accept this, life will be made much easier for us all. *(Laughter)* We will close this contact and hope that in the future that he is cooperative as he is *(inaudible)*. I am Hatonn.

(M channeling)

I am Hatonn. I am now with this instrument. Although she is normally very talkative, she refuses to tell more than one of my ideas and I have been flooding her with ideas. I would like for her to say that all the beautiful things that happen to you come through with you. Any flower that you smell the scent of never dies, any baby's laughter that you hear rings on forever. The people of your planet are not collecting beauty to bring with them. The sunset

that you see never dies, but the ones you don't bother to see for you [remain.] Collect beautiful moments. True, your planet has its problems. It has acid rain, but the flowers still grow. Some day things may be barren, but if you have these flowers growing in your mind you will have beauty that comes with you. How many times do you pass something beautiful, something happy, something wonderful and ignore it? Your world has many beautiful things and your people seem to be immune to them. They like highways, they like to go fast, but all beautiful things take time. Walking in the grass, hearing a bird sing, these are beautiful things to take with you. When you leave this planet don't just take its trouble. You really have many wonderful things. Collect them. Cherish them and remember that anything that you remember never dies.

This instrument will not give anymore of my ideas. I will leave this instrument. I am Hatonn.

(Carla channeling)

I am Hatonn. I am again with this instrument. We thank the one known as M for opening wider the channel that is indeed a gift to which we are grateful to avail ourselves.

The sensitivity that this new instrument shows to manifest so quickly, we are having a chuckle at the delightful rapidity of the movement of energy within your group. We would again, if we may, attempt to close our contact through the instrument known as D2. I am Hatonn.

(D2 channeling)

I am Hatonn. I am again with this instrument. We are pleased that this instrument immediately recognized the conditioning and signal of contact. We may reassure this instrument that we will be as patient with him as he is with us and look forward with working with him again in the future. We leave this group [saying] as always in the love and the light of the infinite Creator. We are known to you as Hatonn. Adonai. Adonai vasu borragus.

(Jim channeling)

I am Latwii, and I greet you, my friends, in the love and in the light of the one infinite Creator. We are most privileged to be asked once again by this group to serve in our capacity of attempting to answer your queries. We would, therefore, at this time open this meeting to the queries that may be asked. Is there a question at this time?

M: Yes. I was listening to the radio this morning and it was a review of the news of the recent past, in fact, this past week and one of comments was that it's time for this planet to get its act together, and the next statement was that this planet is a grain of sand in the galaxy and the commentator said he believes there are people on other planets. The thought that came to mind was that this person is probably from the fourth density or maybe even the fifth density because he seemed to have better understanding than most commentators.

I am Latwii, and I am aware of your query, my sister. We find it somewhat humorous to be asked to serve as the commentator upon a commentator. But, my friends, is this not the role which each plays upon your planet? For are not all of your entities the one Creator and does not each comment upon its particular status and experience of the one Creator? Whether it knows it or not, this is what it does. Some of your entities have for great periods of what you call time searched deep within their being and deep within the illusion for the meaning of both. Some, therefore, have drawn unto themselves those portions of their great self which they have sought. The revelations, intuitions, the piecing together of the meaning of the life, of the nature of the one Creator and the functioning of your illusion comes little by little, yet it comes in some form to all.

Many upon your planet, whether they be those known to you as the wanderers, the teachers, the avatars, or whether they be those who are native to this planet or other planet similar to it, have found portions of the Creator in the form by which the entity could understand that which has been found. You will see in the days which follow rapidly the increasing recognition by more and more entities upon your plant of the nature of their existence. For the time and the cycle of this planet does indeed grow short and the act is being gotten together, for the players are those old souls upon your planet who have had many such roles and this is the grand finale. The learnings of each incarnation shall be distilled and shall be radiated to all who have ears to hear. Yes, my friends, great understanding is coming to your planet. Greater understanding shall come to each entity and through each entity in the days which are to come.

May we answer you further, my sister?

M: No, that's fine. Thank you.

I am Latwii. We thank you very much. Is there another question at this time?

Questioner: I have a question or two. In your answer you spoke of very old souls. Could you speak a little on them? I'm not really sure what you mean, are there varying types of ages or anything?

I am Latwii, and I am aware of your query, my sister. In truth, all are one being. This one being, as you know, has chosen to evolve by dividing Itself into many portions. Each portion, therefore, given the freewill, evolves at its own pace, learning those lessons within the framework of what you call space and time, at a pace which is chosen by the entity. For those upon your planet come from many sources, for this planet, which is now finishing its third density experience, has collected into its influence those from many other planets from the third density upon their conclusion of third density, those souls who were unable to achieve the graduation at that time. These entities have come to this planetary influence in order that they might have, once again, the opportunity to learn the lessons of love to the degree necessary to welcome the light of that known as the fourth density of love and understanding. Therefore, the few upon your planet that have evolved from your planet's second density of plant and animal life, could be in one sense considered younger than those who have come to this planet from another third density planet. Yet all are one. In their evolution and by their free choice, entities determine the pace at which they pursue their return to the one Creator.

May we answer you further, my sister?

Questioner: No, thank you, not at this time.

I am Latwii, and I thank you. Is there another question at this time?

M: Yes. Why does Hatonn talk to me when he knows I am not going to say these things? Time's over; is it for next Sunday? Why does he keep talking to me?

I am Latwii, and am aware of your query, my sister. It is a common practice for Confederation members to provide the conditioning vibration to those requesting it as new instruments for as long as the instrument continues to express a desire for this vibration. [Some] of those who do not choose to serve as instruments feel this vibration as a deepening of their meditative state; [some] of those, on the other hand, who are new instruments, not only feel the possibility of the deepening meditation, but are aware of the possibility of transmitting thoughts at that time.

Sensitive instruments, when also being a new instrument, oftentimes are unable to determine the appropriate moment for initiating the contact. This is not unusual. With practice, each instrument may become aware of when the contact is indeed being initiated. The one known as Hatonn has, through your instrument, spoken various thoughts due to the facility with which Hatonn has been able to utilize your instrument. The one known as Hatonn has attempted to build thought upon thought through your channel. There has been the ease of contact with your instrument, coupled with the desire to purely transmit that which is felt by yourself. This desire to purely transmit the thoughts has also provided somewhat a limit to the length of the contact. It is this limit which the one known as Hatonn has offered you the opportunity to lengthen. The opportunity is always there. Your ability to discriminate the appropriate moment for initiating the contact will increase with practice.

May we answer you further, my sister?

M: No, I think you've answered it.

I am Latwii. We are grateful for the opportunity to be of service. Is there another question at this time?

Carla: I have a question sparked by the previous question. When Confederation members send a carrier wave, are there concepts involved in the basic carrier wave? In other words, is there a kind of conceptualized transmission that is answering the subconscious level which may be seeking such information that goes on pretty much all the time, if we open ourselves to it? Or is this carrier wave without concept and M's experience is just a specialized case where she continued to desire the conditioning and, consequently, the sensitive thoughts as well?

I am Latwii, and am aware of your query, my sister. This is not entirely easy to answer, for each experience is most unique. In general, we may say that when the Confederation entities attempt to initiate contact with any instrument there is, by the very nature of the entity involved, a framework, shall we say, of information which is available. Those of Hatonn deal primarily with the concepts of love. When such a contact is initiated, this general framework then is blended, not only with the combined vibrations, shall we say, of the group which is being spoken to, but also is blended with the instrument being utilized; specifically, with the instrument's desires, knowledge, whether conscious or sub-conscious, and the instrument's facility with your language. Therefore, the carrier wave may activate within an instrument a message which blends the Confederation's thoughts, the desires of the group, and the abilities of the instrument. An instrument which desires contact and desires to be of service in this manner may increase the contribution which it makes to that contact if its desire is great. This is acceptable to each Confederation member as long as the instrument also remains open to further communication so concepts may be built upon concepts and a balanced message might be given.

May we answer you further, my sister?

Carla: Yes. I'm sorry to be such a pest, but I've been working with this contact since … twenty years ago, [and] this is the first time this has really come up and I'm fascinated by it. Given that there is another instrument as sensitive as M, I would like to know what's going on next time better. OK. How is a person as sensitive as this new instrument to determine clearly the proper time to initiate contact if the contact is of such a completely comfortable nature that communication is possible on a continual basis? This is not usually true of new instruments and the length is one little by little until a person can communicate a series of concepts. As I understand it, the difficulty is exactly the opposite here where the new instrument is capable of continuing to communicate and continuing to receive and, consequently, how or by what mechanism can such a sensitive new instrument be able to discriminate the proper moment to initiate contact?

I am Latwii, and am aware of your query, my sister. We greatly appreciate the opportunity to comment upon this subject, for, indeed, it is true that seldom do we have the instrument which is both new and quite sensitive and able to perceive our contact with ease. It is therefore recommended to each new instrument that some form of sign be asked for by the new instrument from the Confederation member when contact is to be verbalized. This might take any form comfortable to the instrument, whether it be the gradual opening of the mouth, seemingly at the control of the Confederation member, or the concept within the mind that it is now time to begin to verbalize the concepts, or a feeling of pulsing between the eyebrows, the feeling of energy rushing through the chest, or any other sensation which is acceptable to the instrument. This will allow the new instrument to differentiate between the conditioning vibration, which aids the deepening of the meditation and the initiation of contact through the verbalization of concepts.

May we answer you further, my sister?

Carla: Only if you could give me any other pointers as a person who offers meditations for new instruments in order that I might in any other way be able to help any other new instrument who came to me with the questions M has.

I am Latwii. My sister, we feel that this group has for a great period of what you call time become most familiar with the mechanics of contact of the telepathic nature, therefore, at this time we feel that there has been ample recognition of the nature of the contact by each new instrument and that as new circumstances arise in what you call your future that each entity be asked to query upon any particular problem which is encountered. The asking of the questions concerning the contact should always be encouraged so that the intricacies of this contact might be made known to each entity.

May we answer you further, my sister?

Carla: No, I thank you

I am Latwii. I am grateful to you as well. Is there another question at this time?

A: I have a question. *(Inaudible)*. During meditation sessions, say when you, Latwii, are channeling an answer through an instrument, is it possible for others present to receive or [communicate] with others of, say, Hatonn during, say, your channeling?

I am Latwii, and I am aware of your query my sister. All things are quite possible. We hope that this is not too impossible to digest. If an entity during a meditation, such as this meditation, desires a contact from another Confederation member while a contact is ongoing and being verbalized at that moment, this might occur upon the mental, telepathic level.

Usually such a contact is only felt as the conditioning vibration so that the meditation is deepened, allowing the entity to perceived the concepts being verbalized with as deep a portion of the subconscious mind as possible. This allows the fuller comprehension of the concepts to be enjoyed by the entity.

To seek a contact of a telepathic nature in which concepts are transmitted during a meditation in which verbalized channeling is occurring is possible but not recommended, for though your mind has great potential it is able to focus the attention only upon one train of thought at a time while in the meditative state. Therefore, a choice must be made and it is always recommended that each entity within the circle of meditation focus the energy and the attention upon those verbalized concepts being shared by all, so that the channel may be held as clear and steady as possible, thereby aiding the group as much as is possible. To *(inaudible)* the attention and energy from the concepts being verbalized is to create gaps in the circle of light which sustains the contact.

May we answer you further, my sister?

A: So you're saying also that most likely someone from the Confederation would not initiate mental contact during a meditation. Is this true?

I am Latwii, and I am aware of your query, my sister. This is basically correct, for it is well recognized by each Confederation member that there is a need to keep the focus of attention one-pointed during such telepathic transmission of thoughts. The entities within the circle, however, by the exercise of their free will might at any time request a contact and when called, Confederation members answer in the manner which is most appropriate.

May we answer you further, my sister?

A: No, not at this time, thank you.

I am Latwii. Is there another question at this time?

Questioner: Yes, Latwii. During a Friday session, *(inaudible)* of this group known as M attempted to channel an answer to a question that was in opposition to his own personal bias concerning the subject matter. He had difficulty in transmitting the answer and immediately after had a great deal of difficulty removing the control of his body from the entity channeling through him and regaining the control of his body for himself. Would you please discuss this situation, as it was you initially that was speaking through him?

I am Latwii, and am aware of your query, my brother. When speaking through an instrument such as the one known as M and utilizing concepts which are in opposition to the instrument's beliefs, there is frequently created a situation in which the instrument provides a barrier to the smooth flowing of concepts. Though the instrument's desire may be strong to serve as an instrument, the consternation felt at the information which is being transmitted may for a time cause the instrument to lose the control of its process of receiving the information and block the full reception of the concepts. This can result in another entity's utilization of the instrument for the further diverting of the concepts involved.

This group has, by the very brilliance of the light which emanates from it, attracted the attention of those of the opposite polarity, which is the natural balancing function and, therefore, it is recommended that the most careful tuning be utilized by, not only the group, but by each entity serving as instrument so that the efforts might be kept most pure. When concepts are blocked by the desire of the instrument to transmit only a certain set of thoughts there is set up then the possibility that this blockage might be utilized by other entities. This is quite unusual for most groups do not attract the attention that this group has.

May we answer you further, my brother?

Questioner: Yes. Is this particular instrument known as M possessed of an unusual susceptibility of which he and the others of the group should be aware concerning this potential for displacement and is there any reason that you might suggest that this instrument not channel, or, further, is there any particular process you would recommend for the protection of this individual instrument?

I am Latwii, and am aware of your query, my brother. Instruments, which are sensitive in whatever degree their sensitivity is expressed, are, therefore, sensitive to contact by any entity whose vibratory levels fall within that range of sensitivity, be the entity positive or negative who is attempting to transmit thoughts. It is through the tuning mechanism utilized by the group and by the instrument itself that the choice is made between the positive and negative vibrations. It is, therefore, most helpful [that] the group not only utilize the greatest care in its tuning before the session has begun, but that each instrument utilize some means of determining the nature of the entities wishing to transmit thoughts through their instruments. It is recommended, therefore, that each new instrument create some form of challenge to an entity who wishes to utilize its instrument in the transmission of thoughts. The challenge may take any form which is meaningful to the new instrument. The basic nature of the challenge is to ask that the entity wishing to transmit thoughts whether it is of the Confederation, whether it comes in the name of the Christ or the Christ consciousness, or the positive polarity of service to others. Each Confederation member appreciates this challenge and will answer in the affirmative. Those entities not of the Confederation or not of positive polarity are not able to meet this challenge or answer this query, and therefore, must retire.

Therefore, we once again suggest the tuning of the group and the development of each new instrument of some means of challenging those entities wishing to transmit thoughts through their instrument.

May we answer you further, my brother?

Questioner: Yes, one final question. The information that you have given in response to my questions has been given to me previously, immediately after that session. Could you define for me the source of that information at that time?

I am Latwii, and am aware of your query, my brother. In this case we find that we are bound by that Law of Confusion, also known as the respecting of free will. We find it necessary to recommend that you ponder this query in your meditations and consider its source for yourself.

May we answer further, my brother?

Questioner: No, for myself and my brother M, I thank you.

I am Latwii. We are most grateful to you. Is there another question at this time?

Carla: I would like to apologize to the instrument, but I do have a couple of questions here about M's experience. First of all, is it possible that M's long time fear that precisely this thing would happen to him attracted this experience to him?

I am Latwii, and am aware of your query, my sister. We shall relay your apologies to the instrument. To respond to your query, it is indeed quite possible that what one fears shall be drawn unto the entity until the fear is balanced with acceptance. For …

(Tape ends.) ☙

SUNDAY MEDITATION
JUNE 26, 1982

(M channeling)

I am Hatonn, and I am now with this instrument. I greet you with the love and the light of the infinite Creator. I would like to explain what happened last Sunday. I was not with this instrument when she translated the concept into words. She is not aware that she does not understand words. I will explain this to you. If you say right to her, she cannot understand it. She will say mentally, "You mean turn the machine not to the left but to the right?" This is a concept and she can understand it and follow it. I would not suggest that you say "fire" to her because she has to translate it into, "The building is on fire," into a concept and then she will respond. If I gave her words she would have to translate the words into a concept and translate the concept back into words. It is much easier for me to give her a concept. I will not give her a concept late in the meeting. She may be involved that she forgets to translate it into words. This would not happen again because she would understand that she was translating the concept after I left. She was so fascinated with the concept that she wanted to tell you what I had told her.

I was explaining to her that television machines and cooling systems are negative influences. Before television and cooling systems people sat on their front porch and became involved with their other selves. The drama was not as condensed on the front porch but it was real, and they did not feel isolated the way they do in front of their TV set. Even refrigeration is negatively oriented. In the days of the icebox people went down to the drugstore for ice cream. They went to the grocery store because perishables would not keep. They became involved with their other selves. These machines are negatively oriented. You must be very careful not to use them extensively. That is one reason that there is so much crime on the streets. People are isolated. They do not care. Be aware of the negative influence of these machines and make a point of not using them too much.

I now leave this instrument. I am Hatonn.

(Carla channeling)

I am Hatonn, and am now with this instrument. I greet you once again in the love and in the light of our infinite Creator. It was not our original intention to speak through this instrument at this time, but as we have communications of two types to offer we shall take this opportunity to do so. We would first say to our sister, M, that the brilliance and the clarity of this instrument's personality is quite unusual among your peoples upon this planet. Unlike many of your peoples who seek, this instrument's seeking takes place in an atmosphere which you may call the brightest of noons, and is not shadowed by the many shadings of doubt and confusion that complicate the seeking of many of your peoples.

This has both aided and, may we say, somewhat hindered our initiation of contact with this gifted instrument. It has aided our contact in that we are able to communicate so openly, for this instrument has been well tuned, shall we say, to a specific spiritual frequency of positivity, love and light for a great portion of this instrument's incarnation. However, we would caution the instrument known as M that we, as Confederation members, never instruct but always suggest, that we always desire to leave the room for the doubting, the pause for the consideration. Therefore, when this instrument receives a portion of a concept that is a conclusion that brooks no contrary opinion, this communication contains a large portion of that which is the loving and brilliant deeper mind of the instrument. We desire to keep as a part of all free will channeling a portion of that character that makes each entity a unique and inspiring instrument. However, we say to you, my sister, and to all new channels, we do not wish to instruct your peoples, for we are your brothers and sisters. Therefore, if you receive such, shall we say, cut and dried concepts, ask for more clarity. Ask for a purer contact and we shall be there making the adjustment necessary to blend our thoughts with yours in order that the love and the light of the infinite Creator may be offered to your peoples in words that inspire without the ordering.

We would, in addition, wish to continue that message which was begun so that we may express through each instrument the same thought that you may perceive in two ways—one intention and one meaning. We spoke to you, my friends, of some of what you may call your gadgets—your televisions and your refrigeration. My friends, we could go on and remind you of many of the elements of those days which are in your memory or in the memories of those who bore you into this incarnation, memories of the time when there were more than two or three in a household, where domiciled together there were many more other selves, and where, because of the relative lack of movement geographically among your peoples, there was a far longer term of interaction between yourself and those to whom each person was close. In this particular time, as you call it, your peoples lacked the luxury of those several other selves with whom to

spend an incarnation. And we say a luxury, my friends, because each entity who reflects a loved one in love and without stint or grudge becomes a mirror so that the growth of the entity may accelerate greatly.

For example, my friends, you may hear the babe crying and feel some emotion when that babe is part of a drama upon your television, but need you go and comfort it? Need you nurture it? No, my friends. It is gone to be replaced by another which likewise will only touch you briefly. But to hear the babe crying and to go to it—ah, my friends, there lies service. There lies the opportunity.

There are some of you who come in contact with many, many other selves in your daily lives and yet do not receive the mirror until you meet those other selves that cause you concern, that cause you to ponder, to meditate, to pray, and to care. We ask that you thank the Creator for each opportunity that you have to experience the contact with other selves that teaches you your nature, that gives you the mirror for yourself.

It has been said in your holy works that the love of money is the root of all evil. We would paraphrase this and say that the love of distraction is the root of the slowing of the spirit. It is not that anything is negative in itself, but if an inanimate object, if a convenience, if that which gives you solitude, is loved and sought when you have the opportunity to look in the mirror of your other self, then, my friends, that inanimate object has become a blockage to the positive growth of yourself as a seeker. Seek ye then that truth and that love which can only be found in the experiences of meditation and of the serious consideration of all those thoughts that concern you in your dealings and in your attempts to be of service to your brothers and your sisters.

In closing we thank you for your patience and we thank the one known as M. Indeed, we do not wish to seem to be giving this instrument a hard time but because of this instrument's ability we have a desire to aid this instrument in its nurturing that those words which through her come may be to the fullest extent be that which she wishes—a true channel for the love and the light, and it is in that Creator and in that creation that we leave you. I am Hatonn. Adonai vasu borragus. ⸙

L/L Research is a subsidiary of
Rock Creek Research &
Development Laboratories, Inc.

P.O. Box 5195
Louisville, KY 40255-0195

L/L RESEARCH

www.llresearch.org

Rock Creek is a non-profit
corporation dedicated to
discovering and sharing
information which may aid in
the spiritual evolution of
humankind.

THE LAW OF ONE, BOOK IV, SESSION 91
JUNE 26, 1982

Ra: I am Ra. I greet you in the love and in the light of the one infinite Creator. We communicate now.

Questioner: Could you first please give me the condition of the instrument?

Ra: I am Ra. It is as previously stated.

Questioner: I have listed the different minds and would like to know if they are applied in this particular aspect: first, we have the cosmic mind which is, I would think, the same for all sub-Logoi like our sun. Is this correct?

Ra: I am Ra. This is correct.

Questioner: A sub-Logos such as our sun, then, in creating Its own particular evolutionary experience, refines the cosmic mind or, shall we say, articulates it by Its own additional bias or biases. Is this the correct observation?

Ra: I am Ra. It is a correct observation with the one exception that concerns the use of the term "addition" which suggests the concept of that which is more than the all-mind. Instead, the archetypical mind is a refinement of the all-mind in a pattern peculiar to the sub-Logo's choosing.

Questioner: Then the very next refinement that occurs as the cosmic mind is refined is what we call the archetypical mind. Is this correct?

Ra: I am Ra. Yes.

Questioner: Then this creates, I would assume, the planetary or racial mind. Is this correct?

Ra: I am Ra. No.

Questioner: What is the origin of the planetary or racial mind?

Ra: I am Ra. This racial or planetary mind is, for this Logos, a repository of biases remembered by the mind/body/spirit complexes which have enjoyed the experience of this planetary influence.

Questioner: Now, some entities on this planet evolved from second density into third and some were transferred from other planets to recycle in third density here. Did the ones who were transferred here to recycle in third density add to the planetary or racial mind?

Ra: I am Ra. Not only did each race add to the planetary mind but also each race possesses a racial mind. Thus we made this distinction in discussing this portion of mind. This portion of mind is formed in the series of seemingly non-simultaneous experiences which are chosen in freedom of will by the mind/body/spirit complexes of the planetary influence. Therefore, although this Akashic, planetary, or racial mind is indeed a root of mind it may be seen in sharp differentiation from the deeper roots of mind which are not a function of altering memory, if you will.

We must ask your patience at this time. This channel has become somewhat unclear due to the movement of the cover which touches this instrument. We ask that the opening sentences be repeated and the breath expelled.

(The microphones attached to the cover upon the instrument were pulled slightly as a rug was being placed over a noisy tape recorder. The Circle of One was walked; breath was expelled two feet above the instrument's head from her right to her left; and the Circle of One was walked again as requested.)

Ra: I am Ra. We communicate now.

Questioner: Were we successful in re-establishing clear contact?

Ra: I am Ra. There was the misstep which then needed to be re-repeated. This was done. The communication is once again clear. We enjoyed the humorous aspects of the necessary repetitions.

Questioner: What occurred when the microphone cords were slightly moved?

Ra: I am Ra. The link between the instrument's mind/body/spirit complex and its yellow-ray, chemical, physical vehicle was jarred. This caused some maladjustment of the organ you call the lungs and, if the repair had not been done, would have resulted in a distorted physical complex condition of this portion of the instrument's physical vehicle.

Questioner: What kind of distortion?

Ra: I am Ra. The degree of distortion would depend upon the amount of neglect. The ultimate penalty, shall we say, for the disturbing of the physical vehicle is the death, in this case by what you would call the congestive heart failure. As the support group was prompt there should be little or no distortion experienced by the instrument.

Questioner: Why does such a very minor effect like the slight movement of the microphone cord result in this situation, not mechanically or chemically, but philosophically, if you can answer this question?

Ra: I am Ra. We can only answer mechanically as there is no philosophy to the reflexes of physical vehicular function.

There is what you might call the silver cord reflex; that is, when the mind/body/spirit complex dwells without the environs of the physical shell and the physical shell is disturbed, the physical shell will reflexively call back the absent enlivener; that is, the mind/body/spirit complex which is connected with

what may be metaphysically seen as what some of your philosophers have called the silver cord. If this is done suddenly the mind/body/spirit complex will attempt entry into the energy web of the physical vehicle without due care and the effect is as if one were to stretch one of your elastic bands and let it shrink rapidly. The resulting snap would strike hard at the anchored portion of the elastic band.

The process through which you as a group go in recalling this instrument could be likened unto taking this elastic and gently lessening its degree of tension until it was without perceptible stretch.

Questioner: To get back to what we were talking about, would the different races of this planet be from different planets in our local vicinity or the planets of nearby Logoi which have evolved through their second-density experiences, and would they create the large number of different races that we experience on this planet?

Ra: I am Ra. There are correctnesses to your supposition. However, not all races and sub-races are of various planetary origins. We suggest that in looking at planetary origins one observes not the pigmentation of the integument but the biases concerning interactions with other-selves and definitions regarding the nature of the self.

Questioner: How many different planets have supplied the individuals which now inhabit this planet?

Ra: I am Ra. This is perceived by us to be unimportant information, but harmless. There are three major planetary influences upon your planetary sphere, besides those of your own second-density derivation, and thirteen minor planetary groups in addition to the above.

Questioner: Thank you. One more question before we start on the specific questions in regard to archetypes. Do all Logoi evolving after the veil have twenty-two archetypes?

Ra: I am Ra. No.

Questioner: Is it common for Logoi to have twenty-two archetypes or is this relatively unique to our Logos?

Ra: I am Ra. The system of sevens is the most articulated system yet discovered by any experiment by any Logos in our octave.

Questioner: What is the largest number of archetypes, to Ra's knowledge, used by a Logos?

Ra: I am Ra. The sevens plus The Choice is the greatest number which has been used, by our knowledge, by Logoi. It is the result of many, many previous experiments in articulation of the one Creator.

Questioner: I assume, then, that twenty-two is the greatest number of archetypes. I also ask is it the minimum number presently in use by any Logos to Ra's knowledge?

Ra: I am Ra. The fewest are the two systems of five which are completing the cycles or densities of experience.

You must grasp the idea that the archetypes were not developed at once but step by step, and not in order as you know the order at this space/time but in various orders. Therefore, the two systems of fives were using two separate ways of viewing the archetypical nature of all experience. Each, of course, used the Matrix, the Potentiator, and the Significator for this is the harvest with which our creation began.

One way or system of experimentation had added to these the Catalyst and the Experience. Another system if you will, had added Catalyst and Transformation. In one case the methods whereby experience was processed was further aided but the fruits of experience less aided. In the second case the opposite may be seen to be the case.

Questioner: Thank you. We have some observations on the archetypes which are as follows. First, the Matrix of the Mind is depicted in the Egyptian tarot by a male and this we take as creative energy intelligently directed. Will Ra comment on this?

Ra: I am Ra. This is an extremely thoughtful perception seeing as it does the male not specifically as biological male but as a male principle. You will note that there are very definite sexual biases in the images. They are intended to function both as information as to which biological entity or energy will attract which archetype and also as a more general view which sees polarity as a key to the archetypical mind of third density.

Questioner: The second observation is that we have a wand which has been seen as the power of the will. Will Ra comment?

Ra: I am Ra. The concept of will is indeed pouring forth from each facet of the image of the Matrix of the Mind. The wand as the will, however, is, shall we say, an astrological derivative of the out-reaching hand forming the, shall we say, magical gesture. The excellent portion of the image which may be seen distinctly as separate from the concept of the wand is that sphere which indicates the spiritual nature of the object of the will of one wishing to do magical acts within the manifestation of your density.

Questioner: The hand downward has been seen as seeking from within and not from without and the active dominance over the material world. Would Ra comment on that?

Ra: I am Ra. Look again, O student. Does the hand reach within? Nay. Without potentiation the conscious mind has no inwardness. That hand, O student, reaches towards that which, outside its unpotentiated influence, is locked from it.

Questioner: The square cage represents the material illusion and is an unmagical shape. Can Ra comment on that?

Ra: I am Ra. The square, wherever seen, is the symbol of the third-density illusion and may be seen either as unmagical or, in the proper configuration, as having been manifested within; that is, the material world given life.

Questioner: The dark area around the square, then, would be the darkness of the subconscious mind. Would Ra comment on that?

Ra: I am Ra. There is no further thing to say to the perceptive student.

Questioner: The checkered portion would represent polarity?

Ra: I am Ra. This also is satisfactory.

Questioner: The bird is a messenger which the hand is reaching down to unlock. Can Ra comment on that?

Ra: I am Ra. The winged visions or images in this system are to be noted not so much for their distinct kind as for the position of the wings. All birds are indeed intended to suggest that just as the Matrix figure, the Magician, cannot act without reaching its winged spirit, so neither can the spirit fly lest it be released into conscious manifestation and fructified thereby.

Questioner: The star would represent the potentiating forces of the subconscious mind. Is this correct?

Ra: I am Ra. This particular part of this image is best seen in astrological terms. We would comment at this space/time that Ra did not include the astrological portions of these images in the system of images designed to evoke the archetypical leitmotifs.

Questioner: Are there any other additions to Card Number One other than the star that are of other than the basic archetypical aspects?

Ra: I am Ra. There are details of each image seen through the cultural eye of the time of inscription. This is to be expected. Therefore, when viewing the, shall we say, Egyptian costumes and systems of mythology used in the images it is far better to penetrate to the heart of the costumes' significance or the creatures' significance rather than clinging to a culture which is not your own.

In each entity the image will resonate slightly differently. Therefore, there is the desire upon Ra's part to allow for the creative envisioning of each archetype using general guidelines rather than specific and limiting definitions.

Questioner: The cup represents a mixture of positive and negative passions. Could Ra comment on that?

Ra: I am Ra. The otic portions of this instrument's physical vehicle did not perceive a significant portion of your query. Please requery.

Questioner: There is apparently a cup which we have as containing a mixture of positive and negative influences. However, I personally doubt this. Could Ra comment on this, please?

Ra: I am Ra. Doubt not the polarity, O student, but release the cup from its stricture. It is indeed a distortion of the original image.

Questioner: What was the original image?

Ra: I am Ra. The original image had the checkering as the suggestion of polarity.

Questioner: Then was this a representation of the waiting polarity to be tasted by the Matrix of the Mind?

Ra: I am Ra. This is exquisitely perceptive.

Questioner: I have listed here the sword as representing struggle. I am not sure that I even can call anything in this diagram a sword. Would Ra comment on that?

Ra: I am Ra. Doubt not the struggle, O student, but release the sword from its stricture. Observe the struggle of a caged bird to fly.

Questioner: I have listed the coin represents work accomplished. I am also in doubt about the existence of the coin in this diagram. Could Ra comment on that please?

Ra: I am Ra. Again, doubt not that which the coin is called to represent, for does not the Magus strive to achieve through the manifested world? Yet release the coin from its stricture.

Questioner: And finally, the Magician represents the conscious mind. Is this correct?

Ra: I am Ra. We ask the student to consider the concept of the unfed conscious mind, the mind without any resource but consciousness. Do not confuse the unfed conscious mind with that mass of complexities which you as students experience, as you have so many, many times dipped already into the processes of potentiation, catalyst, experience, and transformation.

Questioner: Are these all of the components, then, of this first archetype?

Ra: I am Ra. These are all you, the student, see. Thusly the complement is complete for you. Each student may see some other nuance. We, as we have said, did not offer these images with boundaries but only as guidelines intending to aid the adept and to establish the architecture of the deep, or archetypical, portion of the deep mind.

Questioner: How is the knowledge of the facets of the archetypical mind used by the individual to accelerate his evolution?

Ra: I am Ra. We shall offer an example based upon this first explored archetype or concept complex. The conscious mind of the adept may be full to bursting of the most abstruse and unimaginable of ideas, so that further ideation becomes impossible and work in blue ray or indigo is blocked through over-activation. It is then that the adept would call upon the new mind, untouched and virgin, and dwell within the archetype of the new and unblemished mind without bias, without polarity, full of the magic of the Logos.

Questioner: Then you are saying, if I am correct in understanding what you have just said, that the conscious mind may be filled with an almost infinite number of concepts but there is a set of basic concepts which are what I would call important simply because they are the foundations for the evolution of consciousness, and will, if carefully applied, accelerate the evolution of consciousness, whereas the vast array of concepts, ideas, and experiences that we meet in our daily lives may have little or no bearing upon the evolution of consciousness except in a very indirect way. In other words, what we are attempting to do here is find the motivators of evolution and utilize them to move through our evolutionary track. Is this correct?

Ra: I am Ra. Not entirely. The archetypes are not the foundation for spiritual evolution but rather are the tool for grasping in an undistorted manner the nature of this evolution.

Questioner: So for an individual who wished to consciously augment his own evolution, an ability to recognize and utilize the archetypes would be beneficial in sorting out that which he wishes to seek from that which would be not as efficient a seeking tool. Would this be a good statement?

Ra: I am Ra. This is a fairly adequate statement. The term "efficient" might also fruitfully be replaced by the term "undistorted." The archetypical mind, when penetrated lucidly, is a blueprint of the builded structure of all energy expenditures and all seeking without distortion. This, as a resource within the deep mind, is of great potential aid to the adept.

We would ask for one more query at this space/time as this instrument is experiencing continuous surges of the distortion you call pain and we wish to take our leave of the working while the instrument still possesses a sufficient amount of transferred energy to ease the transition to the waking state, if you would call it that.

Questioner: Since we are at the end of the Matrix of the Mind I will just ask if there is anything that we can do to make the instrument more comfortable or to improve the contact?

Ra: I am Ra. Each is most conscientious. The instrument might be somewhat more comfortable with the addition of the swirling of the waters with spine erect. All other things which can be performed for the instrument's benefit are most diligently done.

We commend the continual fidelity of the group to the ideals of harmony and thanksgiving. This shall be your great protection. All is well, my friends. The appurtenances and alignments are excellent.

I am Ra. I leave you glorying in the love and in the light of the one infinite Creator. Go forth, then, rejoicing in the power and the peace of the one infinite Creator. Adonai. ☩

SUNDAY MEDITATION
JULY 4, 1982

(Carla channeling)

[I am Hatonn,] and I greet you, my friends in the love and the light of our infinite Creator. We would speak through this instrument in order to express your compassion and that of the Confederation of Planets in the Service of the Infinite Creator for your planet. We are aware as we look into the thoughts of this instrument that this day has meaning to your nation. It is a day called Independence Day, won, my friends, as so many things have been won upon your planet, by killing and forcing one group's opinion upon another in what seems to be a planetary love of hostile struggle. We know that you as well grieve for those strangers who you have never met, who die violently in unknown lands mouthing the ideals that have been taught them. We know that within your thoughts there lies great concern for those who have killed but have not been killed.

My friends, in the end, the victors and the victims merge into one pitiable panorama of carnage and experience, hard won. We would not say to you, my friends, that those who are the victims of what you call war have not profited in their spiritual growth, for all experience is useful, and death is but the end of a parenthesis in endlessness. But we would say to you, my friends, that because of the nationwide preoccupation with ideals that presuppose hostile actions, and because of planetary belief systems which are likewise dangerous, your planet is in great need of healing and in potential need of far more healing, for there are many within your planetary sphere who would not be adverse to global warfare.

Therefore, as your hearts go out to those of whom you may know who have died attempting to be of service by killing and being killed, we take this opportunity to suggest to you that at any time that you may feel this compassion which we share for your planet that you share with your planet your peace and your love. Peace, my friends, is not a word used to indicate a positive [force] but rather the absence of a negative. Peace has been used by your peoples to mean an absence of active hostility. My friends, there is a peace that is an active principle. It is the other face of power, and it is part of the nature of the unity of all creation. That peace is no weak alternative to an ideal. That peace offers power of a spiritual kind which dissolves the seeming impossibilities of your geographical enmities and their rapprochement. We ask you to call upon that peace, that active and living principle of a Creator of love. Whenever you see brother against brother, may we suggest that you become inwardly active, invoking that principle of peace. The power of that principle is as great as your ability to comprehend the functions, the activities, and the being of yourself and all about you as one thing.

At this time, my brother Laitos shall begin conditioning each newer instrument, and we shall transfer this contact to the one known as S1. I am Hatonn.

(S1 channeling)

I am Hatonn. I am with this instrument, and I greet you again, my brothers and sisters, in the love and the light of the infinite Creator. My friends, this love is a blessed thing—to share this love with your brothers and sisters no matter who they are or where you meet them, in your work day, in your daily lives, on the streets of your world, in the structures of your planet, remember they are your other selves, your brothers and sisters, and share this love which you feel within this group, this small number of entities. Think on this, my friends. Were you to share with one other entity this feeling and they were to share, how quickly the feeling would grow and become larger and larger toward the end which we all seek and strive for.

My friends, remember as you go about your daily lives that we are with you, should you ever call—correction—should you but ask our assistance, and it will be joyfully and cheerfully given, for we know that in your density the striving is quite difficult at times, and the confusion of your world tends to get you down, so to speak. But, my friends, the love that we have for you and share with you this evening is always there. Our humble words that we share with you through these instruments are only given to guide you and help you along your way. They are not meant to direct you or confidently tell you how your path should or must be. For only you, my friends know what your path is and what you are most comfortable with. This is beginning to know yourself and know your desires and where your path leads.

My friends, our love is always with you at a thought. We share your dreams, my friends. I leave you now, quietly, peacefully, as we hope your day has been, as we hope all your days will be, my brothers and sisters. I am known to you as Hatonn. Adonai, my friends. Adonai vasu borragus.

(M channeling)

I am Hatonn. I am now with this instrument. I greet you with the love and the light of the infinite Creator. I have been with this instrument for some time. She loves to talk with me and I know that she will tell it to you, even though she prefers not to. We have been discussing freedom, as it is your day of freedom. Freedom is an interesting concept. Plants, trees and flowers have limited freedom because they cannot move. They can only live, die, become smaller or larger. But animals such as the squirrel has more freedom, but he can only be a squirrel. He cannot be a cat or a dog. You as a human have much more freedom than a squirrel. You have the opportunity to understand larger ideas. You can choose, but many of your choices are not consequential. It is similar to choosing vanilla or chocolate. In the long run it really doesn't matter.

Many people feel they have great freedom. But part of their freedom is ignorance. They do not realize that they were patterned as a squirrel and flower. The other people are their other selves. They can hurt them. They can help them. They can learn at a slow rate, a fast rate, or whatever is their rate. But they are linked to the Creator. They are linked with their other selves, and this does limit their freedom, as a squirrel's freedom is limited to being a squirrel. The more knowledge they see, the less freedom they really have. Freedom is precious in one sense and dangerous in another. Everything you do affects other people. If you have the freedom to love, you are directed in a positive way. You also have the freedom to hate, and that is not necessarily bad. It certainly is negative, and you are hurting your other selves. You do have these choices. So your freedom is large in some sense and very small in others. I am Hatonn. I now leave this instrument.

(S1 channeling)

I am Laitos, and I greet you, my brothers and sisters, in the love and light of our infinite Creator. I come this evening to share with you our conditioning vibration and to blend our vibration with yours in the hopes that we may be of service to you, brothers and sisters. In blending our vibrations and sending our conditioning to you, you allow us to be of service, and our love is strongly visible in this way.

My friends, this day on your planet has been one of seeking in the hearts of many for the meaning of freedom—of freedom of will, freedom of your countries, and the dangers they face in the upcoming times. Many peoples on your planet wish to know the joy of freedom that you experience this evening within this group—the freedom and joy of loving one another, of sharing yourselves with one another, and being as one. So many of your peoples, my loved ones, do not share this feeling, this source of freedom. To love and share that love with one another is a source of freedom.

We wished only to say a few words through this instrument and will now leave you in the love and light of the Creator. But remember, my dear ones, should you but ask, and we will be with you to share our conditioning vibration to help you in your meditation, to share our love with you. Should you but ask with your mind, and we will be there. We leave you now, that our brothers and sisters of Latwii may perform their service of answering any questions you may have brought with you this evening. In so doing, you allow them also to serve you in the love and light. Again, my friends of our infinite Creator, we leave you now. I am Laitos.

(Carla channeling)

I am Latwii, and I greet you, my friends, in the love and in the light of the one infinite Creator. We are adjusting to relax this instrument's neck. We do not wish to be a pain in the neck. We enjoy channeling through this instrument and seldom have a reason to do so especially, but wished to aid our brothers and sisters in this meeting which we have been witnessing with our usual enjoyment and anticipation of our art. We are aware that each instrument wishes to know the progress of its opening of its instrument, and we wish to assure that we have refrained from working with the ones known as D and S2 this evening due to feelings that it would be more efficacious in an intensive session, as there were some thoughts that were called for by the group this evening, and we wished to have, what you call, the time to express them without wearing out your seats.

We would say to the instrument known as S1 that we look forward to working with this instrument, and commend this instrument on the quality of its work. It is proceeding quite accurately and needs only release a very small bit more of the personality to flesh out our concept in order to be re—we correct this instrument, which has a tied tongue—in order to reach the desired ration of deeper self to Confederation concept.

To the one known as M we would also commend the conscientious and continuing efforts. We would, however, attempt to clarify this evening's experience, that this gifted instrument may learn the techniques of what you may call the surrender of the personality in order that the appropriate ratio of Confederation concept may be reached. The conditioning was of the one known as Laitos. We are aware that this is difficult sometimes for the new instrument to perceive, that is, which entity is contacting it. But it is well to request identification. Also, there are often clues in the rhythm of the meetings, such as the statement by our brothers and sisters of Hatonn that the Laitos entities were working with the new instruments. Also, it is rare for our somewhat professorial brothers and sisters of Hatonn to leave a meeting with the appropriate closing and then immediately return as if they had left their spectacle case.

These are intended to be helpful, and not to be critical, for as the instrument known as M may see to, we hope, her delight, the gist of the message was as given by Laitos with only the exception of the portion given by the entity, S1. This portion was a substantial portion, as it redefined freedom moving from that fixed position which each entity finds itself in in a very thick illusion and transferring the concept of freedom to the vastness of the inward reaches of self and its identification with love. In love and in service, my friends, there is perfect freedom. This is a patent paradox. It is only in the working out of this paradox that the experience of true freedom is found.

We thank this instrument and all the new instruments for the great service that they provide us, and, as always, offer to you our heartfelt joy at being requested to share our thoughts with you. Since this instrument is restricted from the question and answer portion, we have the privilege of using another instrument at this time, one whose patience with us is well known. We therefore would transfer this contact at this time to the instrument known as Jim. I am Latwii.

(Jim channeling)

I am Latwii, and am with this instrument. We greet you once again in love and light. It is our privilege at this time to offer ourselves in the capacity of attempting to answer your queries. Are there any queries at this time?

S2: Yes, Latwii. Excuse me for being vague, but this is a rather private question. I have a perception that is bothering me quite a bit. Can you tell me if this perception is correct? If you cannot do that, can you give me any information about it?

I am Latwii, and am aware of your query, vague though it be. To private queries we give general responses. We say firstly that …

(Side one of tape ends.)

(Jim channeling)

I am Latwii, and am with this instrument once again. The supposition which you have perceived is that which may provide for you a catalyst for further growth, my sister. To look upon such a possibility with the eyes of the usual responses and perceptions of your culture is to see only within strict boundaries. May we say, these boundaries are not necessary. There is the possibility of a great freedom which also is paramount within this perception. We hope that we have not been too vague, but this is our lot in such a situation.

May we respond further, my sister?

S2: Yes. Am I incorrect in perceiving this as potentially dangerous?

I am Latwii, and am aware of your query, my sister. We can only respond by suggesting that though the danger may exist, its manifestation is not necessarily the outcome of the situation which you have perceived. There are other possibilities included.

May we answer you further, my sister?

S2: I'll have to think on it for a minute. Thank you.

We are most grateful to you for allowing us this service. Is there another question at this time?

Carla: Well, I'd like to follow up this vague question that I couldn't figure out much of a general answer to. So let's just say for the sake of a possible other question that someone has a perception of some metaphysical stumbling block or even a metaphysical difficulty which may be seen as negative. You said that anything which may be perceived as dangerous may also be perceived as not dangerous. There would seem to be suggested some transformation. Is this in the mind of the perceiver?

I am Latwii. My sister, we feel that you have grasped the heart of our response. We apologize for the vagueness that is necessitated by the type of query which we have responded to. Any perception which an entity has within the mind, whether it be that which seems most unavoidable and imminent within the future, as you call it, or that which is vaguely feared as a possibility at a distant date, there is the possibility within the entity's mind to rearrange the thinking, shall we say, by looking at that which is feared. There is the possibility of allowing that feared perception to grow in the mind, run its full course, and find the balance within the same mind so that no longer is fear the response towards the possible occurrence. Thus, indeed, might a transformation occur within an entity's mind, for all experiences upon your planet within this illusion have the purpose of transformation.

May we answer you further, my sister?

Carla: Not on that point. That's a great answer. Thank you. I would like to ask you a question that's not vague, in that I don't mind talking about it, but it's kind of hard to put into words. In the past month or so I've been feeling an increasing desire to have a vacation of some kind after about a year and a half of pretty steady, heavy-duty metaphysical work with the Ra contact, and I'm dealing with a lot of feelings of guilt at the thought of just letting the Ra contact go for the amount of time it would take me to be away for awhile, and to a lesser extent, the feeling of just not being available for the people that might need to talk with me or be with me. I wonder if you could talk to me about the concept of selfishness and service because I'm not feeling balanced on that point, and even after meditation I'm not feeling balanced.

I am Laitos, and am aware of your query, my sister. To respond most helpfully, we feel that we should begin by suggesting that the configuration of the mind is that which determines the entity's responses, perceptions and actions. It is this configuration of the mind that each entity has incarnated to work upon in a balanced manner. The activities which an entity undertakes to be of whatever service it can be are activities which have been determined before the incarnation. Therefore, when an entity gives itself to a service which it hopes will be of benefit to others, there is then the feeling within the entity that a completion of purpose has been accomplished. Along the path of this service, however, it might be noted that the entity may discover certain needs that from time to time may apparently detract from that service if the needs are fulfilled. To an entity who sincerely desires to be of service to others, it is often the case that the personal needs become neglected, for an entity does not wish frequently to focus overly much on those needs that may at first seem somewhat selfish. Yet, must not an entity maintain its being in a manner which is able to serve others most efficiently? Can one ask the self to never consider its own needs, and yet continue to serve others? In many cases, the answer is obvious.

Would you refuse to eat when your body needs nourishment in order that one more effort be made in the service of another? This could be done for some portion of your time. It could not be continued overly long. Would you refuse the sleep that is necessary for the maintenance of your physical vehicle? Again, only for a limited time. Each entity must look within the self to discover those needs which indeed are unique to its own being. It may be that an entity would be greatly benefited, and the service it performs benefited as well by the variation of the pace, shall we say, in the service to others. It is often the case that an entity becomes overly idealistic in the serving of others, and gets in its own way, shall we say, by refusing to see that the self has needs which must be met.

May we answer you further, my sister?

Carla: That's a really helpful answer, but how do you tell when those are needs that have to be met, and when those are needs that are just sort of whimsical or extra or selfish?

I am Latwii. My sister, when you do not eat, how often does your body tell you that you are hungry? When you do not sleep, how often do you hear a call of sleep until, indeed, you do sleep? Any need which strikes to the core of your being, and continues in its call may be considered that which is not of a frivolous nature, for those needs of a frivolous nature tend to come and go with the wind, with time, and with forgetting.

May we answer you further, my sister?

Carla: No, thank you, Latwii. That did it. Thank you.

I am Latwii. We thank you. Is there another query at this time?

M: Yes, Latwii. Could you tell me why my messages are different than other people?

I am Latwii, and am aware of your query, my sister. Each entity which wishes to serve as an instrument for the Confederation of Planets in the Service of the One Infinite Creator is quite unique. Most entities who wish this service, as you are aware, begin a process which is somewhat different than your own,

though each is quite unique. Your process, as has been observed by our brothers and sisters of Hatonn, is one which is quite open and available. This openness allows for a much easier contact and the fluid transmission of concepts, but at the same time offers a difficulty in that due to your desire to transmit clearly those thoughts which you receive, you have the need to, shall we say, become aware of a greater amount of the message before you are willing to act as instrument and transmit the concepts. This desire on your part is respected by each Confederation entity, for it is of paramount importance that the free will of each instrument be maintained.

In your particular case, as we have mentioned, this desire to transmit clearly which has resulted in the desire to know the major portion of the message before its transmission, allows for a clear perception of transmission, yet puts certain boundaries upon that transmission, for to add to those concepts which you have become aware of is then difficult after you have initiated the contact, since additions lie beyond the boundaries which are acceptable to you. It is therefore quite easy for the shorter message of a unique nature to be transmitted through your instrument, but is more difficult for the development of concepts. This creates the bright star effect, shall we say, where the contact blooms rapidly and then ends as rapidly. We might suggest, if you wish to expand these gifted abilities, that in subsequent contacts, when you feel the message is near its end as you perceive it, remain with the contact. Allow the mind to become completely blank, virgin, unblemished with any preconceived idea. And then speak those concepts which begin to appear upon the horizon of your mind. This then will allow the development of concepts which would not be possible otherwise.

May we answer you further, my sister?

M: No. I think you've answered me very well. Thank you.

I am Latwii. We are most grateful to you. Is there another question at this time?

S1: Yes, Latwii. Why would someone not remember their dreams?

I am Latwii, and am aware of your query, my sister. That state of your being known as the dream state is seldom given much value by the entities upon your planet. There is a great cultural bias which suggests that dreams be ignored as being unreal and useless. Therefore, it takes a great deal of effort on the part of any entity wishing to utilize this state of your being for growth to utilize it. An entity needs to make the inner commitment each night before retiring to your sleep that it shall remember those events in which it partakes during its sleeping time. When this commitment has been intensified to the sufficient degree that the subconscious is convinced that the conscious mind wishes a communication with it, then the subconscious mind shall aid in the remembering of the dreams.

May we answer you further, my sister?

S1: Well, I have a question for a friend. Is there any spiritual value in, or could spiritual value be applied in developing the area of telekinesis in an individual?

I am Latwii, and am aware of your query, my sister. Each area which is of potential interest to an entity, whatever the area, does indeed have the possibility of providing spiritual sustenance, for is not the one creation the one Creator, and does not all experience teach this simple lesson? But we must also say, my sister, that there are certain areas which some of your peoples find of interest only for the novelty that that area offers. Those abilities described as telekinetic by your parapsychological researchers are of such a nature. Most entities, in attempting to research or develop such abilities, lose sight of the relationship between that ability and the evolution of the mind, the body, and the spirit. It is as though a trinket were placed in front of the eyes and the entity became hypnotized, and was unable to see beyond the trinket. If an entity enters into such an endeavor to study this particular area, or any other, with the desire to seek the truth, to use the study to seek the means to enhance that seeking, then the seeking indeed may well be enhanced. In short, may we suggest that it is the attitude of the entity which determines whether fruits shall be found upon one tree or another.

May we answer you further, my sister?

S1: No, thank you, Latwii.

I am Latwii. We thank you. Is there another question at this time?

Questioner: Yes, Latwii. When in the dream state, does the subconscious mind leave the three dimensional plane, and, if so, where is it? Does it leave the body and the three dimensional plane, and, if so, where does it go during the dream state?

I am Latwii, and am aware of your query, my sister. That known to your peoples as the subconscious mind exists in realms and reaches far greater than has ever been perceived by those who have studied the phenomenon of dreams. Your conscious mind dwells in this illusion for the purpose of utilizing the catalyst which may teach it the lessons necessary for the graduation. The subconscious mind, on the other hand, is directly linked to the creative forces which are the foundation not only of this illusion but of all illusions within this octave of experience. The subconscious mind, therefore, includes a great array of resources which the conscious mind might draw upon for inspiration and information to expand the boundaries of its perception. The subconscious mind has the basic purpose of allowing this expansion of perception and increase in the ability to learn by providing the catalysts which provoke, shall we say, new lessons and learnings. The subconscious mind is directly connected to the planetary mind, that is, the mind that contains the total experiences of all entities who inhabit your planet at this time. Beyond this are reaches of the mind which are greater yet. These mind reaches included that known to your peoples as the basic motivating force of the universe, that being the Logos or love. It is through this connection that each individual upon your planet reproduces the nature of the one infinite Creator, that is, to experience and to grow from experience. Therefore, each entity is connected to the one Creator through the deep reaches of the mind as though the one creation could be seen as a great wheel with each spoke being a portion of yet another entity's deep mind.

May we answer you further, my sister?

Questioner: Well, that gives me a lot to think about. But I must have missed the answer to my question, and right at this point in time I'm not exactly sure what my question was. What I really think I was getting at was where … I feel like when I'm in the dream state I do have some recall of dreams, but they're usually disjointed and fragmented and very bizarre and confusing and they seem to surpass time, the dimension of time as I know it, and I don't see what it can teach me or where, and I feel like I'm some place else when I'm dreaming. And I can't really seem to piece together or interpret anything from my dreams other than the little fragments I remember as being very bizarre, things happening to people I know, or very unrealistic or unreal. Well, that's all I can come up with right now. I can't remember what my question was.

I am Latwii. We shall, if it is agreeable with you, attempt once again to phrase our response in a manner which might be more helpful. The subconscious mind in the dream state operates within the framework which you might call the metaphysical. The illusion which you inhabit in your conscious waking state is the physical. It is that which provides the catalysts and experiences which teach. In the metaphysical or time/space portion of your being, all things are possible, for thoughts are things. This is not normally so in your waking consciousness. Your subconscious mind is able to show to the conscious mind the lessons which have not been well learned or which have been ignored. Yet, to preserve the free will of the conscious mind, these lessons must be in symbolic form in most cases.

Therefore, each entity who wishes to utilize the dream state for accelerating growth must make a concerted effort to determine what the language and landscape of its subconscious mind represents. Each entity has conscious memories of experiences which were vivid and imprinted within its past. One entity, for example, might see a bug as being a symbol of fear. Another entity might see the same bug as being a symbol of its nature or survival instincts. Each entity has language which its subconscious uses in expressing those lessons which might be of benefit if looked at in another manner.

When you are in that dreaming state, you are indeed beyond the normal space/time continuum. You exist at that time within a realm which is quite fluid and flexible, and your subconscious mind may then utilize the great power of its being to express its perception of your progress in the evolution of your mind, your body, and your spirit.

May we answer you further, my sister?

Questioner: Not at this time. Thank you for your answer.

I am Latwii. We are most grateful to you. Is there another question at this time?

S1: Yes, Latwii. Would you elaborate a little on one of your opening statements about releasing the

personality in order to grasp the Confederation concept?

I am Latwii, and am aware of your query, my sister. In regard to your instrument, this statement was meant to suggest that in your desire to be a clear channel, you have restricted somewhat the additions to the message which your deeper self could offer, for each contact with new instruments begins to approach the ideal percentage ratio when the new instrument is comfortable enough with the contact to speak clearly those concepts which appear in its mind, whether these concepts are recognized as being a portion of the instrument's own experience, or are recognized as being other than the instrument's experience. New instruments are often hesitant to speak those concepts which are familiar to them, for they fear they speak only their own minds, and are fabricating the entire contact.

In your particular case, it was our suggestion that you are restricting those portions of your deeper mind which could add to and make more unique the contact that is transmitted through you from Confederation sources.

May we answer you further, my sister?

S1: I would suppose that only through meditation and prayer and contemplation would this be opened a little faster, right? Is this correct?

I am Latwii, and am aware of your query, my sister. These techniques may indeed prove quite useful. One might also benefit from simply relaxing, and not worrying about the process.

May we answer you further, my sister?

S1: No, thank you.

I am Latwii. We thank you. Is there another question at this time?

Carla: What color are you in tonight?

I am Latwii. The color in which we find ourselves this evening is that which you would describe as a light chartreuse. We examine this color for its healing properties.

May we answer you further, my sister?

Carla: No, thank you.

I am Latwii. We thank you. Is there another question at this time?

Carla: When engaged in planetary healing, is this a good color to image?

I am Latwii. For the healing of the planetary entity it might be more useful to envision the white light encircling the planet, and continue this image in the mind for as long as it comfortable.

May we answer you further, my sister?

Carla: No. Silly me, I knew that. Thank you.

I am Latwii. We thank you very much for your silliness. Is there another question at this time?

Questioner: Latwii, may I have a few suggestions about getting rid of self-consciousness and awareness of self so that I can more readily open my mind and be less aware of who I am, or who I think I am in this particular density, third density?

I am Latwii, and am aware of your query, my sister. We might suggest that there is a great difficulty in simply ridding the self of a perception of the self. We might instead suggest that in your meditative state you look at that image which seems to be yourself, expand upon it in every degree …

(Tape ends.)

L/L Research is a subsidiary of
Rock Creek Research &
Development Laboratories, Inc.

P.O. Box 5195
Louisville, KY 40255-0195

L/L RESEARCH

www.llresearch.org

Rock Creek is a non-profit
corporation dedicated to
discovering and sharing
information which may aid in
the spiritual evolution of
humankind.

The Law of One, Book IV, Session 92
July 8, 1982

Ra: I am Ra. I greet you in the love and in the light of the one infinite Creator. We communicate now.

Questioner: Could you first please give me the condition of the instrument?

Ra: I am Ra. The condition of this instrument is slightly more distorted towards weakness in each respect since the previous asking.

Questioner: Is there a specific cause for this and could you tell us what it is?

Ra: I am Ra. The effective cause of the increased physical distortions has to do with the press of continuing substantial levels of the distortion you call pain. Various vehicular distortions other than the specifically arthritic have been accentuated by psychic greeting and the combined effect has been deleterious.

The continued slight but noticeable loss of the vital energies is due to the necessity for the instrument to call upon this resource in order to clear the, shall we say, way for a carefully purified service-to-others working. The use of the will in the absence of physical and, in this particular case, mental and mental/emotional energies requires vital energies.

Questioner: We have been trying to figure out how to provide the instrument with the swirling waters, and we hope to do that soon. Is there any other thing that we can do to improve this situation?

Ra: I am Ra. Continue in peace and harmony. Already the support group does much. There is the need for the instrument to choose the manner of its being-ness. It has the distortion, as we have noted, towards the martyrdom. This can be evaluated and choices made only by the entity.

Questioner: What is the present situation with the negative fifth-density visitor?

Ra: I am Ra. It is with this group.

Questioner: What prompted it to return?

Ra: I am Ra. The promptings were duple. There was the recovery of much negative polarity upon the part of your friend of fifth density and at the same approximate nexus a temporary lessening of the positive harmony of this group.

Questioner: Is there anything that we can do about the instrument's stomach problem or constipation?

Ra: I am Ra. The healing modes of which each is capable are already in use.

Questioner: In the last session we discussed the first tarot card of the Egyptian type. Are there any distortions in the cards that we have that Ra did not originally intend or any additions that Ra did intend in this particular tarot?

Ra: The distortions remaining after the removal of astrological material are those having to do with the mythos of the culture to which Ra offered this teach/learning tool. This is why we have suggested approaching the images looking for the heart of the image rather than being involved overmuch by the costumes and creatures of a culture not familiar to your present incarnation. We have no wish to add to an already distorted group of images, feeling that although distortion is inevitable there is the least amount which can be procured in the present arrangement.

Questioner: Then you are saying that the cards that we have here are the best available cards.

Ra: I am Ra. Your statement is correct in that we consider the so-called Egyptian tarot the most undistorted version of the images which Ra offered. This is not to intimate that other systems may not, in their own way, form an helpful architecture for the adept's consideration of the archetypical mind.

Questioner: I would like to make an analogy of when a baby is first born. I am assuming that the Matrix of the Mind is new and undistorted and veiled from the Potentiator of the Mind and ready for that which it is to experience in the incarnation. Is this correct?

Ra: I am Ra. Yes.

Questioner: I will read several statements and ask for Ra's comments. The first is: Until an entity becomes consciously aware of the evolutionary process the Logos or intelligent energy creates the potentials for an entity to gain the experience necessary for polarization. Would Ra comment on that?

Ra: I am Ra. This is so.

Questioner: Then, this occurs because the Potentiator of the Mind is directly connected, through the roots of the tree of mind, to the archetypical mind and to the Logos which created it and because of the veil between the Matrix and Potentiator of the Mind allows for the development of the will. Will Ra comment on that?

Ra: I am Ra. Some untangling may be needed. As the mind/body/spirit complex which has not yet reached the point of the conscious awareness of the process of evolution prepares for incarnation it has programmed for it a less than complete, that is to say a partially randomized, system of learnings. The amount of randomness of potential catalyst is proportional to the newness of the mind/body/spirit complex to third density. This, then, becomes a portion of that which you may call a potential for

incarnational experience. This is indeed carried within that portion of the mind which is of the deep mind, the architecture of which may be envisioned as being represented by that concept complex known as the Potentiator.

It is not in the archetypical mind of an entity that the potential for incarnational experience resides but in the mind/body/spirit complex's insertion, shall we say, into the energy web of the physical vehicle and the chosen planetary environment. However, to more deeply articulate this portion of the mind/body/spirit complex's being-ness this archetype, the Potentiator of the Mind, may be evoked with profit to the student of its own evolution.

Questioner: Then are you saying that the source of preincarnatively programmed catalyst is the Potentiator of the Mind?

Ra: I am Ra. No. We are suggesting that the Potentiator of the Mind is an archetype which may aid the adept in grasping the nature of this preincarnative and continuingly incarnative series of choices.

Questioner: The third statement: Just as free will taps intelligent infinity which yields intelligent energy which then focuses and creates the densities of this octave of experience, the Potentiator of the Mind utilizes its connection with intelligent energy and taps or potentiates the Matrix of the Mind which yields the Catalyst of the Mind. Is this correct?

Ra: I am Ra. This is thoughtful but confused. The Matrix of the Mind is that which reaches just as the kinetic phase of intelligent infinity, through free will, reaches for the Logos or, in the case of the mind/body/spirit complex the sub-sub-Logos which is the free will potentiated being-ness of the mind/body/spirit complex; to intelligent infinity, Love, and all that follows from that Logos; to the Matrix or, shall we say, the conscious, waiting self of each entity, the Love or the sub-sub-Logos spinning through free will all those things which may enrich the experience of the Creator by the Creator.

It is indeed so that the biases of the potentials of a mind/body/spirit complex cause the catalyst of this entity to be unique and to form a coherent pattern that resembles the dance, full of movement, forming a many-figured tapestry of motion.

Questioner: The fourth statement: When the Catalyst of the Mind is processed by the entity the Experience of the Mind results. Is this correct?

Ra: I am Ra. There are subtle misdirections in this simple statement having to do with the overriding qualities of the Significator. It is so that catalyst yields experience. However, through free will and the faculty of imperfect memory catalyst is most often only partially used and the experience thus correspondingly skewed.

Questioner: Then, the dynamic process between the Matrix, Potentiator, Catalyst, and Experience of the Mind forms the nature of the mind or the Significator of the Mind. Is this correct?

Ra: I am Ra. As our previous response suggests, the Significator of the Mind is both actor and acted upon. With this exception the statement is largely correct.

Questioner: As the entity becomes consciously aware of this process it programs this activity itself before the incarnation. Is this correct?

Ra: I am Ra. This is correct. Please keep in mind that we are discussing, not the archetypical mind, which is a resource available equally to each but unevenly used, but that to which it speaks: the incarnational experiential process of each mind/body/spirit complex. We wish to make this distinction clear for it is not the archetypes which live the incarnation but the conscious mind/body/spirit complex which may indeed live the incarnation without recourse to the quest for articulation of the processes of potentiation, experience, and transformation.

Questioner: Thank you. And finally, as each energy center becomes activated and balanced, the Transformation of the Mind is called upon more and more frequently. When all of the energy centers are activated and balanced to a minimal degree, contact with intelligent infinity occurs; the veil is removed; and the Great Way of the Mind is called upon. Is this correct?

Ra: I am Ra. No. This is a quite eloquent look at some relationships within the archetypical mind. However, it must be seen once again that the archetypical mind does not equal the acting incarnational mind/body/spirit complex's progression or evolution.

Due to the first misperception we hesitate to speak to the second consideration but shall attempt clarity. While studying the archetypical mind we may suggest that the student look at the Great Way of the Mind, not as that which is attained after contact with intelligent infinity, but rather as that portion of the archetypical mind which denotes and configures the particular framework within which the Mind, the Body, or the Spirit archetypes move.

Questioner: Turning, then, to my analogy or example of the newborn infant and its undistorted Matrix of the Mind, this newborn infant has its subconscious mind veiled from the Matrix of the Mind. The second archetype, the Potentiator of the Mind, is going to act at some time through the veil—though I hesitate to say through the veil since I don't think that is a very good way of stating it—but the Potentiator of the Mind will act to create a condition such as the example I mentioned of the infant touching a hot object. The hot object we could take as random catalyst. The infant can either leave its hand on the hot object or rapidly remove it. My question is, is the Potentiator of the Mind involved at all in this experience and, if so, how?

Ra: I am Ra. The Potentiator of Mind and of Body are both involved in the questing of the infant for new experience. The mind/body/spirit complex which is an infant has one highly developed portion which may be best studied by viewing the Significators of Mind and Body. You notice we do not include the spirit. That portion of a mind/body/spirit complex is not reliably developed in each and every mind/body/spirit complex. Thusly the infant's significant self, which is the harvest of biases of all previous incarnational experiences, offers to this infant biases with which to meet new experience.

However, the portion of the infant which may be articulated by the Matrix of the Mind is indeed unfed by experience and has the bias of reaching for this experience through free will just as intelligent energy in the kinetic phase, through free will, creates the Logos. These sub-sub-Logoi, then, or those portions of the mind/body/spirit complex which may be articulated by consideration of the Potentiators of Mind and Body, through free will, choose to make alterations in their experiential continuum. The results of these experiments in novelty are then recorded in the portion of the mind and body articulated by the Matrices thereof.

Questioner: Are all activities that the entity has from the state of infancy a function of the Potentiator of the Mind?

Ra: I am Ra. Firstly, although the functions of the mind are indeed paramount over those of the body, the body being the creature of the mind, certainly not all actions of a mind/body/spirit complex could be seen to be due to the potentiating qualities of the mind complex alone as the body and in some cases the spirit also potentiates action. Secondly, as a mind/body/spirit complex becomes aware of the process of spiritual evolution, more and more of the activities of the mind and body which precipitate activity are caused by those portions of the mind/body/spirit complex which are articulated by the archetypes of Transformation.

Questioner: The Matrix of the Mind is depicted as a male on the card and the Potentiator as female. Could Ra state why this is and how this affects these two archetypes?

Ra: I am Ra. Firstly, as we have said, the Matrix of the Mind is attracted to the biological male and the Potentiator of the Mind to the biological female. Thusly in energy transfer the female is able to potentiate that which may be within the conscious mind of the male so that it may feel enspirited.

In a more general sense, that which reaches may be seen as a male principle. That which awaits the reaching may be seen as a female principle. The richness of the male and female system of polarity is interesting and we would not comment further but suggest consideration by the student.

Questioner: In Card #2, the Potentiator of the Mind, we see a female seated on a rectangular block. She is veiled and sitting between two pillars which seem to be identically covered with drawings but one is much darker than the other. I am assuming that the veil represents the veil between the conscious and subconscious or Matrix and Potentiator of the Mind. Is this correct?

Ra: I am Ra. This is quite correct.

Questioner: I am assuming that she sits between the different colored columns, with the dark one on her left, to indicate at this position an equal opportunity for the potentiation of the mind to be of the negative or positive nature. Would Ra comment on this?

Ra: I am Ra. Although this is correct it is not as perceptive as the notice that the Priestess, as this figure has been called, sits within a structure in which polarity, symbolized as you correctly noted by the light and dark pillars, is an integral and necessary part. The unfed mind has no polarity just as intelligent infinity has none. The nature of the sub-sub-sub-Logos which offers the third-density experience is one of polarity, not by choice but by careful design.

We perceive an unclear statement. The polarity of Potentiator is there not for the Matrix to choose. It is there for the Matrix to accept as given.

Questioner: In other words, this particular illusion has polarity as its foundation which might be represented by the structural significance of these columns. Is this correct?

Ra: I am Ra. This is correct.

Questioner: It seems to me that the drawings on each of these columns are identical but that the left-hand column, that is the one on the Priestess's left, has been shaded much darker indicating that the events and the experiences may be identical in the incarnation but may be approached, viewed, and utilized with either polarity. Is this correct?

Ra: I am Ra. This is correct. You will note also, from the symbol denoting spirit in manifestation upon each pillar, that the one infinite Creator is no respecter of polarity but offers Itself in full to all.

Questioner: There seems to be a book on the Priestess's lap which is half hidden by a robe or material that covers her right shoulder. It would seem that this indicates that knowledge is available if the veil is lifted but is not only hidden by the veil but is hidden partially by her very garment which she must somehow remove to become aware of the knowledge which she has available. Is this correct?

Ra: I am Ra. In that the conceit of the volume was not originated by Ra we ask that you release the volume from its strictured form. Your perceptions are quite correct.

The very nature of the feminine principle of mind which, in Ra's suggestion, was related specifically to what may be termed sanctified sexuality is, itself, without addition, the book which neither the feminine nor the male principle may use until the male principle has reached and penetrated, in a symbolically sexual fashion, the inner secrets of this feminine principle.

All robes, in this case indicating the outer garments of custom, shield these principles. Thusly there is great dynamic tension, if you will, betwixt the Matrix and the Potentiator of the Mind.

Questioner: Are there any other parts of this picture that were not given by Ra?

Ra: I am Ra. The astrological symbols offered are not given by Ra.

Questioner: The fact that the Priestess sits atop the rectangular block indicates to me that the Potentiator of the Mind has dominance or is above the material illusion. Is this in any way correct?

Ra: I am Ra. Let us say, rather, that this figure is immanent, near at hand, shall we say, within all manifestation. The opportunities for the reaching to the Potentiator are numerous. However, of itself the Potentiator does not enter manifestation.

Questioner: Would the half moon on the crown represent the receptivity of the subconscious mind?

Ra: I am Ra. This symbol is not given by Ra but it is not distasteful for within your own culture the moon represents the feminine, the sun the masculine. Thusly we accept this portion as a portion of the image, for it seems without significant distortion.

Questioner: Was the symbol on the front of the Priestess's shirt given by Ra?

Ra: I am Ra. The crux ansata is the correct symbol. The addition and slight distortion of this symbol thereby is astrological and may be released from its stricture.

Questioner: Would this crux ansata then be indicating the sign of life as the spirit enlivening matter?

Ra: I am Ra. This is quite correct. Moreover, it illuminates a concept which is a portion of the archetype which has to do with the continuation of the consciousness which is being potentiated, in incarnation, beyond incarnation.

Questioner: Were the grapes depicted on the cloth over her shoulder of Ra's communication?

Ra: I am Ra. Yes.

Questioner: We have those as indicating the fertility of the subconscious mind. Is that correct?

Ra: I am Ra. This is correct, O student, but note ye the function of the mantle. There is great protection given by the very character of potentiation. To bear fruit is a protected activity.

Questioner: The protection here seems to be depicted as being on the right-hand side but not the left. Would this indicate that there is protection for the positive path but not for the negative?

Ra: I am Ra. You perceive correctly an inborn bias offering to the seeing eye and listing ear information concerning the choice of the more efficient polarity. We would at this time, as you may call it, suggest one more full query.

Questioner: I will attempt an example of the Potentiator of the Mind acting. As the infant gains time in incarnation would it experience the Potentiator offering both positive and negative potential thoughts, shall I say, for the Matrix to experience which then begin to accumulate in the Matrix and color it one way or the other in polarity depending upon its continuing choice of that polarity? Is this in any way correct?

Ra: I am Ra. Firstly, again may we distinguish between the archetypical mind and the process of incarnational experience of the mind/body/spirit complex.

Secondly, each potentiation which has been reached for by the Matrix is recorded by the Matrix but experienced by the Significator. The experience of the Significator of this potentiated activity is of course dependent upon the acuity of its processes of Catalyst and Experience.

May we ask if there are briefer queries before we leave this instrument?

Questioner: Is there anything that we can do to make the instrument more comfortable or to improve the contact?

Ra: I am Ra. The support group is functioning well. The instrument, itself, might ponder some earlier words and consider their implications. We say this because the continued calling upon vital energies, if allowed to proceed to the end of the vital energy, will end this contact. There is not the need for continued calling upon these energies. The instrument must find the key to this riddle or face a growing loss of this particular service at this particular space/time nexus.

All is well. The alignments are exemplary.

I am Ra. I leave you, my friends, in the love and the light of the one infinite Creator. Go forth, then, rejoicing in the power and in the peace of the one infinite Creator. Adonai. ✸

L/L Research is a subsidiary of
Rock Creek Research &
Development Laboratories, Inc.

P.O. Box 5195
Louisville, KY 40255-0195

www.llresearch.org

Rock Creek is a non-profit
corporation dedicated to
discovering and sharing
information which may aid in
the spiritual evolution of
humankind.

INTENSIVE MEDITATION
JULY 15, 1982

(M channeling)

[I am Hatonn.] I am with this instrument. We greet you, brothers and sisters, in the love and the light of the infinite Creator. It is a great pleasure for us to be with you this evening. We always rejoice at the opportunity to share this time with you, to feel your vibrations, to share your love. We look forward this evening to working with each of the new instruments in their endeavor to learn to pick up our channeled messages. It is a great service you perform, each of you perform for us, to give us this opportunity to, in a sense, speak to many more brothers and sisters upon your planet. We are most eager for this opportunity. We are not infallible, of course, but we do have an understanding of some concepts of the Creator which we want to share with you, and you, through your channeling, give us the opportunity to reach others who are seeking who might otherwise not have the benefit of our years of learning similar lessons as we passed through the density of separation.

We are pleased with the progress that each of you have made at your attempts at channeling. Your strong desire, my brothers and sisters, has been the key to your rapid success. This intense desire coupled with the intense love you have for your fellow man truly makes you effective instruments of the Creator, a potential to perform a valuable service for your fellow man. We are all too pleased to have this opportunity to work with such as you.

At this time, we will pass to another instrument, so they may practice the pursuance of this contact. We leave this instrument in the love and the light of the infinite Creator. I am Hatonn.

(A channeling)

I am Hatonn, and we are now with this instrument, and we greet you again in the love and the light of our infinite Creator. My brothers and sisters, we wish to say to you a few words that might help ease you on your journey along the path, for at times you may become tired, and the path may look longer than it has in some time. But do not worry, for even though it may seem to get harder and the climb to be steeper, you will know that which you need to know, for you know that the future will come, and that time will not stop.

And so, as you move on your journey …

We will start again, and we thank this instrument for pausing. For as you go on this journey through what you know as time, you feel that time will not stop, and that you must go on. And for you this is true. But at all times you are one with the Creator, and all you must do is ask and the love will be there. And if you become tired and confused, we suggest that meditation might be of aid in easing the confusion of living in this time.

We would now like to say to this instrument we are pleased that she finished our thought and started over so that we might more completely give our message. And that it was okay to stop and to rechallenge our contact.

And now we will transfer this contact so as to exercise the other instruments present. We leave you again in the love and the light of the infinite Creator. I am Hatonn.

(S1 channeling)

I am Hatonn. It is a pleasure, my friends, to greet you once more this evening in the love and the light of the one infinite Creator. It seems that often we greet you several times during one evening, but each time we indeed feel the love and the light that we greet you in. We are pleased to feel the love surrounding all of us as we join together in our efforts to serve the one infinite Creator. It is a journey that we are on as well as you, for are we not all walking in the same direction? Are we not all seeking the same thing? Do we not all see the same light and enjoy the same love? And we are always aware that you are with us. And we also hope that you are aware that we are with you. We are honored by the calls we receive from each of you and are indeed pleased to spend some of what you call time with you, as it is very rewarding for us. It lets us know that we are serving in our way, and we are indeed happy for the opportunity that you allow us. For, were there no seekers that were calling upon us, we would indeed be in somewhat of a fix, for we would have no one to aid. It is in this—correction—it is for this reason we are indeed humbly grateful to you for sharing your love, your light, your time, and your meditations with us. May we thank you once again.

We would leave this instrument at this time in the same love and light that we have greeted and left you many times this evening. I am Hatonn.

(S2 channeling)

I am Hatonn, and I greet you once again, my brothers and sisters, in the love and the light of the one infinite Creator. My friends, my loved ones, your purpose this evening is to serve your many brothers and sisters through the act of channeling. Many of these brothers and sisters have never heard

of this act of service which you perform—and perform so well, we might add. But in the coming years time grows short and more and more of your peoples, your brothers and sisters in the light, will be becoming aware of the light, in different stages perhaps, but all will reach the point they are destined to reach, and you, my loved ones, our brothers and sisters of the Creator, and in the Creator, will help those many peoples that are now in darkness. Will help them to become aware that there is a glorious and beautiful love and happiness awaiting each and every one at the end of a sometimes dark and weary road that somehow never seems to end. Until one day, you will say, "I can see the light. I am one with the light."

My brothers and sisters, we are still striving for this also. We are not very much further along that path than you. That is why, in your act of channeling, in your service of channeling, you allow us to share with you that little knowledge we have gained a little further along the path. My friends, the love and light of the Creator is a glorious thing to share with your brothers and sisters. Be happy and do so. Share, and it will be returned many times over.

I leave you now that our brothers and sisters of Latwii may have the chance to serve in their fashion of answering your many questions. We leave you softly and gently in love, deeply felt for each of you, my friends. We leave you in the love and the light of the one infinite Creator. Adonai vasu borragus.

(Jim channeling)

I am Latwii, and I greet you, my friends, in the love and in the light of our infinite Creator. What an honor it is to once again be asked to blend our vibrations with yours. We cannot thank you enough for this wonderful opportunity, and it is our privilege to once again ask if there might be a question at this time which we could attempt to answer?

S2: Latwii, I have a question, but it's quite difficult. Now, I realize that we all are a part of the Creator, but, if some one entity, an individual, says that they are channeling God, how should we react to this?

I am Latwii; I am God. My sister, there is no difference. When an entity partakes of any activity, you see the Creator in movement. You see the movements as the Creator. You see all about you as the Creator. When you see an entity which then says that it has, shall we say, the corner on the market of the Creator, then you know there is some type of distortion apparent within that perception, for each entity at all times channels the Creator. We do not suggest that you render any judgment whatsoever towards one who might be of this distortion, for it is not necessary to rank the levels of distortion of those about you, and to separate in your mind further one entity from another. The separation of your illusion is most efficient, and will provide you with the learning catalyst that you need.

It is the task of each entity within your illusion to seek and find the Creator within all beings. Each entity begins at a certain point of viewing, shall we say. The growth of the entity is determined by its ability to move from that point, and to see the Creator in all other points of viewing. This is the process of the growth of the soul, of your mind, your body, and your spirit. Therefore, observe the entities about you in their various distortions. Learn to love each, for each is a pure expression of the one Creator, whether it calls its expression "God" or "Fred."

May we answer you further, my sister?

S2: No. Thank you very much, Latwii.

I am Latwii. We are most grateful to you, my sister. Is there another question at this time?

S1: Yes, Latwii. Lately, I have, in my conditioning at these meditations, every once in a while received what I might call a false alarm. Can you give me any information about this?

I am Latwii, and am aware of your query, my sister. The new instrument will most often find some difficulty in determining when contact has been made for the purpose of the vocal channeling as opposed for the—we correct this instrument—as opposed to the conditioning which is necessary when asked for as a preparation for this vocal channeling. We suggest, therefore, that each new instrument ask for some type of signal from the Confederation entity providing the conditioning vibration that will signify to the new instrument that the vocalizing of the thoughts is now appropriate. This may be a simple intensification of the contact in whatever means it has been experienced, a dropping of the jaw, a rushing of the pulse of the heart, an increase in the sensations of the forehead. Whatever is a new instrument's unique

configuration, then let this be that signal for the beginning of the contact in its vocalized form.

Do not be discouraged, my sister, if this technique also takes time to learn. The new instrument that is full to the brim with the desire to be of service in this manner has opened itself to such a degree that the sensitivity is quite finely tuned, and therefore the next step becomes necessary, that is, the discrimination of the sensations which are experienced. With practice, you shall become most adept at this as well.

May we answer you further, my sister?

S1: I thought that was what was going on, but thank you for confirming it for me.

I am Latwii. We thank you, my sister, for the service which you provide. Is there another question at this time?

M: Yes, Latwii. I'm not quite sure how to ask it. I've got a couple, but the first has to do with how one should react perhaps to a given condition. The situation that I'm thinking of is there are a couple of people in my life that I'm no longer in contact with on a daily basis that were very difficult people to interact with, and I would think of them in all the love and light of the infinite Creator, and think of them as my brother, and really try to shed a lot of light on the situation, and in my meditations I could do that and feel good about them. But in daily contact, they were such negative people that I really could not enjoy their company, and yet I felt like somewhere along the way I was missing the concept of brotherhood and being one by not being able to love them even when I was around them. I don't even know what I'm asking, other than, is it a distortion of the oneness to not be able to feel close to everyone when you desire to?

I am Latwii, and am aware of your query, my brother. Of course, my brother, it is a distortion. This density of illusion is most useful in that it allows each entity to refine the distortions of the one Creator into a seeking of great purity. Do not be discouraged, my brother, when you meet those challenges in your daily round of activities which you are unable to successfully, shall we say, complete, for if you were always able to love without end each entity and situation [that] presented itself to you, where then would you find the opportunity for growth?

There must be for each entity the full range of experience so that there might be those times of knowing the love and unity for and with all your creation. There must be those times where for the moment you falter, so that you might see yet one more way in which to be of service. There must also be those times for each seeker in which great despair is felt. For, are you not all things and do you not seek to know the Creator, which is all things? Can you not then see the opportunities presented to you in what you call failure, in what might be a momentary stumbling on that path of the pure seeking?

My friends, this illusion was not created to be a smooth experience. A catalyst within your illusion is most intense, and by this we mean to say, it seems from time to time there is no unity. It seems there is no love. It seems that each is separate, struggling and full of despair, and that your world falls to pieces. It is an illusion, my friends, for in truth, there is only unity. But to know that unity in its fullest extent, you must then experience its polarity, that is, the illusion of the separation. To experience that illusion is to prepare the foundation within your being to know the unity, for it is all one, my friends.

May we answer you further, my brother?

M: That was real purty, Latwii. Thank you.

I am Latwii. We are pleased with your pleasure as well. Is there another question at this time?

M: One, perhaps you can answer briefly. Tonight I've been experiencing, I guess it's conditioning, that feels different than any conditioning I've ever received before. Could you shed some light on that?

I am Latwii, and am aware of your query, my brother. We would suggest with any new conditioning that the entity so experiencing the conditioning begin that process which you have lately come to know as the challenge. Offer unto that entity which conditions your instrument the challenge so that it might itself reveal to you its source. We cannot, as you know, provide that service for you, for to do so would be to rob you of the opportunity of growth that each such situation presents.

May we answer you further, my brother?

M: No, thank you.

I am Latwii. We are most grateful to you. Is there another question at this time?

(Pause)

I am Latwii. We see that our silver words have been replaced …

(Tape ends.) ☙

L/L RESEARCH

L/L Research is a subsidiary of Rock Creek Research & Development Laboratories, Inc.

P.O. Box 5195
Louisville, KY 40255-0195

www.llresearch.org

Rock Creek is a non-profit corporation dedicated to discovering and sharing information which may aid in the spiritual evolution of humankind.

ADVANCED MEDITATION
JULY 18, 1982

(C channeling)

I am Hatonn, and am now with this instrument. We greet you, my friends, in the love and the light of the one infinite Creator. It is indeed a privilege to work with those who seek to improve their abilities to receive and channel the humble messages that we of the Confederation speak to you. We would like to begin, as we have before, [by] beginning a story through one instrument and would then switch our contact to another to continue the story with the first and end it.

My friends, there was once a tree which was situated by the side of a trail at a point where it branched. The tree was not of great stature, and in fact was in its years of decline, becoming softer and starting to hollow and at this time it still stood. The leaves still sprouted and its sap of its life still flowed within. We would now transfer.

(L channeling)

The tree, although it declined, was still capable of bearing fruit and those who passed by, though selecting either path that branched before the tree, would often select a piece of fruit from the tree and bear it with them as they continued their journey down one path or the other and found nourishment and satisfaction from the fruits of this hollow tree. It may be said that the tree in its offerings [of] its fruits

was able to travel both journeys while remaining at the branch in the path. We would now transfer.

(Carla channeling)

The season passed. The tree sent its roots with less and less energy into the life-giving soil and turned its leaves in fewer and fewer numbers to the warmth of the sun and the gentle cleansing and nourishment of the rain, and the path became empty. So rich and so perfect was each piece of fruit, and yet so apparently uneaten, unused, unappreciated. This was of no importance to the tree, for it was in rhythm with its own cycle and it flourished, flowered, bloomed and faded as the seasons rattled the leaves of fall, sifted the snows of winter, warmed the earth of spring, and brightened the skies of summer. We will now transfer this contact.

(Jim channeling)

It was felt by many who passed the tree on their journey that there could be no further purpose for the tree, for it seemed that the usefulness had perished with its fruitfulness. There was the feeling of the travelers upon both paths that the tree had fulfilled its purpose and that travelers would now be left without the fruit to take with them upon their journey. But there also were those who saw the season of the tree as providing but one type of fruit, as was understood by those who had been nourished by that fruit. And yet, some said, is there not still a purpose for such a tree, even though its fruit has long since passed? There became an effort to discern what that purpose could be. We will how transfer this contact.

(C channeling)

The purpose of the tree when the fruit was gone became an ever-increasing concern of many who walked past. Instead of looking at other sources or simply ignoring other sources, some of the people began to mourn for the tree, and instead of continuing along their chosen paths, stopped and stayed at that place. Others, however, knew that they could no longer depend upon this single tree for the food to sustain them on their journey [and] decided to seek further along the path for other sources of sustenance. We will now transfer.

(Carla channeling)

And to those who listened to the tree, the tree seemed to say to them, "My friends, there was a great period when no one passed by. Not to the right, not to the left. But I did not think, because of your absence for a moment of your time, that the path would be forever empty, for I knew that pilgrims, though each may walk alone, forever walk in a great company. No matter that the way be barren and the seekers seemingly absent for awhile, yet still another generation passed by.

"Just so, pilgrims, because I have found the cycle in my being of stillness, does that not mean the chance for another generation of trees to offer you shade and beauty and truth? For did not your fathers eat from me and drop the seeds where they root upon each path?" I would now transfer this contact.

(Jim channeling)

"And does not the one Creator who made us all provide for us in seasons of plenty and of scarcity? Does not that one Creator provide the nourishment for life and the means by which the pilgrim of either path might travel through the mystery of the creation? My friends, I lived for much of your time at the fork of these paths and through me did not the Creator show an equal love for all? And now, in this season of my stillness, cannot each pilgrim find the stillness within itself as once was found the nourishment of the outer being? Therefore, my friends, does not the one Creator nourish each entity both within and without, no matter which path is chosen?" We shall now transfer this contact.

(C channeling)

Each is nourished. Each partakes of that which they need: the fruit to nourish, the shade to rest, the branch for a staff to support, the sign that life is renewed. The theme exists, a cyclic harmony that for each creation there is a place along the journey that points the choice, a decision. There are sources such as the tree which offers itself to the traveler in what way it can. Those who partake of the fruit of the tree serve to aid in the scattering of the seed and new sources of sustenance may grow and may in turn be available to the journeyer. We will transfer.

(L channeling)

It is the opportunity of all to serve in a multitude of ways throughout the cycle of their lifespan. At certain points along the curve it may be possible to serve by providing a comfort and the relaxation, the easing of the soul that comes from allowing an other self to rest for awhile within one's shadow and to support that other self as they lean against you to recover their strength and determination. At another point on the curve, one might be blessed with the opportunity to provide sustenance, and in so doing to sweeten another's life, no matter their intention or their destination. As the cycle continues, one's purpose—correction—one's service might be limited to providing a staff, a source of stability and rigidity that an other self requires to complete their journey, for there are a number who must spend their lives in close contact with an unyielding determination to enable themselves to partake of that determination and so complete their journey and finally, as the circle completes, as the cycle begins anew, one's service might be to foreshadow the sweetness of the fruits that lie ahead for those who follow either path. We will now transfer.

(Carla channeling)

My friends, as you experience the continuum of your incarnation, of your cycle, and as you seek to be of service, know that wherever you are, to others you appear to be a stationary object at the branching of two paths. You can never know what service you may provide. One may see your beauty and the sweet blossoms that are lit with the sunshine of springtime. One may find the solace of your shade and take from you that rest which is nourishment to the weary soul. One in hunger may find that gracious and perfect fruit which, unbeknownst to you in your inward life, you have produced and have offered. And one may take a little piece of your being, your words, your thoughts, your actions, and use that image as a staff.

But, my friends, never forget your greatest gift, your greatest service. That is your hollowness, your stillness, your final beingness, for there you stand and there you witness to the great panorama of the creation, our Father. I would transfer at this time.

(Jim channeling)

I would now open this meeting to questions, if any present would desire to query upon any topic of importance. Is there a question?

C: Hatonn, I've noticed there seems to be an increase in frequency with which my son awakens, and his cries withdraw me from my meditation. Is there any information you can offer as to the cause or any suggestions you could make to prevent this occurrence?

I am Hatonn, and can suggest that the young being has a growing desire for your presence due to its own desire to experience that which you can teach it. The young entity is more and more able to perceive that there are opportunities for its own expression to expand which you might be of service in the facilitating of. The meditations which you have found somewhat disturbed by this increased …

(Tape ends.) ❧

L/L Research is a subsidiary of Rock Creek Research & Development Laboratories, Inc.

P.O. Box 5195
Louisville, KY 40255-0195

www.llresearch.org

Rock Creek is a non-profit corporation dedicated to discovering and sharing information which may aid in the spiritual evolution of humankind.

SUNDAY MEDITATION
JULY 18, 1982

(S channeling)

[I am Hatonn,] and I greet you, my brothers and sisters, in the love and in the light of our infinite Creator. My friends, your meeting this evening is especially blessed with the birth of a new entity into your plane of existence. This life will sow many things. It will reap many things. The guidance that is given this child through its parents, its friends, its loved ones, in this group and other groups will sow many lifetimes of learning. The reaping is upon each and every one that is here. The learning that is now culminating in these last few years will experience many things.

We apologize, my brothers and sisters. This instrument is having difficulty this evening and would prefer not to finish the message we have started. We appreciate her efforts and would at this time transfer to another contact. I am Hatonn.

(Carla channeling)

I am Hatonn, and am with this instrument. We would apologize, my friends, through this instrument, for the circumstances that cause us to, at this particular time, request each instrument to continuously tune towards the appropriate amplitudes and harmonies of love and light. It is not, my friends, a usual difficulty that we of the Confederation of Planets experience when we are working with free will groups such as this one, but

we say to you that we are experiencing at this time an interference, not of each of you in this group, but rather of the group itself in its identity, as that group which functions as messenger for the Confederation entity known as Ra. This group has undertaken work which has borne fruit in the form of a blossoming of light, and for such light much thanksgiving may be given. Within this particular group, however, you are experiencing, without any conscious request or intent, visits from those of what you would call a darker polarity, whose desires can have no effect upon the properly tuned instrument, but whose effects can disturb the, shall we say, morale of a group such as this one.

We therefore sympathetically apologize for the inconvenience. But, my friends, as light shines in darkness, it is said in your holy works that the darkness does not know it. Yet that darkness, my friends, is the darkness of ignorance. There are those who do know the light and wish to absorb it. They shall never succeed. For as love vanquishes all that comes before it, so shall the light never be extinguished unless it is with the conscious choice of entities such as yourselves to cease the careful tuning of which we have spoken so often in these last few meetings.

We would not presume to predict the actions of other entities, but we believe that you shall find, as those who have worked with the Ra entities have found, that these disturbances are only visits, that they are the visits of entities who are friends, brothers and sisters, entities to whom love may be given, unqualified and full. As you experience the offering of love in positive oneness with these visitors, they shall rapidly become less interested in experiencing contact with this group, for love, my friends, is to one which desires cold and darkness an uncomfortable and unhappy reaction.

We are sorry to have spent so much time, as you call it, speaking on this subject, but without giving it too much importance, we wish to give you assurances as to our continued contact in answer to your continued calling, and as to your own ability, through the love and the light of the infinite One, to bear with grace and beauty those small difficulties which are caused by the unfamiliar greetings of friends whom you might not think [of as such.] They are one with the Creator, and if you can, see them, greet them, bless them, and send them on their way knowing that you cannot help them, nor they you. Your rest in the Christ consciousness, as this instrument would call it, will grow and expand and become more articulated from this experience so that you will learn more about love. Not the love of man, my friends, but the love of the Creator.

We would continue to speak upon the subject of the thanksgiving that we share with you at the birth of the young entity who bides now at his mother's breast. So much, my friends, is before each entity in incarnation, and as you cast your mind backwards in time, you too can recapture those moments before each decision was made which caused you to be the entity which you are at this moment. My friends, we would ask you to look now at yourself as that newborn, for you have the same incredible possibilities in your grasp as does the young one, just opening its eyes in this incarnation. As you grow in years and experience, you, or at least many of your peoples, became convinced that there is a rigidity to existence that demands certain behavior, exhibits certain truths, and delineates the human possibility. My friends, the spirit within you does not know any limits. That which governs your heart, your life, and your soul throughout eternity does not speak the language of society, family, government or even planetary considerations. It recognizes a law that is so far beyond the laws of your science and the dogmas of your religion that most have great difficulty in grasping the mechanisms of the spirit.

The one known to you as Jesus the Christ offered the heart or ethic of this law, saying, "Love your God with all your heart, all your mind, all your soul, and all your strength; and love your neighbor as yourself." The law, my friends, is love. It is a law of freedom, not restriction, of flexibility, not rigidity, of wisdom, not knowledge, of possibilities, not dogma. And we ask that as you give thanksgiving for this wondrous miracle, this infinite, immortal and precious spirit that has come among you to be cherished, to be guided and to be set free, that you see yourself also as infinitely precious and infinitely miraculous. Do you lift up your heart in thanksgiving at a baby? No less lift it up for yourselves, for your neighbors, for your brothers and sisters, for are you not each eternal facets of the one infinite Creator?

We would at this time transfer the contact gratefully back to the one known as S, that this instrument may feel more clarity and reassurance as to the accuracy and the stability of this contact. We thank each of you for the continuous tuning that you have been doing. We would now transfer this contact. I am Hatonn.

(S channeling)

I am Hatonn, and greet you once again through this instrument. We are sorry to have had the difficulty previously and would want this instrument to realize that it is not to be taken upon herself the total blame for this difficulty.

We appreciate the efforts of all the new instruments within this group for channeling our thoughts and helping to spread the message of the Creator and His love and light. This instrument wishes very much to serve in this fashion, as do the other new instruments within this room and the pleasure we share with each is quite extensive, my friends. Our joy is unbounded. We will now leave this instrument in order that we may exercise the other instruments within this group. Your continuing efforts are encouraged, even though you may have doubts. We would urge you to continue in your service. I am Hatonn.

(Carla channeling)

I am Hatonn. I am again with this instrument and greet each again in the love and the light of the infinite Creator. Having worked with the one known as K and the one known as M, we find requests from each to pass them by at this particular time that they may do the working which they desire to do in this particular service at what you would call a later time. We find within the one known as A [the] same confusion, but a desire to speak. Therefore, we would ask that the group join once again in the one light while we condition the instrument known as A. We would then close our message through this instrument. We thank each instrument for fidelity, for laughter, for joy, and for the dedication to seeking which is our life light and in whose pursuit we are here in service to each of you. We would now transfer. I am Hatonn.

(A channeling)

I am Hatonn. I am now with this instrument, and greet you once again in the love and the light of the one infinite Creator. We would just like to speak a few words and a closing through this instrument so as to reaffirm our contact with her, for there was some confusion as to if it was our vibration she felt. We are appreciative to the tuning we are given, for it aids in the contact through which our thoughts may be sent.

And now we will close in saying that we are always there and you but need to ask for our presence. I am Hatonn. Adonai, my friends. Adonai vasu borragus.

(Jim channeling)

I am Latwii, and I greet you, my friends, in the love and in the light of the one infinite Creator. We are most honored to join your group this evening and we extend to each the blessings which are sent forth from this group, for it makes our contact a great joy and privilege to pursue. Again it is our honor to present ourselves in the capacity of attempting to answer your queries. Therefore, may we ask if there be a query at this time?

C: Not a question, but I would like to say thank you for yours and the presence of the other members of the Confederation whose aid was felt at the hospital. So I just want to say thank you.

I am Latwii. My brother, an honor such as aiding a new entity to enter into the illusion which you now inhabit is an honor which we cannot describe, but for which our gratitude is also immeasurable. We thank you. Is there a question at this time?

A: Yes, Latwii, I have a question. I was wondering what is the significance of the blue light?

I am Latwii, and am aware of your query, my sister. As each entity pursues the path of the seeker there is the awakening, step by step, of various levels of perception, shall we say. These have been codified and described by many of your peoples as the system of chakras or energy centers, which when activated and balanced each with the other, culminate in the Christ identity. As an entity releases those blockages which inhibit this full functioning of each energy center, there is, according to the center being worked upon, the experience of various sensations, according to the nature of the center.

The blue light which might be experienced in meditation or seen as a symbol within the dreams is a correspondence which emanates from the throat chakra, that energy center which has as its basic characteristic the clear communication of an entity with fellow entities and with itself. This center is most important for the transmission of thoughts in as undistorted a manner as possible for entities upon your planet. It is a center not frequently worked upon by many of your peoples, for the lessons of your illusion deal primarily with the center of the heart and the green-ray vibrations of universal love, compassion, forgiveness and understanding. These lessons of the heart, when mastered to a sufficient degree, may then be communicated as a form of inspiration to others by an entity's very being as well as the more obvious words and deeds of that entity.

May we answer you further, my sister?

A: No, thank you.

I am Latwii. We thank you. Is there another question at this time?

Carla: Yes. The information that I heard while I was channeling it from Hatonn about there being some so-called negative interference with members of the group besides Jim, me and Don has me a little puzzled. I can understand why they would want to communicate to us and lessen our polarity, but I cannot understand why they would want to do that to the people in this group which will never sit in a Ra session. Seems like they're just picking on people. Could you comment?

I am Latwii, and am aware of your query, my sister. We find in this situation that the entities who sit within this meditation seek ever more purely the one Creator. These entities, then, create a beacon of light and this beacon of light shines to those who call for service to others. Yet this group is part of yet another effort which also is as a beacon of light. Both beacons of light call …

(Side one of tape ends.)

(Jim channeling)

I am Latwii, and am once again with this instrument. To continue. The calling of both beacons of light to those of positive polarity is answered, and this group has its guides and protectors. Yet such a beacon of light also serves to attract the attention of those of negative polarity, for there is the necessity of the balance within the density of forgetting which you inhabit.

Those entities, therefore, of the dark light seek in whatever manner presents itself to depolarize and to extinguish those lights, for as you are aware, it is the way of the negative polarity to seek control and mastery over others that others might serve the self. There is power in the light of a magical nature. To then take that power and attempt to control it, if successful, would give to the negative entities an increase in their own polarity and power. Any target of opportunity, shall we say, is quite the fair game, for where there is the love for others and concern for others, then there is the possibility that that concern might be utilized to cause the worry, the frustrations and the eventual detuning of various entities within the group. Therefore, this group becomes as a body, a unit, each entity forming a portion of the wall of light. Therefore, any entity might also become a target for the light to be dimmed.

May we answer you further, my sister?

Carla: Well, I'd just, to clarify, then, what you're basically correcting is my assumption that because these people are not physically present at Ra sessions, they are not part of the Ra sessions. What you're saying is everyone in this living room, in this meeting, because of the fact that we love each other, we are the Ra group, all of us. Is this what you're trying to tell me, because the reality seen in terms of light is metaphysical, not physical. Is that correct?

I am Latwii. My sister, this is correct. You have within this group a family of light beings and each, therefore, has the opportunity to accelerate its polarity and its evolution by means of the utilization of the information generated in these meditations and in the meditations which have resulted in the Ra contact. Therefore, the Law of Responsibility holds

sway, so that where the opportunity to accelerate evolution upon the positive path comes into being, there must also be the balancing opportunity for the entity to choose the opposite path.

May we answer you further, my sister?

Carla: Yes. Carrying that further then, anyone who studies this material carefully and conscientiously works with it, therefore becomes a part of this same opportunity for increased spiritual evolution and also increased opportunities to view the other opportunities, the other polarities. Is that correct?

I am Latwii. My sister, this is quite correct. The burden of the seeker is that it shall bear the responsibility for the purity of its seeking. The path in union with the one Creator is a path which is hard-won, the traveling of which is not always easy. The pearl of great price, as it has been called, has as its price the constant seeking and the constant choosing to be of that positive polarity. To refine the seeking to the purity necessary to achieve the pearl requires that there be the constant opportunity to have a choice, the constant opposing force, shall we say against which to push. It is a testing. It is a choosing. It is a seeking and a refining. And those of the positive path rejoice in this process, for each opposing force which acts within the life of the seeker presents yet one more opportunity to increase the desire to seek the truth. If there were no force against which to push, there would be no motion, no movement, no evolution. Rejoice, then, my friends, for your opportunities of seeking are greatly enhanced, yet you must bear the responsibility of this seeking and of the increased opportunities.

May we answer you further, my sister?

Carla: No, thank you, Latwii.

I am Latwii. We thank you, my sister. Is there another question at this time?

K: Yeah, to follow that just one step further. Are you saying that the more we seek, the more likely we are to encounter a stumbling block that may at times appear, well, too difficult, or at least at times it seems that we've had a real set-back, so the harder we seek, the … well, I guess, what I'm trying to say and I'm not doing it very well, the more we seek and the greater the desire, the more likely we are to encounter a real stumbling block. Is that right?

I am Latwii, and am aware of your query, my sister. In general, we might agree that you are quite correct, for when the seeker seeks, what is it that the seeker seeks? Do you not wish to know the truth more clearly? Do you not wish to increase the purity of your seeking? If this be true, then how can that truth be known? How can that purity be gained if there not be that obstacle which tests the ability of the seeker to continue to seek and to refine the purity?

May we answer you further, my sister?

K: No, that helps a great deal. I think I understand.

I am Latwii. Is there another question at this time?

M: Yeah, Latwii. I have an opportunity to perhaps help some people and I'm not just sure how to do it. I'm working in a situation where a company's offering a great sum of money for blue sky research. I've got an opportunity to push some blue sky ideas. I want to somehow be able to get in touch with some part of my being that's—that can somehow help me conceptually understand something that would be of benefit to the people of this world, rather than something that's just going to earn more money for the stockholders, so to speak. I want to be able to get in touch with that creative part of me to come up with something the world really needs while that opportunity is here. How can I do that?

I am Latwii, and am aware of your query, my brother. It is only in the general sense in which we may respond—we correct this instrument—in which we may respond to this query, for to specifically guide the footsteps of the seeker is to walk the path for the seeker. Therefore, may we suggest that in your meditations you begin each meditation which is dedicated to the solution of this problem, shall we say, with the consideration of what it is you wish to do and with what given opportunities you have to work. Consider well the boundaries of your situation. Analyze to the best of your intellectual ability how to proceed. You have within the experience of your being many remembrances which will be helpful. Blend them, my brother. Then let them go and seek within your meditative state the inspiration from your higher self, your guides, or whatever forces of light you wish to call upon. Wait for that inspiration that will guide your own actions.

My brother, to simply say, "Look within," seems much too simple for the seeker. Many people upon your planet have devised the most intricate of procedures by which to decide upon one action over another. Most entities dwell within the details and confusions of the mind that consciously attempts to figure and calculate, weigh, balance and scheme. We suggest to the seeker that the simple removing of the self into meditation so that those matters of import might rise from the subconscious levels of your being as inspirational insights that might then be acted upon. Seek within, my brother. Your direction is well known to you.

May we answer you further?

M: No, thank you, Latwii.

I am Latwii. We thank you. Is there another question at this time?

K: Yes, one more. As I've watched the news and the terrible destruction in Beirut and Lebanon, the thought has occurred to me—did those people who have suffered and are still suffering so much, did they choose to incarnate in order to experience that suffering?

I am Latwii, and am aware of your query, my sister. Each entity before the incarnation draws up the general guidelines, shall we say, of the upcoming incarnation. These plans may call for the entity to bear a great deal of that known as unhappiness or suffering in order that the entity might find the love of the Creator within that suffering, for the Creator's love is not absent from any moment or situation. It may not be specifically planned that the suffering shall result from that which you know as warfare. It may be that such suffering can be beneficially experienced as a disease of the body, a disease of the mind, a condition of strained relationships with those near and close to the entity's heart. It may be that such suffering can be achieved by an entity who feels great empathy for a world in pain. That such suffering is programmed before the incarnation is quite correct. How it shall be encountered is often not specifically delineated.

May we answer you further, my sister?

K: No, that answered it. Thank you.

I am Latwii. We are most grateful to you. Is there another question at this time?

(Pause)

I am Latwii. My friends, we cannot express in a complete enough sense our great joy at being able to join you this evening. The path each of you travels is one which is pointed surely and steadily at the one Creator. Your path has many pitfalls; it is so for each true seeker. We rejoice with each of your efforts. They are most valiant, for the conditions under which you labor are conditions which hide a great portion of the truth from you. The truth of your oneness with each of your brothers and sisters, the truth of your oneness with the Creator, and the truth of the love and the light and the power of that one Creator within each of your beings is a truth which is hidden from you so that your desire to find it might be enhanced. We rejoice with each of you as you rekindle that desire. Seek, my brothers and sisters, for as you seek, so shall you surely find, for that which you seek is already within your being.

We leave you now, as always, in the love and the light of the one Creator Who is the All. We are known to you as Latwii. Adonai vasu borragus. ❧

L/L RESEARCH

L/L Research is a subsidiary of
Rock Creek Research &
Development Laboratories, Inc.

P.O. Box 5195
Louisville, KY 40255-0195

www.llresearch.org

Rock Creek is a non-profit
corporation dedicated to
discovering and sharing
information which may aid in
the spiritual evolution of
humankind.

SUNDAY MEDITATION
JULY 25, 1982

(C channeling)

I am Hatonn, and am now with this instrument. We greet you, as always, my friends, in the love and the light of the one infinite Creator. It is indeed a great privilege for us to welcome the new participants in this group tonight and to welcome an old friend returned. Groups this large are indeed rare and we treasure every opportunity to speak our few humble words to them.

Tonight we would seek to remind each and all that by the fact that there are so many in this one place tonight that you are not alone. You have many brothers and sisters to walk with you, near you on your journey. You need not put excessive burdens upon yourself, for there are those who would, if you would but open yourself to them, help. The journey is so much more pleasant when the burden is shared. Each offers opportunities to learn and each offers opportunities to teach, to share. We of the Confederation would at any time, when in your meditations you request, join with you and aid, as we may, your journey. As you grow, your awareness of the light and of the love of the infinite Creator increases, and as your awareness grows, so grows that light within you, the love that is you. Reach out and touch others, and bring to you ever more opportunities to learn, to share and grow.

We of Hatonn can feel many requests this evening for us to work with various instruments within this group who are seeking to enhance their ability to receive our vibration, and would at this time transfer our contact to the instrument known as M1 so that we may continue through him. If he would but relax. I am Hatonn.

(M1 channeling)

I am Hatonn. I am with this instrument. We greet you, my brothers, again in the love and the light of the infinite Creator. As always, [it is] our pleasure to work with each of the new instruments, for we delight in seeing them grow in their abilities. My brothers, we are here tonight with each to share, to learn, and to grow in every experience with you. For in teaching, surely we learn, and in giving, surely we receive. In sharing each experience with you, are you not sharing your experience with us? These are opportunities we rejoice in—the opportunity to gain a oneness with you, one portion of the creation.

It is such a beautiful experience that you are living in, one certainly difficult to appreciate at times, as the experience grows ever so challenging. But each challenge placed before you, my friends, is an opportunity to triumph, to grow at an ever faster rate, to grow closer to that oneness with the infinite Creator, the awareness of that oneness with the one infinite Creator. My friends, whenever possible when facing the challenges, the roadblocks, the problems along the way that appear to make you stumble, look at them always as opportunities. The barrier is not a wall, but a stepping stone, and take each one that way. For each is an opportunity given you, even requested by you long before coming here. It is an opportunity for you to grow.

At this time we transfer this contact. I am Hatonn.

(M2 channeling)

I am Hatonn. I am now with this instrument. I greet you with the love and the light of the infinite Creator. Change is very good for everybody. A film is lifted from your eyes. When you go to some other place than your usual habitat, you look, you really see. You smell, you feel. And when you return home you have clearer eyes, a sharper smell, and a greater sense of touch. So much of life passes you by when you stay in the same place. You forget to look up at the sky. You don't smell the scent of the forest. You don't touch those. When you come home you see them all with these new eyes. If you can't travel, it might be fun for one day a week to think that you will only be able to see for this day. You will only be able to smell for this day. You will only be able to touch for this day. If one day every week you could bring this excitement into your life, you would see the beauty you are missing. So much of the wonders of the world are taken for granted. On a trip the same sky looks different because your eyes are different. Make a point of seeing the beauty of the world. Don't let it pass you by.

I now leave this instrument. I am Hatonn.

(D channeling)

I am Hatonn. I am with this instrument. It is a pleasure to speak once again through this instrument, and we wish to speak of the wealth that each of you possess. In your world there are many types of wealth, but that which is most desirable is the wealth of knowledge within your inner being, and the greatest tool that you possess is the ability to go within yourself, to learn of your true existence, to learn of the origin from which you have come. Any man living upon your planet that has gone within himself and come to rest and knows that he is of the Father, or the Creator, then he is the most wealthy of all. For that of your world, that which you touch, is only a tool. It is only a toy, and as you pass through this life you lay many of them aside and desire others. But constantly man looks for something, knowing not what it is until he looks within himself.

You seek to know what there is other than that which you have learned upon this planet, and for that reason you are here. To seek is the first step. But to participate and to turn within yourself in a group such as this is an even greater step, for together your energies can mesh and accomplish a great deal more than you can alone. Yet we of the Confederation stress that if you truly seek to know the Creator, if you seek the wealth of the universe, seek it with your friends as well as alone. Both are vital. For within a group as this, you receive information upon an intellectual basis as well as spiritual energies, as you might call them. But when you are alone, and you go within yourself, and you reach the core of your being, you are all people and all things. You are in unison with the Creator. And His words shall not be heard; they shall emanate within your life. His energies can flow freely as you open the doors and cross the barriers that you have placed between you and the universe.

My friends, your life is but a mask that you wear. It is good for your growth. But it is only a tiny portion of the truth that you seek. Learn the lesson of love while upon this planet and you shall graduate into an environment that is love. Seek and ye shall find. Seek love, my friends, and your reward shall be that.

I shall now leave this instrument. I am Hatonn.

(Carla channeling)

I am Hatonn, and am now with this instrument. We would condition the instrument known as K, and would after that close our message through the one known as S. But first we wish, along with our brother Laitos, to touch the unique vibratory essences which comprise each of those here who may wish to feel our presence at this time. We may say to the one known as A that the one known as Latwii will be working with that instrument. We would pause now that this conditioning may take place for each of those who may mentally request it. I am Hatonn.

(Pause)

(K channeling)

I am Hatonn. Again we greet you, my friends, in the love and the light of the infinite Creator. And again, we wish to emphasize the joy that we feel of being with this group, and of the sincere efforts of each one and especially of the new instruments. We wish to go with each one of you this week so that you may rejoice in the infinite Creator, perhaps in a greater sense than you have before.

I now leave this instrument and transfer the contact.

(S channeling)

I am Hatonn, and am now with this instrument. We would like once more this evening, my brothers and sisters, to greet you in the love and in the light of the one infinite Creator. My friends, many times have we spoken this phrase this evening, and many more will we speak it. For to know the love and the light of the Creator is why you are here. The love and the light of the one Creator is the reason we speak through each of these instruments, for their wish to serve is culminated in this service to the Creator. Each one in their daily lives serves many people and many things in small ways, my friends. Ways that may not at the moment seem worth anything, but by serving the smallest of the creation you serve the Creator. Microcosm affects the macrocosm, my friends. The least that you do will blossom, though you may not see or know the end result of your action.

Ah, my friends, what good you could do by thinking one beautiful thought towards another self, towards doing one small service to another self. My friends, by doing this you serve yourself, for everything is one. We are all one within the One, and this purpose is what we seek and why you are here this evening, drawn by things you may not realize, reasons beyond your comprehension at the moment. You are drawn to serve the Creator, my friends. Remember the saying of your holy book, "Do unto others as you would have them do unto you." So simple, my friends, and so true. Think upon this as you go about your daily lives, for love is so very simple, and yet at the end of a life you may consider full of struggles and strife, by seeking the one Creator and striving to serve the Creator, you will find this very simple message of love.

We leave you now in this same love and light, and wish you every happiness that can be bestowed by the Creator. I am known to you as Hatonn. Adonai, my friends. Adonai vasu borragus.

(S channeling)

I am Latwii, and am very pleased to be here this evening. We would thank this instrument, even though we caught her by surprise, we think, and would say we appreciate her picking up our vibration, but only do so to accustom her a bit more to our vibrations, and will not continue this contact any longer. We thank her again, and would now transfer this contact. I am Latwii.

(Jim channeling)

I am Latwii, and am with this instrument. We greet you, my friends, in the love and the light of the one infinite Creator. Again may we thank our sister known as S for her great desire to be of service, and may we congratulate her on her ability to perceive our vibrations. As always, it is a great privilege to be asked to join this group in the capacity of attempting to answer those queries which those present may have the value in the requesting. Therefore, may we ask if there are any questions at this time?

C: Latwii, I'm having difficulties here of late when attempting to meditate privately. I think my main problem is really a matter of tuning, but I was wondering if you could make any comments about what it is I am doing wrong, because it leaves me quite drained and really quite irritable afterwards.

I am Latwii, and am aware of your query, my brother. We may suggest, my brother, that at any time you wish to pursue your seeking through meditation, that the first portion of your meditation be given to some inward devotion to the one Creator. Whether this be a prayer, a chant, a mantra, a visualization, makes no difference. Use this device to refine your desire to seek the truth in the positive sense. If then you have but a moment in which to meditate, fear not that time is too short, for a moment given to the one Creator cannot be measured in time. Rest in that moment as you surrender your small self and your will to the will of the Father. Know that in that moment you have drunk of the essence of your being. Then go forth, refreshed, full and whole. Your desire, my brother, will see you through. You have no shortage of that most important ingredient.

May we answer you further, my brother?

C: Yes. In visualization, I've had a vision that I had before I knew what meditation was, and continue to use. But I'm having doubts as to this particular visualization actually being beneficial. I guess the doubts arise from the various feelings the visualization is a part of. The other visualization, when it started occurring to me, was simply a matter of falling, but has developed into a falling, not bodily, but simply a motion through some sort of tone at an extreme rate of speed. Whenever this occurs to me, which it does without conscious trying, it results in a feeling of really almost of rushing from myself. Is this causing part of my problem?

I am Latwii, and am aware of your query, my brother. As always, it is our lot to make only the general comment for the specific practice of the seeker. In this regard, therefore, may we suggest that if you find the visualization which you have used to be of an unsettling nature in any degree, that you investigate each portion of the experience and replace those portions which have the unsettling effect. It is the seeker's responsibility to determine the nature and content of all practices which are used in seeking. You have within your conscious mind the information which is necessary for the construction of a technique which will be most useful in your seeking. We do not mean to be shy of information, but feel we might be of the most service at this time by directing your query back to your own being.

May we answer you further, my brother?

C: Not at the moment. And I'm fully aware of that what you may say, and I only hoped for general information so that I may really gain some reassurance. Thank you.

I am Latwii. My brother, we are most grateful to you. Is there another question at this time?

M2: I'd like to inquire a little more about the same thing. Could he be experiencing a negative influence?

I am Latwii, and am aware of your query, my sister. As this group is well aware, there are those influences of the negative nature which accompany this group, and any seeker which has sought in a purified fashion the truth of the one Creator. We cannot say for any seeker whether such and such an experience …

(Side one of tape ends.)

(Jim channeling)

I am Latwii, and am once again with this instrument. To conclude our response, it is necessary for each seeker to find the path which is the purest expression of its positive polarity. We remind each in this group that the offerings which are made to you by those sources and forces which you might describe as negative are great services, my friends, for each offers you the opportunity to choose once again to serve the one Creator in a positive fashion.

May we answer you further, my sister?

M2: Thank you. I think you've answered my question very well.

I am Latwii. We are pleased that we have been of service. We thank each for each query that offers us this opportunity. Is there another question at this time?

Carla: Latwii, could you speak to love, wisdom and martyrdom?

I am Latwii, and am aware of your query, my sister. You have asked a query which covers a great deal of ground, shall we say. We hesitate for a moment to find the focus. The love which is the salvation of your density of illusion is that love which sees creation as one being. This being has many facets. This being is in each face, is in each experience, and any pain, sorrow or suffering that an entity observes in an other self then resounds to that entity who feels the love of the Creator as a pain, a sorrow, a suffering which must needs be attended. The entity feeling this love, then, if it feels the love purely and without any addition of wisdom, seeks by whatever means are deemed possible to heal the suffering, to calm the sorrow, and to make whole that which was broken. The self which gives this love to the other self that suffers is willing to give all with no reservations in order that an other portion of the creation might be healed and soothed.

The entity, on the other hand, which seeks and experiences the ways of wisdom also sees each portion of the one creation as being indeed the one Creator, but differs somewhat from the entity viewing this creation in love in that it sees sorrow and suffering as being a perfect means whereby the entity's experience in the sorrow and suffering might learn those lessons which they have determined before the incarnation to undertake. Each experience, therefore, is seen as a perfect portion of an illusion which has but one purpose, and that is to teach love.

The entity which sees the creation purely through the eyes of love without the eye of wisdom may, in the service to others, became that known as the martyr, for the self is given without reservation, and without the discernment which would allow the perception of the perfection of all suffering, sorrow and tragedy in the lives of those who experience these traumas. The entity who travels the path of the martyr cannot be said to serve less well than the entity who travels the path of wisdom. Each path sees Creator and the creation in unity. The martyr is the perfect expression of love for the Creator and the creation in each other self. The martyr, however, limits the amount of service or the quality, shall we say, if it completes its service in the path of martyrdom, giving of itself until there is no self left within the illusion to give.

The entity who balances the love of all with wisdom, therefore, has an additional tool to utilize in the serving of others in that the entity is able to see that indeed there is service that can be given to others, but there are times when it is of a greater service, shall we say, to allow others to experience the illusion in such and such a way, whether it include sorrow or not, in order that they might most purely learn their lessons. The wisdom to know when to serve is most helpful to an entity who wishes to serve in the deepest pattern possible for it.

May we answer you further, my sister?

Carla: No. Latwii. I really needed to hear those words. I'm working on that subject and I would ask especially for your aid in my meditations in the coming weeks.

I am Latwii. My sister, as always, it is our honor to address this subject, for we realize that you and each within this group seeks to be of the greatest service possible, and that type of service is not always obvious. We shall indeed be with you and with each as requested.

Is there another question at this time?

M2: Yes, then in that context, Jesus could have been of greater service had he not chosen to be a martyr, is that right?

I am Latwii, and am aware of your query, my sister. The response which we made to the previous query

was a general response which is not always applicable to specific situations. The entity known to your peoples as Jesus had a specific purpose for its incarnation. As you are aware, this entity was that known as a wanderer, and incarnated for the purpose of giving a pattern to your peoples that would be useful in the daily round of activities for many of your years to come. The pattern was that of love of other selves in as pure a fashion as possible. To make this statement in a fashion which would have the necessary force, shall we say, to survive throughout your ages, the one known as Jesus determined before incarnation to travel the path of love in as pure a fashion as possible. This fashion, as we have mentioned, is that of the martyr.

Indeed, it has been said that greater love hath no man than he who would lay down his life for another. It was the determination of the one known as Jesus that the peoples of your planet needed a pattern such as he determined finally to offer in order that some distortion of that pattern would remain and have an influence upon those who would follow, in some portion, his footsteps. If the entity had decided, for example, not to complete the purpose of its mission and become that known as the martyr, then there would be much less emphasis given to those teachings which the entity offered during its incarnation. This entity had a specific purpose in its incarnation and fulfilled it well. We cannot say what is most appropriate for any one entity, but only give those guidelines which each entity then may interpret in his or her own fashion.

May we answer you further, my sister?

M2: No, that answered me quite well. Thank you.

I am Latwii. We thank you, my sister. Is there another question at this time?

M2: Latwii, do you think the cat eating the string was an accident or a planned event?

I am Latwii, and am aware of your query, my sister. We find some degree of humor in this particular query, for there are indeed those activities which are of the unusual nature occurring within this group which might be said to have a planned and somewhat negative influence. But we find the young entity of the feline variety is without the necessary mental apparatus to allow such programming, therefore we might suggest that this young entity was pursuing its trade as a cat, which will eat almost anything.

May we answer you further, my sister?

M2: No, thank you, Latwii.

I am Latwii. We are most grateful to you. Is there another question at this time?

K: Yes. I guess this is a little humorous also, but we'll try it anyway. My daughter was ill on the trip. She had a sore throat and her nose stopped up and she couldn't breathe, so I had to see that she got to the emergency room at the hospital, and it cost her seventy dollars plus the tax. And about three or four nights later we were at Las Vegas, and she won seventy dollars playing a little game called Keno on the first try. And it did seem a little odd that she should have one expense of seventy dollars, and then win seventy dollars. Was that accident?

I am Latwii, and am aware of your query, my sister. We might suggest to each entity, as that journey is traveled which culminates in the various lessons being learned, there shall appear from time to time those co-incidences which may suggest to the entity that there are indeed no such things as accidents. There are, to the seeker, a continuing array and panorama of events which seem random until the heart of the event is determined. To an entity such as your daughter, it might be considered appropriate from time to time to learn of certain lessons by the method which you have described. It might be, for instance that such an entity might need to know that the creation supports it, and the Creator is within it, and there is no need to fear the chance happening, shall we say, of the injury or loss to self in any degree, for there is always that portion of the Creator which stands ready to teach the opposite lesson.

It might be helpful, therefore, for such an entity to receive this information within its own experience in a fairly short period of what you call time in order to become aware of the essence of balance within the creation. This occurs for each entity from time to time as the deeper portions of the self determine that it is appropriate to present the lessons in this fashion.

May we answer you further, my sister?

K: No, that answered it. And she really did need to learn that lesson, and I think she learned it. So I'm glad to hear that explanation. Thank you.

I am Latwii. We thank you, my sister. Is there another question at this time?

M2: You might answer one question for me. Why is my happy little fellow—that's the only name I know for him—dancing around Hatonn's words when two of the people spoke, but not quite coming in?

I am Latwii, and am aware of your query, my sister. We cannot always present those explanations which are what you might call perfectly clear, for entities of this nature. For each entity has that known as free will, and does present itself to those open to its vibrations in such and such a manner. It might be its choice to act in this manner in order to, shall we say, capture your attention, and present the riddle of sorts.

May we answer you further, my sister?

M2: No, thank you. I think you've answered it.

I am Latwii. We thank you. Is there another question at this time?

A: Yes, Latwii, I have a question I hope you can answer. Lately I've been confused and hurting, and I don't know if you can help, but the question I have is, why?

I am Latwii, and am aware of your query, my sister. We also hope that we might be of service in this regards, but we find that such an experience of pain and confusion is one which has great lessons to teach, and to speak too specifically would rob the seeker of those lessons. May we then suggest that if it is possible within your meditations or within your conscious contemplation upon this experience of pain and confusion that you look as from above upon yourself within the situation in which the pain and confusion is generated. See those forces in motion. Look at them in their symbolic form, if possible, without becoming lost in specific identities. See yourself as actor, and as that which is acted upon. Look at the result of the action. If possible, intensify in your mind that activity so that its logical conclusion, shall we say, might be experienced within your being.

As you find portions of this experience which have meaning to you on your journey, meditate upon them to unlock further keys and understandings, that your journey might continue. For, my sister, there is no experience within your illusion that does not have the purpose of teaching a certain lesson and opening yet another door, that you might pass through and continue your journey. Look, my sister, then within yourself and within that experience, and you shall find those treasures which at present are covered and hidden. Yet do not doubt that treasures await, for your illusion is filled with them, yet they are camouflaged to many.

May we answer you further, my sister?

A: No, thank you.

I am Latwii. We are most grateful to you. Is there another question at this time?

Questioner: Latwii, are members of your Confederation aware of channeling with Michael Pacc and panel?

I am Latwii, and am aware of your query. We of the Confederation of Planets in the Service of the One Infinite Creator do observe those activities which you describe. There are many such activities occurring at this time upon the surface of your planet for the sole purpose of awakening those entities who seek the message of love that they might know in further degree the truth of love, light and unity with the one Creator. We are most honored to be but a small portion of that awakening.

May we answer you further?

Questioner: Yes. Is this channeling always positive?

I am Latwii, and am aware of your query. We find that in answering this query we are restricted by that great Law of Confusion that prohibits the infringement upon the free will of any other being. We cannot determine, therefore, for any such instrument or channel the positive or negative nature of the experience, for this is most important to each seeker, and especially to those who serve as instruments. It is necessary that each seeker be able to discriminate for itself the nature of information which is garnered, whatever its source might be. In this way the pearls of wisdom, shall we say, truly then belong to the seeker, for they have been won by the seeker's own efforts.

May we answer you further, my sister?

Questioner: Thank you. I think that's all right.

I am Latwii. We are most grateful to you. Is there another question at this time?

M2: Yes. I've had some unpleasant experiences happen to me, and I really think I should be

miserable. But I don't seem to be able to hold on to misery. Is there something wrong with me?

I am Latwii, and am aware of your query, my sister. And in one sense, we rejoice with you, for it would seem that to be unable to retain the experience of misery would be a most desired state of being. It might, on the other hand, be determined by another portion of yourself that another try, shall we say, be made so that you might experience that known as misery, not to become distorted towards unhappiness within yourself, but perhaps to be able to feel compassion for others who experience the distortion known as misery. We cannot say what the particular purpose of your inability to retain this state of being is, but can only suggest that there are no mistakes, and your ability or lack of same has its own purpose and you are learning this well.

May we answer you further, my sister?

M2: Thank you.

I am Latwii. We thank you. Is there another query at this time?

M2: If no one else has a question, do you think I'm taking my misery too lightly?

I am Latwii, and am aware of your query. We cannot make such a judgment for it would be an infringement, my sister, upon your free will to make that discernment for yourself.

May we answer you further?

M2: No. I guess you mean I have to figure it out for myself.

I am Latwii. You state it much better than [I do.]

(Group laughter.)

R: I've had some problems arising in a new business, and these problems that have arisen have been brought on by one or two people, not that they're vindictive or anything. One particular person brought me to a standstill, but I was able to acquire what I needed through another company, and we just received them. And the first one that stopped me and brought me to a standstill now seems to be having some worries about what he'd done. Will he be successful in carrying on?

I am Latwii, and am aware of your query, my brother. We feel we might be of most aid in this regard by responding in a general sense. My brother, it is an illusion which you inhabit, an illusion in which you have forgotten, as do each—we correct this instrument—as does each entity which passes through this illusion, that it is the one Creator. It is most helpful to forget this great truth, in order that experiences of a great variety might then be available to teach this truth in a manner which reaches to the depth of the being. When difficulties, as you call them, are encountered of any nature, you might then look at the situation as a situation which has an opportunity for growth, for within the difficulty is a lesson. Each such lesson, though it be uniquely tailored, has the purpose of teaching the ability to be tolerant, the ability for the light touch, shall we say, and the ability to find the love and the light of the one Creator within each experience, and each entity one encounters. Therefore, we would suggest that it is of small concern as to whether or not successes will be encountered in this or that endeavor. For what does your illusion teach? To love, my brother. To know love, to give love, to be love, and in that endeavor we can assure you that each shall be most successful.

May we answer you further, my brother?

R: *(Inaudible).*

Is there another question at this time?

(Pause)

I am Latwii. We thank each present this evening for asking that we join our vibrations with yours during your meditation. As always, it is the greatest of honors for us to participate with your group in seeking the love, the light, and the unity of the one Creator. We remind each entity that we are but brothers and sisters who travel the same path that you now tread. It may be true that we have traveled somewhat further upon this trail than you have at this time, and it is therefore our honor to share our insights, and those lessons which have been most useful to us, as you request them. But we do remind each that we are not in any way infallible. We are your brothers and sisters in the truest sense. We share what truths we have found. We seek yet further, and we know that we are all one. We leave you now in the love and in the light of the one infinite Creator who resides within all. We are known to you as Latwii. Adonai, my friends. Adonai vasu borragus.

(Carla channeling)

I am Nona. I greet you, my friends, in the love and in the light of the infinite Creator. We have been conditioning this instrument, as she was reluctant to lengthen the communiqué. However, there is a request from the inner planes and from some of those present for the healing of our sound vibrations. We would ask each of you to visualize one who has recently passed from your illusion as we sing through this instrument one melody which has great meaning for this entity's guide, and one melody which has great influence upon the moving into greater realms for the entity passing.

(Carla channels a melody from Nona.) ✣

L/L RESEARCH

L/L Research is a subsidiary of Rock Creek Research & Development Laboratories, Inc.

P.O. Box 5195
Louisville, KY 40255-0195

www.llresearch.org

Rock Creek is a non-profit corporation dedicated to discovering and sharing information which may aid in the spiritual evolution of humankind.

ABOUT THE CONTENTS OF THIS TRANSCRIPT: This telepathic channeling has been taken from transcriptions of the weekly study and meditation meetings of the Rock Creek Research & Development Laboratories and L/L Research. It is offered in the hope that it may be useful to you. As the Confederation entities always make a point of saying, please use your discrimination and judgment in assessing this material. If something rings true to you, fine. If something does not resonate, please leave it behind, for neither we nor those of the Confederation would wish to be a stumbling block for any.

CAVEAT: This transcript is being published by L/L Research in a not yet final form. It has, however, been edited and any obvious errors have been corrected. When it is in a final form, this caveat will be removed.

SUNDAY MEDITATION
AUGUST 8, 1982

(Carla channeling)

[I am Hatonn, and] I greet you, my friends, in the love and the light of the infinite Creator. To be with you is exquisite pleasure, and we thank you for requesting our presence. The opportunity to share our thoughts with you is the greatest opportunity for which we could hope. We should like to offer philosophical thoughts framed in parable this evening, and we shall move from one channel to another with some frequency. Therefore, we suggest that if you have tuned and challenged us mentally that you may dispense with the beginning and ending greetings until the end of the message.

Once upon a time there was a wooded copse, a beautiful leafy glade, and within that small forest lived many creatures that you would call spirits of nature; others have called them fairies and elves. To them, the smallest peony was as a towering tree and the red clover was enough to make a roof for their house. We shall transfer.

(C channeling)

This world was to this fairy an idyllic place of beauty of peace and harmony between yourself and nature. They took not but they couldn't give back and lived in quiet serenity for some time.

We will transfer.

(Jim channeling)

These entities felt the great peace of oneness, yet in that peaceful unity, there was something that was missing, for though their daily routine provided all that was needed for their simple sustenance, there still was felt in each the yearning for something more, and on certain occasions these entities would gather in what you might call a council circle. There were at these times, shall we say, certain ritualized celebrations. Yet the heart of the council was the attempt to resolve the matter of what was lacking in the lives which seemed so rich and full of pleasure, of harmony, and of peace.

We shall now transfer.

(C channeling)

Into this setting at times creatures other than the small fairy folk would enter. Most were passive forest dwellers seeking sustenance from nature with whom which [the] small fairy folk existed harmoniously. But it came that into this setting entered one different from any the small fairy folk had ever encountered. It seemed strange to them, for instead of harmony it seemed to emote a discord.

We will transfer.

(Carla channeling)

This entity, so unlike the forest denizens, stood upright and was even taller than the peony bush. It was a five-year-old boy, and he was deeply troubled because he saw things he did not understand. But he was unafraid, and knelt down and put his face very close to the ground to speak with it. "Who are you?" he asked. All the nature spirits laughed and said, "Oh, we are the spirits of nature. Call us the folk of Fairy. We cause your flowers to bloom, your trees to grow tall, your grass to smile in the sunshine. We tell the butterflies when to pop from their cocoons and we speak to the busy insects. We have converse with all that is within our ken." "Oh," said the little boy. "You are so beautiful. Can you fly with your wings?" "Of course," said the fairies, "Would you like to see us?" And they took a gigantic flight all the way up to the top of the peony bush and back down again. "Ohh!" said the little boy, clapping his hands and making thunder roll for the fairies. "That was splendid. And can you show me where I lost my marbles last year, for I was shooting near here." "Of course," said the fairies, if you speak of those huge boulders that we cannot move." "Yes, yes," said the little boy.

We will transfer.

(Unknown channeling)

The little boy was delighted that he had found beings such as the fairy folk, and his troubled mind at their unusual nature was soon put to rest by their gleeful acceptance of his questions and presence. He had many questions for them concerning how he saw his world, questions that the five-year-old mind ponders frequently and with much determination. He asked if they grew old, and when they replied that they grew very old and did not die, he compared their situation to the one he knew was true for his family and friends, where death had been known once or twice. And he asked what was the meaning of the life and the meaning of the death. And they began to explain that in their lives meaning was found in the services which they provided to the various plants and animals which appreciated assistance in carrying out their normal functions of growing and blooming, living and dying.

We shall now transfer.

(S channeling)

As the little boy pondered the growth and blooming and death of the flowers and the other things that were found in this fairyland, he seemed to become somewhat less fearful, for had not the flowers brought beauty to his world and to the world of the fairies, and had they not returned that which had been given to them by the little ones who had aided in its growth and development? The little boy pondered similar, and wondered if he too might be as this flower who would grow and become strong and with the help of many from his own world be able to return that which was done for him. He thought of the many times he had been caressed when he had fallen and skinned a knee. He thought of the many kisses planted on his cheek so that he might sleep feeling safe, secure and loved, and he thought of the happy faces which greeted him in the morning and prepared his breakfast and sent him off to school.

And he wondered if he had been returning all the smiles and warmth and love that was brought to him by those around him. And he thought to himself, "Perhaps I am not showing my appreciation for these gifts that I am indeed so grateful for. Perhaps I should make my gratitude known so that those who are dear to me will realize that I appreciate the caresses, the kisses, the smiling faces, and the touch of one who loves me." He pondered similar and made up his mind to return home and plant a kiss on his mother's cheek, though she was not going to bed, and give her a big hug, though she had not skinned her knee, and to tell her he loved her for no apparent reason other than he wanted to be sure that she knew.

We will transfer.

(Carla channeling)

Before he left the glade that day, he thanked the folk of Fairy and told them of his plans. They laughed merrily as they so often did, and one of them said to him a bit shyly, "Perhaps you do not need to speak of where you found this wisdom." "Oh perhaps," said the boy rather absentmindedly. He jingled his clanking marbles together in his pocket, and practiced whistling all the way home. His mother was in the kitchen. "Hi, mom." "Hello, dear," was the reply. "Bend down, mom, because I'm going to plant a kiss on your cheek, just like you plant the roses in the garden." Laughing, the mother bent down. "And I am going to give you a big hug," he said. "This is my lucky day," laughed his mother. "I love you, mom," said the little boy.

His mother, glad enough to have the embrace, looked at him and smiled. "Now, what put that in your head?" said his mother. "Oh, the little people." "What?" said the mother. Then the little boy remembered what the fairy had said: "Do not tell them of us." But the mother had heard. "What little people?" Said the boy, "Oh, just little people in the forest that make things grow and found my marbles that I lost last year." His mother sat him down carefully. "Now, listen son," she said, "I'm very happy that you found them, but you know there are no such thing as little people in the forest."

We shall transfer.

(C channeling)

The boy's mother was unable to understand what the little boy's openness and innocence had allowed him to see in the forest. She was afraid that because the small boy was seeing and hearing entities in the forest, that he was not living in the real world but in one of imagination.

We will transfer.

(Jim channeling)

The little boy had discovered that those things and thoughts of most importance to himself were often not exactly shared by those around him, and he began to realize the wisdom of the fairy creature's warning not to speak of the presence of little folks in the woods. He began to consider that what he had learned of love and of expressing it to those whom he dearly loved could be done better than it could be described. And thus, he began to show what he knew in his actions and to be somewhat shy with his words. Yet, his being radiated the love which the little folks had aided in its growth just as they aided the growth of the flowers, the trees, and the birthing of the butterflies.

We shall now transfer.

(Carla channeling)

One …

(Side one of tape ends.)

(Carla channeling)

One day he put down his school books, for he had become older and begun school, and went as he so often had before to the lovely copse where he had so often spent a happy hour. He could no longer find the little people. "Where are you," he cried, "Where are you?" Carefully he got down upon his knees and began to peer under the clover. "I am so afraid I will step on you", he said. The fairy folk watched him, knowing that the world had finally become more real to him than the kingdom of the Creator. Safe in their own dimension from any stepping feet, and filled with the greatest of love, they watched their young friend, the giant among them. His blond hair picked leaves from the bushes, and his eyes were blue and wide with distress. "Where are you, where are you?" he cried. His tears began to fall. "My friends," said the king of the folk of Fairy, "It is for this divine gift that we sit in circle and do our rituals, for as wise as we are, we do not have the gift of tears. We do not have the love that cries for loss, for all has become one to us. And yet we remember. Mark well, my people, as you grow old but do not die, this precious gift."

We shall transfer.

(C channeling)

The fairy folk watched the boy, saw that he was experiencing something they were unable to know, for to them was given all they needed to exist in a finely arranged harmony, but [he] existed within a harmony they were denied, an aspect of love that enabled love to search within, to draw forth the deeper understanding of the Creator. They had not the opportunity to grow by experience.

We transfer.

(Carla channeling)

We shall close through this instrument, as we find the energies are somewhat variable and would suggest retuning after this contact.

We of the Confederation of Planets in the Service of the Infinite Creator are full of sorrow as we gaze upon your people. We hope to inspire you and aid the butterfly within you to be birthed and the flower within you to bloom, yet we cannot quiet you. It is you who may bring to the service of your planet the gift of your tears. You are those who have faith in things unseen, in the ideals of love and truth, and you gaze upon that which is not there. That which is not there gives you the desire to manifest love, radiance to glow, to grow, and the feeling that there is more, far more balance, far more holiness than is visible to the objective beholder of circumstance. You bring to your planet the gift of your perception, the gift of your faith. Can you cry out for fear lest you lose those things, lest those about you lose those things? Can you cry out that those about you deny them, and live and die with no knowledge of perfection?

The ideals which you seek in meditation have enabled you to find that which you had lost; to love and reach and give. Remember the gift of tears. You who are in the illusion, whose spirits dwell in flesh, are full of wonder and full of folly. Which will you choose? How much do you care? You may do a service that we cannot with all our knowledge. We encourage you to remain open and innocent and childlike, no matter what cynicism greets you, no matter what horror awaits you in the illusion. Leave your consciousness in the hands of love and truth and give to a planet desperate for your light, that powerful fire—your caring, your salt tears of remembrance and faith.

We are those of Hatonn. We thank each of you for the great gift of your service in working with us to create thoughts which may be of aid to those among your peoples who seek love and truth. We leave you in that love and in the light of our infinite Creator. Adonai vasu borragus. ✸

L/L RESEARCH

L/L Research is a subsidiary of Rock Creek Research & Development Laboratories, Inc.

P.O. Box 5195
Louisville, KY 40255-0195

www.llresearch.org

Rock Creek is a non-profit corporation dedicated to discovering and sharing information which may aid in the spiritual evolution of humankind.

INTENSIVE MEDITATION
AUGUST 12, 1982

(S channeling)

I am Hatonn, and I greet you, my brothers and sisters, in the love and in the light of the one infinite Creator. We are extremely happy to be here this evening. It has been long since we have been with this group in what you call the intensive session. It is our pleasure and great joy to be with you this evening, and to exercise the instruments so that they, through their desire to serve, can perfect or attempt to perfect the technique of channeling. We are pleased to see the one known as G this evening and to feel and blend with her vibration. She is at this time not quite sure of the process known as channeling, so we will condition and work with her and we thank her sincerely for the opportunity.

At this time we would transfer this contact to the one known as A in order to exercise the instrument. I am known to you as Hatonn.

(A channeling)

I am Hatonn, and once again we greet you through this instrument. On this night we wish to work with the new instruments, for they feel they are out of practice and have lost some of their touch on channeling. We wish to say that if the desire is there, there is no need to worry about losing the touch. We are happy to be here tonight so that we may learn *(inaudible)* our vibrations with each, and to also bring forth a small message to all. It is a message of

peace and of hope, and it is as a small reminder that you are all on this planet by choice, and that while you are here you have many, many lessons to experience, to learn from, to grow from. Be patient and do not try to figure out the whole future at once. It is there and it is now, and so we ask of each of you to be patient with those things that you do not understand. Once you have overcome the confusion you will very easily see the lesson that was at hand.

We have made this message short, or shall we say, this reminder short and would now wish to transfer this contact. I am Hatonn.

(Carla channeling)

I am Hatonn. We ask your pardon for the delay, but were requesting as to whether the channel known as Don might be available for work with us at this time. This instrument prefers to listen at this time, and so we are very pleased to speak through this instrument to close the message. For indeed it has been some time since we spoke through this instrument, and it is a privilege to speak through this as through all of the instruments.

We would like to say a few words in particular to the one known as G, but, in general, towards the subject of dedication. When an entity such as each of these instruments decides that he or she desires to be of service by receiving concepts and passing them on, these concepts being of a recognized spiritual quality, the decision for this service has an emotional content. In some cases this emotional content is not great, and in these cases, as the novelty wears off, the instrument ceases that particular service and moves on. This is, of course, perfectly acceptable to us and we are grateful for being able to work with any instrument for any length of time.

Others who come to recognize our vibrations discover within themselves an emotion which can be described as dedication. In these particular instruments there has been developed a love of service which does not grow on compliments nor fatten on praise, but rests instead on the desire to be of service as each instrument has been served in his or her own turn. And we say to the one known as G, and to each, it does not matter greatly whether or not an entity determined to be of service by learning the skill of more and more precisely tuning the receiver so as to transmit our messages. What matters, my friends, is that in whatever service you are attempting to perform, there lie beneath the surface an inner dedication that is not a veneer which washes away with constant use nor is rubbed away with idle chatter and stray thoughts, but instead remains, a kind of inner lodestar, [guiding] the servant on to seek an ever more precise rendition of whatever service he or she has undertaken to perform.

The array of services in your illusion, my friends, is staggering. The emotion with which one faces any service is a constant. In the vicissitudes of your daily round, look then to that which lies below the surface of your reactions. Analyze carefully the depth of your dedication to service. And, my friends, if you are not satisfied, continue to seek from within that great sun service of love and hope and strength which will give you the energy of vital and careful dedication.

In being so serious, my friends, we do not wish to unbalance your lives as you ponder the mysteries of service, for indeed very often the greatest service you can offer another is your own smile, your own light word, your own cheerful touch. Therefore, let your dedication be careful and deep. But do not forget to let the sunshine flow through all your thinking, and lighten it that your service may be pleasant and of good cheer. For it is with those about you that you shall wend your way as pilgrims. It is with those about you that the ever-changing present will come. Therefore, my friends, let your souls be merry and

glad together, that in loving the one infinite Creator you may love each other with the gentleness and forbearance requisite for each unique being in your life.

We thank you for requesting our presence at this meeting, and at this time will take our leave through this instrument. We leave you riding upon the winds of the present moment. Lift your arms, my friends, and ride those winds with the grace with which you are capable, with the faith which is within you, with the love and the light which are yours as part of an infinite creation of love and light. In that unity, we leave you. We are known to you as Hatonn. Adonai, my friends. Adonai vasu borragus.

(Jim channeling)

I am Latwii, and I greet you, my friends, in love and light. We are most privileged once again to be able to blend our vibrations with yours. We are always honored to be asked to join your meditations and offer ourselves in the capacity of attempting to answer your queries if it be within our capabilities. May we then ask at this time if there is a question?

Carla: I have a question, but I'm not sure if it makes any sense or not. I was recently gone for two weeks, and my oldest cat was repeatedly reported to have suffered. Did Gandalf indeed suffer in some way that I could have helped, because of my two week's absence?

I am Latwii, and am aware of your query, my sister. We find that the entity known to you as Gandalf has a great deal of what your peoples describe as devotion for your presence and your care. You are not unfamiliar with this quality in this being, and should not be discouraged to discover that when you have removed yourself for a period of time from his presence that there is the feeling of loss within this entity. You yourself know that feeling in a recent manifestation of your own experience. We do not find a particular need for corrective action in this instance, for your presence is once again known to this entity.

May we answer you further, my sister?

Carla: Yes. What I was trying to ask was, is there any way that I could have explained to this second-density entity, who is so bright for being a cat, that I would be back at the end of the two weeks so that he didn't have to worry?

I am Latwii. My sister, we find that there is a limit, shall we say, to the conceptualizations possible for this particular entity, though it is indeed quite, as you would call it, intelligent. The nature of this entity is not a nature which includes the perceiving of time in the same manner in which your peoples describe it. So that, though there is benefit to the entity to have your vibrations assured of your return, it is not perfectly understandable to this entity that a certain period of what you call time must be experienced before the return occurs. Therefore, we feel that it has been well accomplished on your part to impart to this entity, as you did, that you would return.

May we answer you further, my sister?

Carla: No, thank you, Latwii.

I am Latwii. We are grateful to you, as well. May we attempt another query at this time?

(Pause)

I am Latwii. The sounds of your evening are a great source of peace to all present. We rejoice in sharing these vibrations with you. Before we leave, we shall ask for any queries which might be upon the mind, but which have not yet found their way to the tongue.

(Pause)

I am Latwii. My friends, it has been a great honor to join with you this evening, though it has been for but a brief moment, as you would call it. Be not discouraged in any way that any moment be too brief, for within the one creation that we share as one being, all moments are part of the great eternity which opens in every portion of what you call time. We thank you, my friends, for asking for our presence, and we assure each present that we shall be most honored to join you in your private meditations should you but request that we do so. We leave you now in the love and the light of the one infinite Creator, and we rejoice with you in the eternal present. We are known to you as Latwii. Adonai, my friends. Adonai vasu borragus. ☙

L/L RESEARCH

L/L Research is a subsidiary of
Rock Creek Research &
Development Laboratories, Inc.

P.O. Box 5195
Louisville, KY 40255-0195

www.llresearch.org

Rock Creek is a non-profit
corporation dedicated to
discovering and sharing
information which may aid in
the spiritual evolution of
humankind.

ABOUT THE CONTENTS OF THIS TRANSCRIPT: This telepathic channeling has been taken from transcriptions of the weekly study and meditation meetings of the Rock Creek Research & Development Laboratories and L/L Research. It is offered in the hope that it may be useful to you. As the Confederation entities always make a point of saying, please use your discrimination and judgment in assessing this material. If something rings true to you, fine. If something does not resonate, please leave it behind, for neither we nor those of the Confederation would wish to be a stumbling block for any.

CAVEAT: This transcript is being published by L/L Research in a not yet final form. It has, however, been edited and any obvious errors have been corrected. When it is in a final form, this caveat will be removed.

SUNDAY MEDITATION
AUGUST 15, 1982

(C channeling)

I am Hatonn, and I am now with this instrument. We greet you, as always, my friends, in the love and in the light of the one infinite Creator. The sounds we have heard tonight are indeed beautiful—your voices, the voices of the nature that surrounds you, the song of your planet, the harmony that exists. Though there be notes of discord, the theme is there, the parts are all being sung, each part gaining in strength, blending into a sound that fills many of your planet, touches many others, and is whispering to still more, if you will listen, if you take time, quiet time, if you would meditate, if you would be open, if you would but listen, experience. Your planet is growing as are you. You grow together, each drawing strength from the other. As more of your peoples become aware of the love and the light of the Creator, they grow. As the peoples grow, so does the planet, but like all people, it grows at its own rate. Though you are connected with it, it grows at its own rate. It has times when it surges ahead. It has times when it falls back. It has times to remain still.

Your peoples affect your planet's growth. It feels the energies of the lives upon it. It reacts to the energies. Its consciousness develops. With development and awareness, it changes. You are well aware that the time of transition, of harvest, is not that distant. At that time your planet will have changed. We of Hatonn wish to be of service to you. We remain open and willing to share, to aid as we may. My friends, as you meditate, you need but ask and we shall be with you. We listen. We ask that you allow us the time, and listen, feel, for more and more of your peoples have chosen, have started their journeys. We wish that more of your peoples would listen. Take some of your time to listen and feel, for you, your illusion, time, your concept of time, is so short and so limited. We would remind you that time is limited. There is more than enough, more than enough so that you can take that time. Allow yourself to listen. Be open to the light, the love.

We know that …

(C has been speaking with deep intensity of feeling.)

(Carla channeling)

… mentally requests our presence. We wish everyone may know this marvel, to be especially reassured as to it, and as this entity seems to depart to another geographical location, we wish to say there is one creation and one Creator, and we are available to each of you wherever you meet in this illusion which you share, agonizing and enjoying. We have spoken this evening of devout things, of the ability to listen, to feel and to be, and have spoken of allowing those things which are past to be released so that each may live in the present moment with all its infinity and wonder.

My friends, each of you has been given a physical vehicle. You are not disembodied experience. You are embodied, and in these bodies we learn. We stress tonight for each of you the value of acquiring that state of mind and heart wherein you are in the eternal present and your body for the moment makes no demands upon you. The great additions and multiplications and subtractions and divisions of life are gone. Those enemies which you may face are hence from you, and the joys which you contemplate are similarly lost from your world, and you dwell in endless bliss. This is what awaits the inner ear, and we ask you to be content with no less, to continue seeking, if it be until this incarnation's end, for those moments when you are in the present, when you have found eternity. For it is in those moments that you are adding to that eternal self which is you the kind of learning which you shall carry with you beyond this illusion.

And, my friends, after this moment is over and you are back in [the illusion] faced with the great arithmetic of living—its sorrows and its joys—we ask that you consider and constantly analyze why it is that you might be in this body and in this circumstance. Each body is imperfect, and yet are you not all perfect? And are not all circumstances full of the possibilities of perfection, of learning, of gaining knowledge, and of giving to those about you? How important it is, my friends, to be aware of both these things at once—that you are eternal and that your lessons are those of eternity, and that you are in manifestation at this time to learn and to teach. Stand in the present moment, my friends, as much of the time as you can. The public world about you in this illusion will seem to be somewhat negatively polarized. This is the nature of your illusion. This is the nature of your opportunity.

We wish you all of the awareness of love and light that is within you and the amount of that awareness of the original Thought is infinite. It is with infinity that you may meet the arithmetic, the terrible subtractions and additions and disengagements and confrontations of the solution. It is with the infinite Creator that you go forth. Could you in all eternity ask for a better opportunity?

We are your brothers and sisters. How much we have enjoyed sharing this meditation with you. We greet and love each, and so we leave you. We leave you through this instrument in the love and the light of the infinite Creator. Adonai, my friends, Adonai.

(Jim channeling)

I am Latwii, and greet you, my friends, in the love and the light of the one infinite Creator. It is once again our great honor and privilege to join your group in your meditation. As always, it is our honor to be asked the queries upon your mind, and we offer ourselves at this time in that capacity. Is there a question we may attempt to answer?

L: I'd like to ask a question, Latwii. In a recent discussion, a couple of us were in disagreement concerning information that we had received from the Confederation, specifically, should our race attempt a nuclear war that would hypothetically destroy all of our race or the planet itself, would this be allowed to occur?

I am Latwii, and am aware of your query, my brother. We of the Confederation of Planets in the Service of the Infinite Creator observe that Creator in all possible manifestations. And should your planet manifest that condition of the Creator wherein the so-called destructive elements of your nuclear bombs be released, we would with our full abilities attempt to maintain each entity as an entity, and this would be our service. We would allow the expression known to you as destruction by nuclear war, for this is a great lesson, one that teaches much. It has, as you are aware, been begun upon another entity, or as you call it, planetary sphere within your own solar system and seeks now its balance upon your own planet.

May we answer you further, my brother?

L: Yes. I've noticed that there is in our own communications industries a large amount of attention given to the subject of nuclear war. The orientation of this attention seems to have changed in the last few years away from a very non-participatory examination of potential effects to a very self-involved examination of the consequences, a great deal of attention to the likelihood that no one would be likely to survive unscathed. Are we receiving any particular attention or communication on a planetary basis to aid us in realizing more fully the effects of this kind of event?

I am Latwii, and am aware of your query, my brother. As we mentioned in our previous response, there is upon your planet the attempt by many entities to balance actions begun upon other spheres both within and without your own solar system. The third-density illusion which you inhabit offers the opportunity for the choice of any lesson which is found to hold a potential for increasing polarization. Upon your sphere at this time reside those entities who have experienced this devastation upon other spheres. Many now seek the balancing action; many seek to repeat the action. The lessons that have been chosen by each entity will be enacted within the bounds of your illusion with free will offering an infinite array of opportunities. There are many who are aware of the results of such an action. Therefore, these entities from the depths of their being seek another path.

May we answer you further, my brother?

L: No, thank you for your assistance.

I am Latwii. We are grateful to you. Is there another query at this time?

E: I have a query, Latwii, and that is that you said, you indicated that those of us on this planet desire that lesson of nuclear war, or there are many that do. And my question is, would a nuclear war be the war to end all wars? Would we learn to make war no more, that is, would we became polarized towards service to others through such an experience or would we tend to be polarized towards service to self by such an experience, or can you say?

I am Latwii, and am aware of your query, my brother. We see many possibilities for what you call your future. Indeed, the possibilities are infinite, though many have more potential for manifestation than do others. We cannot say what will occur, for free will assures a great variety of possibilities. Indeed, whatever the outcome of this particular path of action, there is always the possibility for the polarization in either direction, the positive or negative.

Indeed, upon your planet at this time, the circumstances of living are becoming altered to the extent where more of what you call the stressful factors are becoming apparent. As the conditions surrounding your survival become more perilous, there is the greater possibility that each entity upon your planet might find the desire to seek within and increase polarization, for as the environment surrounding an entity is less and less supportive, shall we say, the entity then of necessity must seek within the self for the meaning of that experience which it finds itself in. Such seeking offers the

greater possibility that polarization shall be increased.

Do not fear, my friends, that a birthing is not occurring. Though there be pains with the birth, yet the child emerges and shall breathe the air of life and love.

May we answer you further, my brother?

E: No, thank you, not on that. But I do have another question on something else. That is, my radio has been giving me a lot of trouble recently, and it seems as though there is a lot of interference which seems to be coming from the sun, and what I would like to know is, is there any connection between the turmoil that we're going through on this planet and the interference that I seem to be getting from the sun?

I am Latwii, and am aware of your query, my brother. We are aware that there are many factors which affect the peoples of your planet at this time, and though there is indeed an effect which is the result of activity upon the entity known to you as your Sun, we find that the great majority of causes for the actions of your of your peoples resides within the mass mind of your own planet and planetary consciousness, for as your peoples have inhabited this planet for the duration of this cycle in a manner which has been somewhat less than harmonious, these vibrations have became a part of the planet itself and the planetary consciousness, and then, as the transition into that density of love and understanding which approaches occurs, the blending of the vibrations of your planet and this density of love and understanding becomes less than easy. Your planet begins to give off the vibrations which it has been bathed in, shall we say, and finds that there is some difficulty in the releasing of these vibrations.

Therefore, the entities which walk its surface do respond to the accumulated experience of the planetary mind which itself has interacted with the experience of each entity throughout the ages of your planet's third-density experience. Therefore, though there are many effects which originate from without your planet, such as those which you have mentioned, they are quite small in comparison to the causes of the actions of your peoples which are a result of the free will having been exercised in a less than harmonious manner over the many thousands of years of your planet's third-density experience.

May we answer you further, my brother?

E: No, thank you.

We thank you, my brother, and may we say it is with joy that we greet you this evening, as it has been some measure of what you call time since we have had the honor of joining you in this group.

E: Thank you.

Is there another question at this time?

M1: I have something you may not be able to answer, but if you can, I would appreciate it. This whole evening a cold breeze has been on my feet and part way up my legs, and when I decided to ask you about it, it stopped. Is there some particular significance to it?

I am Latwii, and am aware of your query, my sister. Is it not always the case that the symptoms disappear when one approaches the doctor's waiting room? But to be more to the point, my sister, may we suggest that there is, as far as we can tell, no special significance to the various breezes and movements of air which inhabit this dwelling.

May we answer you further?

M1: No, thank you.

I am Latwii. We are grateful to you. Is there another question at this time?

L: Yes, I have one other question. The social memory complex Ra, in one of the books, made what seemed to be some rather ambiguous statements concerning those individuals currently being born into our density who simultaneously maintain a third and fourth density body or vehicle. The question I propose is this. In the transition from third to fourth density for these individuals, would they perceive the release of all third-density vehicles as a physical death?

I am Latwii, and am aware of your query, my brother. Yes, these entities shall experience the physical death as you know it.

May we answer you further?

L: Then, may I assume that all who would pass from third to fourth density in our planetary experience will experience that physical death?

I am Latwii, and am aware of your query, my brother. Again, this is correct. May we answer you further?

L: One final question on the same subject. The time period of approximately thirty years remaining before the transition occurs on our planet has been offered by members of the Confederation. It would then be correct to assume that all of those still possessing physical vehicles in this third density at that time will experience a physical death. Is this correct?

I am Latwii, and am aware of your query, my brother. This is, in general, correct, though one must not assume that the population at that time will include the great numbers that your current population would suggest, for the deaths that shall occur between the present moment and the final harvesting shall accrue, so that the population becomes more slowly reduced due to the harvesting in the various manners.

May we answer you further, my brother?

L: No. I just had same confusion as to what was actually likely to occur. I appreciate your clearing it up for me. Thank you.

I am Latwii. We thank you, my brother. Is there another question at this time?

M2: Yes, along that same line, to make sure I understood it, if someone is born into this world with fourth-density activated physical vehicle, will they make the transition without physical death?

I am Latwii, and am aware of your query, my brother. These entities of the dually activated bodies shall experience the physical death in the same manner as any other third-density entity, yet their transition shall be of a somewhat different nature, for they shall already have been harvested from other planetary spheres, and shall not need to repeat the harvesting procedure, but may then immediately inhabit the fourth-density sphere which your planet is rapidly growing to become.

May we answer you further, my brother?

M2: No, thank you.

I am Latwii. We are thankful to you. Is there another question at this time?

S: Yes, Latwii. This has probably been answered before, but when an entity reaches fourth density, is the veil of forgetting lifted?

I am Latwii, and am aware of your query, my sister. This is correct, although the veil is not such a simple device that one might assume its removal would be as simply accomplished as the pulling of a curtain. Various portions of the mind/body/spirit complex of each entity upon your planet have been veiled, shall we say, so that the knowledge, experience and expression of the self as the Creator is hidden from the entity. There are various portions that shall be revealed in their due course. When the entity has fully passed into that density of love and understanding, known as the fourth density, then shall all veils be removed so that the entity is more fully aware of its beingness as the one infinite Creator.

May we answer you further, my sister?

S: No, thank you …

(Side one of tape ends.)

(A question was asked by M1 prior to the tape recorder being turned back on.)

(Jim channeling)

I am Latwii. We are once again with this instrument. We are aware of your query, my sister, and may respond by suggesting that certain entities are more able to express the nature of the physical body's polarity, for there are various portions of your physical vehicle which are positively and negatively charged, this in the electrical sense. Therefore, the emanations which proceed from the right hand are of a positive nature, and may affect certain devices within your illusion such as the television mechanism. The right hand emitting these positive vibrations of electrical nature, therefore, might in some cases enhance the colored nature of your television in its projecting of the image. The left hand, then, might, through its receptive abilities remove these same particles, thereby causing the appearance of the lack of color. Many upon your planet might experience this phenomenon if the proper experiment was attempted.

May we answer you further, my sister?

M1: No, thank you, I think you've answered me very well.

I am Latwii. We thank you, my sister. Is there another question at this time?

Questioner: I have a question. Is there a Confederation brother or sister by the name of,

something like Ritonn, I don't think that's right, but it sounds something like that? Or Rittye?

I am Latwii, and am aware of your query, my sister. We cannot be one hundred per cent accurate in the reproduction of sound vibration complexes of Confederation members, for various members choose various sound vibration complexes for the transmission of thoughts to various groups, as various groups are more receptive to certain of the names, as you call them. The naming procedure is not always chosen by Confederation members. Indeed, most exist without that which you call the name or sound vibration complex, the name being chosen primarily for use in the communication with entities upon your sphere or similar spheres of the third density. Therefore, we cannot be accurate by suggesting that such a entity does or does not exist as a Confederation member.

May we answer you further, my sister?

Questioner: No, thank you.

I am Latwii. We thank you. Is there another question at this time?

M1: Yes, I've been visiting in a nursing home, and the nurse has given me a patient who does not even know her last name, and she asks the same question over again and again, for instance, she asks me where I live several times while I'm with her. And just generally, what can be the value of a visit with someone who—I guess senile is the word, I suppose—who is as senile as this?

I am Latwii, and am aware of your query, my sister. The value of such offering of love cannot often be seen in such a situation, but do not doubt that the love which you offer such an entity is felt. Many times those entities which inhabit the homes for the aged within the state of mind known to your peoples as senility are attempting to make an orientation upon another plane while remaining within the physical vehicle. Therefore, their awareness has been withdrawn to the outer eye and dwells in other realms, so that the entity might become familiar with certain lessons and recapitulations of lessons of the life which is drawing to a close.

Therefore, when one such as yourself visits and shares love with an entity who is not apparently aware of a large variety of beingness, there is, nevertheless, an absorption and appreciation of that love, for though the awareness of the entity is not fully with the physical vehicle, yet it is nourished by the love given to that vehicle.

May we answer you further, my sister?

M1: Well, then, does the visit make her transition easier, or does it help her in her transition to another, well, in preparation for death?

I am Latwii. My sister, love is always a great enabler and enobler of all beings at all times. May we answer you further?

M1: No, that answers it. It seems so useless, but I can see your point of view. I can understand. Thank you.

I am Latwii. We thank you. Is there another question at this time?

M1: I have a question. If people die singly, or in the millions, many millions at one time, does it affect their advancement in any way?

I am Latwii. May we ask that the query be restated. We have some difficulty in penetrating the heart of your query.

M1: I want to know if large numbers of people, millions of people die at once, or if a person dies in the normal course of their life, one person at a time, does it affect their advancement? Can millions of people be advanced at the same time, or is it better if they go one at a time?

I am Latwii, and am aware of your query, my sister. We are not aware of any effect of the number of people dying which would be a factor in the advancement or the progress upon the evolutionary path, for upon your planet each day, thousands of your entities pass. When looked at as a whole, your planet passes many entities each day, though each entity might make the transition as an individual.

May we answer you further, my sister?

M1: No, thank you.

I am Latwii. We thank you. Is there another query at this time?

Carla: I have a question concerning questions. Don Elkins has suggested to me that we make a change in the questioning and limit the questions only to philosophical questions in order that we might further improve the contact and the quality of the material that you are able to convey to us. Could

you comment on the suggestion, especially concerning its merit?

I am Latwii, and am aware of your query, my sister. The factor which affects the type of information which we may share with groups such as this group is the tuning of the group as a whole, which is in turn affected by the tuning of each individual with the group. By tuning, my friends, we mean that each entity focuses the attention of the mind upon a certain point or array of points. When the group is summed or looked at as a whole, the focus of each entity is seen to lend itself in the formation of the focus of the group. When you join in love and light and sing or chant or pray, you continue a tuning that has begun in each entity's personal life. When each entity, then, refines that tuning through whatever means of a personal nature have meaning, the tuning thus is further enhanced.

The tuning may further be affected by the types of queries which are offered, for we may give only that information which is a response to the interests of the group, and which does not infringe upon the free will of any within the group. Therefore, the suggestion that questions of a philosophical nature only be offered is a suggestion which would enhance the type of information which we of the Confederation might then offer. This is assuming, of course, that by enhancement one would agree that the evolution of mind, body and spirit is the primary purpose for which each entity has incarnated. But we cannot suggest to this group that this be done or that any other particular path be chosen, for it is the free will of this group that is paramount as we transmit our thoughts to you through instruments such as are gathered here this evening.

May we answer you further, my sister?

Carla: No, thank you, Latwii. I think we'll probably have to talk about it as a group.

I am Latwii. We thank you. Is there another question at this time?

(Pause)

I am Latwii. My friends, it has been a very great honor to be asked to join your group this evening. As always, it is our privilege to do so. We remind you once again that a simple request for our presence in your meditations is all that is necessary for us to join you there. We leave this group at this time in the love and in the light of the one infinite Creator.

Be merry, my friends. Rejoice in your beingness. The opportunities for your growth are ever more abundant. We are known to you as Latwii. Adonai vasu borragus. ♣

L/L Research is a subsidiary of
Rock Creek Research &
Development Laboratories, Inc.

P.O. Box 5195
Louisville, KY 40255-0195

L/L RESEARCH

www.llresearch.org

Rock Creek is a non-profit
corporation dedicated to
discovering and sharing
information which may aid in
the spiritual evolution of
humankind.

© 2009 L/L RESEARCH

THE LAW OF ONE, BOOK IV, SESSION 93
AUGUST 18, 1982

Ra: I am Ra. I greet you in the love and in the light of the one infinite Creator. We communicate now.

Questioner: Could you first please give me the condition of the instrument?

Ra: I am Ra. The physical complex distortions of this instrument far more closely approach what you might call the zero mark; that is, the instrument, while having no native physical energy, is not nearly so far in physical energy deficit distortions. The vital energy distortions are somewhat strengthened since the last asking.

Questioner: What is the position and condition of our fifth-density, negatively oriented visitor?

Ra: I am Ra. This entity is with this group but in a quiescent state due to some bafflement as to the appropriate method for enlarging upon its chosen task.

QUESTIONER Thank you. You have stated previously that the foundation of our present illusion is the concept of polarity. I would like to ask, since we have defined the two polarities as service-to-others and service-to-self, is there a more complete or eloquent or enlightening definition of these polarities or any more information that we don't have at this time that you could give on the two ends of the poles that would give us a better insight into the nature of polarity itself?

Ra: I am Ra. It is unlikely that there is a more pithy or eloquent description of the polarities of third

density than service-to-others and service-to-self due to the nature of the mind/body/spirit complexes' distortions towards perceiving concepts relating to philosophy in terms of ethics or activity. However, we might consider the polarities using slightly variant terms. In this way a possible enrichment of insight might be achieved for some.

One might consider the polarities with the literal nature enjoyed by the physical polarity of the magnet. The negative and positive, with electrical characteristics, may be seen to be just as in the physical sense. It is to be noted in this context that it is quite impossible to judge the polarity of an act or an entity, just as it is impossible to judge the relative goodness of the negative and positive poles of the magnet.

Another method of viewing polarities might involve the concept of radiation/absorption. That which is positive is radiant; that which is negative is absorbent.

Questioner: Now, if I understand correctly, prior to the veiling process the electrical polarities, the polarities of radiation and absorption, all existed in some part of the creation, but the service-to-others/service-to-self polarity with which we are familiar had not evolved and only showed up after the veiling process as an addition to the list of possible polarities in the creation. Is this correct?

Ra: I am Ra. No.

Questioner: Would you correct me on that?

Ra: I am Ra. The description of polarity as service-to-self and service-to-others, from the beginning of our creation, dwelt within the architecture of the primal Logos. Before the veiling process the impact of actions taken by mind/body/spirits upon their consciousness was not palpable to a significant enough degree to allow the expression of this polarity to be significantly useful. Over the period of what you would call time this expression of polarity did indeed work to alter the biases of mind/body/spirits so that they might eventually be harvested. The veiling process made the polarity far more effective.

Questioner: I might make the analogy, then, in that when a polarization in the atmosphere occurs to create thunderstorms, lightening, and much activity, this more vivid experience could be likened to the polarization in consciousness which creates the more vivid experience. Would this be appropriate as an analogy?

Ra: I am Ra. There is a shallowness to this analogy in that one entity's attention might be focused upon a storm for the duration of the storm. However, the storm producing conditions are not constant whereas the polarizing conditions are constant. Given this disclaimer, we may agree with your analogy.

Questioner: With the third tarot card we come to the first addition of archetypes after the veiling process, as I understand it. I am assuming that this third archetype is, shall I say, loaded in a way so as to create the possible polarization since that seems to be one of the primary objectives of this particular Logos in the evolutionary process. Am I in any way correct on that?

Ra: I am Ra. Before we reply to your query we ask your patience as we must needs examine the mind complex of this instrument in order that we might attempt to move the left manual appendage of the instrument. If we are not able to affect some relief from pain we shall take our leave. Please have patience while we do that which is appropriate.

(Thirty second pause.)

I am Ra. There will continue to be pain flares. However, the critical portion of the intense pain has been alleviated by repositioning.

Your supposition is correct.

Questioner: There seems to be no large hint of polarity in this drawing except for the possible coloration of the many cups in the wheel. Part of them are colored black and part are colored white. Would this indicate that each experience has within it the possible negative or positive use of that experience that is randomly generated by this seeming wheel of fortune?

Ra: I am Ra. Your supposition is thoughtful. However, it is based upon an addition to the concept complex which is astrological in origin. Therefore, we request that you retain the concept of polarity but release the cups from their strictured form. The element you deal with is not in motion in its original form but is indeed the abiding sun which, from the spirit, shines in protection over all catalyst available from the beginning of complexity to the discerning mind/body/spirit complex.

Indeed you may, rather, find polarity expressed, firstly, by the many opportunities offered in the material illusion which is imaged by the not-white and not-dark square upon which the entity of the image is seated, secondly, upon the position of that seated entity. It does not meet opportunity straight on but glances off to one side or another. In the image you will note a suggestion that the offering of the illusion will often seem to suggest the opportunities lying upon the left-hand path or, as you might refer to it more simply, the service-to-self path. This is a portion of the nature of the Catalyst of the Mind.

Questioner: The feet of the entity seem to be on an unstable platform that is dark to the rear and light to the front. I am guessing that possibly this indicates that the entity standing on this could sway in either direction, to the left or to the right-hand path. Is this correct?

Ra: I am Ra. This is most perceptive.

Questioner: The bird, I am guessing, might be a messenger of the two paths depicted by the position of the wings bringing catalyst which could be used to polarize on either path. Is this in any way correct?

Ra: I am Ra. It is a correct perception that the position of the winged creature is significant. The more correct perception of this entity and its significance is the realization that the mind/body/spirit complex is, having made contact with its potentiated self, now beginning its flight towards that great Logos which is that which is sought by the adept.

Further, the nature of the winged creature is echoed both by the female holding it and the symbol of the female upon which the figure's feet rest; that is, the nature of catalyst is overwhelmingly of an unconsciousness, coming from that which is not of the mind and which has no connection with the intellect, as you call it, which precedes or is concomitant with catalytic action. All uses of catalyst by the mind are those consciously applied to catalyst. Without conscious intent the use of catalyst is never processed through mediation, ideation, and imagination.

Questioner: I would like, if possible, an example of the activity we call Catalyst of the Mind in a particular individual undergoing this process. Could Ra give an example of that?

Ra: I am Ra. All that assaults your senses is catalyst. We, in speaking to this support group through this instrument, offer catalyst. The configurations of each in the group of body offer catalyst through comfort/discomfort. In fact all that is unprocessed that has come before the notice of a mind/body/spirit complex is catalyst.

Questioner: Then presently we receive catalyst of the mind as we are aware of Ra's communication and we receive catalyst of the body as our bodies sense all of the inputs to them, but could Ra then describe catalyst of the spirit, and are we at this time receiving that catalyst and if not, could Ra give an example of that?

Ra: I am Ra. Catalyst being processed by the body is catalyst for the body. Catalyst being processed by the mind is catalyst for the mind. Catalyst being processed by the spirit is catalyst for the spirit. An individual mind/body/spirit complex may use any catalyst which comes before its notice, be it through the body and its senses or through mediation or through any other more highly developed source, in its unique way to form an experience unique to it, with its biases.

Questioner: Would I be correct in saying that the archetype for the Catalyst of the Mind is the Logos's model for its most efficient plan for the activity or use of the catalyst of the mind?

Ra: I am Ra. Yes.

Questioner: Then the adept, in becoming familiar with the Logos's archetype in each case, would be able to most efficiently use the Logos's plan for evolution. Is this correct?

Ra: I am Ra. In the archetypical mind one has the resource of not specifically a plan for evolution but rather a blueprint or architecture of the nature of evolution. This may seem to be a small distinction, but it has significance in perceiving more clearly the use of this resource of the deep mind.

Questioner: Then Ra presented the images which we know now as the tarot so that the Egyptian adepts of the time could accelerate their personal evolution. Is this correct, and was there any other reason for the presentation of these images by Ra?

Ra: I am Ra. You are correct.

Questioner: Are there any other uses at all of tarot cards other than the one I just named?

Ra: I am Ra. To the student the tarot images offer a resource for learn/teaching the processes of evolution. To any other entity these images are pictures and no more.

Questioner: I was specifically thinking of the fact that Ra, in an earlier session, spoke of the tarot as a system of divination. Would you tell me what you meant by that?

Ra: I am Ra. Due to the influence of the Chaldees, the system of archetypical images was incorporated by the priests of that period into a system of astrologically based study, learning, and divination. This was not a purpose for which Ra developed the tarot.

Questioner: The third card also shows the wand, I am assuming it is, in the right hand. The ball atop the wand is the round magical shape. Am I in any way correct in guessing that the Catalyst of the Mind suggests the possible eventual use of the magic depicted by this wand?

Ra: I am Ra. The wand is astrological in its origin and as an image may be released from its stricture. The sphere of spiritual power is an indication indeed that each opportunity is pregnant with the most extravagant magical possibilities for the far-seeing adept.

Questioner: The fact that the clothing of the entity is transparent indicates the semi-permeability of the veil for the catalytic process. Is this correct?

Ra: I am Ra. We again must pause.

(Fifteen second pause.)

I am Ra. We continue under somewhat less than optimal conditions. However, due to the nature of this instrument's opening to us our pathway is quite clear and we shall continue. Because of pain flares we must ask you to repeat your last query.

Questioner: I was just wondering if the transparency of the garments on the third card indicates the semi-permeable nature of the veil between the conscious and unconscious mind?

Ra: I am Ra. This is a thoughtful perception and cannot be said to be incorrect. However, the intended suggestion, in general, is an echo of our earlier suggestion that the nature of catalyst is that of the unconscious; that is, outward catalyst comes through the veil.

All that you perceive seems to be consciously perceived. This is not the correct supposition. All that you perceive is perceived as catalyst unconsciously. By the, shall we say, time that the mind begins its appreciation of catalyst, that catalyst has been filtered through the veil and in some cases much is veiled in the most apparently clear perception.

Questioner: I'm at a loss to know the significance of the serpents that adorn the head of the entity on this drawing. Are they of Ra and, if so, what do they stand for?

Ra: I am Ra. They are cultural in nature. In the culture to which these images were given the serpent was the symbol of wisdom. Indeed, to the general user of these images perhaps the most accurate connotation of this portion of the concept complexes might be the realization that the serpent is that which is powerful magically. In the positive sense this means that the serpent will appear at the indigo-ray site upon the body of the image figures. When a negative connotation is intended one may find the serpent at the solar plexus center.

Questioner: Is there any significance to the serpent? Is there any polarity to the serpent as we experience it in this illusion?

Ra: I am Ra. We assume that you question the serpent as used in these images rather than the second-density life form which is a portion of your experience. There is a significance to the serpent form in a culture which coexists with your own but which is not your own; that is, the serpent is symbol of that which some call the kundalini and which we have discussed in previous material.

Questioner: Is there any other aspect of this third card that Ra could comment on at this time?

Ra: I am Ra. There may be said to be many aspects which another student might note and ponder in this image. However, it is the nature of teach/learning to avoid trespass into the realms of learn/teaching for the student. We are quite agreed to comment upon all observations that the student may make. We cannot speak further than this for any student.

We would add that it is expected that each student shall naturally have an unique experience of perception dealing with each image. Therefore, it is not expected that the questioner ask comprehensively for all students. It is, rather, expected and accepted that the questioner will ask a moiety of questions which build up a series of concepts concerning each archetype which then offer to each succeeding student the opportunity for more informed study of the archetypical mind.

May we ask for one more query at this time. We are pleased to report that this instrument has remembered to request the reserving of some transferred energy to make more comfortable the transition back to the waking state. Therefore, we find that there is sufficient energy for one more query.

Questioner: I am assuming that you mean one full question. I'll make that question in this form. I'd like to know the significance of the shape of the crux ansata, and if that's too much of an answer I'll just ask if there is anything that we can do to make the instrument more comfortable or to improve the contact?

Ra: I am Ra. There are mathematical ratios within this image which may yield informative insights to one fond of riddles. We shall not untangle the riddle. We may indicate that the crux ansata is a part of the concept complexes of the archetypical mind, the circle indicating the magic of the spirit, the cross indicating that nature of manifestation which may only be valued by the losing. Thus the crux ansata is intended to be seen as an image of the eternal in and through manifestation and beyond manifestation through the sacrifice and the transformation of that which is manifest.

The support group functions well. The swirling waters experienced by the instrument since our previous working have substantially aided the instrument in its lessening of the distortion of pain.

All is well. The alignments are well guarded.

We leave you, my friends, in the love and the light of the infinite One. Go forth, therefore, rejoicing in the power and in the peace of the one infinite and glorious Creator. Adonai. ☥

L/L Research is a subsidiary of
Rock Creek Research &
Development Laboratories, Inc.

P.O. Box 5195
Louisville, KY 40255-0195

L/L RESEARCH

www.llresearch.org

Rock Creek is a non-profit
corporation dedicated to
discovering and sharing
information which may aid in
the spiritual evolution of
humankind.

SUNDAY MEDITATION
AUGUST 22, 1982

(Unknown channeling)

(Inaudible). I greet you, my friends, in the love and the light of the infinite Creator. It has been a joy to observe the bounties of the new life that has come into your midst. Your love and your light will be very helpful to this young life, and you will be rewarded by watching him grow in the love and light of the infinite Creator. Your love and your light can also be a great help to C and D. We appreciate the opportunity of exercising this instrument and we will now leave this instrument for another contact.

(Unknown channeling)

I am Hatonn, and I greet you through this instrument also in the love and the light of our infinite Creator. It is indeed a benediction and a blessing for our vibrations to blend with yours as you attempt with your whole hearts the beginning of a spiritual experience that will last a lifetime for the little being known as B. Because this has been attempted this evening, my friends, with such love and such sincerity we would ask that you consider some aspect of living a life in which your spirit is continuously conscious. My friends, your entire people and their culture have a marked tendency towards the appreciation of convenience and quickness in all things. And this tendency to expect and look for *(inaudible)* to bear no searching *(inaudible)*. In each case we are aware that these gaps

are many and that the reasons for them are overwhelming, for your illusion is indeed a difficult one. But each place where the spirit is not is a missed opportunity for learning, for radiating the love and the light of the one Creator and for appreciating the thoroughness and the unity of that one great original Thought of love. My friends, it is the nature of your physical manifestation that you shall seek comfort and for us to ask you to actively seek discomfort could scarcely be called a bid for popularity nor do we suggest that a life lived in constant consciousness of the Creator is not joyful. We suggest only that in order to grow in that life, as you wish to do, to learn those things which you have come into this sphere to learn it is necessary to cultivate that divine discomfort which is called inward seeking.

This eve you have promised to aid another being in his life of seeking. Perhaps the greatest aid that you can be to this small entity is to continue in all ways to seek, at whatever cost, the path of love and service to others. Your mistakes will be myriad, for the illusion guarantees misunderstanding. The moments in which you lack confidence will be many, for no entity can hope to see through your illusion more than imperfectly. And yet if you are willing to take upon yourself what seems to be the greatest burden that we could describe to you, the burden of yourself, if you take it well—thoroughly and truly—

you shall find an ever expanding experience and ever further reaching journey of seeking.

It is not within our grasp to express to you the joy, the fruit, the bliss and the peace of total commitment to seeking, and to ask that is to ask far more than any may accomplish in one incarnation, but we recommend the attempt, my friends, for the merest shadow of such an attempt has a stature that is great among your peoples.

In your meditations, if you wish, we shall be with you, as always, but know also that there is another great being with you. There is a portion of the Creator with you which has been perfect and whole and wise since the beginning of creation. That being, my friends, is you, for each of you is part of one infinite and perfect Creator. Seek that aid and then as you come out of meditation, as you live your life, call from that meditation not merely comfort, but strength—strength to delight and to be overjoyed and to bless all those about you, all that you see and all that is you.

My friends, in your holy works it is written that when the one known as Jesus told his disciples what was expected of them, many, being unequal to such a great charge, left this teacher, never to return. It is written that the one known as Jesus then asked the one known as Peter, "And will you also leave me?" And the one known as Peter replied, "I have no choice. Yours is the only voice that speaks of the spirit and of life."

My friends, we cannot urge upon you any effort, any conditions or any thoughts that are not yours, born within you and truly thought by you, but we do wish to inspire not only the realization of the enormous comfort and healing and protection of the Creator, but the stringent challenge that a life as a disciple of the truth shall offer you. Take you this challenge then, my friends? We can but hope that you will give our humble words some consideration. We will wish to close through the one known as M. We shall transfer at this time. I am Hatonn.

(M channeling)

I am Hatonn, and am with this instrument. My brothers and sisters, it is such great pleasure for us to share this event with you this evening, to be among you as each of you share your blessings with another coming into this world. We are with you each as you participated in this sacred loving blessing as we will

be with each of you tomorrow and the next day and the day after. And we will be with B tomorrow and the day after as long as he wishes our presence, our support, and our love. We can scarcely express the joy we feel in sharing these beautiful moments with you. This group *(inaudible)* indeed fortunate that each of you have come to know enough about yourselves, about the Creator, about the truth to share love in this manner. If only the rest of the peoples of your world could share in such an experience *(inaudible)*. Our blessings are with each of you tonight and our blessings are especially with the one known as B—a new life, a brilliant new life, experiencing a sunrise upon this precious planet. We leave you, my friends, in the love and the light of the one infinite Creator. *(Inaudible)*.

(Unknown channeling)

I am Hatonn. I am now with this instrument. I greet you in the love and the light of the infinite Creator. The beginning of life and the ending of life is a time of great rejoicing and a little fear. A new adventure is starting. White is the slate which has not been used. Only he can write on it. During his lifetime many people will try to pick up his chalk and write. You can influence him, but you cannot write on his slate. Many times his friends and family will try to erase what he's written, but only B can erase it. It's B's story and B's song. It's an exciting time and a fearful time. His whole lifetime will be an original creation. Many times you will not understand what he has written. Many times you will not agree with him. But when his life is ended it will be an original manuscript. It will be B's song. It will be his story. At this time I will leave this instrument.

(Jim channeling)

I am Latwii, and greet you in the love and the light of the one infinite Creator, for we are again most honored to be asked to join your group this evening and we offer ourselves, as always, in the capacity of attempting to answer your queries. We see that there are many who have joined this evening bringing the queries upon the minds. We would then ask if there would be a question at this time?

Questioner: Yes, I have a question about the evolution of consciousness. I was at the horse show last night and I was amazed at how the rider and the horse were able to communicate and the thought came to me as I watched this process, is it possible that these horses that receive so much care and so much love, is it possible that they can … after they die that they can be human even as we are, and take on … or could they be reincarnated again as a human being rather than a horse because of the care and the love that's been given to them?

I am Latwii, and am aware of your query, my sister. Indeed, this means of the investing of the second-density creature with the vibrations of love from a third-density entity is one of the principle means for the evolution of the second-density entities. The great spiral of light that travels the journey throughout all of creation seeking the One begins in the great unformed chaos that precedes the solidification and orbiting of your spheres known as planets and then throughout the great reaches of time as you know it, life seeds itself within the red-ray density which is the foundation for all which is to come. The simple awareness is refined within the second density known to your peoples as the forms of life that are plants and animals. This great spiral of light continues the path of seeking the One and is aided in many cases when the second-density creatures share in habitation of a sphere with the third-density entities such as yourselves. When the third-density entities then begin a specific relationship with that creature of second density and invests that creature with love so that the creature become inspirited, shall we say, and its pace of evolution quickened, there are those entities presently upon your planet at this time who have evolved from the second density of this planet. At this time, as your cycle draws to an end, there are many creatures of the second density which have indeed become invested to a sufficient degree with the vibrations of love that their individualization will now allow expression within a third-density illusion. But at this time upon your planet, the third density's remaining period is so short that such second-density entities shall be forced to find a third-density planet beginning its cycle of third density on which to incarnate for upon your planet at this time are placed those entities who have the greatest opportunity of making the harvest, shall we say, into the fourth-density vibrations which rapidly surround your sphere, and a second-density creature just beginning this cycle of evolution would not be, shall we say, in line for an incarnation upon this planet at this time, as you call it.

May we answer you further, my sister?

Questioner: No, I believe not right now.

I am Latwii. We thank you for your concern and your query. Is there another question at this time?

Questioner: I have a question, Latwii. And that is, I'm wondering, if one's meditation can be aided by a form … by sitting in a form like a band-shell.

I am Latwii, and am aware of your query, my brother. Throughout the ages of your planet's evolution, the mystics, as you call them, and seekers of truth, have sought the rounded shape such as the cave, the dome, the arch, and the pyramid, for such entities have, through long seeking, become aware that the love/light that is the one Creator that is omnipresent within your illusion is focused by the rounded arched shape. The focus of this which others of your cultures have called prana is that effect which intensifies the seeking of the entity experiencing it. Therefore, for the greatest effect, the shell of which you speak would need to be made whole—that is, completed in a dome-like manner. There would be, however, some small resonance precipitated by the shape which you have spoken of which would be of aid in reducing the, as you may call it, the static from your meditative state.

May we answer you further, my brother?

Questioner: Yes, just one more question on that and that is how would one determine the best place to be within the space for meditating?

I am Latwii, and before answering your query [we] must determine if we speak of the band-shell or of the completed dome.

Questioner: Band-shell.

I am Latwii, and am now aware of your query, my brother. The most efficient means [of] determining this position would be a series of experiments so that in your own meditations you might notice the effect of one position in relation to another position upon your meditation. There may be a position which is most efficient for general use and there may be a position which is most useful for your own use, therefore it is necessary that you make the experiments and then the choice yourself.

May we answer you further, my brother?

Questioner: Just one more. I've noted that sound was most intense at one particular point and wonder whether or not that point wouldn't be something of a focal point in the space and if so whether that might not be the best place to be while meditating?

I am Latwii, and am aware of your query, my brother. The vibrations of sound which you have noticed to be focused in a certain position impinge upon the sphere from a definite direction. The energy with which you deal in meditation, that energy of the prana, as we have spoken, is an energy which emanates from each point in a 360 degree solid angle, therefore it impinges from all directions simultaneously and your experimentation with meditation in various positions may yield a somewhat variant position.

May we answer you further, my brother?

Questioner: No, you've been very helpful. Thank you very much.

I am Latwii. We are most grateful to you, my brother. Is there another query at this time?

Questioner: Yes. On a couple of nights this week I was out under a lot of trees just as the sun … well, the sun had just gone down and I didn't know whether I was delusional or what happened, but it seemed like I felt something like energy rising from the ground through my body. I've never experienced anything like that before and I began to think, "Is the ground conscious of my being here? Are the trees conscious of my being here?" Because I know always one … but anyway that was a new experience. Have you got any comment about that?

I am Latwii, and am aware of your query, my sister. Indeed, my sister, as you are aware, the entire creation is alive and as you move within this creation you interact with it on levels which are only dimly perceptible to your five senses. As you move throughout your life within this illusion, the web of energy which is the essence of your being and which is fed by the configuration of your mind, as you think and as you be, is that interaction which is noticed and responded to by each portion of the creation through which you move. There are times when an entity such as yourself may for a moment remove unconsciously all blockages from the energy centers or plexi and allow an interaction with the creation which is quite ecstatic in that the very power of being is for that moment experienced. Indeed, my sister, the entire creation nourishes you and feeds you with the love and light of the one Creator at all times when a certain stimulus such as the beauty of the setting sun or the grandeur …

(Side one of tape ends.)

(Jim channeling)

I am Latwii, and am again with this instrument. And opens your centers of energy for that moment you experience a truer picture of the nature of your illusion and the interaction of its portions.

May we answer you further, my sister?

Questioner: Yes, just one further. The thought came to me … well, this energy that I'm feeling is healing energy … not only physically but emotionally and in every respect. This must be healing energy. Is that true?

I am Latwii, and am aware of your query, my sister. Indeed, the love and light of the one Creator which is ever present and available to each entity is a healing energy, for to become aware, in even a distorted degree, of the nature of this love and light is to experience the wholeness and the healingness of the one Creator.

May we answer you further, my sister?

Questioner: No, no that's fine. Thank you.

I am Latwii. We thank you. Is there another query at this time?

Questioner: I have another question. I know of a person who has multiple personalities. I've spoken to you of this before but I'd like to speak again of it. My question is … well, let me explain. This individual has several adult personalities and many children personalities, all of which have different talents and skills and experiences: four languages, two are painters, and there are many children and they're all housed in one body but the body doesn't have any control over which personality it is at any moment and so is undergoing therapy in which they're trying to eliminate the personalities by fusing them together and hopefully will end up with one personality, but the problem is that the one personality will have lost all the experiences and skills and talents of the many individuals that seem to inhabit this body now. And my question is, is there not … is there no way for this entity to become integrated without losing all this … all that she now has, or is there some way in which she might be able to control the many entities that live in her and keep the skills and the experience and the talents?

I am Latwii, and am aware of your query, my brother. Such an entity is quite, quite unique among your peoples and the experience of the third-density illusion for such an entity has called upon the deeper portions of the mind which are usually veiled from entities within your illusion. The calling when the results [are] what appear to be a randomized traumatic event is a calling which does not carry the skills of the adept, shall we say, and therefore the partial removing of that veil between the conscious and unconscious minds happens in a pattern which seems to be random and which is most usually beyond the effecting or control of the conscious entity experiencing the joining of its consciousness with the, as you have called them, personalities which dwell deep within its own subconscious mind. Therefore, when the attempt is made to, as you have called it, fuse the various uncontrollable personalities with the original conscious personality, what is occurring is not, in truth, a fusion, but is more correctly a replacing of the veil, piece by piece, so that the entity more closely approaches the normal experience within your third-density illusion. That is, the experience of one overriding personality which itself has various portions that have attained greater or lesser degrees of what your peoples call maturity. When an entity such as the one which you have spoken of experiences the variety of personalities which have penetrated this veil there is the uncontrollable nature which is most likely to remain uncontrollable for the entity has not engaged itself in a conscious program of self-exploration and has not developed consciously the means of contacting deeper portions of its own mind and previous experiences. Therefore, the normal, if we can use that term in this situation, procedure is for a replacing of the veil instead of the continuing conscious use of the skills of the various personalities.

May we answer you further, my brother?

Questioner: Yes. You're saying that it is best that she lose these personalities because she would not be able to control them?

I am Latwii, and am aware of your query, my brother. We refrain from using—we correct this instrument—from utilizing any terms of judgment such as best or better, but suggest only that it is more nearly inevitable that either the entity shall have the variety of personalities and their correspondent skills or shall have its veil repaired and replaced and lose, shall we say, the access to these personalities and skills, for the entity has not called

upon this portion of the deep mind in a conscious fashion but has, through a traumatic experience, found that there are certain holes, shall we say, within the veil which separates its conscious and unconscious minds.

May we answer you further, my brother?

Questioner: I'm still not clear on whether or not she can go on being as she is and gain control over her resources, or whether she has to lose them?

I am Latwii, and am aware of your query, my brother. It is possible for such an entity, through long practice of the disciplining of the personality, to gain what you call the control over these aspects of its deeper mind. This type of study is usually reserved to those who seek quite intensively upon the path of the evolution of mind, body and spirit. Entities with such a determination and strength of will can indeed [find] such as would be required for this entity to obtain the control of its many randomly generated personalities.

May we answer you further, my brother?

Questioner: I don't believe that she's ever been exposed to any higher consciousness material. What I'm trying to say, I think, is I'm wondering if she shouldn't at least be given the option of taking the path of discipline and of the personality rather than losing her abilities. My question is what … what form of discipline would she need to perform?

I am Latwii. May we suggest the resolving of this second-density conflict?

(At least one cat was hissing during the last question and this answer. Sounds of shuffling, laughter and then the following exchange.)

Questioner: Pause the tape recorder (laughter) …

(Pause)

Questioner: I thought it was my question.

Questioner: (Inaudible) developing another personality.

(Jim channeling)

I am Latwii, and we greet you once again, my friends, in love and light. We are appreciative of the efforts at the achieving of a more harmonious condition. We thank each for your great good humor and we shall proceed, if it is agreeable to the feline counterparts.

Questioner: I don't think they're here anymore.

The entity of which you speak has many options, as you may call them. It is not possible, nor appropriate, to describe a certain course of study for such an entity, for to carry weight the course of study would need to come from that entity's own choosing. It is quite possible for any to present this entity with materials which are felt to be of potential use. Many are the choices available to such an entity wishing to be of this service. We cannot suggest for any the path which is most appropriate for the seeking.

May we answer you further, my brother?

Questioner: I have one more question and I apologize for taking up so much time. The question is: is there any danger involved in encouraging her in any way to seek some other solution rather than con … repairing the holes in her unconscious that are allowing this to happen? In other words, she's undergoing therapy and I'm concerned if it were suggested that she read some material that might indicate another path that it might be more … do more damage than good.

I am Latwii, and am aware of your query, my brother. Such an entity as this one of which you speak, is an entity which is in what we may call a quite delicate position, for already there is the fragmenting of its focus of consciousness. To suggest a certain course of action to such an entity would have potential damaging effects, in any case, for the consciousness of this entity seeks in many directions and may not continue that which is begun, thereby utilizing such suggestions as partial courses of action. It is not an easy position through which to experience your illusion. And we cannot make any suggestion for such an entity for our great desire not to infringe upon the free will of any is enhanced manyfold when dealing with such an entity for this entity already experiences an illusion which is so much more intense, shall we say, than the one which most here experience, that to tamper with such a delicate balance is to offer a great potential for imbalance. The sending of the love and light and the prayers and the visualizations of peace and wholeness for such an entity may be all that most could ever do to be of aid. The type of aid which this entity could profit most from is not the type which is well known to the peoples of this planet, therefore we would suggest the enveloping of this entity in love and in light and the remembering and the prayers.

May we answer you further, my brother?

Questioner: No, thank you. Thank you very much. You've been very helpful.

I am Latwii. We thank you, my brother. Is there another question at this time?

Carla: I'd like to follow that a little further but first I'd like to ask you as to the instrument's condition. Is he fatigued enough that we should continue questioning at another time?

I am Latwii, and aware of your query, my sister. We find this instrument is not greatly fatigued and is quite capable of continuing.

Carla: OK. I've been fascinated by this case too and because my mother was a psychologist and has dealt for years with schizophrenics. This is just an extreme case of schizophrenia and she's often noted to me the talents and the psychic nature sometimes of the split personality and it's occurred to me to wonder whether the portion of the deep mind—when the veil is lifted and that person becomes a schizophrenic and goes into another personality—might not be from a previous incarnation and that there is a portion of the deeper mind that consists of our previous incarnational experiences. Could you confirm this?

I am Latwii, and am aware of your query, my sister. It is often the case with what you have called the multiple personalities that indeed those experiences of previous incarnations have been recalled to this particular incarnation for there is some aspect of the current incarnation which is able to make use of these previous aspects of the self. It is also possible that portions of the multiple personality are from what we might also call parallel existences. These existences are in dimensions that are adjoining your own within other universes. There is occasionally the opening of the door between universes within the being also occurring within the deep portions of the unconscious mind and these openings may then allow another aspect of this entity to experience the illusion which adjoins the illusion from whence it came. It is also possible that portions of the entity's future being, as you would call it, may make up a part of the multiple personalities, for it is only within your illusion that time is perceived as sequential and linear. It is in truth more clearly and correctly stated that all of what you know of as creation occurs simultaneously. Just as there are many entities within each city, as you call it, going about their business at one time, so it is with each individual. The many portions of the self which seem to exist in what you call the past, the present, and the future are as the many entities inhabiting the city of the self and it is possible for entities from time to time to become aware of and experience these portions of the self. Usually such occurrences take place within what you would call your dreaming state and occasionally within your meditative state of being. When this door is opened in the veil, shall we say, between the conscious and unconscious minds and allows this new, shall we say, personality to enter and become part of the waking self then there is what is called by your psychologists the split personality or the multiple personality or the schizophrenic personality, each description being a distorted attempt to describe the addition to, rather than the fragmenting of, a conscious personality.

May we answer you further, my sister?

Carla: Yes. Then past selves, parallel present selves, and future selves are all a functional portion of the deeper mind. Is that correct?

I am Latwii, and am aware of your query, my sister. This is in general quite correct for your unconscious mind extends throughout great spans of what you space and time and has known the creation of the one infinite Creator in ways quite imperceptible to the normal waking consciousness. When these experiences of the self which you are become available in what may be called an unbidden fashion, then there is what your psychologists call the breakdown of the personality in one fashion or another, as we have mentioned. It is not truly a breaking down but an addition to of an awareness which may be seen to be quite non-understandable to the normal consciousness.

May we answer you further, my sister?

Carla: OK. When the living consciousness is pushed past its limits so that without conscious control it escapes and finds these selves, these parts of itself, then it is considered pathological. But would it not be true that when an entity in its incarnation is able to develop the gifts which the past, parallel present, or future may have, then the person is simply considered extraordinarily gifted or a genius or

talented. In other words, does the phenomenon that we know of as genius or great talent represent an integrated movement from the conscious into the unconscious with the veil intact but with the will and the faith of the entity making these resources available safely? Could this be considered to be true?

I am Latwii, and am aware of your query, my sister. We may use the analogy of the television, as you call it. The illusion which you inhabit is likened unto one channel or station. Most entities are not able to change the channel or station, but must experience the offerings of your illusion and work with them in a disciplined manner before they are able to penetrate the nature of your illusion and change the stations by an act of their own will. An entity which through some seeming random or abnormal and usually traumatic circumstance experiences the changing of the station without conscious control of that changing, then there is what your psychologists and so forth describe as a pathological state of consciousness. Indeed, many of those entities described as genius or mystic in nature have been able through some discipline of their own personalities to change to another station momentarily or perhaps for greater portions of what you call time. The entities which are able to change their stations and states of awareness at will are quite, quite rare upon your planet.

May we answer you further, my sister?

Carla: No, thank you. I think it throws a whole new light on Itzhac Perlman and people like that who seem to come into this incarnation already knowing how to do something that's incredibly difficult. I thank you.

I am Latwii. We thank you, my sister. Is there another query at this time?

Questioner: You've really worked on that question hard and I don't want to make this difficult but let me see if I can summarize something for my own benefit. If it were not for the veil of forgetting which occurs when we take on this physical body, if it were not for that forgetting, would not all of us be schizophrenic, as we use the word schizophrenia?

I am Latwii, and am aware of your query, my sister. This is in one sense correct and in another incorrect. The correctness lies in the fact that without the veil each entity would be aware of every experience of every incarnation ever experienced, but would not be, shall we say, at the mercy *(inaudible)* the experiences would be quite *(inaudible)* able to be affected by the *(inaudible)* conscious choice, therefore there would not be *(inaudible)*.

Is there another question at this time?

(The sound of crickets can be heard.)

I am Latwii. Before we take our leave of this instrument and this group may we suggest that the leaving of the circle of seeking creates another type of hole within the tuning of this group. It is somewhat more difficult to maintain clear contact when there is the movement to and from this circle. We mention this in order that those present who are desirous of increasing their seeking and in strengthening the tuning might have yet one more tool in accomplishing this desire. We thank each of you, my brothers and sisters, for your great desire and your increasing devotion to seeking the love and light of the one infinite Creator. We are greatly honored to have been able to have blended our vibrations with yours for this short span of what you call time. We thank each present for allowing us this great privilege. Our gratitude is boundless. We shall leave this group now rejoicing in love and light and we leave each in that same love and light which the one infinite Creator has provided with an unending joy of being. We are known to you as Latwii. We leave you now, my friends. Adonai vasu borragus. ♣

L/L Research is a subsidiary of
Rock Creek Research &
Development Laboratories, Inc.

P.O. Box 5195
Louisville, KY 40255-0195

L/L RESEARCH

www.llresearch.org

Rock Creek is a non-profit
corporation dedicated to
discovering and sharing
information which may aid in
the spiritual evolution of
humankind.

INTENSIVE MEDITATION
AUGUST 26, 1982

(S channeling)

I am Hatonn, and I greet you, my brothers and sisters, in the love and in the light of the one infinite Creator. We are pleased, as always, to be called among you to be of service in this method you refer to as the channeling technique. We gladly offer our services in exercising the new channels as their desire deepens and grows with each day that passes on your planet. We often hear your calls to us, my friends, in each day as you progress as through the rounds of your daily activities that make up your life and experiences. We hear your calls and we are with you in each moment that your desire is open to us for our service, for our love, we are there. Never doubt that our presence is always close to those who strive as continually and with such diligence as the ones who are gathered this evening. We are always close, my friends, always close enough should you ever put out a mental hand, a thought, and we are there. We know your desire is strong to serve in this fashion of channeling, to spread the light among the peoples in the service of your planet. Time grows short and ever more often there are people who see and seek the light. There has been much done and much still that needs to be done. But even if one person is reached, my friends, then that has been a job well done. For in reaching only one person and sharing your light with that one person you have done a great service to mankind.

At this time we would transfer this contact to another. I am known to you as Hatonn.

(M1 channeling)

I am Hatonn. I am with this instrument. We are happy to be working with this instrument this evening as we are pleased to be with each of you this evening. My brothers and sisters, we are here among you to work with you, to help you develop in the service of channeling, the service of love, and at times, the service of self-sacrifice for those around you, a sacrifice that may at times seem that you are ever giving and you do not receive and it is this way in everything you do through each day that you serve, you are also being served. For each person you interact with, do you not interact with yourself? For as you teach, as you not learning? As you reach to help one along by the hand, are they not in fact pulling you along? The opportunity for you to be of service is so great, especially at this time. There are so many with needs, they are all around you. And as you look at each person, my friends, look within, recognize that the need they manifest is actually you and your need. So as you help them over that stumbling block, whatever it may be, you are in fact, my friends, learning to scale that barrier yourselves, moving along the path together arm in arm with those who are going along the same path, a very similar path, as different as it may appear in this, your illusion. Each person ultimately has the same goal, that of being one with the Creator, each person traveling that path experiencing the growth, the joy, the fulfillment together with you. They are you. Such a splendid opportunity you have. And we rejoice that you are eager to take this opportunity and grow the most from it. You have a gift, my brothers and sisters. Not a gift [different than] that those around you have, for of course they have it too, but you do recognize, more so than many of the others of your world, who you are and what you are capable of. You [are] vested with a great deal of power, self-assurance, confidence, a faith, so to speak, a faith strong enough to accomplish all, to accomplish each and every desire. [This is] a combination of factors, my friends, that offers you the opportunity for great growth, great growth for those that are around you. We rejoice in seeing you grow, where possible, helping those around you grow. But you are not able to save your whole world, my friends. Everyone will have a chance to learn the lessons they came to learn. Should they not, then they will get the opportunity to again. If you have learned the lessons you came to learn you will get an opportunity [from there on]. Such is the path. Our blessings go with you, my friends. We will transfer this contact. I am Hatonn.

(A channeling)

I am Hatonn. I am now with this instrument and we greet you once again in the love and the light of our one Creator. We wish to say just a few words through this instrument, for it has been some time since we have spoken through her. Remember that as you live in this world with all that you see, with all that you know, that there is always love and light. That power, that energy that comes from the love and light is strong and is always there. You are aware of it. Do not forget it. This instrument is tired. We will transfer the contact to another. I am Hatonn.

(K channeling)

I am Hatonn, and I am now with this instrument. There are times, my friends, when you feel that your service to your fellow man is limited and that you are not rendering very much service. If you wish to serve, you have but to ask and the door will be opened before you. You need never doubt that the things you do for someone else are worthwhile. We have but to remember the words of the one known as Jesus who did nothing more than going about doing good. When you have a tendency to become

discouraged, you have but to look about you, my friends, and see the beauty of nature and it will most surely restore you. There is sufficient beauty in a sunset to give you encouragement when you have need. It has been a great joy and a great pleasure to be with you. I am Hatonn.

(M2 channeling)

I am Hatonn. I am now with this instrument. I greet you with the love and the light of the infinite Creator. Always keep an open mind. Gather new ideas with wild abandon. If you cannot use them, gather them and store them as a miser stores gold. My friends, they are as valuable as gold. When an occasion comes that you need one of these ideas, you have them in reserve and can withdraw them and enlighten your problem. Find as much excitement in new ideas as you find in wealth. They are your true wealth. Look for them everywhere. Understand situations that you meet. Look at them from many angles. Love things that are different. You grow by understanding differences. I am Hatonn. I leave this instrument.

(Carla channeling)

I am Hatonn. I shall close through this instrument, offering many thanks to each instrument. We no longer call those present new instruments, for each is capable now of communicating not simply our identification, but our concepts. We most humbly and heartily thank you, each and every instrument present, for we are aware, at least to some small degree, of the many demands upon your time and your energy and we know the hours that you have spent privately and in meetings with a group such as this one working on your service to others.

We speak one single basic message. And in each instrument it has its own overtones and harmonies so that as many as possible might hear some portion, some version, some idea of our great fundamental theme of love and service and be inspired thereby to the wild and perilous belief that such a thing as love does exist in the world. To the casual eye, such a belief may seem foolhardy. We encourage you in your foolhardiness. It is the path, well trodden by pilgrims from the beginning of creation. It is the one path, call it what you will, which circles back to the source of all that there is.

Think now upon each other, my friends. Picture one by one those faces who have become dear to you that are circled in the gentle light of evening as your planet's sun moves beneath the rim of your sphere. Do you find one entity wise because of the age or the experience? Another wise because of a gift or a talent? Another wise because of some great service? Another wise because of some extraordinary amount of determination to seek? We suggest that you cease finding any wise. There is no wisdom in age for all are children of one Creator. Nor is there wisdom in gifts, for those are given, not understood. There is no wisdom in service. That is an action like any other. Nor is there the wisdom in determination, for many have been determined for many reasons.

These beloved faces, my friends, are all the faces of one being, each in a marvelous disguise. Each is the face of the Creator. Each mouth speaks the words of the Creator. Spend your love then, as brother and sister, encouraging, aiding, comforting. But know always what entity it is whom you serve. You serve the Creator, my friends, as do we, as do each of you in your mental vibratory configurations. We find each a perfect and wondrous delight and leave each of you our blessing. We shall be with you as always.

We leave this instrument at this time in that love and that light which is the emanation of each of you that is the one Creator. Adonai vasu.

(Jim channeling)

I am Latwii, and I greet you, my friends, in love and light. We are most privileged to be asked to join your group this evening. We thank each of you, for it is our great honor to be asked to provide the humble service of attempting to answer your queries. Remember always, my friends, we are your brothers and sisters and know only a small amount concerning the mystery of the creation which we share with you. Gladly though do we share that pittance that is ours. May we ask if there might be a question at this time?

K: Yes. In a former session, maybe a couple of weeks ago, something was said, I'm not sure that I got it accurate, about the planet is growing, or something about the growth of the planet and after I got home I wasn't sure of the meaning. It seems to me the planet is being destroyed rather than growing. Did I get that wrong?

I am Latwii, and am aware of your query, my sister. Your planet undergoes a process of evolution as does each entity upon its surface. Many entities

throughout this process of evolution may incur those difficulties which seem to be the stoppage of growth, the decay, the disease, the trauma that threatens to cease the experience of the illusion. Yet do not all entities make a progress through such circumstances and find, shall we say, the light at the end of the long and dark tunnel? So then, my sister, does your planet itself make progress and become transformed through the many experiences which the entities as cultures and races upon its surface experience. This entity which is your planet is having what might be called a difficult labor. There are the wars and rumors of wars as you call them. There are the changes in the garment of the surface of your planet. There are the personal difficulties of the inhabitants of each culture upon your planet's surface. There are the difficulties in the harmonizing of the vibrations of the density which you leave and the density which you enter. Yet your planet grows. And yet your planet shall be born anew and shall be a new entity, as will those entities be new which remain with it.

May we answer you further, my sister?

K: Yes, let me see if I can understand it a little better. What we see and which looks like destruction, revolution, etc., etc., is really an illusion. There is still an evolutionary process going on that is growth? Fairly accurately?

I am Latwii. My sister, your statement is most accurate. From the ashes does the phoenix rise.

May we answer you further?

K: No, thank you.

I am Latwii. We are most grateful to you. Is there another question at this time?

S1: Yes, Latwii, I have a question. For the past week and a half or two weeks the one known as G and I have been experiencing an extreme state of physical fatigue even though we have both been getting enough rest and that sort of thing. Could this fatigue be due to a draining of or a scattering of the vital energies?

I am Latwii, and am aware of your query, my sister. Indeed, it is possible for entities who seek a solution to the mysteries of being and who are willing to undergo those transformations which present themselves as opportunities to the seeker for an experience of that which might be called a spiritual weariness. The path of the seeker is a path which has its price, that is to say, from time to time there is the expenditure of much energy so that understanding, to use a poor term, might be enlarged, the bounds of the being might be expanded to include a new way. This might be likened unto those growing pains, that you call them, for the physical vehicle during the early parts of the incarnation. The spiritual seeker, like the young entity of your illusion, finds new capabilities opening up within the being as the seeking increases in intensity. As these new ways of being, perceiving and thinking continue to be experienced by the seeker, there is the effort that is necessary to procure them and seek them within the being of the seeker. Such an effort is primarily of a spiritual nature, but does have its mental, emotional and physical counterparts so that the stretching of the being in all these complexes then on occasion cause the entity to experience that which is commonly known to your peoples as weariness. Be not discouraged in any degree or sense by this weariness for it is simply that that which you have reached for is now a part of your being. And as it becomes more uniformly a part of your being, then you shall grow new spiritual muscles, shall we say.

May we answer you further, my sister?

S1: No, thank you very much, Latwii.

We are most grateful to you, my sister. Is there another question at this time?

Carla: Latwii, if we're light on questions tonight, I would like to ask a question for my friend S2. S2 is a wanderer who continues seeking all by herself year after year with no help or support from any close kin and only the love and support of friends like me and like you to aid her. She has wondered whether she might not be a part of a kind of experiment in wanderers, a part of an experiment which places wanderers in various positions. She's very weary of waiting and although she knows that she's equal to the necessity of continuing to wait for years and years if necessary, her real fear is that she will completely miss her ability to perform her mission. I have the feeling that there are many wanderers who have become aware that they have come to this Earth for a reason but as yet do not have any guidance as to what it is and are in similar circumstances of mind as to how to. Could you comment on her plight and the possibility of what she calls the experiment?

I am Latwii and am aware of your query, my sister. May we begin by suggesting that this entity, as all entities, is supported daily by the creation which it inhabits. No entity, in truth, is without support, for the entire creation is alive with the original Thought of the experiencing …

(Side one of tape ends.)

(Jim channeling)

I am Latwii, and am with this instrument once again. The original Logos, shall we say, began this octave of creation. Each entity travels a path which it has chosen before it entered the incarnation. The nature of the path varies from entity to entity so that in truth it might be said each entity experiments with its own beingness. Those entities which have recently been called upon your planet the wanderers are entities which not only come to grow within the bounds of their own being, but to aid those of your planet which seek the lessons of love for the first time. Each so-called wanderer has the desire to be of a certain type of service besides the general desire to serve. Whether the talents of each are developed to a finely tuned degree, shall we say, is the determination of each entity during the incarnation. For each is presented with that programming, as you may call it, which wells up from the deeps of the unconscious mind.

Each entity, then, sees about it the catalyst which provokes and promotes the remembering or reconfiguring of the original intent. Many become distracted for greater or lesser periods of time by the illusion which they inhabit, for the illusion is an intense one and is most easily able to redirect the attention of many who seek to be of service within it.

We are unable to determine any specific experiment for the one which you have called S2 apart from the experiment which each entity undertakes as the third-density illusion is entered and utilized for growth and service. We suggest to each entity which questions in this regard that the meditation upon those queries will bring those responses and glimpses of truth from the great depths of being of the unconscious mind. And by so seeking shall the entity be able to rest the conscious mind and know that there are in truth no mistakes. There are only opportunities to be of service and to expand the experience of the one infinite Creator.

May we answer you further, my sister?

Carla: Yes, just a bit. First I would like to thank you for that answer. I know my sister S2 well enough to say that she will continue wondering beyond any bounds what she is to do, but your words of comfort will undoubtedly help her. I would like to ask just one little detail of the experiment thing that she was working on in her last letter. She said during her regression she at one point referred to her teachers and said that she was their [seed.] This is part of her experiment idea. These teachers were beautiful, wise, golden beings whom she loved dearly and who loved her as dearly in another density and in another time. Would you comment on her feeling on that relationship for her?

I am Latwii and am aware of your query, my sister. The planetary entities which form the various members of the Confederation of Planets in the Service of the One Infinite Creator are as one being, each unto themselves, though they are many in number. Each portion of such a social memory complex, as you have come to known them, is therefore, a seed of that grouping or social memory complex. As each portion then is sent out to be that which you have called the wanderer, then the seeds of that complex are sown throughout the universe of the one infinite Creator. The seeds of light are planted within the darkness. There it is hoped that there shall be the nourishment of the great central sun from which all springs so that the growth, the eventual flowering and fruiting of these entities might be accomplished, and that those who dwell in the so-called darkness might then have the opportunity to taste of the love and light of the one Creator. In this way each entity, therefore, is the seed.

May we answer you further, my sister?

Carla: Just to clarify it for my understanding. What you're saying then, is what she perceived as teachers were part of her social memory complex, that she found herself being separated from as seed when she made the decision to come here as a wanderer. Is that right?

I am Latwii and am aware of this query, my sister. This is, in general, correct. There is, of course, within each social memory complex the variety of relationships which you might expect to find within any grouping of entities, where some teach in certain areas and learn in yet others, all being teachers and

all being students, yet in certain areas of service, might one find teachers tutoring students who then undertake the laboratory experiment, shall we say.

May we answer you further, my sister?

Carla: No. I'll send that off to S2 and ask questions only if she asks me to. Thank you so much, Latwii.

I am Latwii. We are most grateful to you, my sister. Is there another question at this time?

M1: Yes, Latwii. I think you've already answered it, but I want to try it on you for size. I'll be making some decisions here and I recognize there are no mistakes and there are no detours, but is there a watchword of sorts which you might have that I should perhaps key on in the rest of my search for the rest of my path here for the near future?

I am Latwii and am aware of your query, my brother. We hesitate to give the word in any sense which would direct your attention away from those concerns which are unique to your being at this time. We wish to be of service without infringing upon free will and feel that we might be of the best aid by suggesting that you look in meditation within your being at the purpose for the life. Look then as well to the opportunities which present themselves. Find the balance which is unique to your seeking and to your being.

May we answer you further, my brother?

M1: I think you did pretty well. In fact, that was a better answer than I'm used to getting from you, pardner. Thank you.

I am Latwii and am most appreciative of your compliment, my brother. We are not always able to earn them, as you are aware. May we ask if there might be another query at this time?

(Pause)

I am Latwii. We thank you, my brothers and sisters for allowing us to join with you this evening. Your vibrations have been most delicious, shall we say. To taste of the seeking that is pure, clear and intensified through what you call time is to taste of the very essence of the one infinite Creator. To grow, to know, to share, and to be, by these modes do you in your incarnations reproduce the nature of the one Creator. We are privileged to be but a small part of this process. We thank each of you for allowing us to blend our vibrations with yours on evenings such as this one. We are with you whenever requested. We shall at this time take our leave of this group, though in truth, always are we one. Then in that love and light do we leave you now. We are known to you as Latwii. Adonai, my friends. Adonai, vasu, borragus.

♣

L/L Research is a subsidiary of
Rock Creek Research &
Development Laboratories, Inc.

P.O. Box 5195
Louisville, KY 40255-0195

www.llresearch.org

Rock Creek is a non-profit
corporation dedicated to
discovering and sharing
information which may aid in
the spiritual evolution of
humankind.

The Law of One, Book IV, Session 94
August 26, 1982

Ra: I am Ra. I greet you in the love and in the light of the one infinite Creator. I communicate now.

Questioner: Could you first please give me the condition of the instrument?

Ra: I am Ra. There is some small increase in physical energy deficit. It is not substantial. All else is as at the previous asking.

Questioner: From the previous session the statement was made that much is veiled to the most apparently clear observation. Would Ra expand on what was meant by that statement? I assume that this means the veiling of all that which is outside of the limits of what we call our physical perception having to do with the spectrum of light, etc., but I also intuit that there is more than that veiled. Would Ra expand on that concept?

Ra: I am Ra. You are perceptive in your supposition. Indeed, we meant not any suggestions that the physical apparatus of your current illusion was limited as part of the veiling process. Your physical limits are as they are.

However, because of the unique biases of each mind/body/spirit complex there are sometimes quite simple instances of distortion when there is no apparent cause for such distortion. Let us use the example of the virile and immature male who meets and speaks clearly with a young female whose physical form has the appropriate configuration to cause, for this male entity, the activation of the red-ray sexual arousal.

The words spoken may be upon a simple subject such as naming, information as to the occupation, and various other common interchanges of sound vibratory complex. The male entity, however, is using almost all the available consciousness it possesses in registering the desirability of the female. Such may also be true of the female.

Thusly an entire exchange of information may be meaningless because the actual catalyst is of the body. This is unconsciously controlled and is not a conscious decision. This example is simplistic.

Questioner: I have drawn a small diagram in which I simply show an arrow which represents catalyst penetrating a line at right angles to the arrow, which is the veil, depositing in one of two repositories which I would call the right-hand path and the left-hand path, and I have labeled these two repositories the Experience. Would this be a very rough analogy of the way the catalyst is filtered through the veil to become experience?

Ra: I am Ra. Again, you are partially correct. The deeper biases of a mind/body/spirit complex pilot the catalyst around the many isles of positivity and negativity as expressed in the archipelago of the deeper mind. However, the analogy is incorrect in that it does not take into account the further polarization which most certainly is available to the conscious mind after it has perceived the partially polarized catalyst from the deeper mind.

Questioner: It seems to me that the Experience of the Mind would act in such a way as to change the nature of the veil so that catalyst would be filtered so as to be acceptable in the bias that is increasingly chosen by the entity. For instance, if he had chosen the right-hand path the Experience of the Mind would change the permeability of the veil to accept more and more positive catalyst. Also the other would be true for accepting more negative catalyst if the left-hand path were the one that was chosen. Is this correct?

Ra: I am Ra. This is not only correct but there is a further ramification. As the entity increases in experience it shall, more and more, choose positive interpretations of catalyst if it is upon the service-to-others path and negative interpretations of catalyst if its experience has been of the service-to-self path.

Questioner: Then the mechanism designed by the Logos of the action of catalyst resulting in experience was planned to be self-accelerating in that it would create this process of variable permeability. Is this an adequate statement?

Ra: I am Ra. There is no variable permeability involved in the concepts we have just discussed. Except for this, you are quite correct.

Questioner: Now I can understand, to use a poor term again, the necessity for the archetype of Catalyst of the Mind but what is the reason for having a blueprint or model for the Experience of the Mind other than this simple model of dual repositories for negative and positive catalyst? It seems to me that the first distortion of free will would be better served if no model for experience was made. Could you clear that up for me?

Ra: I am Ra. Your question is certainly interesting and your confusion hopefully productive. We cannot learn/teach for the student. We shall simply note, as we have previously, the attraction of various archetypes to male and to female. We suggest that this line of consideration may prove productive.

Questioner: In the fourth archetype the card shows a male whose body faces forward. I assume that this indicates that the Experience of the Mind will reach for catalyst. However, the face is to the left which indicates to me that in reaching for catalyst, negative

catalyst will be more apparent in its power and effect. Would Ra comment on this?

Ra: I am Ra. The archetype of Experience of the Mind reaches not, O student, but, with firm authority, grasps what it is given. The remainder of your remarks are perceptive.

Questioner: The Experience is seated upon the square of the material illusion which is colored much darker than in Card Number Three. However, there is a cat inside of this square. I am guessing as experience is gained the second-density nature of the illusion is understood and the negative and positive aspects separate. Would Ra comment on this?

Ra: I am Ra. This interpretation varies markedly from Ra's intention. We direct the attention to the cultural meaning of the great cat which guards. What, O student, does it guard? And with what oriflamme does it lighten that darkness of manifestation? The polarities are, indeed, present; the separation nonexistent except through the sifting which is the result of cumulative experience. Other impressions were intended by this configuration of the seated image with its milk-white leg and its pointed foot.

Questioner: In Card Number Three the feet of the female entity are upon the unstable platform, signifying the dual polarity by its color. In Card Number Four one foot is pointed so that if the male entity stands on the toe it would be carefully balanced. The other foot is pointed to the left. Would Ra comment on my observation that if the entity stands on this foot it will be very, very carefully balanced?

Ra: I am Ra. This is an important perception, for it is a key to not only this concept complex but to others as well. You may see the T-square which, at times riven as is one foot from secure fundament by the nature of experience yet still by this same nature of experience, is carefully, precisely, and architecturally placed in the foundation of this concept complex and, indeed, in the archetypical mind complex. Experience[9] has the nature of more effectively and poignantly expressing the architecture of experience, both the fragility of structure and the surety of structure.

_____

[9] Card Number Four.

Questioner: It would seem to me, from the configuration of this male entity in Card Number Four, who looks to the left with the right foot pointed to the left, that this card would indicate you must be in a defensive position with respect to the left-hand path, but there is no need to concern yourself about protection with respect to the right-hand path. Would Ra comment on that?

Ra: I am Ra. Again, this is not the suggestion we wished to offer by constructing this image. However, the perception cannot be said to be incorrect.

Questioner: The magical shape is on the right edge of the Card Number Four which indicates to me that the spiritual experience would be on the right-hand path. Could Ra comment on that?

Ra: I am Ra. Yes. The figure is expressing the nature of experience by having its attention caught by what may be termed the left-hand catalyst. Meanwhile, the power, the magic, is available upon the right-hand path.

The nature of experience is such that the attention shall be constantly given varieties of experience. Those that are presumed to be negative, or interpreted as negative, may seem in abundance. It is a great challenge to take catalyst and devise the magical, positive experience. That which is magical in the negative experience is much longer coming, shall we say, in the third density.

Questioner: Both the third and fourth archetypes, as I see it, work together for the sole purpose of creating the polarity in the most efficient manner possible. Is this correct?

Ra: I am Ra. This cannot be said to be incorrect. We suggest contemplation of this thought complex.

Questioner: Then prior to the veiling process that which we call catalyst after the veiling was not catalyst simply because it was not efficiently creating polarity, because this loading process, you might say, that I have diagrammed, of catalyst passing through the veil and becoming polarized experience, was not in effect because the viewing of what we call catalyst by the entity was seen much more clearly as the experience of the one Creator and not something that was a function of other mind/body/spirit complexes. Would Ra comment on that statement?

Ra: I am Ra. The concepts discussed seem without significant distortion.

Questioner: Thank you. Then we're expecting, in Card Number Four, to see the result of catalytic action and, therefore, a greater definition between the dark and the light areas. In just glancing at this card we notice that it is more definitely darkly colored in some areas and more white in others in a general sense than in Card Number Three, indicating to me that the separation along the two biases has occurred and should occur in order to follow the blueprint for experience. Could Ra comment on that?

Ra: I am Ra. You are perceptive, O student.

Questioner: The bird in Card Number Three now seems to be internalized in the center of the entity in Card Number Four in that it has changed from its flight in Card Number Three. The flight has achieved its objective and has become a part, a central part, of the experience. Could Ra comment on that?

Ra: I am Ra. This perception is correct, O student, but what shall the student find the bird to signify?

Questioner: I would guess that the bird signifies that a communication that comes as catalyst signified in Card Number Three is accepted by the female and, used, becomes a portion of the experience. I'm not sure of that at all. Am I in any way correct?

Ra: I am Ra. That bears little of sense.

Questioner: I'll have to work on that.

Then I am guessing that the crossed legs of the entity in Card Four have a meaning similar to the crux ansata. Is this correct?

Ra: I am Ra. This is correct. The cross formed by the living limbs of the image signifies that which is the nature of mind/body/spirit complexes in manifestation within your illusion. There is no experience which is not purchased by effort of some kind, no act of service-to-self or others which does not bear a price, to the entity manifesting, commensurate with its purity. All things in manifestation may be seen in one way or another to be offering themselves in order that transformations may take place upon the level appropriate to the action.

Questioner: The bird is within the circle on the front of the entity on Card Four. Would that have the same significance of the circular part of the crux ansata?

Ra: I am Ra. It is a specialized form of this meaningful shape. It is specialized in great part due to the nature of the crossed legs of manifestation which we have previously discussed.

Questioner: The entity on Card Four wears a strangely shaped skirt. Is there a significance to the shape of this skirt?

Ra: I am Ra. Yes.

Questioner: The skirt is extended toward the left hand but is somewhat shorter toward the right. There is a black bag hanging from the belt of the entity on the left side. It seems to me that this black bag has a meaning of the acquiring of the material possessions of wealth as a part of the left-hand path. Would Ra comment on that?

Ra: I am Ra. Although this meaning was not intended by Ra as part of this complex of concepts we find the interpretation quite acceptable.

(Thirty second pause.)

I am Ra. As we observe a lull in the questioning we shall take this opportunity to say that the level of transferred energy dwindles rapidly and we would offer the opportunity for one more full question at this working, if it is desired.

Questioner: I would just state that this card, being male, would indicate that as experience is gained the mind becomes the motivator or that which reaches or does more than the simple experiencer it was prior to the gaining of the catalytic action. There is a greater tendency for the mind to direct the mind/body/spirit complex, and other than that I would just ask if there is anything that we can do to make the instrument more comfortable or to improve the contact?

Ra: I am Ra. In the context of your penultimate query we would suggest that you ponder again the shape of the garment which the image wears. Such habiliment is not natural. The shape is significant and is so along the lines of your query.

The support group cares well for the instrument. We would ask that care be taken as the instrument has been offered the gift of a distortion towards extreme cold by the fifth-density friend which greets you.

Although you may be less than pleased with the accouterments, may we say that all was as carefully prepared as each was able. More than that none can do. Therefore, we thank each for the careful alignments. All is well.

We leave you, my friends, in the love and in the light of the one glorious infinite Creator. Go forth, then, rejoicing in the power and in the peace of the One. Adonai. ✤

L/L Research is a subsidiary of
Rock Creek Research &
Development Laboratories, Inc.

P.O. Box 5195
Louisville, KY 40255-0195

L/L RESEARCH

www.llresearch.org

Rock Creek is a non-profit
corporation dedicated to
discovering and sharing
information which may aid in
the spiritual evolution of
humankind.

THE LAW OF ONE, BOOK V, SESSION 94, FRAGMENT 45
AUGUST 26, 1982

Jim: The first few questions and responses in this session are more of the nuts and bolts maintenance which we constantly found ourselves having to deal with in keeping up with both Carla's arthritic flare-ups of pain and our fifth-density negative friend's accentuating of these difficulties.

Toward the beginning of Session 92 in Book Four of *The Law Of One*, one of Ra's responses was "There is the need for the instrument to choose the manner of its beingness. It has the distortion, as we have noted, towards the martyrdom. This can be evaluated and choices made only by the entity." And at the end of that same session, Ra added "The instrument, itself, might ponder some earlier words and consider their implications. We say this because the continued calling upon vital energies, if allowed to proceed to the end of the vital energy, will end this contact. There is not the need for continued calling upon these energies. The instrument must find the key to this riddle or face a growing loss of this particular service at this particular space/time nexus." The last part of the personal material from Session 94 consists of a query from Carla upon which she pondered long concerning the riddle which Ra had presented in Session 92. The riddle was Ra's way of maintaining Carla's free will and at the same time giving her a direction for thought which might enhance both her own growth and the service of the contact to others.

Carla: As time went on, we fiddled around more and more with clothing and such, trying to maximize my comfort and the length of sessions. I was warmly clothed, all in white, with the white comforter placed so it did not drag down the arms, and then my hands were gloved, and the kind of tubing used to vent washer/dryers went over both hands up to about the elbow, to keep the weight of the cover off them completely. It was a job just getting dressed for the sessions. It seems almost funny when one looks back on it, that we kept on with such perseverance. But at the time, there was only one thought between us three, and that was to continue this contact and learn all we could. I think if it happened again, I'd do the same thing again: give my utmost. And I imagine Jim would say the same. Without question Don was also absolutely single-minded about pursuing the questioning with Ra. He felt that this was the culmination of his life's work. If we were somewhat wearied and even battered by the conditions we had to work in, that was acceptable. And we did indeed all feel the weariness.

I appreciate the point those of Ra make concerning my gift of faith. It has been true for as long as I can remember that I have enjoyed that attitude of faith and hope. It may well be why I am alive today, while Don is a soldier fallen in the spiritual battle. Don was a person of infinite dignity, intelligence and ethical purity, but always a somewhat melancholy man under the mask of polite courtesy, efficiency and professorial charm that he wore to meet the world. Much has been given me in this life in the way of gifts, but this is surely the most precious.

Doesn't Ra offer a marvelous perspective to the myopic spiritual eye, in suggesting that I was only looking at what still needed doing, rather than giving thanks for what had come around already? I have often taken their advice and pondered the merits of judging as the stern critic that would have everything just so. Life is messy, and often things are very much untidy, and that needs to be released, forgiven and accepted.

And Ra's final thought is truly a jewel. What, after all, is all our striving in the end, including this contact and all human thought, but a vain and empty folly? We cannot move from illusion to truth in this body, on this plane of existence. So where is our truest and central service? Not in the doing but in the being, in allowing the true self, that open-hearted lover of all things in creation, to share its essence with the world, and to allow the love and light of the Infinite One to pass through it and radiate into the planetary consciousness. That is our true geste, *all of us who have come here at this time to be of service: being, living a devotional and devoted life.*

Session 94, August 26, 1982

Questioner: I have questions here from the instrument. The first one is, "Is our fifth-density friend responsible for the instrument's extreme distortion towards pain during and just after sessions?"

Ra: I am Ra. Yes.

Questioner: Is there anything that we can do that we are not doing to remedy this situation so that the instrument does not experience this pain, or as much pain?

Ra: I am Ra. There Is little that can be done due to a complex of pre-existing distortions. The distortions are triple in the source.

There is the, shall we say, less than adequate work of your chirurgeons which allows for various distortions in the left wrist area.

There is the distortion called systemic lupus erythematosus which causes the musculature of the lower left and right arms to allow for distortions in the normal, shall we say, configuration of both.

Lastly, there is the nerve damage, more especially to the left, but in both appendages from the thoracic outlet.

In the course of the waking behavior the instrument can respond to the various signals which ring the tocsin of pain, thus alerting the mind complex, which in turn moves the physical complex in many and subtle configurations which relieve the various distortions. Your friend greets these distortions, as has been stated before, immediately prior to the beginning of the working. However, during the working the instrument is not with its yellow-ray chemical vehicle and thusly the many small movements which could most effectively aid in the decrease of these distortions are not possible. Ra must carefully examine thc mental configurations of the mind complex in order to make even the grossest manipulation. It is not our skill to use a yellow-ray vehicle.

The weight of the cover has some deleterious effect upon these distortions in some cases and thus we mentioned that there was a small thing which could be done; that is, the framing of that which lifted the coverlet from the body slightly. In order to compensate for loss of warmth the wearing of material warming the manual appendages would then be indicated.

Questioner: I immediately think of the instrument wearing long underwear under the robe that it now wears and an extremely light, white cover. Would this be satisfactory?

Ra: I am Ra. Due to this instrument's lack of radiant physical energy the heavier cover is suggested.

Questioner: In your statement, at the beginning of it, you said "less than adequate work of" and then there was a word that I didn't understand at all. Are you familiar with the word that I am trying to understand?

Ra: I am Ra. No.

Questioner: Then we'll have to wait until we transcribe the material. I assume that our fifth-density negative friend docsn't cause these distortions all of the time because he wishes to emphasize the fact that the instrument is going to be distorted only if she attempts one of these service-to-others workings and, therefore, attempts to stifle the workings. Is this correct?

Ra: I am Ra. This is partially correct. The incorrect portion is this: The entity of which you speak has found its puissance[10] less than adequate to mount a continuous assault upon this instrument's physical vehicle and has, shall we say, chosen the more effective of the space/time nexi of this instrument's experience for its service.

Questioner: Could you tell me why I have felt so tired on several recent occasions?

Ra: I am Ra. This has been covered in previous material.

The contact which you now experience costs a certain amount of the energy which each of the group brought into manifestation in the present incarnation. Although the brunt of this cost falls upon the instrument, it is caparisoned by pre-incarnative design with the light and gladsome armor of faith and will to a far more conscious extent than most mind/body/spirit complexes are able to enjoy without much training and initiation.

Those of the support group also offer the essence of will and faith in service to others, supporting the instrument as it releases itself completely in the service of the one Creator. Therefore, each of the support group also experiences a weariness of the spirit which is indistinguishable from physical energy deficit except that if each experiments with this weariness each shall discover the physical energy in its usual distortion.

Questioner: Thank you. I didn't mean to go over previous material. I should have phrased my question more carefully. That is what I expected. I was trying to get a confirmation of my suspicion. I suspected that. I will try to be more careful in questioning.

The second question from the instrument says, "While on vacation I uncovered a lot about myself not consciously known before. It seems to me that I have coasted a lot on the spiritual gifts given at birth and never have spent any time getting to know my human self which seems to be a child, immature and irrational. Is this so?"

Ra: I am Ra. This is partially correct.

Questioner: Then she says, "If this is so, this seems to be part of the riddle about the manner of my beingness that Ra spoke of. I fear that if I do not work successfully on my human distortions I shall be responsible for losing the contact. Yet also Ra suggests the over-dedication to any outcome is unwise. Could Ra comment on these thoughts?"

Ra: I am Ra. We comment in general first upon the query about the contact which indicates once again that the instrument views the mind/body/spirit complex with jaundiced eye. Each mind/body/spirit complex that is seeking shall almost certainly have the immature and irrational behaviors. It is also the case that this entity, as well as almost all seekers, has done substantial work within the framework of the incarnative experience and has indeed developed maturity and rationality. That this instrument should fail to see that which has been accomplished and see only that which remains to be accomplished may well be noted. Indeed, any seeker discovering in itself this complex of mental and mental/emotional distortions shall ponder the possible non-efficacy of judgment.

As we approach the second portion of the query we view the possibility of infringement upon free will. However, we believe we may make reply within the boundaries of the Law of Confusion.

This particular instrument was not trained, nor did it study, nor worked it at any discipline in order to contact Ra. We were able, as we have said many times, to contact this group using this instrument because of the purity of this instrument's dedication to the service of the one infinite Creator and also because of the great amount of harmony and acceptance enjoyed each by each within the group; this situation making it possible for the support group to function without significant distortion.

We are humble messengers. How can any thought be taken by an instrument as to the will of the Creator? We thank this group that we may speak through it, but the future is mazed. We cannot know whether our *geste* may, after one final working, be complete. Can the instrument, then, think for a moment that it shall cease in the service of the one infinite Creator? We ask the instrument to ponder these queries and observations. ⚡

_____

[10] puissance: The power to accomplish or achieve; potency [<OF].

L/L RESEARCH

L/L Research is a subsidiary of
Rock Creek Research &
Development Laboratories, Inc.

P.O. Box 5195
Louisville, KY 40255-0195

www.llresearch.org

Rock Creek is a non-profit
corporation dedicated to
discovering and sharing
information which may aid in
the spiritual evolution of
humankind.

ABOUT THE CONTENTS OF THIS TRANSCRIPT: This telepathic channeling has been taken from transcriptions of the weekly study and meditation meetings of the Rock Creek Research & Development Laboratories and L/L Research. It is offered in the hope that it may be useful to you. As the Confederation entities always make a point of saying, please use your discrimination and judgment in assessing this material. If something rings true to you, fine. If something does not resonate, please leave it behind, for neither we nor those of the Confederation would wish to be a stumbling block for any.

CAVEAT: This transcript is being published by L/L Research in a not yet final form. It has, however, been edited and any obvious errors have been corrected. When it is in a final form, this caveat will be removed.

Sunday Meditation
August 29, 1982

(C channeling)

I am Hatonn, and I am now with this instrument. My friends, it is always an honor and a privilege for us to speak to you. It is somewhat easier when you journey with another along the path. It may at times seem easier, but so much is lost when there is not the sharing and the learning that is generated by the interaction with others. Energies of a group strengthens forces. When you share freely, give your energies, your love, you form a more powerful vehicle in which to journey.

As you know, at this time on your planet the number of entities is increasing rapidly. Entities striving to complete lessons. As the number of entities increases you may see an increase in those who seek to separate themselves from all other entities. They will try, but ever increasing numbers will act to bring those seeking to separate themselves to look at the self through different eyes. For each is separate; each is also one with the Creator and increasing numbers are inclined to offer to all the chance to give themselves to their brothers and sisters for the needs …

I am Hatonn, and would now pause, for our contact is not a good one, and this instrument has been receiving another contact as well as our own. We are adjusting. I am Hatonn. We have now readjusted our contact, and this instrument has pulled himself

back. We would ask that this group please retune themselves for the various stages of alertness are causing the energies to wane. If you would retune, we would again try to speak to you. I am Hatonn.

Carla: *(Chanting, with group.)* Omm.

(M channeling)

I am Hatonn. I am now with this instrument. I greet you with the love and the light of the infinite Creator. You have been especially among people very healthy. *(inaudible)* Some of your people get so disturbed over insignificant situations. They treat them as life and death matters where it should be considered a [new] life and a *(inaudible)* experience. They so overcharge their emotions that they do not learn from the experience. When they return to a normal state they need to re-experience the situation. The forgetting process is necessary for learning. But if you can take the long view of the situation, you can learn as you first experience it. It is not healthy to over-involve yourself in a situation. Remember that your whole life is a learning experience. The insignificant details are there to teach but not to overcome.

I am Hatonn. I now leave this instrument.

(C channeling)

I am Hatonn, and am once again with this instrument. We regret the interference, but now we seem to have a much better contact. We would caution those who seek to act in the service of channeling to always remain within themselves. To channel, you need not surrender. To channel is an act of free will. If the one seeking to channel begins to drift, so to speak, to reach out beyond and separate even partially from the physical being, then that instrument is open to others who would speak. The interference could quite possibly be to information that would harm instead of help. We know that you wish to be of service to all, but caution you to remain in position where you choose, where you are not used. Your free will is extremely important to your learning, to your experiencing freely the lessons that you have chosen to learn in this incarnation.

If at any time as you act as a channel you seem pulled, please take time. Collect yourself. As you begin channeling, we and my brothers and sisters of Laitos suggested that you open yourself to speak freely without doubt and analysis, but as you speak any of the words, the thoughts are not comfortable, take time …

Carla: Who is speaking, Hatonn? C, answer to your name. C?

C: Yes.

Carla: Okay. Get close enough to L to put your hand under his leg or under his arm or hold his hand or something like that. L, don't hold on to him hard or anything, just keep contact.

C, do you feel all right?

C: *(Inaudible).*

Carla: Okay. Relax. There is no longer any possibility that you will leave your body. You're grounded to L. That's why I always hold hands with Jim. Does anybody else feel any problem? Excuse me, Hatonn, please go on through another channel and let C relax for the remainder of the evening.

(L channeling)

I am Hatonn. I am now with this instrument. We are appreciative of these difficulties being experienced by the one known as C, and extend our apologies for over-using the instrument that he so generously provided for the purpose of our communication. We were unaware of the extent of disorientation resultant from the higher disturbance caused by a negatively-polarized entity seeking

simultaneously to be of service. We commend the one known as Carla for her perception, and are also appreciative of her service. It is apparent to ourselves and an increasing number of those present that there has been a sustained effort toward the disruption of the efforts towards positive polarization of this group this evening. We are confident of the ability of this group to sustain both its polarization and self-possession, so to speak, and would desire to continue with our message. However, if any present desire a cessation for any reason, we shall pause at this time to reopen this possibility for the expression verbally. Are there any present who desire the cessation of this contact?

Carla: I don't desire the cessation of the contact, Hatonn, but I would appreciate the opportunity to give C some remark.

C: Hatonn?

(L channeling)

I am Hatonn.

C: Would it be better if I left the circle for awhile? Would it help *(inaudible)*?

I am Hatonn. My friend, the strength that has sustained you in [the] recent past is that strength which also sustains those present and is a benefit to those present that your presence is included. However, we would not desire to imply that your presence is required, should it be your desire to depart.

C: I don't want to interfere, so I'm going to go outside for a little while.

I am Hatonn. We thank you for your decision.

(C leaves.)

We would suggest that consideration be given to some accompaniment for the one known as C.

(Another person leaves the room.)

I am Hatonn. I am again with this instrument. My brothers and sisters, here is a force that feeds upon and is strengthened by itself. If you would desire, the continuation of that sensation would be a wise choice to maintain a conscious—correction—consciousness of that which you fear and thus be rewarded by its reinforced presence. However, should your desire be to flip that fear behind yourself and progress beyond it, a wise selection might be to extend—correction—cease extending your life force to the support of that construct. The universe within which you live, my brothers and sisters, is of your creation, and responds to that which you reinforce.

At this time we shall relinquish our use of this instrument that our brothers and sisters of Latwii might extend their service as well. I am known to you as Hatonn. Adonai, my friends.

(L channeling)

I am Latwii, and I greet you, my brothers and sisters, in the love and light of the infinite Creator. And might we suggest, my friends, that attention be extended to the maintenance by all present of the attunement, or variations of a severe nature may be accomplished in the attunement of the group by a reduction in concentration among those present. At this time we would offer ourselves in the service of answering questions, if there are any questions tonight.

K: Yes, Latwii, I have a question. We were talking about the poltergeist tonight on our way out, and we continued talking about it a little bit in here. Could these thoughts have been a distraction and could that have been a … had some part in what happened in the group tonight?

I am Latwii, and I am aware of your question. My sister, the variation in attunement experience was the result of several factors. However, we would downplay the significance of the conversations on this particular subject prior to the attunement.

May we answer you further?

K: No, thank you.

We thank you, my sister. Is there another question?

Carla: I'm aware that the relaxation technique caught an extremely good hypnotic subject by surprise in C, and wonder if it would be going beyond the bounds of free will if you would scan the group and let me know if there is anyone else in the group …

(Side one of tape ends.)

[I am Latwii, and am aware of your]) question and your concern, my sister. We may say that we are quite confident that at this point we have the vast majority of each individual present's attention at this moment due to unforeseen circumstances. We might suggest however, that in addition to the entity known as C encountering some difficulty, the

instrument we are currently using "went right under" in his terms, but was able to make a gradual comeback.

May we answer you further?

Carla: Does he need further aid?

I am Latwii. We have examined this instrument quite carefully prior to setting foot inside, so to speak, and it is not only wide awake, but curiously well rested.

May we answer you further?

Carla: Oh, good. Thank you.

As always, we thank you. Is there another question?

Carla: Did you have a message for us tonight? I'm really missing the spiritual inspiration.

I am Latwii. I am aware of your question. We had not planned on the delivery of an impromptu sermonette, and in all sincerity find that the current atmosphere is perhaps too highly keyed for our liking for such an undertaking. We would prefer to beg off until a more suitable time might occur, if that would be acceptable.

Carla: I'll take a light check.

We thank you, and may we say, that was lightly put. Is there another question?

K: Yes. I'm … Having worked in a mental hospital for a long time, and observed how—what can happen to human beings, it's my belief that too much thinking can break the barrier between, shall we say, the barrier between reality and non-reality. Would we not be better off if we had a little more levity, and a little more humor to counterbalance the seeking? I don't know if I've made myself clear. If not, I'll try it again.

I am Latwii. My sister, a significant facet of love is humor, for it is through humor that we encounter the exuberance of the Creator and His creation. There are many among your peoples who seek deeply and earnestly, yet manage to overlook the simplicity of that within which they exist. It is possible to travel from one point to another by many routes and arrive quite exhausted and depressed by many of the longer routes, yet we find that there is a strong correlation on the path we have traveled between lightness and levity.

May we answer you further, my sister?

K: You may not be able to answer this, and that's quite all right. As you scan my life, didn't I go through a period when I was about to go off the deep end, so to speak, and maybe lose contact with reality on this plane? And I'll understand if you don't want to answer that.

I am Latwii. As you surmised, my sister, we are very reluctant to undertake the extension of interpretation of an individual's life path. However, we would be willing to say in general that most individuals who consciously follow a path will often encounter side roads that seem quite attractive until traveled sufficiently to reveal their potential destination. At this point, many will simply retrace their steps to their original path, and continue to follow it.

May we answer you further?

K: No, that's fine. Thank you.

We thank you. Is there another question?

Carla: I have a couple of observations, but I would enjoy your confirmation or comments on them if that is possible. Thinking about what K said. First of all, I've known several people that came through this group that were pathologically mentally ill either during or after the experience with the group, either for a small amount of time or permanently. And it was my observation that the seeking that they displayed in my group was entirely different from the seeking displayed by those who are, in the context of their lives as a whole, going at it day by day, week after week, in that it was almost a symptom. It was a compulsion that they had sort of caught on, and what it was doing to them had almost nothing to do with what they said that they were seeking, but was driving them into an intensity beyond which the mind cannot rebound. Which really has nothing at all to do with seeking, it has to do with intensity. Can you comment or confirm this at all?

I am Latwii. We again are reluctant to undertake the description of individual cases known to those present. However, we would observe that there are many forms of addiction within your world and very few of our vantage points seem to be of a contributory nature.

May we answer you further?

Carla: That was a good comment. Thank you.

We thank you, my sister.

Carla: The other observation that K sparked off in me—I was thinking back through what happened to me since I consciously determined to live a life of seeking. And what's happened to me within various periods, there has been what almost might be called an initiation period where things were very, very difficult for a time, there was something I had to learn. Once I figured out what it was I had to learn, sometimes I had to dwell within that learning for awhile to indicate to myself that I did learn it indeed, and then it was over and the path was free and easy again. But I would not be surprised if every seeker didn't go through these times that are simply a part and parcel of the transformational process as you work through change. And change is never completely easy. Would you comment on that?

I am Latwii. As many present are aware, it is quite difficult to establish a new path through dense undergrowth that requires large amounts of sustained effort. However, once the path has been firmly established and used quite regularly for a period of time, one might leave that particular path through the undergrowth and perform other tasks for an extended length of time and return to find the path still easily trodden.

May we answer you further?

Carla: No, thank you.

We thank you. Is there another question?

M: Yes. If new channels remained opened too long, doesn't it give negative entities a chance to enter where they are not experienced enough to have the real intensity necessary?

If any channel, no matter how well intentioned, should overextend its abilities, the potential is always present for an interruption or confusion to be interspersed with the message attempting to be channeled.

May we answer you further?

M: Well, I think you mean then that new channels can became overextended more easily than more experienced channels. Is that correct?

I am Latwii. As your original query was concerned with the possibility for distortion to occur, we desired to indicate that that possibility was present when any individual desiring to be of service as a channel for messages overextended their energies. We acknowledge that in most instances the lesser experienced individual seeking to be of service in this manner will tire more quickly, and thus be more rapidly accessible to distortion, but we would not suggest that this be regarded as a—correction—as an inflexible rule, for there are many factors which can affect the endurance of one seeking to serve in this fashion.

May we answer you further?

M: No, thank you. That answers my question.

We thank you, my sister. Is there another question?

K: Yes. One other question. Regarding the positive polarity and the negative polarity. Since I've been in this group and I've thought about this more, it seems to me that what we are seeing in the Middle East is simply—well, I don't want to use the word conflict … well, I'll use that word anyway—a conflict between the positive and negative polarities. Is that true?

I am Latwii. My sister, the answer could well be true or false with its outcome dependent upon the perspective of that individual who evaluates the situation to which you refer. From our own perspective we perceive that the majority of those participants are neither positively nor negatively polarized to any appreciable extent, and from that perspective would feel it correct to state that your assumption was false. However, as with any situation such as the one to which you refer, there is always an effort by those of a negative polarization to take advantage of the situation to extend their own services and, as you might well guess, there are those of the positive polarization who simultaneously seek to be of service, as the objectives of each polarity is the same, that is, to be of service, but their efforts are directly at odds, so to speak. One might also interpret the situation as a struggle between the positive and negative polarities. We would suggest as an overview that the awareness that both positive and negative polarities are based on service.

May we answer you further?

K: No. That helps. But I can assume, then, that the preponderance of entities in that area are just not polarized in either direction, or the large majority of entities in the Middle East are not polarized in either direction. Is that assumption right?

I am Latwii. We would agree with that statement, and extend it to include the majority of the population of your planet. May we answer you further?

K: No, I think maybe that's why we're all crazy. Maybe that's why we're in such a mess. Thank you very much.

We thank you, my sister. Is there another question?

Carla: Would the term "mixed polarity" be more accurate, in that many people who are fighting on both sides believe that God is on their side, which is positive. They believe that they are being patriotic and doing the right thing in helping their buddies and saving lives, their buddies. And on the other hand they are shooting people which is not right, so they sort of cancel themselves out. So would the term "mixed polarity" be part of what you mean by saying they are polarized in neither direction?

I am Latwii. We find your observations of the confusion existent within the given situation to be particularly apt. However, we will graciously refrain from supplying any labels because of the potential for personal distortion that so often occurs.

May we answer you further?

Carla: No, thank you, Latwii.

Is there another question at this time?

(Pause)

I am Latwii. As there are no further questions, we will take our leave at this time. Adonai, my friends. We are known to you as Latwii. ⚜

L/L Research is a subsidiary of
Rock Creek Research &
Development Laboratories, Inc.

P.O. Box 5195
Louisville, KY 40255-0195

L/L RESEARCH

www.llresearch.org

Rock Creek is a non-profit
corporation dedicated to
discovering and sharing
information which may aid in
the spiritual evolution of
humankind.

© 2009 L/L RESEARCH

THE LAW OF ONE, BOOK IV, SESSION 95
SEPTEMBER 2, 1982

Ra: I am Ra. I greet you, my friends, in the love and in the light of the one infinite Creator. We communicate now.

Questioner: Could you first please give me the condition of the instrument?

Ra: I am Ra. It is as previously stated.

Questioner: Thank you. What is the situation with respect to our fifth-density negative associate?

Ra: I am Ra. The aforenamed entity has chosen various means to further its service and though each is effective in itself, none leads to the lessening of the dedication to service for others or the valuing of harmonious interaction. Therefore, the entity, though not quiet as it has been, is somewhat depolarized on balance.

Questioner: There seems to be an extremely high probability that we will move from this position to another residence. If we move from this residence and cease using this room for workings with Ra, is there a magically appropriate ritual for closing the use of this place of working, or is there anything that we should do with respect to leaving this particular place?

Ra: I am Ra. It would be appropriate to remove from this room and, to a lesser extent, from the dwelling, the charging of what you might call the distortion towards sanctity. To remove this charge it is valuable either to write upon your paper your own working or to use existing rituals for the deconsecration of a sacred place such as one of your churches.

Questioner: Thank you. The new room that we choose for this working will of course be carefully cleaned and marred surfaces made well. We shall also use the Banishing Ritual of the Lesser Pentagram prior to a working. Is there anything else that Ra could suggest? I would like, also, to know if there is anything in particular that you might suggest with respect to the particular place that has been chosen for our new location?

Ra: I am Ra. We scan the recent memory configurations of the questioner. Firstly, there have been some less than harmonious interactions within this dwelling. The dynamics of this interaction were potent enough to attract a lesser thought-form. Therefore, we suggest the salting and ritual cleansing by blessed water of all windows and doorways which offer adit into the domicile or any out-buildings thereof.

Further, we suggest the hanging of the cut garlic clove in the portion of the room which has accommodated those whose enjoyment has turned into a darker emotion centering upon the area we find you call the wet bar, also the room intended for the sleeping which is found near the kitchen area. The appropriate words used to bid farewell to those of the lower astral shall be used in connection with the hanging of the garlic cloves for the period of approximately 36 of your hours. We believe that this is equivalent to two of your night periods and one of your lit periods. This should cleanse the house as you find it to the extent that it is neutral in its vibrations of harmony, love, and thanksgiving which this group shall then, as the incarnation experience proceeds, offer to the domicile.

Questioner: I am assuming that we would prepare the blessed water the same as we prepare the water for the instrument to drink after a session and would then wipe the windows and doors with this water. This would probably have to be done in a bucket. I would like to know if this is correct, and what was meant by salting the windows and doors?

Ra: I am Ra. Firstly, you may bless the water yourselves or may request so-called holy water from any blessed place; that is, blessed by intention. Secondly, the water shall be carefully shaken from the fingers along the sills of all windows and doors as they have been opened. Thirdly, prior to the sprinkling of this cleansing, blessing sacrament of water, the salt shall be trailed along these sills in a line and again allowed to exist in this configuration for 36 to 48 hours. Then the virgin broom may ritually sweep the salt out of each window and doorway, sweeping with each stroke the less fortunate of the vibrations within the dwelling which might find coexistence with group difficult.

Questioner: I assume that you mean that we should put the salt only on the outer doorway sills and not on the inner doorway sills in the house. Is that correct?

Ra: I am Ra. This is correct. We cannot express the nature of salt and water and garlic with clarity enough to inform you as to the efficacy with which salt absorbs vibrations which have been requested to move into salt when salt has been given water. We cannot express the full magical nature of your water, nor can we express the likeness and attractiveness of the garlic cut to lower astral forms. The attractiveness is negative and no service-to-self astral form will accept coexistence with the cut garlic.

Therefore, we offer the suggestions. We also request, carefully, that the broom be clean and that the garlic be burned. The virginity of the broom is most efficacious.

Questioner: Let me see if I have the scenario correctly in mind. I'll repeat my version of it. We would hang fresh-cut garlic in the area of the wet bar and in the area of the bedroom that is adjacent to the kitchen area. We would salt all window sills and all outer wall door sills and then sprinkle blessed water from our fingers on the salted areas. We would then say the appropriate words to bid farewell to lower astrals. Those words I am not sure of. Would Ra comment on the scenario that I have stated?

Ra: I am Ra. Your grasp of our suggestions is good. We note that the salt be poured in the straight line with no gaps. There are various ritual words of blessing and farewell to entities such as you are removing. We might suggest the following.

When the salt is laid you may repeat "We praise the one Creator which gave to salt the ability to enable those friends, to which we wish to bid farewell, to find a new home."

As the water is sprinkled you may say "We give thanks to the one Creator for the gift of water. Over it the Creator moves Its hand and stirs Its will to be done."

The hanging of the cut garlic may be accompanied by the words "We praise the one Creator for the gift of garlic and bless its ability to offer to those friends to whom we wish to bid farewell the arrow which points their way of egress."

When the sweeping is done you may say "We praise the one Creator and give thanksgiving for the spiritual cleanliness of this dwelling place."

As the garlic is burned you may say "We give thanks to the one Creator for the gift of spiritual cleanliness in our dwelling place and seal the departure of all those who have left by this exit by the consuming of this substance" .

Questioner: Is there any place more appropriate than any other to hang the garlic in the room; for instance, over the windows or anything like that? I know that it is supposed to be hung in the area of the bar but I meant in the bedroom. Is there any more appropriate place than another?

Ra: I am Ra. The windows and the doorways are most appropriate and, in addition, we suggest the salting and sprinkling of any door which may lead elsewhere than out of the dwelling in order to afford to the entities the understanding that they are not desired elsewhere within the dwelling.

Questioner: I understand that the garlic is to be used at the bar area and the bedroom that is close to the kitchen and has an exit onto the carport. If I am correct, those are the only two places that it is to be used. This is correct, isn't it?

Ra: I am Ra. This is correct.

Questioner: We would like to pick the most appropriate room for sanctifying for the Ra contact. Is there any room that would be most appropriate that Ra could name?

Ra: I am Ra. When you have finished with your work the dwelling shall be as a virgin dwelling in the magical sense. You may choose that portion of the dwelling that seems appropriate and once having chosen it you may then commence with the same sort of preparation of the place with which you have been familiar here in this dwelling place.

Questioner: I am assuming that the newly chosen place meets the parameters for the best contact with Ra on the exterior of the house and I would like to ask Ra at this time if there are any suggestions with respect to the exterior of the house?

Ra: I am Ra. The dwelling seems surrounded with the trees and fields of your countryside. This is acceptable. We suggest the general principle of preparing each part of your environment as it best suits each in the group with the beauty which each may feel to be appropriate. There is much of blessing in the gardening and the care of surroundings, for when this is accomplished in love of the creation the second-density flowers, plants, and small animals are aware of this service and return it.

Questioner: On one end of the house are four stalls that have been occupied by horses. Would it be appropriate or necessary to modify in any way the condition of that area even though it is outside the living area?

Ra: I am Ra. There has been no undesirable negative energy stored in this area. Therefore, it is acceptable if physically cleaned.

Questioner: Is there any other comment about our new location that Ra could make?

Ra: I am Ra. We are gratified that this query was offered to us for there has been a concentration of negative thought patterns at a distance north to 10° of north, approximately 45 of what you call yards extending therefrom to all four directions in a rectangular but irregular shape.

We ask that the garlic be strung approximately 60-70 feet beyond the far verge of this area which is approximately 57 yards from the dwelling on a bearing north to 10° of north. We suggest that the garlic be hung in the funnel so that the energies are drawn into the south small end of the funnel and traduced northward and away from the dwelling. The procedure of the hanging will be one for testing your ingenuity but there are several ways to suspend the substance and it is well to do so.

Questioner: I envision a cardboard funnel approximately three feet in length and then a small cardboard of the same configuration inside of that funnel, the garlic placed between the two cardboard surfaces so that the garlic actually makes a funnel itself held in place by the two cardboard cones. The smaller end of the cone would be toward the house and the larger end would be away from the house.

I would also like to know that I am accurately aware of the position that we are talking about. Taking a specific point on the house such as the front door, I suspect that the direction is up toward the road that leads out of the property. An exact measurement from the doorknob to the center of the area of negativity of which we speak would be helpful. Would Ra comment on that?

Ra: I am Ra. We were working from the other side of the dwelling. However, the exact distance is not important due to the generalized nature of the astral leavings. The heading would be approximately 10° east of north to 5° east of north. This is not a heading in which absolute fastidiousness needs be paramount. The yardage is approximately as given. As to the hanging of the garlic, it must be able to be blown by the wind. Therefore, the structure which was envisioned is less than optimal. We might suggest the stringing between two placed posts on either side of the funnel of the strung cloves.

Questioner: Would a wire framework such as chickenwire which has a small inch-square mesh or something like that shaped into a cone with the garlic attached to the cone with the small end toward the house and the open end away from the house strung between two poles be appropriate?

Ra: I am Ra. That is appropriate. You see in this case the center of the negativity is as described, but there will be a general cleansing of the dwelling and its acreage by this means. One action you might take in order to improve the efficacy of the cleansing of the environment is the walking of the perimeter with the opened clove in hand, swinging the clove. No words need be said unless each wishes to silently or verbally speak those words given for garlic previously.

Questioner: Is there any other thing that we can do to prepare this new place that Ra could mention at this time?

Ra: I am Ra. There are no more specific suggestions for the specific location you contemplate. In general, the cleanliness is most helpful. The removal from the mind complex of those thoughts not of harmony is most helpful and those practices which increase faith and will that the spirit may do its work are most helpful.

Questioner: After the suggestions are accomplished with respect to cleansing of the property, does Ra anticipate our contact with Ra will be as efficient there as in this particular place?

Ra: I am Ra. All places in which this group dwells in love and thanksgiving are acceptable to us.

Questioner: Thank you. A question has been asked which I will ask at this time. In processing the catalyst of dreams is there a universal language of the unconscious mind which may be used to interpret dreams, or does each entity have a unique language in its own unconscious mind which it may use to interpret the meaning of dreams?

Ra: I am Ra. There is what might be called a partial vocabulary of the dreams due to the common heritage of all mind/body/spirit complexes. Due to each entity's unique incarnational experiences there is an overlay which grows to be a larger and larger proportion of the dream vocabulary as the entity gains experience.

Questioner: Thank you. In the last session you indicated in the statement about the immature male meeting the immature female that the information exchanged was quite different with respect to what occurred because of the veil. Would you give an example of the information exchange prior to the veil for the same case?

Ra: I am Ra. Given this same case; that is, the random red-ray sexual arousal being activated in both male and female, the communication would far more likely have been to the subject of the satisfying of that red-ray, sexual impulse. When this had occurred other information such as the naming

could be offered with clear perception. It is to be noted that the catalyst which may be processed by the pre-veil experience is insignificant compared to the catalyst offered to the thoroughly bemused male and female after the veil. The confusion which this situation, simplistic though it is, offers is representative of the efficiency of the enlargement of the catalytic processes occurring after the veiling.

Questioner: For the condition of meeting after the veiling process, either entity will choose, as a function of its previous biases or Card Four, the experience and the way in which it will handle the situation with respect to polarity, therefore probably producing more catalyst for itself along the chosen path of polarization. Would Ra comment on this statement?

Ra: I am Ra. This statement is correct.

Questioner: In Card Four in the last session we spoke of the shape of the skirt and it has occurred to us that the skirt of the entity representing the archetype of the Experience of the Mind is extended to the left to indicate that other-selves would not be able to get close to this entity if it had chosen the left-hand path. There would be a greater separation between it and other-selves, whereas if it had chosen the right-hand path there would be much less of a separation. Would Ra comment on that observation?

Ra: I am Ra. The student is perceptive.

Questioner: And it seems that the square upon which the entity sits, which is almost totally black, is a representation of the material illusion and the white cat is guarding the right-hand path which is now separated in experience from the left. Would Ra comment on that observation?

Ra: I am Ra. O student, your sight almost sees that which was intended. However, the polarities need no guardians. What, then, O student, needs the guard?

Questioner: What I meant to say was that the entity is guarded along the right-hand path, once it has chosen this path, from effects of the material illusion that are of the negative polarity. Would Ra comment on that?

Ra: I am Ra. This is an accurate perception of our intent, O student. We may note that the great cat guards in direct proportion to the purity of the manifestations of intention and the purity of inner work done along this path.

Questioner: From that statement I interpret the following. If the Experience of the Mind has sufficiently chosen the right-hand path, and as total purity is approached in the choosing of the right-hand path, then total imperviousness from the effect of the left-hand catalyst is also approached. Is this correct?

Ra: I am Ra. This is exquisitely perceptive. The seeker which has purely chosen the service-to-others path shall certainly not have a variant apparent incarnational experience. There is no outward shelter in your illusion from the gusts, flurries, and blizzards of quick and cruel catalyst.

However, to the pure, all that is encountered speaks of the love and the light of the one infinite Creator. The cruelest blow is seen with an ambiance of challenges offered and opportunities to come. Thusly, the great pitch of light is held high above such an one so that all interpretation may be seen to be protected by light.

Questioner: I have often wondered about the action of random and programmed catalyst with respect to the entity with the very strong positive or negative polarization. Would either polarity be free to a great extent from random catalyst such as great natural catastrophes or warfare or something like that which generates a lot of random catalyst in the physical vicinity of a highly polarized entity? Does this great cat, then, have an effect on such random catalyst on the right-hand path?

Ra: I am Ra. In two circumstances this is so. Firstly, if there has been the preincarnative choice that, for instance, one shall not take life in the service of the cultural group, events shall fall in a protective manner. Secondly, if any entity is able to dwell completely in unity the only harm that may occur to it is the changing of the outward physical, yellow-ray vehicle into the more light-filled mind/body/spirit complex's vehicle by the process of death. All other suffering and pain is as nothing to one such as this.

We may note that this perfect configuration of the mind, body, and spirit complexes, while within the third-density vehicle, is extraordinarily rare.

Questioner: Am I to understand, then, that there is no protection at all if the Experience of the Mind has chosen the left-hand path and that path is traveled? All random catalyst may affect the negatively polarized individual as a function of the statistical nature of the random catalyst. Is this correct?

Ra: I am Ra. This is correct. You may note some of those of your peoples which, at this space/time nexus, seek places of survival. This is due to the lack of protection when service to self is invoked.

Questioner: The possibility of the legs of the entity of Card Four being at right angles was linked with the tesseract[11], mentioned in a much earlier session by Ra, as the direction of transformation from space/time into time/space and I was thinking that possibly it was also linked with the crux ansata. Am I in any way correct in this observation?

Ra: I am Ra. This shall be the last query of this working, as transferred energy wanes. The observation of the right angles and their transformational meaning is most perceptive, O student. Each of the images leading to the Transformations of Mind, Body, and Spirit and ultimately to the great transformative Choice has the increasing intensity of increasing articulation of concept; that is to say, each image in which you find this angle may increasingly be seen to be a more and more stridently calling voice of opportunity to use each resource, be it experience as you now observe or further images, for the grand work of the adept which builds towards transformation using the spirit's bountiful shuttle to intelligent infinity. Please ask any brief queries at this space/time.

Questioner: Is there anything that we can do to make the instrument more comfortable or to improve the contact?

Ra: I am Ra. We observe some small worsening of the distortions of the dorsal side. This is due to the nature of the beginning use of the swirling waters. The difficulties are physically accentuated as the swirling waters begin to aid the musculature surrounding the nexi of distortions. We encourage the swirling waters and note that complete immersion in them is somewhat more efficacious than the technique now used .

We ask that the support group attempt to aid the instrument in remembering to preserve the physical energies and not expend them upon movements associated with the packing, as you call this activity,

---

[11] tesseract: in speculative mathematics, a cube which has developed at least one additional dimension.

and the movement between geographical locations upon your sphere.

The alignments are excellent. All is well.

We leave you glorying in the love and in the light of the one infinite Creator. Go forth, therefore, rejoicing in the mighty peace of the one infinite Creator. Adonai. 🜚

L/L RESEARCH

L/L Research is a subsidiary of
Rock Creek Research &
Development Laboratories, Inc.

P.O. Box 5195
Louisville, KY 40255-0195

www.llresearch.org

Rock Creek is a non-profit
corporation dedicated to
discovering and sharing
information which may aid in
the spiritual evolution of
humankind.

SUNDAY MEDITATION
SEPTEMBER 5, 1982

(M1 channeling)

[I am Hatonn.] I am now with this instrument. I greet you, my friends, with the love and the light of the infinite Creator. One reason you have so much trouble with pollution on your planet, you do not stop to enjoy the beauty of the streams, the beauty of your parks, the beauty of your sunset. People who see the beauty do not throw things in the streams, do not cause pollution. You are worried about your pollution, but your lack of appreciation of the beauty in the world is the cause of your pollution. Your young children should be taught to see the beauty of nature, the beauty of human beings. People would not be mistreated if the original nature of each person was appreciated. When a channel is lowest from abuse, that particular individual will never come again. People who love beauty know how to treat it. Never be so busy that you don't stop to enjoy the beauty of the flowers, the beauty of the trees and the beauty of the sunset. I am Hatonn. I leave this instrument.

(C channeling)

I am Hatonn, and I am with this instrument. We greet you again, especially those new and those who have been away but have rejoined the group. We would this evening speak but briefly through as many of the new instruments as wish to practice this evening so as to further [their] confidence and hone their abilities. We are always indeed more than grateful when allowed to aid any who seek to serve in the capacity of vocal channeling, for each aids us in that our few meager words may aid those of your planet who are searching and seeking the knowledge of the love and the light that is the one infinite Creator.

We would now switch our contact to another, speak a few words, pass on. We now transfer. I am Hatonn.

(A channeling)

I am Hatonn. I am now with this instrument, and we greet you again this evening. As we said, we wish to just speak a few words through this new instrument—correction—this instrument. We wish to say that as you work your lives on this planet, that you remember that you are indeed alive, living in what some call an illusion. But if it was not for this illusion, you would miss getting to learn some of the greatest lessons in learning to love and to care.

You do not need to wish to be somewhere else, for look about you. Is not where you are a great and beautiful place? Do not be quick to see what is not good, for in all things there is a purpose and a reason, no matter how bleak you may see it. Therefore, we say in closing, remember to live, because you are alive and you are here and you chose to be. We now wish to transfer to another instrument. I am Hatonn.

(M1 channeling)

I am Hatonn. I am now with this instrument. I greet you again in the love and the light of the infinite Creator. Expanding our earlier conversation—make yourself larger with beauty, with friendship, with love. Did you see something beautiful today? Did you stop to admire it? Did it make you bigger? Were you with your friends? Did you feel their affection, and did they feel yours? Did you see someone that you truly love? These are the things that expand your soul. Do not become so involved in the physical that the beauty of your life and your soul are left unfulfilled. I am Hatonn. I leave this instrument.

(Carla channeling)

I am Hatonn, and I greet you once again, my friends, in the love and the light of the infinite Creator. We had intended to move to M2, and found that this instrument was receiving the signals in a particularly sensitive manner, so that it would perhaps be appropriate to use this instrument and then move on to the one known as M2 and the one known as S. We would like at this time to pause so that the brothers and sisters of Laitos may move among you if you would mentally request their presence. It is their especial honor to be an assistant to those who wish to deepen their meditative state, and to feel the presence of the Confederation of Planets. We shall pause for them at this time.

(Pause)

(Carla channeling)

I am Hatonn, and I am again with this instrument. It gives us pleasure to speak to this instrument as we are aware that our opportunities to speak to these, our beloved friends, through this instrument are few. My friends, we speak to you of the beauties and the opportunities of living a full and generous life, and indeed that is the great first part of the lesson of love—to apprehend the nature of your surroundings, of your environment, of your opportunities and of yourself; to apprehend the one infinite Creator in all that lies about you from the smallest particle to the farthest sound of the distant car driven by a stranger to a place unknown to you. Wherever that stranger goes, so do you go. You are with all beings. You are a part of all that there is, yet the opportunities for the learning of the lessons of love are inexhaustible.

There is a great second part that we would speak to you about, and that is the part of the hand that cuts the flower, of the reaper that harvests the grain. My friends, if you are too comfortable in your thinking about life, about truth, and about the Creator, reexamine your circumstances and find out where your challenge lies, for there is no still and unlearned place in the pilgrimage of the soul. You shall be forever learning, forever blessed with the challenge. Indeed, my friends, there is a strength, a placid calm, the deepest night unlit by any star within your being into which you may go for comfort and wisdom. But from that great source of love and strength and power there comes a time when you must get up from your meditation and go forward.

Try, if you can, my friends, to know that feeling that the harvest [of] each day represents to you. Each day, my friends, those things which you have sown in the past may come into bloom. Each day, something that you could not do before, or have prayed to be able to do may finally come into bloom, and each day, you must examine the possibility that there is something that you may reap and offer to the creation. Perhaps not to the part of creation that you would wish, perhaps to an entity or a situation that you would far rather were not as it were. But as we said previously, there is no circumstance without its purpose.

Investigate your own flowering abilities as each day brings its situation and challenges, for you did not come into this illusion to gaze idly by while others learned. No, my friends, you came to walk a path that has been walked by many and shall be walked by many more. We came seeking; we are with you as you seek. But your greatest resource is your own carefully and beautifully intentioned past. Whatever has been done ill, whatever error you may have committed, you have also sown many thoughts, many ideas, many intentions, many desires for the truth, for love, for the Creator. Each thought will flower in its time and each flower will be needed, so watch your garden.

We would now leave this instrument and transfer to the one known as K. I am Hatonn.

(K channeling)

I am Hatonn. I am now with this instrument, and I would say a few words along the ones that have already been spoken. We read in your scriptures about the light that is set on a hill for all to see. A light shining in darkness is really quite easy to see. My friends, as you go about the routine which is oftentimes seemingly unimportant, and perhaps even dull and boring, if you would practice serenity and peace and joy, all of which are deep inside you as has already been indicated, you will indeed be like that light set on a hill. This may be difficult to learn, but practice is necessary for anything that you accomplish, and so I encourage you to practice these attributes in your daily life. You will not only be of help to others about you, but you will grow in the process. I now leave this instrument. I am Hatonn.

(S channeling)

I am Hatonn, and we greet you once again this evening in the love and the light of our one infinite Creator. Many times this evening have we done so, and this greeting, my brothers and sisters, can never be spoken enough or felt within your souls enough. We say this not only to greet you, but to instill in you the feeling of the light and love of the Creator. For this love and this light, my friends, is that which all of you have chosen to seek and to find in your lives and to spread throughout your world to help the peoples of this planet see this love and this light that is shared so intensely among you. You are so very bright. It should not be hard for anyone to let their light shine, to see in the future how one moment of light could change and bring about so many changes in so many peoples' lives on your planet.

My friends, we have spoken long this evening. It was our great pleasure and great joy to be called among so many. We would want you to know, as we have said in the past, that we are with you if but you call in a moment of need or a moment of quiet reflection to aid your meditation, to aid you in any way we can in your particular search for the light and for the path leading to that light. We realize that there are times when you feel very much alone, but, my friends, you are never alone. Look around you. Feel the Creator in everything you touch, everything you see. Feel His grace, His love. There is nothing that does not exude His light. And if you can but see and be aware, you will never need feel lonely or without the support that you feel you need to grow or to sustain you in your search.

We would at this time leave this instrument and transfer this contact. I am known to you as Hatonn.

(M2 channeling)

I am Hatonn. I am with this instrument. We greet you again in the love and the light of the infinite Creator. We will say just a few words through this instrument in closing because this instrument is fatigued. It is again, as always, a great joy for us to share this time and our thoughts with you. We are forever at your beck and call. Just think our names, and we are with you in your meditations and in your daily routine. Our thoughts go with you. We leave you now in the love and the light. I am Hatonn.

(M1 channeling)

I am Hatonn. I am now with this instrument. I greet you with the love and the light of the infinite Creator. You cannot imagine how much it means to us to speak to M2. It is not easy, but for some reason he had a special meaning for us. *(Inaudible).* Nourish your body because it houses your soul. The physical is very important. But remember, it is a temporary covering for your soul. Each day nourish yourself. Nourish the souls of your friends. When you are speaking with your friends and you compliment them, this is a greater favor than inviting them to dinner. Feeding them physically is a temporary thing. Expanding their soul is permanent. Try to see the good in everybody, but never forget to tell them. Many times you appreciate attractive things about your friends and you forget to tell them. This gives you no chance to expand their soul. Remember your soul and the souls of your friends are very important. Help them to expand their soul and never let a day go by that you are not conscious that your soul will go on. The physical is very good for helping the soul, but it really is what you people call a [whirlwind.] You feel you need three meals a day, but how many of you stop and feed your soul? When you go to bed at night, do you think of the food that you have given your soul? Are you involved with growing? Keep your soul as the valuable thing. All other things are [vapid.] Basically, in the long run, they are unimportant. I am Hatonn. I leave this instrument.

(Jim channeling)

I am Latwii, and I greet you, my friends, in the love and the light of the one infinite Creator. We are most honored once again to be allowed to join this group and to offer ourselves in the capacity of attempting to answer those queries which have value to you. May we then ask if there might be a query with which we might begin?

K: I would like to ask one, some thoughts on a subject that all of us are going to be concerned with soon, and that is moving from one place to another. I understand that you learn from that and meet new people and grow. The difficulty that I have is with feeling sad about leaving friends and family that are loved ones, and I could use some help with this.

I am Latwii, and am aware of your query, my sister. May we begin by suggesting that though there are what you call periods of time which seem to remain unchanging, the true nature of your illusion is one of constant change. Each moment is a treasure which offers the opportunity …

(Side one of tape ends.)

(Jim channeling)

I am Latwii, and am once again with this instrument. These moments offer the opportunity for you to expand your experience of yourself, and therefore the one Creator as well. As you move through each moment, there is an unending variety of opportunities to find love, to know wisdom, to feel unity, or to make whatever response is yours to make. Each moment builds upon the experience which is significant for each to undertake in the incarnation. Each moment, therefore, offers the opportunity for the type of growth which you might call a transformation of your being, so that constantly you have the opportunity to live within the moment, to allow the old to pass from your being, to experience a tiny death, and to be born again into yet another moment.

For each entity there are also those times of greater significance and larger transformations. There are various ways in which each entity experiences such transformations. The joining of couples in marriage, the birthing of children, the forming of communities, and the moving of the family or group from one location to another are obvious examples of these types of transformations. These experiences offer the entity a new beginning, and offer the entity not only growth which has been accomplished, but the opportunity to make the self new once again.

As you look about you, whether you are in the position of moving, having moved, or remaining in the location which you have known for some period of what you call time, you may see that which you call your past as having yielded the fruits which make you now what you are. Bless those experiences, my friends, for they have been well accomplished and have done their duty, shall we say. But also look to what you call your future so that there might be the symbolic opening within yourself to yet further experiences, for your life was not meant to become as the stagnant pool, but is meant to flow as the river.

May we answer you further, my sister?

K: No, thank you.

We thank you. Is there another question at this time?

E: I have a question, Latwii. It refers to the interminable questions I was asking last week, and that is, I know of an entity that has multiple personalities, and I was of the understanding that it would be very difficult for her ever to integrate her personalities. And last week I learned that one of her personalities is teaching another how to play the violin, and I would like you to comment on that, and how it relates to her possibility of putting herself back together, if you know what I mean.

I am Latwii, and am aware of your query, my brother. This entity has, as is true for each entity, incarnated for specific reasons. In general, each entity may be seen as the one infinite Creator in search of Itself. As this entity of which you speak makes that journey of seeking for the self, it has found a quite unique experience available to it. There are portions of each entity which remain hidden during what you call the incarnation, and yield their fruits, their skills, only in subliminal fashion. For this entity, these portions are not so hidden. As we mentioned before, this entity has experienced other portions of itself entering through what we then called tears or holes in the veil which separates the conscious and unconscious minds. As these portions or personalities of this entity's greater self begin to find an integration, then there is a finding of greater portions of the self for this entity. And as this particular experience which you refer to occurs, there is the melding of the self as portions which seemed divorced begin what might be termed a communication, one with the other. This is the fulfillment of a portion of this entity's purpose of its incarnation.

May we answer you further, my brother?

E: No, not at the time, thank you.

We thank you. Is there another question at this time?

K: Yes. Scripture tells about Jesus casting out devils and the disciples talked about casting out devils. Would you comment on the meaning of this?

I am Latwii, and am aware of your query, my sister. For those entities upon your planet who have sought the meaning of life, and the nature of truth, there has been the answer to the calling in an infinite variety of ways. Those works which you refer to as the holy scriptures of your Bible are but one example of an answer, or more correctly, a series of answers to a series of callings. Each answer, therefore, is made understandable by the one answering the call for the one who calls. Therefore, you might note that different terms can be used for those entities which are described in this work as devils or evil spirits.

Forget not, my friends, that there is one Creator and one creation, and many portions of that creation are of what is normally called the darker side, for there is night and there is light and together they make the day. Those entities of the negative nature are those entities which pursue the polarity of serving the self, which is to say, they draw unto the self the light which surrounds them and do not reflect it or radiate it unto others, for such radiation is of the positive polarity. Entities of the so-called negative nature, therefore, might seem at times to be in opposition, as you might call it, to entities of a positive polarity. Yet, my friends, in truth, this is not so. Each serves the other so that the one Creator which resides in both might know Itself in greater varieties and intensities and manners of being.

Yet, with the, shall we say, short run of time there might be the inharmonious joining of positive and negative. When entities of a positive nature are hindered in their attempts to be of service to others, this hindrance is a portion of the dance of the Creator. And another portion of that dance might include the entities of positive polarity seeking a purification of their being, of their place or location, and of those types of service which they seek to render in such purification or such casting out of demons, as it is called in these scriptures. It is

recognized by those of purely positive polarity that though they ask those of the negative nature to remove themselves from the immediate surroundings, yet all are seen as the one Creator. Within certain levels of the illusions which create the densities of being, it is more appropriate from time to time for such purifications to occur. Yet, all action is the Creator which is experiencing Itself.

May we answer you further, my sister?

K: Yes, just one clarification to see if I understand. If one entity is seeking the love and the light and seeking to be the light set on a hill and another is of the negative polarity, or as you say, the negative nature, then sometimes it would be good for the ones seeking to absent themselves from the one that is of the negative nature, shall I say?

I am Latwii, and am aware of your query, my sister. In general, this is a correct summary of our suggestions and comments. We would only add that as the illusion of the separations of the two polarities takes place through the means of purification, it is most purely accomplished when it is realized that in truth there is no separation. This may seem a paradox, and indeed the illusion which you inhabit has many of these seeming paradoxes to offer.

May we answer you further, my sister?

K: I believe that answers the question. Thank you.

I am Latwii. We are most grateful to you. Is there another question at this time?

E: I have another question, Latwii, and it concerns the Bible. And that is, in the story of Adam and Eve, when their children are of age, they are instructed to go out and marry amongst the tribes, and my question is, who are these beings that they go out and marry, and where do they come from?

I am Latwii, and am aware of your query, my brother. We find you have discovered a point which many who read your book called the Holy Bible have not noticed or given great attention to. It is often felt that the descriptions made in the first few books of this work are descriptions only of an allegorical nature, when this is not in truth the case.

There were at the time in which this story was written, many entities inhabiting your planet. These entities were those who had been transferred from another within your own solar system to the planet Earth to complete the third-density cycle which they were unable to complete upon that planet which you call Mars. Their inability to complete that cycle upon their home planet was due to the bellicose nature of the means in which their societies interacted. Such warring natures created an environment upon that planet which did not permit the completing of its cycle without a great period of what you call time devoted to the healing of the entity that is that planet. Therefore, the transfer was undertaken by entities of the Confederation of Planets in Service to the Infinite Creator who felt that not only the transfer, but the genetic mixing, shall we say, of their beingness with the beingness of the entities being transferred to your planet would be helpful to these entities who had undergone what might be called much stress upon their home planet and who were in somewhat of a state of confusion, shall we say.

Therefore, your planet began its third-density experience 75,000 of your years in the past as you measure time, not with only its own third-density population which had evolved from the second-density life forms, but also had added unto these entities those of the planet which your peoples call Mars.

May we answer you further, my brother?

E: No, thank you.

I am Latwii. We thank you. Is there another question at this time?

K: Yes, that reminds me of the Urantia book. Would you comment on the validity of the book?

I am Latwii, and am aware of your query, my sister. This book, which your peoples call the Urantia book, was compiled by entities existing within the so-called inner planes of your planet. These entities sought to be of service by explaining in their terms, yet using some veiling of explanation, the nature of creation and the nature of evolution upon this planet. These entities sought to be of this service in response to a call of the third-density entities of your planet many, many of your years in your past. As with all answers to those who call, the information offered is stated in such a way as to speak only to those who call. Therefore, the information might be seen to be of a limited use, as is any information communicated in this manner, including the information which we have to offer.

May we answer you further, my sister?

K: Then I'm assuming this is true of what we call the Bible also.

I am Latwii, and am aware of your query, my sister. To our knowledge, this is true of any information offered by any source to any who call. For any information is a distortion of that which is attempted in the transmission, that is to say, the nature of truth, the nature of creation, the nature of the Creator is as it is. There are those who have traveled the path of seeking who have discovered more and more about truth, shall we say, but to attempt to describe it in what you call words is not to reveal the truth, but to point a direction towards the truth. Words are not the experience, therefore, all words are distortion of the experience.

May we answer you further, my sister?

K: Yes. I think I understand that then, it would be proper to say that as consciousness evolves, then truth is constantly evolving also?

I am Latwii, and am aware of your query, my sister. In one respect, this is correct, for what is true to any entity is only true as it is perceived. What is true for one changes, therefore the truth for the one changes. Yet the nature of all that is does not in its essence change. For all that is is as it is. Yet the one Creator is a being which seeks experience of Itself. There is a portion of the one Creator which this group has come to know as intelligent infinity which is not created, for it is not a portion of the creation, but is that from which the creation springs. Its nature is as it is. Yet, what springs from it constantly evolves and seems to add to it. Yet, in that addition there is no true change. This again is a paradox which we cannot resolve for you using the language of words, but we are hindered in this respect, for at this time this is our means of communication with you. We apologize for the inability that we recognize, that is, our inability to express the heart of this concept.

May we answer you further, my sister?

K: No, that helps a lot. I think that's enough for right now. Thank you.

I am Latwii. We are most grateful to you, my sister. Is there another question at this time?

A: Yes, Latwii, I have a question. In this group of meditation we put forth work in tuning so as to open [more] to one center thought of light, and it has sometimes been necessary during the meditation for people to leave the group, and you have mentioned that this causes a disruption in the circle. And I'm wondering if there's anything that can be done to cause less of a disruption if someone needs to leave?

I am Latwii, and am aware of your query, my sister. Should it occur that one must remove the self from the circle of seeking for a short period of time, as you call it, the easiest method to utilize for the remaining and retaining of the unified seeking is to leave as silently as possible. And prior to the leaving, to image within the mind the circle of light which is the group, and to see that position which you are leaving as sealed by light. Then, upon the reentry into the group, seeing that circle reinforced once again, and to make the circle of light stronger within your mind, and to feel once again your unity in seeking with the group.

May we answer you further, my sister?

A: No, thank you.

I am Latwii. We thank you. Is there another question at this time?

M1: I have a question, Latwii, concerning multiple personalities. Is it good for the personality to become integrated or is it better for them to remain separate?

I am Latwii, and am aware of your query, my sister. We cannot make a general statement which covers each separate case, for there are entities who experience the phenomenon which you call the multiple personality for the reasons that are knowable only to the entity, and perhaps shall not be known fully for the entire span of the incarnation. It might be thought more helpful for an entity to have the unified focus of its being to work upon its evolution of mind, of body, and of spirit, and for most upon your planet this is indeed so. But it is also possible that for some entities there is the need to splinter, shall we say, a portion of the self from another portion of the self so that through the dynamic tension which is created between the portions which are split, a certain series of experiences and lessons might be had.

Each entity upon your planet from time to time experiences some form of this splitting, for such a splitting, when accomplished within certain boundaries, shall we say, is a means for the enhancing of the experience of the entity in that certain portions of the self are then able to express their characteristics in more profound manners, and therefore might be more easily noticed by the entity as a whole or unified being. Each entity within this group this evening has at some time felt a portion of its own being moving, shall we say, away from the greater portion of the self. This frequently occasions the feelings of schizophrenia, shall we say, or the feelings of losing the control of the self for a period of time. These instances are often helpful in what you call the long run, for they enable experiences to occur which then add to the lessons which are set forth by the entity.

May we answer you further, my sister?

M1: No, that's very good. Thank you.

I am Latwii. We thank you. Is there another question at this time?

(Pause)

I am Latwii. Since we do not perceive further queries, may we say it has been a great honor to be asked to join your group this evening. We are most grateful for each opportunity to share our meager thoughts with those seekers who ask those queries which have meaning on their journey. We remind each that we are but your brothers and your sisters, and the thoughts we offer have no degree of infallibility. We suggest the contemplation and the acceptance of those which have meaning, and the discarding of any thoughts which have no value. At any time, should you ask our presence for your meditations, we would be most honored to join you. We leave you now, my friends, rejoicing in the love and in the light of the one infinite Creator. We are known to you as Latwii. Adonai vasu borragus. ✦

L/L Research is a subsidiary of
Rock Creek Research &
Development Laboratories, Inc.

P.O. Box 5195
Louisville, KY 40255-0195

www.llresearch.org

Rock Creek is a non-profit
corporation dedicated to
discovering and sharing
information which may aid in
the spiritual evolution of
humankind.

INTENSIVE MEDITATION
SEPTEMBER 9, 1982

(Jim channeling)

I am Hatonn, and greet you, my friends, in the love and the light of the one infinite Creator. It is our great privilege to be able to join your group this evening. We thank each entity present for the desire we feel within each to be of the service which you have called the vocal channeling. We would begin the process this evening with the newer instruments so that we might devote the greatest amount of what you call time to their initial contact. We shall be working with our brothers and sisters of Laitos this evening, and at this time, for each new instrument who is desirous of feeling the initial contact from the Confederation, our brothers and sisters of Laitos shall pass among you and begin the conditioning process. A mental request is all that is necessary for the conditioning vibration to be experienced. You may notice any one of a variety of manifestations of this vibration. Simply request that contact be made and then allow yourself to experience the result. If at any time this process should be uncomfortable in any way, simply ask that the vibration be reduced, and if comfort is not immediately noticed, then request that the vibration be removed and it shall be done immediately.

We would first begin by conditioning the one known as N, if this entity would wish to receive our vibrations, and after a few moments of this conditioning would then attempt to make our initial contact with this entity. It is most helpful to rest the mind in its analytical processes so that the thoughts which become apparent to the inner eye may be spoken clearly. To attempt any determination as to whether the thoughts are of the Confederation or are from the entity's own subconscious is not helpful. This process is helpful at a later time after the meditation has been completed. Therefore, the simple speaking of whatever thoughts are apparent is that which shall aid the beginning of the telepathic contact.

At this time we shall attempt to speak our identification through the one known as N. We shall repeat, "I am Hatonn," until this instrument has been able to perceive our thoughts. We would at this time transfer this contact to the one known as N. I am Hatonn.

(Jim channeling)

I am Hatonn, and am once again with this instrument. We feel that we have been successful in making our initial contact with the one known as N, but find that there is some doubt on this entity's mind that the thoughts were indeed from our contact. This is quite a normal beginning, and we would reassure the entity that there is no great trick or difficulty associated with the telepathic contact and the simple speaking of our thoughts is all that is necessary to initiate and continue it. We shall attempt once again therefore to speak our identification through the one known as N. I am Hatonn.

(Jim channeling)

I am Hatonn, and am with this instrument once again. We thank the one known as N for her great desire to be of this service, and we assure her that though she has not been able to vocalize our initial thoughts, we are most pleased with the ease which we have found in making our first contact with this instrument. We also reassure her that a simple period of practice, shall we say, is all that is necessary for this process to find a home within this entity. We shall now move to those instruments who have somewhat more experience in this process and therefore shall not identify the instrument to whom the contact shall be transferred. I am Hatonn.

(M1 channeling)

I am Hatonn. I am now with this instrument. I greet you with the love and the light of the infinite Creator. The people of your density have something called depression. There are many ways to overcome the situation. If you can pretend you are back in the second density as an animal and look at your life, and find that you have food, shelter, and animal conveniences, you would realize that your life is not as bad as you think it is. You can also go into the fourth density in your mind and look at your life as an observer. You will see that the things that bother are not immediate. You have the comfort that you saw as an animal. You have food, shelter and the necessities for today. If you can get out of yourself, and look at yourself as you someday will be, you will be able to leave some of your depression.

Depression is a condition seen mostly in the third density. The forgetting process keeps you from seeing the total picture, but because you imagine you see the total picture, you become depressed. If you could see the total picture, you would realize that the problems that are bothering you are only a small part of the total picture. It is very helpful to go either direction—back to the second density or imagine yourself beyond the third density. Either of these outlooks will help your depression. I am Hatonn. I leave this instrument.

(K channeling)

I am Hatonn. I greet you, my friends, again in the love and the light of the infinite Creator. Again it gives us great joy to be with this group. At the end of the day at the time of sunset, if you can but look back upon the day and count your blessings, you will find more to be thankful for than you had imagined. If you continue this practice, to look back on the day, you will find that the little things seem to fall away, and there are more things to be thankful for. As your days pass, you learn how to use the energies now available to you to bring about the good things, not only within your own life, but in the lives of those about you. The understanding of how to use the energies that are yours each day is very important. All the energy that you need is available if it is requested, and as has been indicated in times past, the beauty of the sunset and the quietness at the end of the day restores the soul.

Again we would like to express the joy we feel at being in the midst of this group. We now transfer the contact. I am Hatonn.

(A channeling)

I am Hatonn, and we greet you once again, my brothers and sisters, in the love and the light of the one infinite Creator. We do so enjoy coming to your group to feel the love you share, to see the joy. We also watch and see the joyous occasions that you have. We also see the concern of those needing. It also seems to be a worry because of the fear of losing close friends. But you live in an illusion, one which seems to be a time of separation. But is it really? Where can people go so that they are totally separated? Since we all are one, there seems to be no need to worry of losing something. But much can be gained from learning the lessons in your illusion, and we are sometimes envious of the lessons you can learn. We are joyous though, in being able to watch you grow, to learn to love, and if ever you wish our presence, you need but ask. We shall be there. We are more than happy to serve you in this manner.

We shall now transfer this contact to another instrument. I am Hatonn.

(S channeling)

I am Hatonn, and once again we greet you, our brothers and sisters, in the love and in the light of our one infinite Creator. This evening we have spoken of love that is shared between friends, between others like yourselves who have similar interests. But, my friends, do you take that extra step to share that love with the people whom you meet in your everyday lives, to share that love that is so abundant among you? To share the light, the Creator's love? Is this so hard to do? We have spoken of sharing among your families, as indeed you are a family. And to include others in that family would be an accomplishment along the path which you seek, for that path is service.

This entity—we correct this instrument. This instrument is fatigued this evening and having trouble maintaining our contact. Therefore at this time, we would transfer to another instrument. I am Hatonn

(M1 channeling)

I am Hatonn, and am once again with this instrument. I greet you with the love and the light of the infinite Creator. I know in your heart you are uneasy because the more established instruments are leaving. If letters or tapes could be sent back and forth, if part of a letter or part of a tape could be read at the beginning of a meeting, or if the instruments who are leaving would set aside this time to be with you in spirit for a short time until you feel more comfortable alone, it would be very helpful. If they could set aside fifteen minutes on a Sunday evening, you would not feel so alone. They would be with you in spirit. If they could send the thoughts they have during that time to you, you would know you are not alone. You will not feel so uncomfortable and can continue the spirit of the meeting. I leave this instrument. I am Hatonn.

(M2 channeling)

I am Hatonn, and I greet you again in the love and the light of the infinite Creator. We are pleased to see the progress of each of the channels. You are no longer new channels. You have grown in confidence. Your desire has been steady. You have worked and prayed to attain as pure a channel as possible. You have an opportunity, brothers and sisters, before you to use this channel medium to continue to share with those that are around you. Your group will grow and it will become small. It will grow and become small again, perhaps. For such is the nature of your group, to always be willing to serve others that pass through; to always have the watchful eye for someone in need; to always have the helping hand for someone who may have stumbled.

You have grown strong, especially through the bonding of the friendships and your love with one

another. While many of you will be physically separated, surely you know by now that you are not separated at all. But just as we are with you at your call, your brothers and sisters in the spirit of your cause are also with you at your call. They share in your joy, they share in your sorrow, and especially they share in your strength. And this is the strength that will help you carry on many times when the distractions are great or the interest wanes, and you wonder, "Is there still a need for this type of service?"; when weeks may pass and many of the members that have frequented this road of learning have gone their separate ways. But your desire is strong, my brothers and sisters, and it will always bring you back. Bring you back together. You are a family in unison who will serve those in need. Each time you come together you grow in the strength of your commitment to serve. A legacy of sorts is left to you, and [as] a very able and willing group you are to take it upon your shoulders. Our blessings are on all of you.

We leave this instrument. I am Hatonn.

(Jim channeling)

I am Hatonn, and greet you all once again in love and light. Before we take our leave of this group, we would perform what is for us somewhat of an unusual honor, and that is the attempting to answer your queries on this evening. We usually are not asked to perform this task, for it is most often our brothers and sisters of Latwii who are requested to perform this service, but it is our honor this evening, for there are the needs upon our vibration of love which we feel we might be most able to fulfill. May we ask if there is a question which we might make an answer to at this time?

S: I have a question. My question is, how will I know when it is you in my consciousness and not my own input? I am fearful to say what is on my mind and not what is knowledge from you.

I am Hatonn. My sister, your concern is indeed well-founded, for it is most helpful for the desire of each new instrument to be strong in purity. This you have achieved. May we also then suggest that in order to initiate the vocalized channeling process that you speak those thoughts which appear in your mind while you are meditating within a group which has devoted itself to this type of service. You will not know with any degree of what you call certainty that the thoughts belong to us or belong to you. This is necessary so that each contact is what we call free will contact. That is, no truth of any reproducible or certain nature may be given. This aids the new instruments and each entity much more in what you call the long run than having absolute proof that the thoughts belong to us and not to you, for the exercise of faith and will together are most helpful to any entity's growth. To have the work done or the proof given without some doubt being overcome, shall we say, on the part of the entity is not most helpful, for it does not take any faculty of will or faith for an entity to have proven for it that such and such a phenomenon exists. Therefore, we suggest that while you are attempting to make the contact with any member of the Confederation of Planets that you speak those thoughts which appear in your mind, and only later attempt to analyze their origin.

May we answer you further, my sister?

S: No, thank you.

I am Hatonn. We thank you. Is there another question at this time?

M1: I have a question. Is it possible that some of us knew you before this incarnation?

I am Hatonn. My sister, all things are quite possible. May we answer you further?

M1: Thanks for that answer to my question.

I am Hatonn. We thank you. Is there another question at this time?

K: Yes. I'd like for you to comment on an experience I had this week. My daughter has trouble sleeping. She came over two nights ago, at 2:30 in the morning, and touched me and scared me half to death, and she said, "Mother, I can't sleep." And because of having to teach the next day, she almost panics when she has trouble sleeping. And so I made a pallet for her, and she lay down on the floor, and I tried to put some energy from my own hands into the solar plexus to help her calm down, and then I got back on the bed, and I found that I couldn't rest. And I thought, well, we're both in a dilemma now, 'cause I don't know what to do. It seemed like I was supposed to be doing something. And so I imagined light beginning at her head and just going down and covering her like a cocoon. And I still couldn't relax myself, and I was afraid my anxiety was going to make her anxiety worse. And then the thought occurred to me. I will seal that light so that it's …

she is completely sealed in this light of peace and rest, and with that thought, I was totally relaxed myself, and I went to sleep and she went to sleep.

And the next morning I thought, I didn't know if she'd been asleep, I know I went to sleep. The next morning I wondered how she was going to be, and she came in before she went to school, and I've never seen her so excited. And I just wondered if that little thing of sealing the light …

(Side one of tape ends.)

(Jim channeling)

I am Hatonn. We have had a small difficulty in perceiving the point of the query which we feel has some merit. May we ask for a summary?

K: Why did … I didn't get relief, and couldn't relax myself until I sealed the light about her. Now, why was that significant for me?

I am Hatonn, and we feel we have a better grasp now of the gist of your query, my sister. It is often the case that those upon your planet who have entered the relationships of a family have ties which are quite close in the experience of your illusion. That your daughter sought your comfort in a period of her own discomfort is the expression of the yearning for the love of the parent, and your response was the completion of that cycle of being. That you sought to seal that cycle's completion was most appropriate, for both of you were engaged in a process of growth which was symbolic in nature, that of the giving and receiving of love. To seal that symbolic learning was indeed to seat it within your being, and was of great aid to your daughter, for she was then more able to feel the love living within her being, and it was then able to provide a new type of perception or energetic being for her.

May we answer you further, my sister?

K: No. That was a good explanation, thank you.

I am Hatonn. We are most grateful to you, my sister. May we attempt another query at this time?

Carla: I have a question from K's question. She so often gets me started on something. I've noticed that sometimes people try the laying on of hands as if they were attempting to take the pain unto themselves. And there is another kind of healing in which a person seems to realize that the healing comes through them and not from them, and therefore they don't take the pain unto themselves, they just allow themselves to be channels of light. And the feeling that one gets from that type of a healing may or may not do anything on the physical plane, but it seems to be a more permanent and a more peaceful feeling.

So I was wondering when K touched her daughter on her solar plexus if she had not taken some of her daughter's discomfort unto herself in the desire to heal her daughter because she loved her, and when she made that symbolic sealing it was as if she released that healing to the Creator. In other words, I'm trying to see the thing in a larger light, so that I can understand it in more different circumstances than just this one. Would this sort of be a relatively accurate understanding of the dynamic of it?

I am Hatonn. My sister, we find your perception quite adequate to describe this phenomenon. The process which the one known as K undertook, the taking on of her daughter's discomfort, is one which is in itself and in its place quite appropriate to one who serves as what you might call the mother in the protective capacity that might be required in order to complete a certain portion of learning for both the mother and the daughter. The sealing in light of the love and light of the one Creator which the one known as K then undertook as her final portion of that action is the demonstration of a more universal principle, that of the one who does indeed turn to the one Creator as the source of all beingness and gives up the will, shall we say, the small will that wishes for one thing or another for the daughter, and allows the one Creator to act through the small will and transform it, that the will of the one Creator might be manifested. Thus, you have types of activity which occurred, each appropriate to the lessons that were being learned.

May we respond further, my sister?

Carla: No, thank you.

I am Hatonn. We are grateful to you as well, my sister. May we respond to another query at this time?

K: Yes. Let me just push that on a little bit further. I didn't know what happened, but that … the explanation was excellent, but, since that, I have felt a sense of humility, even though I was unaware exactly what happened, but I have felt the sense of humility and almost—how do I—a glow since that

experience. Is that the result of the experience of love, or why has it affected me since then?

I am Hatonn. My sister, the greatest humility is felt by those who are vessels for the one Creator and who do not claim that what proceeds from their being is a portion of their small being, but who know and express their knowledge that the one Creator moves through their being. To be such a vessel is the greatest of honors, and causes within such a vessel the greatest humility, for such an one knows that of itself no such power is possible, but to open the being to the one Creator is to allow the greatest of possibilities of knowing love for all creation to flow through the being, and for that love to exercise its healing power. Therefore, humility is always the result.

May we answer you further, my sister?

K: No, thank you.

I am Hatonn. We thank you, my sister. Is there another query at this time?

S: I have a question, Hatonn. I don't know whether you can answer it or not. In the past three or four days, G and I have felt an entity in our new home and are curious as to whether it's left over, so to speak, or if we have drawn the entity there since we have been in [town]?

I am Hatonn. My sister, we find that there is somewhat of a residue which exists with the entity which has become your new dwelling. This is most frequently the case when the dwelling place is inhabited for a portion of time, that certain thought forms shall be created by the inhabitants, and shall remain with the place of dwelling should the inhabitants leave. Therefore, it is often most helpful to initiate some type of ritual ceremony to purify the new place of dwelling so that it might then be more receptive to those harmonics or vibrations of its new inhabitants.

May we answer you further, my sister?

S: Well, yes, a little bit. The entity, being the presence, does not seem negative or malevolent at all. Should we not welcome him, or by going through the ritual of purifying the house, would that not be in itself a negative act, by trying to control or, what would be, remove him?

I am Hatonn. My sister, we find that it is frequently most helpful for those who have chosen the positive path of service to others to perform such a ritual in any new dwelling place so that the environment which shall nourish such entities might be most purely positive. To perform such a ritual does not then ask all entities to leave, but only requests those of the negative sense depart. Those of the positive nature shall know they have found a good home. To exercise such discrimination within the bounds of one's dwelling is not to attempt the control that which might be viewed as negative, but is to attempt the purity which then nourishes most effectively those of the positive nature who wish to be of service to others. It is the choice of how to tend the garden. The choice of allowing the weeds to persist or to remove the weeds, and to then water the garden.

May we answer you further, my sister?

S: No, thank you. I hadn't quite seen it in that perspective. I feel a lot better now.

I am Hatonn. We are most grateful to you, my sister. Is there another query at this time?

A: Yes, Hatonn, I have one, an inquiry that goes along the lines of S's. I'm curious—is the ritual the same as the one Jim and Don and Carla would use on their new home?

I am Hatonn. My sister, this ritual which you have referred to is quite efficient in its ability to banish, shall we say, the lesser vibratory rates of beings, and may not be necessary in most cases. A ritual which has meaning to these entities which would then include those elements of the nature of the salt or the garlic or the water or the burning cedar might also be helpful. The intent is that which is most important. The intent of purification so that positive vibrations might be enhanced, and the praise of the one Creator for providing the opportunities for service are most helpful in this regard.

May we answer you further, my sister?

A: Yes, but now to another house. Where I am living does not seem to be the most positive place, and I'm finding I have problems studying there, and just basically finding peace of mind there. But since I have someone living in the other part of the house, is it possible just to do part of the house, or if I do the whole house, will whatever his vibrations are counteract, or how can it be done to, say, bring a house more positively when both people in it might not be towards the same goal?

I am Hatonn. My sister, in such a case, you indeed have more to work with in the way of obstacles and barriers. It is possible to purify a portion of a dwelling, but those entities which create thought forms at variance with your own then intrude from time to time and affect the tuning which you have achieved. In such cases there is the need for the repetition of such rituals, and this is recommended in such a situation.

May we answer you further, my sister?

A: Yes. I do not wish to cause him any problems, and from what I recall, a Ra session says that entities may not leave the house, but just go to another portion, and I would not wish to cause him any problems by sending mine to his half of the house. So, would that happen? Would that be a concern?

I am Hatonn. In this case, my sister, we find that these entities or thought forms would simply be returning to their source. You would not be providing any new additions to the other dwellers of this place.

May we answer you further?

A: No, thank you.

I am Hatonn. Is there another question at this time?

Carla: One quick question that you probably can't answer. Is there any reason that I'm not supposed to sing songs for this young women's prayer group?

I am Hatonn. We are not aware of any reason. May we answer you further?

Carla: No, thank you. No, I just wondered. I've been trying a lot.

I am Hatonn. We thank you, my sister. At this time we shall take our leave of this group, for we find there is some discomfort within this instrument, and it would be most appropriate at this time for us to take our leave. We thank each within the group for the dedication to the service of the one Creator by developing that skill which you have come to call the vocal channeling. We assure each that we shall be with you whenever requested. We assure the new instruments that the desire and the dedication and the practice will result in the sharpening of the skills which are new. We leave each of you, my friends, in the love and in the light of the one infinite Creator. We are known to you as Hatonn. Adonai, my friends. Adonai vasu borragus. ﻌ

THE LAW OF ONE, BOOK IV, SESSION 96
SEPTEMBER 9, 1982

Ra: I am Ra. I greet you in the love and in the light of the one infinite Creator. We communicate now.

Questioner: Could you first please give me the condition of the instrument?

Ra: I am Ra. The physical energy deficit is significantly greater than the last asking. There has been substantive lessening also of the vital energies, although the perquisite degree of energy for mental/emotional distortions of normalcy are yet available.

Questioner: The instrument asks if the house which is to be our new location is capable of being transformed by painting and cleaning? We don't plan to put down all new carpets. Would cleaning the carpets that are there now be acceptable?

I want to bring this particular house up to acceptable limits so that it is neutral after we do the salting. I have a concern only for the conditions for our work there. The physical location isn't that important. In fact I don't consider that important at all. Could Ra comment on this?

Ra: I am Ra. It is, of course, the preference of this group which is the only consideration in the situation for the contact with Ra.

The domicile in question has already been offered a small amount of blessing by this group through its presence and, as we have previously stated, each of your days spent in love, harmony, and thanksgiving will continue transforming the dwelling.

It is correct, as we have previously stated, that physical cleanliness is most important. Therefore, the efforts shall be made to most thoroughly cleanse the dwelling. In this regard it is to be noted that neither in the dwelling as a whole wherein you now reside or in the chamber of this working is there an absence of your dust, earth, and other detritus which is in toto called dirt. If the intention is to clean, as much as is physically possible, the location, the requirements for physical cleanliness are fulfilled. It is only when a lower astral entity has, shall we say, placed portions of itself in the so-called dirt that care should be taken to remove the sentient being. These instructions we have given.

May we note that just as each entity strives in each moment to become more nearly one with the Creator but falls short, just so is physical spotlessness striven for but not achieved. In each case the purity of intention and thoroughness of manifestation are appreciated. The variance between the attempt and the goal is never noted and may be considered unimportant.

Questioner: The sequence of events that I am considering is first the painting and then the cleaning, then the moving in of the furniture, then the salting and use of garlic. Is this as good as any other sequence or would another sequence be better?

Ra: I am Ra. Any sequence which results in the cleansing is acceptable. It is to be noted that the thresholds are not to be crossed during the cleansing.

Since such stricture upon use of the limen may affect your considerations we make note of this.

Questioner: Would Ra comment on the technique of blessing the water that we will use to sprinkle the salt? I assume that we just sprinkle the water directly off of our finger tips onto the line of salt. How much water, in general, should be sprinkled on the salt? How wet should we get it? I would like to get this done right.

Ra: I am Ra. The blessing of the water may be that one we have previously given, or it may be that one which is written within the liturgy of this instrument's distortion of the worship of the one Creator, or it may simply be obtained from what you call your Catholic Church in the form of holy water.

The intention of blessing is the notable feature of blessed water. The water may be sprinkled not so that all salt is soaked but so that a goodly portion has been dampened. This is not a physical working. The substances need to be seen in their ideal state so that water may be seen to be enabling the salt.

Questioner: I have planned to re-draw the tarot cards omitting the extraneous additions by those who came after Ra and I would like quickly to go through those things that I intend to eliminate from each card and ask Ra if there is anything else that should be eliminated to make the cards as they were before the astrological and other appendages were added.

I would eliminate all of the letters from the edge of the card with the possible exception of the number of the card. That would be the case for all of the cards. In Card Number One I would eliminate the star, the wand in the Magician's hand, and I understand that the sphere remains but I am not really sure where it should be. Would Ra comment on that please?

Ra: I am Ra. Firstly, the elimination of letters is acceptable. Secondly, the elimination of stars is acceptable in all cases. Thirdly, the elimination of the wand is appropriate. Fourthly, the sphere may be seen to be held by the thumb and index and second finger.

Fifthly, we would note that it is not possible to offer what you may call a pure deck, if you would use this term, of tarot due to the fact that when these images were first drawn there was already distortion in various and sundry ways, mostly cultural.

Sixthly, although it is good to view the images without the astrological additions, it is to be noted that the more general positions, phases, and characteristics of each concept complex are those which are significant. The removal of all distortions is unlikely and, to a great extent, unimportant.

Questioner: I didn't think that we could ever remove all distortions but it is very difficult to work with or interpret these cards because of the quality of the drawing, and as we go through them we get a better idea of what some of these things are and how they should be drawn. I think that we can improve on the quality of the cards and also remove some of the extraneous material that is misleading.

On the second card we should remove the letters and the stars. At the center of the female form here she is wearing something that looks something like a crux ansata and we should change that. Is that correct?

Ra: I am Ra. We perceive an incomplete query. Please requestion.

Questioner: I think that I should put a crux ansata in the place of this thing that looks a little like a crux ansata on the front of the female. Is that correct?

Ra: I am Ra. This is correct.

Questioner: Then as to the thing that she wears on her head, that, I believe, is a bit confusing. What should it be shaped like?

Ra: I am Ra. We shall allow the student to ponder this point. We note that although it is an astrologically based addition to the concept complex it is not entirely unacceptable when viewed with a certain feeling. Therefore, we suggest, O student, that you choose whether to remove the crown or to name its meaning in such a way as to enhance the concept complex.

Questioner: Would Ra please give me any information possible on the ratios of dimensions, and the shape of the crux ansata as it should be made or drawn?

Ra: I am Ra. No.

Questioner: In Card Number Three we will remove all the letters and the stars and I assume that the little cups around the outside of the rays representing the sun should be removed? Is that correct?

Ra: I am Ra. Yes

Questioner: In Card Number Four we will remove all the letters and the stars and it seems that again we have a situation of removing the wand and putting the sphere in the hand. Is that correct?

Ra: I am Ra. Again, this is a matter of choice. Though astrological in nature, this particular scepter has possibilities of relevance in the originally intended concept complex.

This instrument is experiencing some small lack of that distortion which you call proper breathing due to the experience of your near past, as you perceive it. Therefore, as this instrument has requested a substantial enough amount of transferred energy to be retained that it might effect a comfortable re-entry, we shall at this time ask for one more query, after noting the following.

We did not complete our statement upon the dimensions of the crux ansata. It is given in many places. There are decisions to be made as to which drawing of this image is the appropriate one. We may, of course, suggest viewing the so-called Great Pyramid if the puzzle is desired. We do not wish to work this puzzle. It was designed in order that in its own time it be deciphered. In general, of course, this image has the meaning previously stated.

Questioner: Is there anything that we can do to make the instrument more comfortable or to improve the contact?

Ra: I am Ra. Continue in harmony, communication, praise, and thanksgiving.

We would note that this instrument's distortions would be lessened were it to refrain from the speaking to some extent for a diurnal period or perhaps two if the difficulty remains. We would also recommend against the activity such as running which would cause rapid respiration. This after-effect of the greeting is not necessarily long-lasting. However, as this instrument has some blood vessels in the forward regions of the skull; that is, the integument covering the skull, which are greatly swollen at this time and since this instrument has the distortion known as the streptococcal infection, it is best to be full of care for a short period in order that

the distortions do not catapult the entity into longer-term after-effects.

All is well. We find the alignments satisfactory.

I am Ra. I leave you in the love and light of the infinite One. Go forth, therefore, rejoicing in the power and in the peace of the one infinite Creator. Adonai. ☥

L/L RESEARCH

L/L Research is a subsidiary of
Rock Creek Research &
Development Laboratories, Inc.

P.O. Box 5195
Louisville, KY 40255-0195

www.llresearch.org

Rock Creek is a non-profit
corporation dedicated to
discovering and sharing
information which may aid in
the spiritual evolution of
humankind.

THE LAW OF ONE, BOOK V, SESSION 96, FRAGMENT 46
SEPTEMBER 9, 1982

Jim: Don's job as a pilot for Eastern Airlines saw him based in Atlanta. Commuting to and from Atlanta became more and more wearing on him and reduced the amount of time available for Ra sessions due to his absence and due to the time needed for him to recover from his weariness when he was home. Thus, in the fall of 1982 we found a house near the airport in Atlanta that we thought we would move to so Don's commuting time would be reduced. It had previously been inhabited by people who had trafficked in illegal drugs and who had apparently had numerous disharmonious experiences within the dwelling that was to become our new home. These unfortunate experiences by the former tenants had apparently attracted elementals and lower astral entities into the house which Carla was somewhat able to perceive.

She wanted very much to move into the house because it would have greatly helped Don to be that close to his work. She wanted to buy new carpeting to replace the soiled one, or failing that, to begin scrubbing the carpet to cleanse the house of the undesirable presences, but the limitations of our budget and her arthritis made that impossible. Thus a blue-ray blockage of communication occurred which, two days later while she was on her daily walk, was entered by our fifth-density, negative friend and enhanced in the magical sense until she was unable to breathe for about thirty seconds. This was symbolic of her inability to talk to Don about what the house needed. Keeping calm during the

distress saw her through it, and talking to Don about the house cleared the blockage.

The queries about the malfunctioning tape recorder refer to strange sounds that came from it a few days later when Carla was trying to record some of her singing to send to a friend.

The last portion of this session returns to the subject of the house next to the airport in Atlanta that was to become our new home. In our personal and fallible opinions it is from this point that the difficulties that eventually led to Don's death may be traced. When we returned to our home in Louisville from looking at the new home-to-be in Atlanta, we had just walked in the front door when, all of the sudden, a hawk with a wing span of at least four feet landed outside of our kitchen window, remained for a few moments, and then flew off over the tree tops. Carla and I took the appearance of the hawk as a sign confirming the desirability of the house in Atlanta as our new home. Don, however, was not sure that the hawk was a good sign, and he began to doubt whether we should move to the house after all.

Carla: I cannot tell you just how sorry I was that the Atlanta "farm" they were talking about here did not work out as a dwelling place for us. In it, Don was just three miles from the airport. It was a very nice place, although peculiar in that the house simply ended with no wall between it and the adjoining horse barn. It was less expensive to rent than the place we had in

Louisville, it was a milder climate, and there was room for Jim to stretch out and have his own place, and Don and me to do likewise. What foiled it was an attitude of Don's that was deeply characteristic, and I imagine stemmed from growing up in the depression. He did not want to spend the money to get the place really clean. The dirtiness of the place was everywhere, it had been neglected for some time, dusted and vacuumed occasionally, but any spills were left as they fell, and there was the slight patina of ground-in dirt that only good soap would get, and much hard scrubbing. The most logical solution to me was simply to replace the floor covering throughout the dirtied area. Barring that, hiring a good cleaning agency with professional equipment would have sufficed. Don wished to do neither of these things.

When the hawk flew, and Don took it as a bad omen, that was it. There was no more to discuss, as far as Don was concerned. At that point, as Jim has said, there was a definite shift in Don's peace of mind. He was more concerned about having enough energy to work as a pilot than ever, and yet everything seemed to be too much trouble. When we tried to buy the Louisville house from its owner, there was a $5,000.00 dispute that the owner and Donald developed that put the quietus on that deal. So we had to move somewhere, as the owner of the Louisville property was selling it out from under us. Don eventually OK'd a lovely and pricey house on Lake Lanier, about 40 bad miles from the airport. What we hadn't realized was that Atlanta traffic is terrible; after the Olympics were held there, the whole nation became aware of that. And Don had to drive from the extreme north of the traffic tangle to the extreme south, where the airport lay. He spent more time getting there from the lake house than he had done from Louisville, since all he had to do in Louisville was take a short drive to the airport and commute for an hour to Atlanta. The driving from the lake was always an hour and a half to two hours, because of the traffic. There simply seemed no relief and no solution at that house. And so began a difficult experience for all three of us, who somehow had no safe place to be.

If Donald had been normal, he would have been talking a good deal about his various fears. But Don was Don, a wonderful, wise, charming, funny and truly great man, but an unique man who had from an early age pretended he had no preferences and was only an observer. After his death I found out that he was developing real fears about losing me to Jim. But to me

he said nothing, following his usual practice of behaving as though he had no preferences. So I was utterly confused. I figured he was just upset about having the right place, and spent countless hours poring over newspaper ads trying to find him a place he felt good about, but to no avail. From this point on, we were never at peace. And little by little, I realized at a deep level that something serious was going wrong with Don. He began acting very unlike himself, being unwilling to leave my presence to the point of listening to my music rehearsals, watching me exercise, sleeping in my room, all things the usual Don would scorn. I did not take these things as positive, for I truly loved the irascible and indifferent Don and longed to have him back.

I was grieving for Donald for months while he was still alive, for he quickly changed to the point that neither I not he himself could recognize him. This was a time of the most profound distress for Don and for me. Jim was deeply concerned about both of us, but was pretty stable. Both Don and I went rather quickly beyond the bounds of normalcy. I suffered a breakdown. I asked for and got help from family, friends and therapists. So I walked through my nervous breakdown, continuing to function at a basic level. Don suffered a breakdown also, but his came with a real break from reality, and he was in a place where it seemed no one, most of all I, could help him.

Session 96, September 9, 1982

Questioner: Could you tell me the cause of the lessening of the physical and vital energies?

Ra: I am Ra. We found the need of examining the mental configurations of the instrument before framing an answer due to our reluctance to infringe upon its free will. Those concepts relating to the spiritual contemplation of personal catalyst have been appreciated by the entity so we may proceed.

This entity has an habitual attitude which is singular; that is, when there is some necessity for action the entity is accustomed to analyzing the catalyst in terms of service and determining a course. There was a most unusual variation in this configuration of attitude when this instrument beheld the dwelling which is to be inhabited by this group. The instrument perceived those elementals and beings of astral character of which we have spoken. The instrument desired to be of service by achieving the domicile in question but found its instincts reacting to the unwelcome presences. The division of mind configuration was increased by the continuing catalyst of lack of control. Had this entity been able to physically begin cleansing the dwelling the, shall we say, opening would not have occurred.

Although this entity attempted clear communication upon this matter, and although each in the support group did likewise, the amount of blue-ray work necessary to uncover and grasp the nature of the catalyst was not affected. Therefore, there was an opening quite rare for this mind/body/spirit complex and into this opening the one which greets you moved and performed what may be considered to be the most potent of its purely magical manifestations to this present nexus, as you know time.

It is well that this instrument is not distorted towards what you may call hysteria, for the potential of this working was such that had the instrument allowed fear to become greater than the will to persevere when it could not breathe, each attempt at respiration would have been even more nearly impossible until the suffocation occurred which was desired by the one which greets you in its own way. Thus the entity would have passed from this incarnation.

Questioner: Does this threat, shall I say, still exist and, if so, is there something that we can do to alleviate it?

Ra: I am Ra. This threat no longer exists, if you wish to phrase this greeting in this manner. The communication which was affected by the scribe and then by the questioner did close the opening and enable the instrument to begin assimilating the catalyst it had received.

Questioner: Was the unusual sound on the instrument's tape recorder that occurred while she was trying to record her singing a greeting from our fifth-density, negative associate?

Ra: I am Ra. No. Rather it was a greeting from a malfunctioning electronic machine.

Questioner: There was no catalyst for that machine to malfunction from any of the negative entities then. Is that right? It was only a function of the random malfunction of the machine. Am I correct?

Ra: I am Ra. No.

Questioner: What was the origin of this malfunction?

Ra: I am Ra. There are two difficulties with the machine. Firstly, this instrument has a strong effect upon electromagnetic and electronic machines and instruments, and likely, if continued use of these is desired, should request that another handle the machines. Also, there was some difficulty from physical interference due to the material you call tape catching upon adjoining, what you would call, buttons when the "play" button, as you call it, is depressed.

Questioner: How is Ra able to know all of this information? This is somewhat of an unimportant question, but it is just amazing to me that Ra is able to know all of these trivial things. What do you do, move in time/space and inspect the problem or what?

Ra: I am Ra. Your former supposition is correct, your latter unintelligible to us.

Questioner: You mean that you move in time/space and inspect the situation to determine the problem. Is that correct?

Ra: I am Ra. This is so.

Questioner: Was there a significance with respect to the hawk that landed the other day just outside the kitchen window?

Ra: I am Ra. This is correct. We may note that we find it interesting that queries offered to us are often already known. We assume that our confirmation is appreciated.

Questioner: This seems to be connected with the concept of the bird being messengers in the tarot and this was a demonstration of this concept. I was wondering about the mechanics, you might say, of this type of message. I assume that the hawk was a messenger, and I assume that as I thought of the possible meaning of this with respect to our activities I was, in the state of free will, getting a message in the appearance of this very unusual bird, unusual, I say, in that it came so close. I would be very interested to know the origin of the message. Would Ra comment on this, please?

Ra: I am Ra. No.

Questioner: I was afraid that you would say that. Am I correct in assuming that this is the same type of communication as depicted in Card Number Three of the Catalyst of the Mind?

Ra: I am Ra. We may not comment due to the Law of Confusion. There is an acceptable degree of confirmation of items known, but when the recognized subjective sigil[12] is waved and the message not clear, then it is that we must remain silent. ♣

---

[12] sigil: A seal or signet; a mark or sign supposed to exercise occult power [< L *siggilum* seal].

THE LAW OF ONE, BOOK IV, SESSION 97
SEPTEMBER 15, 1982

Ra: I am Ra. I greet you in the love and in the light of the one infinite Creator. We communicate now.

Questioner: Could you first please give me the condition of the instrument?

Ra: I am Ra. It is as previously stated.

Questioner: What is the situation with our fifth-density negative friend?

Ra: I am Ra. It is as previously stated.

Questioner: Are there any items in the first four cards not of Ra's intention that we could remove to present a less confusing card as we make our new drawings?

Ra: I am Ra. We find much material in this query which would constitute repetition. May we suggest rephrasing the query?

Questioner: Possibly I didn't phrase that the way I meant to. We had already determined the items that should be removed from the first four cards and my question was: had I missed anything that should be removed that was not of Ra's original intention?

Ra: I am Ra. We shall repeat our opinion that there are several concepts which, in each image, are astrologically based. However, these concepts are not without merit within the concept complex intended by Ra, given the perception by the student of these concepts in an appropriate manner.

We wish not to form that which may be considered by any mind/body/spirit complex to be a complete and infallible series of images. There is a substantial point to be made in this regard. We have been, with the questioner's aid, investigating the concept complexes of the great architecture of the archetypical mind. To more clearly grasp the nature, the process, and the purpose of archetypes, Ra provided a series of concept complexes. In no way whatsoever should we, as humble messengers of the one infinite Creator, wish to place before the consideration of any mind/body/spirit complex which seeks its evolution the palest tint of the idea that these images are anything but a resource for working in the area of the development of the faith and the will.

To put this into perspective we must gaze then at the stunning mystery of the one infinite Creator. The archetypical mind does not resolve any paradoxes or bring all into unity. This is not the property of any source which is of the third-density. Therefore, may we ask the student to look up from inward working and behold the glory, the might, the majesty, the mystery, and the peace of oneness. Let no consideration of bird or beast, darkness or light, shape or shadow keep any which seeks from the central consideration of unity.

We are not messengers of the complex. We bring the message of unity. In this perspective only may we affirm the value to the seeker of adepthood of the grasping, articulating, and use of this resource of the deep mind exemplified by the concept complex of the archetypes.

Questioner: Thank you. Card Number Five, the Significator of the Mind, indicates, firstly, as I see it, simply a male within a rectangularly structured form which suggests to me that the Significator of the Mind in third density is well bounded within the illusion, as is also suggested by the fact that the base of the male is a rectangular form showing no ability for movement. Would Ra comment on that?

Ra: I am Ra. O student, you have grasped the barest essence of the nature of the Significator's complete envelopment within the rectangle. Consider for the self, O student, whether your thoughts can walk. The abilities of the most finely honed mentality shall not be known without the use of the physical vehicle which you call the body. Through the mouth the mind may speak. Through the limbs the mind may affect action.

Questioner: The entity looks to the left, indicating that the mind has the tendency to notice more easily catalyst of a negative essence. Would Ra comment on that observation?

Ra: I am Ra. This is substantially correct.

Questioner: There are two small entities at the bottom, one black and one white. I will first ask Ra if this drawing is correct in the coloring? Is the black one in the proper position with respect to Ra's original drawings?

Ra: I am Ra. That which you perceive as black was first red. Other than this difference, the beings in the concept complex are placed correctly.

Questioner: The red coloration is a mystery to me. We had originally decided that these represented the polarization of the mind. Would Ra comment on that?

Ra: I am Ra. The indications of polarity are as presumed by the questioner. The symbolism of old for the left-hand path was the russet coloration.

We shall pause at this time if the questioner will be patient. There are fairly serious difficulties with the instrument's throat. We shall attempt to ameliorate the situation and suggest the rewalking of the Circle of One.

(The Circle of One was rewalked and breath expelled two feet above the instrument's head.)

Ra: I am Ra. Please continue.

Questioner: What was the nature of the problem?

Ra: I am Ra. The fifth-density entity which greets this instrument affected a previous difficulty distorting the throat and chest area of the instrument. Some fraction of this distortion remained unmentioned by the instrument. It is helpful if the instrument speaks as clearly as possible to the support group of any difficulties that more care may be taken.

However, we find very little distortion left in the chest area of the instrument. However, immediately preceding the working the instrument was offered an extreme activation of what you may call the allergies and the mucous from the flow which this distortion causes began to cause difficulty to the throat. At this juncture the previous potential for the tightening of the throat was somewhat activated by reflex of the yellow-ray, chemical body over which we have only gross control.

We would appreciate you reminding us to cause this instrument to cough before or after each query for the remainder of this working. Once conscious, this instrument should have no serious difficulty.

Questioner: I was wondering why the dark entity was on the right side of the card in relation to the Significator. Could Ra comment on that after making the instrument cough?

Ra: *(Cough)* The nature of … We pause.

(Ten second pause.)

I am Ra. There was a serious pain flare. We may now continue.

The nature of polarity is interesting in that those experiences offered to the Significator as positive frequently become recorded as productive of biases which may be seen to be negative, whereas the fruit of those experiences apparently negative is frequently found to be helpful in the development of the service-to-others bias. As this is perhaps the guiding characteristic of that which the mind processes and records, these symbols of polarity have thusly been placed.

You may note that the hands of the central image indicate the appropriate bias for right and left-hand working; that is, the right hand gestures in service-to-others, offering its light outward. The left hand attempts to absorb the power of the spirit and point it for its use alone.

Questioner: The eight cartouches at the bottom would possibly signify the energy centers and the evolution through those centers with the possibility for positive or negative polarization because of the white and black coloration of the figures. Would Ra comment on that after making the instrument cough?

Ra: *(Cough)* I am Ra. The observations of the student are perceptive. It is informative to continue the study of octaves in association with this concept complex. Many are the octaves of a mind/body/spirit complex's beingness. There is not one that does not profit from being pondered in connection with the considerations of the nature of the development of polarity exemplified by the concept complex of your Card Number Five.

Questioner: Do the symbols on the face of each of these little cartouches such as the birds and the other symbols have a meaning in this card that is of value in considering the archetypes? Could you answer that after making the instrument cough?

Ra: *(Cough)* I am Ra. These symbols are letters and words much as your language would receive such an entablature. They are, to a great extent, enculturated by a people not of your generation. Let us, in the rough, suggest that the information written upon these cartouches be understood to be such as the phrase, "And you shall be born again to eternal life."

Questioner: Thank you. I thought that the wings on top of the card might indicate the protection of the spirit over the process of evolution. Would Ra comment on that after having the instrument cough?

Ra: *(Cough)* I am Ra. We shall end this session for we are having considerable difficulty in using the sympathetic nervous system in order to aid the instrument in providing sufficient of your air for its respiration. Therefore, we prematurely suggest ending this session.

Is there any brief query before we leave this instrument?

Questioner: It's not necessary to answer this if you want to end right now for the instrument's benefit, but is there anything that we can do to improve the contact or make the instrument more comfortable?

Ra: I am Ra. All is well. The support group functions well.

It is suggested that the instrument be encouraged to take steps to recover completely from the distortion towards the aching of the throat and, to a lesser extent, the chest. There is no way in which we or you may remove that working which has been done. It simply must be removed by physical recovery of the normal distortion. This is not easy due to this instrument's tendency towards allergy.

The alignments are being carefully considered.

I am Ra. I leave you, my friends, glorying and rejoicing in the love and the light of the infinite Creator. Go forth, then, in the great dance, empowered by the peace of the one infinite Creator. Adonai.

(Session #98, September 24, 1982, contains only personal material and was, for that reason, removed from The Law of One, Book IV.) ❦

L/L RESEARCH

L/L Research is a subsidiary of
Rock Creek Research &
Development Laboratories, Inc.

P.O. Box 5195
Louisville, KY 40255-0195

www.llresearch.org

Rock Creek is a non-profit
corporation dedicated to
discovering and sharing
information which may aid in
the spiritual evolution of
humankind.

THE LAW OF ONE, BOOK V, SESSION 97, FRAGMENT 47
SEPTEMBER 15, 1982

Jim: After more thought on the subject of the hawk, Don again queried Ra about its significance. Since Ra did not wish to infringe upon Don's free will by clearly explaining the meaning of the hawk—and thus making Don's decision to move or not move to the house for him—the most Ra could do was speak in an indirect sense, in a kind of riddle that required that Don, and each of us, make our own determinations. The extreme desire on the part of any positive entities such as Ra to maintain the free will of each person on our third-density planet is due to the fact that if an entity such as Ra gives information that could change one's future choices, that entity, then, has not only taught the third-density being but has learned for it. By learning for it, it has removed the spiritual strength that comes to one who struggles and finally learns for him/herself. In the larger view this is not seen as a service but as a disservice. Because of Don's doubt about the appropriateness of the house in Atlanta as our next home, we did not move to that house but remained in Louisville for another year. It was the fall of 1983 before we finally found another house in the Atlanta area and moved there. By that time Don's weariness had increased to the critical point and he had begun worrying more and more about whether he was even going to have a job since Eastern airlines was rapidly failing financially.

Carla: Ah, to be able to read aright the little hints that the Creator always seems to be offering us! Both Jim and I thought the hawk was simply a confirmation of that location. But Don was the boss, and he really felt unsure, to the point that he left, for a time, the idea of moving completely, and tried to purchase the house we were renting. As I mentioned, the difference of about 4% of the house's cost was in dispute, and Donald did not see his way clear to giving the rather greedy owner an extra bonus for having us over the barrel of "buy or move." So in the end we were forced to move somewhere, either in Louisville or Atlanta. It was a fateful move, attended from the beginning by struggles and problems. The sad tale of our demise as a group able to contact Ra was beginning.

Session 97, September 15, 1982

Questioner: I've been doing some consideration of the appearance of the hawk and have made this analysis of the bird in Card Number Three. The bird is a message from the higher self, and the position of the wings on Card Three, one pointing toward the female, indicates that it is a message to the female acting as catalyst for the mind. The position of the downward wing indicates that the message is of a negative nature or of a nature indicating the inappropriateness of certain mental activity or plans. Would Ra comment on that?

Ra: I am Ra. No.

Questioner: Is the reason for this lack of comment the first distortion?

Ra: I am Ra. This is correct.

Questioner: I have analyzed the hawk that I saw immediately after returning from the house in Atlanta as a message, probably from my higher self, indicating that the plan of moving was not the best or not too appropriate since, without the hawk, we would have continued as planned with no added catalyst. This single catalyst of a remarkable nature then, logically, from my point of view, could only mean that there was a message as to the inappropriateness of the plan for some reason yet to be discovered. Would Ra comment on that?

Ra: I am Ra. We tread as close as possible to the Law of Confusion in suggesting that not all winged creatures have an archetypical meaning. We might suggest that the noticing of shared subjectively notable phenomena is common when, in another incarnational experience, work significant to the service of increased polarity has been shared. These subjectively interesting shared phenomena then act as a means of communication, the nature of which cannot be discussed by those outside of the shared incarnational experience without the interference with the free will of each entity involved in the complex of subjectively meaningful events.

Questioner: Can Ra tell us the source of the unusual odor in this room this morning?

Ra: I am Ra. There are two components to this odor. One is, as has been surmised, the decomposing physical vehicle of one of your second-density Rodentia. The second is an elemental which is attempting to take up residence within the putrefying remains of this small creature.

The cleansing of the room and the burning of the incense has discouraged the elemental. The process of decomposition shall, in a short period of your space/time, remove the less than harmonious sensations provided for the nose.

Questioner: I find myself presently in a difficult position of decision, primarily because of the appearance of the aforementioned hawk upon our return from Atlanta. The only objective of any value at all is the work that we are doing which includes not only the contact but communication and dissemination of this material to those who might request it. Since a move was connected with that, and since the hawk was, to me, obviously a function of that process, I am presently in a quandary with respect to the optimal situation since I have not yet definitely decided on the significance of the hawk or

the advantages or the efficaciousness of the move and do not want to create any process which is basically irreversible if it is going to result in a lack of our ability to be of service to those who would seek that which we are able to manifest in our efforts. Would Ra comment on that situation?

Ra: I am Ra. The questioner presumes much, and to comment is an infringement upon its free will. We may suggest the pondering of our previous comments regarding the winged creatures of which you speak. We repeat that any place of working, properly prepared by this group, is acceptable to Ra. The discrimination of choice is yours. ✣

L/L RESEARCH

L/L Research is a subsidiary of Rock Creek Research & Development Laboratories, Inc.

P.O. Box 5195
Louisville, KY 40255-0195

www.llresearch.org

Rock Creek is a non-profit corporation dedicated to discovering and sharing information which may aid in the spiritual evolution of humankind.

SUNDAY MEDITATION
SEPTEMBER 19, 1982

(C channeling)

I am Hatonn, and I am now with this instrument. We greet you in the love and in the light of the one Creator. *(Inaudible).* It is the time in your season's change when one season *(inaudible)* people of your day …

(About one third of side one is inaudible. Portions that are audible indicate a story of a man and a tree.)

I am Hatonn. I will now pause so that my brothers and sisters of Laitos may pass among those here wishing to deepen their meditation. I am Hatonn.

(M1 channeling)

I am Hatonn. I am now with this instrument. I greet you with the love and the light of the infinite Creator. The people of your planet live too much in the past. They judge their own shortcomings and the shortcomings of their friends. They remember unpleasant things that they did and unpleasant things that were said to them. This is similar to your expression, "beating a dead horse." You can never bring it back. When people die, they are no longer with you. Your past days are no longer with you. Of course, you could say that it helps you predict the future, but this is not always accurate. In your holy book, Saul, through inspiration and through forgiveness, was changed into Paul. Jacob, who took his brother Esau's birthright, became Israel.

If you will start your day with a clean slate and give your friends and your so-called enemies the same privilege, you may inspire yourself and others to change. The past is as dead as the trees in winter. The only difference is the trees will return each spring, but the past is gone. Giving yourself a clean slate helps you to change for the better. Giving your friends a clean slate and also your enemies inspires them not to repeat their mistakes. The only real good thing about the past are the good times. They will help you and teach you. But negative influences, judging people, and judging yourself will keep you *(inaudible)*. Wake up each day giving yourself and your friends a clean slate. That day cannot help but be finer. And that day is all you have.

I am Hatonn and I leave this instrument.

(L channeling)

I am Hatonn, and I greet you again, my brothers and sisters, in the love and the light of the infinite Creator. My friends, there will be times in your lives when the extension of love and understanding will be difficult, for, as you are aware, those experiences in which learning are obtained are frequently uncomfortable. My friends, we would urge those of you who seek to make the path of service less difficult to spend more of your own time in solitude, for it is the times in which you detach yourself from the illusion that much of your growth may be accomplished.

We realize that our use of the word solitude is misunderstood by some here, for it is not our advice to seek aloneness, but rather oneness. We therefore suggest that those present who desire to progress along the path of service to others avail themselves of the opportunity to meditate, to seek the solitude of oneness with their other selves.

At this time we will relinquish our use of this instrument, that our brothers and sisters of Latwii may perform their service. I am known to you as Hatonn.

(Pause)

(L channeling)

I am Latwii, and I greet you once again, my brothers and sisters, in the love and in the light of the infinite Creator. At this time, it is our desire to be of service to those who would pose questions that we might seek to enlighten those areas of confusion. Is there a question at this time?

C: What do babies dream?

I am Latwii. My brother, the use of the term "dream" is not precise in defining those experiences which occur within the consciousness of your young, for it is not their need to sharply define sharply their perceptions of that which you term imaginative from that which you term real. It must be remembered, therefore, that those recently entering your world of illusion do not have imprinted within their consciousness the affirmation that that which they see is real. For your young, their world consists of a series of lessons, of perceptions, some of which pertain to the world into which they have recently been ejected, so to speak, and much of [what] concerns our young [is] adjustment to the physical vehicle and the sensations of that vehicle.

Within the consciousness of the child or newly arrived individual is a constant barrage of stimuli. The newly arrived entity, being unfamiliar with its sensory apparati, is initially incapable of distinguishing those signals generated externally, and those which originate through the process you know as imagination. It would therefore be more accurate to state that to a large extent the newly arrived entity dreams of the illusion which he or she has chosen to enter.

May we answer you further, my brother?

C: Yes. I was thinking about the—the thought that hit me, would that being newly incarnated and not having been bombarded by years of existence in its illusion whether or not it is unconscious—if they still are—had—well, that they still had actually ties to their previous life, and that some parts of it still stimulate the input in these periods of ease?

I am Latwii, and we shall assume that your statements are indicative of a question, and will attempt to respond. In a majority of individuals newly arrived to your illusion, the combination of factors most significant to the entity are the new physical vehicle and the recent *(inaudible)*. Consider, if you will, the individual to whom you refer [to] as an amnesiac who suddenly awakens to illness, to a life of illness. It is difficult for one in that situation to pose to themselves the question, "How might I improve upon my functions of this day?" for it is most frequently an understanding of the present that dominates the learning experience.

The newly arrived entity is suddenly within a physical vehicle after a period of existence in a form of unawareness within the womb. The assumption of a physical vehicle has been likened to an act of imprisonment and this reflection *(inaudible)* but you can appreciate the *(inaudible)* from the new vehicle and its barrage of stimuli, but coupled with the forgetting that accompanies entry to your illusion. The philosophical bent of the entity is quite often ignored in the start in the struggle to survive as a stranger in a strange world.

May we answer you further?

C: No, thank you.

We thank you, my brother. Is there another question?

E: I have a question, Latwii. It concerns a subject which you enlightened us on last week and the week before about pyramids, bandshells and other structures that focus energy. And my question is, can hilltops also be included in those forms that focus energy?

I am Latwii. My brother, consider your own history, that of your predecessors who wrote of the significance of him whom you called Moses, who returned from the mountain; of him you called Mohammed, who spent time of enlightenment within a cave; of him whom you call Jesus Christ, who was transfigured on a mountain; of the tendency of your peoples to erect mountains of their own in their seeking of that which they call God. These structures, my brother, have the potential of focusing much power, and the significance of the structure has been long understood by your religious leaders the significance of the structure. Many variations are attempted to [tame] the power they describe, ranging from the construction of vast cathedrals, basilicas, pyramids or the construction of edifices upon the mountains themselves as in that area which you call Tibet.

May we answer you further?

E: No, thank you.

We thank you. Is there another question?

M1: I have a question, but I'm not sure I understand it. Maybe Hatonn gets through to us in different ways, but why did he give me the impression he was going speak through K and A and S and M2, and he hasn't spoke?

I am Latwii, and I am aware of your question. My sister, our brothers and sisters of Hatonn will often allow their communications to one another or communal thoughts to bleed through to the attentive listener. In this particular situation, consideration was being given to the availability of willing instruments as well as the need to exercise those instruments choosing to make themselves available. As this particular instrument was willing to channel, as you say, and had fallen somewhat into disuse, our brothers and sisters of Hatonn elected to avail themselves of the opportunity to do a bit of housecleaning, so to speak, and assist the instrument in retuning itself. In the accomplishment of this task, our brothers and sisters of Hatonn completed their message and evaluated the remaining instruments as being sufficiently attuned that no adjustments were necessary.

May we answer you further?

M1: No, thank you.

We thank you, my sister. Is there another question?

K: Yes. You mentioned the mountains of Tibet, and I'm assuming that it is the power of the mountains that draws so many of the adepts of the East into the mountains. And then that leads me to ask this

question. If one does not have a mountain available, what's the next best thing?

I am Latwii. My sister, if we might be allowed a bit of frivolity, we would simply quote a passage from your own literature in that if Mohammed cannot go to the mountain …

(Side one of tape ends.)

(L channeling)

In a more serious vein of communication, however, we would point out that the necessity for the mountain is non-existent, for it is within the individual that the power referred to may be tapped successfully. Such appliances as mountains or pyramids may be used to accomplish specific tasks but one must not make the mistake of regarding the mountain or the structure as the significant factor in one's growth, for is not the mountain itself part of the illusion?

It is within the archetype of the Fool to seek high places that they might step forward unafraid into space, for this is a portion of yourself and all others, to seek the unknown heights. As the mountain is a reflection of your seeking within the physical plane, it, in echoing your ambition, focuses your attention upon that facet of your character, and provides an attractive force which is often mistaken for attraction to the mountain itself rather than that which the mountain represents. However, we would conclude that if the mountain serves the purpose of adequately enabling one to focus one's striving, then perhaps the impartation of that which you referred to as Mt. Everest might be in order.

May we answer you further?

K: Then it would be conceivable that a coin or an inspirational work of art or something of that nature could serve the same purpose as a mountain?

I am Latwii. That is not only correct but astute, my sister.

K: Thank you.

We thank you. Is there another question?

M1: Carrying the thing one bit further, could you be inspired in a deep hole and in a cave as well?

I am Latwii. My sister, if your physical vehicle resides within the cave or the well, but your consciousness is upon the mountain top, where then, are you?

M1: I'm in the hole.

I am Latwii. My sister, one must remember that the illusion presents many entanglements that encourage one to accept limitation, for it is only in exceeding those limitations that one attains growth. Your existence is defined not by your physical vehicle's location, but rather by the path upon which you strive. If you tread the path of service consciously, then there is no prison, no cavern, that may contain you, for your service may be extended in infinite directions to infinite distance. For it is the location of your awareness, of your attention, that truly defines the location of your self, and learning as well as service may occur no matter where your physical vehicle may reside.

May we answer you further?

M1: No, I think you've answered it, but I think my attention would be down in the hole. Probably down there. I don't think I could get up. I don't need a map but at least I need to get out of the hole.

I am Latwii. My sister, we agree with you wholeheartedly, and would suggest the avoidance of the hole.

Is there another question?

(Pause)

I am Latwii. As there are no further questions, we will take our leave with the reminder that our service and the service of our brothers and sisters of the Confederation are available at any time to any person who simply asks. In the love and the light of the infinite Creator we bid you adonai. I am known to you as Latwii. ❧

INTENSIVE MEDITATION
SEPTEMBER 24, 1982

(Carla channeling)

I am Hatonn, and I greet you, my friends, in the love and in the light of the infinite Creator. It is a great pleasure to speak to this group. We have been working with each and find ourselves in the position of several instruments being eager to courteously step aside for each other's practice. This, my friends, is a very good practice except when carried to the extent that there is no message due to an excess of courtesy. We would like to work with each instrument. We would first like to work with the instrument known as D. This instrument is a very stable instrument, however, the group dynamics of the larger groups in what you would call your recent meetings have not been propitious for this instrument to practice with a great degree of self-confidence. Therefore, we are most pleased that the instrument has availed himself in an intensive session that we may continue building upon the contact which we have so that in good time the instrument will feel the nature of our contact regardless of the variety of groups that may desire to hear Confederation philosophy, and so gather about instruments such as are here this evening.

This is not easy, my friends. If you are a conscientious instrument, you will find that each group with which you meet flavors and colors the vibrations of the, shall we say, the atmosphere of the contact. It is then a more advanced ability to be able to have the inner personal tuning that allows for communication if there is a group desire for this communication, regardless of the variation in the group dynamics.

We pause in the light at this time in order to more firmly make our contact with the one known as D, and then would say a few words through this instrument. I am Hatonn.

(Jim channeling)

I am Hatonn. I am now with this instrument. We are having some difficulty in making our thoughts perceptible to the one known as D. It is often the situation that a new instrument will perceive the first few words of our greeting as being of personal origin and then be unable to determine whether this perception is correct. We would therefore advise each new instrument to simply speak those words which are well known as our greeting so that the words which are not as well known, and may be more fully understood to be of our origin, might then proceed into the consciousness of the new instrument. We would at this time attempt once again to speak through the one known as D, if he would relax the analysis and speak easily. We would transfer this contact. I am Hatonn.

(D channeling)

I am Hatonn. We felt the need to prod this instrument as he is again reluctant to speak those words which enter. We will pause. I am Hatonn.

(Pause)

We felt the need to refamiliarize this instrument with our presence as he is still somewhat uncomfortable. However, with practice this will be made much easier. We will continue to condition this instrument as we pass on to the other instruments. I am Hatonn.

(S1 channeling)

I am Hatonn, and am with this instrument. We would like to greet you once again in the love and light of the infinite Creator, and once again we were experiencing each instrument willingly and gladly wishing to serve their brothers by allowing them to speak first. Once again we would like to say this is indeed a noble and service-oriented trait. However, at times it is best to take the bit between the teeth, so to speak. We would only wish to say a few words through each instrument this evening, for the one known as M, the one known as S2, and the one known as S1, through which we speak, are no longer new instruments and are here solely for the purpose of reaffirming the contact and gaining more self-confidence in themselves, for they at times do not see the results as more experience channels, yet each has the capability and most of all the desire to serve in this manner, and as we have said many times, the desire to serve is the main facet of this work.

At this time we would transfer this contact. I am Hatonn

(S2 channeling)

I am Hatonn, and I again greet you, my brothers and sisters, in the love and the light of the infinite Creator. As we have said before, we would only speak a few words through each instrument, for they are primarily here to reaffirm their confidence and their contact with us. We have always said that desire is important for this contact, and that if the desire is strong enough, there will be a strong contact, and we know that there is a strong desire on your part. We would at this time like to transfer this contact to another who has the desire. I am Hatonn.

(M channeling)

I am Hatonn. I am with this instrument. We are pleased to have had the opportunity to work with each of you tonight, and rejoice in your desire for service to one another and to many of your brothers. We are always at your service, always prepared to be with each of you at your call. We are only a thought away, and your calling for our assistance or our message is indeed a great service to us, for it gives us the opportunity for us to share with you the bounty of our own experiences. Our advice, or our words to you, rather than advice, are certainly fallible. They are true to the best of our understanding, and we thank each of you for allowing us this opportunity to serve.

At this time we would like the opportunity to work briefly once again with the instrument known as D if he would still be interested in our contact. We leave this instrument in the love and the light. I am Hatonn.

(D channeling)

I am Hatonn, and am once again with this instrument. We have been making some slight adjustments and sweeping out a few cobwebs. Our contact is much better now and we look forward to further communication in the future. We must leave this group now. We look forward to another such gathering in the near future. We leave you, as always, in the love and light. I am Hatonn.

(S2 channeling)

I am Latwii, and I wish to greet you again, my brothers, in the love and the light of the infinite Creator. And as always, we would like to answer any questions that your group may have this evening. We will ask if there are any questions.

D: Yes, I have a question. Several years ago at a meeting a strong attempt—or what felt like a strong attempt—was made to contact me, the first time that it ever happened was not requested by me. If this is a free will contact, how are those attempts made?

I am Latwii, and I am aware of your question. For the experience that you inquire about, it is a free will contact, as you have said. It was felt that for you to feel our presence at that time was not a violation of your free will, but was in hopes for you to become more familiar and comfortable with our contact.

May we answer you further?

D: Well, it was announced that contact was—an attempt was being made at contact by another source. A name was never given, and the contact was never made, because I didn't allow it. Does this happen often?

I am Latwii, and I am aware of your question. As we have said, it was hoped that the contact you felt was not intended to distress you, but it was hoped that you would feel the love and the light that was intended. Rarely do we ever force ourselves upon the unwilling, but, as we have suggested, that that contact was intended, that contact was intended to show our love and so that you would be able to make that decision for yourself for what path you wished to take.

May we answer you further?

D: No, thank you very much.

And as always, we thank you, my brother. Is there another question we may answer?

(Pause)

I am Latwii, and at this time we would like to transfer this contact so that the instrument with the contact may have the opportunity to ask any questions that he may have. I am Latwii.

(Jim channeling)

I am Latwii, and I greet you again, my brothers and sisters, in love and light. We at this time shall ask if there might be another query that we might attempt to answer.

S2: I have a question, if I could decide upon which one it is. In the past I have asked several questions about the time-regressed hypnosis. Are there any suggestions—now that it appears that I will be able to make an attempt at it—are there any suggestions you might make that might help us in that endeavor?

I am Latwii, and am aware of your query, my brother. We have found that suggestions are frequently taken as more than suggestions. Therefore, we must speak most generally. Each course of action which one takes has the opportunity for growth. We can only recommend that whatever course one might take to realize the greatest growth, it is helpful to seek as purely for the purpose of growth in the spirit, in the mind, and in the body, so that what is awaiting the entity might be able then to come forth purely, having been purely called. The various phenomena which the seeker encounters upon the journey which attract the attraction for but the moment, though intriguing for that moment, sometimes lack in lasting value. Therefore, we simply recommend the seeking with the heart of the goal in mind.

May we answer you further, my brother?

S2: No, I think you've helped me a lot, thank you.

I am Latwii. We thank you, my brother. May we answer another question at this time?

(Pause)

I am Latwii. We perceive the great silence of the being of this group and rejoice in the peace. We thank you for allowing us the opportunity to speak with you, to blend our vibrations with you. It is an honor which we treasure and look forward to at each gathering of this group. We leave this group now, rejoicing in love and light, and as always, we leave you in that love and light. We are known to you as those of Latwii. Adonai, my brothers and sisters. Vasu borragus. ✣

L/L Research is a subsidiary of
Rock Creek Research &
Development Laboratories, Inc.

P.O. Box 5195
Louisville, KY 40255-0195

L/L RESEARCH

www.llresearch.org

Rock Creek is a non-profit
corporation dedicated to
discovering and sharing
information which may aid in
the spiritual evolution of
humankind.

THE LAW OF ONE, BOOK V, SESSION 98, FRAGMENT 48
SEPTEMBER 24, 1982

Jim: Session 98 is presented in total here. Our experiences were beginning to become a little more unusual and difficult at this point in our lives. We had difficulty agreeing on how to proceed concerning the house near the airport in Atlanta, and this is the difficulty of blue-ray blockage which Ra speaks of in the very long response to Carla's compound question. Since our difficulties were freely chosen by us, they were fair game for our negative companion of fifth density to intensify.

In querying about how once again to aid our long-time pet and companion, Gandalf, in another tumor removal operation, we found that second-density creatures are also subject to causing cancer by creating unresolved anger within themselves—the same process that applies for third-density beings.

And, finally, we found when one constructs the artifacts, clothing, or structures with which one accomplishes service-to-others work, there is a great investment of love and magical potential which may result from such homemade and heartmade artifacts.

Carla: As we prepare this personal material for publication, I am sitting at the computer, and am very tempted to rub my eyes, because the gardening I did earlier placed me in one of many environments to which I'm allergic. I think these allergies are often a complaint of Wanderers, and have to do at least partially with the mismatch of vibrations between this earth world and the world of origin. Often the more uncomplaining the Wanderer, the more the body shall

act out the difficulties we may have emotionally and mentally with the vibrations here. Certainly this is true of myself. I do see the psychosomatic nature of these allergies, and by long practice have developed a fair resistance to them, which allows me to do some of the too many things I enjoy, whether it be patting the cats or pulling henbit out of the ivy. Or eating one of many foods, or dusting, or getting the mold out of something I find at church on one of my housekeeping forays. I doubt I could duck these no matter what my attitude, but I hope they are as little a part of my awareness as possible, and feel that the attitude really is key.

What it shows me is just how carefully balanced we are, as we come into incarnation here. I was given just these distortions, largely in order that I would have plenty of forced time to become more contemplative. It may seem that I am a thoroughgoing mystic, and certainly during many years of forced stillness, I have always found a depth of faith and a joy that illumined my life from within. It is almost as though the adversity of illness or limitation is a teacher, taking you out of the old ways of doing, and introducing you to the contemplative life. I have wanted to be here every day of my life, with the exception of some sorry time during early puberty when I lost all faith and decided if I couldn't be of help to anyone, I might as well go on. Which my body obligingly did not six months later, throwing itself into kidney failure brought on by an allergic reaction. And the allergies are there because of the mismatch in vibratory complexes. See how neatly this works. Such is catalyst. it's a wonderful world.

As I got up from the sickbed at last during 1992, I vowed not to lose this love of stillness. But I also love to do, busy bee that I am. Of course I love to help L/L Research with correspondence and writing and channeling, and my church and singing. These are like the footers for the building I live in, real pillars of renewing spirit within. But there's more. I love the company of women and go out of my way to have that gal's night out in my schedule. I love to cook, and do as much as I can cram in, and an extension of that is that I take a morning each week to go through the parish where I worship in community and just go around straightening, washing out, putting away and making ready, especially in the church kitchen but really all over the building. It is a joy being a servant in the Lord's house.! And I could continue till you were exhausted of any possible interest. There are so many good things to do, so many needs I hear and wish to respond to. Too many to accomplish, sadly. The plight of the nineties: no time!

What this is all in aid of is simply to demonstrate how deeply bred in the bone my love of helpful activity is. Activity at whatever level I can accomplish it is inevitable. It is part of who I am, and some would say that is a born martyr. Perhaps this is somewhat true. I only know we live and then we are gone, and while I am here, I want to respond as deeply as I can. This means I am always pushing the envelope, and always prey to psychic greeting. I have not ceased being greeted. It is just that I deal with it, as does Jim, with respect, in acknowledging it, and discipline, in allowing it to pass quickly without judgment, knowing the negative essence behind it as part of myself that I love. Acceptance and forgiveness simply move the situation forward, and the crises pass. This is hard-won wisdom. I encourage any groups who get into a situation where psychic greeting is occurring to study the ways of forgiveness and acceptance of this seemingly opposing energy. In claiming the higher truth that all is one, we place ourselves in that finer, fuller light, and the difficulties ease away as we simply persevere in living without fear of these greetings. For those who might be interested, I do have a chapter on psychic greeting and psychic self-defense in my Channeling Handbook. *The essence of that advice: fear not and lean on prayer and keeping the self aligned in open-hearted love.*

My recovery from the bad throat infection discussed above was accomplished by a 6-week course of antibiotics taken with lots of buttermilk, not a substance I enjoy. It did, however, work.

Gandalf was a very special little person. Given to me by an old friend in 1968, he was a kitten when Donald and I began our life together. He adored Don, and would play retriever with him, repeatedly fetching the peppermint candy wrappers Don would tie in a little bow-tie and throw, and putting them in Don's shoes, which were always off if he was at home. His devotion was intense. If we were sitting, he was almost always upon one of us. Don loved to walk around with Gandalf hanging over his shoulder, and I can still see them clearly, doing their daily tour of the rooms of our apartment. Gandalf expressed such love! As he became quite old, he got both arthritis and cancer, but until the moment he died, he was fiercely determined to be here and as close to us as possible. I feel that he has now reincarnated in our beautiful cat, "Mo," who expresses much the same energy. I am thankful we have had more time with this soul, who is certainly harvestable to third density.

Session 98, September 24, 1982

Ra: I am Ra. I greet you in the love and in the light of the one infinite Creator. We communicate now.

Questioner: Could you first please give me the condition of the instrument?

Ra: I am Ra. The physical energy deficit has somewhat increased. The vital energy distortions are somewhat improved.

Questioner: We eliminated our meditation prior to the session. Would Ra comment on that?

Ra: I am Ra. The purpose of preparation for a working is the purification of each entity involved with the working. The removal of a portion of this preparation has a value determined by the purity of each which takes part in the working has achieved without that particular aid.

Questioner: I had just taken a wild guess that possibly it was during that meditation prior to the working that was used by our fifth-density, negative friend to create the allergic reactions and other reactions in the instrument. Was I correct in that assumption, or was I incorrect?

Ra: I am Ra. This entity greets the instrument as close to the working in your space\ time continuum as is practicable. The elimination of that preparation caused the fifth-density entity to greet this instrument at this juncture of decision not to meditate. The greeting does not take what you would call a noticeable amount of your time.

Questioner: Was the greeting as effective as it would have been if meditation had been done?

Ra: I am Ra. Yes.

Questioner: I have a question from the instrument. It states: "Could Ra tell us what factors are allowing our fifth-density, negative companion to be able to continue greeting the instrument in the throat area as well as with other unusual sensations such as dizziness, the smelling of orange blossoms, the feeling of stepping on imaginary creatures, and what can be done to lessen these greetings? Also, why do the greetings occur on walks?"

Ra: I am Ra. There are various portions of the query. We shall attempt answer to each. We tread close to the Law of Confusion, saved only by the awareness that given lack of information this instrument would, nonetheless, continue to offer its service.

The working of your fifth-density companion which still affects the instrument was, as we have stated, a potent working. The totality of those biases which offer to the instrument opportunities for increased vital and physical strength, shall we say, were touched by the working. The blue-ray difficulties were not entirely at an end after the first asking. Again, this group experienced blockage rare for the group; that is, the blue-ray blockage of unclear communication. By this means the efficacy of the working was reinforced.

The potential of this working is significant. The physical exercising, the sacred music, the varieties of experience, and indeed simple social intercourse are jeopardized by a working which attempts to close the throat and the mouth. It is to be noted that there is also the potential for the loss of this contact.

We suggest that the instrument's allergies create a continuous means whereby the distortion created by the magical working may be continued. As we have stated, it shall be necessary, in order to remove the working, to completely remove the distortion within the throat area caused by this working. The continuous aggravation of allergic reactions makes this challenging.

The orange blossom is the odor which you may associate with the social memory complex of fifth-density positive which is known to you as sound vibration, Latwii. This entity was with the instrument as requested by the instrument. The odor was perceived due to the quite sensitive nature of the instrument due, again, to its, shall we say, acme in the eighteen-day cycle.

The sensation of stepping upon the small animal and killing it was a greeting from your fifth-density, negative companion also made possible by the above circumstance.

As to the removal of the effects of the magical working, we may make two suggestions, one immediate, and one general. Firstly, within the body of knowledge which those healers known among your peoples as medical doctors have is the use of harsh chemical substances which you call medicine. These substances almost invariably cause far more changes than are intended in the mind/body/spirit complex. However, in this instance the steroids or, alternately, the antibiotic family might be useful in the complete removal of the difficulty within which the working is still able to thrive. Of course, the allergies would persist after this course of medicine were ended, but the effects of the working would no longer come into play.

The one you call Jerome might well be of aid in this somewhat unorthodox medical situation. As allergies are quite misunderstood by your orthodox healers, it would be inappropriate to subject the instrument to the services of your medical doctors which find the amelioration of allergic effects to be connected with the intake of these same toxins in milder form. This, shall we say, treats, the symptom. However, the changes offered to the body complex are quite inadvisable. The allergy may be seen to be the rejection upon a deep level of the mind complex of the environment of the mind/body/spirit complex. Thus the allergy may be seen in its pure form as the mental/emotional distortion of the deeper self.

The more general recommendation lies with one which does not wish to be identified. There is a code name prayer wheel. We suggest ten treatments from this healer and further suggest a clear reading and subsequent following upon the part of the instrument of the priorities of allergy, especially to your foodstuffs.

Lastly, the effects of the working become apparent upon the walking when the body complex has begun to exert itself to the point of increased respiration. Also a contributing factor is the number of your second-density substances to which this instrument is allergic.

Questioner: Thank you. The second question is: "Our oldest cat, Gandalf, has a growth near his spine. Is there anything that makes the surgical removal of this growth less appropriate than the surgical removal of the growth that we had performed a year ago last April, and would the most appropriate action on our part to aid his recovery be the visualization of light surrounding him during the surgery and the repeating of ritual phrases periodically while he is at the veterinarians'?"

Ra: I am Ra. No. There is no greater cause for caution than previously and, yes, the phrases of which you speak shall aid the entity. Although this entity is, in body complex, old and, therefore, liable to danger from what you call your anesthetic, its mental, emotional, and spiritual distortions are such that it is strongly motivated to recover that it might once again rejoin the loved one. Keep in mind that this entity is harvestable third density.

Questioner: Would you explain why you said "Keep in mind that this entity is harvestable third density" and tell me if you have any other specific recommendations with respect to the proposed operation on the growth?

Ra: I am Ra. We stated this in order to elucidate our use of the term "spirit complex" as applied to what might be considered a second-density entity. The implications are that this entity shall have far more cause to abide and heal that it may seek the presence of the loved ones.

Questioner: Is there any additional recommendation that Ra could make with respect to the proposed operation?

Ra: I am Ra. No.

Questioner: I was wondering if I was correct in my assumption for the reason for the growth was a state of anger in the cat, Gandalf, because of the addition of the newer cats in his environment? Was I correct?

Ra: I am Ra. The original cause of what you call cancer was the distortion caused by this event. The proximate cause of this growth is the nature of the distortion of the body cells which you call cancer.

Questioner: Are there any other cancerous growths at this time in Gandalf?

Ra: I am Ra. Yes.

Questioner: Can we alleviate those and, if so, how and where are they?

Ra: I am Ra. None can be alleviated at this space/time nexus. One is located within the juncture of the right hip. Another which is very small is near the organ you call the liver. There are also small cell distortions under the, we may call it, arm, to distinguish the upper appendages, on both sides.

Questioner: Is there anything that we can do to alleviate these problems that are other than surgical to help Gandalf?

Ra: I am Ra. Continue in praise and thanksgiving, asking for the removal of these distortions. There are two possible outcomes. Firstly, the entity shall dwell with you in contentment until its physical vehicle holds it no more due to distortions caused by the cancerous cells. Secondly, the life path may become that which allows the healing. We do not infringe upon free will by examining this life path although we may note the preponderance of life paths which use some distortion such as this to leave the physical body which in this case is the orange-ray body.

Questioner: Does the cat, Fairchild, have any of these same type of problems?

Ra: I am Ra. Not at this space/time nexus.

Questioner: Was it necessary for the cat Gandalf to be a mind/body/spirit complex and harvestable third density to have the anger result in cancer?

Ra: I am Ra. No.

Questioner: Then any mind/body complex can develop cancer. Is this correct?

Ra: I am Ra. This is correct.

At this time we would break our routine by making an observation. We observe the following coincidence. Firstly, the congestion of this instrument's throat due to the flow of mucous caused by energized allergic reaction has, at this point, become such that we may safely predict the probability/possibility vortex approaching certainty that within one-half of an hour we shall need to depart from this working. Secondly, as we noted the above the sound vibration made by one of your sound vibration recording devices was audible to us. If this group desires, it may choose to have sessions which are brought to an ending soon after this sound vibration occurs. This decision would ensure the minimal distortions within the instrument towards the discomfort/comfort within the throat until the effects of the magical working of your fifth-density companion have been removed.

Questioner: That is perfectly fine with us. That noise occurs at the forty-five minute time period since the tapes are forty-five minutes on a side. I would just ask as the final question, then, if the new table that Jim has built for the appurtenances is satisfactory to hold them since it will give us more room to walk around the bed, and is it better to leave it in its natural condition, or is it better to coat it with linseed oil, varnish, or paint?

Ra: I am Ra. We view this appurtenance. It sings with joy. The pine vibrates in praise. Much investment of this working in wood has been done. It is acceptable. We may suggest it be left either as it is or rubbed with the oil which also is easily magnetized and holds the proffered vibration to a profound extent.

Questioner: I was wondering if this would be an appropriate time to end since the tape recorder clicked some time ago?

Ra: I am Ra. This is a matter for your discrimination. The instrument remains open to our use although, as we have noted, the physical distortions begin to mount.

Questioner: Then we had better close to protect the instrument's physical energy, and I will ask if there is anything that we can do to improve the contact or to make the instrument more comfortable?

Ra: I am Ra. All is well. We find your concerns appropriate.

We leave you in the love and in the light of the one infinite Creator. Go forth, therefore, rejoicing in the power and in the peace of the One. Adonai. ⚬

L/L Research is a subsidiary of
Rock Creek Research &
Development Laboratories, Inc.

P.O. Box 5195
Louisville, KY 40255-0195

L/L RESEARCH

www.llresearch.org

Rock Creek is a non-profit
corporation dedicated to
discovering and sharing
information which may aid in
the spiritual evolution of
humankind.

SATURDAY MEDITATION
SEPTEMBER 25, 1982

(A1 channeling)

I am Hatonn, and I greet you in the love and in the light of the one infinite Creator. I am pleased to be called to your group once again so that we might bring forth a message. It is just a small message with great meaning to some. It deals with living in your illusion, and with coping with those many, many lessons you have chosen to learn. There are always those times which seem to have no meaning but at times there must be endurance so as to get to a bigger and better time. But care should be taken to look at every detail of the lesson, and to be aware of many facets which it holds. It could be wanting—not having loved another—to love oneself, it could be the lesson of patience or of endurance, it could be learning to see God in each person, seeing the oneness of the world. There are many things the lessons have to offer and in those times when there seems to be no point in staying in that one particular lesson you might want to look at it one more time. It is like looking in the mirror one more time to see yourself again to make sure you are there, and that you have forgotten to pardon yourself. When you see yourself, see the other, know that there is a oneness with all, and remember with patience and with the will to learn the lessons you have chosen to experience will be beneficial, and you will grow in oneness with the Creator.

We would at this time like to transfer this contact to another present in the group. I am known to you as Hatonn.

(L channeling)

I am Hatonn, and I greet you once again, my brothers and sisters, in the love and light of the infinite Creator. My friends, it is often difficult to experience those passages of time in which one seems to have lost an awareness of the path which one treads. For as those of you [who] have traveled through the forests of your planet are aware, the most pleasurable segments of your travels are those within which events of significance are discerned: a particularly beautiful flower, a joyous song, a passing bird, an impressive outcropping of stones—each of these is an easily discernible landmark of your journey, one which may be easily reexperienced at a later date. But, my friends, was not the greater value of the journey acquired as one quieted oneself in anticipation of that which was to come? Is it not true that the greatest value derived from such a trip is not determined by those seemingly significant objects or experiences, but rather the balance one retains through the journey?

So also, my friends, is the path you tread, on which you periodically encounter the beauty of re-experiencing to a greater or lesser degree the oneness with your other selves. It is this oneness that is the sharing of the Creator's love, the perception of the Creator's light that makes your path worth seeking. Yet, my friends, do not be dismayed if your path reveals few landmarks. Rather, be attentive to the fact that in following the path one opens oneself to listen, to see that which is often overlooked, to be that which one has the potential to be. My friends, the glory of your journey lies not in its landmarks or its completion but rather in its undertaking. It is the constant undertaking of oneness, the constant desire to be that which is, instead of that which appears, that is the true reward of the path you follow. Therefore, my friends, be not dismayed that your path has many persistent stretches between the sharpened pines and the regrettable ravines, for each step can only be taken with consciousness and each step, my friends, is a step closer to oneness.

At this time we will take our leave, that our brothers and sisters of Latwii may perform their service. Adonai, my friends. We are known to you as Hatonn.

(L channeling)

I am Latwii, and I greet you, my friends, in the love and the light of the infinite Creator, and we desire to communicate to those present that it is an exquisite pleasure to be able to strut our stuff before such an elite group. For it is never so frequent an experience to have visitors as to become humdrum, as you might say, and we are at this moment relishing the task of undertaking to display our eloquence. We assume that the gentle peals of laughter are merely vociferations of anticipation, and we shall hold you in suspense no longer. Is there a question we might answer?

A1: Well, Latwii, I have a question. Since we're so eager to be with you tonight, and you're so glad to perform, I was wondering if you have any small message which you would like to share with us at this time?

I am Latwii. I am aware of your question. We desire to communicate to those present that we are—and speaking for our brethren and sistren of the Confederation as well as ourselves—quite pleased that those of this cadre who have traveled such a great distance have displayed such dedication to the hobbling of their personal paths and desire to commend them for their attentiveness to the task which they undertook in entering your illusion.

Is there another question?

A1: I have a question about those who come into the world to aid others and how do they—it seems like some people come in groups, such as in families, but the group seems to go its separate ways and come back again. How does this separating and gathering disturb the energy of the family or does it?

My sister, if we may be allowed an analogy, we would refer to those cycles on your planet which are called by you seasons within in which many things are accomplished as that which presently exists seems to be in a process of splitting asunder. The order of creation is in a sense circular in nature, yet the circle must not be too constricted in nature or those who the circle serves will become stale and less perceptive. In the situations such as you describe it is often possible for two tasks to be accomplished: the service rendered unto others as you have described, as well as the service rendered unto others that is accomplished when the entity withdraws so as to extend the entity's own series of growth experiences. As you pointed out, quite frequently the growth experiences enable the entity to approach the former work or a new type of service with a renewed enthusiasm, and a rejuvenated desire to serve.

May we answer you further, my sister?

A1: No, thank you.

We thank you. Is there another question?

S: We have been gifted with a new entity. Although I speak with maternal bias, this entity seems very special. Do you have a suggestion as to how we can provide an environment which will further enable this entity to flower?

I am Latwii. I am aware of your question and would extend our commendation for the sincerity of your intention. While we are aware that this subject has been the object of much soul-searching for yourself, we would suggest, generally speaking, that the newly arrived entity has perceptions quite dissimilar from those who have occupied your illusion for a length of time, for this is the case with all newly arrived entities. It is the process of daily education through interaction with brothers and sisters of your planet that tends to distort the perceptions of the newly arrived entity. As you are aware, it is the will of the occupants of your illusion that establish the parameters within which you and your other selves exist. Therefore we would suggest that for any individual who seeks to assist a newly arrived entity the maintenance of an awareness of the potential for unity between oneself and one's other selves be attempted, for the newly arrived entity has chosen its date of arrival to participate in the harvest which will occur, and will be greatly assisted by being initially programmed, so to speak, with the correct data. The atmosphere of love without judgment is strongly recommended and the emphasis upon an awareness of the Creator's role in all areas of life would also be recommended, for the young entity would be benefited by such assistance in overcoming the distortions that will later be encountered.

May we answer you further?

S: I wish so much to learn, not only for myself but that the information I pass on be accurate information. I know so few other ways than to attempt to figure things out for myself. Have you any suggestion?

I am Latwii. My sister, the striving of which you speak is the catalyst that will promote communication between the universe, so to speak, and you own subconscious as you consciously attempt to decipher that which is confusing or that which is not understood. It is wise to determine intuitively whether one is satisfied with the answer arrived at in the logical fashion to which you refer. If there is within one's soul, so to speak, an instant awareness of the truth of the answer arrived at, one may safely rely on that information. However, if there is some question in regards to the accuracy or the completeness of that which is determined by the logical process, we would recommend that one simply drop the pursuit through logic for a period of time so that the communication of the desired information may be accomplished by the subconscious mind. When reexamined later one may often find that the conscious mind has quite suddenly developed additional and surprisingly accurate information.

May we answer you further?

S: Thank you. You have been surprisingly helpful. I will contemplate your response.

I am Latwii. We are grateful for your response, and we would add in the words of this instrument the rejoinder, "Shucks, ma'am, twarn't nothin." Is there another question?

A2: Yes, Latwii. Is there anything you can say, comment on, shed some light on in the area of what's been going on with A1's physical problems that have been coming up, and any way she could see how this is a catalyst, and see direction and ways in which to use this?

I am Latwii. I am aware of your question. As you are aware, it is undesirable in our manner of service or in the manner of striving which each of you pursues to provide free answers to the pop quizzes. However, we will extend ourselves a bit upon the limb by making some general observations on this subject of physical impairments. The nature of the physical impairment is the key to the spiritual imbalance or lesson that must be learned or addressed. Each of you is able to formulate within your own awareness such examples. We would therefore suggest that the entity known as A1 consider the nature of the physical impairment as well as the locations which are affected, for this entity is oriented toward the perception of symbolism and therefore is capable of afflicting herself within specific regions of the physical vehicle so as to provide clues in the deciphering of the lesson.

If we might return to generalized comments we would offer such examples as difficulty in the legs or feet might often refer, might often indicate a weakness or refusal in understanding. The affliction of the hands, for example, might be indicative of a resistance or imbalance in the manner in which one communicates with one's other selves, for as you are aware, the hands, next to the tongue, are essential organs of communication, and an imbalance between that which is a spiritual lesson and that which is the path naturally being followed in a situation may result in the production of pain that attention may be drawn to the imbalance.

May we answer you further?

A2: I'm sure the answer is very much appreciated. I thank you very much, and I have one further question which might be specific so I would appreciate whatever generalities you could offer. I am unclear in areas in which I have very strong ideas, and they are so clear for me that it is difficult for me to see where most, many other people are coming from, and I wish to share with them what would serve them best. Do you have any comments on what type of sharing is most easily assimilated or used by others?

I am Latwii. If we may be allowed to be succinct, we would respond that that sharing which is most useful to others or most easily assimilated by others is that which is sought.

May we answer you further?

A2: Does this mean that I should wait and simply answer questions?

I am Latwii. My sister, the desire to communicate that which one has uncovered or that which has been revealed to one is a powerful drive, for as your chosen path appears to be that of service to others, the desire to progress along that path by sharing such revelations is a powerful force. However, one must first consider the value of service performed in extending to another self that which is unsought, perhaps undesired, yet on revelation is that which is unavoidable. For example, that which is revealed untimely to another self, however well-intentioned, becomes a revelation that the other …

(Side one of tape ends.)

(L channeling)

… becomes a revelation for which that other self is suddenly made responsible for incorporating into their awareness. If the child is suddenly pressed in the position of making the moral decisions of an adult the difficulty and trauma may be well imagined. If this is coupled with the child being made responsible for actions resulting from information which the child is incapable of assimilating fully a substantial amount of damage may occur.

We would therefore suggest, my sister, that your own intuitive perceptions will allow you to identify those other selves who are upon a path similar in nature to your own which may accord growth through the acquisition of the information you possess. However, we would caution that in most cases it would be better for yourself and the other self who seeks, to await the indication in some form by the other self that a conscious request for information pertinent to personal growth is made. In this manner the other self consciously elects to accept the information and the responsibility for the information that will be received. Obviously, in making this decision the entity cannot kick and scream at will [at] that which it is willing to accept and be responsible for. As you are aware, the selection of a path holds many surprises. However, it

is essential that the other self consciously elect to seek that which you desire to reveal.

May we answer you further?

A2: No, thank you very much.

We thank you my sister. Is there another question?

A1: Well, Latwii, I just want to say thanks for answering my sister's question. But I need a little clarity. I understood the symbolism of the hands but I was a little confused on the symbolism of the legs and understanding. Could you kind of clarify this a little?

I am Latwii, and as this was a generalized statement we will joyfully attempt to clarify for you. The physical vehicle itself is possessed of many symbols which allow the diagnosis of the true spiritual cause of illnesses or physical impairments so that the spiritual renouncing may be attempted, for as you are aware it is the spiritual growth that is the motivation for assuming a physical vehicle. Therefore if an individual is of the mental structure to perceive symbols and use these symbols to determine physical imbalances and their spiritual origins, one might realize that the legs and feet are that from which one stands, and might read a symbolism in an imbalance in these areas as an imbalance in understanding. One might examine the feet and realize that the feet are one's contact with that which is most substantial of your physical world, the earth itself. An impairment in this area might be interpreted as a refusal to accept that physical illusion upon which one physically stands.

There are no hard and fast rules for the interpretation of the various symbolisms for the individual originates his or her own physical imbalances in such a pattern as to match the individual's own style, so to speak, of creating symbols. One who regards the physical vehicle as completely non-symbolic, for example, and who relies heavily upon the maintenance structures for physical vehicles and their mechanics, or hospitals and doctors, would have very little use for a symbolic revelation, and instead might create a physical imbalance that would leave oneself bedridden for extensive periods of time that a greater opportunity for contemplation could be provided. It is the individual who creates the physical imbalance, and it is to the individual's particular bent of interpretation that the symbols are structured.

May we answer you further?

A1: Just in one small, little thing. So then, you kind of can mean someone with a broken leg in some cases [it could] be a symbol of great imbalance?

I am Latwii. As you surmise, a broken leg, by one who perceives symbolism, would be perceivable or interpretable as a grave imbalance. However, the same broken leg by one who is oblivious to such symbolism might be interpreted as a general tendency for clumsiness.

May we answer you further?

A1: No, thank you. What you said has great meaning. I see a lot of truth about my beliefs. Thank you.

We thank you, my sister, for the opportunity to give service. Is there another question?

J: Yes, Latwii. To carry this discussion a little farther, once a person is able to perceive what the body's symbol is trying to tell them, and are able to learn the lesson, then does the body go ahead and become healed in regard to the physical manifestation of the problem?

I am Latwii. My sister, the suggestion or interpretation which you offer in many cases is correct. However, we would caution that the individual might have chosen prior to incarnation to experience a debilitating illness, for example, that would, in reducing the entity's ability toward activity, increase the individual's tendency toward contemplation or meditation. If this is indeed the situation, an awareness of cause and effect may have no bearing on the continuation of the impairment, for on a higher level, so to speak, the entity may have previously decided to avoid the possibility of self-repair to the detriment of one's spiritual growth.

The case may also occur in which the entity develops spontaneously the impairment, and in deciphering the cause of the impairment may correct the cause but maintain the impairment because additional facility may be derived from the impairment. For example, there are present in your own knowledge several entities who are physically blind yet have accomplished great works in the field generally and often erroneously referred to as entertainment. The blind individual in many cases might be able to acquire physical eyesight yet elects not to acquire their physical vision out of a fear that the distraction might be sufficient to deter their performance of service in their musical creations.

May we answer you further?

J: Could you speak a little generally to the symbolism of other afflictions: depression, tummy aches, skin allergies, and bladder problems for instance—you know, pick and choose, one or all, whatever. Just generally, give me some more help if you can.

I am Latwii. My sister, we would preface our general discussion with the reminder that we seek to offer service in the understanding of the true universe and the Creator's will, and are reluctant to undertake the opening of a clinic in that it might restrict our other efforts. Therefore, we would caution against the mistake of applying our generalized comments to specific individual's illness, for as we have previously explained the symbology is specific to the entity.

To address a few of those physical impairments to which you referred we would suggest first examining the interaction of the specific physical component with the role within which it exists. For example, the stomach is that which takes in or digests specifically chosen facets or components of your world. Would it not be fitting therefore in many cases to use this organ as a lodestone which indicates that which one erroneously for growth refuses to take upon oneself or to make a part of oneself?

The skin is both a communicator and a barrier, for is not the skin that which insulates oneself from the outside world, yet in proximity or contact is used to communicate sharing or acceptance. Therefore, one might, generally speaking, assume that a skin disorder could be a potential indicator of one's reluctance to accept contact with their world or one's over-extension of oneself to the point of abuse.

The area which you describe as the knees could be for one entity interpreted as a portion [of] that which we have previously discussed as understanding. In another entity's situation the ailment might be generated to indicate an unyielding nature, a lack of flexibility or openness to the revelations of the subconscious mind due perhaps to a over-reliance upon the rigid, unyielding logic.

May we answer you further?

J: No, thank you, not on that, Latwii. Hi. How are you? I feel like I get to talk with you just all the time because I get to transcribe the tapes. Are you with me when I'm sitting at the typewriter and listening to the tape recorder?

I am Latwii. My sister, we are in the third seat to the left, three rows forward. In a more serious vein, my sister, we would simply acknowledge that your calling makes our presence available, and the frequency of your calling is quite pleasurable for us as well, and we are grateful that you would seek our companionship so readily, and we thank you for this, my sister.

J: I thank you, and I'm glad to know that. I am always aware when you and Hatonn say, you know, that if we ask for you in our meditations you will aid us and help us. How do we experience your aid?

I am Latwii. My sister, we would humbly point out that you are currently experiencing our aid.

J: I see. I have another question. Can you give me a—tell me what the words of closing mean when you say—I know what "adonai" means, but "vasu borragus"?

I am Latwii. My sister, we are aware that many clear, definitive translations have been offered for these expressions. However, we regret to be the informers that they are not literal translations of our statements, but rather tools, as are all words, to communicate with as little distortion as possible our intended messages. Therefore, the statements, "good-bye, see you again, have a good time," might readily serve if they conveyed the appropriate message through the distortive tendencies of those who channel our messages, for as you are aware, it is quite unlikely that you will encounter an undistorted message. Therefore, if we were to explain our reliance upon these particular terms we would do so in terms again of the channeling individual's preference in expressing as closely as possible our intended messages. If the instrument believes the word to convey a specific message, then we will use that instrument's vocabulary to accomplish the delivery of a certain message.

In brief, we would conclude that our closing is generally composed of a combination of several messages, such as the equally familiar statement, "In the love and the light of the infinite Creator"; the statement, "We love you"; the statement, "We appreciate our communion with you and desire to be of service again whenever possible." Each of these

is an equally valid translation of our intended message at a given time. The preference of those receiving the messages to interpret the specific words, "Adonai vasu borragus" to convey these messages is the major factor in our selection of these terms.

May we answer you further?

J: No, that was almost more than I could understand. I have one last question briefly. Do you have any suggestions about any appropriate good way for us to invoke a special blessing on our new car?

I am Latwii.

(Snickers from group.)

I am Latwii, and we appreciate the editorial comment, for as you are aware we are always interested in those messages which are conveyed to us. We would extend the following suggestion for the preservation of your motorized vehicle and its occupants. The vehicle itself is, as you are aware, a part of your physical illusion. We are in turn aware that this makes the motorized vehicle dear to your hearts. Therefore, we would suggest that an awareness that the motorized vehicle is protected from all non-growth creating encounters with other motorized vehicles would be most valuable in sustaining those physical attributes of that vehicle which you so admire.

May we answer you further?

J: I'm not sure that you understood me correctly. Not that I admire this motorized vehicle as much, that I want it to be endowed with as much—the valuation in it to be—that it be used in love and light and for the protection and well-being of all who ride in it or come in contact with it in any way. You know, a blessing that it be a blessing. Not that it has inherent value in itself as a bucket of bolts.

I am Latwii. My sister, we apologize for our misinterpretation. We would suggest that our comprehension was somewhat tainted by conflicting perceptions of your value in the physical vehicle existent within this room. We would therefore suggest, my sister, that you be aware that the physical vehicle will take upon itself or be imbued with your own personal atmospheres. If you would seek to make it a tool of service to others it will become rapidly pervaded with the aura of your striving. This, we feel, is the vibration which you desire your motor vehicle to transmit. We would suggest further that in those periods of operation of this vehicle which are most stressful, such as delays in travel caused by unforeseen circumstances or other vehicle operators who appear to be performing their operation in a substandard manner, [those] be regarded with an openhearted acceptance as expressions of the full range of potential of the Creator's creation, for the intensity of emotion projected during these times of stress often become the dominant vibration within a vehicle such as you describe. An amount of wisdom or perspective during these times of stress would be beneficial to maintaining the vibration within your vehicle that you seek.

May we answer you further?

J: No, thank you. That was an answer that really satisfies me because it is the way I thought it was. Thanks for all the time you've taken for me. See you at the typewriter.

I am Latwii. My sister, we are heartily grateful for the time you've taken for us. Is there another question?

A1: Yes, how is the instrument doing?

I am Latwii. The instrument is functioning well as a result of its capacity to draw upon energy resources that are not commonly available. The instrument is capable of this accomplishment because of the interest and attentiveness of those present which maintains a stable and beneficial rate of communal vibration which in turn minimizes the distortion of our efforts to communicate. In short, your communal attentiveness results in a minimal amount of stretching or searching for the instrument, and the instrument is therefore capable of simultaneously resting the physical vehicle and tapping other sources of energy to perform this service.

May we answer you further?

A1: No, I just wanted to make sure he wasn't growing too fatigued. Thank you.

We thank you, my sister. Is there another question?

S: I feel that you have answered many questions, both those vocalized and unvocalized. I sense that you wear the cloak of modesty yet you have honored us. I sense now and again in the evening that you

would honor us further. Is there a message that you desire to express?

I am Latwii. I am aware of your communication. It is our desire to communicate to those present that we are in many ways humbled by the intensity of the love and selflessness that has drawn you together on this night. My friends, the illusion in which you function is dominated by the desires of its occupants, and regrettably within your illusion a large number desire that such intensities of love, of sharing, and of service should not exist. We are therefore …

(Tape ends.) ♣

38787834R20225

Made in the USA
Lexington, KY
26 January 2015